101 Speed Tests

for

Indian Railways (RRB)

Assistant Loco Pilot

- **Corporate Office :** 45, 2nd Floor, Maharishi Dayanand Marg, Corner Market,
  Malviya Nagar, New Delhi-110017
  Tel. : 011-49842349 / 49842350

Typeset by Disha DTP Team

Printed at Repro Knowledgecast Limited, Thane

DISHA PUBLICATION

For further information about books from DISHA,
Log on to **www.dishapublication.com** or email to **info@dishapublications.com**

CONTENTS

NUMBER SYSTEM

101 SPEED TEST — 1

Max. Marks : 20   **No. of Qs. 20**   **Time : 20 min.**   **Date : ..../........./...............**

1. $1.236 \times 10^{15} - 5.23 \times 10^{14}$ is equal to :
   (a) 7.13×10^{14} (b) 7.13×10^{15}
   (c) 71.3×10^{14} (d) -3.994

2. If $\sqrt{5} = 2.236$, then the value of $\dfrac{\sqrt{5}}{2} - \dfrac{10}{\sqrt{5}} + \sqrt{125}$ is equal to :
   (a) 7.826   (b) 8.944   (c) 5.59   (d) 10.062

3. The unit's digit in the product $7^{35} \times 3^{71} \times 11^{55}$ is :
   (a) 1   (b) 3   (c) 7   (d) 9

4. What is the missing figure in the expression given below ?
   $$\frac{16}{7} \times \frac{16}{7} - \frac{*}{7} \times \frac{9}{7} + \frac{9}{7} \times \frac{9}{7} = 1$$
   (a) 1   (b) 7   (c) 4.57   (d) 32

5. $9^6 + 7$, when divided by 8, would have a remainder :
   (a) 0   (b) 6
   (c) 5   (d) None of these

6. Taking $\sqrt{2} = 1.414$, $\sqrt{3} = 1.732$, $\sqrt{5} = 2.236$ and $\sqrt{6} = 2.449$, find the value of $\dfrac{9+\sqrt{2}}{\sqrt{5}+\sqrt{3}} + \dfrac{6-\sqrt{2}}{\sqrt{5}-\sqrt{3}}$ to the three places of decimal.
   (a) 9.2321   (b) 13.716   (c) 11.723   (d) 15.892

7. The sum of the digits of a 3 digit number is subtracted from the number. The resulting number is always :
   (a) divisible by 7   (b) not divisible by 7
   (c) divisible by 9   (d) not divisible by 9

8. Rs. 6500 were divided equally among a certain number of persons. Had there been 15 more persons each would have got Rs 30 less. Find the original number of persons.
   (a) 45   (b) 50   (c) 55   (d) 48

9. If 11,109,999 is divided by 1111, then what is the remainder?
   (a) 1098   (b) 11888   (c) 1010   (d) 1110

10. Find the whole number which when increased by 20 is equal to 69 times the reciprocal of the number:
    (a) 7   (b) 5   (c) 3   (d) 2.5

11. The sum of the place values of 3 in the numbers 50, 35 and 35 is
    (a) 3300   (b) 6   (c) 60   (d) 3030

12. The number of two digit numbers exactly divisible by 3 is
    (a) 33   (b) 32   (c) 31   (d) 30

13. Two times a two-digit number is 9 times the number obtained by reversing the digits and sum of the digits is 9. The number is
    (a) 72   (b) 54   (c) 63   (d) 81

14. A six digit number is formed by repeating a three digit number. For example 245245. Any number of this form is always divisible by
    (a) 7   (b) 11
    (c) 13   (d) All of the above

15. What is the digit in the hundred place in the product of first 45 even natural numbers.
    (a) 6   (b) 5   (c) 4   (d) 0

16. The unit digit of $(7^{95} - 3^{58})$ is
    (a) cube of 2   (b) lies between 6 and 10
    (c) 6   (d) lies between 3 and 6

17. Unit place digit in the product of first 40 odd natural number is
    (a) 6   (b) 0   (c) 5   (d) 8

18. The sum of two numbers is 90 and the greater number exceeds thrice the smaller number by 14. The number is
    (a) 18, 72   (b) 19, 71   (c) 20, 70   (d) 15, 75

19. Two numbers are in the ratio 5 : 3. If they differ by 18, then numbers are
    (a) 45, 27   (b) 25, 15   (c) 35, 21   (d) 65, 39

20. The sum of three consecutive multiples of 8 is 888, then multiples are
    (a) 160, 168, 176   (b) 288, 296, 304
    (c) 320, 328, 336   (d) 264, 272, 280.

RESPONSE GRID

1. ⓐⓑⓒⓓ	2. ⓐⓑⓒⓓ	3. ⓐⓑⓒⓓ	4. ⓐⓑⓒⓓ	5. ⓐⓑⓒⓓ
6. ⓐⓑⓒⓓ	7. ⓐⓑⓒⓓ	8. ⓐⓑⓒⓓ	9. ⓐⓑⓒⓓ	10. ⓐⓑⓒⓓ
11. ⓐⓑⓒⓓ	12. ⓐⓑⓒⓓ	13. ⓐⓑⓒⓓ	14. ⓐⓑⓒⓓ	15. ⓐⓑⓒⓓ
16. ⓐⓑⓒⓓ	17. ⓐⓑⓒⓓ	18. ⓐⓑⓒⓓ	19. ⓐⓑⓒⓓ	20. ⓐⓑⓒⓓ

HCF & LCM

101 SPEED TEST 2

Max. Marks : 20 **No. of Qs. 20** **Time : 20 min.** **Date : ..../........./.................**

1. The LCM and HCF of two numbers are 84 and 21, respectively. If the ratio of two numbers be 1 : 4, then the larger of the two numbers is :
   (a) 21 (b) 48 (c) 84 (d) 108

2. The LCM of two numbers is 4800 and their HCF is 160. If one of the numbers is 480, then the other number is :
   (a) 16 (b) 16000 (c) 160 (d) 1600

3. Three numbers are in the ratio 3 : 4 : 5 and their L.C.M. is 2400. Their H.C.F is
   (a) 40 (b) 80 (c) 120 (d) 200

4. The HCF and LCM of two numbers are 11 and 385 respectively. If one number lies between 75 and 125, then that number is
   (a) 77 (b) 88 (c) 99 (d) 110

5. Let 'K' be the greatest number that will divide 1305, 4665 and 6905, leaving the same remainder 25 in each case. Then sum of the digits of 'K' is
   (a) 7 (b) 5 (c) 6 (d) 8

6. The least number, which when divided by 48, 60, 72, 108, 140 leaves 38, 50, 62, 98 and 130 remainders respectively, is
   (a) 11115 (b) 15110 (c) 15120 (d) 15210

7. HCF of first 200 prime numbers which are of the form $10p + 1$ is
   (a) 10 (b) 7
   (c) 6 (d) None of these

8. The LCM of $\frac{1}{3}, \frac{5}{6}, \frac{2}{9}, \frac{4}{27}$ is:
   (a) $\frac{1}{54}$ (b) $\frac{10}{27}$
   (c) $\frac{20}{3}$ (d) None of these

9. If HCF $(a, b) = 12$ and $a \times b = 1800$, then LCM $(a, b) =$
   (a) 900 (b) 150 (c) 90 (d) 3600

10. There are 264 girls and 408 boys in a school. These children are to be divided into groups of equal number of boys and girls. The maximum number of boys or girls in each group will be
    (a) 11 (b) 17 (c) 24 (d) 36

11. Three bells begin tolling at the same time and continue to do so at intervals of 21, 28 and 30 seconds respectively. The bells will toll together again after
    (a) 7 seconds (b) 420 seconds
    (c) 630 seconds (d) 1764 seconds

12. The ratio of two numbers is 3 : 4 their HCF is 4. Their LCM is:
    (a) 12 (b) 16 (c) 24 (d) 48

13. Product of two co-prime numbers is 117. Their LCM should be
    (a) 1 (b) 117
    (c) equal to their HCF (d) 0

14. Which of the following pairs of fraction adds up to a number more than 5?
    (a) $\frac{5}{3}, \frac{3}{4}$ (b) $\frac{7}{3}, \frac{11}{5}$ (c) $\frac{11}{4}, \frac{8}{3}$ (d) $\frac{13}{5}, \frac{11}{6}$

15. The length and breadth of rectangular field are 55 m and 45 m respectively. The length of the largest rod (in m) that can measure the length and breadth of the field exactly, is
    (a) 11 m (b) 9 m (c) 5 m (d) 10 m

16. One pendulum ticks 57 times in 58 seconds and another 608 times in 609 seconds. If they started simultaneously, find the time after which they will tick together.
    (a) $\frac{211}{19}$ s (b) $\frac{1217}{19}$ s (c) $\frac{1218}{19}$ s (d) $\frac{1018}{19}$ s

17. Four runners started running simultaneously from a point on a circular track they took 200 sec, 300 sec, 360 sec and 450 sec to complete one round, after how much time do they meet at the starting point for the first time?
    (a) 1800 sec (b) 3600 sec
    (c) 2400 sec (d) 4800 sec

18. The numbers 11284 and 7655, when divided by a certain number of three digits, leave the same remainder. Find that number of three digits.
    (a) 161 (b) 171 (c) 181 (d) 191

19. Three bells toll at intervals of 9, 12 and 15 minutes respectively. All the three begin to toll at 8 a.m. At what time will they toll together again?
    (a) 8.45 a.m. (b) 10.30 a.m.
    (c) 11.00 a.m. (d) 1.30 p.m.

20. Four bells begin to toll together and toll respectively at intervals of 6, 5, 7, 10 and 12 seconds. How many times they will toll together in one hour excluding the one at the start ?
    (a) 7 times (b) 8 times
    (c) 9 times (d) 11 times

<table>
<tr><td rowspan="4">RESPONSE GRID</td><td>1. (a)(b)(c)(d)</td><td>2. (a)(b)(c)(d)</td><td>3. (a)(b)(c)(d)</td><td>4. (a)(b)(c)(d)</td><td>5. (a)(b)(c)(d)</td></tr>
<tr><td>6. (a)(b)(c)(d)</td><td>7. (a)(b)(c)(d)</td><td>8. (a)(b)(c)(d)</td><td>9. (a)(b)(c)(d)</td><td>10. (a)(b)(c)(d)</td></tr>
<tr><td>11. (a)(b)(c)(d)</td><td>12. (a)(b)(c)(d)</td><td>13. (a)(b)(c)(d)</td><td>14. (a)(b)(c)(d)</td><td>15. (a)(b)(c)(d)</td></tr>
<tr><td>16. (a)(b)(c)(d)</td><td>17. (a)(b)(c)(d)</td><td>18. (a)(b)(c)(d)</td><td>19. (a)(b)(c)(d)</td><td>20. (a)(b)(c)(d)</td></tr>
</table>

SIMPLIFICATION

101 SPEED TEST 3

Max. Marks : 20   **No. of Qs. 20**   **Time : 20 min.**   **Date : ..../........./.................**

1. If $x = \dfrac{1}{2+\sqrt{3}}$, find the value of $x^3 - x^2 - 11x + 3$
   (a) 0   (b) 3   (c) x   (d) x+3

2. If $x = 3\sqrt{3} + \sqrt{26}$ find the value of $\dfrac{1}{2}\left(x + \dfrac{1}{x}\right)$
   (a) $\dfrac{1}{2}$ (b) $\sqrt{3}$ (c) 3   (d) $3\sqrt{3}$

3. If $x = 2 + 2^{1/3} + 2^{2/3}$ find $x^3 - 6x^2 + 6x - 2$.
   (a) 0   (b) 1   (c) 2   (d) 6

4. Express $1.272727..... = 1.\overline{27}$ in the form $\dfrac{p}{q}$, where p and q are integers and $q \neq 0$.
   (a) $\dfrac{1}{27}$ (b) $\dfrac{1}{11}$ (c) $\dfrac{14}{11}$ (d) $\dfrac{14}{27}$

5. The value of x, when $2^{x+4} \cdot 3^{x+1} = 288$.
   (a) 1   (b) -1 (c) 0   (d) None

6. When simplified the product
   $$\left(1+\dfrac{1}{2}\right)\left(1+\dfrac{1}{3}\right)\left(1+\dfrac{1}{4}\right)........\left(1+\dfrac{1}{n}\right)$$ becomes
   (a) n (b) $\dfrac{n-1}{2}$ (c) $\dfrac{n+1}{2}$ (d) $\dfrac{n}{2}$

7. If $a = 2 + \sqrt{3}$ and $b = 2 - \sqrt{3}$ then $\dfrac{1}{a^2} + \dfrac{1}{b^2}$ is equal to
   (a) 14   (b) -14 (c) $8\sqrt{3}$ (d) $-8\sqrt{3}$

8. Rationalizing factor of $(2 + \sqrt{3}) =$
   (a) $2 - \sqrt{3}$ (b) $\sqrt{3}$ (c) $2 + \sqrt{3}$ (d) $3 + \sqrt{3}$

9. Which of the following is eaual to x ?
   (a) $x^{\frac{12}{7}} - x^{\frac{5}{7}}$ (b) $\sqrt[12]{\left(x^4\right)^{\frac{1}{3}}}$ (c) $\left(\sqrt{x^3}\right)^{\frac{2}{3}}$ (d) $x^{\frac{12}{19}} + x^{\frac{7}{19}}$

10. If $\dfrac{1}{x+1} + \dfrac{1}{x+4} = 0$ then $x =$
    (a) $2\dfrac{1}{2}$ (b) $-2\dfrac{1}{2}$ (c) 3   (d) -3

11. If $\dfrac{x}{pq} + \dfrac{x}{qr} + \dfrac{x}{pr} = p + q + r$, then $x =$
    (a) pqr (b) $\dfrac{pq}{r}$ (c) $\dfrac{p}{qr}$ (d) $\dfrac{q}{pr}$

12. The equation $\dfrac{12x+1}{4} = \dfrac{13x-1}{5} + 3$ is true for
    (a) $x = \dfrac{1}{8}$ (b) $x = 2$ (c) $x = 5/8$ (d) $x = \dfrac{3}{4}$

13. If $\dfrac{a}{2} + b = 0.8$ and $\dfrac{7}{a + \dfrac{b}{2}} = 10$, then (a, b) are
    (a) (0.2, 0.4)   (b) (0.3, 0.5)
    (c) (0.4, 0.6)   (d) (0.4, 0.5)

14. A bag contains 50P, 25P and 10P coins in the ratio 2:3:4: amounting to Rs 129. Find the number of coins of each type
    (a) 120, 180, 240   (b) 180, 150, 200
    (c) 200, 180, 120   (d) 180, 200, 140

15. Monthly incomes of two persons are in the ratio 4 : 5 and their monthly expenses are in the ratio 7 : 9. If each saves Rs. 50 per month, their monthly incomes (in rupees) are :
    (a) (500, 400)   (b) (300, 600)
    (c) (400, 500)   (d) none of these

16. If $6x + 3y = 7xy$ and $3x + 9y = 11xy$, then the value of x and y are
    (a) $\left(1, \dfrac{3}{2}\right)$ (b) $\left(2, \dfrac{3}{2}\right)$ (c) $\left(\dfrac{3}{2}, 1\right)$ (d) $\left(\dfrac{3}{2}, 2\right)$

17. The angle A of a triangle ABC is equal to the sum of the two other angles. Also the ratio of the angle B to angle C is 4 : 5. The three angles are
    (a) $90°, 40°, 50°$ (b) $90°, 55°, 35°$
    (c) $90°, 60°, 30°$ (d) None of these

18. If a is a natural number then $a^2 + \dfrac{1}{a^2}$ is always greater than or equal to
    (a) 5   (b) 4   (c) 3   (d) 2

19. If $\sqrt{0.04 \times 0.4 \times a} = 0.4 \times 0.04 \times \sqrt{b}$, then value of $\dfrac{b}{a}$ is
    (a) 0.016   (b) $\dfrac{125}{2}$ (c) 0.16   (d) None of these.

20. If 'x' is any natural number, then $x^3 - \dfrac{1}{x^3}$ will always be greater than or equal to
    (a) $x + \dfrac{1}{x}$ (b) $3\left(x - \dfrac{1}{x}\right)$ (c) $3\left(x + \dfrac{1}{x}\right)$ (d) $\left(x^3 + \dfrac{1}{x^3}\right)$

<table>
<tr><td rowspan="4">RESPONSE GRID</td><td>1. ⓐⓑⓒⓓ</td><td>2. ⓐⓑⓒⓓ</td><td>3. ⓐⓑⓒⓓ</td><td>4. ⓐⓑⓒⓓ</td><td>5. ⓐⓑⓒⓓ</td></tr>
<tr><td>6. ⓐⓑⓒⓓ</td><td>7. ⓐⓑⓒⓓ</td><td>8. ⓐⓑⓒⓓ</td><td>9. ⓐⓑⓒⓓ</td><td>10. ⓐⓑⓒⓓ</td></tr>
<tr><td>11. ⓐⓑⓒⓓ</td><td>12. ⓐⓑⓒⓓ</td><td>13. ⓐⓑⓒⓓ</td><td>14. ⓐⓑⓒⓓ</td><td>15. ⓐⓑⓒⓓ</td></tr>
<tr><td>16. ⓐⓑⓒⓓ</td><td>17. ⓐⓑⓒⓓ</td><td>18. ⓐⓑⓒⓓ</td><td>19. ⓐⓑⓒⓓ</td><td>20. ⓐⓑⓒⓓ</td></tr>
</table>

SURDS, INDICES

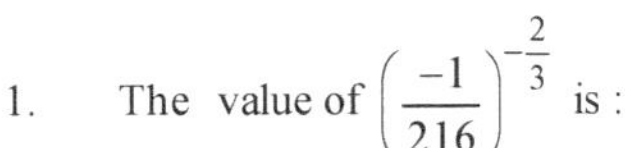

101 SPEED TEST — 4

Max. Marks : 20   **No. of Qs. 20**   **Time : 20 min.**   **Date : ..../........./.................**

1. The value of $\left(\dfrac{-1}{216}\right)^{-\frac{2}{3}}$ is :

   (a) $\dfrac{1}{36}$ (b) $-\dfrac{1}{36}$ (c) -36 (d) 36

2. The value of $\left(\dfrac{1}{4}\right)^{-2}$ is :

   (a) 2 (b) $-\dfrac{1}{2}$ (c) $-\dfrac{1}{16}$ (d) 16

3. Simplify : $13^{\frac{1}{5}} \cdot 17^{\frac{1}{5}}$

   (a) 221 (b) $\sqrt{221}$ (c) $\sqrt[5]{221}$ (d) $\dfrac{1}{5}$

4. Simplify: $\left(\dfrac{2^a}{2^b}\right)^{a+b}\left(\dfrac{2^b}{2^c}\right)^{b+c}\left(\dfrac{2^c}{2^a}\right)^{c+a}$

   (a) 0 (b) 1 (c) 2 (d) $(2)^{a+b+c}$

5. Show that : $\dfrac{x^{a(b-c)}}{x^{b(a-c)}} \div \left(\dfrac{x^b}{x^a}\right)^c = ?$

   (a) 0 (b) 1 (c) x (d) $2^{(a+b+c)}$

6. If $\left[\left\{\left(\dfrac{1}{7^2}\right)^{-2}\right\}^{-1/3}\right]^{\frac{1}{4}} = 7^m$, then find the value of m.

   (a) $m = 1$ (b) $m = \dfrac{1}{3}$ (c) $m = -\dfrac{1}{3}$ (d) $m = -7$

7. When simplified the product

   $\left(1+\dfrac{1}{2}\right)\left(1+\dfrac{1}{3}\right)\left(1+\dfrac{1}{4}\right)\ldots\ldots\left(1+\dfrac{1}{n}\right)$ becomes

   (a) n (b) $\dfrac{n-1}{2}$ (c) $\dfrac{n+1}{2}$ (d) $\dfrac{n}{2}$

8. Evaluate $\sqrt[3]{\left(\dfrac{1}{64}\right)^2}$

   (a) 4 (b) 16 (c) $\dfrac{1}{4}$ (d) $\dfrac{1}{16}$

9. $\dfrac{2^{n+2}-2(2^n)}{2^{(2n+2)}}$ when simplified is

   (a) $1-2(2^n)$ (b) $2^{n+3}-\dfrac{1}{4}$ (c) $\dfrac{1}{2^{n+1}}$ (d) $\dfrac{1}{2^{n-1}}$

10. Simplify : $\left[5\left(8^{\frac{1}{3}}+27^{\frac{1}{3}}\right)^3\right]^{\frac{1}{4}}$

    (a) 0 (b) 1 (c) 5 (d) 2

11. Simplify : $\sqrt[3]{2}+\sqrt[4]{64}+\sqrt[4]{2500}+\sqrt[6]{8}$

    (a) $\sqrt{2}$ (b) $2\sqrt{2}$ (c) $11\sqrt{2}$ (d) $9\sqrt{2}$

12. If abc = 1, then $\left(\dfrac{1}{1+a+b^{-1}}+\dfrac{1}{1+b+c^{-1}}+\dfrac{1}{1+c+a^{-1}}\right) = ?$

    (a) 0 (b) 1 (c) $\dfrac{1}{ab}$ (d) ab

13. $\dfrac{(243)^{\frac{n}{5}}\times 3^{2n+1}}{9^n\times 3^{n-1}} = ?$

    (a) 1 (b) 3 (c) 9 (d) 3^n

14. If $27^k = \dfrac{9}{3^k}$, then value of $\dfrac{1}{k^2}$ is

    (a) $\dfrac{1}{4}$ (b) 4 (c) $\dfrac{1}{2}$ (d) 2

15. If $\dfrac{3^x}{1+3^x}=\dfrac{1}{9}$, the value of $\dfrac{9^x}{1+9^x}$ is

    (a) $\dfrac{1}{27}$ (b) $\dfrac{1}{64}$ (c) $\dfrac{1}{65}$ (d) None of these.

16. If $a = x^{\frac{1}{3}}+x^{-\frac{1}{3}}$ then $a^3-3a =$

    (a) $x-x^{-1}$ (b) $2x$ (c) $x+x^{-1}$ (d) 0

17. On simplification $\left[\dfrac{x^{\frac{a}{a-b}}}{x^{\frac{a}{a+b}}}\div\dfrac{x^{\frac{b}{b-a}}}{x^{\frac{b}{b+1}}}\right]^{a+b}$ reduces to

    (a) 1 (b) -1 (c) 0 (d) None of these.

18. If $4^{\sqrt{x}^{\sqrt{x}}} = 256$ then the value of x is

    (a) 2 (b) 16 (c) 4 (d) $\sqrt{2}$

19. If $3^{2x^2}-2.3^{x^2+x+6}+3^{2(x+6)}=0$ then the values of x are

    (a) $x = -3, -2$ (b) $x = 3, 2$ (c) $x = -3, 2$ (d) $x = 3, -2$

20. Value of $\dfrac{991\times991\times991+9\times9\times9}{991\times991-991\times9+9\times9}$ is

    (a) 991 (b) 9 (c) 1000 (d) 991×9

RESPONSE GRID					
	1. ⓐⓑⓒⓓ	2. ⓐⓑⓒⓓ	3. ⓐⓑⓒⓓ	4. ⓐⓑⓒⓓ	5. ⓐⓑⓒⓓ
	6. ⓐⓑⓒⓓ	7. ⓐⓑⓒⓓ	8. ⓐⓑⓒⓓ	9. ⓐⓑⓒⓓ	10. ⓐⓑⓒⓓ
	11. ⓐⓑⓒⓓ	12. ⓐⓑⓒⓓ	13. ⓐⓑⓒⓓ	14. ⓐⓑⓒⓓ	15. ⓐⓑⓒⓓ
	16. ⓐⓑⓒⓓ	17. ⓐⓑⓒⓓ	18. ⓐⓑⓒⓓ	19. ⓐⓑⓒⓓ	20. ⓐⓑⓒⓓ

SQUARE ROOTS & CUBE ROOTS

101 SPEED TEST

Max. Marks : 20 **No. of Qs. 20** **Time : 20 min.** **Date : ..../........./.................**

1. The smallest number by which 136 must be multiplied so that it becomes a perfect square is
   - (a) 2
   - (b) 17
   - (c) 34
   - (d) None of these

2. The smallest number by which 3888 must be divided so that the resulting number is a perfect square is
   - (a) 2
   - (b) 6
   - (c) 3
   - (d) None of these.

3. The product of two numbers is 1936. If one number is 4 times the other, the numbers are
   - (a) $16, 121$
   - (b) $22, 88$
   - (c) $44, 44$
   - (d) None of these.

4. The least square number exactly divisible by 4, 6, 10, 15 is
   - (a) 400
   - (b) 100
   - (c) 25
   - (d) 900

5. The least 6 digit number which is perfect square is
   - (a) 100000
   - (b) 100144
   - (c) 100489
   - (d) 100225

6. The least number to be subtracted from 24136 to make it a perfect square
   - (a) 155
   - (b) 111
   - (c) 156
   - (d) None of these.

7. What must be added to 24136 to make it a perfect square?
   - (a) 100
   - (b) 200
   - (c) 111
   - (d) None of these.

8. Area of a square field is 22500 m^2. A man cycles along its boundary at 15 km/ hr. The time will be taken by a man to return to starting point, is
   - (a) 2 min 24 sec.
   - (b) 3 min 12 sec.
   - (c) 4 mins.
   - (d) None of these.

9. The value of $\sqrt{388 + \sqrt{127 + \sqrt{289}}}$ is
   - (a) 17
   - (b) 12
   - (c) 20
   - (d) None of these.

10. A gardener arranges plants in rows to form a square. He finds that in doing so 15 plants are left out. If the total number of plants are 3984, the number of plants in each row are,
    - (a) 62
    - (b) 63
    - (c) 64
    - (d) None of these.

11. The area of a circular play ground is $\dfrac{3168}{7}$ m^2. The diameter of the ground is
    - (a) 12 m
    - (b) 22 m
    - (c) 24 m
    - (d) 6 m

12. A least four digit perfect square whose first two digits and last two digits taken separately are also perfect squares, is:
    - (a) 6481
    - (b) 4925
    - (c) 3625
    - (d) 1681

13. You have a rectangular frame that is 40 cm by 60 cm. Can you put a square picture that has an area of 800 cm^2 completely inside the frame?
    - (a) Yes
    - (b) No
    - (c) Can't say
    - (d) Data insufficient

14. The hypotenuse of an isosceles right angled triangular field has a length of $30\sqrt{2}$ m, the length of other side is
    - (a) $30\sqrt{2}$
    - (b) 30 m
    - (c) 25 m
    - (d) None of these

15. The smallest number which when multiplied with 7200 will make the product a perfect cube, is
    - (a) 10
    - (b) 20
    - (c) 30
    - (d) None of these.

16. The three numbers are in the ratio 2 : 3 : 4. The sum of their cubes is 33957. The numbers are,
    - (a) $6, 9, 12$
    - (b) $4, 6, 8$
    - (c) $12, 18, 24$
    - (d) $14, 21, 28$

17. Value of $\sqrt[3]{392} \times \sqrt[3]{448}$ is
    - (a) 50
    - (b) 52
    - (c) 54
    - (d) 56

18. A $8 \times 6 \times 4$ cm^3 metallic cube is melted. The minimum volume of molten metal which should be added to mould it into a cube whose edge is 'x' where 'x' is an integer, is
    - (a) 20 cm^3
    - (b) 21 cm^3
    - (c) 23 cm^3
    - (d) 24 cm^3

19. The volumes of two cubes are in the ratio 343 : 1331, the ratio of their edges, is
    - (a) 7 : 10
    - (b) 7 : 11
    - (c) 7 : 12
    - (d) None of these.

20. The square of a natural number when subtracted from its cube results in 48. The number is
    - (a) 6
    - (b) 5
    - (c) 4
    - (d) 8

RESPONSE GRID	1. ⓐⓑⓒⓓ	2. ⓐⓑⓒⓓ	3. ⓐⓑⓒⓓ	4. ⓐⓑⓒⓓ	5. ⓐⓑⓒⓓ
	6. ⓐⓑⓒⓓ	7. ⓐⓑⓒⓓ	8. ⓐⓑⓒⓓ	9. ⓐⓑⓒⓓ	10. ⓐⓑⓒⓓ
	11. ⓐⓑⓒⓓ	12. ⓐⓑⓒⓓ	13. ⓐⓑⓒⓓ	14. ⓐⓑⓒⓓ	15. ⓐⓑⓒⓓ
	16. ⓐⓑⓒⓓ	17. ⓐⓑⓒⓓ	18. ⓐⓑⓒⓓ	19. ⓐⓑⓒⓓ	20. ⓐⓑⓒⓓ

RATIO, PROPORTION & PARTNERSHIP

101 SPEED TEST — 6

Max. Marks : 20 **No. of Qs. 20** **Time : 20 min.** **Date : ..../........./.................**

1. There is a ratio of 5 : 4 between two numbers. If 40 % of the first number is 12 then what would be the 50% of the second number?
   (a) 12
   (b) 24
   (c) 18
   (d) None of these.

2. An amount of money is to be distributed among P, Q and R in the ratio of 5 : 8 : 12 respectively. If the total share of Q and R is four times that of P, what is definitely P's share?
   (a) Rs. 3000
   (b) Rs. 5000
   (c) Rs. 8000
   (d) Data insufficient.

3. The numerator and denominator of a fraction are in the ratio of 2 : 3. If 6 is subtracted from the numerator, the result is a fraction that has a value 2/3 of the original fraction. The numerator of the original fraction is
   (a) 6
   (b) 18
   (c) 27
   (d) 36

4. If $A : B : C = 2 : 3 : 4$. then $\dfrac{A}{B} : \dfrac{B}{C} : \dfrac{C}{A}$ is equal to
   (a) $4 : 9 : 16$
   (b) $8 : 9 : 12$
   (c) $8 : 9 : 16$
   (d) $8 : 9 : 24$

5. In a school, the ratio of boys to girls is 4 : 5. When 100 girls leave the school, the ratio becomes 6 : 7. How many boys are there in the school?
   (a) 1600
   (b) 1500
   (c) 1300
   (d) None of these

6. A person distributes his pens among four friends A, B, C, D in the ratio $\dfrac{1}{3} : \dfrac{1}{4} : \dfrac{1}{5} : \dfrac{1}{6}$. The minimum number of pens that the person should have is
   (a) 59
   (b) 58
   (c) 57
   (d) 50

7. What least number must be subtracted from each of the numbers 21, 38, 55, 106 so that they becomes in proportional.
   (a) 2
   (b) 3
   (c) 4
   (d) 5

8. The third proportional between $\left(a^2 - b^2\right)$ and $(a + b)^2$ is
   (a) $\dfrac{a+b}{a-b}$
   (b) $\dfrac{a-b}{a+b}$
   (c) $\dfrac{(a-b)^2}{a+b}$
   (d) $\dfrac{(a+b)^3}{a-b}$

9. If $\dfrac{5x-3y}{5y-3x} = \dfrac{3}{4}$, then value of $\dfrac{x}{y}$ is
   (a) 2 : 9
   (b) 7 : 2
   (c) 7 : 9
   (d) None of these.

10. Some 1 rupee, 50 paisa and 25 paise coins make up ₹ 93.75 and their number are in proportion 3 : 4 : 5. The number of each type of coins, are
    (a) 40, 70, 75
    (b) 46, 58, 75
    (c) 42, 56, 70
    (d) 45, 60, 75

11. If $(a+b) : (b+c) : (c+a) = 6 : 7 : 8$ and $a + b + c = 14$, then the value of 'c' is
    (a) 8
    (b) 7
    (c) 6
    (d) 12

12. The monthly salary of A, B and C is in the proportion 2 : 3 : 5. If C's monthly salary is ₹ 1200 more than A's monthly salary then B's annual salary is
    (a) ₹ 14400
    (b) ₹ 24000
    (c) ₹ 1200
    (d) ₹ 2000

13. In 30 litres mixture of milk and water, the ratio of milk and water is 7 : 3. Find the quantity of water to be added in the mixture in order to make this ratio 3 : 7.
    (a) 30 litres
    (b) 40 litres
    (c) 20 litres
    (d) 10 litres

14. The ratio of three numbers is 3 : 4 : 5 and sum of their squares is 1250. The sum of the numbers is
    (a) 30
    (b) 50
    (c) 60
    (d) 90

15. The sum of three numbers is 98. If the ratio of first to the second is 2 : 3 and that of the second to the third is 5 : 8, then the second number is
    (a) 20
    (b) 30
    (c) 48
    (d) 58

16. Two whole numbers whose sum is 72 cannot be in the ratio
    (a) 5 : 7
    (b) 4 : 5
    (c) 3 : 5
    (d) 3 : 4

17. Seats for mathematics, physics and biology in a school are in the ratio 5 : 7 : 8. There is a proposal to increase these seats by 40 %, 50% and 75% respectively. The ratio of increased seats will be
    (a) 2 : 3 : 4
    (b) 6 : 8 : 9
    (c) 6 : 7 : 8
    (d) None of these.

18. The ages of A and B are in the ratio 3 : 1. 15 year hence the ratio will be 2 : 1. Their present ages are
    (a) 45 yrs, 15yrs
    (b) 60 yrs, 20 yrs
    (c) 30 yrs, 10 yrs
    (d) 21 yrs, 7 yrs

19. The sides of a triangle are in the ratio $\dfrac{1}{2} : \dfrac{1}{3} : \dfrac{1}{4}$ and its perimeter is 104 cm. The length of the longest side is
    (a) 48 cm
    (b) 32 cm
    (c) 26 cm
    (d) 52 cm.

20. If $(x + 4) : (3x + 15)$ is the triplicate of 2 : 3, then the value of x is
    (a) 1
    (b) 3
    (c) 4
    (d) None of these

RESPONSE GRID	1. ⓐⓑⓒⓓ	2. ⓐⓑⓒⓓ	3. ⓐⓑⓒⓓ	4. ⓐⓑⓒⓓ	5. ⓐⓑⓒⓓ
	6. ⓐⓑⓒⓓ	7. ⓐⓑⓒⓓ	8. ⓐⓑⓒⓓ	9. ⓐⓑⓒⓓ	10. ⓐⓑⓒⓓ
	11. ⓐⓑⓒⓓ	12. ⓐⓑⓒⓓ	13. ⓐⓑⓒⓓ	14. ⓐⓑⓒⓓ	15. ⓐⓑⓒⓓ
	16. ⓐⓑⓒⓓ	17. ⓐⓑⓒⓓ	18. ⓐⓑⓒⓓ	19. ⓐⓑⓒⓓ	20. ⓐⓑⓒⓓ

Max. Marks : 20   **No. of Qs. 20**   **Time : 20 min.**   Date : ..../........./................

1. The average age of the family of five members is 24. If the present age of youngest member is 8 yr, then what was the average age of the family at the time of the birth of the youngest member ?
   (a) 20 yr   (b) 16 yr   (c) 12 yr   (d) 18 yr

2. The sum of five numbers is 924. The average of first two numbers is 201.5 and the average of last two number is 196. What is the third number ?
   (a) 133   (b) 129
   (c) 122   (d) Cannot be determined

3. The average marks of 65 students in a class was calculated as 150. It was later realised that the marks of one of the students was calculated as 142, whereas his actual marks were 152. What is the actual average marks of the group of 65 students ? (Rounded off to two digits after decimal)
   (a) 151.25   (b) 150.15   (c) 151.10   (d) 150.19

4. The average marks in Science subject of a class of 20 students is 68. If the marks of two students were misread as 48 and 65 of the actual marks 72 and 61 respectively, then what would be the correct average ?
   (a) 68.5   (b) 69   (c) 69.5   (d) 70

5. The average weight of A, B and C is 84 kg. If D joins the group, the average weight of the group becomes 80 kg. If another man E who weighs 3 kg more than D replaces A, then the average of B, C, D and E becomes 79 kg. What is the weight of A?
   (a) 64 kg   (b) 72 kg   (c) 75 kg   (d) 80 kg

6. The average of 11 results is 50. If the average of first 6 results is 49 an that of last 6 is 52, find the 6th result.
   (a) 50   (b) 52   (c) 56   (d) 60

7. The average of 30 observations is 45. If three new observations 42, 44 and 48 be added, find the new average.
   (a) 42.9   (b) 40.1   (c) 42.4   (d) 44.9

8. Average of two numbers is 14.5 and square root of their product is 10. What are the numbers?
   (a) 25, 4   (b) 20, 5
   (c) 10, 15   (d) Cannot be determined

9. If average of 25 numbers is 30. If each no. decrease by 10. Then find new average of these no.
   (a) 15   (b) 20   (c) 30   (d) 40

10. A person divides his total route of journey into three equal parts and decides to travel the three parts with speeds of 40, 30 and 15 km/hr respectively. Find his average speed during the whole journey.
    (a) 14 km/hr   (b) 24 km/hr
    (c) 34 km/hr   (d) 44 km/hr

11. The average age of a lady and her daughter is 28.5. The ratio of their ages is 14 : 5 respectively. What is the daughters age?
    (a) 12 years   (b) 15 years
    (c) 18 years   (d) Cannot be determined

12. The age of a man is 4 times that of his son. 5 yrs ago, the man was nine times as old as his son was at that time. What is the present age of the man?
    (a) 28 yrs   (b) 32 yrs   (c) 40 yrs   (d) 42 yrs

13. After 5 yrs, the age of a father will be thrice the age of his son, whereas five years ago, he was 7 times as old as his son was. What are their present ages?
    (a) 30 yrs   (b) 40 yrs   (c) 50 yrs   (d) 60 yrs

14. The ratio of the father's age to the son's age is 4 : 1. The product of their ages is 196. What will be the ratio of their ages after 5 years?
    (a) 7 : 3   (b) 14 : 9   (c) 11 : 4   (d) 17 : 3

15. A man's age is 125% of what it was 10 years ago, but $83\frac{1}{3}\%$ of what it will be after 10 years. What is his present age?
    (a) 30 yrs   (b) 40 yrs   (c) 50 yrs   (d) 60 yrs

16. In a family, a couple has a son and daughter. The age of the father is three times that of his daughter and the age of the son is half of his mother. The wife is nine years younger to her husband and the brother is seven years older than his sister. What is the age of the mother?
    (a) 40 years   (b) 45 years   (c) 50 years   (d) 60 years

17. Abhay's age after six years will be three-seventh of his father's age. Ten years ago, the ratio of their ages was 1 : 5. What is Abhay's father's age at present?
    (a) 30 yrs.   (b) 40 yrs.   (c) 50 yrs.   (d) 60 yrs.

18. Tanya's grandfather was 8 times older to her 16 years ago. He would be 3 times of her age 8 years from now. Eight years ago, what was the ratio of Tanya's age to that of her grandfather?
    (a) 1 : 2   (b) 1 : 5   (c) 3 : 8   (d) 11 : 53

19. The sum of the ages of 5 children born at the intervals of 3 years each is 50 years. What is the age of the youngest child?
    (a) 4 years   (b) 8 years   (c) 10 years   (d) 12 years

20. Eighteen years ago, a father was three times as old as his son. Now the father is only twice as old as his son. Then the sum of the present ages of the son and the father is:
    (a) 54   (b) 72   (c) 105   (d) 108

RESPONSE GRID	1. ⓐⓑⓒⓓ	2. ⓐⓑⓒⓓ	3. ⓐⓑⓒⓓ	4. ⓐⓑⓒⓓ	5. ⓐⓑⓒⓓ
	6. ⓐⓑⓒⓓ	7. ⓐⓑⓒⓓ	8. ⓐⓑⓒⓓ	9. ⓐⓑⓒⓓ	10. ⓐⓑⓒⓓ
	11. ⓐⓑⓒⓓ	12. ⓐⓑⓒⓓ	13. ⓐⓑⓒⓓ	14. ⓐⓑⓒⓓ	15. ⓐⓑⓒⓓ
	16. ⓐⓑⓒⓓ	17. ⓐⓑⓒⓓ	18. ⓐⓑⓒⓓ	19. ⓐⓑⓒⓓ	20. ⓐⓑⓒⓓ

PERCENTAGE

101 SPEED TEST — 8

Max. Marks : 20   **No. of Qs. 20**   **Time : 20 min.**   **Date : ..../........./................**

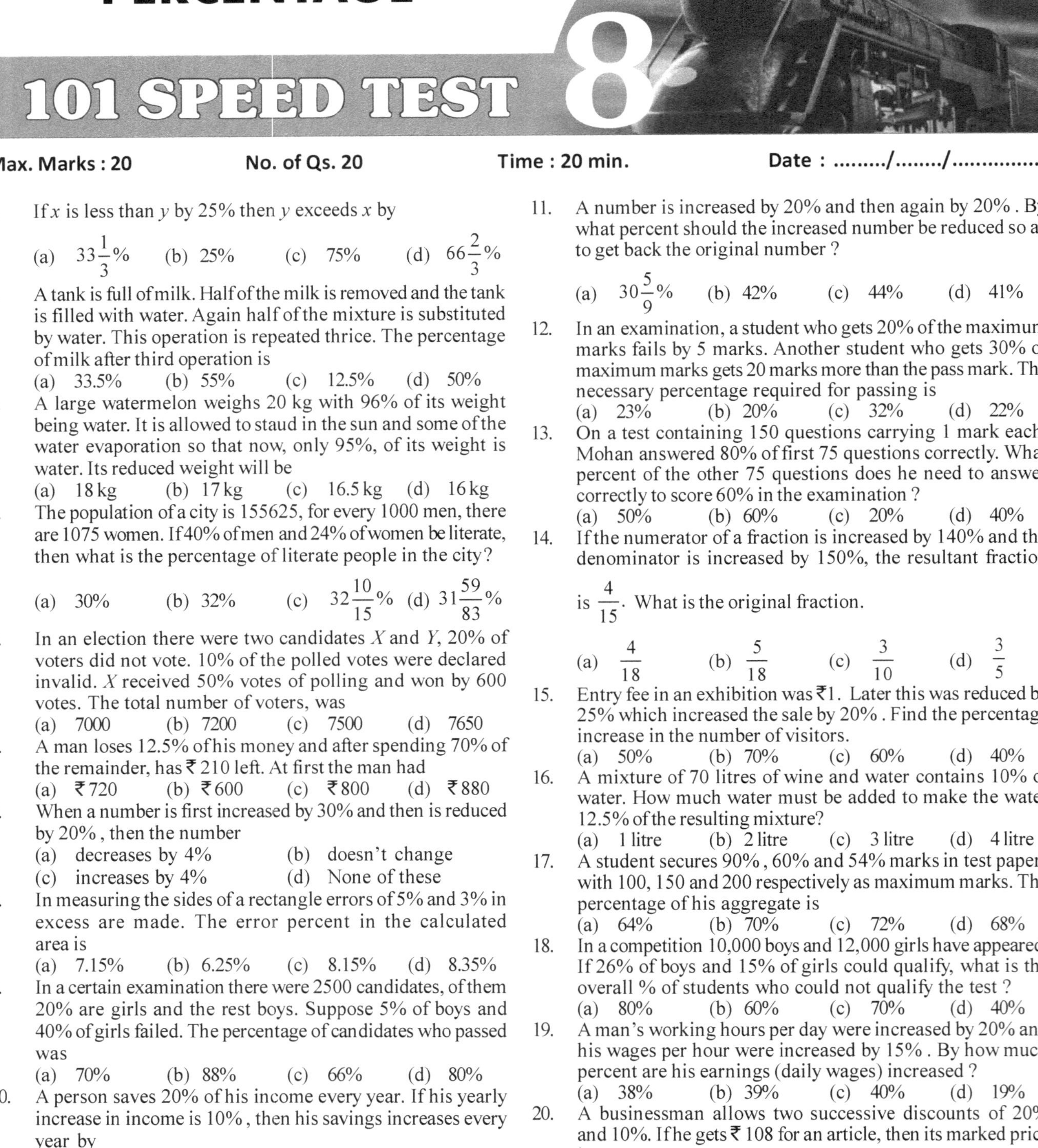

1. If x is less than y by 25% then y exceeds x by
   (a) $33\frac{1}{3}\%$ (b) 25%   (c) 75%   (d) $66\frac{2}{3}\%$

2. A tank is full of milk. Half of the milk is removed and the tank is filled with water. Again half of the mixture is substituted by water. This operation is repeated thrice. The percentage of milk after third operation is
   (a) 33.5%   (b) 55%   (c) 12.5%   (d) 50%

3. A large watermelon weighs 20 kg with 96% of its weight being water. It is allowed to staud in the sun and some of the water evaporation so that now, only 95%, of its weight is water. Its reduced weight will be
   (a) 18 kg   (b) 17 kg   (c) 16.5 kg   (d) 16 kg

4. The population of a city is 155625, for every 1000 men, there are 1075 women. If 40% of men and 24% of women be literate, then what is the percentage of literate people in the city?
   (a) 30%   (b) 32%   (c) $32\frac{10}{15}\%$ (d) $31\frac{59}{83}\%$

5. In an election there were two candidates X and Y, 20% of voters did not vote. 10% of the polled votes were declared invalid. X received 50% votes of polling and won by 600 votes. The total number of voters, was
   (a) 7000   (b) 7200   (c) 7500   (d) 7650

6. A man loses 12.5% of his money and after spending 70% of the remainder, has ₹210 left. At first the man had
   (a) ₹720   (b) ₹600   (c) ₹800   (d) ₹880

7. When a number is first increased by 30% and then is reduced by 20%, then the number
   (a) decreases by 4%   (b) doesn't change
   (c) increases by 4%   (d) None of these

8. In measuring the sides of a rectangle errors of 5% and 3% in excess are made. The error percent in the calculated area is
   (a) 7.15%   (b) 6.25%   (c) 8.15%   (d) 8.35%

9. In a certain examination there were 2500 candidates, of them 20% are girls and the rest boys. Suppose 5% of boys and 40% of girls failed. The percentage of candidates who passed was
   (a) 70%   (b) 88%   (c) 66%   (d) 80%

10. A person saves 20% of his income every year. If his yearly increase in income is 10%, then his savings increases every year by
    (a) 10%   (b) 6%   (c) 5%   (d) 4%

11. A number is increased by 20% and then again by 20%. By what percent should the increased number be reduced so as to get back the original number?
    (a) $30\frac{5}{9}\%$ (b) 42%   (c) 44%   (d) 41%

12. In an examination, a student who gets 20% of the maximum marks fails by 5 marks. Another student who gets 30% of maximum marks gets 20 marks more than the pass mark. The necessary percentage required for passing is
    (a) 23%   (b) 20%   (c) 32%   (d) 22%

13. On a test containing 150 questions carrying 1 mark each, Mohan answered 80% of first 75 questions correctly. What percent of the other 75 questions does he need to answer correctly to score 60% in the examination?
    (a) 50%   (b) 60%   (c) 20%   (d) 40%

14. If the numerator of a fraction is increased by 140% and the denominator is increased by 150%, the resultant fraction is $\frac{4}{15}$. What is the original fraction.
    (a) $\frac{4}{18}$ (b) $\frac{5}{18}$ (c) $\frac{3}{10}$ (d) $\frac{3}{5}$

15. Entry fee in an exhibition was ₹1. Later this was reduced by 25% which increased the sale by 20%. Find the percentage increase in the number of visitors.
    (a) 50%   (b) 70%   (c) 60%   (d) 40%

16. A mixture of 70 litres of wine and water contains 10% of water. How much water must be added to make the water 12.5% of the resulting mixture?
    (a) 1 litre   (b) 2 litre   (c) 3 litre   (d) 4 litre

17. A student secures 90%, 60% and 54% marks in test papers with 100, 150 and 200 respectively as maximum marks. The percentage of his aggregate is
    (a) 64%   (b) 70%   (c) 72%   (d) 68%

18. In a competition 10,000 boys and 12,000 girls have appeared. If 26% of boys and 15% of girls could qualify, what is the overall % of students who could not qualify the test?
    (a) 80%   (b) 60%   (c) 70%   (d) 40%

19. A man's working hours per day were increased by 20% and his wages per hour were increased by 15%. By how much percent are his earnings (daily wages) increased?
    (a) 38%   (b) 39%   (c) 40%   (d) 19%

20. A businessman allows two successive discounts of 20% and 10%. If he gets ₹108 for an article, then its marked price is
    (a) ₹124   (b) ₹140   (c) ₹150   (d) ₹170

RESPONSE GRID	1. ⓐⓑⓒⓓ	2. ⓐⓑⓒⓓ	3. ⓐⓑⓒⓓ	4. ⓐⓑⓒⓓ	5. ⓐⓑⓒⓓ
	6. ⓐⓑⓒⓓ	7. ⓐⓑⓒⓓ	8. ⓐⓑⓒⓓ	9. ⓐⓑⓒⓓ	10. ⓐⓑⓒⓓ
	11. ⓐⓑⓒⓓ	12. ⓐⓑⓒⓓ	13. ⓐⓑⓒⓓ	14. ⓐⓑⓒⓓ	15. ⓐⓑⓒⓓ
	16. ⓐⓑⓒⓓ	17. ⓐⓑⓒⓓ	18. ⓐⓑⓒⓓ	19. ⓐⓑⓒⓓ	20. ⓐⓑⓒⓓ

PROFIT & LOSS

101 SPEED TEST

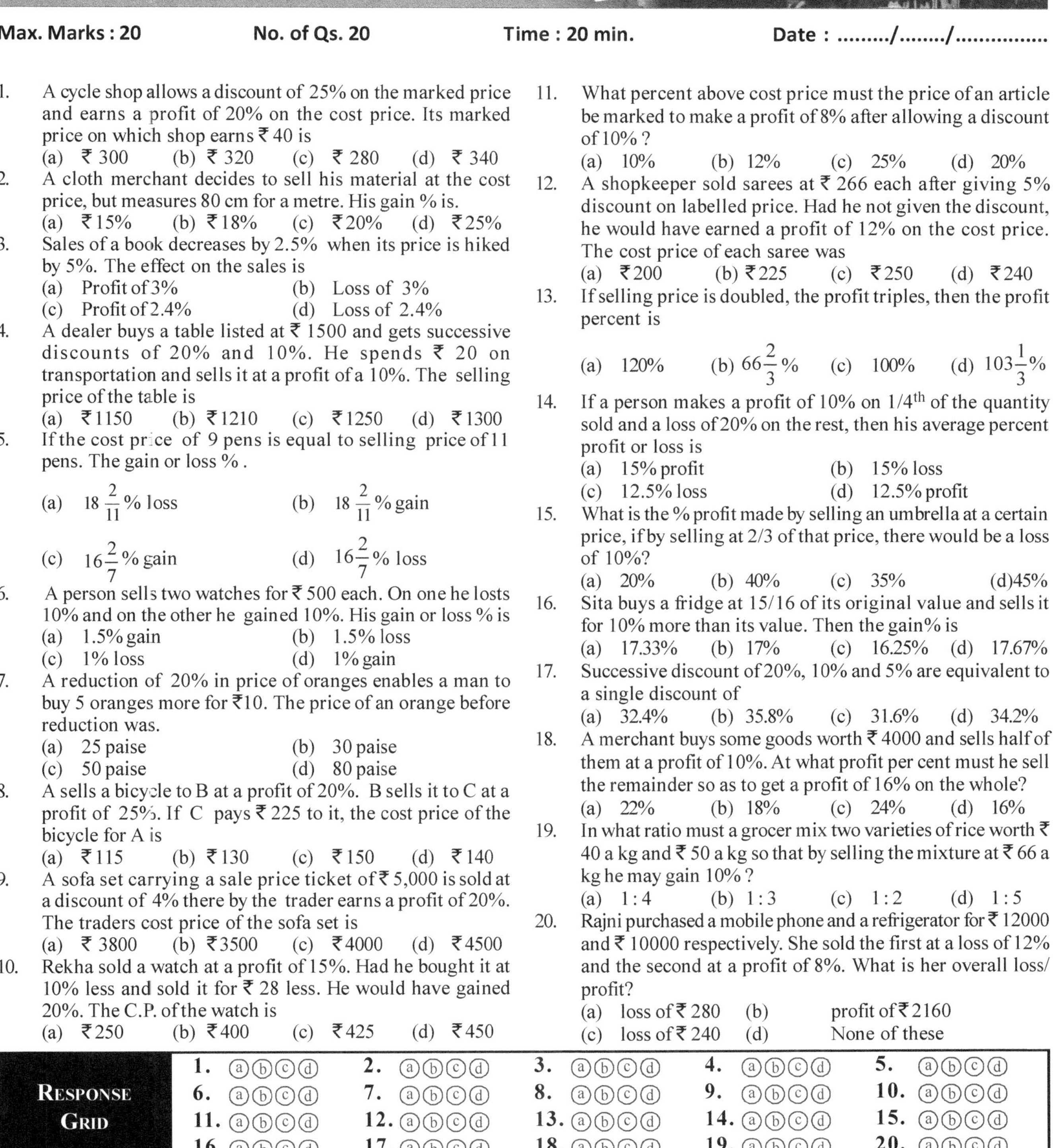

Max. Marks : 20   **No. of Qs. 20**   **Time : 20 min.**   Date : ..../........./...............

1. A cycle shop allows a discount of 25% on the marked price and earns a profit of 20% on the cost price. Its marked price on which shop earns ₹ 40 is
   (a) ₹ 300   (b) ₹ 320   (c) ₹ 280   (d) ₹ 340

2. A cloth merchant decides to sell his material at the cost price, but measures 80 cm for a metre. His gain % is.
   (a) ₹ 15%   (b) ₹ 18%   (c) ₹ 20%   (d) ₹ 25%

3. Sales of a book decreases by 2.5% when its price is hiked by 5%. The effect on the sales is
   (a) Profit of 3%   (b) Loss of 3%
   (c) Profit of 2.4%   (d) Loss of 2.4%

4. A dealer buys a table listed at ₹ 1500 and gets successive discounts of 20% and 10%. He spends ₹ 20 on transportation and sells it at a profit of a 10%. The selling price of the table is
   (a) ₹ 1150   (b) ₹ 1210   (c) ₹ 1250   (d) ₹ 1300

5. If the cost price of 9 pens is equal to selling price of 11 pens. The gain or loss % .
   (a) $18\frac{2}{11}\%$ loss   (b) $18\frac{2}{11}\%$ gain
   (c) $16\frac{2}{7}\%$ gain   (d) $16\frac{2}{7}\%$ loss

6. A person sells two watches for ₹ 500 each. On one he losts 10% and on the other he gained 10%. His gain or loss % is
   (a) 1.5% gain   (b) 1.5% loss
   (c) 1% loss   (d) 1% gain

7. A reduction of 20% in price of oranges enables a man to buy 5 oranges more for ₹10. The price of an orange before reduction was.
   (a) 25 paise   (b) 30 paise
   (c) 50 paise   (d) 80 paise

8. A sells a bicycle to B at a profit of 20%. B sells it to C at a profit of 25%. If C pays ₹ 225 to it, the cost price of the bicycle for A is
   (a) ₹ 115   (b) ₹ 130   (c) ₹ 150   (d) ₹ 140

9. A sofa set carrying a sale price ticket of ₹ 5,000 is sold at a discount of 4% there by the trader earns a profit of 20%. The traders cost price of the sofa set is
   (a) ₹ 3800   (b) ₹ 3500   (c) ₹ 4000   (d) ₹ 4500

10. Rekha sold a watch at a profit of 15%. Had he bought it at 10% less and sold it for ₹ 28 less. He would have gained 20%. The C.P. of the watch is
    (a) ₹ 250   (b) ₹ 400   (c) ₹ 425   (d) ₹ 450

11. What percent above cost price must the price of an article be marked to make a profit of 8% after allowing a discount of 10% ?
    (a) 10%   (b) 12%   (c) 25%   (d) 20%

12. A shopkeeper sold sarees at ₹ 266 each after giving 5% discount on labelled price. Had he not given the discount, he would have earned a profit of 12% on the cost price. The cost price of each saree was
    (a) ₹ 200   (b) ₹ 225   (c) ₹ 250   (d) ₹ 240

13. If selling price is doubled, the profit triples, then the profit percent is
    (a) 120%   (b) $66\frac{2}{3}\%$ (c) 100%   (d) $103\frac{1}{3}\%$

14. If a person makes a profit of 10% on 1/4th of the quantity sold and a loss of 20% on the rest, then his average percent profit or loss is
    (a) 15% profit   (b) 15% loss
    (c) 12.5% loss   (d) 12.5% profit

15. What is the % profit made by selling an umbrella at a certain price, if by selling at 2/3 of that price, there would be a loss of 10%?
    (a) 20%   (b) 40%   (c) 35%   (d)45%

16. Sita buys a fridge at 15/16 of its original value and sells it for 10% more than its value. Then the gain% is
    (a) 17.33%   (b) 17%   (c) 16.25%   (d) 17.67%

17. Successive discount of 20%, 10% and 5% are equivalent to a single discount of
    (a) 32.4%   (b) 35.8%   (c) 31.6%   (d) 34.2%

18. A merchant buys some goods worth ₹ 4000 and sells half of them at a profit of 10%. At what profit per cent must he sell the remainder so as to get a profit of 16% on the whole?
    (a) 22%   (b) 18%   (c) 24%   (d) 16%

19. In what ratio must a grocer mix two varieties of rice worth ₹ 40 a kg and ₹ 50 a kg so that by selling the mixture at ₹ 66 a kg he may gain 10% ?
    (a) 1 : 4   (b) 1 : 3   (c) 1 : 2   (d) 1 : 5

20. Rajni purchased a mobile phone and a refrigerator for ₹ 12000 and ₹ 10000 respectively. She sold the first at a loss of 12% and the second at a profit of 8%. What is her overall loss/profit?
    (a) loss of ₹ 280   (b) profit of ₹ 2160
    (c) loss of ₹ 240   (d) None of these

RESPONSE GRID	1. ⓐⓑⓒⓓ	2. ⓐⓑⓒⓓ	3. ⓐⓑⓒⓓ	4. ⓐⓑⓒⓓ	5. ⓐⓑⓒⓓ
	6. ⓐⓑⓒⓓ	7. ⓐⓑⓒⓓ	8. ⓐⓑⓒⓓ	9. ⓐⓑⓒⓓ	10. ⓐⓑⓒⓓ
	11. ⓐⓑⓒⓓ	12. ⓐⓑⓒⓓ	13. ⓐⓑⓒⓓ	14. ⓐⓑⓒⓓ	15. ⓐⓑⓒⓓ
	16. ⓐⓑⓒⓓ	17. ⓐⓑⓒⓓ	18. ⓐⓑⓒⓓ	19. ⓐⓑⓒⓓ	20. ⓐⓑⓒⓓ

TIME & WORK

101 SPEED TEST — 10

Max. Marks : 20 **No. of Qs. 20** **Time : 20 min.** **Date : ..../........./................**

1. If 30 men do a piece of work in 27 days, in what time can 18 men do another piece of work 2 times as great ?
   (a) 80 days (b) 70 days
   (c) 90 days (d) None of these

2. If 18 binders bind 900 books in 10 days, how many binders will be required to bind 660 books in 12 days ?
   (a) 14 (b) 13 (c) 22 (d) 11

3. If a family of 7 persons can live on Rs.8400 for 36 days, how long can a family of 9 persons live on Rs.8100 ?
   (a) 27 days (b) 37 days (c) 36 days (d) 24 days

4. If 1000 copies of a book of 13 sheets required 26 reams of paper, how much paper is required for 5000 copies of a book of 17 sheets ?
   (a) 270 reams (b) 170 reams
   (c) 180 reams (d) 140 reams

5. 5 horses eat 18 quintals of oats in 9 days, how long at the same rate will 66 quintals last for 15 horses ?
   (a) 99 days (b) 93 days (c) 92 days (d) 91 days

6. If the carriage of 810 kg for 70 km costs Rs.112.50, what will be the cost of the carriage of 840 kg for a distance of 63 km at half the former rate ?
   (a) Rs.50.5 (b) Rs.52 (c) Rs.52.5 (d) Rs.53

7. If 27 men take 15 days to mow 225 hectares of grass, how long will 33 men take to mow 165 hectare ?
   (a) 9 days (b) 18 days (c) 6 days (d) 12 days

8. If 6 men can do a piece of work in 30 days of 9 hours each, how many men will it take to do 10 times the amount of work if they work 25 days of 8 hours each ?
   (a) 81 men (b) 80 men (c) 79 men (d) 82 men

9. A gang of labors promise to do a piece of work in 10 days, but 5 out of them become absent. If the rest of the gang do the work in 12 days, find the original number of men.
   (a) 30 (b) 40 (c) 25 (d) 35

10. If 10 masons can build a wall 50 meters long in 25 days of 8 hours each, in how many days of 6 hours each will 15 masons build a wall 36 metres long ?
    (a) 15 days (b) 24 days (c) 18 days (d) 16 days

11. X and Y can do a piece of work in 72 days. Y and Z can do it in 120 days. X and Z can do it in 90 days. In how many days all the three together can do the work ?
    (a) 100 days (b) 150 days (c) 60 days (d) 80 days

12. 8 men and 2 children can do a work in 9 days. A child takes double the time to do a work than the man. In how many days 12 men can complete double the work ?

    (a) $16\frac{1}{2}$ days (b) $10\frac{1}{2}$ days (c) 14 days (d) 21 days

13. P is 3 times more efficient than Q, and is therefore able to complete a work in 60 days earlier. The number of days that P and Q together will take to complete the work is

    (a) $22\frac{1}{2}$ (b) 30 (c) 25 (d) $27\frac{1}{2}$

14. A can do $\frac{1}{2}$ work in 5 days. B can do $\frac{3}{5}$ of same work in 9 days and C can do $\frac{2}{3}$ of that work in 8 days. In how many days can three of them together do the work.

    (a) 5 days (b) $4\frac{1}{2}$ days (c) 3 days (d) 4 days

15. If 6 men and 8 boys can do a piece of work in 10 days and 26 men and 48 boys can do the same work in 2 days, the time taken by 15 men and 20 boys to do the same type of work will be
    (a) 6 days (b) 4 days (c) 8 days (d) 7 days.

16. A and B can do a piece of work in 40 days. After working for 10 days they are assisted by 'C' and work is finished in 20 days more. If 'C' does as much work as B does in 3 days, in how many days A alone can do the work.
    (a) 52 days (b) 48 days (c) 64 days (d) 35 days

17. To complete a work, A takes 50% more time than B. If together they take 18 days to complete the work, how much time shall B take to do it?
    (a) 30 days (b) 42 days (c) 50 days (d) 48 days

18. 12 men can complete a piece of work in 36 days. 18 women can complete the same piece of work in 60 days. 8 men and 20 women work together for 20 days. If only women were to complete the remaining piece of work in 4 days, how many women would be required?
    (a) 30 (b) 70 (c) 44 (d) 65

19. A garrison of 3000 men has provision for 30 days. If after 10 days, they are reinforced by 1000 men, how long will the provision last?
    (a) 21 days (b) 15 days (c) 12 days (d) 16 days

20. The work done by man, a woman and a boy are in the ratio 3 : 2 : 1. There are 24 men, 20 women and 16 boys in a factory whose weekly wages amount to ₹ 224. What will be the yearly wages of 27 men, 40 women and 15 boys.
    (a) ₹16366 (b) ₹16466 (c) ₹16066 (d) ₹16016

RESPONSE GRID					
	1. ⓐⓑⓒⓓ	2. ⓐⓑⓒⓓ	3. ⓐⓑⓒⓓ	4. ⓐⓑⓒⓓ	5. ⓐⓑⓒⓓ
	6. ⓐⓑⓒⓓ	7. ⓐⓑⓒⓓ	8. ⓐⓑⓒⓓ	9. ⓐⓑⓒⓓ	10. ⓐⓑⓒⓓ
	11. ⓐⓑⓒⓓ	12. ⓐⓑⓒⓓ	13. ⓐⓑⓒⓓ	14. ⓐⓑⓒⓓ	15. ⓐⓑⓒⓓ
	16. ⓐⓑⓒⓓ	17. ⓐⓑⓒⓓ	18. ⓐⓑⓒⓓ	19. ⓐⓑⓒⓓ	20. ⓐⓑⓒⓓ

PIPES & CISTERNS

101 SPEED TEST — 11

Max. Marks : 20   **No. of Qs. 20**   **Time : 20 min.**   **Date : ..../........./................**

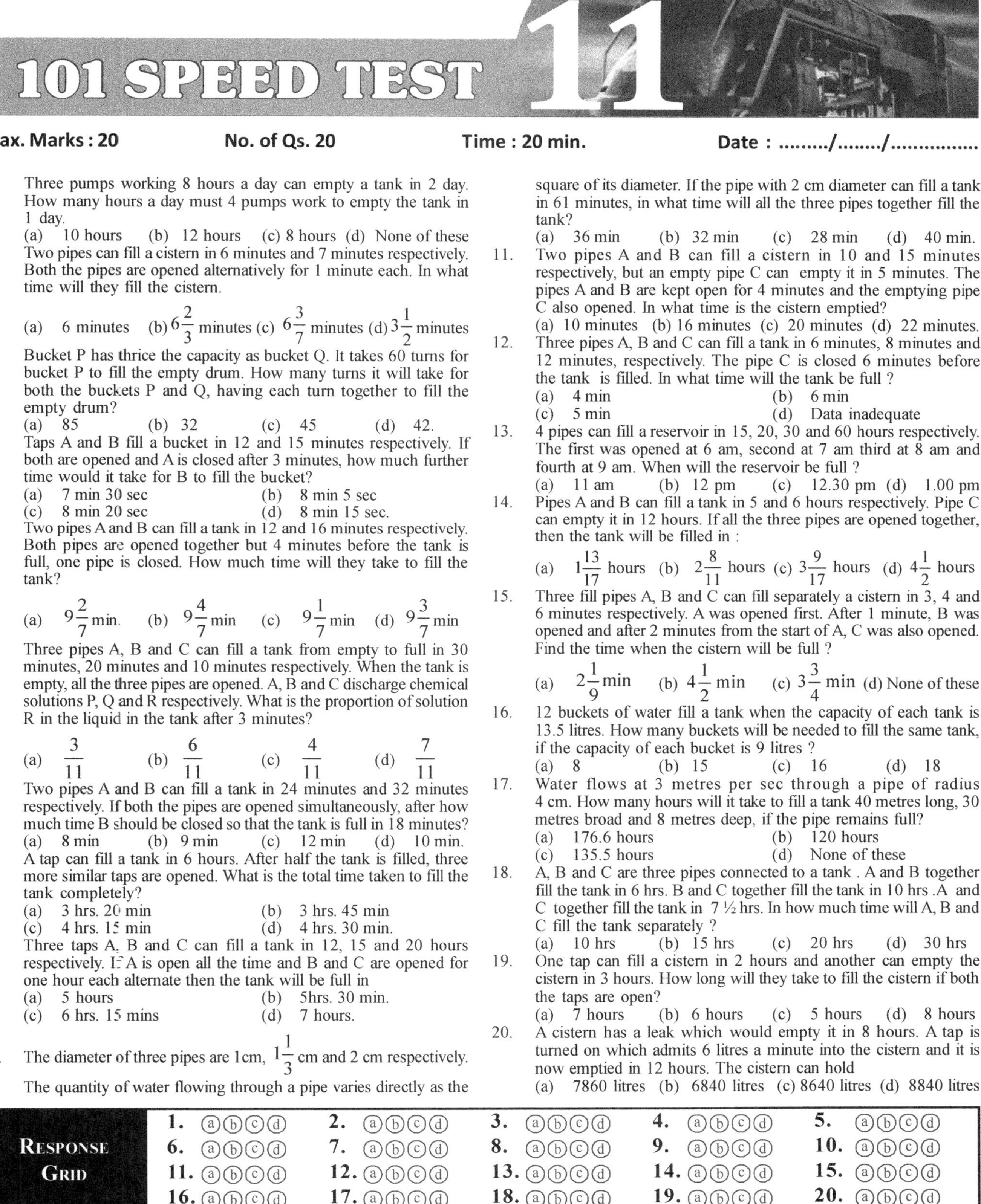

1. Three pumps working 8 hours a day can empty a tank in 2 day. How many hours a day must 4 pumps work to empty the tank in 1 day.
   (a) 10 hours   (b) 12 hours   (c) 8 hours   (d) None of these

2. Two pipes can fill a cistern in 6 minutes and 7 minutes respectively. Both the pipes are opened alternatively for 1 minute each. In what time will they fill the cistern.
   (a) 6 minutes   (b) $6\frac{2}{3}$ minutes   (c) $6\frac{3}{7}$ minutes   (d) $3\frac{1}{2}$ minutes

3. Bucket P has thrice the capacity as bucket Q. It takes 60 turns for bucket P to fill the empty drum. How many turns it will take for both the buckets P and Q, having each turn together to fill the empty drum?
   (a) 85   (b) 32   (c) 45   (d) 42.

4. Taps A and B fill a bucket in 12 and 15 minutes respectively. If both are opened and A is closed after 3 minutes, how much further time would it take for B to fill the bucket?
   (a) 7 min 30 sec   (b) 8 min 5 sec
   (c) 8 min 20 sec   (d) 8 min 15 sec.

5. Two pipes A and B can fill a tank in 12 and 16 minutes respectively. Both pipes are opened together but 4 minutes before the tank is full, one pipe is closed. How much time will they take to fill the tank?
   (a) $9\frac{2}{7}$ min.   (b) $9\frac{4}{7}$ min   (c) $9\frac{1}{7}$ min   (d) $9\frac{3}{7}$ min

6. Three pipes A, B and C can fill a tank from empty to full in 30 minutes, 20 minutes and 10 minutes respectively. When the tank is empty, all the three pipes are opened. A, B and C discharge chemical solutions P, Q and R respectively. What is the proportion of solution R in the liquid in the tank after 3 minutes?
   (a) $\frac{3}{11}$ (b) $\frac{6}{11}$ (c) $\frac{4}{11}$ (d) $\frac{7}{11}$

7. Two pipes A and B can fill a tank in 24 minutes and 32 minutes respectively. If both the pipes are opened simultaneously, after how much time B should be closed so that the tank is full in 18 minutes?
   (a) 8 min   (b) 9 min   (c) 12 min   (d) 10 min.

8. A tap can fill a tank in 6 hours. After half the tank is filled, three more similar taps are opened. What is the total time taken to fill the tank completely?
   (a) 3 hrs. 20 min   (b) 3 hrs. 45 min
   (c) 4 hrs. 15 min   (d) 4 hrs. 30 min.

9. Three taps A, B and C can fill a tank in 12, 15 and 20 hours respectively. If A is open all the time and B and C are opened for one hour each alternate then the tank will be full in
   (a) 5 hours   (b) 5hrs. 30 min.
   (c) 6 hrs. 15 mins   (d) 7 hours.

10. The diameter of three pipes are 1cm, $1\frac{1}{3}$ cm and 2 cm respectively. The quantity of water flowing through a pipe varies directly as the square of its diameter. If the pipe with 2 cm diameter can fill a tank in 61 minutes, in what time will all the three pipes together fill the tank?
    (a) 36 min   (b) 32 min   (c) 28 min   (d) 40 min.

11. Two pipes A and B can fill a cistern in 10 and 15 minutes respectively, but an empty pipe C can empty it in 5 minutes. The pipes A and B are kept open for 4 minutes and the emptying pipe C also opened. In what time is the cistern emptied?
    (a) 10 minutes   (b) 16 minutes   (c) 20 minutes   (d) 22 minutes.

12. Three pipes A, B and C can fill a tank in 6 minutes, 8 minutes and 12 minutes, respectively. The pipe C is closed 6 minutes before the tank is filled. In what time will the tank be full ?
    (a) 4 min   (b) 6 min
    (c) 5 min   (d) Data inadequate

13. 4 pipes can fill a reservoir in 15, 20, 30 and 60 hours respectively. The first was opened at 6 am, second at 7 am third at 8 am and fourth at 9 am. When will the reservoir be full ?
    (a) 11 am   (b) 12 pm   (c) 12.30 pm   (d) 1.00 pm

14. Pipes A and B can fill a tank in 5 and 6 hours respectively. Pipe C can empty it in 12 hours. If all the three pipes are opened together, then the tank will be filled in :
    (a) $1\frac{13}{17}$ hours   (b) $2\frac{8}{11}$ hours   (c) $3\frac{9}{17}$ hours   (d) $4\frac{1}{2}$ hours

15. Three fill pipes A, B and C can fill separately a cistern in 3, 4 and 6 minutes respectively. A was opened first. After 1 minute, B was opened and after 2 minutes from the start of A, C was also opened. Find the time when the cistern will be full ?
    (a) $2\frac{1}{9}$ min   (b) $4\frac{1}{2}$ min   (c) $3\frac{3}{4}$ min   (d) None of these

16. 12 buckets of water fill a tank when the capacity of each tank is 13.5 litres. How many buckets will be needed to fill the same tank, if the capacity of each bucket is 9 litres ?
    (a) 8   (b) 15   (c) 16   (d) 18

17. Water flows at 3 metres per sec through a pipe of radius 4 cm. How many hours will it take to fill a tank 40 metres long, 30 metres broad and 8 metres deep, if the pipe remains full?
    (a) 176.6 hours   (b) 120 hours
    (c) 135.5 hours   (d) None of these

18. A, B and C are three pipes connected to a tank . A and B together fill the tank in 6 hrs. B and C together fill the tank in 10 hrs .A and C together fill the tank in 7 ½ hrs. In how much time will A, B and C fill the tank separately ?
    (a) 10 hrs   (b) 15 hrs   (c) 20 hrs   (d) 30 hrs

19. One tap can fill a cistern in 2 hours and another can empty the cistern in 3 hours. How long will they take to fill the cistern if both the taps are open?
    (a) 7 hours   (b) 6 hours   (c) 5 hours   (d) 8 hours

20. A cistern has a leak which would empty it in 8 hours. A tap is turned on which admits 6 litres a minute into the cistern and it is now emptied in 12 hours. The cistern can hold
    (a) 7860 litres   (b) 6840 litres   (c) 8640 litres   (d) 8840 litres

RESPONSE GRID	1. ⓐⓑⓒⓓ	2. ⓐⓑⓒⓓ	3. ⓐⓑⓒⓓ	4. ⓐⓑⓒⓓ	5. ⓐⓑⓒⓓ
	6. ⓐⓑⓒⓓ	7. ⓐⓑⓒⓓ	8. ⓐⓑⓒⓓ	9. ⓐⓑⓒⓓ	10. ⓐⓑⓒⓓ
	11. ⓐⓑⓒⓓ	12. ⓐⓑⓒⓓ	13. ⓐⓑⓒⓓ	14. ⓐⓑⓒⓓ	15. ⓐⓑⓒⓓ
	16. ⓐⓑⓒⓓ	17. ⓐⓑⓒⓓ	18. ⓐⓑⓒⓓ	19. ⓐⓑⓒⓓ	20. ⓐⓑⓒⓓ

TIME, SPEED & DISTANCE

101 SPEED TEST — 12

Max. Marks : 20   **No. of Qs. 20**   **Time : 20 min.**   **Date : ..../......./...............**

1. A car moves 300 km at a speed of 45 kmph and then it increases its speed to 60 kmph to travel another 500 km. Find average speed of car.
   (a) $23\dfrac{1}{3}$ km/h   (b) $53\dfrac{1}{3}$ km/h   (c) 67 km/h   (d) 73 km/h

2. A man travels three-fifths of a distance AB at a speed of 3a and remaining at the speed of 2b. If he goes from B to A and back at a speed of 5c in the same time then
   (a) $\dfrac{1}{a}+\dfrac{1}{b}=\dfrac{2}{c}$ (b) $\dfrac{1}{a}+\dfrac{1}{b}=2c$
   (c) $a+b=c$ (d) None of these

3. A car complete a journey in 10 hours. He travels first half of the journey at the rate of 21 km/hr and second half at the rate of 24 km/hr. The total journey in km is
   (a) 224   (b) 230   (c) 234   (d) 220

4. My mother left for Nasik from Pune at 5.20 AM. She travelled at the speed of 50 km/hr for 2 hour 15 minutes. After that the speed was reduced to 60 km/hr. If the distance between two cities is 350 km, at what time did she reach Nasik?
   (a) 9.25 AM   (b) 9.35 AM
   (c) 9.20 AM   (d) None of these

5. In covering a certain distance, the speeds of A and B are in the ratio of 3 : 4. A takes 30 minutes more than B to reach the destination. The time taken by 'A' to reach the destination is
   (a) 1 hr   (b) 2 hrs   (c) $2\dfrac{1}{2}$ hrs   (d) $1\dfrac{1}{2}$ hrs

6. Two cars P and Q start at the same time from A and B which are 120 km apart. If the two cars travels in opposite directions, they meet after one hour and if they travel in same direction from A towards B, then P meets Q after 6 hours. The speed of car P is
   (a) 70 km/hr   (b) 120 km/hr (c) 60 km/hr (d) None of these

7. A man travels 600 km by train at 80 km/hr, 800 km by ship at 40 km/hr, 500 km by aeroplane at 400 km/hr and 100 km by car at 50 km/hr. The average speed for entire distance is
   (a) 70 km/hr   (b) $70\dfrac{5}{123}$ km/hr
   (c) $65\dfrac{5}{123}$ km/hr   (d) 72 km/hr

8. If a person walks at 14 km/hr instead of 10 km/hr, he would have walked 20 km more. The actual distance travelled by him is
   (a) 56 km   (b) 80 km   (c) 70 km   (d) 50 km

9. Excluding stoppages, the speed of a bus is 54 km/hr and including stoppages, it is 45 km/hr, for how many minutes does the bus stop per hour?
   (a) 12 minutes   (b) 8 minutes
   (c) 10 minutes   (d) None of these

10. A farmer travelled a distance of 61 km in 9 hours. He travelled partly on foot at the rate of 4 km/hr and partly on bicycle at rate of 9 km/hr. The distance travelled on foot is
    (a) 15 km   (b) 17 km   (c) 14 km   (d) 16 km

11. A car travelling with $\dfrac{5}{7}$ of its actual speed covers 42 km in 1 hr 40 min 48 sec. The actual speed of car is
    (a) 25 km/hr   (b) 28 km/hr
    (c) 35 km/hr   (d) $24\dfrac{3}{7}$ km/hr

12. With a uniform speed a car covers a distance in 8 hours. Had the speed been increased by 4 km/hr, the same distance could have been covered in $7\dfrac{1}{2}$ hours. The distance covered is
    (a) 400 km   (b) 450 km   (c) 480 km   (d) 380 km

13. The speed of a car increases by 2 kilometer after every one hour. If the distance travelled in the first one hour was 35 kilometers, then the total distance travelled in 12 hours was
    (a) 460 km   (b) 552 km   (c) 483 km   (d) 572 km

14. The jogging track in a stadium as 726 m in circumference. Rakesh and Ismail start from the same point and walk in opposite direction at 4.5 kmph and 3.75 kmph respectively. They will meet for the first time in
    (a) 4.7 min   (b) 5.65 min   (c) 5.28 min   (d) 6.2 min

15. Starting from his house, one day a student walks at a speed of $2\dfrac{1}{2}$ km / hr and reaches his school 6 minutes late. Next day he increases his speed by 1 km/hr and reaches the school 6 minutes early. How far is the school from his house?
    (a) 1.5 km   (b) 1.75 km   (c) 2.25 km   (d) 2.5 km

16. A boy goes to his school from his house at a speed of 3 kmph and returns at a speed of 2 kmph. If he takes 5 hours in going and coming, then the distance between his house and school is
    (a) 4 km   (b) 4.5 km   (c) 3 km   (d) 6 km

17. A man travelled from the village to post office at the rate of 25 kmph and walked back at the rate of 4 kmph. If the whole journey took 5 hr 48 min, then the distance of post office from the village is
    (a) 20 km   (b) 22 km   (c) 28 km   (d) 28.5 km

18. A car travels a distance of 170 km in 2 hours partly at a speed of 100 km/hr and partly at 50 km/hr. Find the distance travelled at speed of 100 km/hr.
    (a) 100 km   (b) 70 km   (c) 140 km   (d) 160 km

19. A truck travels a distance of 240 km in 6 hours, partly at a speed of 60 km/hr and partly at 30 km/hr. Find the time for which it travels at 60 km/hr.
    (a) 1 H   (b) 2 H   (c) 3 H   (d) 5 H

20. An increase in the speed of car by 10 km per hour saves 1 hour in a journey of 200 km, find the initial speed of the car.
    (a) 20 km/h   (b) 30 km/h   (c) 36 km/h   (d) 40 km/h

RESPONSE GRID	1. (a)(b)(c)(d)	2. (a)(b)(c)(d)	3. (a)(b)(c)(d)	4. (a)(b)(c)(d)	5. (a)(b)(c)(d)
	6. (a)(b)(c)(d)	7. (a)(b)(c)(d)	8. (a)(b)(c)(d)	9. (a)(b)(c)(d)	10. (a)(b)(c)(d)
	11. (a)(b)(c)(d)	12. (a)(b)(c)(d)	13. (a)(b)(c)(d)	14. (a)(b)(c)(d)	15. (a)(b)(c)(d)
	16. (a)(b)(c)(d)	17. (a)(b)(c)(d)	18. (a)(b)(c)(d)	19. (a)(b)(c)(d)	20. (a)(b)(c)(d)

TRAINS

101 SPEED TEST — 13

Max. Marks : 20   **No. of Qs. 20**   **Time : 20 min.**   **Date : ..../........./................**

1. Two trains each of length 90 m, run on parallel tracks. When running in the same direction, the faster train passes the slower train completely in 18 seconds, but when they are running in opposite directions at speeds same as before, they cross each other in 9 seconds. The speed of second train is
(a) 5 m/s   (b) 15 m/s   (c) 8 m/s   (d) 6 m/s

2. A running train crosses a stationary pole in 4 seconds and a platform 75 m long in 9 seconds. The speed of the train and its length is
(a) 42 m, 15 m/s   (b) 50 m, 15 m/s
(c) 60 m, 15 m/sec   (d) 45 m, 10 m/s

3. Two goods trains each 500 m long are running in opposite directions on paralleled tracks. Their speeds are 45 km/hr and 30 km/hr respectively. The time taken by the slower train to pass the driver of the faster train is
(a) 24 sec   (b) 48 sec   (c) 60 sec   (d) 12 sec

4. Two trains start from stations A and B travel toward each other at speeds of 50 km/hr and 60 km/hr respectively. At the time of their meeting the second train has travelled 120 km more than the first. The distance between A and B, is
(a) 1500 km   (b) 1300 km   (c) 1150 km   (d) 1320 km

5. Two trains of equal length take 10 seconds and 15 seconds respectively to cross a telegraph post. If the length of each train be 120 m, in what time (in seconds) will they cross each other travelling in opposite directions ?
(a) 12 sec   (b) 8 sec   (c) 11 sec   (d) 15 sec

6. A train does a journey without stopping in 8 hours. If it had travelled 5 km an hour faster, it would have done the journey in 6 hours 40 min, its slower speed is
(a) 32 km/hr   (b) 25 km/hr   (c) 28 km/hr   (d) 40 km/hr

7. MS express left Nagpur for Mumbai at 14:30 hours, travelling at a speed of 60 km/hr and VB express left Nagpur for Mumbai on the same day at 16:30 hrs, travelling at a speed of 80 km/hr. How far away from Nagpur will the two trains meet.
(a) 150 km   (b) 200 km   (c) 400 km   (d) 480 km

8. Trains are running with speeds 30 km/hr and 58 km/hr in the same direction. A man in the slower train passes the faster train in 18 seconds. The length of faster train is
(a) 125 m   (b) 140 m   (c) 150 m   (d) 160 m

9. A train 300 m long is running at a speed of 90 km/hr. How many seconds will it take to cross a 200 m long train running in the opposite direction at a speed of 60 km/hr ?
(a) 9 sec   (b) 15 sec   (c) 18 sec   (d) 12 sec

10. A train travels at the speed of 65 km/hr and halts at 8 junctions for a certain time. It covers a distance of 1300 km in 1 day. How long does the train stop at each junction, if it stops for the same period of time at all the junctions?
(a) 30 min   (b) 35 min   (c) 42 min   (d) 20 min

11. A man sitting in a train travelling at the rate of 50 km/hr observes that it takes 9 seconds for a goods train travelling in the opposite direction to pass him. If the goods train is 187.5 m long, then its speed is
(a) 48 km/hr   (b) 28 km/hr   (c) 38 km/hr   (d) 25 km/hr

12. A train consists of 12 boggies, each boggie 15 metres long. The train crosses the telegraph post in 18 seconds. Due to some problems, two boggies were detached. The train now crosses the telegraph post in
(a) 12 sec   (b) 15 sec   (c) 10 sec   (d) None of these

13. A Jogger running at 9 km/hr along side a railway track is 240 metres ahead of the engine of a 120 metre long train running at 45 km/hr in the same direction. In how much time will the train pass the jogger?
(a) 15 sec   (b) 24 sec   (c) 30 sec   (d) 36 sec

14. A passenger train runs at the rate of 72 km/hr. It starts from station P at same time. After 5 hours a goods train leaves the station Q. The passenger train overtakes the goods train after 4 hours. The speed of goods train is
(a) 24 km/hr   (b) 32 km/hr   (c) 40 km/hr   (d) 52 km/hr

15. Two trains running in opposite directions cross a man standing on the platform in 27 sec and 17 sec respectively. They cross each other in 23 sec. The ratio of their speeds is
(a) 1 : 2   (b) 2 : 1   (c) 3 : 2   (d) 2 : 3

16. A goods train leaves a station at a certain time and at a fixed speed. After 6 hours, an express train leaves the same station and moves in the same direction at a uniform speed of 90 kmph. This train catches up the goods train in 4 hours. Find the speed of the goods train.
(a) 36 kmph   (b) 40 kmph   (c) 30 kmph   (d) 42 kmph

17. Without stoppages, a train travels certain distance with an average speed of 80 km/h, and with stoppages, it covers the same distance with an average speed of 60 km/h. How many minutes per hour the train stops ?
(a) 15   (b) 18   (c) 10   (d) None of these

18. A train running between two stations A and B arrives at its destination 10 minutes late when its speed is 50 km/h and 50 minutes late when its speed is 30 km/h. What is the distance between the stations A and B ?
(a) 40 km   (b) 50 km   (c) 60 km   (d) 70 km

19. A train 108 m long moving at a speed of 50 km/h crosses a train 112 m long coming from the opposite direction in 6 seconds. The speed of the second train is
(a) 48 km/h   (b) 54 km/h   (c) 66 km/h   (d) 82 km/h

20. A train 100 m long passes a bridge at the rate of 72 km/h per hour in 25 seconds. The length of the bridge is :
(a) 150 m   (b) 400 m   (c) 300 m   (d) 200 m

RESPONSE GRID	1. ⓐⓑⓒⓓ	2. ⓐⓑⓒⓓ	3. ⓐⓑⓒⓓ	4. ⓐⓑⓒⓓ	5. ⓐⓑⓒⓓ
	6. ⓐⓑⓒⓓ	7. ⓐⓑⓒⓓ	8. ⓐⓑⓒⓓ	9. ⓐⓑⓒⓓ	10. ⓐⓑⓒⓓ
	11. ⓐⓑⓒⓓ	12. ⓐⓑⓒⓓ	13. ⓐⓑⓒⓓ	14. ⓐⓑⓒⓓ	15. ⓐⓑⓒⓓ
	16. ⓐⓑⓒⓓ	17. ⓐⓑⓒⓓ	18. ⓐⓑⓒⓓ	19. ⓐⓑⓒⓓ	20. ⓐⓑⓒⓓ

BOATS & STREAMS

101 SPEED TEST

14

Max. Marks : 20   **No. of Qs. 20**   **Time : 20 min.**   **Date : ..../........./................**

1. The speed of a boat in still water is 15 km/h and the rate of stream is 5 km/h. The distance travelled downstream in 24 minutes is
(a) 4 km   (b) 8 km   (c) 6 km   (d) 16 km

2. A man rows upstream 24 km and downstream 36 km taking 6 hours each. Find the speed of current.
(a) 0.5 km/h   (b) 1 km/h   (c) 1.5 km/h   (d) 2 km/h

3. A motor boat whose speed is 15 km/h in still water goes 30 km downstream and comes back in four and a half hours. The speed of the stream is :
(a) 46 km/h   (b) 6 km/h   (c) 7 km/h   (d) 5 km/h

4. A boat goes 24 km upstream and 28 km downstream in 6 hours. It goes 30 km upstream and 21 km downstream in 6 hours and 30 minutes. The speed of the boat in still water is :
(a) 10 km/h   (b) 4 km/h   (c) 14 km/h   (d) 6 km/h

5. If a man's rate with the current is 12 km/hr. and the rate of the current is 1.5 km/hr, then man's rate against the current is –
(a) 9 km/hr   (b) 6.75 km/hr   (c) 5.25 km/hr   (d) 7.5 km/hr

6. The speed of a motor boat to that of the current of water is 36 : 5. The boat goes along with the current in 5 hours 10 minutes. It will come back in
(a) 5 hours   (b) 6 hours 15 min
(c) 6 hours 30 min   (d) 6 hours 50 min

7. A steamer goes downstream from one part to another in 4 hours. It covers the same distance upstream in 5 hours. If the speed of stream is 2 km/hr, the distance between the two ports is
(a) 45 km   (b) 64 km   (c) 68 km   (d) 80 km

8. A boat takes half the time in moving a certain distance downstream than upstream. The ratio between rate in still water and rate of current is
(a) 1 : 4   (b) 1 : 2   (c) 3 : 1   (d) 3 : 2

9. A person can row a boat d km upstream and the same distance downstream in 5 hours 15 mins. Also he can row the boat 2d km upstream in 7 hours. How long will it take to row the same distance 2d km downstream.

(a) $7\frac{2}{3}$ hours   (b) $7\frac{3}{4}$ hours

(c) 8 hours   (d) $\frac{7}{2}$ hours

10. The speed of a boat in still water is 8 km/hr. It can travel 20 km downstream at the same time as it can travel 12 km upstream, the rate of stream (in kmph) is
(a) 0.5   (b) 2   (c) 2.5   (d) 2.75

11. A man swimming in a stream which flows 1.5 km/hr, finds that in a given time he can swim twice as fast with the stream as he can against it. At what rate does he swim ?
(a) 4.5 km/hr   (b) 5.25 km/hr
(c) 6 km/hr   (d) None of these

12. A man swims downstream 40 km in 4 hours and upstream 24 km in 3 hours. His speed in still water is
(a) 8 km/hr   (b) 8.5 km/hr   (c) 9 km/hr   (d) 9.5 km/hr

13. A man can row three-quarters of a kilometer against the water stream in $11\frac{1}{4}$ minutes and along the stream in $7\frac{1}{2}$ minutes respectively. The speed in (km/hr) of the man in still water is
(a) 3.5   (b) 2.5   (c) 5   (d) 6.5

14. A man rows 10 km upstream and back again to the starting point in 55 min. If the speed of stream is 2 km/hr, then the speed of rowing in still water is
(a) 22 km/hr   (b) 19 km/hr   (c) 21 km/hr   (d) 25 km/hr

15. A boat covers 24 km upstream and 36 km downstream in 6 hours, while it covers 36 km upstream and 24 km downstream in $6\frac{1}{2}$ hour. The velocity of the current is
(a) 2.4 km/hr   (b) 2 km/hr   (c) 3 km/hr   (d) 0.75 km/hr

16. A man takes twice as long to row a distance against the stream as to row the same distance in favour of the stream. The ratio of the speed of the boat (in still water) and the stream is
(a) 3 : 1   (b) 4 : 3   (c) 2 : 1   (d) 3 : 2

17. A boat takes 19 hours for travelling downstream from point A to point B and coming back to point C, mid way between A and B. If the velocity of the stream is 4 km/hr and the speed of the boat in still water is 14 km/hr. then the distance between A & B is
(a) 200 km   (b) 160 km   (c) 180 km   (d) 190 km

18. A man can row a boat 120 km with stream in 5 hours. If speed of the boat is double the speed of the stream, then the speed of stream is
(a) 6 km/h   (b) 8 km/h   (c) 9 km/h   (d) 12 km/h

19. A man rows a distance downstream in 45 min and the same distance upstream in 75 min. What is the ratio of speed of the stream to the boat in still water ?
(a) 1 : 2   (b) 1 : 3   (c) 1 : 4   (d) 2 : 3

20. A man can row 5 kmph in the still water. If the river is running at 2 kmph, it takes him 5 hours to row up to a place and come down. How far is the place?
(a) 6 km   (b) 8 km   (c) 10 km   (d) 14 km

101 SPEED TEST 15

Max. Marks : 20 **No. of Qs. 20** **Time : 20 min.** **Date : ..../........./................**

1. A sum of money, at compound interest, yields ₹ 200 and ₹ 220 at the end of first and second year respectively. The rate % is
   (a) 20 (b) 15 (c) 10 (d) 5

2. ₹ 12500 lent at compound interest for two years at 10% per annum fetches ₹.... more, if the interest was payable half yearly than if it was payable annually
   (a) zero (b) ₹ 10.48 (c) ₹ 38.50 (d) ₹ 68.82

3. Nanoo and Meenu borrowed ₹ 400 each at 10% interest per annum. Nanoo borrowed at compound interest while Meenu borrowed at simple interest. In both the cases, the interest was calculated half yearly. At the end of one year.
   (a) Both paid the same amount as interest
   (b) Nanoo paid ₹ 1 more as interest
   (c) Meenu paid ₹ 5 more as interest
   (d) Meenu paid ₹ 5 less as interest

4. The difference between S.I. and C.I. on a sum for 2 years at 8% per annum is ₹ 160. If the interest were compounded half yearly, the difference in interests in two years will be nearly
   (a) ₹ 246.50 (b) ₹ 240 (c) ₹ 168 (d) ₹ 160

5. An amount is lent at 15% p.a. compound interest for 2 years. The percent increase in the amount at the end of 2 years is
   (a) 22.5% (b) 30% (c) 32.25% (d) 35.5%

6. The population of a village increases @ 5% p.a.. If present population is 8000, after how many years the population will be 9261?
   (a) 2 years (b) 3 years (c) $3\frac{1}{2}$ years (d) 4 years

7. A father divides ₹ 5100 between his two sons, Mohan and Sohan who are 23 and 24 at present in such a way that if their shares are invested at compound interest @ 4% p.a., they will receive equal amount on attaining the age of 26 years. Mohan's share is
   (a) ₹ 2400 (b) ₹ 2500 (c) ₹ 2550 (d) ₹ 2600

8. Population of a town increases at a certain rate per cent per annum. Present population of the town is 3600 and in 5 years it becomes 4800. How much will it be in 10 years ?
   (a) 5000 (b) 6000 (c) 6400 (d) 7000

9. Of a certain sum, $\frac{1}{3}$ rd is invested at 3%, $\frac{1}{6}$ th at 6% and the rest at 8%. If the SI for 2 years from all these investments amounts to ₹ 600, then the original sum was
   (a) ₹ 2000 (b) ₹ 3000 (c) ₹ 4000 (d) ₹ 5000

10. In what time will ₹ 72 become ₹ 81 at $6\frac{1}{4}$% p.a. SI?
   (a) $1\frac{1}{2}$ year (b) $2\frac{1}{2}$ years
   (c) 2 years (d) None of these

11. Bhanu borrowed a certain sum of money at 12% per annum for 3 years and Madhuri borrowed the same sum at 24% per annum for 10 years. The ratio of their amounts, is
   (a) 1 : 3 (b) 2 : 1 (c) 2 : 3 (d) 2 : 5

12. Gopi borrowed ₹ 1800 at 12% per annum for 2 years and Krishna borrowed ₹ 1200 at 18% per annum for 3 years. Then the ratio of interests paid by them is
   (a) 1 : 2 (b) 2 : 3 (c) 3 : 1 (d) 2 : 1

13. Compound interest on ₹ 1600 at 2.5% p.a. for 2 years is
   (a) ₹ 80 (b) ₹ 81 (c) ₹ 82 (d) ₹ 1681

14. Compound interest on ₹ 25000 at 20% p.a. for $2\frac{1}{2}$ years, if interest is compounded annually, is
   (a) ₹ 39600 (b) ₹ 14600 (c) ₹ 37500 (d) ₹ 12500

15. A certain sum of money invested at a certain rate of compound interest doubles in 5 years. In how many years will it become 4 times?
   (a) 10 years (b) 12 years (c) 15 years (d) 20 years

16. If compound interest for second year on a certain sum at 10% p.a. is ₹ 132, the principal is,
   (a) ₹ 600 (b) ₹ 1000 (c) ₹ 1100 (d) ₹ 1200

17. A man invested ₹ 16000 at compound interest for 3 years, interest compounded annually. If he got ₹ 18522 at the end of 3 years, then the rate of interest is
   (a) 4% (b) 5% (c) 6% (d) 7%

18. The compound interest on ₹ 2000 for 9 months at 8% per annum being given when the interest is compunded quarterly is
   (a) ₹ 122 (b) ₹ 130 (c) ₹ 150 (d) ₹ 145

19. A man had ₹ 1200, part of which he lent at 5% and the remaining at 4% he got ₹ 106 as interest after 2 years. The amount lent at 5% is
   (a) ₹ 700 (b) ₹ 800 (c) ₹ 500 (d) ₹ 400

20. The difference between CI and SI on ₹ 8000 for 3 yrs at 2.5% p.a. is
   (a) ₹ 15.125 (b) ₹ 10.125 (c) ₹ 18.125 (d) ₹ 19.125

RESPONSE GRID	1. ⓐⓑⓒⓓ	2. ⓐⓑⓒⓓ	3. ⓐⓑⓒⓓ	4. ⓐⓑⓒⓓ	5. ⓐⓑⓒⓓ
	6. ⓐⓑⓒⓓ	7. ⓐⓑⓒⓓ	8. ⓐⓑⓒⓓ	9. ⓐⓑⓒⓓ	10. ⓐⓑⓒⓓ
	11. ⓐⓑⓒⓓ	12. ⓐⓑⓒⓓ	13. ⓐⓑⓒⓓ	14. ⓐⓑⓒⓓ	15. ⓐⓑⓒⓓ
	16. ⓐⓑⓒⓓ	17. ⓐⓑⓒⓓ	18. ⓐⓑⓒⓓ	19. ⓐⓑⓒⓓ	20. ⓐⓑⓒⓓ

MENSURATION

101 SPEED TEST

Max. Marks : 20   **No. of Qs. 20**   **Time : 20 min.**   **Date : ..../........./................**

1. The sides of a triangle are in the ratio 3:4:5. If its perimeter is 36 cm then the area of the triangle is
   (a) 54 sqm   (b) 56.5 sqm   (c) 57 sqm   (d) None of these

2. Two sides of a plot measure 32 m and 24 m and angle between them is perfect right angle. The other two sides measure 25 m each and the other three angles are not right angles. The area of plot (in m^2) is
   (a) 534   (b) 754   (c) 705   (d) 684

3. A room of size 6.75 m long and 5.75 m wide is to be paved with square tiles. The minimum number of square tiles required is
   (a) 630   (b) 430   (c) 621   (d) 421

4. A square is converted into a rectangle by increasing its length by 20% and decreasing its width by 20%. Which of the following statement is true ?
   (a) Area of square = Area of rectangle
   (b) Area of square = 10% Area of rectangle
   (c) Area of rectangle = 10% Area of square
   (d) Area of rectangle = 96% Area of square

5. The length and breadth of a rectangular plot of a land are in the ratio 5 : 3. The owner spent ₹ 3000 for surrounding it from all the sides at the rate of ₹ 7.5 per meter. The difference between the length and breadth of the plot is
   (a) 75 m   (b) 50 m   (c) 90 m   (d) 60 m

6. The area of a square with side 9 cm is one sixth of the area of a rectangle, whose length is six-times its breadth. The perimeter of the rectangle is
   (a) 104 cm   (b) 52 cm   (c) 78 cm   (d) 126 cm

7. The ratio of length and breadth of a rectangle is 5 : 4. If the breadth is 20 m less than the length then. Its perimeter is
   (a) 280 m   (b) 325 m   (c) 360 m   (d) 380 m

8. The ratio of area of a square to another a square drawn on its diagonal is
   (a) 3 : 4   (b) 4 : 5   (c) 2 : 3   (d) 1 : 2

9. An athletic track 14 m wide consists of two straight sections 120 m long joining semi-circular ends whose inner radius is 35 m. The area of the track is
   (a) 7056 m^2 (b) 7016 m^2 (c) 7076 m^2 (d) 7006 m^2

10. A path of uniform width runs round the inside of a rectangular field 38 m long and 32 m wide. If the path occupies 600 cm^2, then the width of the path is
    (a) 5 m   (b) 8 m   (c) 7.5 m   (d) 9 m

11. If the radius of a circle is increased by 1 cm, its area increases by 22 cm^2, then original radius of the circle is
    (a) 4 cm   (b) 3 cm   (c) 3.5 cm   (d) 5 cm

12. The area of the ring between two concentric circles, whose circumferences are 88 cm and 132 cm is
    (a) 700 cm^2 (b) 720 cm^2 (c) 750 cm^2 (d) 770 cm^2

13. Four horses are tethered at four corners of a square plot of side 63 m so that they just cannot reach one another. The area left ungrazed is
    (a) 858.5 m^2 (b) 850.5 m^2 (c) 798.8 m^2 (d) 901.5 m^2

14. If the length and the breadth of a rectangle are increased by x% and y% respectively, then the area of rectangle will be increased by
    (a) $(x + y)$%
    (b) $(x \times y)$%
    (c) $\left(x + y + \dfrac{xy}{100} \right)$%
    (d) $\left(x + y - \dfrac{xy}{100} \right)$%

15. In the figure ABCD is a square with side 10. BFD is an arc of a circle with centre C. BGD is an arc of a circle with centre A. The area of the shaded region is

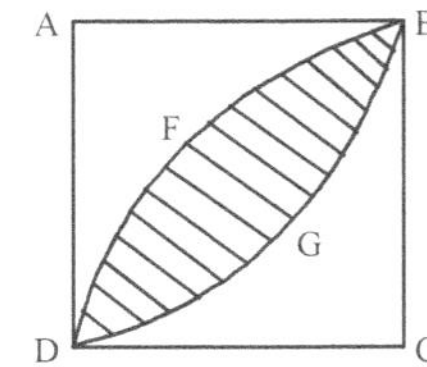

    (a) $50 - 50\,\pi$
    (b) $100 - 75\,\pi$
    (c) $50\pi - 100$
    (d) $100\pi - 75$

16. Area of the shaded region of the below given figure is
    (a) 10 m^2 (b) 11 m^2 (c) 15 m^2 (d) 19 m^2

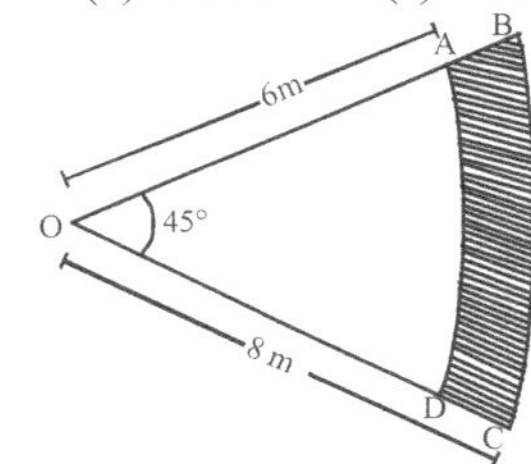

    (Take $\pi = \dfrac{22}{7}$ unless otherwise mentioned)

17. A hemisphere of radius 6 cm is cast into a right circular cone of height 75 cm. The radius of the base of the cone is
    (a) 2.4 cm   (b) 2.8 cm   (c) 3.5 cm   (d) 3.8 cm

18. The diameter of a garden roller is 1.4 m and it is 2 m long. How much area will it cover in 5 revolutions?
    (a) 44 m^2 (b) 33 m^2 (c) 66 m^2 (d) 88 m^2

19. The diameters of two cones are equal and their slant heights are in the ratio 5 : 4. If the curved surface of the larger cone is 200 cm^2, then the curved surface of the larger cone is
    (a) 240 cm^2 (b) 250 cm^2 (c) 260 cm^2 (d) 280 cm^2

20. A measuring jar of internal diameter 10 cm is partially filled with water. Four equal spherical balls of diameter 2 cm, each are dropped in it and they sink down in the water completely. What will be the increase in the level of water in the jar.
    (a) $\dfrac{16}{75}$ cm   (b) $\dfrac{16}{51}$ cm   (c) 15 cm   (d) $\dfrac{16}{5}$ cm

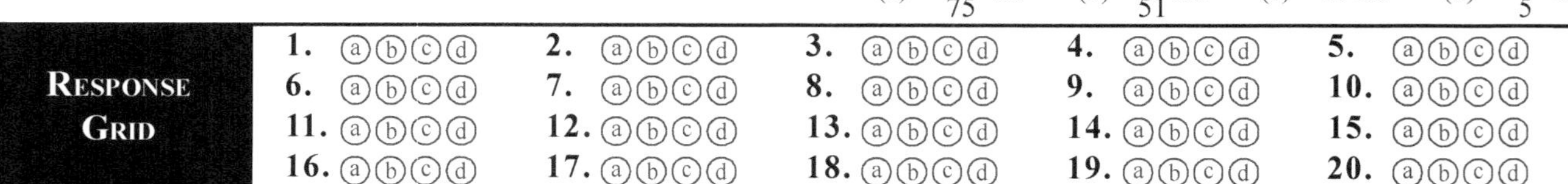

MATHEMATICS SECTION TEST-I

101 SPEED TEST

Max. Marks : 20   **No. of Qs. 20**   **Time : 20 min.**   **Date : ..../........./................**

1. The value of $(0.\overline{6} + 0.\overline{7} + 0.\overline{8})$ is
   (a) $\dfrac{21}{10}$ (b) $\dfrac{19}{9}$ (c) $\dfrac{7}{3}$ (d) None of these

2. The HCF and LCM of two numbers are 11 and 385 respectively. If one number lies between 75 and 125, then that number is
   (a) 77   (b) 88   (c) 99   (d) 110

3. Unit place digit in the product of first 40 odd natural number is
   (a) 6   (b) 0   (c) 5   (d) 8

4. In a zoo, the total number of Lions and Peacocks is 50 and the total number of their legs is 140. Find the number of Loins and Peacocks.
   (a) 10, 20   (b) 20, 30   (c) 30, 40   (d) 40, 50

5. The value of $\sqrt{388 + \sqrt{127 + \sqrt{289}}}$ is
   (a) 17   (b) 12
   (c) 20   (d) None of these.

6. If $\dfrac{5x - 3y}{5y - 3x} = \dfrac{3}{4}$, then value of $\dfrac{x}{y}$ is
   (a) $2 : 9$ (b) $7 : 2$
   (c) $7 : 9$ (d) None of these.

7. The ages of A and B are in the ratio 3 : 1. 15 year hence the ratio will be 2 : 1. Their present ages are
   (a) 45 yrs, 15 yrs   (b) 60 yrs, 20 yrs
   (c) 30 yrs, 10 yrs   (d) 21 yrs, 7 yrs

8. $\left(\dfrac{x^b}{x^c}\right)^{b+c-a} \times \left(\dfrac{x^c}{x^a}\right)^{c+a-b} \times \left(\dfrac{x^a}{x^b}\right)^{a+b-c} = ?$
   (a) x^{abc} (b) 1
   (c) x^{a+b+c} (d) $x^{ab+bc+ca}$

9. The sides of a triangle are in the ratio 3:4:5. If its perimeter is 36 cm then the area of the triangle is
   (a) 54 sqm   (b) 56.5 sqm
   (c) 57 sqm   (d) None of these

10. Find the volume of a sphere whose surface area is 2464 cm^2.
    (a) 11560.43 cm^3 (b) 11498.67 cm^3
    (c) 10248 cm^3 (d) 11398.67 cm^3

11. If the area of the three adjacent faces of a cuboidal box are 120 cm^2, 72 cm^2 and 60 cm^2 respectively. The volume of the box is
    (a) 720 cm^3 (b) 780 cm^3 (c) 728 cm^3 (d) 798 cm^3

12. With a uniform speed a car covers a distance in 8 hours. Had the speed been increased by 4 km/hr, the same distance could have been covered in $7\dfrac{1}{2}$ hours. The distance covered is
    (a) 400 km   (b) 450 km   (c) 480 km   (d) 380 km

13. Starting from his house, one day a student walks at a speed of $2\dfrac{1}{2}$ km / hr and reaches his school 6 minutes late. Next day he increases his speed by 1 km/hr and reaches the school 6 minutes early. How far is the school from his house?
    (a) 1.5 km   (b) 1.75 km   (c) 2.25 km   (d) 2.5 km

14. A running train crosses a stationary pole in 4 seconds and a platform 75 m long in 9 seconds. The speed of the train and its length is
    (a) 42 m, 15 m/s   (b) 50 m, 15 m/s
    (c) 60 m, 15 m/sec   (d) 45 m, 10 m/s

15. The speed of a motor boat to that of the current of water is 36 : 5. The boat goes along with the current in 5 hours 10 minutes. It will come back in
    (a) 5 hours   (b) 6 hours 15 min
    (c) 6 hours 30 min   (d) 6 hours 50 min

16. $3 \div \left[(8-5) \div \left\{ (4-2) \div \left(2 + \dfrac{8}{13} \right) \right\} \right]$ equals :
    (a) $\dfrac{13}{17}$ (b) $\dfrac{68}{13}$ (c) $\dfrac{17}{13}$ (d) $\dfrac{13}{68}$

17. The value of $1 + \dfrac{1}{1 + \dfrac{1}{1 + \dfrac{1}{9}}}$ is:
    (a) $\dfrac{29}{19}$ (b) $\dfrac{10}{19}$ (c) $\dfrac{29}{10}$ (d) $\dfrac{10}{9}$

18. If 5% more is gained by selling an article for ₹ 350 than by selling it for ₹ 340, the cost of the article is :
    (a) ₹ 50   (b) ₹ 160   (c) ₹ 200   (d) ₹ 225

19. By selling 12 oranges for one rupee a man loses 20%. How many for a rupee should he sell to get a gain of 20%?
    (a) 5   (b) 8   (c) 10   (d) 15

20. A sum of money becomes Rs. 756 in two years and Rs. 873 in 3.5 years. The annual rate of simple interest is :
    (a) 13%   (b) 11%   (c) 17%   (d) 19%

RESPONSE GRID

1. ⓐⓑⓒⓓ	2. ⓐⓑⓒⓓ	3. ⓐⓑⓒⓓ	4. ⓐⓑⓒⓓ	5. ⓐⓑⓒⓓ
6. ⓐⓑⓒⓓ	7. ⓐⓑⓒⓓ	8. ⓐⓑⓒⓓ	9. ⓐⓑⓒⓓ	10. ⓐⓑⓒⓓ
11. ⓐⓑⓒⓓ	12. ⓐⓑⓒⓓ	13. ⓐⓑⓒⓓ	14. ⓐⓑⓒⓓ	15. ⓐⓑⓒⓓ
16. ⓐⓑⓒⓓ	17. ⓐⓑⓒⓓ	18. ⓐⓑⓒⓓ	19. ⓐⓑⓒⓓ	20. ⓐⓑⓒⓓ

MATHEMATICS SECTION TEST-II

101 SPEED TEST

18

Max. Marks : 20   No. of Qs. 20   Time : 20 min.   Date : ..../........./................

1. $(41)^2 + (38)^2 \times (0.15)^2 = ?$
   - (a) 3125.0225
   - (b) 1713.49
   - (c) 3125.15
   - (d) 59204.0225

2. $434.43 + 43.34 + 3.44 + 4 + 0.33 = ?$
   - (a) 421.45
   - (b) 455.54
   - (c) 485.54
   - (d) 447.45

3. By how much is $\frac{3}{4}$th of 968 less than $\frac{7}{8}$th of 1008 ?
   - (a) 154
   - (b) 156
   - (c) 165
   - (d) 158

4. A number when subtracted by $\frac{1}{7}$ of itself gives the same value as the sum of all the angles of a triangle. What is the number ?
   - (a) 224
   - (b) 210
   - (c) 140
   - (d) 350

5. $(0.064) \times (0.4)^7 = (0.4)^? \times (0.0256)^2$
   - (a) 17
   - (b) 2
   - (c) 18
   - (d) 3

6. $\left(\sqrt{6}+1\right)^2 = ? + 2\sqrt{6}$
   - (a) 7
   - (b) $\sqrt{6}$
   - (c) $4\sqrt{6}+7$
   - (d) $4\sqrt{6}$

7. If $\sqrt{21025} = 145$, then the value of $\sqrt{210.25} + \sqrt{2.1025} = ?$
   - (a) 0.1595
   - (b) 1.595
   - (c) 159.5
   - (d) 15.95

8. The value of $1.\overline{34} + 4.\overline{12}$ is :
   - (a) $\frac{133}{99}$
   - (b) $\frac{371}{90}$
   - (c) $\frac{5169}{990}$
   - (d) $\frac{5411}{990}$

9. $2 - \frac{11}{39} + \frac{5}{26} = $ _____.
   - (a) $\frac{149}{39}$
   - (b) $1 + \frac{71}{78}$
   - (c) $\frac{149}{76}$
   - (d) $\frac{149}{98}$

10. Given that $\frac{-6p-9}{3} = \frac{2p+9}{5}$, find the value of p.
    - (a) -4
    - (b) -2
    - (c) 3
    - (d) 5

11. $\sqrt{2\sqrt{2\sqrt{2\sqrt{2\sqrt{2}}}}} = ?$
    - (a) 0
    - (b) 1
    - (c) 2
    - (d) $2^{31/32}$

12. The difference in SI and CI on a certain sum of money in 2 years at 15% p.a. is Rs. 144. The sum is:
    - (a) ₹6,000
    - (b) ₹6,200
    - (c) ₹6,300
    - (d) ₹6,400

13. The CI on a certain sum for 2 years is Rs. 410 and SI is Rs. 400. The rate of interest per annum is:
    - (a) 10%
    - (b) 8%
    - (c) 5%
    - (d) 4%

14. The area of a rhombus is 28 cm^2 and one of its diagonals is 4 cm. Its perimeter is:
    - (a) $4\sqrt{53}$ cm
    - (b) 36 cm
    - (c) $2\sqrt{53}$ cm
    - (d) none of these

15. If the altitude of an equilateral triangle is $\sqrt{6}$ cm, its area is
    - (a) $2\sqrt{3}$ cm^2
    - (b) $2\sqrt{2}$ cm^2
    - (c) $3\sqrt{3}$ cm^2
    - (d) $6\sqrt{2}$ cm^2

16. If the circumference of a circle is $\frac{30}{\pi}$ then the diameter of the circle is:
    - (a) 60π
    - (b) $\frac{15}{\pi}$
    - (c) $\frac{30}{\pi^2}$
    - (d) 30

17. If $\frac{1}{5} : \frac{1}{x} = \frac{1}{x} : \frac{1}{1.25}$, then the value of x is :
    - (a) 1.5
    - (b) 2
    - (c) 2.5
    - (d) 3.5

18. 36 men can complete a piece of work in 18 days. In how many days will 27 men complete the same work?
    - (a) 12
    - (b) 18
    - (c) 22
    - (d) 24

19. The average age of three boys is 25 years and their ages are in the ratio 3 : 5 : 7. The age of the youngest boy is:
    - (a) 21 years
    - (b) 18 years
    - (c) 15 years
    - (d) 9 years

20. In a camp, 95 men had provision food for 200 days. After 5 days, 30 men left the camp. For how many days will the remaining food last now?
    - (a) 180
    - (b) 285
    - (c) $139\frac{16}{19}$
    - (d) None of these

<table>
<tr><td rowspan="3">RESPONSE GRID</td><td>1. ⓐⓑⓒⓓ</td><td>2. ⓐⓑⓒⓓ</td><td>3. ⓐⓑⓒⓓ</td><td>4. ⓐⓑⓒⓓ</td><td>5. ⓐⓑⓒⓓ</td></tr>
<tr><td>6. ⓐⓑⓒⓓ</td><td>7. ⓐⓑⓒⓓ</td><td>8. ⓐⓑⓒⓓ</td><td>9. ⓐⓑⓒⓓ</td><td>10. ⓐⓑⓒⓓ</td></tr>
<tr><td>11. ⓐⓑⓒⓓ</td><td>12. ⓐⓑⓒⓓ</td><td>13. ⓐⓑⓒⓓ</td><td>14. ⓐⓑⓒⓓ</td><td>15. ⓐⓑⓒⓓ</td></tr>
<tr><td></td><td>16. ⓐⓑⓒⓓ</td><td>17. ⓐⓑⓒⓓ</td><td>18. ⓐⓑⓒⓓ</td><td>19. ⓐⓑⓒⓓ</td><td>20. ⓐⓑⓒⓓ</td></tr>
</table>

Max. Marks : 20   **No. of Qs. 20**   **Time : 20 min.**   Date : ..../........./................

In each of the following questions. select the related word/letters/number from the given alternatives :

1. Safe : Secure : : Protect : ?
   (a) Conserve   (b) Sure
   (c) Guard   (d) Lock

2. Conference : Chairman : : Newspaper : ?
   (a) Reporter   (b) Distributor
   (c) Printer   (d) Editor

3. Pantry : Store : : Scullery : ?
   (a) Cook   (b) Kitchen
   (c) Utensils   (d) Wash

4. Eye : Myopia : : Teeth : ?
   (a) Pyorrhoea   (b) Cataract
   (c) Trachoma   (d) Eczema

5. Flower : Bud : : Plant : ?
   (a) Seed   (b) Taste
   (c) Flower   (d) Twig

6. Vegetable : Chop : : Body : ?
   (a) Cut   (b) Amputate
   (c) Peel   (d) Prune

7. Circle : Circumference : : Square : ?
   (a) Volume   (b) Area
   (c) Diagonal   (d) Perimeter

8. Ink : Pen : : Blood : ?
   (a) Donation   (b) Vein
   (c) Accident   (d) Doctor

9. Victory : Encouragement : : Failure : ?
   (a) Sadness   (b) Defeat
   (c) Anger   (d) Frustration

10. South : North-west : : West : ?
    (a) South-west   (b) North-east
    (c) East   (d) South

11. 42 : 56 : : 110 : ?
    (a) 18   (b) 132
    (c) 136   (d) 140

12. 48 : 122 : : 168 : ?
    (a) 215   (b) 225
    (c) 290   (d) 292

13. 2 : 7 : : 3 : ?
    (a) 8   (b) 12
    (c) 26   (d) 28

14. NUMBER : UNBMRE : : GHOST : ?
    (a) HOGST   (b) HOGTS
    (c) HGOST   (d) HGSOT

15. DRIVEN : EIDRVN : : BEGUM : ?
    (a) EUBGM   (b) MGBEU
    (c) BGMEU   (d) UEBGM

16. QYGO : SAIQ : : UCKS : ?
    (a) WDMV   (b) VFNU
    (c) WDLU   (d) WEMU

17. YAWC : UESG : : QIOK : ?
    (a) MINC   (b) MIKE
    (c) KOME   (d) MMKO

18. In a certain code BRIGHT is written as JSCSGG. How is JOINED written in that code?
    (a) HNIEFO   (b) JPKEFO
    (c) JPKMDC   (d) None of these

19. '34' is related to '12' in the same way as '59' is related to
    (a) 45   (b) 14
    (c) 42   (d) 38

20. 'Mustard' is related to 'Seed' in the same way as 'Carrot' is related to
    (a) Fruit   (b) Stem
    (c) Flower   (d) Root

ANALOGY-II

101 SPEED TEST 

Max. Marks : 20   **No. of Qs. 20**   **Time : 20 min.**   **Date : ..../........./...............**

1. Which of the following has the same relationship as that of Money : Wealth
   (a) Pity : Kindness
   (b) Cruel : Anger
   (c) Wise : Education
   (d) Pride : Humility

2. Which of the following is related to 'Melody' in the same way as 'Delicious' is related to 'Taste'?
   (a) Memory
   (b) Highness
   (c) Tongue
   (d) Voice

3. In a certain way 'Diploma' is related to 'Education'. Which of the following is related to 'Trophy' in a similar way?
   (a) Sports   (b) Athlete   (c) Winning   (d) Prize

4. 'Clock' is related to 'Time' in the same way as 'Vehicle' is related to which of the following?
   (a) Driver
   (b) Road
   (c) Passenger
   (d) Journey

5. "Illness" is related to "Cure" in the same way as "Grief" is related to
   (a) Happiness
   (b) Ecstasy
   (c) Remedy
   (d) Solicitude

6. 'Necklace' is related to 'Jewellery' in the same way as 'Shirt' is related to
   (a) Cloth   (b) Cotton   (c) Apparel   (d) Thread

7. 'Bouquet' is related to 'Flowers' in the same way as 'sentence' is related to
   (a) Letters
   (b) Paragraph
   (c) Content
   (d) Words

8. Which of the following relates to FLOWER in the same way as RTERBN relates to SECTOR?
   (a) RWLGPF
   (b) EOFKUQ
   (c) EOFMXS
   (d) RWLEND

9. 'Income' is related to 'Profit' in the same way as 'Expenditure' is related to
   (a) Sale
   (b) Receipts
   (c) Surplus
   (d) Loss

10. 'Electricity' is related to 'Wire' in the same way as 'Water' is related to
    (a) Bottle   (b) Jug   (c) River   (d) Pipe

11. 'Hospital' is related to 'Nurse' in the same way as 'Court' is related to
    (a) Justice
    (b) Lawyer
    (c) Judgement
    (d) Trial

12. By following certain logic 'THEIR' is written as 'TRIHE' and 'SOLDIER' is written 'SROLIED'. How is CUSTOM written in that logic?
    (a) UTSOMC
    (b) CTSUOM
    (c) CUTSOM
    (d) YUSOMC

Directions : In each of the following questions, there are two words / set of letters / numbers to the left of the sign :: which are connected in some way. The same relationship obtains between the third words / set of letters / numbers and one of the four alternatives under it. Find the correct alternative in each question.

13. PRLN : XZTV :: JLFH : ?
    (a) NPRT   (b) NRPT   (c) NTRP   (d) RTNP

14. DRIVEN : EIDRVN :: BEGUM : ?
    (a) EUBGM
    (b) MGBEU
    (c) BGMEU
    (c) UEBGM

15. ACFJ : OUZJ :: SUXB : ?
    (a) GNSA   (b) GLQZ   (c) GKPY   (d) GMRB

16. ACE : HIL :: MOQ : ?
    (a) XVT   (b) TVX   (c) VTX   (d) TUX

17. Foresight : Anticipation :: Insomnia : ?
    (a) Treatment
    (b) Disease
    (c) Sleeplessness
    (d) Unrest

18. CG : EI :: FJ : ....
    (a) LM   (b) IJ   (c) GK   (d) HL

19. Ocean : Pacific :: Island : ?
    (a) Greenland
    (b) Ireland
    (c) Netherland
    (d) Borneo

20. Tuberculosis : Lungs :: Cataract : ?
    (a) Ear   (b) Throat   (c) Skin   (d) Eye

<table>
<tr><td rowspan="4">RESPONSE GRID</td><td>1. ⓐⓑⓒⓓ</td><td>2. ⓐⓑⓒⓓ</td><td>3. ⓐⓑⓒⓓ</td><td>4. ⓐⓑⓒⓓ</td><td>5. ⓐⓑⓒⓓ</td></tr>
<tr><td>6. ⓐⓑⓒⓓ</td><td>7. ⓐⓑⓒⓓ</td><td>8. ⓐⓑⓒⓓ</td><td>9. ⓐⓑⓒⓓ</td><td>10. ⓐⓑⓒⓓ</td></tr>
<tr><td>11. ⓐⓑⓒⓓ</td><td>12. ⓐⓑⓒⓓ</td><td>13. ⓐⓑⓒⓓ</td><td>14. ⓐⓑⓒⓓ</td><td>15. ⓐⓑⓒⓓ</td></tr>
<tr><td>16. ⓐⓑⓒⓓ</td><td>17. ⓐⓑⓒⓓ</td><td>18. ⓐⓑⓒⓓ</td><td>19. ⓐⓑⓒⓓ</td><td>20. ⓐⓑⓒⓓ</td></tr>
</table>

Max. Marks : 20   **No. of Qs. 20**   **Time : 20 min.**   **Date : ..../........./................**

DIRECTIONS (Qs. 1-14) : In each of the following questions, four words have been given, out of which three are alike in some manner and the fourth one is different. Choose out the odd one.

1. (a) Car   (b) Autorickshaw
   (c) Van   (d) Taxi
2. (a) Fingers   (b) Palm
   (c) Knee   (d) Wrist
3. (a) Ear   (b) Kidney
   (c) Lungs   (d) Liver
4. (a) Teach   (b) Instruct
   (c) Educate   (d) Explain
5. (a) Probe   (b) Exploration
   (c) Deliberation   (d) Investigation
6. (a) Sugarcane   (b) Coffee
   (c) Tobacco   (d) Rice
7. (a) Mother   (b) Grandfather
   (c) Father   (d) Wife
8. (a) Electricity   (b) Telephone
   (c) Telegram   (d) Post
9. (a) Herb   (b) Flower
   (c) Tree   (d) Shrub
10. (a) Saw   (b) Axe
    (c) Hammer   (d) Screw-driver
11. (a) ACDF   (b) FGKL
    (c) HIVW   (d) TUOP
12. (a) JIHG   (b) OPNM
    (c) SRQP   (d) ZYXW
13. (a) JKST   (b) GHQR
    (c) ABKL   (d) DENO
14. (a) FJOU   (b) EINT
    (c) JNRX   (d) ADHM

DIRECTIONS (Qs. 15 - 17) : In each of the following questions, four pairs of words are given out of which the words in three pairs bear a certain common relationship. Choose the pair in which the words are differently related.

15. (a) Atom : Electron   (b) Train : Engine
    (c) House : Room   (d) Curd : Milk
16. (a) Crime : Punishment   (b) Judgment : Advocacy
    (c) Enterprise : Success   (d) Exercise : Health
17. (a) Broad : Wide   (b) Light : Heavy
    (c) Tiny : Small   (d) Big : Large

DIRECTIONS (Qs. 18 - 20) : One set of numbers in each of the following questions is different from the rest four that are formed under certain norms. Find the odd set.

18. (a) 7, 4, 9   (b) 13, 36, 7
    (c) 5, 25, 9   (d) 11, 16, 7
19. (a) 72, 60   (b) 108, 96
    (c) 84, 72   (d) 60, 36
20. (a) 12, 8   (b) 6, 16
    (c) 18, 6   (d) 32, 3

RESPONSE GRID					
	1. ⓐⓑⓒⓓ	2. ⓐⓑⓒⓓ	3. ⓐⓑⓒⓓ	4. ⓐⓑⓒⓓ	5. ⓐⓑⓒⓓ
	6. ⓐⓑⓒⓓ	7. ⓐⓑⓒⓓ	8. ⓐⓑⓒⓓ	9. ⓐⓑⓒⓓ	10. ⓐⓑⓒⓓ
	11. ⓐⓑⓒⓓ	12. ⓐⓑⓒⓓ	13. ⓐⓑⓒⓓ	14. ⓐⓑⓒⓓ	15. ⓐⓑⓒⓓ
	16. ⓐⓑⓒⓓ	17. ⓐⓑⓒⓓ	18. ⓐⓑⓒⓓ	19. ⓐⓑⓒⓓ	20. ⓐⓑⓒⓓ

Max. Marks : 20 **No. of Qs. 20** **Time : 20 min.** **Date : ..../........./.................**

1. Which combination of alphabets would come in the position of the question mark in the following sequence ?
   ABP, CDQ, EFR, ?
   (a) GHS
   (b) GHT
   (c) HGS
   (d) GHR

2. Which of the following will come next in the series given below ?
   nsi, org, pqe, qpc, ?
   (a) pqa
   (b) rqd
   (c) aor
   (d) roa

3. The next term in the series
   13, 25, 51, 101, 203, ... is
   (a) 405
   (b) 406
   (c) 407
   (d) 411

4. The next term in the series
   4, 8, 28, 80, 244, ... is
   (a) 278
   (b) 428
   (c) 628
   (d) 728

5. What is the missing element in the sequence represented by the question mark ?
   P 3 C, R 5 F, T 8 I, V 1 2 L, ?
   (a) Y 11 7 O
   (b) X 17 M
   (c) X 17 O
   (d) X 16 O

DIRECTIONS (Qs. 6 - 13) : Find the next term in the given series in each of the questions below.

6. 198, 194, 185, 169, ...
   (a) 136
   (b) 144
   (c) 9
   (d) 92

7. 6, 9, 7, 10, 8, 11, ...
   (a) 12
   (b) 13
   (c) 9
   (d) 14

8. 5, 6, 8, 9, 11, ...
   (a) 15
   (b) 12
   (c) 17
   (d) 20

9. 35, 30, 25, 20, 15, 10, ...
   (a) 15
   (b) 10
   (c) 5
   (d) 2

10. 0, 2, 6, 12, 20, ...
    (a) 38
    (b) 30
    (c) 45
    (d) 60

11. 5, 7, 9, 11, 13, ...
    (a) 15
    (b) 10
    (c) 8
    (d) 6

12. 125, 80, 45, 20, ...
    (a) 8
    (b) 12
    (c) 10
    (d) 5

13. 198, 202, 211, 227, ...
    (a) 210
    (b) 212
    (c) 252
    (d) 27

DIRECTIONS (Qs. 14- 17) : Complete the following series :

14. ... ab ... b .. bc ... ca ..
    (a) cacab
    (b) abcca
    (c) abacb
    (d) accbb

15. a...bb a...b...a...b...
    (a) aabab
    (b) ababb
    (c) bbaba
    (d) baaba

16. Complete the series below :
    10, 18, 34, ..., 130, 258
    (a) 32
    (b) 60
    (c) 68
    (d) 66

17. Find out right letters for the questions marks :
    A M B N E I F J C O D P G K ??
    (a) M N
    (b) L M
    (c) IE
    (d) None of these

DIRECTIONS (Qs. 18- 20) : For the questions below, what is the missing element in the sequence represented by the question mark ?

18. A, G, L, P, S, ?
    (a) X
    (b) Y
    (c) W
    (d) U

19. 625, 5, 125, 25, 25, ? 5
    (a) 125
    (b) 5
    (c) 25
    (d) 625

20. 2, 12, 30, 56, ? 132, 182
    (a) 116
    (b) 76
    (c) 90
    (d) 86

101 SPEED TEST

23

Max. Marks : 20   **No. of Qs. 20**   **Time : 20 min.**   **Date : ..../........./................**

DIRECTIONS (Qs. 1 - 13) : In each of the following questions various terms of a series are given with one term missing as shown by (?). Choose the missing term.

1. P 3 C, R 5 F, T 8 I, V 12 L, ?
    - (a) Y 17 O
    - (b) X 17 M
    - (c) X 17 O
    - (d) X 16 O

2. C4X, F9U, I16R, ?
    - (a) L25P
    - (b) L25O
    - (c) L27P
    - (d) None of these

3. 2Z5, 7Y7, 14X9, 23W11, 34V13, (?)
    - (a) 27U24
    - (b) 45U15
    - (c) 47UI5
    - (d) 47V14

4. J2Z, K4X, I7V, ?, H16R, M22P
    - (a) I11T
    - (b) L11S
    - (c) L12T
    - (d) L11T

5. Q1F, S2E, U6D, W21C, ?
    - (a) Y66B
    - (b) Y44B
    - (c) Y88B
    - (d) Z88B

6. K – 11, M – 13, P – 16, T – 20, ?
    - (a) V – 22
    - (b) U – 21
    - (c) Y – 25
    - (d) W – 25

7. C - 2, E - 3, G - 4, I - 5, ?
    - (a) H - 6
    - (b) K - 6
    - (c) J - 8
    - (d) L - 7

8. KM5, IP8, GSl1, EV14, ?
    - (a) BY17
    - (b) BX17
    - (c) CY17
    - (d) CY18

9. 2 A 11, 4 D 13, 12 G 17 ?
    - (a) 36 J 21
    - (b) 36 I 19
    - (c) 48 J 21
    - (d) 48 J 23

10. 5G7 7H10 10I14 14J19 ?
    - (a) 16 K 20
    - (b) 17 K 21
    - (c) 18 K 21
    - (d) 19 K 25

11. J 15 K M21N ? S39T V51W
    - (a) N 24 P
    - (b) P 27 Q
    - (c) P 29 Q
    - (d) P 25 Q

12. D23F H19J L17N ? T11V
    - (a) P15R
    - (b) P14R
    - (c) P13R
    - (d) P12R

13. Z70B D65F H60J ? P50R
    - (a) K55L
    - (b) L55M
    - (c) L55N
    - (d) L55P

DIRECTIONS (Qs. 14 - 20) : A series is given with one/two term(s) missing. Choose the correct alternative from the given ones that will complete the series.

14. A3E, F5J, K7O, ?
    - (a) T9P
    - (b) S9T
    - (c) P9T
    - (d) P11S

15. D9Y, J27S, P81M, V243G, ?
    - (a) A324B
    - (b) C729B
    - (c) B729A
    - (d) A729B

16. cx fu ir ? ol ri
    - (a) lo
    - (b) mn
    - (c) no
    - (d) op

17. C2E, E5H, G12K, I27N, ?
    - (a) I58P
    - (b) J58Q
    - (c) K58Q
    - (d) I57Q

18. ZA_5, Y_4B, XC_6, W_3D, ?
    - (a) VE_7
    - (b) E_7V
    - (c) V_2E
    - (d) VE_5

19. b – 0, y – 3, c – 8, x – 15, d – 24, ?.
    - (a) e – 48
    - (b) w – 35
    - (c) w – 39
    - (d) v – 30

20. C – 3, E – 5, G – 7, I – 9 , ?, ?.
    - (a) M – 18, K – 14
    - (b) X – 24, M – 21
    - (c) K – 11, M – 13
    - (d) O – 15, X – 24

RESPONSE GRID					
	1. ⓐⓑⓒⓓ	2. ⓐⓑⓒⓓ	3. ⓐⓑⓒⓓ	4. ⓐⓑⓒⓓ	5. ⓐⓑⓒⓓ
	6. ⓐⓑⓒⓓ	7. ⓐⓑⓒⓓ	8. ⓐⓑⓒⓓ	9. ⓐⓑⓒⓓ	10. ⓐⓑⓒⓓ
	11. ⓐⓑⓒⓓ	12. ⓐⓑⓒⓓ	13. ⓐⓑⓒⓓ	14. ⓐⓑⓒⓓ	15. ⓐⓑⓒⓓ
	16. ⓐⓑⓒⓓ	17. ⓐⓑⓒⓓ	18. ⓐⓑⓒⓓ	19. ⓐⓑⓒⓓ	20. ⓐⓑⓒⓓ

Max. Marks : 20　　　**No. of Qs. 20**　　　**Time : 20 min.**　　　**Date : ..../........./................**

1. A trader in order to code the prices of article used the letters of PSICHOLAZY in the form of '0 to 9' respectively. Which of the following code stands for ₹ 875.50?
   (a) AIL.HP
   (b) AIL.HS
   (c) ZYA.HO
   (d) None of these

2. If B is coded as 8, F is coded as 6, Q is coded as 4, D is coded as 7, T is coded as 2, M is coded as 3, and K is coded as 5, then what is the coded form of QKTBFM?
   (a) 452683
   (b) 472683
   (c) 452783
   (d) None of these

3. In a certain code language GAME is written as '$ ÷ * %' and BEAD is written as '# % ÷ ×'. How will the word MADE be written in that code language?
   (a) $ ÷ × %　(b) * ÷ $ %　(c) * ÷ × %　(d) # ÷ × %

4. In a certain code language BORN is written as APQON and LACK is written as KBBLK. How will the word GRID be written in that code language?
   (a) FQHCD　(b) FSHED　(c) HSJED　(d) FSHCD

5. In a certain code language STREAMLING is written as CGTVUHOJMN. How will the word PERIODICAL be written in that language?
   (a) PJSFQMNBJE
   (b) QKTGRMBDJE
   (c) QKTGRMCEKF
   (d) PJSFQMBDJE

6. In a certain code language GEOPHYSICS is written as IOPDHZRJBT. How is ALTIMETE₹ written in that code'?
   (a) NHULBFSDQT
   (b) NIUKBFSDQT
   (c) NHUKCFSDQT
   (d) None of these

7. If W means White, Y means Yellow, B means Black, G means Green, R means Red, which of the following will come next in the sequence given below?
   W W Y W Y B W Y B G W Y B G R W W Y W Y B W Y B
   (a) Red　(b) White　(c) Green　(d) Yellow

8. In a certain code 'CLOUD' is written as 'GTRKF'. How is SIGHT written in that code?
   (a) WGJHV　(b) UGHHT　(c) UHJFW　(d) WFJGV

9. In a certain code AROMATIC is written as BQPLBSJB. How is BRAIN written in that code?
   (a) CQBJO　(b) CSBJO　(c) CQBHO　(d) CSBHO

10. If 'yellow' means 'green', 'green' means 'white', white means 'red', 'red' means 'black', 'black' means 'blue' and 'blue' means 'violet', which of the following represents the colour of human blood?
    (a) black
    (b) violet
    (c) red
    (d) None of these

11. In a code language "1357" means "We are very happy", "2639" means "They are extremely lucky", and "794" means "Happy and lucky". Which digit in that code language stands for "very"?
    (a) 1
    (b) 5
    (c) 7
    (d) Data inadequate

12. In a certain code language 'CREATIVE' is written as 'BDSBFUJS'. How is 'TRIANGLE' written in that code?
    (a) BSHSFHKM
    (b) BHSSMHHF
    (c) BSSHFMKH
    (d) BHSSFKHM

13. In a certain code OVER is written as 'PWFSQ' and BARE is written as 'CBSFD'. How is OPEN written in that code?
    (a) PQFOM
    (b) NODMO
    (c) PQFOO
    (d) POFMM

14. If 'white' is called 'rain', 'rain' is called 'green', 'green' is called blue', 'blue', is called 'cloud', 'cloud' is called 'red', 'red' is called 'sky', 'sky' is called 'yellow' and 'yellow' is called' 'black', what is the colour of 'blood'?
    (a) Red
    (b) Blue
    (c) Cloud
    (d) Sky

15. In a certain code language 'POETRY' is written as 'QONDSQX' and 'OVER' is written as 'PNUDQ'. How is 'MORE' written in that code?
    (a) NNNQD　(b) NLPQD　(c) NLNQD　(d) LNNQD

16. In a certain code language 'MOTHERS' is written as 'OMVGGPU'. How is 'BROUGHT' written in that code?
    (a) CPRTIEV
    (b) DPQSIFV
    (c) DPRTIDV
    (d) DPQTIFV

17. In a certain code 'PENCIL' is written as 'RCTAMJ' then in that code 'BROKEN' is written as
    (a) SPFLIM
    (b) SVFLIN
    (c) FVSMGL
    (d) None of these

18. In a certain code language the word FUTILE is written as HYVMNI. How will the word PENCIL be written in that language?
    (a) OIFRLT
    (b) OIFRLS
    (c) OLFRIT
    (d) None of these

19. In a certain code language the word 'NUMBER' is written as 'UMHTEL'. How will the word 'SECOND' be written in that language?
    (a) CTQDRB　(b) GRQDRB　(c) CTQFRB　(d) GRQFRB

20. In a certain code 'SENSITIVE' is written as 'QHLVGWGYC'. How is 'MICROSOFT' written in that code?
    (a) KGAPMQMDT
    (b) QKETQUQHV
    (c) KLAUMVMIR
    (d) LKBTNUNHS

CODING AND DECODING-II

101 SPEED TEST — 25

Max. Marks : 20　　**No. of Qs. 20**　　**Time : 20 min.**　　Date : ..../......../................

1. If LOSE is coded as 1357 and GAIN is coded as 2468, what do the figures 84615 stand for?
   (a) NAILS　(b) SNAIL　(c) LANES　(d) SLAIN
2. If DANCE is coded as GXQZH then how will RIGHT be coded?
   (a) UFJEW　　　　(b) SGKFX
   (c) UFJWE　　　　(d) UFWJE
3. EXCURTION is coded as CXEURTNOI, SCIENTIST will be coded in the same manner as :
   (a) TSIICSNTE　　　(b) ICSNTETSI
   (c) ICSTNETSI　　　(d) ICSNTEIST
4. If in a certain code, RAMAYANA is written as PYKYWYLY, then how MAHABHARATA can be written in that code?
   (a) NBIBCIBSBUB　　　(b) LZGZAGZQZSZ
   (c) MCJCDJCTCVC　　　(d) KYFYZFYPYRY
5. If MEKLF is coded as 91782 and LLLJK as 88867, then how can IGHED be coded?
   (a) 97854　(b) 64521　(c) 53410　(d) 75632
6. If DELHI is coded as 73541 and CALCUTTA as 82589662, then how can CALICUT be coded?
   (a) 5279431　　　(b) 5978013
   (c) 8251896　　　(d) 8543691
7. If in a certain language, PLAYER is coded as QNDCJX, then how SINGER will be coded in the same language?
   (a) TKQKJX　　　(b) TKJKQX
   (c) TKQKXJ　　　(d) TKQXJK
8. If $\alpha\,\delta\,\gamma\,\chi\,\epsilon$ is decoded as ARGUE and $\sigma\,\phi\,\lambda\,\pi\,\epsilon$ is SOLVE, what is $\pi\,\alpha\,\gamma\,\chi\,\epsilon\,\lambda\,\omega$?
   (a) VAGUELY　　　(b) VAGRAT
   (c) VAGUELE　　　(d) VAGUER
9. If in a certain code language INSTITUTION is coded as NOITUTITSNI, then how will PERFECTION be coded in that code language?
   (a) NOITEERPFC　　　(b) NOITCEFREP
   (c) NOITCFERPE　　　(d) NOTICEFRPE
10. In a certain code COMPUTER is written as OCPMTURE. In that code which alternative will be written as OHKCYE?
    (a) HCOKEY　　　(b) HYKOCE
    (c) HOCKEY　　　(d) HOYECK
11. In a certain code, 'CAPITAL' is written as 'CPATILA'. How is 'PERSONS' written in that code?
    (a) PSONRES　　　　(b) PONSRES
    (c) PESONRS　　　　(d) PREOSSN
12. If SISTER is coded as 20, 10, 20, 21, 6, 19, then the code for BROTHER is
    (a) 2, 15, 16, 21, 9, 5, 18　　(b) 3, 19, 16, 21, 9, 6, 19
    (c) 4, 20, 15, 18, 8, 7, 9　　(d) 3, 18, 16, 20, 9, 7, 19
13. If PEAR is written a GFDN, how is REAP written in this code?
    (a) FDNG　　　　(b) NFDG
    (c) DNGF　　　　(d) NDFG
14. If FLATTER is coded as 7238859 and MOTHER is coded as 468159, then how is MAMMOTH coded?
    (a) 4344681　　　　(b) 4344651
    (c) 4146481　　　　(d) 4346481
15. If SEARCH is coded as TFBSDI, how will PENCIL be coded?
    (a) RGPEN　　　　(b) LICNEP
    (c) QFODJM　　　　(d) QDMBHK
16. If TRAIN is coded as WUDLQ, how is the word BUS coded?
    (a) EXU　　　　(b) DWU
    (c) EXV　　　　(d) VXE
17. If ASHA equals 79, then VINAYBHUSHAN = ?
    (a) 211　(b) 200　(c) 144　(d) 180
18. If MATCH is coded as NCWGM and BOX as CQA, then which of the following is coded as OQWIGUVS?
    (a) NOTEBOOK　　　(b) NOTEBOKE
    (c) NOTFBOPE　　　(d) MOKEBOOT
19. If in a certain code, ADVENTURE is coded as BFYISZBZN, how is COUNTRY coded in that code?
    (a) DPVOUSZ　　　(b) DQXRYXF
    (c) EQWPVTA　　　(d) BNTMSQX
20. In a certain code, SURFER is written as RUSREF. How is KNIGHT written in that code?
    (a) THGINK　　　(b) GHTINK
    (c) INKTHG　　　(d) THINKG

<table>
<tr><td rowspan="4">RESPONSE GRID</td><td>1. ⓐⓑⓒⓓ</td><td>2. ⓐⓑⓒⓓ</td><td>3. ⓐⓑⓒⓓ</td><td>4. ⓐⓑⓒⓓ</td><td>5. ⓐⓑⓒⓓ</td></tr>
<tr><td>6. ⓐⓑⓒⓓ</td><td>7. ⓐⓑⓒⓓ</td><td>8. ⓐⓑⓒⓓ</td><td>9. ⓐⓑⓒⓓ</td><td>10. ⓐⓑⓒⓓ</td></tr>
<tr><td>11. ⓐⓑⓒⓓ</td><td>12. ⓐⓑⓒⓓ</td><td>13. ⓐⓑⓒⓓ</td><td>14. ⓐⓑⓒⓓ</td><td>15. ⓐⓑⓒⓓ</td></tr>
<tr><td>16. ⓐⓑⓒⓓ</td><td>17. ⓐⓑⓒⓓ</td><td>18. ⓐⓑⓒⓓ</td><td>19. ⓐⓑⓒⓓ</td><td>20. ⓐⓑⓒⓓ</td></tr>
</table>

WORD FORMATION

101 SPEED TEST — 26

Max. Marks : 20   **No. of Qs. 20**   **Time : 20 min.**   **Date : ..../........./................**

1. If it is possible to make a meaningful word with the second, the fourth, the sixth and the ninth letters of the word PERMEABILITY, which of the following will be the first letter of that word? If no such word can be formed give 'N' as the answer. If only two such words can be formed give 'D' as the answer and if more than two such words can be formed give 'Z' as the answer.
   (a) M   (b) L   (c) N   (d) Z

2. How many such pairs of digits are there in the number 95137248 each of which has as many digits between them in the number as when they are arranged in ascending order?
   (a) None   (b) One   (c) Two   (d) Three

3. Find the two letters in the word EXTRA which have as many letters between them in the word as in the alphabet. If these two letters are arranged in alphabetical order which letter will come second?
   (a) E   (b) X   (c) T   (d) R

4. If it is possible to make only one meaningful English word from the sixth, the fifth, the twelfth and the fourth letters of the word IMAGINATIONS, using each letter only once, the **second** letter of that word is your answer. If no such word can be made mark 'X' as your answer, and if more than one such word can be formed mark 'M' as your answer.
   (a) I   (b) N   (c) S   (d) M

5. If each of the letters in the English alphabet is assigned odd numerical value beginning A = 1, B = 3 and so on, what will be the total value of the letters of the word 'INDIAN'?
   (a) 96   (b) 89   (c) 88   (d) 86

6. If it is possible to make a meaningful word with the third, the fifth, the sixth and the eleventh letters of the word MERCHANDISE, using each letter only once, which of the following will be the third letter of that word? If no such word can be formed, give 'X' as answer and if more than one such word can be formed, mark 'T' as answer.
   (a) H   (b) E   (c) R   (d) X

7. If it is possible to make a meaningful word with the first, the fifth, the ninth and the eleventh letters of the word PENULTIMATE, using each letter only once, which of the following will be the third letter of that word? If no such word can be made give 'N' as the answer and if more than one such word can be formed give 'D' as the answer.
   (a) E   (b) P   (c) L   (d) D

8. How many such pairs of letters are there in the word CREDIBILITY each of which has only one letter between them in the word as also in the alphabet?
   (a) None   (b) One   (c) Two   (d) Three

9. If the letters in the word POWERFUL are rearranged as they appear in the English alphabet, the position of how many letters will remain unchanged after the rearrangement?
   (a) None   (b) One   (c) Two   (d) Three

10. How many such pairs of letters are there in the word PRODUCTION each of which has as many letters between them in the word as in the English alphabet?
    (a) None   (b) One   (c) Two   (d) Three

11. If it is possible to make only one meaningful word with the fourth, the fifth, the seventh and the eleventh letters of the word PREDICTABLE, which of the following will be the first letter of that word? If only two such words can be formed, give 'P' as the answer; if three or more than three such words can be formed, give 'Z' as the answer; and if no such word can be formed, give 'X' as the answer.
    (a) D   (b) T   (c) P   (d) Z

12. If it is possible to make a meaningful word from the first, the fourth, the eighth, the tenth and the thirteenth letters of the word ESTABLISHMENT, using each letter only once, the last letter of that word is your answer. If more than one such word can be formed write 'P' as your answer and if no such word can be formed write 'X' as your answer.
    (a) X   (b) P   (c) T   (d) E

13. The positions of the first and the eighth letters in the word WORKINGS are interchanged. Similarly, the positions of the second and the seventh letters are interchanged, the positions of the third letter and the sixth letter are interchanged, and the positions of the remaining two letters are interchanged with each other. Which of the following will be the third letter to the left of *R* after the rearrangement?
    (a) G   (b) S   (c) I   (d) N

14. If it is possible to make only one meaningful word with the second, the seventh, the tenth and the eleventh letters of the word 'TRADITIONAL', what will be the second letter of the word? If no such word can be formed, give 'X' as the answer. If only two such words can be formed give 'Y' as the answer and if more than two such words can be formed give 'Z' as the answer.
    (a) L   (b) I   (c) X   (d) Z

15. How many pairs of letters are there in the word SPONTANEOUS which have number of letters between them in the word one less than the number of letters between them in Engiish alphabet?
    (a) Five   (b) One   (c) Four   (d) Two

16. If it is possible to make a meaningful word from the fifth, seventh, eighth, ninth and thirteenth letters of the word 'EXTRAORDINARY' using each letter only once, write the second letter of that word as your answer. If no such word can be formed write 'X' as your answer and if more than one such word can be formed, write 'M' as your answer.
    (a) A   (b) I   (c) R   (d) M

17. The letters of the name of a vegetable are I, K, M, N, P, P, U. If the letters are rearranged correctly, then what is the last letter of the word formed ?
    (a) M   (b) N   (c) K   (d) P

18. If it is possible to make a meaningful word with the third, the fifth, the seventh and the tenth letters of the word 'PROJECTION' which of the following is the third letter of that word? If no such word can be made, give X as the answer. If more than one such word can be made, give M as the answer.
    (a) O   (b) N   (c) X   (d) None of these

19. If the first three letters of the word COMPREHENSION are reversed, then the last three letters are added and then the remaining letters are reversed and added, then which letter will be exactly in the middle. ?
    (a) H   (b) N   (c) R   (d) S

20. How many independent words can 'HEARTLESS' be divided into without changing the order of the letters and using each letter only once ?
    (a) Two   (b) Three   (c) Four   (d) None of these

BLOOD RELATION

101 SPEED TEST — 27

Max. Marks : 20   **No. of Qs. 20**   **Time : 20 min.**   **Date : ..../........./................**

1. B is D's mother and C is D's brother. H is E's daughter whose wife is D. How are E and C related?
   - (a) Father-in-law
   - (b) Brother-in-law
   - (c) Uncle
   - (d) Brother

2. In a joint family there are father, mother, 3 married sons and one unmarried daughter. Of the sons, 2 have 2 daughters each, and one has a son. How many female members are there in the family?
   - (a) 2
   - (b) 3
   - (c) 6
   - (d) 9

3. A is father of C and D is son of B. E is brother of A. If C is sister of D how is B related to E?
   - (a) Sister-in-law
   - (b) Sister
   - (c) Brother
   - (d) Brother-in-law

4. M is the son of P. Q is the granddaughter of O who is the husband of P. How is M related to O?
   - (a) Son
   - (b) Daughter
   - (c) Mother
   - (d) Father

5. X and Y are brothers. R is the father of Y. S is the brother of T and maternal uncle of X. What is T to R?
   - (a) Mother
   - (b) Wife
   - (c) Sister
   - (d) Brother

   Considering the given options, it may be assumed that T is wife of R.

6. A is the father of B, C is the daughter of B, D is the brother of B, E is the son of A. What is the relationship between C and E?
   - (a) Brother and sister
   - (b) Cousins
   - (c) Niece and uncle
   - (d) Uncle and aunt

7. Vinod introduces Vishal as the son of the only brother of his father's wife. How is Vinod related to Vishal?
   - (a) Cousin
   - (b) Brother
   - (c) Son
   - (d) Uncle

8. Rahul and Robin are brothers. Pramod is Robin's father. Sheela is Pramod's sister. Prema is Pramod's niece. Shubha is Sheela's granddaughter. How is Rahul related to Shubha?
   - (a) Brother
   - (b) Cousin
   - (c) Uncle
   - (d) Nephew

9. A husband and a wife had five married sons and each of them had four children. How many members are there in the family?
   - (a) 32
   - (b) 36
   - (c) 30
   - (d) 40

10. Arun said, "This girl is the wife of the grandson of my mother". Who is Arun to the girl?
    - (a) Grandfather
    - (b) Husband
    - (c) Father-in-law
    - (d) Father

11. Mohan is the son of Arun's father's sister. Prakash is the son of Reva, who is the mother of Vikas and grandmother of Arun. Pranab is the father of Neela and the grandfather of Mohan. Reva is the wife of Pranab. How is the wife of Vikas related to Neela?
    - (a) Sister
    - (b) Sister-in-law
    - (c) Niece
    - (d) None of these

12. A man pointing to a photograph says, "The lady in the photograph is my nephew's maternal grandmother and her son is my sister's brother-in-law. How is the lady in the photograph related to his sister who has no other sister?
    - (a) Mother
    - (b) Cousin
    - (c) Mother-in-law
    - (d) Sister-in-law

13. Pointing to a boy, Urmila said, "He is the son of my grandfather's only daughter." How is Urmila related to the boy?
    - (a) Mother
    - (b) Maternal Aunt
    - (c) Paternal Aunt
    - (d) None of these

14. Madhu said, 'My mother's only son Ashok has no son'. Which of the following can be concluded?
    - (a) Ashok has only daughters
    - (b) Ashok is not married
    - (c) Ashok does not have a father
    - (d) None of these

15. D is brother of B. M is brother of B. K is father of M. T is wife of K. How is B related to T?
    - (a) Son
    - (b) Daughter
    - (c) Son or Daughter
    - (d) Data inadequate

16. Pointing to a girl, Arun said, "She is the only daughter of my grandfather's son." How is the girl related to Arun?
    - (a) Daughter
    - (b) Sister
    - (c) Cousin sister
    - (d) Data inadequate

17. Pointing to a photograph, Rasika said "He is the grandson of my grandmother's only son". How is the boy in photograph related to Rasika?
    - (a) Son
    - (b) Nephew
    - (c) Brother
    - (d) Cannot be determined

18. A, B, C, D, E, F and G are members of a family consisting of 4 adults and 3 children, two of whom, F and G are girls. A and D are brothers and A is a doctor. E is an engineer married to one of the brothers and has two children. B is married to D and G is their child. Who is C ?
    - (a) G's brother
    - (b) F's father
    - (c) E's father
    - (d) A's son

19. Examine the following relationships among members of a family of six persons *A, B, C, D, E* and *F.*
    1. The number of males equals that of females
    2. A and *E* are sons of *F.*
    3. *D* is the mother of two, one boy and one girl
    4. *B* is the son of *A*
    5. There is only one married couple in the family at present
    Which one of the following inferences can be drawn from the above?
    - (a) *A, B* and *C* are all females
    - (b) *A* is the husband of *D*
    - (c) *E* and *F* are children of *D*
    - (d) *D* is the grand daughter of *F*

20. There is a family of 6 persons A, B, C, D, E and F. There are two married couples in the family. The family members are lawyer, teacher, salesman, engineer, accountant and doctor. D, the salesman is married to the lady teacher. The doctor is married to the lawyer. F, the accountant is the son of B and brother of E. C, the lawyer is the daughter-in-law of A. E is the unmarried engineer. A is the grandmother of F. How is E related to F?
    - (a) Brother
    - (b) Sister
    - (c) Father
    - (d) Cannot be established (cannot be determined)

<table>
<tr><td rowspan="4">RESPONSE GRID</td><td>1. ⓐⓑⓒⓓ</td><td>2. ⓐⓑⓒⓓ</td><td>3. ⓐⓑⓒⓓ</td><td>4. ⓐⓑⓒⓓ</td><td>5. ⓐⓑⓒⓓ</td></tr>
<tr><td>6. ⓐⓑⓒⓓ</td><td>7. ⓐⓑⓒⓓ</td><td>8. ⓐⓑⓒⓓ</td><td>9. ⓐⓑⓒⓓ</td><td>10. ⓐⓑⓒⓓ</td></tr>
<tr><td>11. ⓐⓑⓒⓓ</td><td>12. ⓐⓑⓒⓓ</td><td>13. ⓐⓑⓒⓓ</td><td>14. ⓐⓑⓒⓓ</td><td>15. ⓐⓑⓒⓓ</td></tr>
<tr><td>16. ⓐⓑⓒⓓ</td><td>17. ⓐⓑⓒⓓ</td><td>18. ⓐⓑⓒⓓ</td><td>19. ⓐⓑⓒⓓ</td><td>20. ⓐⓑⓒⓓ</td></tr>
</table>

Max. Marks : 20   **No. of Qs. 20**   **Time : 20 min.**   Date : ..../........./................

1. Meghna drives 10 km towards South, takes a right turn and drives 6 km. She then takes another right turn, drives 10 km and stops. How far is she from the starting point?
   (a) 16 km   (b) 6 km   (c) 4 km   (d) 12 km

2. Vikas walked 10 metres towards North, took a left turn and walked 15 metres, and again took a left turn and walked 10 metres and stopped walking. Towards which direction was he facing when he stopped walking?
   (a) South   (b) South-West
   (c) South-East   (d) Cannot be determined

3. Mohan walked 30 metres towards South, took a left turn and walked 15 metres. He then took a right turn and walked 20 metres. He again took a right turn and walked 15 metres. How far is he from the starting point?
   (a) 95 metres   (b) 50 metres
   (c) 70 metres   (d) Cannot be determined

4. P, Q, R, S and T are sitting in a straight line facing North. P sits next to S but not to T. Q is sitting next to R who sits on the extreme left corner. Who sits to the left of S if T does not sit next to Q?
   (a) P   (b) Q   (c) R   (d) T

5. Roma walked 25 metre towards south, took a right turn and walked 15 metre. She then took a left turn and walked 25 meter. Which direction is she now from her starting point?
   (a) South-east   (b) South
   (c) South-west   (d) North-west

6. A man starts from a point and walks 2 km towards north. He turns right and walks 3 km. Then he turns left and travels 2 km. What is the direction he is now facing?
   (a) East   (b) West   (c) South   (d) North

7. Kamu walks 5 kms straight from her house towards west, then turns right and walks 3 kms. Thereafter she takes left turn and walks 2 km. Further, she turns left and walks 3 km. Finally, she turns right and walks 3 kms. In what direction she is now from her house?
   (a) West   (b) North   (c) South   (d) East

8. Sandhya walks straight from point A to B which is 2 kms away. She turns left, at 90° and walks 8 kms to C, where she turns left again at 90° and walks 5 kms to D. At D she turns left at 90° and walks for 8 kms to E. How far is she from A to E?
   (a) 2   (b) 3   (c) 5   (d) 8

9. A man starts from a point, walks 4 miles towards north and turns left and walks 6 miles, turns right and walks for 3 miles and again turns right and walks 4 miles and takes rest for 30 minutes. He gets up and walks straight 2 miles in the same direction and turns right and walks on mile. What is the direction he is facing?
   (a) North   (b) South   (c) South-east (d) West

10. From her home Prerna wishes to go to school. From home she goes toward North and then turns left and then turns right, and finally she turns left and reaches school. In which direction her school is situated with respect to her home?
    (a) North-East   (b) North-West
    (c) South-East   (d) South-West

11. Vijit walks 10 metres westward, then turns left and walks 10 metres. He then again turns left and walks 10 metres. He takes a 45 degree turn rightwards and walks straight. In which direction is he walking now?
    (a) South   (b) West
    (c) South-East   (d) South-West

12. A man started walking West. He turned right, then right again and finally turned left. Towards which direction was he walking now?
    (a) North   (b) South   (c) West   (d) East

13. One evening, Raja started to walk toward the Sun. After walking a while, he turned to his right and again to his right. After walking a while, he again turned right. In which direction is he facing?
    (a) South   (b) East   (c) West   (d) North

14. Five boys A, B, C, D, E are sitting in a park in a circle. A is facing South-west, D is facing South-East, B and E are right opposite A and D respectively and C is equidistant between D and B. Which direction is C facing?
    (a) West   (b) South   (c) North   (d) East

15. Ganesh cycles towards South-West a distance of 8 m, then he moves towards East a distance of 20 m. From there he moves towards North-East a distance of 8 m, then he moves towards West a distance of 6 m. From there he moves towards North-East a distance of 2 m. Then he moves towards West a distance of 4 m and then towards South-West 2 m and stops at that point. How far is he from the starting point?
    (a) 12 m   (b) 10 m   (c) 8 m   (d) 6 m

16. From my house I walked 5 km towards North. I turned right and walked 3 km. Again I went one km to the south. How far am I from my house?
    (a) 7 km   (b) 6 km   (c) 4 km   (d) 5 km

17. Jaya started from house with son Rakesh and moved to North. Before signal point, Rakesh's school bus took him to the right side. Jaya continued in the same line and got petrol filled in the scooter. Then she turned to her left and entered a supermarket. In which direction is the supermarket located from the petrol pump?
    (a) East   (b) South   (c) North   (d) West

18. Daily in the morning the shadow of Gol Gumbaz falls on Bara Kaman and in the evening the shadow of Bara Kaman falls on Gol Gumbaz exactly. So in which direction is Gol Gumbaz of Bara Kaman?
    (a) Eastern side   (b) Western side
    (c) Northern side   (d) Southern side

19. A man starts from his house and walked straight for 10 metres towards North and turned left and walked 25 metres. He then turned right and walked 5 metres and again turned right and walked 25 metres. Which direction is he facing now?
    (a) North   (b) East   (c) South   (d) West

20. Village A is 20 km to the north of Village B. Village C is 18 km to the east of Village B, Village D is 12 km to the west of Village A. If Raj Gopal starts from Village C and goes to Village D, in which direction is he from his starting point ?
    (a) North-East   (b) North-West
    (c) South-East   (d) North

CLOCK & CALENDAR

101 SPEED TEST 29

Max. Marks : 20   **No. of Qs. 20**   **Time : 20 min.**   Date : ..../......../................

1. If the day before yesterday was Thursday, when will Sunday be?
   (a) Tomorrow
   (b) Day after tomorrow
   (c) Today
   (d) Two days after today

2. Raju and Nirmala celebrated their first wedding anniversary on Sunday, the 5th of December 1993. What would be the day of their wedding anniversary in 1997?
   (a) Wednesday
   (b) Thursday
   (c) Friday
   (d) Tuesday

3. Mrs. Susheela celebrated her wedding anniversary on Tuesday, 30th September 1997. When will she celebrate her next wedding anniversary on the same day?
   (a) 30 September 2003
   (b) 30 September 2004
   (c) 30 September 2002
   (d) 30 October 2003

4. A clock gains five minutes every hour. What will be the angle traversed by the second hand in one minute?
   (a) 360°
   (b) 360.5°
   (c) 390°
   (d) 380°

5. If John celebrated his victory day on Tuesday, 5th January 1965, when will be celebrate his next victory day on the same day?
   (a) 5th January 1970
   (b) 5th January 1971
   (c) 5th January 1973
   (d) 5th January 1974

6. After 9'O clock at what time between 9 p.m and 10 p.m. will the hour and minute hands of a clock point in opposite direction?
   (a) 15 minutes past 9
   (b) 16 minutes past 9
   (c) $16\frac{4}{11}$ minutes past 9
   (d) $17\frac{1}{11}$ minutes past 9

7. Suresh was born on 4th October 1999. Shashikanth was born 6 days before Suresh. The Independence Day of that year fell on Sunday. Which day was Shashikanth born?
   (a) Tuesday
   (b) Wednesday
   (c) Monday
   (d) Sunday

8. At what time are the hands of clocks together between 6 and 7?
   (a) $32\frac{8}{11}$ minutes past 6
   (b) $34\frac{8}{11}$ minutes past 6
   (c) $30\frac{8}{11}$ minutes past 6
   (d) $32\frac{5}{7}$ minutes past 6

9. In the year 1996, the Republic day was celebrated on Friday, On which day was the Independence day celebrated in the year 2000?
   (a) Tuesday
   (b) Monday
   (c) Friday
   (d) Saturday

10. In Ravi's clock shop, two clocks were brought for repairs. One clock has the cuckoo coming out every sixteen minutes, while the other one has the cuckoo coming out every eighteen minutes. Both cuckoos come out at 12.00 noon. When will they both come out together again?
    (a) 2.06 pm
    (b) 2.08 pm
    (c) 2.24 pm
    (d) 2.32 pm

11. A watch reads 7.30. If the minute hand points West, then in which direction will the hour hand point?
    (a) North
    (b) North East
    (c) North West
    (d) South East

12. March 1, 2008 was Saturday. Which day was it on March 1, 2002?
    (a) Thursday
    (b) Friday
    (c) Saturday
    (d) Sunday

13. How many times are an hour hand and a minute hand of a clock at right angles during their motion from 1.00 p.m. to 10.00 p.m.?
    (a) 9
    (b) 10
    (c) 18
    (d) 20

14. At what time between 3 and 4 O' clock, the hands of a clock coincide?
    (a) $16\frac{4}{11}$ minutes past 3
    (b) $15\frac{5}{61}$ minutes past 3
    (c) $15\frac{5}{60}$ minutes to 2
    (d) $16\frac{4}{11}$ minutes to 4

15. It was Sunday on Jan 1, 2006. What was the day of the week on Jan 1, 2010?
    (a) Sunday
    (b) Saturday
    (c) Friday
    (d) Wednesday

16. The calendar for the year 2007 will be the same for the year.
    (a) 2014
    (b) 2016
    (c) 2017
    (d) 2018

17. Today is Monday. After 61 days, it will be
    (a) Wednesday
    (b) Saturday
    (c) Tuesday
    (d) Thursday

18. What was the day of the week on 17th June, 1998?
    (a) Monday
    (b) Tuesday
    (c) Wednesday
    (d) Thursday

19. If 21st July, 1999 is a wednesday, what would have been the day of the week on 21st July, 1947 ?
    (a) Monday
    (b) Sunday
    (c) Thursday
    (d) Saturday

20. A watch is a minute slow at 1 p.m. on Tuesday and 2 minutes fast at 1 p.m. on Thursday. When did it show the correct time ?
    (a) 1:00 a.m. on Wednesday
    (b) 5:00 a.m. on Wednesday
    (c) 1:00 p.m. on Wednesday
    (d) 5:00 p.m. on Wednesday

<table>
<tr><td rowspan="4">RESPONSE GRID</td><td>1. ⓐⓑⓒⓓ</td><td>2. ⓐⓑⓒⓓ</td><td>3. ⓐⓑⓒⓓ</td><td>4. ⓐⓑⓒⓓ</td><td>5. ⓐⓑⓒⓓ</td></tr>
<tr><td>6. ⓐⓑⓒⓓ</td><td>7. ⓐⓑⓒⓓ</td><td>8. ⓐⓑⓒⓓ</td><td>9. ⓐⓑⓒⓓ</td><td>10. ⓐⓑⓒⓓ</td></tr>
<tr><td>11. ⓐⓑⓒⓓ</td><td>12. ⓐⓑⓒⓓ</td><td>13. ⓐⓑⓒⓓ</td><td>14. ⓐⓑⓒⓓ</td><td>15. ⓐⓑⓒⓓ</td></tr>
<tr><td>16. ⓐⓑⓒⓓ</td><td>17. ⓐⓑⓒⓓ</td><td>18. ⓐⓑⓒⓓ</td><td>19. ⓐⓑⓒⓓ</td><td>20. ⓐⓑⓒⓓ</td></tr>
</table>

LOGICAL VENN DIAGRAM-1

101 SPEED TEST

30

Max. Marks : 10   **No. of Qs. 10**   **Time : 10 min.**   **Date : ..../........./................**

1. Which diagram correctly represents the relationship between politicians, poets and women?

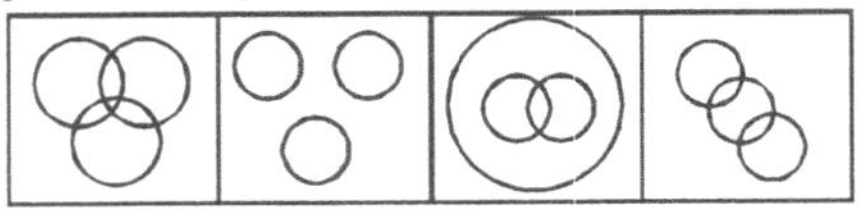

   (a)   (b)   (c)   (d)

2. There are 80 families in a small extension area. 20 percent of these families own a car each. 50 per cent of the remaining families own a motor cycle each. How many families in that extension do not own any vehicle?
   (a) 30   (b) 32   (c) 23   (d) 36

3. Which one of the following diagrams represent the correct relationship among 'Judge', 'Thief' and 'Criminal'?

   (a) 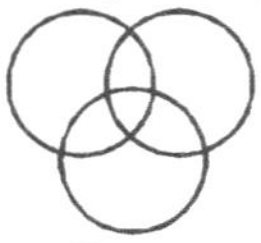   (b)

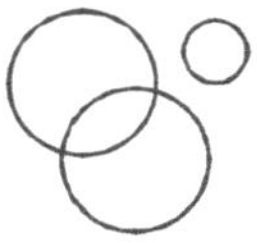

   (c) 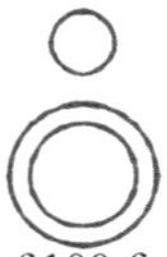   (d)

4. Out of 100 families in the neighbourhood, 50 have radios, 75 have TVs and 25 have VCRs. Only 10 families have all three and each VCR owner also has a TV. If some families have radio only, how many have only TV?
   (a) 30   (b) 35   (c) 40   (d) 45

5. Which diagram correctly represents the relationship between Human beings, Teachers, Graduates?

   (a) 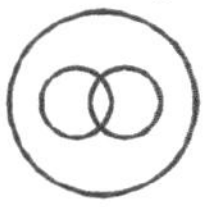   (b)

   (c) 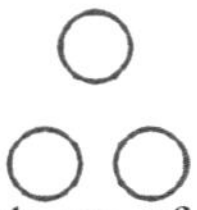   (d)

6. Which one of the following Venn diagram represents the best relationship between Snake, Lizard, Reptiles?

   (a)   (b)

   (c)   (d)

7. Which one of the following diagrams best depicts the relationship among Tiger, Lions and Animals?

   (a)    (b)

   (c)    (d)

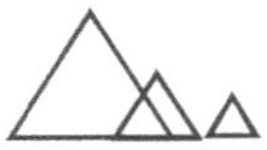

8. How many students take Maths and Physics but not Spanish?

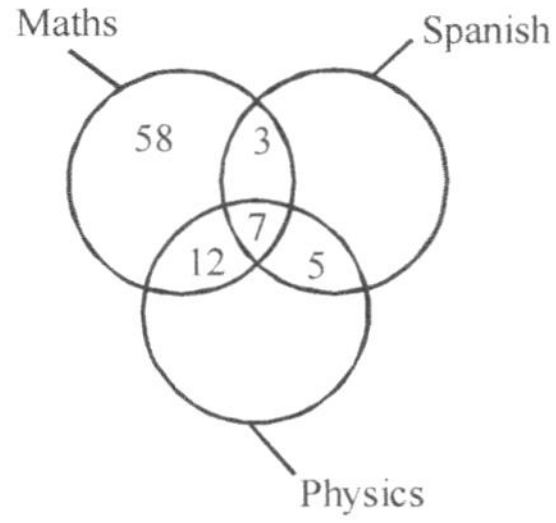

   Maths   Spanish

   58   3   7   12   5

   Physics

   (a) 12   (b) 7   (c) 3   (d) 5

9. Which figure represent the relationship among Sun, Moon, Molecule?

   (a) 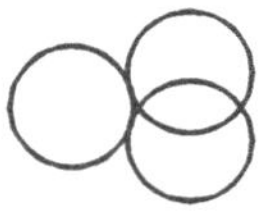   (b)

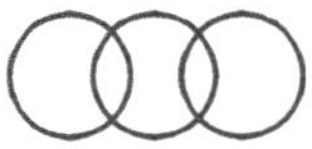

   (c)    (d)

10. In the following figure ◯ represents hardworking . △ represents sincere and ☐ represents intelligent. Find out the hardworking who are intelligent but not sincere.

    5   4   1   2   7   6   3

    (a) 1   (b) 2   (c) 3   (d) 4

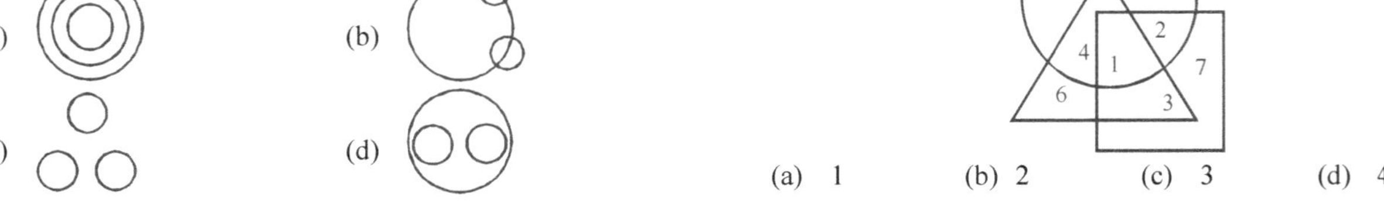

RESPONSE GRID					
	1. ⓐⓑⓒⓓ	2. ⓐⓑⓒⓓ	3. ⓐⓑⓒⓓ	4. ⓐⓑⓒⓓ	5. ⓐⓑⓒⓓ
	6. ⓐⓑⓒⓓ	7. ⓐⓑⓒⓓ	8. ⓐⓑⓒⓓ	9. ⓐⓑⓒⓓ	10. ⓐⓑⓒⓓ

Max. Marks : 15   **No. of Qs. 15**   **Time : 15 min.**   **Date : ..../........./................**

1. Which one of the following diagrams represents the correct relationship among Poison, Bio-products and Food?

(a) 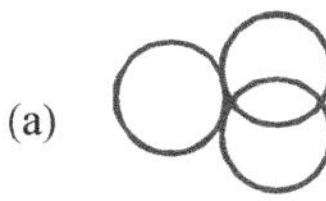   (b) 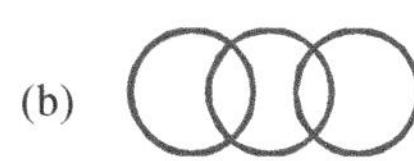

(c) 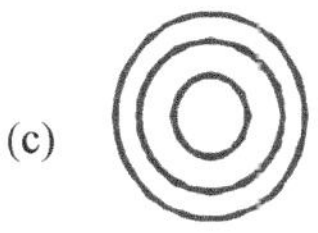   (d)

2. In the given figure the triangle represents people who visited Mysore, the circle represents people who visited Ooty, the square represents people who visited Munnar. The portion which represents people who visited both Mysore and Ooty is

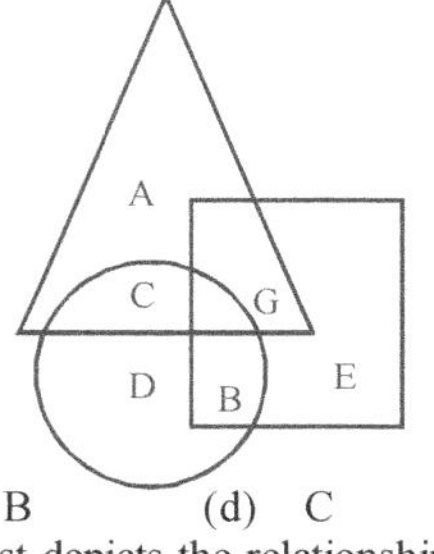

(a) D   (b) G   (c) B   (d) C

3. Which one of the following diagrams best depicts the relationship among pen, pencils, stationery?

(a) 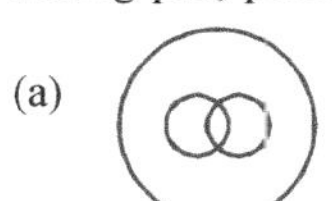   (b) 

(c)    (d) 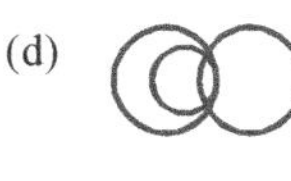

4. Indicate which figure will best represent the relationship amongst the three:
   Legumes Seeds, Peas, Kidney Beans

(a)    (b)

(c) 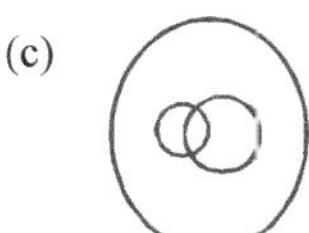   (d) 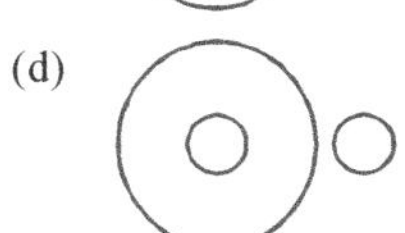

5. Which one of the following diagrams best depicts the relationship among Boys, Students and Athletes?

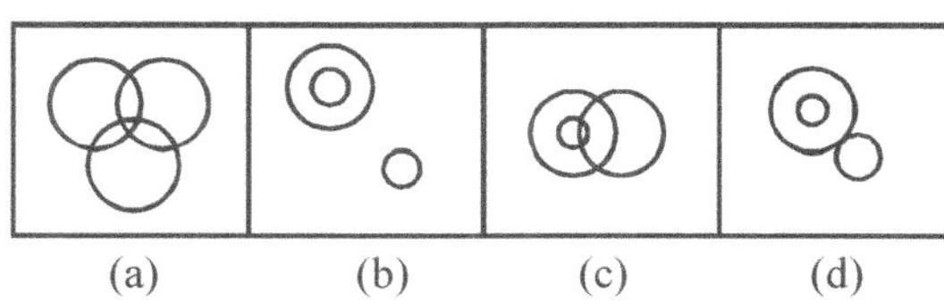

(a)   (b)   (c)   (d)

6. In the following figure, how many educated people are employed?

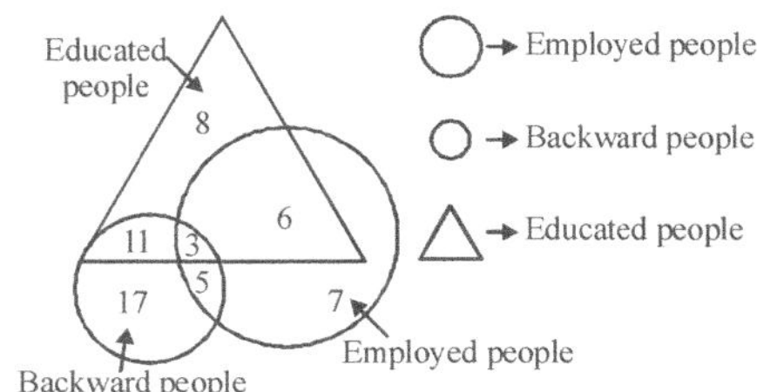

(a) 18   (b) 20   (c) 15   (d) 9

7. Which of the answer figure indicates the best relationship between milk, goat, cow, hen ?

Answer figures :

(a) 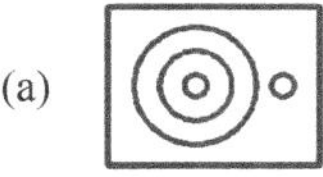   (b) 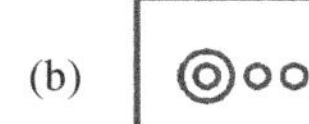

(c)    (d) 

Directions (Qs. 34-49) : In each of these questions, three words are related in some way. The relationship among the words in question can best represents by one of the five diagram.

(a) 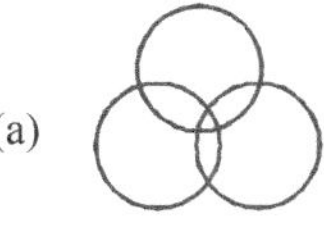   (b) 

(c)    (d)

8. People, Women, Mother
9. Tree, Plant, House
10. Fish, Herring, Animal living in water
11. Hospital, Nurse, Patient.
12. Nose, Hand, Body.
13. Rings, Ornaments, Diamond Rings.
14. Furniture, Table, Books.
15. Indoor games, Chess, Table tennis.

SYLLOGISMS

101 SPEED TEST 32

Max. Marks : 20   **No. of Qs. 20**   **Time : 20 min.**   **Date : ..../........./................**

Directions: In each of the following question, one, two or more statements are given followed by conclusion I, II or more. You have to consider the statements to be true, even if they seem to be at variance from commonly known facts. You are to decide which of the given conclusions definitely follows from the given statements.

1. **Statements:**
   1. All poets are intelligent.
   2. All singers are intelligent.
   Conclusions:
   I. All singers are poets.
   II. Some intelligent persons are not singers.
   (a) Only conclusion I follows.
   (b) Only conclusion II follows.
   (c) Either conclusion I or II follows.
   (d) Neither conclusion I nor II follows.

2. **Statements:**
   1. All students are boys.
   2. No boy is dull.
   Conclusions:
   I. There are no girls in the class.
   II. No student is dull.
   (a) Only conclusion I follows.
   (b) Only conclusion II follows.
   (c) Both conclusions I and II follows.
   (d) Neither conclusion I nor conclusion II follows.

3. **Statements:**
   1. All children are students.
   2. All students are players.
   Conclusions:
   I. All cricketer are students
   II. All children are players.
   (a) Only conclusion I follows.
   (b) Only conclusion II follows.
   (c) Both conclusions I or II follows.
   (d) Neither conclusion I nor conclusion II follows.

4. **Statements:**
   1. No teacher comes to the school on a bicycle.
   2. Anand comes to the school on a bicycle.
   Conclusions:
   I. Anand is not a teacher.   II. Anand is a student.
   (a) Conclusion I alone can be drawn.
   (b) Conclusion II alone can be drawn.
   (c) Both Conclusions can be drawn.
   (d) Both Conclusions can not be drawn.

5. **Statements:**
   1. Some food are sweet.   2. Some food are sour.
   Conclusions:
   I. All food are either sweet or sour.
   II. Some sweets are sour.
   (a) Only Conclusion I follows.
   (b) Only conclusion II follows.
   (c) Both Conclusions I and II follows.
   (d) Neither conclusion I nor II follows.

6. **Statements:**
   1. Science teachers do not use plastic bags.
   2. Plastic bags are not use by some engineers.
   Conclusions:
   I. All Science teachers are engineers.
   II. All Engineers do not use plastic bags.
   (a) Only conclusion I follows.
   (b) Only conclusion II follows.
   (c) Both conclusions I and II follow.
   (d) Neither conclusion I nor II follows.

7. **Statements:**
   1. All students are girls.   2. No girl is dull.
   Conclusions:
   I. There are no boys in the class.
   II. No student is dull.
   (a) Only conclusion II follows.
   (b) Both conclusions I and II follow.
   (c) Neither conclusion I nor conclusion II follows.
   (d) Only conclusion I follows.

8. **Statements:**
   1. All teachers are aged.
   2. Some women are teachers.
   Conclusions:
   I. All aged are women.   II. Some women are aged.
   (a) Only conclusion I follows.
   (b) Only conclusion II follows.
   (c) Neither conclusion I nor II follows.
   (d) Both conclusions I and II follow.

9. **Statements:**
   1. All skaters are good swimmers.
   2. All good swimmers are runners.
   Conclusions:
   I. Some runners are skaters.
   II. Some skaters are good swimmers.
   (a) Only conclusion I follows.
   (b) Only conclusion II follows.
   (c) Both conclusions I and II follow.
   (d) Neither conclusion I nor II follows.

10. **Statements:**
    1. All lawyers are liars.
    2. Some women are lawyers.
    Conclusions:
    I. Some women are liars.   II. All liars are women.
    (a) Neither conclusion I nor II follows.
    (b) Both conclusions I and II follow.
    (c) Only conclusion I follow.
    (d) Only conclusion II follows.

11. **Statements:**
    1. All stones are men.   2. All men are tigers.
    Conclusions:
    I. All stones are tigers.   II. All tigers are stones.
    III. All men are stones.   IV. Some tigers are stones
    (a) Only conclusion II and III follow.
    (b) Only conclusion II and IV follow.
    (c) All conclusions follow.
    (d) Conclusions I, II and IV follow.

12. **Statements:**
    1. All books are pens.   2. Some pens are scales.
    Conclucions:
    I. Some books are scales.   II. Some scales are books.
    III. Some scales are pens.   IV. Some pens are books.
    (a) Only conclusions I and II follows.
    (b) Only conclusion II and III follow.
    (c) Only conclusions III and IV follow.
    (d) Only conclusions I and IV follow.

13. **Statements:**
    1. All cities are towns.   2. Some cities are villages.
    Conclusions:
    I. All villages are towns.   II. No village is a towns.
    III. Some villages are town.
    (a) Only conclusions III follows
    (b) Only conclusion I follows
    (c) Only conclusion II follows
    (d) None of these

14. **Statements:**
    1. Some birds are clouds.   2. Horse is a bird.
    Conclucions:
    I. Some clouds are birds.
    II. Horse is not a cloud.
    (a) Only conclusion I follows.
    (b) Only conclusion II follows.
    (c) Either conclusion I or II follows.
    (d) Neither conclusion I nor II follows.

15. **Statements:**
    1. Ravi has five pens.
    2. No one else in the class has five pens.
    Conclusions:
    I. All students in the class have pens.
    II. All students in the class have five pens each.
    III. Some of the students have more than five pens.
    IV. Only one student in the class has exactly five pens.
    (a) Only conclusion I follows.
    (b) Only conclusion III follows.
    (c) Only conclusion II follows.
    (d) Only conclusions IV follows.

16. **Statements:**
    1. Some ladies are beautiful.
    2. Some beautifuls are honest.
    3. All honest are sensitives.
    Conclucions:
    I. Some sensitivies are beautifuls.
    II. Some honest are ladies.
    III. Some sensitives are ladies.
    (a) None of the Conclusion follows.
    (b) Only conclusion I follows.
    (c) Only conclusion I and II follow.
    (d) All Conclusions follow.

17. **Statements:**
    1. Some years are decades.
    2. All centuries are decades.
    Conclusions:
    I. Some centuries are years.
    II. Some decades are years.
    III. No century is a year.
    (a) Only conclusion either I or III follows.
    (b) Only conclusion I and II follow.
    (c) Only conclusion I and III follow.
    (d) Only conclusions I follows.

18. **Statements:**
    1. Ankit is a singer.   2. All the singers are fat.
    Conclucions:
    I. Ankit is fat.
    II. All fat men are singers.
    III. Fat men are not singers.
    IV. Ankit is not fat.
    (a) Only conclusion I follows.
    (b) Only conclusion II follows.
    (c) Only conclusion III follows.
    (d) Only conclusion IV follows.

19. **Statements:**
    1. Some cats are dogs.   2. No dog is a toy.
    Conclusions:
    I. Some dogs are cats.
    II. Some toys are cats.
    III. Some cats are not toys.
    IV. All toys are cats.
    (a) Only Conclusions I and III follow.
    (b) Only Conclusions II and III follow.
    (c) Only Conclusions I and II follow.
    (d) Only Conclusion I follows.

20. **Statements:**
    1. Some keys are locks, some locks are numbers.
    2. All numbers are letters, all letters are words.
    Conclusions:
    I. Some words are numbers.
    II. Some locks are letters.
    (a) Conclusion I follows.
    (b) Conclusion II follows.
    (c) Conclusion I and II follow.
    (d) None of the conclusion follows.

<table>
<tr><td rowspan="3">RESPONSE GRID</td><td>10. ⓐⓑⓒⓓ</td><td>11. ⓐⓑⓒⓓ</td><td>12. ⓐⓑⓒⓓ</td><td>13. ⓐⓑⓒⓓ</td><td>14. ⓐⓑⓒⓓ</td></tr>
<tr><td>15. ⓐⓑⓒⓓ</td><td>16. ⓐⓑⓒⓓ</td><td>17. ⓐⓑⓒⓓ</td><td>18. ⓐⓑⓒⓓ</td><td>19. ⓐⓑⓒⓓ</td></tr>
<tr><td>20. ⓐⓑⓒⓓ</td><td></td><td></td><td></td><td></td></tr>
</table>

Max. Marks : 10   **No. of Qs. 10**   **Time : 20 min.**   **Date : ..../........./................**

Directions (Qs. 1 -5) : In each of the following questions a series begins with an unnumbered figure on the extreme left. One and only one of the five lettered figures in the series does not fit into the series. The two unlabelled figures, one each on the extreme left and the extreme right, fit into the series. You have to take as many aspects into account as possible of the figures in the series and find out the one and only one of the five lettered figures which does not fit into the series. The letter of that figure is the answer.

1.
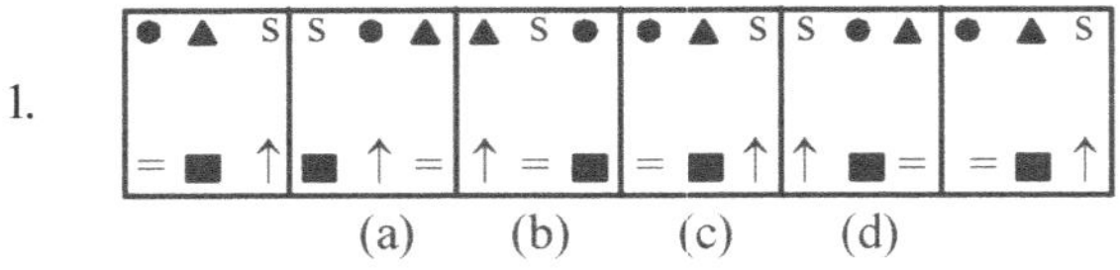
(a)   (b)   (c)   (d)

2.
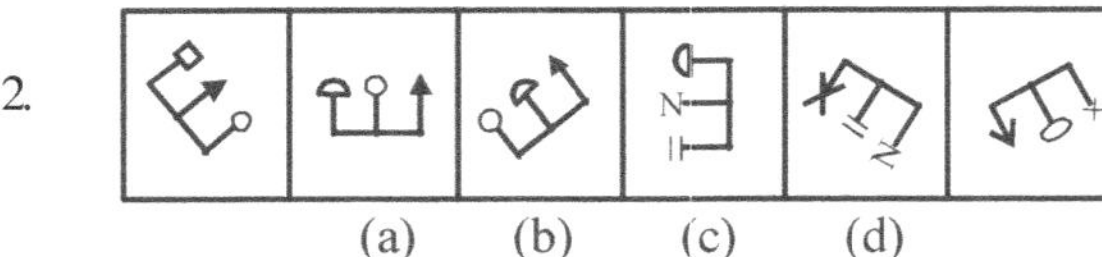
(a)   (b)   (c)   (d)

3.
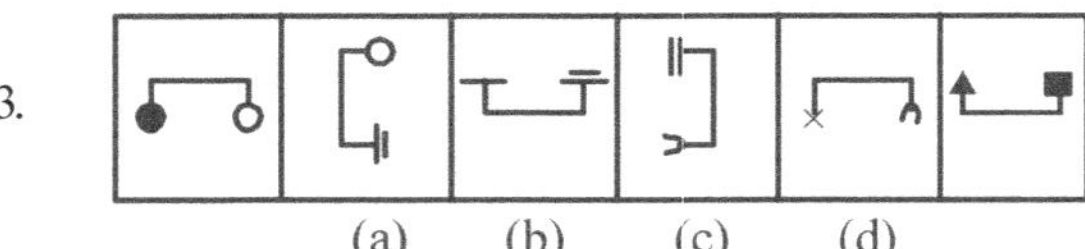
(a)   (b)   (c)   (d)

4.
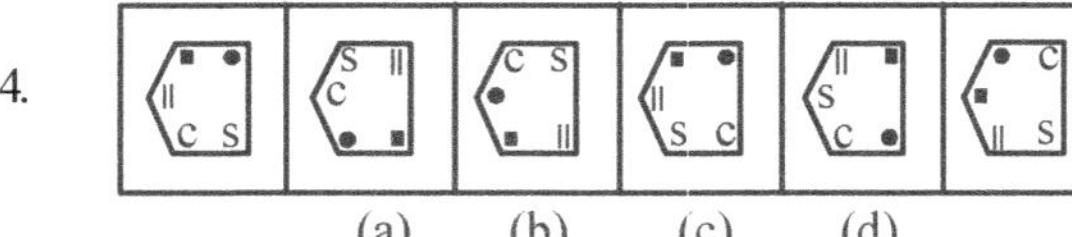
(a)   (b)   (c)   (d)

5.
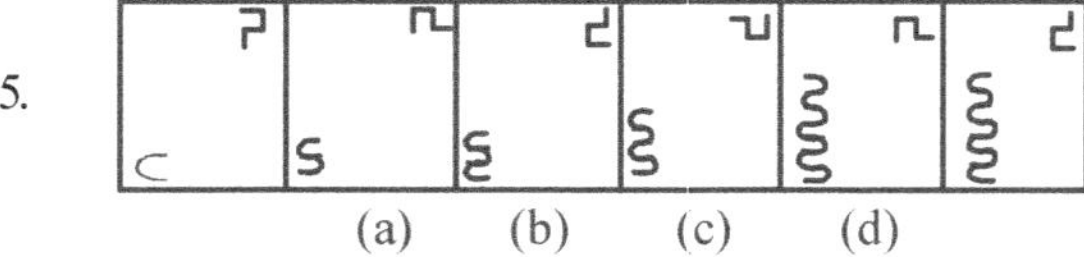
(a)   (b)   (c)   (d)

Directions (Qs. 6-10) : In each of the questions given below which one of the five answer figures on the bottom should come after the problem figures on the top if the sequence were continued?

6. **Problem Figures**
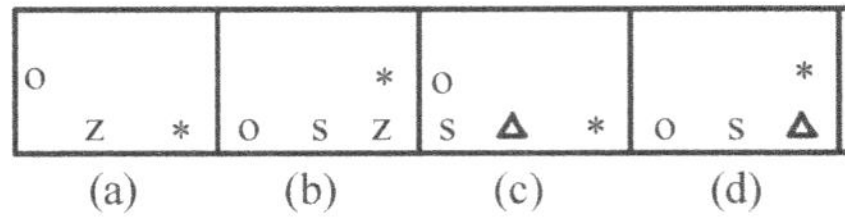

Answer Figures

(a)   (b)   (c)   (d)

7. **Problem Figures**
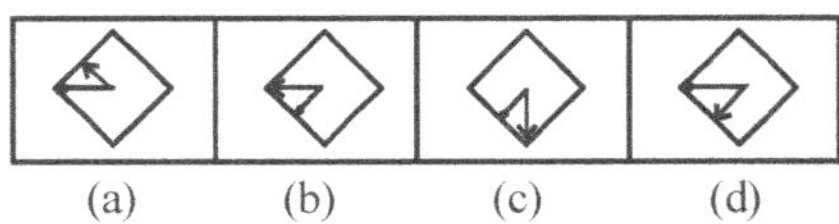

Answer Figures

(a)   (b)   (c)   (d)

8. **Problem Figures**
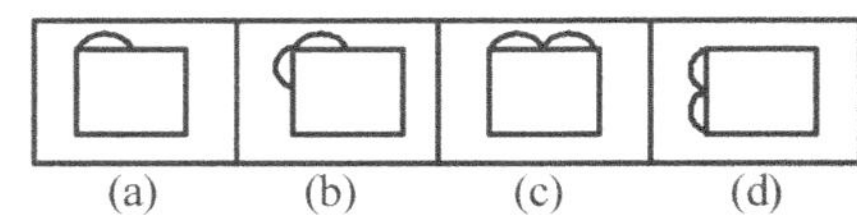

Answer Figures

(a)   (b)   (c)   (d)

9. **Problem Figures**
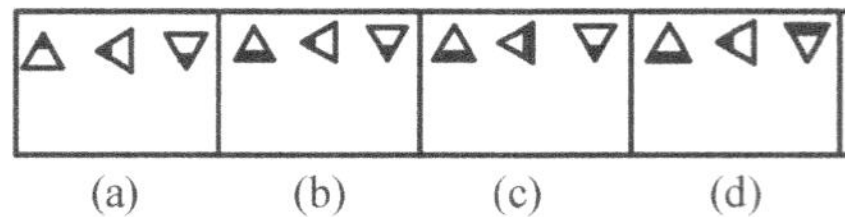

Answer Figures

(a)   (b)   (c)   (d)

10. **Problem Figures**
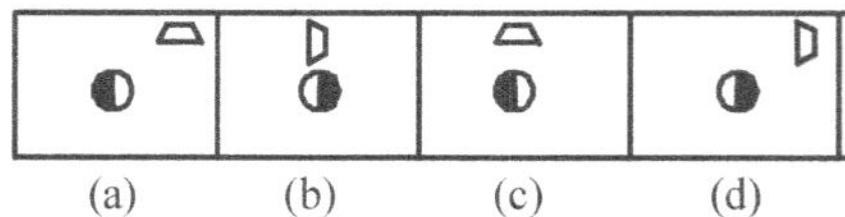

Answer Figures
(a)   (b)   (c)   (d)

RESPONSE	1. ⓐⓑⓒⓓ	2. ⓐⓑⓒⓓ	3. ⓐⓑⓒⓓ	4. ⓐⓑⓒⓓ	5. ⓐⓑⓒⓓ
GRID	6. ⓐⓑⓒⓓ	7. ⓐⓑⓒⓓ	8. ⓐⓑⓒⓓ	9. ⓐⓑⓒⓓ	10. ⓐⓑⓒⓓ

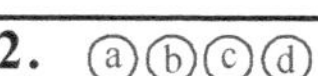
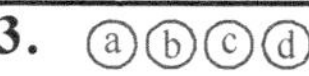
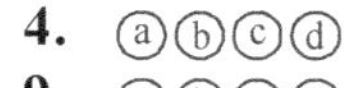

34

Max. Marks : 10   **No. of Qs. 10**   **Time : 15 min.**   **Date : ..../........./................**

1. A 'Square' is related to 'Cube' in the same way as a 'Circle' is related to
   - (a) Sphere
   - (b) Circumference
   - (c) Diameter
   - (d) Area

2. 'Mustard' is related to 'Seed' in the same way as 'Carrot' is related to
   - (a) Fruit
   - (b) Stem
   - (c) Flower
   - (d) Root

3. Four of the following five are alike in a certain way and so form a group. Which is the one that does not belong to that group ?
   - (a) Rose
   - (b) Jasmine
   - (c) Hibiscus
   - (d) Lotus

4. Four of the following five are alike in a certain way and so form a group. Which is the one that does not belong to that group?
   - (a) 21
   - (b) 35
   - (c) 42
   - (d) 49

5. What should come next in the number series given below ?
   1 1 2 1 2 3 1 2 3 4 1 2 3 4 5 1 2 3 4 5 6 1 2 3 4 5 6
   - (a) 5
   - (b) 2
   - (c) 8
   - (d) None of these

6. What should come next in the following letter series?
   A B C D P Q R S A B C D E P Q R S T A B C D E F P Q R S T
   - (a) A
   - (b) V
   - (c) U
   - (d) W

7. How many such pairs of letters are there in the word GOLDEN, each of which has as many letters between them in the word as in the English alphabet?
   - (a) None
   - (b) One
   - (c) Two
   - (d) Three

8. How many three - letter meaningful words can be formed from the word TEAR beginning with 'A' without repeating any letter within that word?
   - (a) One
   - (b) Three
   - (c) Five
   - (d) Two

9. If 'table' is called 'chair'; 'chair' is called `cupboard', 'cupboard' is called 'chalk', 'chalk' is called 'book', 'book'
   is called 'duster' and 'duster' is called 'table', what does the teacher use to write on the black board?
   - (a) book
   - (b) cupboard
   - (c) table
   - (d) duster

10. Saroj is mother-in-law of Vani who is sister-in-law of Deepak. Rajesh is father of Ramesh, the only brother of Deepak. How is Saroj related to Deepak?
    - (a) Mother-in-law
    - (b) Wife
    - (c) Aunt
    - (d) Mother

Max. Marks : 10   **No. of Qs. 10**   **Time : 15 min.**   **Date : ..../........./................**

1. A man pointing to a photograph says, "The lady in the photograph is my nephew's maternal grandmother and her son is my sister's brother-in-law. How is the lady in the photograph related to his sister who has no other sister?
   (a) Mother
   (b) Cousin
   (c) Mother-in-law
   (d) Sister-in-law

2. If 'DO' is written as 'FQ' and 'IN' is written as 'KP' then how would 'AT' be written?
   (a) C V
   (b) B S
   (c) C U
   (d) D V

3. If 8 is written as B, 1 as R, 6 as K, 9 as O, 4 as M, 7 as W and 3 as T, then how, would WROMBT be Written in the numeric form?
   (a) 714983
   (b) 719483
   (c) 769483
   (d) 719486

4. If blue means green, green means black, black means white, white means pink, pink means red and red means orange, then what is the colour of blood?
   (a) Red
   (b) Black
   (c) White
   (d) None of these

5. School children

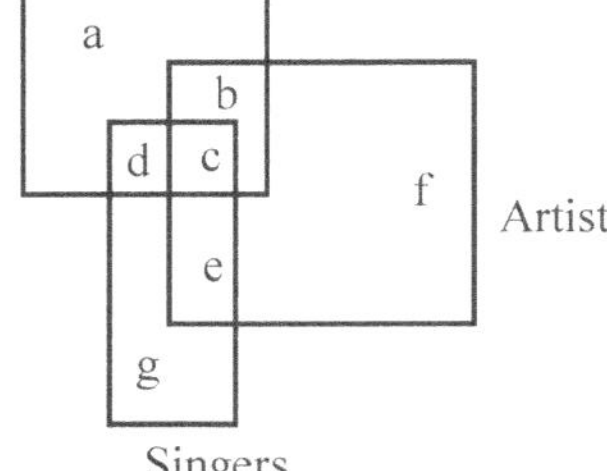

   Above diagram represents school children, artist and singers. Study the diagram and identify the region. Which represents those school children who are artist not singers.
   (a) a
   (b) b
   (c) f
   (d) e

6. In question below are given three statements followed by two conclusions numbered I and II. You have to take the given statements to be true even if they seem to be at variance from commonly known facts. Read both of the conclusions and then decide which of the given conclusions logically follows from the given statements disregarding commonly known facts.

   Statements: Some phones are computers.
   All computers are radios.
   All radios are televisions.

   Conclusions: I. All televisions are computers.
   II. Some radios are phones.
   (a) None follows
   (b) Only I follows
   (c) Only II follows
   (d) Both I and II follow

7. Ram walks 10 m south from his house, turns left and walks 25 m, again turns left and walks 40 m, then turns right and walks 5 m to reach to the school. In which direction the school is from his house ?
   (a) South-west
   (b) North-east
   (c) East
   (d) North

8. How many meaningful five-letter words can be formed with the letters SLIKL using each letter only once ?
   (a) One
   (b) Two
   (c) Three
   (d) More than three

9. The positions of how many alphabets will remain unchanged if each of the alphabets in the word WALKING is arranged in alphabetical order from left to right ?
   (a) None
   (b) One
   (c) Two
   (d) Three

10. Which one of the letters when sequentially placed at the gaps in the given letter series shall complete it?
    a – c a – b c – b c c – b c a
    (a) b b a b
    (b) b a b a
    (c) a a b b
    (d) b b a a

RESPONSE GRID	1. ⓐⓑⓒⓓ	2. ⓐⓑⓒⓓ	3. ⓐⓑⓒⓓ	4. ⓐⓑⓒⓓ	5. ⓐⓑⓒⓓ
	6. ⓐⓑⓒⓓ	7. ⓐⓑⓒⓓ	8. ⓐⓑⓒⓓ	9. ⓐⓑⓒⓓ	10. ⓐⓑⓒⓓ

MECHANICS-I

101 SPEED TEST 36

Max. Marks : 20　　　**No. of Qs. 20**　　　**Time : 20 min.**　　　**Date :** ..../........../................

1. Two bodies of different masses say 1 kg and 5kg are dropped simultaneously from a tower. They will reach the ground
   (a) simultaneously
   (b) the heavier one arriving earlier
   (c) the lighter one arriving earlier
   (d) cannot say, the information is insufficient.

2. The numerical ratio of displacement to distance for a moving object is
   (a) always less than 1　　　(b) always equal to 1
   (c) always more than 1　　　(d) equal to less than 1

3. A man is walking from east to west on a level rough surface. The frictional force on the man is directed
   (a) from the west to east　　　(b) from the east to west
   (c) along the north　　　(d) along the west

4. A parrot is sitting on the floor of a closed glass cage which is in a boy's hand. If the parrot starts flying with a constant speed, the boy will feel the weight of the cage as
   (a) unchanged　　　(b) reduced
   (c) increased　　　(d) nothing can be said

5. The working principle of a washing machine is :
   (a) centrifugation　　　(b) dialysis
   (c) reverse osmosis　　　(d) diffusion

6. If a body is moving at constant speed in a circular path, its
   (a) velocity is constant and its acceleration is zero
   (b) velocity and acceleration are both changing direction only
   (c) velocity and acceleration are both increasing
   (d) velocity is constant and acceleration is changing direction

7. When a motorcar makes a sharp turn at a high speed, we tend to get thrown to one side because
   (a) we tend to continue in our straight line motion
   (b) an unbalanced force is applied by the engine of the motorcar changes the direction of motion of the motorcar
   (c) we slip to one side of the seat due to the inertia of our body
   (d) All of these

8. A hockey player pushes the ball on the ground. It comes to rest after travelling certain distance because
   (a) player stops pushing the ball
   (b) unbalanced force action on the wall
   (c) ball moves only when pushes
   (d) opposing force acts on the body.

9. A body having zero speed
   (i) is always under rest　　　(ii) has zero acceleration
   (iii) has uniform acceleration　　　(iv) always under motion
   (a) (i) and (ii) only　　　(b) (ii) and (iii) only
   (c) (i) and (iii) only　　　(d) (i), (ii) and (iii)

10. Two balls A and B of same masses are thrown from the top of the building. A, thrown upward with velocity V and B, thrown downward with velocity V, then –
    (a) velocity of A is more than B at the ground
    (b) velocity of B is more than A at the ground
    (c) both A and B strike the ground with same velocity
    (d) none of these

11. Which of the following curves do not represent motion in one dimension?

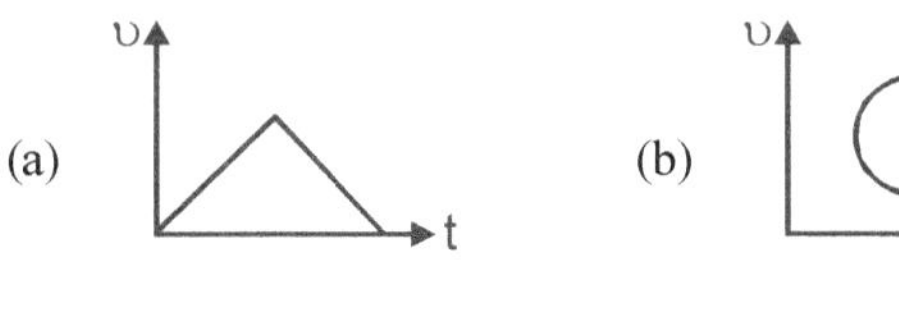

12. A hunter aims at a monkey sitting on a tree at a consideratble distance. At the instant he fires at it, the monkey drops. Will the bullet hit the monkey.
    (a) No　　　(b) Yes
    (c) Sometimes　　　(d) Never

<table>
<tr><td rowspan="3">RESPONSE
GRID</td><td>1. ⓐⓑⓒⓓ</td><td>2. ⓐⓑⓒⓓ</td><td>3. ⓐⓑⓒⓓ</td><td>4. ⓐⓑⓒⓓ</td><td>5. ⓐⓑⓒⓓ</td></tr>
<tr><td>6. ⓐⓑⓒⓓ</td><td>7. ⓐⓑⓒⓓ</td><td>8. ⓐⓑⓒⓓ</td><td>9. ⓐⓑⓒⓓ</td><td>10. ⓐⓑⓒⓓ</td></tr>
<tr><td>11. ⓐⓑⓒⓓ</td><td>12. ⓐⓑⓒⓓ</td><td></td><td></td><td></td></tr>
</table>

13. A car sometimes overturns while taking a turn. When it overturns, it is
    (a) the inner wheel which leaves the ground first
    (b) the outer wheel which leaves the ground first
    (c) both the wheel leave the ground simultaneously
    (d) either wheel will leave the ground first

14. A cyclist taking turn bends inwards while a car passenger taking the same turn is thrown outwards. The reason is
    (a) Car is heavier than cycle
    (b) Car has four wheels while cycle has only two
    (c) Difference in the speed of the two
    (d) Cyclist has to counteract the centrifugal force while in the case of car only the passenger is thrown by this force

15. Which is a suitable method to decrease friction?
    (a) Polishing   (b) Lubrication
    (c) Ball bearing   (d) All of these

16. A cricketer lowers his hands while holding a catch because
    (a) The momentum decreases with time
    (b) The velocity decreases with time
    (c) The force decreases as time increases
    (d) It is a style of holding a catch

17. Depression on sand is more when you are standing than when you are lying down, because
    (a) In standing position, for equal thrust, area is smaller so pressure is more
    (b) In lying position, more area is involved so thrust is less and pressure is more
    (c) Thrust is more in standing position
    (d) Centre of gravity lowers down while lying down, so pressure is more

18. A ladder is more apt to slip when you are high up on its rung than when you are just begin to climb. Why?
    (a) When you are high up, the moment of force tending to rotate the ladder about its base increase, while in the latter case, the moment of inertia is insufficient to cause slipping.
    (b) When you are high up, the ladder is in unstable, equilibrium
    (c) As you climb up, your potential energy increases
    (d) When you are high up, the centre of gravity of the system shifts upwards so the ladder is unstable, while in the latter case the system is more stable

19. Going 50 m to the south of her house, Radhika turns left and goes another 20 m. Then turning to the north, she goes 30 m and then starts walking to her house. In which direction is she walking now ?
    (a) North West   (b) North
    (c) South East   (d) East

20. In which of the following cases, the net force is not zero ?
    (a) A kite skillfully held stationary in the sky.
    (b) A ball falling freely from a height
    (c) An aeroplane rising upwards at an angle of 45° with the horizontal with a constant speed
    (d) A cork floating on the surface of water

MECHANICS-II

101 SPEED TEST 37

Max. Marks : 20   **No. of Qs. 20**   **Time : 20 min.**   **Date : ..../........./................**

1. An artificial satellite orbiting the earth does not fall down because the earth's attraction
    (a) is balanced by the attraction of the moon
    (b) vanishes at such distances
    (c) is balanced by the viscous drag produced by the atmosphere
    (d) produces the necessary acceleration of its motion in a curved path

2. All bodies whether large or small fall with the
    (a) same force   (b) same acceleration
    (c) same velocity   (d) same momentum

3. The weight of a body at the centre of the earth is
    (a) zero   (b) infinite
    (c) same as at other places
    (d) slightly greater than that at poles

4. A boy is whirling a stone tied with a string in an horizontal circular path the string breaks, the stone
    (a) will continue to move in the circular path
    (b) will move along a straight line towards the centre of the circular path
    (c) will move along a straight line tangential to the circular path
    (d) will move along a straight line perpendicular to the circular path away from the boy

5. The weight of an object is the
    (a) Mass of the object
    (b) Force with which it is attracted towards the earth
    (c) Product of its mass and acceleration due to gravity
    (d) Only (b) and (c)

6. Potential energy of your body is minimum when you
    (a) are standing   (b) are sitting on a chair
    (c) are sitting on the ground   (d) lie down on the ground

7. If a running boy jumps on a rotating table, which of the following is conserved.
    (a) Linear momentum   (b) K.E
    (c) Angular momentum   (d) Neither of above

8. An athlete runs some distance before taking a long jump because
    (a) he gains energy to take him through long distance
    (b) it helps to apply large force
    (c) by running action and reaction force increases
    (d) by running the athlete gives himself larger inertia of motion

9. A metal ball hits a wall and does not rebound whereas a rubber ball of the same mass on hitting the wall with the same velocity rebounds back. It can be concluded that
    (a) metal ball suffers greater change in momentum
    (b) rubber ball suffers greater change in momentum
    (c) the initial momentum of metal ball is greater than initial momentum of rubber ball
    (d) both suffer same change in momentum

10. A boy carrying a box on his head is walking on a level road from one place to antoher on a straight road is doing no work. This statement is
    (a) correct   (b) incorrect
    (c) partly correct   (d) insufficient data

11. A man stands at one end of a boat which is stationary in water. Neglect water resistance. The man now moves to the other end of the boat and again becomes stationary. The centre of mass of the 'man plus boat' system will remain stationary with respect to water
    (a) in all cases
    (b) only when the man is stationary initially and finally
    (c) only if the man moves without acceleration on the boat
    (d) only if the man and the boat have equal masses

12. To an astronaut in a space ship the sky appears black due to
    (a) absence of atmosphere in his neighbourhood
    (b) light from the sky is absorbed by the medium surrounding him
    (c) the fact that at height, sky radiations are only in the infra-red and the ultraviolet region
    (d) none of the above

13. When an air bubble at the bottom of a lake rises to the top, it will
    (a) maintain its size   (b) decrease in size
    (c) increase in size
    (d) flatten into a dishlike shape

14. A chair is tilted about two of its legs and then left. It would return to its original position if
    (a) It is tilted through an angle of $60°$
    (b) It centre of gravity falls within the base.
    (c) Its centre of gravity falls outside the base.
    (d) It will never regain its original position.

15. 'Black holes' refers to
    (a) Collapsing object of high density
    (b) Bright spots on the sun
    (c) Holes occuring in heavenly bodies
    (d) Collapsing object of low density

16. Atmospheric pressure exerted on earth is due to the
    (a) Gravitational pull   (b) Revolution of earth
    (c) Rotation of earth   (d) Uneven heating of earth

17. If a toy boat in a tank sinks, the level of water will
    (a) Fluctuate   (b) Decrease
    (c) Increase   (d) Remain the same

18. If we go inside a mine and drop a 10 lb iron ball and 1 lb aluminium ball from the top of a high plaftform
    (a) Both will reach the floor at the same time
    (b) 1 lb weight will reach the floor first
    (c) 10 lb weight will reach the floor first
    (d) It is not possible to indicate which of the two will reach the floor first without further data

19. A man pushes a wall and fails to displace it. He does
    (a) Positive but not maximum work
    (b) negative work
    (c) maximum work   (d) No work at all

20. If the earth losses its gravity then for a body
    (a) weight becomes zero but not the mass
    (b) mass becomes zero but not the weight
    (c) both mass and weight become zero
    (d) Neither mass nor weight become zero.

Max. Marks : 20   **No. of Qs. 20**   **Time : 20 min.**   Date : ..../........./.................

1. An ice block floats in a liquid whose density is less than water. A part of block is outside the liquid. When whole of ice has melted, the liquid level will
   - (a) Rise
   - (b) Go down
   - (c) Remain same
   - (d) First rise then go down

2. The rain drops falling from the sky neither injure us nor make holes on the ground because they move with
   - (a) constant acceleration
   - (b) variable acceleration
   - (c) variable speed
   - (d) constant terminal velocity

3. A liquid flows through a non-uniform pipe. The pressure in the pipe will be
   - (a) lower where the cross-section is smaller
   - (b) the same throughout the pipe
   - (c) higher where the cross-section is smaller
   - (d) higher where velocity of the liquid is smaller

4. The clouds float in the atmosphere because of their low
   - (a) pressure
   - (b) velocity
   - (c) temperature
   - (d) density

5. A small wooden block is floating in a tub of water. The water is gradually heated. The volume of the wooden block visible above the water level
   - (a) Fluctuates
   - (b) Decrease
   - (c) Increases
   - (d) Remains the same

6. Hydraulic brakes are based on
   - (a) Dulong and Petit's law
   - (b) Pascal's law
   - (c) Pressure law
   - (d) Dalton's law of partial pressure

7. Two cubes of equal mass, one made of iron and the other of aluminium are immersed in water and weighed. Under such case
   - (a) The weight of aluminium cube will be less than that of the iron cube
   - (b) The two weights will be equal
   - (c) The weight of the iron cube will be less than that of the aluminium cube
   - (d) The data provided is insufficient

8. An iceberg is floating in the sea. Out of 10 parts of its mass, how many will remain above the surface of the water ?
   - (a) Three parts
   - (b) Two parts
   - (c) One part
   - (d) Five parts

9. The relative densities of three liquids X, Y and Z are 0.7, 1.2 and 1.7 respectively. A small rod floats vertically just fully immersed in the liquid Y. Which of the following set of diagrams illustrates the equilibrium positions of the rod in the liquids X and Z?

(a) 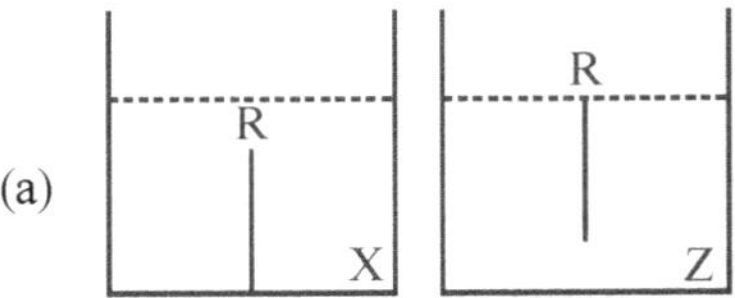

(b) 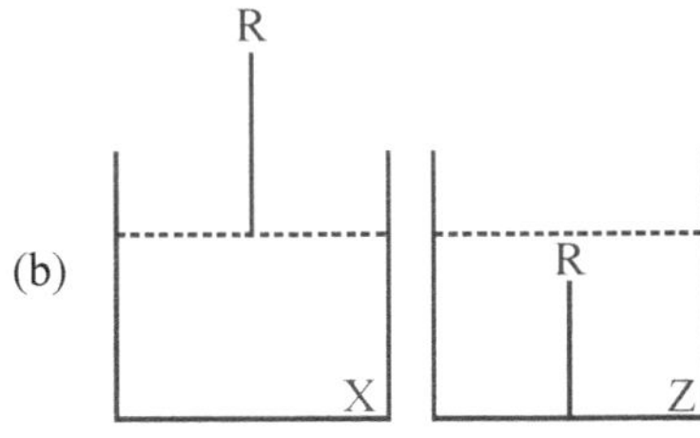

(c) 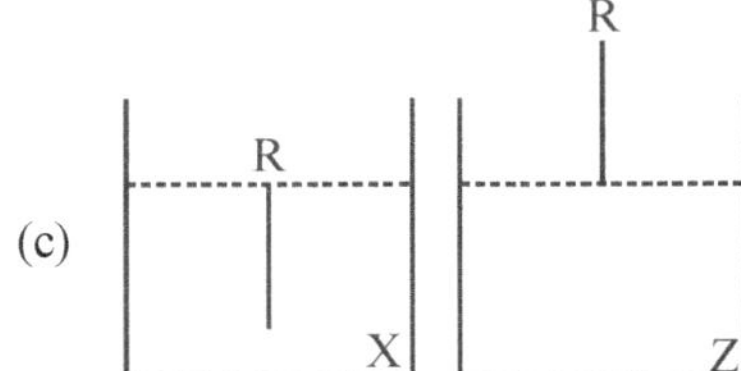

(d) 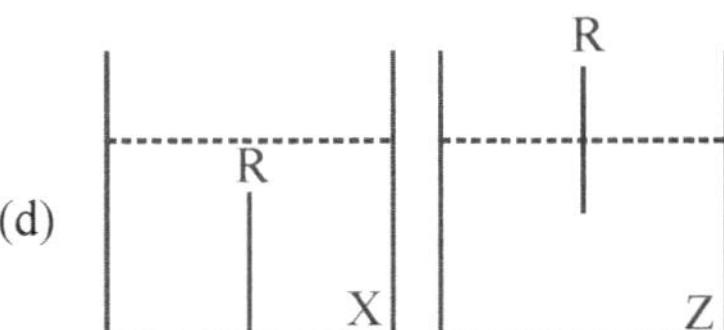

10. Construction of a submarrine is based on
    - (a) Bernoulli's theorem
    - (b) Pascal's law
    - (c) Archimedes's principle
    - (d) None of these

RESPONSE GRID	1. ⓐⓑⓒⓓ	2. ⓐⓑⓒⓓ	3. ⓐⓑⓒⓓ	4. ⓐⓑⓒⓓ	5. ⓐⓑⓒⓓ
	6. ⓐⓑⓒⓓ	7. ⓐⓑⓒⓓ	8. ⓐⓑⓒⓓ	9. ⓐⓑⓒⓓ	10. ⓐⓑⓒⓓ

11. Rain drops are falling with a constant speed by the time they reach the ground because
    (a) Rain drops originate in outer space where the gravitational forces are negligible
    (b) The force due to air resistance increases with the speed of the rain drops until it balances the gravitational force
    (c) Rain drops are too light and hence not affected by acceleration due to gravity
    (d) The force due to air resistance is constant and balances the gravitational force
12. The spherical shape of rain-drop is due to
    (a) Density of the liquid   (b) Surface tension
    (c) Atmospheric pressure   (d) Gravity
13. Air is blown through a hole on a closed pipe containing liquid. Then the pressure will
    (a) Increase on sides
    (b) Increase downwards
    (c) Increase in all directions
    (d) Never increases
14. A large ship can float but a steel needle sinks because of
    (a) Viscosity   (b) Surface tension
    (c) Density   (d) None of these
15. In the following figure is shown the flow of liquid through a horizontal pipe. Three tubes A, B and C are connected to the pipe. The radii of the tubes A, B and C at the junction are respectively 2cm, 1 cm and 2 cm. It can be said that the

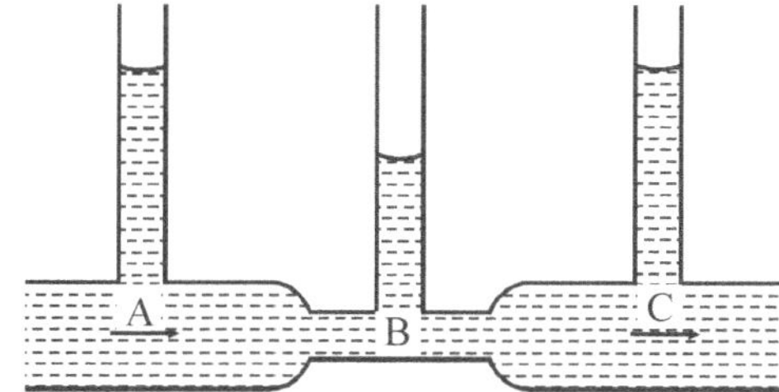

(a) Height of the liquid in the tube A is maximum
(b) Height of one liquid in the tubes A and B is the same
(c) Height of the liquid in the three tubes is the same
(d) Height of the liquid in the tubes A and C is the same
16. The working of an atomizer depends upon
    (a) Bernoulli's theorem
    (b) Boyle's law
    (c) Archimedes principle
    (d) Newton's law of motion
17. Velocity of water in a river is
    (a) Same everywhere
    (b) More in the middle and less near its banks
    (c) Less in the middle and more near its banks
    (d) Increase from one bank to other bank
18. To keep constant time, watches are fitted with balance wheel made of
    (a) Invar
    (b) Stainless steel
    (c) Tungsten
    (d) Platinum
19. Writing on blackboard with a piece of chalk is possible by the property of
    (a) Adhesive force
    (b) Cohesive force
    (c) Surface tension
    (d) Viscosity
20. The most characteristic property of a liquid is
    (a) elasticity
    (b) fluidity
    (c) formlessness
    (d) volume conservation

| **RESPONSE** | 11. ⓐⓑⓒⓓ | 12. ⓐⓑⓒⓓ | 13. ⓐⓑⓒⓓ | 14. ⓐⓑⓒⓓ | 15. ⓐⓑⓒⓓ |
| **GRID** | 16. ⓐⓑⓒⓓ | 17. ⓐⓑⓒⓓ | 18. ⓐⓑⓒⓓ | 19. ⓐⓑⓒⓓ | 20. ⓐⓑⓒⓓ |

HEAT

101 SPEED TEST

39

Max. Marks : 20   **No. of Qs. 20**   **Time : 20 min.**   **Date : ..../........./................**

1. A metal sheet with a circular hole is heated. The hole
   - (a) gets larger
   - (b) gets smaller
   - (c) remains of the same size
   - (d) gets deformed
2. In a pressure cooker the cooking is fast, because
   - (a) the boiling point of water is raised by the increased pressure inside the cooker
   - (b) the boiling point of water is lowered by pressure
   - (c) more steam is available to cook the food at 100°C
   - (d) more pressure is available to cook the food at 100°C
3. Two blocks of ice when pressed together join to form a block because
   - (a) of heat produced during pressing
   - (b) of cold produced during pressing
   - (c) melting point of ice decreases with increase of pressure
   - (d) melting point of ice increases with increase in pressure
4. Which of the following combinations of properties would be most desirable for a cooking pot?
   - (a) high specific heat and low conductivity
   - (b) low specific heat and high conductivity
   - (c) high specific heat and high conductivity
   - (d) low specific heat and low conductivity
5. It is difficult to cook at high altitude, because
   - (a) there is less oxygen in the air
   - (b) due to fall in temperature, one has to give more heat
   - (c) due to decrease in atmosphereic pressure, the boiling point of water decreases
   - (d) of high moisture content at higher altitudes
6. Cryogenic engines find applications in
   - (a) Rocket technology
   - (b) Frost-free refrigerators
   - (c) Sub-marine propulsion
   - (d) Researches in superconductivity
7. A thermometer for measuring very low temperature is called
   - (a) Cryometer
   - (b) Bolometer
   - (c) Pyrometer
   - (d) Platinum resistance thermometer
8. Brick walls are used in the construction of a cold storage because
   - (a) Brick is a bad conductor
   - (b) It is cheaper
   - (c) It is easier to construct
   - (d) None of these
9. When the door of a refrigerator in a room is kept open, the temperature of the room
   - (a) decreases
   - (b) neither (a) nor (b)
   - (c) increases
   - (d) cannot say
10. A closed bottle containing water (at 30°C) is carried in a spaceship and placed on the surface of the moon. What will happen to the water when the bottle is opened ?
    - (a) Nothing will happen to it
    - (b) Water will freeze
    - (c) Water will boil
    - (d) It will decompose into H_2 and O_2
11. Water in an earthen pot cools below the room temperature due to
    - (a) Absence of radiation
    - (b) Evaporation of water from the surface of the pot
    - (c) Insulation
    - (d) Absence of convection
12. Two thin blankets are warmer than a single one of the same thickness because
    - (a) The air layer trapped in between the two blankets is a bad conductor
    - (b) The distance of heat transmission is increased
    - (c) The total mass of the blankets will be more
    - (d) None of these
13. Heat from the sun is received by the earth through
    - (a) Radiation
    - (b) Convection
    - (c) Conduction
    - (d) None of the above
14. 'Green house effect' means
    - (a) Pollution in houses in tropical region
    - (b) Trapping of solar energy due to atmospheric oxygen
    - (c) Trapping of solar energy due to atmospheric carbon dioxide
    - (d) None of the above
15. What is solar prominence ?
    - (a) A relative cool area on the Sun's surface
    - (b) A huge burst of fiery hydrogen gas from the Sun's photosphere
    - (c) An active region of Sun spots
    - (d) All of these
16. Water has maximum density at
    - (a) 0°C
    - (b) 32°F
    - (c) –4°C
    - (d) 4°C
17. A beaker is completely filled with water at 4°C. It will overflow if
    - (a) Heated above 4°C
    - (b) Cooled below 4°C
    - (c) Both heated and cooled above and below 4°C respectively
    - (d) None of the above
18. 540 g of ice at 0°C is mixed with 540 g of water at 80°C. The final temperature of the mixture is
    - (a) 0°C
    - (b) 40°C
    - (c) 80°C
    - (d) Less than 0°C
19. The sprinkling of water reduces slightly the temperature of a closed room because
    - (a) Temperature of water is less than that of the room
    - (b) Specific heat of water is high
    - (c) Water has large latent heat of vaporisation
    - (d) Water is a bad conductor of heat
20. Water is used to cool radiators of engines, because
    - (a) Of its lower density
    - (b) It is easily available
    - (c) It is cheap
    - (d) It has high specific heat

RESPONSE GRID	1. ⓐⓑⓒⓓ	2. ⓐⓑⓒⓓ	3. ⓐⓑⓒⓓ	4. ⓐⓑⓒⓓ	5. ⓐⓑⓒⓓ
	6. ⓐⓑⓒⓓ	7. ⓐⓑⓒⓓ	8. ⓐⓑⓒⓓ	9. ⓐⓑⓒⓓ	10. ⓐⓑⓒⓓ
	11. ⓐⓑⓒⓓ	12. ⓐⓑⓒⓓ	13. ⓐⓑⓒⓓ	14. ⓐⓑⓒⓓ	15. ⓐⓑⓒⓓ
	16. ⓐⓑⓒⓓ	17. ⓐⓑⓒⓓ	18. ⓐⓑⓒⓓ	19. ⓐⓑⓒⓓ	20. ⓐⓑⓒⓓ

SOUND

101 SPEED TEST 40

Max. Marks : 20   **No. of Qs. 20**   **Time : 20 min.**   **Date : ..../........./................**

1. An empty vessel produces louder sound than a filled one because
   (a) The liquid in the filled vessel absorbs the vibrations of the liquid molecules
   (b) The air molecules in empty vessel have greater amplitude and hence greater intensity than liquid molecules in the filled vessel
   (c) The density of air is less than the density of liquid contained in the vessel when filled
   (d) The kinetic energy of particles constituting the air column is greater as compared to the kinetic energy of particles of liquid column

2. Echo is the effect produced due to
   (a) Reflection of sound
   (b) Dispersion of sound
   (c) Absorption of sound
   (d) Refraction of sound

3. A stone is dropped in a well and splash is heard after 1.5 seconds after the stone hits the water surface. If the velocity of sound is 327 m/s, the depth of the well is
   (a) 654.0 m   (b) 490.5 m   (c) 227 m   (d) 981.0 m

4. During thunderstorm lightning is seen first and thunder is heard later on Why?
   (a) First light and then sound is produced
   (b) Light travels faster than sound
   (c) Sound travels faster than light
   (d) Sound becomes feeble due to storm

5. In the microphone, used in the public address system
   (a) Electric signals are first converted into sound waves
   (b) Sound waves are directly transmitted
   (c) Sound waves are converted into electric signals which are amplified and transmitted
   (d) Amplification is not required

6. Sitar maestro Ravi Shankar is playing sitar on its strings, and you, as a physicist (unfortunately without musical ears), observed the following oddities.
   I. The greater the length of a vibrating string, the smaller its frequency.
   II. The greater the tension in the string, the greater is the frequency
   III. The heavier the mass of the string, the smaller the frequency.
   IV. The thinner the wire, the higher its frequency.
   The maestro signalled the following combination as correct one :
   (a) II, III and IV
   (b) I, II and IV
   (c) I, II and III
   (d) I, II, III and IV

7. A big explosion on the Moon cannot be heard on the Earth because
   (a) The explosion produces high frequency sound wave which are inaudiable
   (b) Sound waves require a material medium for propagation
   (c) Sound waves are absorbed in the atmosphere of moon
   (d) Sound waves are absorbed in Earth's atmosphere

8. A man sets his watch by a whistle that is 2 km away. How much will his watch be in error. (speed of sound in air 330 m/sec)
   (a) 3 seconds fast
   (b) 3 seconds slow
   (c) 6 seconds fast
   (d) 6 seconds slow

9. Velocity of sound is maximum in
   (a) Air   (b) Water   (c) Vacuum   (d) Steel

10. Frequency range of the audible sounds is
    (a) 0 Hz – 30 Hz
    (b) 20 Hz – 20 kHz
    (c) 20 kHz – 20,000 kHz
    (d) 20 kHz – 20 MHz

11. On which principle does sonometer works
    (a) Hooke's Law
    (b) Elasticity
    (c) Resonance
    (d) Newton's Law

12. When we hear a sound, we can identify its source from
    (a) Amplitude of sound
    (b) Intensity of sound
    (c) Wavelength of sound
    (d) Overtones present in the sound

13. In the musical octave ' Sa', 'Re', 'Ga'
    (a) The frequency of the note 'Sa' is greater than that of 'Re', 'Ga'
    (b) The frequency of the note 'Sa' is smaller than that of 'Re', 'Ga'
    (c) The frequency of all the notes 'Sa', 'Re','Ga' is the same
    (d) The frequency decreases in the sequence 'Sa', 'Re', 'Ga'

14. In an orchestra, the musical sounds of different instruments are distinguished from one another by which of the following characteristics
    (a) Pitch
    (b) Loudness
    (c) Quality
    (d) Overtones

15. The material used for making the seats in an auditorium has sound absorbing properties. Why?
    (a) It reduces reverberations.
    (b) It makes the quality of sound better
    (c) It makes the sound travel faster
    (d) All of the above

16. Sitar is a
    (a) wind instrument
    (b) stringed instrument
    (c) percussion instrument
    (d) reed instrument

17. Bats can hunt at night
    (a) their eyesight is good
    (b) they can smell their prey
    (c) the high-pitched ultrasonic squeaks of the pat are reflected from the obstacles or prey and returned to bat's ear and thus the bat is able to detect.
    (d) All of the above

18. To hear a distinct echo, the minimum distance of a reflecting surface should be :
    (a) 17 metres
    (b) 34 metres
    (c) 68 metres
    (d) 340 metres

19. Earthquake produces which kind of sound before the main shock wave begins
    (a) ultrasound
    (b) infrasound
    (c) audible sound
    (d) None of the above

20. Speed of sound
    (a) Decreases when we go from solid to gaseous state
    (b) Increases with increase in temperature
    (c) Depends upon properties of the medium through which it travels
    (d) All these statements are correct

RAY OPTICS

101 SPEED TEST 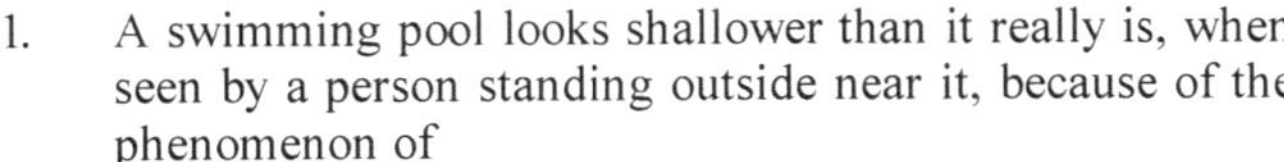 41

Max. Marks : 20 **No. of Qs. 20** **Time : 20 min.** **Date : ..../......../...............**

1. A swimming pool looks shallower than it really is, when seen by a person standing outside near it, because of the phenomenon of
   (a) refraction of light (b) reflection of light
   (c) dispersion of light (d) None of these

2. A student sitting on the last bench can read the letters written on the blackboard but is not able to read the letters written in his textbook. Which of the following statements is correct?
   (a) The near point of his eyes has receded away
   (b) The near point of his eyes has come closer to him
   (c) The far point of his eyes has come closer to him
   (d) The far point of his eyes has receded away

3. Which of the following phenomena of light are involved in the formation of a rainbow?
   (a) Reflection, refraction and dispersion
   (b) Refraction, dispersion and total internal reflection
   (c) Refraction, dispersion and total internal reflection
   (d) Dispersion, scattering and total internal reflection

4. The danger signals installed at the top of tall buildings are red in colour. These can be easily seen from a distance because among all other colours, the red light
   (a) is scattered the most by smoke or fog
   (b) is scattered the least by smoke or fog
   (c) is absorbed the most by smoke or fog
   (d) moves fastest in air

5. Twinkling of a star is due to
   (a) atmospheric refraction of sunlight
   (b) atmospheric refraction of starlight
   (c) lightening in the sky
   (d) none of these

6. Soap bubble looks coloured due to
   (a) dispersion (b) reflection
   (c) interference (d) Any one of these

7. A normal eye is not able to see objects closer than 25 cm because
   (a) the focal length of the eye is 25 cm
   (b) the distance of the retina from the eye-lens is 25 cm
   (c) the eye is not able to decrease the distance between the eye-lens and the retina beyond a limit
   (d) the eye is not able to decrease the focal length beyond a limit

8. Magnification produced by a rear view mirror fitted in vehicles
   (a) is less than one
   (b) is more than one
   (c) is equal to one
   (d) can be more than or less than one depending upon the position of the object in front of it.

9. Figure shows two rays A and B being reflected by a mirror and going as A' and B'. The mirror

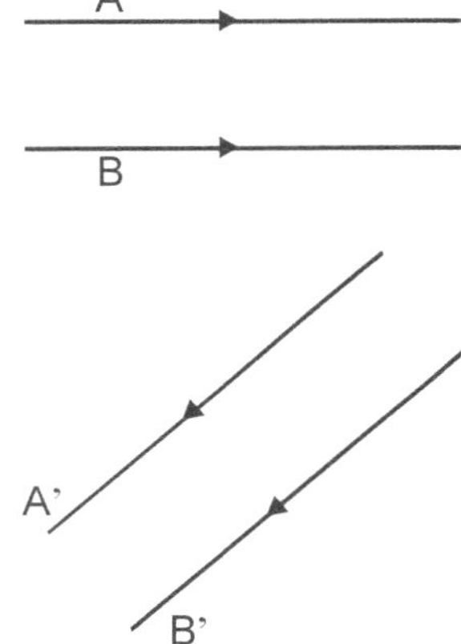

   (a) Is plane
   (b) Is convex
   (c) Is concave
   (d) May be any spherical mirror

10. Endoscopy, a technique used to explore the stomach or other inner parts of the body is based on the phenomenon of
    (a) Diffraction (b) Interference
    (c) Total internal reflection (d) Polarization

---

11. The basic reason for the extraordinary sparkle of a suitably cut diamond is that
    (a) It is very hard
    (b) It has a very high refractive index
    (c) It has a very high transparency
    (d) It has well-defined cleavage planes

12. A person standing in front of a mirror finds that his image is larger than himself. This implies that mirror is
    (a) Covex   (b) Concave
    (c) Plane   (d) Plano convex

13. A plane mirror placed in front of a person is moved parallel to itself at a speed of 0.5 m/s away from the person. Then
    (a) The image moves away from the person at a speed of 1 m/s
    (b) The image moves away from the person at a speed of 0.5 m/s
    (c) The image moves toward the person at a speed of 0.5m/s
    (d) The iamge move towards the person at a speed of 1 m/s

14. Although each eye perceives a separate image, we do not see everything double because
    (a) The inverted image formed by one eye is re-inverted by the other
    (b) The optic nerve fuses the two images
    (c) One eye words at one time
    (d) None of these

15. An object is immersed in a fluid. In order that the object becomes invisible, it should
    (a) behave as a perfect reflector
    (b) Absorb all light falling on it
    (c) Have refractive index one
    (d) Have refractive index exactly matching with that of the surrounding fluid

16. Finger prints on a piece of paper may be detected by sprinkling fluorescent powder on the paper and then looking it into
    (a) Mercury light
    (b) Sunlight
    (c) Infrared light
    (d) ultraviolet light

17. How should people wearing spectacles work with a microscope
    (a) They cannot use the microscope at all
    (b) They should keep on wearing their spectacles
    (c) They should take off spectacles
    (d) b and c is both way

18. The minimum temperature of a body at which it emits light is
    (a) 1200°C   (b) 1000°C
    (c) 500°C   (d) 200°C

19. Stars are not visible in the day time because
    (a) Stars hide behind the sun
    (b) Stars do not reflect sun rays during day
    (c) Stars vanish during the day
    (d) Atmosphere scatters sunlight into a blanket of extreme brightness through which faint stars cannot be visible.

20. If there had been one eye of the man, then
    (a) Image of the object would have been inverted
    (b) Visible region would have decreased
    (c) Image would have not been seen in three dimensional
    (d) b and c both

RESPONSE GRID					
	11. ⓐⓑⓒⓓ	12. ⓐⓑⓒⓓ	13. ⓐⓑⓒⓓ	14. ⓐⓑⓒⓓ	15. ⓐⓑⓒⓓ
	16. ⓐⓑⓒⓓ	17. ⓐⓑⓒⓓ	18. ⓐⓑⓒⓓ	19. ⓐⓑⓒⓓ	20. ⓐⓑⓒⓓ

WAVE OPTICS

101 SPEED TEST 42

Max. Marks : 20 **No. of Qs. 20** **Time : 20 min.** **Date : ..../......../...............**

1. A star is emitting yellow light. If it is accelerated towards earth then to an observer on earth, it will appear
   (a) shinning yellow
   (b) gradually changing to violet
   (c) gradually changing to red
   (d) unchanged

2. Soap bubble looks coloured due to
   (a) dispersion (b) reflection
   (c) interference (d) any one of these

3. Infrared radiation is detected by
   (a) Spectrometer (b) Pyrometer
   (c) Nanometer (d) Photometer

4. The phenomenon of interference is shown by
   (a) Longitudinal mechanical waves only
   (b) Transverse mechanical waves only
   (c) Electromagnetic waves only
   (d) All the above types of waves

5. Illumination of the sun at noon is maximum because
   (a) Scattering is reduced at noon
   (b) Refraction of light is minimum at noon
   (c) Rays are incident almost normally
   (d) The sun is nearer to earth at noon

6. Laser beams are used to measure long distance because
   (a) They are monochromatic
   (b) They are highly polarised
   (c) They are coherent
   (d) They have high degree of parallelism

7. The rectilinear propagation of light in a medium is due to its
   (a) High velocity (b) Large wavelength
   (c) High frequency (d) Source

8. Which of the following is not a property of light
   (a) It requires a material medium for propagation
   (b) It can travel through vacuum
   (c) It involves transportation of energy
   (d) It has finite speed

9. Assuming that universe is expanding, if the spectrum of light coming from a star which is going away from earth is tested, then in the wavelength of light
   (a) There will be no change
   (b) The spectrum will move to infrared region
   (c) The spectrum will seems to shift to ultraviolet side
   (d) None of above

10. It is believed that the universe is expanding and hence the distant stars are receding from us. Light from such a star will show
    (a) Shift in frequency towards longer wavelengths
    (b) Shift in frequency towards shorter wavelength
    (c) No shift in fequency but a decrease in intensity
    (d) A shift in frequency sometimes towards longer and sometimes towards shrter wavelengths

11. Through which character we can distinguish the light waves from sound waves
    (a) Interference (b) Refraction
    (c) Polarisation (d) Reflection

12. If the shift of wavelength of light emitted by a star is towards violet, then this shows that star is
    (a) Stationary
    (b) Moving towards earth
    (c) Moving away from earth
    (d) Information is incomplete.

13. Ozone is found in
    (a) Stratosphere (b) Ionosphere
    (c) Mesosphere (b) Troposphere

14. Heat radiations propagate with the speed of
    (a) α-rays (b) β-rays
    (c) Light waves (d) Sound waves

15. Which of the following are not electromagnetic waves
    (a) Cosmic rays (b) Gamma rays
    (c) β-rays (d) X-rays

16. The region of the atmosphere above troposphere is known as
    (a) Lithosphere (b) Uppersphere
    (c) Lonosphere (d) Stratosphere

17. Which scientist experimentally proved the existence of electromagnetic waves
    (a) Sir J.C. Bose (b) Maxwell
    (c) Marconi (d) Hertz

18. A signal emitted by an antenna from a certain point can be received at another point of the surface in the form of
    (a) Sky wave (b) Ground wave
    (c) Sea wave (d) Both (a) and (b)

19. Which of the following shows green house effect
    (a) ultraviolet rays (b) Infrared rays
    (c) X-rays (d) None of these

20. The ozone layer absorbs
    (a) Infrared radiations (b) ultraviolet radiations
    (c) X-rays (d) γ-rays

RESPONSE GRID	1. ⓐⓑⓒⓓ	2. ⓐⓑⓒⓓ	3. ⓐⓑⓒⓓ	4. ⓐⓑⓒⓓ	5. ⓐⓑⓒⓓ
	6. ⓐⓑⓒⓓ	7. ⓐⓑⓒⓓ	8. ⓐⓑⓒⓓ	9. ⓐⓑⓒⓓ	10. ⓐⓑⓒⓓ
	11. ⓐⓑⓒⓓ	12. ⓐⓑⓒⓓ	13. ⓐⓑⓒⓓ	14. ⓐⓑⓒⓓ	15. ⓐⓑⓒⓓ
	16. ⓐⓑⓒⓓ	17. ⓐⓑⓒⓓ	18. ⓐⓑⓒⓓ	19. ⓐⓑⓒⓓ	20. ⓐⓑⓒⓓ

ELECTROSTATICS

101 SPEED TEST — 43

Max. Marks : 20   **No. of Qs. 20**   **Time : 20 min.**   **Date : ..../........./................**

1. If a body is positively charged, then it has
   - (a) excess of electrons
   - (b) excess of protons
   - (c) deficiency of electrons
   - (d) deficiency of neutrons

4. Among identical spheres A and B having charges as– 5 C and – 16 C
   - (a) – 5C is at higher potential
   - (b) – 16 C is at higher potential
   - (c) both are at equal potential
   - (d) it cannot be said

3. Which of the following is best insulator?
   - (a) Carbon
   - (b) Paper
   - (c) Graphite
   - (d) Ebonite

4. If body is charged by rubbing it, its weight
   - (a) remains precisely constant
   - (b) increases slightly
   - (c) decreases slightly
   - (d) may increase slightly or may decrease slightly

5. A comb run through one's dry hair attracts small bits of paper. This is due to
   - (a) Comb is a good conductor
   - (b) Paper is a good conductor
   - (c) The atoms in the paper get polarised by the charged comb
   - (d) The comb possesses magnetic properties

6. The charge given to any conductor resides on its outer surface, because
   - (a) The free charge tends to be in its minimum potential energy state
   - (b) The free charge tends to be in its minimum kinetic energy state
   - (c) The free charge tends to be in its maximum potential energy state
   - (d) The free charge tends to be in its maximum kinetic energy state

7. Capacitors are used in electrical circuits where appliances need more
   - (a) Current
   - (b) Voltage
   - (c) Watt
   - (d) Resistance

8. When a lamp is connected in series with capacitor, then
   - (a) Lamp will not glow
   - (b) lamp will burst out
   - (c) Lamp will glow normally
   - (d) None of these

9. The net charge on capacitor is
   - (a) 2q
   - (b) q/2
   - (c) 0
   - (d) ∞

10. Two identical conductors of copper and aluminium are placed in an identical electric fields. The magnitude of induced charge in the aluminium will be
    - (a) Zero
    - (b) Greater than in copper
    - (c) Equal to that in copper
    - (d) Less than in copper

11. One metallic sphere A is given positive charge whereas another identical metallic sphere B of exactly same mass as of A is given equal amount of negative charge. Then
    - (a) Mass of A and mass of B still remain equal
    - (b) Mass of A increases
    - (c) Mass of B decreases
    - (d) Mass of B increases

12. There are two metallic spheres of same radii but one is solid and the other is hollow, then
    - (a) Solid sphere can be given more charge
    - (b) Hollow sphere can be given more charge
    - (c) They can be charged equally (Maximum)
    - (d) None of the above

13. A soap bubble is given a negative charge, then its radius
    - (a) Decreases
    - (b) Increases
    - (c) Remains unchanged
    - (d) Nothing can be predicted as information is insulfficient

14. Four metal conductors having difference shapes
    1. A sphere
    2. Cylindrical
    3. Pear
    4. Lighting conductor
    are mounted on insulating sands and charged. The one which is best suited to retain the charges for a longer time is
    - (a) 1
    - (b) 2
    - (c) 3
    - (d) 4

15. When a body is earth connnected, electrons from the earth flow into the body. This means the body is
    - (a) Unchanged
    - (b) Charged positively
    - (c) Charged negatively
    - (d) An insulator

16. Electric potential of earth is taken to be zero because earth is a good
    - (a) Insulator
    - (b) conductor
    - (c) Semiconductor
    - (d) Dielectric

17. An uncharged capacitor is connected to a battery. On charging the capacitor
    - (a) All the energy supplied is stored in the capacitor
    - (b) Half the energy supplied is stored in the capacitor
    - (c) The energy stored depends upon the capacity of the capacitor only
    - (d) The energy stroed depends upon the time for which the capacitor is charged.

18. When we touch the terminals of a high voltage capacitor, even after a high voltage has been cut off, then the capacitor has a tendency to
    - (a) Restore energy
    - (b) Discharge energy
    - (c) Affect dangerously
    - (d) Both (b) and (c)

19. In nature, the electric charge of any system is always equal to
    - (a) Half integral multiple of the least amount of charge
    - (b) Zero
    - (c) Square of the least amount of charge
    - (d) Integral multiple of the least amount of charge

20. Consider two point charges of equal magnitude and opposite sign separated by a certain distance. The neutral point between them
    - (a) Does not exist
    - (b) Will be in mid way between them
    - (c) Lies on the perpendicualr bisector of the line joining the two
    - (d) Will be closer to the negative charge.

RESPONSE GRID					
	1. ⓐⓑⓒⓓ	2. ⓐⓑⓒⓓ	3. ⓐⓑⓒⓓ	4. ⓐⓑⓒⓓ	5. ⓐⓑⓒⓓ
	6. ⓐⓑⓒⓓ	7. ⓐⓑⓒⓓ	8. ⓐⓑⓒⓓ	9. ⓐⓑⓒⓓ	10. ⓐⓑⓒⓓ
	11. ⓐⓑⓒⓓ	12. ⓐⓑⓒⓓ	13. ⓐⓑⓒⓓ	14. ⓐⓑⓒⓓ	15. ⓐⓑⓒⓓ
	16. ⓐⓑⓒⓓ	17. ⓐⓑⓒⓓ	18. ⓐⓑⓒⓓ	19. ⓐⓑⓒⓓ	20. ⓐⓑⓒⓓ

101 SPEED TEST

44

Max. Marks : 20 **No. of Qs. 20** **Time : 20 min.** **Date : ..../........./................**

1. A fuse wire repeatedly gets burnt when used with a good heater. It is advised to use a fuse wire of
   (a) more length (b) less radius
   (c) less length (d) more radius

2. Electric iron uses wires of alloy as
   (a) they do not oxidise at high temperatures
   (b) they do not burn at high temperatures
   (c) both (a) and (b)
   (d) neither (a) or (b)

3. Parameters of electricity supply in India are
   (a) Potential Difference of 220 V, Frequency of 50 hertz and Current Rating of 5A/15A
   (b) Potential Difference of 150 V, Frequency of 40 hertz and Current Rating of 10 A
   (c) Potential Difference of 220 V, Frequency of 60 hertz and Current Rating of 15A
   (d) Potential Difference of 220 V, Frequency of 40 hertz and Current Rating of 5 A

4. Of the two bulbs in a house, one glows brighter than the other. Which of the two has a large resistance?
   (a) The bright bulb (b) The dim bulb
   (c) Both have the same resistance
   (d) The brightness does not depend upon the resistance.

5. Domestic electrical wiring is basically a :
   (a) series connection
   (b) parallel connection
   (c) combination of series and parallel connections
   (d) series connection within each room and parallel connection elsewhere

6. If an electric current is passed through a nerve of a man, then man
   (a) Begins to laugh (b) Begins to weep
   (c) Is excited
   (d) Becomes insensitive to pain

7. The resistance of an incandescent lamp is
   (a) Greate when switched off
   (b) Smaller when switched on
   (c) Greater when switched on
   (d) The same whether it is switched off or switched on

8. Electromotive force is the force which is able to maintain a constant
   (a) Current (b) Resistance
   (c) Power (c) Potential difference

9. A galvanometer can be used as a voltmeter by connecting a
   (a) High resistance in series (b) Low resistance in series
   (c) High resistance in parallel (d) Low resistance in parallel

10. It is easier to start a car engine on a hot day than on a cold day. This is because the internal resistance of the car battery
    (a) Decreases with rise in temperature
    (b) Increases with rise in temperature
    (c) Decreases with a fall in temperature
    (d) Does not change with a change in temperature

11. How much energy in kilowatt hour is consumed in operating ten 50 watt bulbs for 10 hours per day in a month (30 days)
    (a) 1500 (b) 5,000 (c) 15 (d) 150

12. The electric current passing through a metallic wire produces heat because of
    (a) Collisions of conduction electrons with each other
    (b) Collisions of the atoms of the metal with each other
    (c) The energy released in the ionization of the atoms of the metal
    (d) Collisions of the conduction electrons with the atoms of the metallic wires

13. Electric power is transmitted over long distances through conducting wires at high voltage because
    (a) High voltage travels faster (b) Power loss is large
    (c) Power loss is less
    (d) Generator produce electrical energy at a very high voltage

14. Watt-hour meter measures
    (a) Electric energy (b) Current
    (c) Voltage (d) Power

15. Two electric bulbs A and B are rated as 60 W and 100 W. They are connected in parallel to the same source. Then,
    (a) Both draw the same current
    (b) A draws more current than B
    (c) B draws more current than A
    (d) Current drawn are in the ratio of their resistances

16. An electric heater is heated respectively by d.c. and a.c. Applied voltage for both the currents is equal. The heat produced per second will be
    (a) More on heating by a.c. source
    (b) More on heating by d.c. source
    (c) Same for both
    (d) None of the above

17. In charging a battery of motor-car, the following effect of electric current is used
    (a) Magnetic (b) Heating
    (c) Chemical (d) Induction

18. Pick out the wrong statement
    (a) In a simple battery circuit, the point of lowest potential is the negative terminal of the battery
    (b) The resistance of an incandescent lamp is greater when the lamp is switched off
    (c) An ordinary 100 W lamp has less resistance than a 60 W lamp
    (d) At constant voltage, the heat developed in a uniform wire varies inversely as the length of the wire used

19. The value of internal resistance of an ideal cell is
    (a) Zero (b) $0.5\ \Omega$
    (c) $1\ \Omega$ (d) Infinity

20. For goldplating on a copper chain, the substance required in the form of solution is
    (a) Copper sulphate (b) Copper chloride
    (c) Potassium cyanide (d) Potassium aurocyanide

RESPONSE GRID	**1.** ⓐⓑⓒⓓ	**2.** ⓐⓑⓒⓓ	**3.** ⓐⓑⓒⓓ	**4.** ⓐⓑⓒⓓ	**5.** ⓐⓑⓒⓓ
	6. ⓐⓑⓒⓓ	**7.** ⓐⓑⓒⓓ	**8.** ⓐⓑⓒⓓ	**9.** ⓐⓑⓒⓓ	**10.** ⓐⓑⓒⓓ
	11. ⓐⓑⓒⓓ	**12.** ⓐⓑⓒⓓ	**13.** ⓐⓑⓒⓓ	**14.** ⓐⓑⓒⓓ	**15.** ⓐⓑⓒⓓ
	16. ⓐⓑⓒⓓ	**17.** ⓐⓑⓒⓓ	**18.** ⓐⓑⓒⓓ	**19.** ⓐⓑⓒⓓ	**20.** ⓐⓑⓒⓓ

Max. Marks : 20   **No. of Qs. 20**   **Time : 20 min.**   **Date : ..../........./................**

1. A transformer is employed to
   (a) convert A.C. into D.C.
   (b) convert D.C. into A.C.
   (c) obtain a suitable A.C. voltage
   (d) obtain a suitable D.C. voltage

2. To convert mechanical energy into electrical energy, one can use
   (a) DC dynamo   (b) AC dynamo
   (c) motor   (d) (a) & (b)

3. The phenomenon of electromagnetic induction is –
   (a) the process of charging a body.
   (b) the process of generating magnetic field due to a current passing through a coil.
   (c) producing induced current in a coil due to relative motion between a magnet and the coil.
   (d) the process of rotating a coil of an electric motor.

4. At the time of short circuit, the current in the circuit
   (a) reduces substantially   (b) does not change.
   (c) increases heavily   (d) vary continuously

5. For dynamo which one of the following statements is correct
   (a) It converts the electrical energy into light energy
   (b) It converts the kinetic energy into heat energy
   (c) It converts the mechanical energy into electrical energy
   (d) It converts the electrical energy into mechanical energy

6. A conducting wire is dropped along east-west direction, then
   (a) No emf is induced
   (b) No induced current flows
   (c) Induced current flows from west to east
   (d) Induced current flows from east to west

7. Core of transformer is made up of
   (a) Soft iron   (b) Steel   (c) Iron   (d) Alnico

8. Fan is based on
   (a) Electric Motor   (b) Electric dynamo
   (c) Both   (d) None of these

9. The core of a transformer is laminated so that
   (a) Ratio of voltage in the primary and secondary may be increased
   (b) Rusting of the core may be stopped
   (c) Energy losses due to eddy currents may be reduced
   (d) Change in flux is increased

10. Large transformers, when used for some time, become hot and are cooled by circulating oil. The heating of transformer is due to
    (a) Heating effect of current alone   (b) Hysteresis loss alone
    (c) Both the hysteresis loss and heating effect of current
    (d) None of the above

11. Alternating current can not be measured by dc ammeter because
    (a) ac cannot pass through dc ammeter
    (b) Average value of complete cycle is zero
    (c) ac is virtual   (d) ac changes its direction

12. A bulb is connected first with DC and then AC of same voltage it will shine brightly with
    (a) AC   (b) DC
    (c) Brightness will be in ratio 1/1.4
    (d) Equally with both

13. The voltage of domestic AC is 220 volt. What does this represent
    (a) Mean voltage   (b) Peak voltage
    (c) Root mean voltage   (d) Root mean square voltage

14. Radio frequency choke uses core of
    (a) Air   (b) Iron
    (c) Air and Iron   (d) None of these

15. Quantity that remains unchanged in a transformer is
    (a) Voltage   (b) Current
    (c) Frequency   (d) None of the above

16. For high frequency, a capacitor offers
    (a) More reactance   (b) Less reactance
    (c) Zero reactance   (d) Infinite reactance

17. When the number of turns in a coil is doubled without any change in the length of the coil, its self inductance becomes
    (a) Four times   (b) Doubled
    (c) Halved   (d) Unchanged

18. When a metallic plate swings between the poles of a magnet
    (a) No effect on the plate
    (b) Eddy current are set up inside the plate and the direction of the current is along the motion of the plate
    (c) Eddy currents are set up inside the plate and the direction of the current oppose the motion of the plate
    (d) Eddy currents are set up inside the plate

19. A long horizontal metallic rod with length along the east-west direction is falling under gravity. The potential difference between its two ends will be
    (a) Zero   (b) Constant
    (c) Increase with time   (d) Decrease with time

20. What is the function of oil in a transformer?
    (a) It provides insulation   (b) It provides cooling
    (c) It provides smoothness   (d) both (a) and (b)

RESPONSE GRID

1. ⓐⓑⓒⓓ	2. ⓐⓑⓒⓓ	3. ⓐⓑⓒⓓ	4. ⓐⓑⓒⓓ	5. ⓐⓑⓒⓓ
6. ⓐⓑⓒⓓ	7. ⓐⓑⓒⓓ	8. ⓐⓑⓒⓓ	9. ⓐⓑⓒⓓ	10. ⓐⓑⓒⓓ
11. ⓐⓑⓒⓓ	12. ⓐⓑⓒⓓ	13. ⓐⓑⓒⓓ	14. ⓐⓑⓒⓓ	15. ⓐⓑⓒⓓ
16. ⓐⓑⓒⓓ	17. ⓐⓑⓒⓓ	18. ⓐⓑⓒⓓ	19. ⓐⓑⓒⓓ	20. ⓐⓑⓒⓓ

Max. Marks : 20   **No. of Qs. 20**   **Time : 20 min.**   **Date : ..../........./.................**

1. The magnetism in a magnet is mainly due to
   (a) The orbital motion of the electrons
   (b) The spin motion of the electrons
   (c) The nuclear charge
   (d) None of the above

2. Two bars of soft iron exactly same are given. One of them is a magnet. Without using any thing more, how would you find which is a magnet
   (a) By bringing two bars near and noting which one is attracting. The attracting one is a magnet
   (b) By bringing two bars near and noting which one is repelling. One which repels is an ordinary iron.
   (c) By rubbing one bar with the other and noting which becomes magnet. The bar which is magnetised is an ordinary iron
   (d) One bar is placed flat horizontal on the table and the other bar is held vertical with its one end on the middle of first bar. If there is attraction between the two, the vertical bar is magnet otherwise ordinary iron.

3. When a bar magnet is broken into two pieces?
   (a) we will have a single pole on each piece
   (b) each piece will have two like poles
   (c) each piece will have two unlike poles
   (d) each piece will lose magnetism

4. Along the direction of current carrying wire, the value of magnetic field is ?
   (a) Zero   (b) Infinity
   (c) Depends on the length of the wire
   (d) Uncertain

5. A temporary magnet is made of
   (a) cast iron   (b) steel
   (c) soft iron   (d) stainless steel

6. Of dia, para and ferromagnetism, the universal property of all substances is
   (a) Diamagnetism   (b) Paramagnetism
   (c) Ferromagnetism   (d) All the above

7. In a cassette player, materials used for coating magnetic tapes are
   (a) cobalt   (b) $CoFe_2O_4$
   (c) $NiFe_2O_4$ (d) Nickel

8. Curie temperature is the temp. above which
   (a) a ferro magnetic material becomes para magenetic
   (b) a para magnetic material becomes dia magnetic
   (c) a ferro magnetic material becomes dia magnetic
   (d) a para magnetic material becomes ferro magnetic

9. Which one of the following is not a magnetic material?
   (a) Iron   (b) Nickel
   (c) Aluminium   (d) Cobalt

10. If a magnet is dropped into a coil of wire, it will fall with an acceleration
    (a) equal to g   (b) more than g   (c) less than g
    (d) equal to g in the beginning and then more than g

11. A magnet can be demagnetised by
    (a) hammering the magnet
    (b) putting it in the water
    (c) cooling it
    (d) putting it in contact with iron

12. If the horizontal and vertical components of the earth's magnetic field are equal at a certain place, the angle of a dip at that place will be
    (a) 30°   (b) 60°   (c) 45°   (d) 90°

13. An electromagnet is made of
    (a) Copper   (b) Nickel   (c) Soft iron (d) Steel

14. Which of the following instruments is used to measure magnetic field?
    (a) A thermometer   (b) A pyrometer
    (c) A fluxmeter   (d) A hygrometer

15. A moving charge produces
    (a) neither electric field nor magnetic field
    (b) electro-static field only
    (c) magnetic field only
    (d) both magnetic and electro-static field

16. A magnetic field is produced by
    (a) all currents   (b) all charges
    (c) Both (a) and (b)   (d) None of the above

17. Eddy currents are produced when
    (a) A metal is kept in varying magnetic field
    (b) A circular coil is placed in a magnetic field
    (c) A metal is kept in the steady magnetic field
    (d) A current is passed through a circular coil

18. The magnetic compass is not useful for navigation near the magnetic poles. Since
    (a) R = 0   (b) V = 0
    (c) H = 0   (d) $\theta = 0°$

19. The direction of magnetic line of force of a bar magnet is
    (a) from south to north pole
    (b) from north to south pole
    (c) across the bar magnet
    (d) from south to north pole inside the magnet and from north to south pole outside the magnet

20. A bar magnet is cut into two equal halves by a plane parallel to the magnetic axis. Of the following physical quantities the one which remains unchanged is
    (a) pole strength   (b) magnetic moment
    (c) Intensity of magnetisation (d) Moment of inertia

RESPONSE GRID	1. ⓐⓑⓒⓓ	2. ⓐⓑⓒⓓ	3. ⓐⓑⓒⓓ	4. ⓐⓑⓒⓓ	5. ⓐⓑⓒⓓ
	6. ⓐⓑⓒⓓ	7. ⓐⓑⓒⓓ	8. ⓐⓑⓒⓓ	9. ⓐⓑⓒⓓ	10. ⓐⓑⓒⓓ
	11. ⓐⓑⓒⓓ	12. ⓐⓑⓒⓓ	13. ⓐⓑⓒⓓ	14. ⓐⓑⓒⓓ	15. ⓐⓑⓒⓓ
	16. ⓐⓑⓒⓓ	17. ⓐⓑⓒⓓ	18. ⓐⓑⓒⓓ	19. ⓐⓑⓒⓓ	20. ⓐⓑⓒⓓ

SEMICONDUCTOR ELECTRONICS

101 SPEED TEST 47

Max. Marks : 20   **No. of Qs. 20**   **Time : 20 min.**   **Date : ..../........./................**

1. Electric conduction in a semiconductor takes place due to
   (a) Electrons only   (b) Holes only
   (c) Both electrons and holes
   (d) Neither electrons nor holes

2. Let n_p and n_e be the number of holes and conduction electrons in an extrinsic semiconductor. Then
   (a) $n_p > n_e$.   (b) $n_p = n_e$.
   (c) $n_p < n_e$.   (d) $n_p \neq n_e$.

3. If the two ends of a p-n junction are joined by a wire
   (a) There will not be a steady current in the circuit
   (b) There will be a steady current from the n-side to the p-side
   (c) There will be a steady current from the p-side to the n-side
   (d) There may or may not be a current depending upon the resistance of the connecting wire

4. In a transistor
   (a) The emitter has the least concentration of impurity
   (b) The collector has the least concentration of impurity
   (c) The base has the least concentration of impurity
   (d) All the three regions have equal concentrations of impurity

5. What is the resistivity of a pure semiconductor at absolute zero ?
   (a) Zero   (b) Infinity
   (c) Same as that of conductors at room temperature
   (d) Same as that of insulators at room temperature

6. Temperature coefficient of resistance of semiconductor is
   (a) Zero   (b) Constant
   (c) Positive   (d) Negative

7. In a half wave rectifier, the r.m.s. value of the A.C. component of the wave is
   (a) Equal to d.c. value   (b) More than d.c. value
   (c) Less than d.c. value   (d) Zero

8. Zener diode is used for
   (a) Amplification   (b) Rectification
   (c) Stabilisation   (d) All of the above

9. In reverse biasing
   (a) Large amount of current flows
   (b) Potential barrier across junction increases
   (c) Depletion layer resistance decreases
   (d) No current flows

10. The main defference between voltage and power amplifiers is that
    (a) Power amplifier handles current
    (b) Power amplifier handles large voltage
    (c) Power amplifier handles large power
    (d) None of the above

11. In a transistor :
    (a) Both emitter and collector have same length
    (b) Length of emitter is greater than that of collector
    (c) Length of collector is greater than that of emitter
    (d) Any one of emitter and collector can have greater length

12. A d.c. battery of V volt is connected to a series combination of a resistor R and an ideal diode D as shown in the figure below. The potential difference across R will be

    (a) 2V when diode is forward biased
    (b) Zero when diode is forward biased
    (c) V when diode is reverse biased
    (d) V when diode is forward biased

13. The intrinsic semi conductor becomes an insulator at
    (a) 0ºC   (b) 0 K   (c) 300 K   (d) –100ºC

14. In an unbiased p-n junction, holes diffuse from the p-region to n-region because
    (a) free electrons in the n-region attract them
    (b) they move across the junction by the potential difference
    (c) hole concentration in p-region is more as compared to n-region
    (d) All the above

15. In a semiconductor, the concentration of electrons is $8 \times 10^{14}/cm^3$ and that of the holes is $5 \times 10^{12}\ cm^3$. The semiconductor is
    (a) p-type   (b) n-type   (c) intrinsic   (d) pnp type

16. In extrinsic semiconductors
    (a) the conduction band and valence band overlap
    (b) the gap between conduction band and valence band is more than 16 eV
    (c) the gap between conduction band and valence band is near about 1 eV
    (d) the gap between conduction band and valence band will be 100 eV and more

17. Function of rectifier is
    (a) to convert ac into dc   (b) to convert dc into ac
    (c) Both (a) and (b)   (d) None of these

18. An oscillator is nothing but an amplifer with
    (a) positive feedback   (b) negative feedback
    (c) large gain   (d) no feedback

19. To obtain P-type Si semiconductor, we need to dope pure Si with
    (a) Aluminium   (b) Phosphorous
    (c) Oxygen   (d) Germanium.

20. In a full wave rectifiers, input ac current has a frequency 'v'. The output frequency of current is
    (a) v/2   (b) v
    (c) 2v   (d) None of these

	1. ⓐⓑⓒⓓ	2. ⓐⓑⓒⓓ	3. ⓐⓑⓒⓓ	4. ⓐⓑⓒⓓ	5. ⓐⓑⓒⓓ
RESPONSE GRID	6. ⓐⓑⓒⓓ	7. ⓐⓑⓒⓓ	8. ⓐⓑⓒⓓ	9. ⓐⓑⓒⓓ	10. ⓐⓑⓒⓓ
	11. ⓐⓑⓒⓓ	12. ⓐⓑⓒⓓ	13. ⓐⓑⓒⓓ	14. ⓐⓑⓒⓓ	15. ⓐⓑⓒⓓ
	16. ⓐⓑⓒⓓ	17. ⓐⓑⓒⓓ	18. ⓐⓑⓒⓓ	19. ⓐⓑⓒⓓ	20. ⓐⓑⓒⓓ

101 SPEED TEST

48

Max. Marks : 20   **No. of Qs. 20**   **Time : 20 min.**   **Date : ..../........./...............**

1. Which of the following is a chemical change?
   (a) Heating of iron to red hot
   (b) Magnetisation of iron piece
   (c) Rusting of iron
   (d) All of the above

2. Heating of a substance results in
   (a) a physical change
   (b) a chemical change
   (c) a physical or a chemical change
   (d) None of the above

3. Which of the following is a physical change?
   (a) Formation of curd
   (b) Burning of candle
   (c) Rusting of iron rod
   (d) Heating of copper wire by electricity

4. Combustion of a candle is a/an
   (a) physical change   (b) reduction reaction
   (c) endothermic reaction   (d) exothermic reaction

5. Solution of $CaCO_3$ in water forms a
   (a) homogeneous mixture   (b) heterogenous mixture
   (c) azeotropic mixture   (d) None of these

6. An element which is not found in nature is
   (a) Pt   (b) K   (c) Zn   (d) Pm

7. Match the following columns:

List - I		List - II	
A.	mercury	1.	element
B.	oxygen	2.	compound
C.	water	3.	mixture
D.	air	4.	metal

   Codes:

	A	B	C	D
(a)	1	2	3	4
(b)	4	3	2	1
(c)	4	1	2	3
(d)	4	2	3	1

8. Which of the following statements is correct?
   I. german silver is an alloy of silver, copper and zinc
   II. there is no zinc in brass
   III. bronze is an alloy of copper and tin

9. An alloy of .... is used in fountain pen nib tips.
   (a) platinum and silver   (b) platinum and gold
   (c) platinum and iridium   (d) platinum and copper

   (a) I, II and III   (b) only III
   (c) I and III   (d) I and II

10. Which one among the following has been producing/can produce light by a chemical change?
    (a) Sun
    (b) Moon
    (c) Electric bulb
    (d) Lightening and thunder

11. Colloidal solution commonly used in the treatment of eye disease is
    (a) colloidal silver   (b) colloidal gold
    (c) colloidal antimony   (d) colloidal sulphur

12. Match the Column I with the Column II.

	Column I		Column II
A.	Cod liver	1.	Liquid in a gas
B.	Vanishing cream cream	2.	Solid dispersed in gas
C.	Fog	3.	Aqueous emulsion
D.	Smoke	4.	Water in oil emulsion

    Codes:

	A	B	C	D
(a)	1	2	4	3
(b)	3	1	2	4
(c)	4	3	1	2
(d)	2	4	3	1

13. The diagram below shows a magnet near a pile of particles of iron and sulphur. The magnet attracts the iron, separating it from the mixture.

    Based on the diagram, which statement is true?
    (a) The parts of a mixture keep their own properties.
    (b) The elements in a compound keep their own properties.
    (c) The properties of a mixture are different from the properties of its parts.
    (d) The properties of a compound are different from the properties of its elements.

14. The four items below were part of a dinner. Each item is a mixture.

Which of these mixtures is a suspension?
(a) A (b) B (c) C (d) D

15. A water molecule is made up of one oxygen and two hydrogen atoms. Why is water considered a pure substance?
(a) Water can be broken down by physical means.
(b) Water can be combined with other substances by physical means.
(c) Each water molecule is identical.
(d) Water molecules are made up of different types of atoms.

16. A metalloid is a classification of ____________.
(a) atom (b) element
(c) compound (d) mixture

17. Which of these substances is an example of a solution?
(a) Milk (b) Brass
(c) Mercury (d) Concrete

18. Which of the following is a way in which elements and compounds are similar?
(a) Elements and compounds are both pure substances.
(b) Elements and compounds are both listed on the periodic table.
(c) Elements and compounds are both made up of different kinds of atoms.
(d) Elements and compounds can both be broken down by physical changes.

19. In salt water which compound is the solvent?
(a) Water (b) Salt
(c) Oxygen (d) Hydrogen

20. Concentration means
(a) How well two substances mix with each other
(b) The amount of a particular substance in a given mixture
(c) The extent to which a compound chemically combines
(d) The ability of one substance to dissolve in another

Max. Marks : 20   **No. of Qs. 20**   **Time : 20 min.**   **Date : ..../........./...............**

1. Which of the following statements concerning an electron is false?
   (a) It is a particle
   (b) It has wave properties
   (c) Its path is bent by a magnet
   (d) It gives out energy while moving in orbitals

2. When hydrogen nuclei trap neutron, they become
   (a) hydrogen atom
   (b) deuterium
   (c) tritium atom
   (d) beta rays

3. The British physicist who received the 1923 Nobel Prize in Physics for discovering the electron is
   (a) John Dalton
   (b) James Chadwick
   (c) J. J. Thomson
   (d) E. Rutherford

4. The atomic spectra of hydrogen was explained by
   (a) Rutherford's model of the atom
   (b) Hund's rule of maximum multiplicity
   (c) Pauli's exclusion principle
   (d) Bohr's theory

5. Radioactive isotope of hydrogen is
   (a) hydride ion
   (b) tritium
   (c) protium
   (d) deuterium

6. Neutrons are obtained by
   (a) bombardment of radium with α-particles
   (b) bombardment of beryllium with β-particles
   (c) radioactive disintegration of uranium
   (d) None of the above

7. Isobars are produced as a result of the emission of
   (a) α-particles
   (b) γ-rays
   (c) X-rays
   (d) β-particles

8. The de Broglie equation is
   (a) $h/mv = \lambda$
   (b) $h\nu = E_2 - E_1$
   (c) $n\lambda = 2d \sin\theta$
   (d) $c = h\nu$

9. Properties of elements are determined by
   (a) atomic number
   (b) atomic weight
   (c) neutrons
   (d) protons

10. Bohr's theory of fixed orbits contradicts
    (a) Coulomb's law
    (b) Planck's theory
    (c) de Broglie relation
    (d) uncertainty principle

11. Which of the following has the same atomic number and atomic weight?
    (a) hydrogen
    (b) helium
    (c) oxygen
    (d) nitrogen

12. The nucleus of a hydrogen atom consists of
    (a) one proton
    (b) one proton + two neutrons
    (c) one neutron only
    (d) one electron only

13. The names of the scientists, Newland, Mendeleev and Meyer are associated with the development of
    (a) atomic structure
    (b) metallurgy
    (c) periodic table of elements
    (d) discovery of elements

14. The mass number of a nucleus is
    (a) always less than its atomic number
    (b) the sum of the number of protons and neutrons present in the nucleus
    (c) always more than the atomic weight
    (d) a fraction

15. The following are the half-lives of four radio active isotopes. Which one of the following is the most dangerous to handle?
    (a) 3 billion years
    (b) 100 years
    (c) 0.01 minute
    (d) 13 days

16. Anode rays were discovered by
    (a) Goldstein
    (b) J. Stenely
    (c) Rutherford
    (d) Thomson

17. Neutron was discovered by
    (a) Rutherford
    (b) Langnuin
    (c) Chadwick
    (d) Austin

18. Which of the following is the correct sequence in terms of increasing mass?
    (a) Proton, electron, alpha particle, hydrogen atom
    (b) Electron, proton, hydrogen atom, alpha particle
    (c) Hydrogen atom, proton, electron, alpha particle
    (d) Alpha particle, proton, hydrogen atom, electron

19. Neutron are present in all atoms except
    (a) He
    (b) C
    (c) H
    (d) N

20. Which of the following statement is incorrect?
    (a) Isobars possess same chemical properties
    (b) Isotopes occupy same position in Periodic table
    (c) Isotopes possess same atomic number
    (d) In isobars the total number of protons and neutrons in the nucleus is same

Response Grid					
	1. ⓐⓑⓒⓓ	2. ⓐⓑⓒⓓ	3. ⓐⓑⓒⓓ	4. ⓐⓑⓒⓓ	5. ⓐⓑⓒⓓ
	6. ⓐⓑⓒⓓ	7. ⓐⓑⓒⓓ	8. ⓐⓑⓒⓓ	9. ⓐⓑⓒⓓ	10. ⓐⓑⓒⓓ
	11. ⓐⓑⓒⓓ	12. ⓐⓑⓒⓓ	13. ⓐⓑⓒⓓ	14. ⓐⓑⓒⓓ	15. ⓐⓑⓒⓓ
	16. ⓐⓑⓒⓓ	17. ⓐⓑⓒⓓ	18. ⓐⓑⓒⓓ	19. ⓐⓑⓒⓓ	20. ⓐⓑⓒⓓ

Max. Marks : 20   **No. of Qs. 20**   **Time : 20 min.**   **Date : ..../........./...............**

1. The element or elements whose position is anomalous in the periodic table is
   (a) halogens
   (b) Fe, Co and Ni
   (c) inert gases
   (d) hydrogen

2. The energy released when an extra electron is added to a neutral gaseous atom is called
   (a) bond energy
   (b) electron affinity
   (c) ionization potential
   (d) electronegativity

3. The cause of periodicity of properties is
   (a) increasing atomic radius
   (b) increasing atomic weights
   (c) number of electrons in the valency orbit
   (d) the recurrence of similar outer electronic configuration

4. In which of the following groups, are the elements written in the descending order of their respect atomic weights?
   (a) nitrogen, carbon, oxygen, hydrogen
   (b) oxygen, argon, nitrogen, hydrogen
   (c) oxygen, nitrogen, helium, hydrogen
   (d) oxygen, nitrogen, helium, bromine

5. If the electronegativities of two elements are low, the bond between the two is
   (a) ionic
   (b) covalent
   (c) co-ordinate
   (d) a metallic bond

6. The most electronegative element among sodium, bromium, fluorine, and oxygen is
   (a) sodium
   (b) bromium
   (c) fluorine
   (d) oxygen

7. The most electropositive element among the following is
   (a) Na   (b) Ca   (c) K   (d) Cs

8. Rare gases are generally chemically inert because they
   (a) are monoatomic
   (b) have low ionization energy
   (c) have stable electronic configuration
   (d) have a high electron affinity

9. f-block elements are also called
   (a) alkali metals
   (b) inner transition elements
   (c) transition elements
   (d) transuranic elements

10. An element with atomic number 36 belongs to the
    (a) s-block
    (b) p-block
    (c) d-block
    (d) f-block

11. Consider the following statements.
    1. In Modern Periodic Table, the number of periods is 7.
    2. In Modern Periodic Table, the number of groups is 18.
    3. The long form of Periodic Table was developed by Range and Werner.
    Which of the following is/are correct?
    (a) Only 1
    (b) 2 and 3
    (c) 1 and 2
    (d) 1, 2 and 3

12. Which one of the following is not a periodic property i.e., does not show any trend on moving from one side to the other in the Periodic Table?
    (a) Atomic size
    (b) Valency
    (c) Radioactivity
    (d) Electronegativity

13. Which group of Periodic Table contains no metal?
    (a) 1   (b) 13   (c) 17   (d) 7

14. Consider the following statements with reference to the Periodic Table of chemical element.
    1. Ionisation potential gradually decreases along a period.
    2. In a group of element, electron affinity decreases as the atomic weight increases.
    3. In a given period, electronegativity decrease as the atomic number increases.
    Which of these statement(s) is/are correct?
    (a) Only 1   (b) Only 2   (c) 1 and 3   (d) 2 and 3

15. Which of the following properties changes with valency?
    (a) Atomic weight
    (b) Equivalent weight
    (c) Molecular weight
    (d) Density

16. Match the Column I with the Column II.

	Column I		Column II
A.	Modern periodic law	1.	Groups
B.	Father of periodic table	2.	Moseley
C.	Vertical lines in Modern periodic table	3.	Periods
D.	Horizontal lines in Modern periodic table	4.	Mendeleev

Codes:

	A	B	C	D
(a)	3	4	2	1
(b)	4	1	3	2
(c)	2	4	1	3
(d)	2	1	3	4

17. The long form of Periodic Table is based on
    (a) electronegativity
    (b) mass of the atom
    (c) shape of the atom
    (d) atomic number

18. In Periodic Table, metallic elements appear
    (a) in the left-hand columns
    (b) in the top-rows
    (c) in the right-hand columns
    (d) in the bottom rows

19. The first element of rare earth metals is
    (a) cerium
    (b) actinium
    (c) uranium
    (d) lanthanum

20. Which of the following pairs of elements is in the same period of the Periodic Table?
    (a) Na, Ca
    (b) Na, Cl
    (c) Ca, Cl
    (d) Mg, Sb

RESPONSE GRID					
	1. ⓐⓑⓒⓓ	2. ⓐⓑⓒⓓ	3. ⓐⓑⓒⓓ	4. ⓐⓑⓒⓓ	5. ⓐⓑⓒⓓ
	6. ⓐⓑⓒⓓ	7. ⓐⓑⓒⓓ	8. ⓐⓑⓒⓓ	9. ⓐⓑⓒⓓ	10. ⓐⓑⓒⓓ
	11. ⓐⓑⓒⓓ	12. ⓐⓑⓒⓓ	13. ⓐⓑⓒⓓ	14. ⓐⓑⓒⓓ	15. ⓐⓑⓒⓓ
	16. ⓐⓑⓒⓓ	17. ⓐⓑⓒⓓ	18. ⓐⓑⓒⓓ	19. ⓐⓑⓒⓓ	20. ⓐⓑⓒⓓ

Max. Marks : 20　　**No. of Qs. 20**　　**Time : 20 min.**　　**Date : ..../........./...............**

1. Which of the following is acidic in nature?
   - (a) sugar
   - (b) lime
   - (c) baking powder
   - (d) vinegar
2. An element common to all acids is
   - (a) hydrogen
   - (b) oxygen
   - (c) sulphur
   - (d) chlorine
3. Baking soda is also known as
   - (a) sodium bicarbonate
   - (b) sodium carbonate
   - (c) calcium chloride
   - (d) calcium carbonate
4. What is the pH of pure water?
   - (a) 1　　(b) 7　　(c) 5　　(d) 12
5. Match the Column I with the Column II.

Column I	Column II
A. Tartaric acid	1. Red ants
B. Formic acid	2. Grapes
C. Uric acid	3. Apples
D. Maleic acid	4. Urine of mammals

   Codes:

	A	B	C	D
(a)	2	1	4	3
(b)	1	4	3	2
(c)	4	3	2	1
(d)	3	2	1	4

6. Acid turns blue litmus red and base turns red litmus blue. A student tested a liquid with a red litmus paper which remained red with no change. This shows that the liquid
   - (a) is not a base
   - (b) is not an acid
   - (c) is neither an acid nor a base
   - (d) None of these
7. Which one of the following statements is correct?
   - (a) All bases are alkali
   - (b) None of the bases is alkali
   - (c) There are no more bases except the alkalies
   - (d) All alkalies are bases but all bases are not alkalies
8. A base is a substance which
   - (a) is bitter in taste
   - (b) given OH^- ions in aqueous solution
   - (c) can donate electron
   - (d) All of the above
9. The pH of water at 25°C is 7. When it is heated to 100°C, the pH of water
   - (a) increase
   - (b) decreases
   - (c) remains same
   - (d) decreases up to 50° C and then increases

10. Match the Column I with the Column II.

Column I	Column II
A. 10^{-7}	1. pH value of neutral solution
B. >7	2. pH value of acidic solution
C. <7	3. pH value of alkaline solution
D. 7	4. In pure water hydrogen ion concentration

    Codes:

	A	B	C	D
(a)	1	4	3	2
(b)	2	1	4	3
(c)	3	2	1	4
(d)	4	3	2	1

11. Which one of the following is correct? Due to continuous use of calcium superphosphate as fertilizer in soil, the pH of soil becomes
    - (a) more than 7
    - (b) less than 7
    - (c) equal to 7
    - (d) cannot be predicted
12. Consider the following statements
    1. Acids are sour in taste and change the colour of blue litmus to red.
    2. Bases are bitter and change the colour of red litmus to blue.
    3. Litmus is a natural indicator.
    Which of the statements above are correct?
    - (a) 1 and 2
    - (b) 1 and 3
    - (c) 1 and 3
    - (d) 1, 2 and 3
13. Study the following statements
    1. Litmus solution is a purple dye which is extracted from lichen and is commonly used as an indicator.
    2. Red cabbage leaves, turmeric, coloured petals of some flowers indicate the presence of acid or base in a solution.
    3. Some substances whose odour changes in acidic or basic medium are called olfactory indicators.
    Which of the statements given above are correct?
    - (a) 1, 2 and 3
    - (b) 1 and 2
    - (c) 1 and 3
    - (d) 2 and 3

RESPONSE GRID	1. ⓐⓑⓒⓓ	2. ⓐⓑⓒⓓ	3. ⓐⓑⓒⓓ	4. ⓐⓑⓒⓓ	5. ⓐⓑⓒⓓ
	6. ⓐⓑⓒⓓ	7. ⓐⓑⓒⓓ	8. ⓐⓑⓒⓓ	9. ⓐⓑⓒⓓ	10. ⓐⓑⓒⓓ
	11. ⓐⓑⓒⓓ	12. ⓐⓑⓒⓓ	13. ⓐⓑⓒⓓ		

14. Which one of the following can be used as an acid-base indicator by a visually impaired student?
    (a) Litmus
    (b) Vanilla essence
    (c) Turmeric
    (d) Petunia leaves

15. The composition of aqua regia is
    (a) conc. H_2SO_4 and conc. HCl in ratio of 1 : 3
    (b) conc. HNO_3 and conc. HCl in ratio of 1 : 3
    (c) conc. HNO_3 and conc. HCl in ratio of 3 : 1
    (d) conc. H_2SO_4 and conc. HNO_3 in ratio of 3 : 1

16. Which of the following statements is correct about an aqueous solution of an acid and of a base?
    (i) Higher the pH, strong the acid
    (ii) Higher the pH, weaker the acid
    (iii) Lower the pH, stronger the base
    (iv) Lower the pH, weaker the base
    (a) (i) and (iii)
    (b) (i) and (iv)
    (c) (ii) and (iii)
    (d) (ii) and (iv)

17. A sample of soil is mixed with water and allowed to settle. The clear supernatant solution turns the pH paper yellowish orange. Which of the following would change the colour of this pH paper to greenish-blue?
    (a) Lemon juice
    (b) An antacid
    (c) Common salt
    (d) Vinegar

18. The pH of fresh ground water slightly decreases upon exposure to air because
    (a) carbon dioxide from air is dissolved in the water
    (b) oxygen from air is dissolved in the water
    (c) the dissolved carbon dioxide of the ground water escapes into air
    (d) the dissolved oxygen of the ground water escapes into air

19. Match the Column I with the Column II.

	Column I (pH value)		Column II (Product)
A.	7.35 to 7.45	1.	Milk
B.	6.6	2.	Human blood
C.	8.5	3.	Wine
D.	2.8	4.	Sea water

Codes:

	A	B	C	D
(a)	1	4	3	2
(b)	2	1	4	3
(c)	4	3	2	1
(d)	3	2	1	4

20. Human stomach produces acid 'X' which helps in digestion of food. Acid 'X' is
    (a) acetic acid
    (b) methanoic acid
    (c) hydrochloric acid
    (d) citric acid

101 SPEED TEST

52

Max. Marks : 20   **No. of Qs. 20**   **Time : 20 min.**   **Date : ..../......../................**

1. Which one of the following salts when dissolved in water makes the solution basic?
   (a) Sodium chloride   (b) Copper sulphate
   (c) Ferric chloride   (d) Sodium acetate

2. Solution in test tubes containing H_2O and aqueous NaOH can be differentiated with the help of
   (a) red litmus   (b) blue litmus
   (c) Na_2CO_3 (d) HCl (aqueous)

3. Which one among the following is not a property of salt?
   (a) Salts have ordered packing arrangements called lattices
   (b) Salts have low melting points but high boiling points
   (c) Salts are brittle
   (d) Salts conducts electricity when dissolved in water or even in the molten state

4. Consider the following statements
   1. Limestone, chalk and marble are different forms of calcium carbonate
   2. When pH of rain water is less than 5.6, it is called acid rain.
   3. Human body works with in the pH range of 7.0 to 7.8
   Which of the statements given above are correct?
   (a) 1 and 2   (b) 1 and 3
   (c) 2 and 3   (d) 1, 2 and 3

5. A milkman added a small amount of baking soda to fresh milk which had pH close to 6. As a result, pH of the medium
   (a) became close to 2
   (b) became close to 4
   (c) did not undergo any change
   (d) became close to 8

6. The compound used for neutralisation of excess HCl in the stomach is
   (a) $NaHCO_3$ (b) $Mg(OH)_2$
   (c) Both (a) and (b)   (d) None of these

7. The aqueous solution of which of the following salt will have OH^- ions?
   (a) NaCl   (b) Na_2SO_4
   (c) CH_3COONa (d) None of these

8. Which of the following phenomenon occur when a small amount of acid is added to water?
   (i) Ionisation   (ii) Dilution
   (iii) Neutralisation   (iv) Salt formation
   (a) (i) and (ii)   (b) (ii) and (iii)
   (c) (i) and (iii)   (d) (ii) and (iv)

9. Which of the following substances will not give carbon dioxide an treatment with dilute acid?
   (a) Marble   (b) Lime stone
   (c) Lime   (d) Baking soda

10. Identify the substance, having the property of deliquescence
    (a) Gypsum   (b) hydrated calcium chloride
    (c) quick lime   (d) conc. sulphuric acid

11. Which one of the following types of medicines is used for treating indigestion?
    (a) Antibiotic   (b) Antacid
    (c) Analagic   (d) Antiseptic

12. Soda acid fire extinguishes the fire by
    (a) cutting the supply of air
    (b) raising ignition temperature
    (c) removing combustion substance
    (d) None of these

13. The formula of washing soda is
    (a) $NaHCO_3$ (b) $Na_2CO_3 . H_2O$
    (c) Na_2CO_3 (d) $Na_2CO_3 . 10H_2O$

14. The substance which on treating with chlorine, yields bleaching powder is
    (a) quick lime   (b) limestone
    (c) slaked lime   (d) gypsum

15. If tartaric acid is not added in baking powder, the cake will taste bitter due to the presence of
    (a) sodium hydrogen carbonate
    (b) sodium carbonate
    (c) carbon dioxide
    (d) same unreacted tartaric acid

16. Milk of magnesia is
    (a) solid magnesium oxide
    (b) insoluble magnesium hydroxide
    (c) soluble magnesium hydroxide
    (d) insoluble magnesium carbonate

17. Calcium phosphate is present in tooth enamel, its nature is
    (a) basic   (b) amphoteric
    (c) neutral   (d) None of these

18. Which of the following salts does not contain any water of crystallisation?
    (a) Blue vitriol   (b) Washing soda
    (c) Baking soda   (d) Gypsum

19. The role of quick lime in soda lime (mixture) is to
    (a) Absorb moisture present in soda lime
    (b) Increase the efficiency of soda lime
    (c) Absorb moisture present in soda lime
    (d) Take part in reaction with NaOH

20. Which of the following does not form an acid salt?
    (a) Phosphoric acid   (b) Carbonic acid
    (c) Hydrochloric acid   (d) Sulphuric acid

	RESPONSE GRID				
1. ⓐⓑⓒⓓ	**2.** ⓐⓑⓒⓓ	**3.** ⓐⓑⓒⓓ	**4.** ⓐⓑⓒⓓ	**5.** ⓐⓑⓒⓓ
6. ⓐⓑⓒⓓ	**7.** ⓐⓑⓒⓓ	**8.** ⓐⓑⓒⓓ	**9.** ⓐⓑⓒⓓ	**10.** ⓐⓑⓒⓓ
11. ⓐⓑⓒⓓ	**12.** ⓐⓑⓒⓓ	**13.** ⓐⓑⓒⓓ	**14.** ⓐⓑⓒⓓ	**15.** ⓐⓑⓒⓓ
16. ⓐⓑⓒⓓ	**17.** ⓐⓑⓒⓓ	**18.** ⓐⓑⓒⓓ	**19.** ⓐⓑⓒⓓ	**20.** ⓐⓑⓒⓓ

Max. Marks : 20 **No. of Qs. 20** **Time : 20 min.** **Date : ..../........./...............**

1. Which of the following metals is present in the anode mud during the electrolytic refining of copper?
   - (a) Sodium
   - (b) Aluminium
   - (c) Selenium
   - (d) Both (b) and (c)

2. The second most abundant element in the earth's crust is
   - (a) oxygen
   - (b) silicon
   - (c) aluminium
   - (d) iron

3. During smelting, an additional substance is added which combines with impurities to form a fusible product. It is known as
   - (a) slag
   - (b) mud
   - (c) gangue
   - (d) flux

4. Metals are refined by using different methods. Which of the following metals refined by electrolytic refining?
   - (i) Ag
   - (ii) Cu
   - (iii) Na
   - (iv) Al
   - (a) (i) and (ii)
   - (b) (ii) and (iii)
   - (c) (i) and (iii)
   - (d) (iii) and (iv)

5. The method used for reduction of mercuric oxide to mercury is
   - (a) Heating
   - (b) Chemical reduction
   - (c) Tinning
   - (d) Galvanization

6. Which of the following oxides, on reduction with carbon gives metal?
   - (a) Cr_2O_3
   - (b) ZnO
   - (c) MnO_2
   - (d) All of these

7. Identify an ore containing sulphur in it
   - (a) Siderite
   - (b) Fluorspar
   - (c) Iron pyrites
   - (d) Calamine

8. Aluminium is extracted from bauxite
   - (a) by reduction with carbon
   - (b) by reduction with Mg
   - (c) by reduction with CO
   - (d) by electrolysis in molten cryolite

9. Which of the following is always found in a free state in nature?
   - (a) gold
   - (b) silver
   - (c) sodium
   - (d) copper

10. The metal that is usually extracted from sea water is
    - (a) Ca
    - (b) Na
    - (c) K
    - (d) Mg

11. The method of concentrating the ore which makes use of difference in density between ore and impurities is called
    - (a) liquation
    - (b) leaching
    - (c) levigation
    - (d) magnetic separation

12. The most important ore of aluminium is
    - (a) bauxite
    - (b) magnetite
    - (c) haematite
    - (d) monazite

13. The sulphide ores of metals are concentrated by
    - (a) cupellation
    - (b) electrolysis
    - (c) froth flotation
    - (d) calcination

14. Until the nineteenth century, aluminium was almost as expensive as gold. The invention of an inexpensive way to extract this metal by a 22-year-old American made this metal inexpensive subsequently. The investor was
    - (a) Goldschmidt
    - (b) Mond
    - (c) Charles-Martin Hall
    - (d) Parkes

15. A metal obtained directly by roasting of its sulphide ore is
    - (a) Hg
    - (b) Cu
    - (c) Zn
    - (d) Pb

16. Calcination is
    - (a) heating the ore strongly in the absence of any blast of air
    - (b) heating the ore with limestone
    - (c) heating the ore with calcium
    - (d) heating the ore with carbon

17. Which of the following can be purified by the electrolytic method?
    - (a) sodium (Na)
    - (b) selenium (Se)
    - (c) boron (B)
    - (d) chlorine (Cl_2)

18. Which of the following metals can be extracted from the ore called cassiterite?
    - (a) zinc (Zn)
    - (b) mercury (Hg)
    - (c) calcium (Ca)
    - (d) tin (Sn)

19. Malachite, azurite, and chalcopyrite are ores of
    - (a) nickel
    - (b) chromium
    - (c) calcium
    - (d) copper

20. Zone refining is used for the purification of
    - (a) Au
    - (b) Ge
    - (c) Ag
    - (d) Cu

RESPONSE GRID	1. ⓐⓑⓒⓓ	2. ⓐⓑⓒⓓ	3. ⓐⓑⓒⓓ	4. ⓐⓑⓒⓓ	5. ⓐⓑⓒⓓ
	6. ⓐⓑⓒⓓ	7. ⓐⓑⓒⓓ	8. ⓐⓑⓒⓓ	9. ⓐⓑⓒⓓ	10. ⓐⓑⓒⓓ
	11. ⓐⓑⓒⓓ	12. ⓐⓑⓒⓓ	13. ⓐⓑⓒⓓ	14. ⓐⓑⓒⓓ	15. ⓐⓑⓒⓓ
	16. ⓐⓑⓒⓓ	17. ⓐⓑⓒⓓ	18. ⓐⓑⓒⓓ	19. ⓐⓑⓒⓓ	20. ⓐⓑⓒⓓ

Max. Marks : 20   **No. of Qs. 20**   **Time : 20 min.**   **Date : ..../........./................**

1. The first metal to be used by man was
   (a) aluminium   (b) copper
   (c) silver   (d) iron

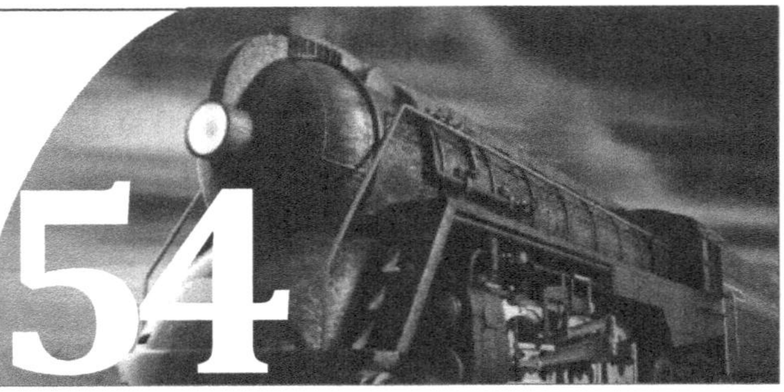

2. The metal that does not give H_2 on treatment with dilute HCl is
   (a) Zn   (b) Fe
   (c) Ag   (d) Ca

3. The metal that is used as catalyst in the hydrogenation of oils is
   (a) Ni   (b) Pb
   (c) Cu   (d) Pt

4. The most malleable metal is
   (a) platinum   (b) silver
   (c) iron   (d) gold

5. Which of the following elements behave chemically, both as a metal and a non-metal?
   (a) argon   (b) carbon
   (c) xenon   (d) boron

6. Which of the following is a non-ferrous metal?
   (a) cobalt   (b) aluminium
   (c) nickel   (d) All of these

7. A metal is left exposed to atmosphere for some time. It becomes coated with green basic carbonate. The metal must be
   (a) Ag   (b) Cu
   (c) Al   (d) Zn

8. White lead is used as a
   (a) dye   (b) vulcanizing agent
   (c) bleaching agent   (d) paint pigment

9. Black lead is
   (a) an allotrope of lead   (b) a lead base pigment
   (c) graphite   (d) a kind of charcoal

10. Calcium metal tarnishes in air due to the formation of
   (a) calcium oxide   (b) calcium bicarbonate
   (c) calcium hydroxide   (d) calcium carbonate

11. Zinc helps in the synthesis of biological protein; this is the basis for using zinc ointment for
   (a) growing more hair
   (b) healing wounds
   (c) increasing body weight
   (d) growing long nails

12. Metals usually form .... oxides.
   (a) acidic   (b) basic
   (c) neutral   (d) saline

13. Silver articles become black on prolonged exposure to air. This is due to the formation of
   (a) Ag_2O (b) Ag_2S
   (c) AgCN   (d) Ag_2O and Ag_2S

14. A student placed an iron nail in copper sulphate solution. He observed the reddish brown coating on the iron nail: Which is
   (a) soft and dull   (b) hard and flading
   (c) smooth and shining (d) rough and granular

15. Which among the following alloys contain non-metal as one of its constituents?
   (a) Brass   (b) Amalgam
   (c) Gun metal   (d) None of these

16. The process of coating of Zn over Fe is known as
   (a) Cathodic protection (b) Metallurgy
   (c) Tinning   (d) Galvanization

17. Which reducing agent is used in chemical reduction:
   (a) C   (b) CO
   (c) Al   (d) All of these

18. Which of the following metals is in a liquid state at normal room temperature?
   (a) sodium   (b) radium
   (c) gallium   (d) silicon

19. Match the following

List-I		List-II
A. calomel	1.	copper sulphate
B. blue vitriol	2.	calcium sulphate
C. gypsum	3.	mercurous chloride
D. normal salt	4.	sodium chloride

Codes:

	A	B	C	D
(a)	1	2	3	4
(b)	4	3	2	1
(c)	3	2	1	4
(d)	3	1	2	4

20. Tellurium is a
   (a) metal   (b) non-metal
   (c) metalloid   (d) transition metal

Max. Marks : 20   **No. of Qs. 20**   **Time : 20 min.**   **Date : ..../........./...............**

1. Which of the following is a greenhouse gas ?
   (a) Methane   (b) Oxygen
   (c) Nitrogen   (d) Hydrogen
2. World Environment Day is celebrated every year on ______ .
   (a) 5th March   (b) 15th April
   (c) 15th May   (d) 5th June
3. Which rays strike on earth due to depletion of ozone layer ?
   (a) Ultraviolet   (b) Infrared
   (c) Visible light   (d) Microwaves
4. Which pollutants are responsible for bronchitis ?
   (a) O_2, CO_2 (b) CO, CO_2
   (c) SO_2, NO_2 (d) Cl_2, H_2S
5. Select the process that does not add particulate materials to air.
   (a) Use of air conditioner
   (b) Burning of fosssil fuels
   (c) Paper industry
   (d) Incomplete combustion of coal
6. The major photochemical oxidant is:
   (a) Ozone
   (b) Hydrogen peroxide
   (c) Nitrogen oxides
   (d) Peroxyl Acetyl Nitrate (PAN)
7. Taj Mahal at Agra may be damaged by:
   (a) Sulphur dioxide (b) Chlorine
   (c) Hydrogen   (d) Oxygen
8. Which of the following is a secondary air pollutant?
   (a) Ozone   (b) Carbon dioxide
   (c) Carbon mono-oxide (d) Sulphur dioxide
9. Air pollution from automobiles can be controlled by fitting:
   (a) Cyclone separator (b) Electrostatic precipitator
   (c) Catalytic converter (d) Wet scrubber
10. Which of the following are likely to be present in photochemical smog?
    (a) Sulphur dioxide (b) Photochemical oxidants
    (c) Chlorofluorocarbon (d) Smog
11. Which of the following on inhalation dissolved in the blood haemoglobin more rapidly than oxygen?
    (a) Sulphur dioxide (b) Carbon mono-oxide
    (c) Ozone   (d) Nitrous oxide
12. Which component present in air as a pollutant is responsible for acid rain?
    (a) Smoke   (b) Dust
    (c) SO_2 (d) NH_3
13. The ozone layer is mainly damaged by
    (a) methane
    (b) CO_2
    (c) sulphur dioxide
    (d) chlorofluoro carbons
14. Which is not a green-house gas?
    (a) CO_2 (b) CH_4
    (c) N_2O (d) Chlorofluorocarbons
15. Main source of lead in air is from
    (a) sewage   (b) leaded gasoline
    (c) tobacco   (d) insecticide
16. Which of the following is the upper most region of the atmosphere?
    (a) Stratosphere   (b) Troposphere
    (c) Exosphere   (d) Thermosphere
17. Higher concentration of nitrogen dioxide in atmosphere air causes
    (a) cancer   (b) corrosion
    (c) bronchitis   (d) nervous depression
18. Global warming may result in
    (a) flood
    (b) cyclone
    (c) decrease in forest productivity
    (d) All of the above
19. The lowest layer of earth's atmosphere is
    (a) troposphere   (b) stratosphere
    (c) mesophere   (d) ionosphere
20. Gradual warming of the atmosphere due to trapping of long wave radiations is called
    (a) air heating   (b) photosynthesis
    (c) air pollution   (d) green house effect

RESPONSE GRID	1. ⓐⓑⓒⓓ	2. ⓐⓑⓒⓓ	3. ⓐⓑⓒⓓ	4. ⓐⓑⓒⓓ	5. ⓐⓑⓒⓓ
	6. ⓐⓑⓒⓓ	7. ⓐⓑⓒⓓ	8. ⓐⓑⓒⓓ	9. ⓐⓑⓒⓓ	10. ⓐⓑⓒⓓ
	11. ⓐⓑⓒⓓ	12. ⓐⓑⓒⓓ	13. ⓐⓑⓒⓓ	14. ⓐⓑⓒⓓ	15. ⓐⓑⓒⓓ
	16. ⓐⓑⓒⓓ	17. ⓐⓑⓒⓓ	18. ⓐⓑⓒⓓ	19. ⓐⓑⓒⓓ	20. ⓐⓑⓒⓓ

Max. Marks : 20   **No. of Qs. 20**   **Time : 20 min.**   **Date : ..../........./................**

1. Biological oxygen demand of _______ is the least.
   (a) sewage   (b) sea water
   (c) pure water   (d) polluted water
2. Due to eutrophication_______.
   (a) BOD increases   (b) BOD decreases
   (c) algae are destroyed (d) water becomes less harmful
3. _______ is the first step of sewage treatment.
   (a) Precipitation   (b) Chlorination
   (c) Sedimentation   (d) Aeration
4. Which of the following is not an environmental problem ?
   (a) Wastage of water   (b) Conservation of water
   (c) Deforestation   (d) Land erosion
5. BOD is _______ in polluted water and _______ in potable water.
   (a) more, less   (b) less, medium
   (c) medium, more   (d) less, more
6. BOD/COD ratio will always be:
   (a) Equal to 1   (b) Less than 1
   (c) More than 1   (d) None of them
7. Biochemical Oxygen Demand measures
   (a) industrial pollution
   (b) air pollution
   (c) soil pollution
   (d) dissolved O_2 needed by microbes to decompose organic waste.
8. Excess fluoride in drinking water is likely to cause:
   (a) Blue baby syndrome
   (b) Fluorosis
   (c) Change in taste and odour
   (d) Intestinal irritation
9. Fluoride pollution mainly affects:
   (a) Kidney   (b) Brain
   (c) Heart   (d) Teeth
10. Which of the following is a non-point source of water pollution?
    (a) Factories
    (b) Sewage treatment plants
    (c) Urban and suburban lands
    (d) All of the above
11. Septic tank is:
    (a) An aerobic attached growth treatment system
    (b) An aerobic suspended growth biological treatment system
    (c) An anaerobic attached growth biological treatment system

(d) An anaerobic suspended growth treatment system
12. Disease caused by eating fish inhabiting mercury contaminated water is:
    (a) Bright's disease   (b) Hiroshima episode
    (c) Mina-mata disease   (d) Osteosclerosis
13. Which of the following is not a marine pollutant?
    (a) Oil   (b) Plastics
    (c) Dissolved oxygen   (d) All of the above
14. Which of the following is a major source of thermal pollution in water bodies?
    (a) Sewage treatment plant
    (b) Solid waste disposal sites
    (c) Thermal power plant
    (d) All of the above
15. In B.O.D. test oxygen plays an important role to
    (a) destroy inorganic matter
    (b) destroy pollution
    (c) destroy waste organic matter
    (d) None of these
16. BOD stands for
    (a) Biological organism death
    (b) Biochemical organic matter decay
    (c) Biotic oxidation demand
    (d) Biochemical oxygen demand
17. Fishes die by sewage because
    (a) of its bad smell
    (b) it replaces food material of fishes
    (c) it increases oxygen competition among fishes
    (d) CO_2 is mixed in large amount in water
18. Which of the following metal is a water pollutant and causes sterility in human being
    (a) As   (b) Mn
    (c) Mg   (d) Hg
19. Eutrophication is caused by
    (a) Acid rain
    (b) Nitrates and phosphates
    (c) Sulphates and carbonates
    (d) CO_2 and CO
20. A lake with an inflow of domestic sewage rich in organic waste may result in
    (a) Drying of the lake very soon due to algal bloom
    (b) An increase production of fish due to lot of nutrients
    (c) Death of fish due to lack of oxygen
    (d) Increased population of aquatic food web organisms

RESPONSE GRID	1. ⓐⓑⓒⓓ	2. ⓐⓑⓒⓓ	3. ⓐⓑⓒⓓ	4. ⓐⓑⓒⓓ	5. ⓐⓑⓒⓓ
	6. ⓐⓑⓒⓓ	7. ⓐⓑⓒⓓ	8. ⓐⓑⓒⓓ	9. ⓐⓑⓒⓓ	10. ⓐⓑⓒⓓ
	11. ⓐⓑⓒⓓ	12. ⓐⓑⓒⓓ	13. ⓐⓑⓒⓓ	14. ⓐⓑⓒⓓ	15. ⓐⓑⓒⓓ
	16. ⓐⓑⓒⓓ	17. ⓐⓑⓒⓓ	18. ⓐⓑⓒⓓ	19. ⓐⓑⓒⓓ	20. ⓐⓑⓒⓓ

101 SPEED TEST 57

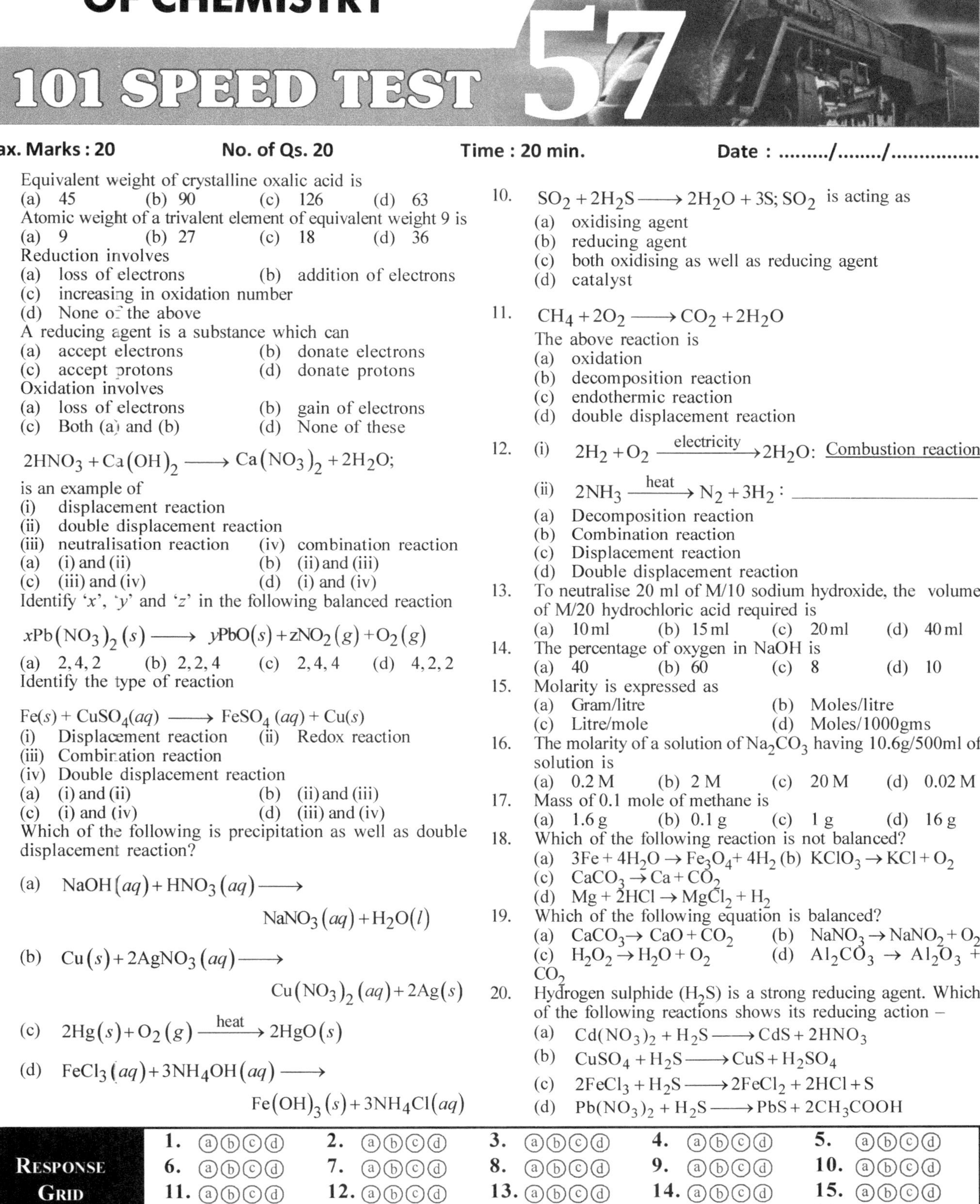

Max. Marks : 20   **No. of Qs. 20**   **Time : 20 min.**   **Date : ..../......../...............**

1. Equivalent weight of crystalline oxalic acid is
   (a) 45   (b) 90   (c) 126   (d) 63
2. Atomic weight of a trivalent element of equivalent weight 9 is
   (a) 9   (b) 27   (c) 18   (d) 36
3. Reduction involves
   (a) loss of electrons   (b) addition of electrons
   (c) increasing in oxidation number
   (d) None of the above
4. A reducing agent is a substance which can
   (a) accept electrons   (b) donate electrons
   (c) accept protons   (d) donate protons
5. Oxidation involves
   (a) loss of electrons   (b) gain of electrons
   (c) Both (a) and (b)   (d) None of these
6. $2HNO_3 + Ca(OH)_2 \longrightarrow Ca(NO_3)_2 + 2H_2O;$
   is an example of
   (i) displacement reaction
   (ii) double displacement reaction
   (iii) neutralisation reaction   (iv) combination reaction
   (a) (i) and (ii)   (b) (ii) and (iii)
   (c) (iii) and (iv)   (d) (i) and (iv)
7. Identify 'x', 'y' and 'z' in the following balanced reaction
   $$xPb(NO_3)_2(s) \longrightarrow yPbO(s) + zNO_2(g) + O_2(g)$$
   (a) 2, 4, 2   (b) 2, 2, 4   (c) 2, 4, 4   (d) 4, 2, 2
8. Identify the type of reaction
   $$Fe(s) + CuSO_4(aq) \longrightarrow FeSO_4(aq) + Cu(s)$$
   (i) Displacement reaction   (ii) Redox reaction
   (iii) Combination reaction
   (iv) Double displacement reaction
   (a) (i) and (ii)   (b) (ii) and (iii)
   (c) (i) and (iv)   (d) (iii) and (iv)
9. Which of the following is precipitation as well as double displacement reaction?

   (a) $NaOH(aq) + HNO_3(aq) \longrightarrow$
   $$NaNO_3(aq) + H_2O(l)$$

   (b) $Cu(s) + 2AgNO_3(aq) \longrightarrow$
   $$Cu(NO_3)_2(aq) + 2Ag(s)$$

   (c) $2Hg(s) + O_2(g) \xrightarrow{heat} 2HgO(s)$

   (d) $FeCl_3(aq) + 3NH_4OH(aq) \longrightarrow$
   $$Fe(OH)_3(s) + 3NH_4Cl(aq)$$

10. $SO_2 + 2H_2S \longrightarrow 2H_2O + 3S;\ SO_2$ is acting as
    (a) oxidising agent
    (b) reducing agent
    (c) both oxidising as well as reducing agent
    (d) catalyst
11. $CH_4 + 2O_2 \longrightarrow CO_2 + 2H_2O$
    The above reaction is
    (a) oxidation
    (b) decomposition reaction
    (c) endothermic reaction
    (d) double displacement reaction
12. (i) $2H_2 + O_2 \xrightarrow{\text{electricity}} 2H_2O$: Combustion reaction
    (ii) $2NH_3 \xrightarrow{\text{heat}} N_2 + 3H_2$: ___________________
    (a) Decomposition reaction
    (b) Combination reaction
    (c) Displacement reaction
    (d) Double displacement reaction
13. To neutralise 20 ml of M/10 sodium hydroxide, the volume of M/20 hydrochloric acid required is
    (a) 10 ml   (b) 15 ml   (c) 20 ml   (d) 40 ml
14. The percentage of oxygen in NaOH is
    (a) 40   (b) 60   (c) 8   (d) 10
15. Molarity is expressed as
    (a) Gram/litre   (b) Moles/litre
    (c) Litre/mole   (d) Moles/1000gms
16. The molarity of a solution of Na_2CO_3 having 10.6g/500ml of solution is
    (a) 0.2 M   (b) 2 M   (c) 20 M   (d) 0.02 M
17. Mass of 0.1 mole of methane is
    (a) 1.6 g   (b) 0.1 g   (c) 1 g   (d) 16 g
18. Which of the following reaction is not balanced?
    (a) $3Fe + 4H_2O \rightarrow Fe_3O_4 + 4H_2$ (b) $KClO_3 \rightarrow KCl + O_2$
    (c) $CaCO_3 \rightarrow Ca + CO_2$
    (d) $Mg + 2HCl \rightarrow MgCl_2 + H_2$
19. Which of the following equation is balanced?
    (a) $CaCO_3 \rightarrow CaO + CO_2$ (b) $NaNO_3 \rightarrow NaNO_2 + O_2$
    (c) $H_2O_2 \rightarrow H_2O + O_2$ (d) $Al_2CO_3 \rightarrow Al_2O_3 + CO_2$
20. Hydrogen sulphide (H_2S) is a strong reducing agent. Which of the following reactions shows its reducing action –
    (a) $Cd(NO_3)_2 + H_2S \longrightarrow CdS + 2HNO_3$
    (b) $CuSO_4 + H_2S \longrightarrow CuS + H_2SO_4$
    (c) $2FeCl_3 + H_2S \longrightarrow 2FeCl_2 + 2HCl + S$
    (d) $Pb(NO_3)_2 + H_2S \longrightarrow PbS + 2CH_3COOH$

RESPONSE GRID					
1. ⓐⓑⓒⓓ	2. ⓐⓑⓒⓓ	3. ⓐⓑⓒⓓ	4. ⓐⓑⓒⓓ	5. ⓐⓑⓒⓓ
6. ⓐⓑⓒⓓ	7. ⓐⓑⓒⓓ	8. ⓐⓑⓒⓓ	9. ⓐⓑⓒⓓ	10. ⓐⓑⓒⓓ
11. ⓐⓑⓒⓓ	12. ⓐⓑⓒⓓ	13. ⓐⓑⓒⓓ	14. ⓐⓑⓒⓓ	15. ⓐⓑⓒⓓ
16. ⓐⓑⓒⓓ	17. ⓐⓑⓒⓓ	18. ⓐⓑⓒⓓ	19. ⓐⓑⓒⓓ	20. ⓐⓑⓒⓓ

101 SPEED TEST

58

Max. Marks : 20   **No. of Qs. 20**   **Time : 20 min.**   **Date : ..../........./................**

1. If glass is cooled suddenly it becomes
   (a) transparent
   (b) soft
   (c) malleable
   (d) brittle
2. Annealing of glass is done to
   (a) make it brittle
   (b) make it opaque
   (c) make it transparent
   (d) None of these
3. Ordinary glass is
   (a) sodium silicate
   (b) borosilicate
   (c) sodium and calcium silicate
   (d) None of the above
4. The principal constituent of pyrex glass is
   (a) Zn   (b) B   (c) Pb   (d) Cl
5. Glass is soluble in
   (a) HF
   (b) H_2SO_4
   (c) $HClO_4$
   (d) Aqua regia
6. Which variety of glass is used for the manufacture of optical lenses?
   (a) Sodium glass
   (b) Quartz
   (c) Flint glass
   (d) Ground glass
7. Silica glass is
   (a) a glass has high coefficient of expansion
   (b) break's up to red hot
   (c) pure SiO_2
   (d) very hard
8. Which one of the following is incorrect about flint glass?
   (a) It is soft and transparent
   (b) It's refractive index is very high
   (c) It is $K_2O . PbO. 6SiO_2$
   (d) It does not breaks on red hot
9. Which one of the following type of glass has a layer of plastic?
   (a) Safety glass
   (b) Ground glass
   (c) Reinforced glass
   (d) Borosilicate glass
10. Percentage of silica
    (a) increases brittleness of glass
    (b) decrease resistivity of glass
    (c) Both (a) and (b)
    (d) None of the above
11. Mortar is a mixture of
    (a) cement + sand + water
    (b) sand + iron
    (c) cement + sand + iron
    (d) None of these
12. Which one among the following is the chemical formula of gypsum, which is an ingredient of cement?
    (a) Ca_2SiO_4
    (b) $CaSO_4.2H_2O$
    (c) CaO
    (d) $CaSO_4.3H_2O$
13. Gypsum is added to clinker during cement manufacturing to
    (a) decrease the rate of setting of cement
    (b) bind the particle of calcium silicate
    (c) facilitate the formation of colloidal gel
    (d) impact strength to cement
14. Match Column I (Type of glass) with Column II (Composition) and select the correct answer using the codes given below the columns.

Column I	Column II
A. Soda glass	1. Mixture of potassium and lead silicates
B. Crown glass	2. Mixture of sodium, barium, zinc and magnesium silicates
C. Flint glass	3. Mixture of sodium, zinc and magnesium silicates
D. Pyrex glass	4. Mixture of sodium and calcium silicates

    Codes:

	A	B	C	D
(a)	4	1	2	3
(b)	3	2	1	4
(c)	4	2	1	3
(d)	3	1	2	4

15. Which one of the following types of glass can cut-off ultraviolet rays?
    (a) Soda glass
    (b) Pyrex glass
    (c) Jena glass
    (d) Crooked glass
16. A major constituent of cement besides lime is
    (a) silica
    (b) alumina
    (c) iron oxide
    (d) magnesia
17. Portland cement is manufactured by using
    (a) limestone, clay and stone
    (b) limestone, gypsum and sand
    (c) limestone, gypsum and alumina
    (d) limestone, clay and gypsum
18. After casting of cement on the wall water is given regularly up to several days because
    (a) setting of cement is exothermic reaction therefore water decreases the temperature
    (b) water absorb the heat from air and supplies to cement for setting
    (c) water helps in complete hydrolysis and setting of cement
    (d) All of the above
19. The cement is usually called Portland cement because
    (a) it can be easily ported
    (b) it is usually prepared near the ports
    (c) when mixed with water it becomes hard like Portland rocks
    (d) None of the above
20. Which is correct about cement?
    (a) Gypsum is added to regulate setting time of cement
    (b) White cement does not contains iron
    (c) Lime is main constituent of cement
    (d) All of the above are correct

RESPONSE GRID	1. (a)(b)(c)(d)	2. (a)(b)(c)(d)	3. (a)(b)(c)(d)	4. (a)(b)(c)(d)	5. (a)(b)(c)(d)
	6. (a)(b)(c)(d)	7. (a)(b)(c)(d)	8. (a)(b)(c)(d)	9. (a)(b)(c)(d)	10. (a)(b)(c)(d)
	11. (a)(b)(c)(d)	12. (a)(b)(c)(d)	13. (a)(b)(c)(d)	14. (a)(b)(c)(d)	15. (a)(b)(c)(d)
	16. (a)(b)(c)(d)	17. (a)(b)(c)(d)	18. (a)(b)(c)(d)	19. (a)(b)(c)(d)	20. (a)(b)(c)(d)

101 SPEED TEST

59

Max. Marks : 20   **No. of Qs. 20**   **Time : 20 min.**   **Date : ..../........./................**

1. Which one of the following is a mixed fertilizer ?
   (a) Urea
   (b) CAM
   (c) Ammonium Sulphate
   (d) NPK

2. When the fats are reacted with alkali, they form 'soaps'. The type of reaction taking place in the formation of soaps is called
   (a) emulsification
   (b) saponification
   (c) halogenation
   (d) oxidation

3. Consider the following statements
   1. Hard soaps (common bar soaps) are the sodium salts of fatty acids.
   2. Soft soaps are the potassium salts of fatty acids and semi-solid in nature
   Which of the statement(s) given above is/are correct?
   (a) Only 1
   (b) Only 2
   (c) Both 1 and 2
   (d) Neither 1 nor 2

4. Consider the following statements
   1. Hardness of water depends upon its soap consuming power.
   2. Temporary hardness is due to bicarbonates of magnesium and calcium.
   3. Permanent hardness of water is due to sulphate and/or chloride of calcium and magnesium.
   4. Permanent hardness can be removed by boiling.
   Which of the statements given above are correct?
   (a) 1, 2, 3 and 4
   (b) 1, 2 and 3
   (c) 2 and 3
   (d) 3 and 4

5. Which of the following statements is not true for soap?
   (a) Soaps are biodegradable.
   (b) Soaps cannot be used in acidic medium.
   (c) Soaps form a white curdy precipitate with hard water.
   (d) Soaps are relatively stronger in their cleansing action than synthetic detergents.

6. Lime is sometimes applied to soil in order to
   (a) increase the acidity of soil
   (b) increase the alkalinity of soil
   (c) make the soil more porous
   (d) restore nitrates of the soil

7. Triple phosphate is a
   (a) mixed fertilizer
   (b) nitrogeneous fertilizer
   (c) potash fertilizer
   (d) none of these

8. The commonly present elements in artificial fertilizers are
   (a) nitrogen, phosphorous and potassium
   (b) nitrogen, phosphorus and sodium
   (c) calcium, potassium and sodium
   (d) all elements of periodic table

9. Which one of the following cannot be used as a nitrogeneous fertilizer?
   (a) $CaCN_2$
   (b) NH_4NO_3
   (c) HNO_3
   (d) NH_2CONH_2

10. Which of the following is known as "muriate of potash"?
    (a) KCl
    (b) K_2SO_4
    (c) KNO_3
    (d) None of these

11. Nodules with nitrogen fixing bacteria are present in
    (a) Mustard   (b) Rice   (c) Gram   (d) Cotton

12. Which of the following nitrogenous fertilizers is not very effective in acidic soil?
    (a) Ammonium sulphate
    (b) Urea
    (c) Nitrolium
    (d) Calcium cyanamide

13. Vitamin A is present in
    (a) cod liver oil
    (b) carrot
    (c) milk
    (d) All of these

14. Ascorbic acid is a
    (a) vitamin
    (b) enzyme
    (c) protein
    (d) carbohydrate

15. The deficiency of vitamin B_1 causes
    (a) Beri-beri
    (b) Scurvy
    (c) Rickets
    (d) Anaemia

16. The deficiency of vitamin-C causes
    (a) Scurvy
    (b) Rickets
    (c) Pyrrohea
    (d) Pernicious Anaemia

17. Deficiency of which vitamin causes rickets
    (a) Vitamin-D
    (b) Vitamin-B
    (c) Vitamin-A
    (d) Vitamin-K

18. The best source of vitamin A is
    (a) Beans   (b) Pulses   (c) Orange   (d) Carrot

19. Which one of the following vitamins is soluble in water
    (a) Vitamin B
    (b) Vitamin E
    (c) Vitamin K
    (d) Vitamin A

20. Toilet soap is a mixture of
    (a) calcium salt of fatty acids
    (b) potassium salt of fatty acids
    (c) fatty acids and alcohol
    (d) phenol and olive oil

RESPONSE GRID	1. ⓐⓑⓒⓓ	2. ⓐⓑⓒⓓ	3. ⓐⓑⓒⓓ	4. ⓐⓑⓒⓓ	5. ⓐⓑⓒⓓ
	6. ⓐⓑⓒⓓ	7. ⓐⓑⓒⓓ	8. ⓐⓑⓒⓓ	9. ⓐⓑⓒⓓ	10. ⓐⓑⓒⓓ
	11. ⓐⓑⓒⓓ	12. ⓐⓑⓒⓓ	13. ⓐⓑⓒⓓ	14. ⓐⓑⓒⓓ	15. ⓐⓑⓒⓓ
	16. ⓐⓑⓒⓓ	17. ⓐⓑⓒⓓ	18. ⓐⓑⓒⓓ	19. ⓐⓑⓒⓓ	20. ⓐⓑⓒⓓ

GENERAL ORGANIC CHEMISTRY

101 SPEED TEST

60

Max. Marks : 20　　　No. of Qs. 20　　　Time : 20 min.　　　Date : ..../......../.................

1. Which one of the following is the correct sequence in increasing order of molecular weights of the hydrocarbons?
   (a) Methane, ethane, propane and butane
   (b) Propane, butane, ethane and methane
   (c) Butane, ethane, propane and methane
   (d) Butane, propane, ethane and methane

2. The father of the aromatic organic compound is
   (a) methane　　　　(b) benzene
   (c) phenol　　　　　(d) aniline

3. The normal butane and isobutane are
   (a) optical isomer　　　(b) chain isomer
   (c) positional isomer　　(d) functional isomer

4. Consider the following statements
   1. The alcohol which is 100% pure is called absolute alcohol.
   2. Ethyl alcohol which cannot be used for the beverage purpose is called denatured alcohol.
   3. The mixture of purified spirit, benzene and petrol is called power alcohol.
   Which of the statements given above are correct?
   (a) 1 and 2　　　　(b) 1 and 3
   (c) 2 and 3　　　　(d) 1, 2 and 3

5. Match Column I with Column II and select the correct answer using the codes given below this columns.

Column I	Column II
(Organic compound)	(Functional group)
A. Alcohol	1. —CHO
B. Aldehyde	2. —OH
C. Carboxylic acid	3. >C = O
D. Ketone	4. —COOH

   Codes:

	A	B	C	D
(a)	2	1	4	3
(b)	1	4	3	2
(c)	4	3	2	1
(d)	3	2	1	4

6. Consider the following statements
   1. Methane is also known as marsh gas.
   2. The main component of the natural gas is methane.
   3. The main component of the LPG is butane.
   Which of the statements given above are correct?
   (a) 1 and 2　　　　(b) 1 and 3
   (c) 2 and 3　　　　(d) 1, 2 and 3

7. The main components of the LPG are
   (a) methane, ethane and hexane
   (b) methane, ethane and nonane
   (c) methane, propane and butane
   (d) ethane, hexane and butane

8. Study the following statements
   1. Benzene and toluene are aromatic hydrocarbons.
   2. In benzene, six carbon atoms are arranged in a closed chain with alternate double and single bonds.
   Which of the above is/are correct?
   (a) Only 1　　　　(b) Only 2
   (c) 1 and 2　　　　(d) None of these

9. Which is the example of branch isomerization

   (a) $C - C - C - C - C$ and $C - \overset{\overset{C}{|}}{C} - C$ (with C below)

   (b) $C - \overset{\overset{C}{|}}{\underset{\underset{C}{|}}{C}} - C$ and $\overset{\overset{C}{|}}{C} - C - C$

   (c) $\overset{C}{\underset{C}{>}}C - C - C$ and $C - C - \overset{\overset{C}{|}}{\underset{\underset{C}{|}}{C}}$

   (d) $C - C - C - C$ and $C - C - \overset{}{\underset{\underset{C}{|}}{C}}$

10. IUPAC name of CH_3CHO is
    (a) Acetaldehyde
    (b) Methyl aldehyde
    (c) Ethanol
    (d) Ethanal

11. IUPAC name of $CH_3 - O - C_2H_5$ is
    (a) Ethoxymethane
    (b) Methoxyethane
    (c) Methylethyl ether
    (d) Ethylmethyl ether

12. Which of the following compound has the functional group – OH
    (a) 1, 2 - ethandiol　　　(b) 2-butanone
    (c) Nitrobenzene　　　　(d) Ethanal

13. Alicylic compounds are
    (a) Aromatic
    (b) Aliphatic
    (c) Heterocyclic
    (d) Aliphatic cyclic

14. The gas emerged through the cigarette lighter is
    (a) butane
    (b) methane
    (c) propane
    (d) redon

15. The methanol is also known by the name of
    (a) rubing alcohol
    (b) grain alcohol
    (c) wood alcohol
    (d) deformed alcohol

16. The wine is prepared by the process of
    (a) fermentation
    (b) catalysation
    (c) conjugation
    (d) displacement

17. Methylated spirit of
    (a) 100% alcohol
    (b) 95.6% alchol + 4.4% water
    (c) 90% alcohol + 9% methanol + pyridine
    (d) power alcohol

18. Consider the following statements
    1. The simplest hydrocarbon is methane (CH_4).
    2. Hydrocarbons support life directly as carbohydrates, proteins, nucleic acids.
    3. Benzene is unsaturated cyclic hydrocarbon.
    Which of the statements given above are correct?
    (a) 1 and 2
    (b) 1 and 3
    (c) 2 and 3
    (d) 1, 2 and 3

19. Study the following statements
    1. The common name of propanone is dimethyl ketone.
    2. An isomer of ethanol is dimethyl ether.
    3. When water vapours are passed over aluminium carbide, we get methane.
    Which of the statements given above are correct?
    (a) 1, 2 and 3
    (b) 1 and 2
    (c) 1 and 3
    (d) 2 and 3

20. To prevent from knocking the substance employed in the car engine is
    (a) ethyl alcohol
    (b) butane
    (c) tetraethyl lead
    (d) white petrol

| **RESPONSE GRID** | 13. (a)(b)(c)(d) | 14. (a)(b)(c)(d) | 15. (a)(b)(c)(d) | 16. (a)(b)(c)(d) | 17. (a)(b)(c)(d) |
| | 18. (a)(b)(c)(d) | 19. (a)(b)(c)(d) | 20. (a)(b)(c)(d) | | |

Max. Marks : 20 **No. of Qs. 20** **Time : 20 min.** **Date : ..../........./................**

1. Nuclear material without cover is found in
   (a) Mycoplasma and Green algae
   (b) Bacteria and Fungi
   (c) Bacteria and Blue green algae
   (d) None of the above

2. Cell theory was proposed by
   (a) Schleiden and Schwann (b) Robert Brown
   (c) Leeuwenhoek (d) Purkinje

3. The suicide bags of the cells are
   (a) Plastids (b) Mitochondria
   (c) Lysosomes (d) Ribosomes

4. The power houses of the cells are
   (a) Mitochondria (b) Plastids
   (c) Golgi complex (d) Ribosomes

5. The energy currency of the cell is
   (a) ADP (b) ATP (c) NADP (d) FADP

6. The organelle that is present only in plant cells is
   (a) mitochondria (b) endoplasmic reticulum
   (c) ribosomes (d) plastids

7. Consider the following statements:
   (i) In living organisms, the mitochondria are the only cell organelle outside the nucleus that contain DNA.
   (ii) Nuclei and mitochondria are surrounded by a double membrane.
   Which of these statement(s) is/are correct ?
   (a) (i) only (b) (ii) only
   (c) Both (i) and (ii) (d) Neither (i) nor (ii)

8. Consider the following statements:
   (i) The ER functions both as a passageway for intracellular transport and as a manufacturing surface.
   (ii) Ribosomes are present in eukaryotic cells only.
   (iii) SER detoxifies many poisons and drugs.
   Which of these statement(s) is/are correct ?
   (a) (i) and (ii) (b) (ii) and (iii)
   (c) (i) and (iii) (d) All are correct

9. Nucleus plays a crucial part in
   (a) metabolism (b) cellular reproduction
   (c) lipid synthesis (d) protein synthesis

10. Which of the following is not present in prokaryotes ?
    (a) Ribosomes (b) Cell wall
    (c) Plasma membrane (d) Nuclear membrane

11. Organelle other than nucleus, containing DNA is
    (a) Endoplasmic reticulum (b) Golgi apparatus
    (c) Mitochondira (d) Lysosome

12. The only cell organelle seen in prokaryotic cell is
    (a) Mitochondria (b) Ribosomes
    (c) Plastids (d) Lysosomes

13. Which organelle is usually found associated with the nucleus of the cell in animals ?
    (a) Centrosome (b) Vacuole
    (c) Chromosome (d) Mitochondria

14. Which animal cell structure is characterized by selective permeability ?
    (a) Chromosome (b) Cell membrane
    (c) Cell wall (d) Ribosomes

15. The process of mitosis is divided into 4 phases. Identify the correct order in which these phases appear in mitosis
    (a) Anaphase, Metaphase, Telophase and Prophase
    (b) Telophase, Anaphase, Metaphase and Prophase
    (c) Metaphase, Prophase, Anaphase and Telophase
    (d) Prophase, Metaphase, Anaphase and Telophase

16. Regarding the sequence of cell cycle, which one is correct?
    (a) G_1, G_2, S and M (b) S, G_1, G_2 and M
    (c) G_1, S, G_2 and M (d) G_2, S, G_1 and M

17. Ribosomes are the centre for
    (a) respiration (b) photosynthesis
    (c) protein synthesis (d) fat synthesis

18. The main difference between Plant and Animal cell is
    (a) Animal cells lack cell wall
    (b) Plant cell has no cell wall
    (c) Animal cell has a rigid cell wall
    (d) Plant cells lack cell membrane

19. The undefined nuclear region in a bacteria is
    (a) Nucleoid (b) Nucleus
    (c) Chromosome (d) Nucleolus

20. The main arena of various types of activities of a cell is
    (a) Plasma membrane (b) Mitochondrian
    (c) Cytoplasm (d) Nucleus

RESPONSE GRID	1. ⓐⓑⓒⓓ	2. ⓐⓑⓒⓓ	3. ⓐⓑⓒⓓ	4. ⓐⓑⓒⓓ	5. ⓐⓑⓒⓓ
	6. ⓐⓑⓒⓓ	7. ⓐⓑⓒⓓ	8. ⓐⓑⓒⓓ	9. ⓐⓑⓒⓓ	10. ⓐⓑⓒⓓ
	11. ⓐⓑⓒⓓ	12. ⓐⓑⓒⓓ	13. ⓐⓑⓒⓓ	14. ⓐⓑⓒⓓ	15. ⓐⓑⓒⓓ
	16. ⓐⓑⓒⓓ	17. ⓐⓑⓒⓓ	18. ⓐⓑⓒⓓ	19. ⓐⓑⓒⓓ	20. ⓐⓑⓒⓓ

TISSUES

101 SPEED TEST 62

Max. Marks : 20   **No. of Qs. 20**   **Time : 20 min.**   **Date : ..../........./................**

1. Blood, phloem and muscle are
   - (a) Tissues
   - (b) Organs
   - (c) Cells
   - (d) Organ system

2. The two kidney shaped cells of the stomata are called
   - (a) Epidermis
   - (b) Guard cells
   - (c) Stoma
   - (d) Phloem

3. The hard matrix of the bone consists of
   - (a) calcium and sodium
   - (b) magnesium and sodium
   - (c) phosphorous and magnesium
   - (d) calcium and phosphorous

4. Which of the following helps in translocation of food is plants?
   - (a) Xylem
   - (b) Phloem
   - (c) Sclerenchyma
   - (d) Collenchyma

5. In plants, which one of the following tissues is dead ?
   - (a) Parenchyma
   - (b) Collenchyma
   - (c) Sclerenchyma
   - (d) Phloem

6. Which of the following bast fibres is of great commercial value?
   - (a) Jute
   - (b) Flax
   - (c) Hemp
   - (d) All of these

7. Average life span of human R.B.C. is
   - (a) 100 days
   - (b) 90 days
   - (c) 120 days
   - (d) None

8. The fibrous tissue which connects the two bone is
   - (a) Connective tissue
   - (b) Tendon
   - (c) Ligament
   - (d) Adipose tissue

9. The main function of the inner bark of a woody plant is to
   - (a) transport minerals and water from the roots to the leaves
   - (b) act as a membrane impermeable to water and gas
   - (c) transport food from the leaves to the other parts of the plant
   - (d) protect the plant from herbivorous animals

10. Meristematic tissues are found in
    - (a) only stems of the plants
    - (b) both roots and stems
    - (c) in all growing tips of the plant body
    - (d) only roots of the plants

11. Which of the following does help in repair of tissue and fills up the space inside the organ?
    - (a) Tendon
    - (b) Adipose tissue
    - (c) Areolar
    - (d) Cartilage

12. Certain parts of a plant can be bent easily without breaking. This flexibility in certain parts, like leaf and stem, can be attributed to the abundance of
    - (a) Parenchyma
    - (b) Collenchyma
    - (c) Sclerenchyma
    - (d) Xylem and phloem

13. Which of the following type of cell junction is not found in animal tissues?
    - (a) Desmosome
    - (b) Tight junction
    - (c) Gap junction
    - (d) Plasmodesmata

14. B and T forms, responsible for the immune response are the type of
    - (a) Thrombocytes
    - (b) Lymphocytes
    - (c) Eosinophils
    - (d) Granulocytes

15. Consider the following statements in relation to plant tissue chlorenchyma :
    1. It is formed by the palisade and spongy mesophyll.
    2. It is a form of parenchyma which contains chloroplasts.
    3. It serves to transport organic solutes made by photo-synthesis.
    4. It is a thin transparent layer which has chiefly a protective function.
    - (a) 1 and 2 only
    - (b) 1, 2 and 4
    - (c) 2 and 3
    - (d) 1 only

16. Bone marrow is absent in
    - (a) Reptilia
    - (b) Amphibia
    - (c) Fishes
    - (d) Birds

17. The hump of camel is made up of which of the following tissues?
    - (a) Areolar tissue
    - (b) Adipose tissue
    - (c) Epithelial tissue
    - (d) Muscular tissue

18. Pernicious anaemia is due to
    - (a) Low RBC count
    - (b) Death of WBC
    - (c) Defective RBC maturation
    - (d) Destruction of young RBC

19. Which of the following are bone forming cells?
    - (a) Osteocytes
    - (b) Osteoblasts
    - (c) Osteoclasts
    - (d) None of these

20. The haemoglobin content per 100 ml of blood of a normal healthy human adult is
    - (a) 5 - 11 g
    - (b) 25 - 30 g
    - (c) 17 - 20 g
    - (d) 12 - 16 g

RESPONSE GRID					
	1. ⓐⓑⓒⓓ	2. ⓐⓑⓒⓓ	3. ⓐⓑⓒⓓ	4. ⓐⓑⓒⓓ	5. ⓐⓑⓒⓓ
	6. ⓐⓑⓒⓓ	7. ⓐⓑⓒⓓ	8. ⓐⓑⓒⓓ	9. ⓐⓑⓒⓓ	10. ⓐⓑⓒⓓ
	11. ⓐⓑⓒⓓ	12. ⓐⓑⓒⓓ	13. ⓐⓑⓒⓓ	14. ⓐⓑⓒⓓ	15. ⓐⓑⓒⓓ
	16. ⓐⓑⓒⓓ	17. ⓐⓑⓒⓓ	18. ⓐⓑⓒⓓ	19. ⓐⓑⓒⓓ	20. ⓐⓑⓒⓓ

101 SPEED TEST 63

Max. Marks : 20   **No. of Qs. 20**   **Time : 20 min.**   Date : ..../........./................

1. The oxygen released during photosynthesis of green plants comes from the breakdown of which one of the following ?
   - (a) Carbon dioxide
   - (b) Fatty acids
   - (c) Carbohydrates
   - (d) Water

2. Which of the following is not performed by root hairs ?
   - (a) Water uptake
   - (b) Oxygen uptake
   - (c) Mineral uptake
   - (d) CO_2 uptake

3. Which pigment is essential for nitrogen fixation by leguminous plants ?
   - (a) Phycocyanin
   - (b) Leghaemoglobin
   - (c) Phycoerythrin
   - (d) Myoglobin

4. Which of the following crops would be preferred for sowing in order to enrich the soil with nitrogen ?
   - (a) Wheat
   - (b) Mustard
   - (c) Sunflower
   - (d) Gram

5. Which of the following is necessary for respiration in plants ?
   - (a) Carbon dioxide
   - (b) Oxygen
   - (c) Chlorophyll
   - (d) Light

6. When dried raisins are put in plain water, they swell up. If put again in brine solution, they shrivel up. This phenomenon indicates the property of
   - (a) Diffusion
   - (b) Perfusion
   - (c) Osmosis
   - (d) Fusion

7. Which of the following is a bacterium involved in denitrification ?
   - (a) *Nitrococcus*
   - (b) *Azotobacter*
   - (c) *Pseudomonas*
   - (d) *Nitrosomonas*

8. Which one of the following doesn't help in molecule transport?
   - (a) Diffusion
   - (b) Osmosis
   - (c) Surface tension
   - (d) Active transport

9. What is the energy currency of a cell ?
   - (a) DNA
   - (b) RNA
   - (c) ATP
   - (d) Minerals

10. Which one among the following Indian scientists proposed a theory for long distance transport of water in plants?
    - (a) J C Bose
    - (b) Birbal Sahni
    - (c) P Maheshwari
    - (d) N S Parihar

11. The response of different organisms to environmental rhythms of light and darkness is called
    - (a) Phototaxis
    - (b) Photoperiodism
    - (c) Phototropism
    - (d) Vernalization.

12. Photosynthetically active radiation is represented by the range of wavelength of
    - (a) 340-450 nm
    - (b) 400-700 nm
    - (c) 500-600 nm
    - (d) 400-950 nm

13. Which one among the following nutrients is a structural component of the cell wall of plants?
    - (a) Manganese
    - (b) Potassium
    - (c) Phosphorus
    - (d) Calcium

14. Excessive elongation of plant stem is due to
    - (a) Cytokinin
    - (b) GA
    - (c) ABA
    - (d) IAA

15. Maximum amount of energy/ATP is liberated on oxidation of
    - (a) fats
    - (b) proteins
    - (c) starch
    - (d) vitamins

16. Which of the following is *not* a micronutrient for a plant?
    - (a) Iron
    - (b) Magnesium
    - (c) Molybdenum
    - (d) Manganese

17. In photosynthesis, oxygen comes from
    - (a) CO_2
    - (b) $C_6H_{12}O_6$
    - (c) H_2O
    - (d) chlorophyll

18. The commonest living, which can respire in the absence of O_2 is
    - (a) *Fish*
    - (b) *Yeast*
    - (c) Potato
    - (d) *Chlorella*

19. Which one of the following is not an essential element for plants ?
    - (a) Potassium
    - (b) Iron
    - (c) Iodine
    - (d) Zinc

20. Plants die from prolonged water-logging because
    - (a) soil nutrients become very dilute.
    - (b) root respiration stops.
    - (c) cell sap in the plants becomes too dilute.
    - (d) nutrients leach down due to excess water.

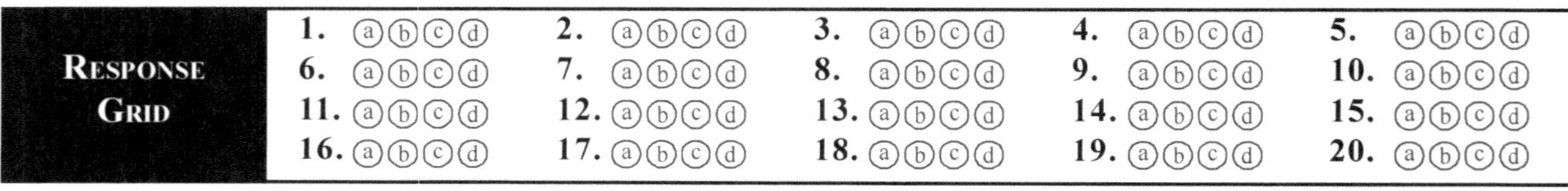

HUMAN PHYSIOLOGY

101 SPEED TEST

64

Max. Marks : 20　　　　**No. of Qs. 20**　　　　**Time : 20 min.**　　　　Date : ..../........../...............

1. In human beings, carbohydrate is stored as glycogen in
   (a) Liver and Muscles　(b) Liver
   (c) Muscles　(d) Spleen

2. The normal blood pressure is
   (a) 160/120 mm Hg　(b) 140/90 mm Hg
   (c) 120/80 mm Hg　(d) 110/70 mm Hg

3. Haemoglobin occurs in
   (a) WBC　(b) RBC
   (c) Blood Platelets　(d) Lymphocytes

4. Which is the element that hardens the tooth enamel?
   (a) Calcium　(b) Fluorine
   (c) Iodine　(d) Sodium

5. The filtration units of kidneys are called
   (a) Ureter　(b) Urethra
   (c) Neurons　(d) Nephrons

6. The instrument used in measuring blood pressure is
   (a) Stethoscope　(b) Sphygomanometer
   (c) Electrocardiograph　(d) Endoscope

7. Skin is an accessory organ of respiration in
   (a) Human　(b) Frog
   (c) Rabbit　(d) Lizard

8. Respiratory structures in the insects are
   (a) Gills　(b) Skin
   (c) Lungs　(d) Tracheae

9. Diabetes insipidus is due to deficiency of hormone
   (a) Insulin　(b) Glucagon
   (c) Anti-diuretic hormone　(d) Thyroxine

10. Number of bones in human body is
    (a) 260　(b) 206
    (c) 306　(d) 203

11. Which one is not a reflex action ?
    (a) Knee jerk
    (b) Coughing
    (c) Closing of eyes on flashing light
    (d) Swallowing

12. During inspiration, diaphragm is
    (a) flattened　(b) arched
    (c) not changed　(d) moved upward

13. Vermiform appendix is a part of
    (a) Alimentary canal　(b) Nervous system
    (c) Vascular system　(d) Reproductive system

14. The fibrous tissue which connects the two bone is
    (a) Connective tissue　(b) Tendon
    (c) Ligament　(d) Adipose tissue

15. The largest gland of the body is
    (a) Liver　(b) Parotid gland
    (c) Pancreas　(d) Mandibular gland

16. In human body, which one of the following harmones regulates blood calcium and phosphate ?
    (a) Glucagon　(b) Growth harmone
    (c) Parathyroid harmone　(d) Thyroxine

17. A pacemaker is meant for
    (a) transporting liver
    (b) transplanting heart
    (c) initiation of heart beats
    (d) regulation of blood flow

18. The function of tongue is to
    (a) help in the act of swallowing
    (b) help in mixing salive with the food
    (c) help in speaking
    (d) All the above

19. Life span of human RBCs is of
    (a) 80 days　(b) 100 days
    (c) 120 days　(d) 150 days

20. Longest cell in human body may be
    (a) Nerve cell　(b) Leg muscle cell
    (c) Bone cell　(d) Heart muscle cell

RESPONSE GRID	1. (a)(b)(c)(d)	2. (a)(b)(c)(d)	3. (a)(b)(c)(d)	4. (a)(b)(c)(d)	5. (a)(b)(c)(d)
	6. (a)(b)(c)(d)	7. (a)(b)(c)(d)	8. (a)(b)(c)(d)	9. (a)(b)(c)(d)	10. (a)(b)(c)(d)
	11. (a)(b)(c)(d)	12. (a)(b)(c)(d)	13. (a)(b)(c)(d)	14. (a)(b)(c)(d)	15. (a)(b)(c)(d)
	16. (a)(b)(c)(d)	17. (a)(b)(c)(d)	18. (a)(b)(c)(d)	19. (a)(b)(c)(d)	20. (a)(b)(c)(d)

GENETICS AND EVOLUTION

101 SPEED TEST 65

Max. Marks : 20   **No. of Qs. 20**   **Time : 20 min.**   Date : ..../........./................

1. There was no free oxygen in the early atmosphere because most of it was tied up in
   - (a) water
   - (b) ammonia
   - (c) methane
   - (d) rock

2. DNA is found primarily
   - (a) in cell nucleus
   - (b) outside the cell nucleus
   - (c) in cell cytoplasm
   - (d) None of these

3. The branch of botany dealing with heredity and variation is called
   - (a) Geobotany
   - (b) Sericulture
   - (c) Genetics
   - (d) Evolution

4. Inheritance of ABO blood grouping is an example of
   - (a) dominance
   - (b) co-dominance
   - (c) incomplete dominance
   - (d) Both (a) and (b)

5. Which one of the following features is closely related with the evolution of humans?
   - (a) Loss of tail
   - (b) Shortening of jaws
   - (c) Binocular vision
   - (d) Flat nails

6. Study of fossils is called
   - (a) Geology
   - (b) Microbiology
   - (c) Paleontology
   - (d) Biology

7. Who proved that DNA is basic genetic material?
   - (a) Griffith
   - (b) Watson
   - (c) Boveri and Sutton
   - (d) Hershey and Chase

8. Which of the following features do humans lack that other primates have ?
   - (a) Forward-facing eyes
   - (b) Short snouts
   - (c) Flexible shoulder and elbow joints
   - (d) Opposable big toes

9. What was the most significant trend in evolution of modern man (*Homo sapiens*) from his ancestors ?
   - (a) Upright posture
   - (b) Shortening of jaws
   - (c) Binocular vision
   - (d) Increasing brain capacity

10. The remains of dead animals or plants that lived in hte remote past are called
    - (a) Homologous organs
    - (b) Analogous organs
    - (c) Vestigial organs
    - (d) Fossils

11. Which of the following is a Test cross?
    - (a) TT × tt
    - (b) Tt × tt
    - (c) Tt × TT
    - (d) tt × tt

12. The book "Origin of species" was written by
    - (a) Lamarck
    - (b) Darwin
    - (c) Mendel
    - (d) De Vries

13. The theory of evolution of species by natural selection was given by
    - (a) Mendel
    - (b) Darwin
    - (c) Morgan
    - (d) Lamarck

14. Which is the example of homologous organs?
    - (a) Forelimbs of man and Wings of bird
    - (b) Wings of birds and Wings of insects
    - (c) Vermiform appendix and Nictitating membrane
    - (d) *Archaeopteryx* and *Balanoglossus*

15. A zygote which has an X-chromosome inherited from the father will develop into a
    - (a) boy
    - (b) girl
    - (c) X-chromosome does not determine the sex of a child
    - (d) either boy or girl

16. In animals sex determination is due to
    - (a) X-chromosome
    - (b) Y-chromosome
    - (c) A-chromosome
    - (d) B-chromosome

17. Evolution of Man is believed to have taken place in
    - (a) Central America
    - (b) Australia
    - (c) Asia
    - (d) Africa

18. Sudden inheritable change is called
    - (a) Recombination
    - (b) Mutation
    - (c) National selection
    - (d) Segregation

19. Mutation rates are affected by
    - (a) temperature
    - (b) X-rays
    - (c) gamma and beta radiation
    - (d) All of the above

20. From heredity point of view which marriage is not suitable?
    - (a) Man Rh (–) and Woman Rh (+)
    - (b) Both Rh (+)
    - (c) Both Rh (–)
    - (d) Man Rh (+) and Woman Rh (–)

RESPONSE GRID	1. (a)(b)(c)(d)	2. (a)(b)(c)(d)	3. (a)(b)(c)(d)	4. (a)(b)(c)(d)	5. (a)(b)(c)(d)
	6. (a)(b)(c)(d)	7. (a)(b)(c)(d)	8. (a)(b)(c)(d)	9. (a)(b)(c)(d)	10. (a)(b)(c)(d)
	11. (a)(b)(c)(d)	12. (a)(b)(c)(d)	13. (a)(b)(c)(d)	14. (a)(b)(c)(d)	15. (a)(b)(c)(d)
	16. (a)(b)(c)(d)	17. (a)(b)(c)(d)	18. (a)(b)(c)(d)	19. (a)(b)(c)(d)	20. (a)(b)(c)(d)

DIVERSITY IN LIVING ORGANISMS

101 SPEED TEST 66

Max. Marks : 20 **No. of Qs. 20** **Time : 20 min.** Date : ..../........./...............

1. Who of the following is known as the Father of Biology?
   (a) Darwin (b) Lamarck
   (c) Aristotle (d) Theophrastus

2. Which of the following does not have blood but undergoes respiration ?
   (a) Cockroach (b) Snail
   (c) *Hydra* (d) Kangaroo

3. Which one of the following is a fungus ?
   (a) *Agaricus* (b) *Funaria*
   (c) *Rhizobium* (d) *Spirogyra*

4. Which one of the following pairs is not correctly matched ?
   (a) *Funaria* : Bryophyta
   (b) *Chlorella* : Pteridophyte
   (c) *Spirogyra* : Algae
   (d) *Cycas* : Gymnosperm

5. The branch of botany under which fungi is studied
   (a) Phycology (b) Mycology
   (c) Ethology (d) Microbiology

6. Which of the following is also called Jelly-Fish ?
   (a) *Hydra* (b) *Physaelia*
   (c) *Aurelia* (d) *Asterias*

7. Which one of the following types of plants produces spores and embryo, but without seeds and vascular tissues?
   (a) Gymnosperms (b) Pteridophytes
   (c) Bryophytes (d) Angiosperms

8. Lichen is a composite combination of two organisms
   (a) Fungi and Bryophyta (b) Fungi and Fern
   (c) Algae and Bryophyta (d) Algae and Fungi

9. The sea horse belongs to the class of
   (a) Fishes (b) Mammals
   (c) Reptiles (d) Molluscs

10. Which of the following plants is referred to as a living fossil ?
    (a) *Ephedra* (b) *Cycas*
    (c) *Ginkgo* (d) *Adiantum*

11. Which of the following is used as an ornamental plant?
    (a) *Psilotum* (b) *Lycopodium*
    (c) *Selaginella* (d) *Pteris*

12. Which of the following is cold blooded?
    (a) Fish (b) Frog
    (c) Lizard (d) All of these

13. To which one of the following types of organism do ferns belong?
    (a) Algae (b) Pteridophytes
    (c) Fungi (d) Lichens

14. Mushrooms is a
    (a) Fungus (b) Alga
    (c) Fern (d) Moss

15. Which one of the following is the largest phylum in the animal kingdom ?
    (a) Annelida (b) Arthropoda
    (c) Chordata (d) Protozoa

16. Which of the following leaf modifications occurs/occur in desert areas to inhibit water loss?
    1. Hard and waxy leaves
    2. Tiny leaves or no leaves
    3. Thorns instead of leaves
    Select the correct answer using the codes given below.
    (a) 1 and 2 only (b) 2 only
    (c) 1 and 3 only (d) 1, 2 and 3

17. Which one of the following is an insectivorous plant?
    (a) Passion flower plant (b) Pitcher plant
    (c) Night queen (d) Flame of the forest

18. Which of the following is an fatty oil yielding plant?
    (a) Sunflower (b) *Acacia*
    (c) *Butea* (d) *Casuarina*

19. Bio-indicator of pollution are
    (a) Lichens (b) Mosses
    (c) Mycorrhiza (d) Toadstools

20. The smallest eggs belong to
    (a) Mammals (b) Fishes
    (c) Amphibians (d) Reptiles

RESPONSE GRID

1. ⓐⓑⓒⓓ	2. ⓐⓑⓒⓓ	3. ⓐⓑⓒⓓ	4. ⓐⓑⓒⓓ	5. ⓐⓑⓒⓓ
6. ⓐⓑⓒⓓ	7. ⓐⓑⓒⓓ	8. ⓐⓑⓒⓓ	9. ⓐⓑⓒⓓ	10. ⓐⓑⓒⓓ
11. ⓐⓑⓒⓓ	12. ⓐⓑⓒⓓ	13. ⓐⓑⓒⓓ	14. ⓐⓑⓒⓓ	15. ⓐⓑⓒⓓ
16. ⓐⓑⓒⓓ	17. ⓐⓑⓒⓓ	18. ⓐⓑⓒⓓ	19. ⓐⓑⓒⓓ	20. ⓐⓑⓒⓓ

HUMAN DISEASES

101 SPEED TEST 67

Max. Marks : 20   **No. of Qs. 20**   **Time : 20 min.**   **Date : ..../........./.................**

1. The organ of the human body directly affected by the disease of hepatitis is
   - (a) Liver
   - (b) Lungs
   - (c) Heart
   - (d) Brain

2. Which of the following disease is caused by Protozoa ?
   - (a) Malaria
   - (b) Cholera
   - (c) Jaundice
   - (d) None of these

3. Which of the following disease is caused by the excessive consumption of alcoholic beverage ?
   - (a) Appendicitis
   - (b) Viral hepatitis
   - (c) Gall stones
   - (d) Liver cirrhosis

4. Emphysema is a disease caused by environmental pollution in which the affected organ of the body is
   - (a) Liver
   - (b) Kidney
   - (c) Lungs
   - (d) Brain

5. In countries where polished rice is the main cereal in their diet, people suffer from
   - (a) Pellagra
   - (b) Beri-beri
   - (c) Scurvy
   - (d) Osteomalacia

6. Accumulation of which one of the following in the muscles leads to fatigue?
   - (a) Lactic acid
   - (b) Benzoic acid
   - (c) Pyruvic acid
   - (d) Uric acid

7. Haemophilia is a genetic disorder which leads to
   - (a) Decrease in haemoglobin level
   - (b) Rheumatic heart disease
   - (c) Decrease in WBC
   - (d) Non-clotting of blood

8. Which one of the following disease is not caused by virus ?
   - (a) Polio
   - (b) Rabies
   - (c) Small pox
   - (d) Diphtheria

9. Which of the following parasites is responsible for 65% of the cases of Malaria in India ?
   - (a) *P. malariae*
   - (b) *P. vivax*
   - (c) *P. falciparum*
   - (d) *P. ovale*

10. The disease in which high levels of uric acid in the blood is detected
    - (a) Meningitis
    - (b) Gout
    - (c) Rheumatism
    - (d) Rheumatic heart

11. Which of the following decrease in number in the human body due to Dengue fever ?
    - (a) Platelets
    - (b) Haemoglobin
    - (c) Sugar
    - (d) Water

12. Which of the following disease is caused by bacteria?
    - (a) Athlete's foot
    - (b) Tuberculosis
    - (c) Ringworm
    - (d) Thrush

13. Which of the following vitamin is effective in blood clotting?
    - (a) Vitamin A
    - (b) Vitamin B
    - (c) Vitamin C
    - (d) Vitamin K

14. Which of the following is a substance available in small quantity in the sea and administered in a certain deficiency disease ?
    - (a) Iron
    - (b) Vitamin A
    - (c) Fluorine
    - (d) Iodine

15. Which one of the following human organs is less susceptible to harmful radiations ?
    - (a) Eyes
    - (b) Heart
    - (c) Brain
    - (d) Lungs

16. Foot and Mouth disease in animals, a current epidemic in some parts of the world, is caused by
    - (a) Bacterium
    - (b) Fungus
    - (c) Protozoan
    - (d) Virus

17. During dehydration, the substance that is usually lost by the body is
    - (a) Sugar
    - (b) Calcium phosphate
    - (c) Sodium chloride
    - (d) Potassium chloride

18. Night blindness is caused by the deficiency of
    - (a) Vitamin A
    - (b) Vitamin B_1
    - (c) Vitamin C
    - (d) Vitamin E

19. Diseases of which of the following pairs are caused by virus?
    - (a) Malaria and Polio
    - (b) Polio and Bird Flu
    - (c) Polio and Tuberculosis
    - (d) Tuberculosis and Influenza

20. The radioisotope used to detect tumours is
    - (a) Iodine-131
    - (b) Cobalt-60
    - (c) Arsenic-74
    - (d) Sodium-24

RESPONSE GRID	1. Ⓐⓑⓒⓓ	2. Ⓐⓑⓒⓓ	3. Ⓐⓑⓒⓓ	4. Ⓐⓑⓒⓓ	5. Ⓐⓑⓒⓓ
	6. Ⓐⓑⓒⓓ	7. Ⓐⓑⓒⓓ	8. Ⓐⓑⓒⓓ	9. Ⓐⓑⓒⓓ	10. Ⓐⓑⓒⓓ
	11. Ⓐⓑⓒⓓ	12. Ⓐⓑⓒⓓ	13. Ⓐⓑⓒⓓ	14. Ⓐⓑⓒⓓ	15. Ⓐⓑⓒⓓ
	16. Ⓐⓑⓒⓓ	17. Ⓐⓑⓒⓓ	18. Ⓐⓑⓒⓓ	19. Ⓐⓑⓒⓓ	20. Ⓐⓑⓒⓓ

PLANT DISEASES

101 SPEED TEST 68

Max. Marks : 20　　　**No. of Qs. 20**　　　**Time : 20 min.**　　　**Date : ..../........./...............**

1. If a disease appear on large scale after a long interval it is
   (a) Epidemic
   (b) Epiphytotic
   (c) Sporadic
   (d) Endemic
2. A disease is abnormal state that may result due to
   (a) Environment
   (b) Mineral
   (c) Pathogen
   (d) All of these
3. Red rot of sugarcane is caused by
   (a) *Puccinia*
   (b) *Helminthosporium*
   (c) *Ustilago*
   (d) *Colletotrichum*
4. Black rust of wheat is caused by
   (a) Yeast
   (b) *Puccinia*
   (c) *Penicillium*
   (d) *Rhizopus*
5. Severe famine of West Bengal of 1942-43 was due to destruction Rice crop by a fungus called
   (a) *Penicillium*
   (b) *Helminthosporium*
   (c) *Rhizopus*
   (d) *Puccinia*
6. Ergot of Rye is caused by
   (a) *Claviceps macrouphala*
   (b) *Claviceps purpurea*
   (c) *Sclerospora graminicola*
   (d) *Erysiphe graminis*
7. Early blight of potato is caused by
   (a) *Phytophthora infestans*
   (b) *Alternaria solani*
   (c) *Helminthosporium oryzae*
   (d) *Albugo candida*
8. Late blight of potato is caused by
   (a) *Alternaria solani*
   (b) *Phytophthora infestans*
   (c) *Albugo candida*
   (d) *Fusarium moniliformae*
9. White Rust of Crucifers is due to
   (a) *Albugo candida*
   (b) *Cercospora personata*
   (c) *Colletotrichum falcatum*
   (d) *Phythium debaryanum*
10. Bunt disease of wheat is due to
    (a) *Tilletia*
    (b) *Puccinia*
    (c) *Ustilago*
    (d) *Cystopus*

11. Loose Smut of Wheat is due to
    (a) *Puccinia graminis tritici*
    (b) *Ustilago tritici*
    (c) *Tilletia tritici*
    (d) *Cystopus candidus*
12. Apple scab is caused by
    (a) *Puccinia*
    (b) *Erysiphe*
    (c) *Ustilago*
    (d) *Venturia*
13. The deadliest mushroom is
    (a) *Agaricus*
    (b) *Amanita*
    (c) *Pleurotus*
    (d) *Volvariella*
14. Tikka disease occurs in
    (a) Rice
    (b) Groundnut
    (c) Wheat
    (d) Sugarcane
15. A plant disease in which the pathogen is seen as cottony growth on the surface of host is called
    (a) Rust
    (b) Smut
    (c) Powdery mildew
    (d) Downy mildew
16. Soft rot disease of Sweet potato is due to
    (a) *Rhizopus stolonifer*
    (b) *Chalmydomonas nivalis*
    (c) *Rhizopus sexualis*
    (d) *Chlamydomonas coccifera*
17. Wart disease caused by *Synchytrium endobioticum* occurs in
    (a) Cabbage
    (b) Pea
    (c) Groundnut
    (d) Potato
18. 'Witches Broom' of legumes is due to
    (a) Mycoplasma
    (b) Bacterium
    (c) Fungus
    (d) Virus
19. Bakane disease of Rice is due to
    (a) *Erysiphe*
    (b) *Gibberella*
    (c) *Phytophthora*
    (d) *Albugo*
20. Rice blast is caused by
    (a) *Taphrina deformis*
    (b) *Puccinia graminis*
    (c) *Pyricularia oryzae*
    (d) *Colletotrichum falcatum*

<table>
<tr><td rowspan="4">RESPONSE GRID</td><td>1. ⓐⓑⓒⓓ</td><td>2. ⓐⓑⓒⓓ</td><td>3. ⓐⓑⓒⓓ</td><td>4. ⓐⓑⓒⓓ</td><td>5. ⓐⓑⓒⓓ</td></tr>
<tr><td>6. ⓐⓑⓒⓓ</td><td>7. ⓐⓑⓒⓓ</td><td>8. ⓐⓑⓒⓓ</td><td>9. ⓐⓑⓒⓓ</td><td>10. ⓐⓑⓒⓓ</td></tr>
<tr><td>11. ⓐⓑⓒⓓ</td><td>12. ⓐⓑⓒⓓ</td><td>13. ⓐⓑⓒⓓ</td><td>14. ⓐⓑⓒⓓ</td><td>15. ⓐⓑⓒⓓ</td></tr>
<tr><td>16. ⓐⓑⓒⓓ</td><td>17. ⓐⓑⓒⓓ</td><td>18. ⓐⓑⓒⓓ</td><td>19. ⓐⓑⓒⓓ</td><td>20. ⓐⓑⓒⓓ</td></tr>
</table>

Max. Marks : 20   **No. of Qs. 20**   **Time : 20 min.**   **Date : ..../........./...............**

1. Mycorrhizal biotechnology has been used in rehabilitating degraded sites because Mycorrhiza enables the plants to
   1. resist drought and increase absorptive area
   2. tolerate extremes of pH
   3. resist disease infestation
   Select the correct answer using the codes given below.
   (a) 1 only
   (b) 2 and 3 only
   (c) 1 and 3 only
   (d) 1, 2 and 3

2. Streptokinase which is used as a 'clot buster' obtained from
   (a) *Streptococcus*
   (b) *Staphylococcus*
   (c) *Lactobacillus*
   (d) Saccharomyces

3. Consider the following organisms:
   1. *Agaricus*   2. *Nostoc*
   3. *Spirogyra*
   Which of the above is/are used as biofertilizer / biofertilizers?
   (a) 1 and 2
   (b) 2 only
   (c) 2 and 3
   (d) 3 only

4. Which one of the micro-organism is used for production of citric acid in industries?
   (a) *Lactobacillus bulgaricus*
   (b) *Penicillium citrinum*
   (c) *Aspergillus niger*
   (d) *Rhizopus nigricans*

5. Yogurt and buttermilk are produced with the use of
   (a) *Saccharomyces*
   (b) *Penicillium*
   (c) *Lactobacillus*
   (d) *Aspergillus*

6. Other than resistance to pests, what are the prospects for which genetically engineered plants have been created?
   1. To enable them to withstand drought
   2. To increase the nutritive value of the produce
   3. To enable them to grow and do photosynthesis in spaceships and space stations
   4. To increase their shelf life
   Select the correct answer using the codes given below :
   (a) 1 and 2 only
   (b) 3 and 4 only
   (c) 1, 2 and 4 only
   (d) 1, 2, 3 and 4

7. Ganga and Yamuna action plan is initiated by
   (a) Ministry of Environment and Forest.
   (b) Ministry of Agriculture.
   (c) Ministry of Wild-life conservation.
   (d) None of these

8. Biogas consists of
   (a) carbon monoxide, methane and hydrogen.
   (b) carbon dioxide, methane and hydrogen.
   (c) carbon monoxide, ethane and hydrogen.
   (d) carbon dioxide, ethane and hydrogen.

9. Given below are the names of four energy crops. Which one of them can be cultivated for ethanol ?
   (a) *Jatropha*
   (b) Maize
   (c) *Pongamia*
   (d) Sunflower

10. The antibiotic "chlorellin" is extracted from the genus
    (a) *Chlamydomonas*
    (b) *Chlorella*
    (c) *Spirogyra*
    (d) *Batrachospermum*

11. The most common species for bee-keeping in india is
    (a) *Apis florae*
    (b) *Apis mellifera*
    (c) *Apis dorsata*
    (d) *Apis indica*

12. Chloramphenicol and Erythromycin (broad spectrum antibiotics) are produced by
    (a) *Streptomyces*
    (b) *Nitrobacter*
    (c) *Rhizobium*
    (d) *Penicillium*

13. The development and flourishment of fishery industry has lead to
    (a) Green revolution
    (b) Blue revolution
    (c) Silver revolution
    (d) White revolution

14. Lactic acid bacteria convert milk into curd and improves its nutritional quality by enhancing
    (a) vitamin A
    (b) vitamin B
    (c) vitamin C
    (d) vitamin D

15. Which gas is responsible for the puffed-up appearance of dough ?
    (a) CO_2
    (b) O_2
    (c) SO_2
    (d) NO_2

16. Vinegar is prepared from alcohol with the help of
    (a) *Lactobacillus*
    (b) *Acetobacter*
    (c) *Azotobacter*
    (d) *Rhizobium*

17. A genetically engineered micro-organism used successfully in bioremediation of oil spills is a species of
    (a) *Pseudomonas*
    (b) *Trichoderma*
    (c) *Xanthomonas*
    (d) *Bacillus*

18. Which of the following fungi is found useful in the biological control of plant disease ?
    (a) *Mucor mucido*
    (b) *Trichoderma viridae*
    (c) *Phytophthora parasitica*
    (d) *Penicillium notatum*

19. *Jatropha* is a
    (a) biodiesel crop
    (b) biopetro crop
    (c) fibre crop
    (d) food crop

20. Lactic acid bacteria convert milk into curd and improves its nutritional quality by enhancing
    (a) Vitamin A
    (b) Vitamin B
    (c) Vitamin C
    (d) Vitamin D

RESPONSE GRID	1. ⓐⓑⓒⓓ	2. ⓐⓑⓒⓓ	3. ⓐⓑⓒⓓ	4. ⓐⓑⓒⓓ	5. ⓐⓑⓒⓓ
	6. ⓐⓑⓒⓓ	7. ⓐⓑⓒⓓ	8. ⓐⓑⓒⓓ	9. ⓐⓑⓒⓓ	10. ⓐⓑⓒⓓ
	11. ⓐⓑⓒⓓ	12. ⓐⓑⓒⓓ	13. ⓐⓑⓒⓓ	14. ⓐⓑⓒⓓ	15. ⓐⓑⓒⓓ
	16. ⓐⓑⓒⓓ	17. ⓐⓑⓒⓓ	18. ⓐⓑⓒⓓ	19. ⓐⓑⓒⓓ	20. ⓐⓑⓒⓓ

Max. Marks : 20 **No. of Qs. 20** **Time : 20 min.** **Date : ..../........./................**

1. In an ecosystem, green plants are known as
   - (a) Primary consumers
   - (b) Secondary consumers
   - (c) Producers
   - (d) Tertiary consumers

2. World environment day is celebrated on
   - (a) 15th March
   - (b) 15th April
   - (c) 4th May
   - (d) 5th June

3. Sound becomes hazardous noise pollution at level
   - (a) above 30 dB
   - (b) above 80 dB
   - (c) above 100 dB
   - (d) above 120 dB

4. Major aerosol pollutant in jet plane emission is
   - (a) sulphur dioxide
   - (b) carbon monoxide
   - (c) methane
   - (d) fluorocarbon

5. As energy is passed from one trophic level to another, the amount of usable energy
   - (a) increases
   - (b) decreases
   - (c) remains the same
   - (d) energy is not passed from one trophic level to another

6. The Taj mahal is threatened due to the effect of
   - (a) oxygen
   - (b) hydrogen
   - (c) chlorine
   - (d) sulphur dioxide

7. CFC are not recommended to be used in refrigerators because they
   - (a) increase temperature
   - (b) affect environment
   - (c) affect aquatic life
   - (d) affect human body

8. Pyramids of energy are
   - (a) always upright
   - (b) always inverted
   - (c) mostly upright
   - (d) mostly inverted

9. The most common indicator organism that represents polluted water is
   - (a) *E. coli*
   - (b) *Pseudomonas*
   - (c) *Chlorella*
   - (d) *Entamoeba*

10. The CO_2 content in the atmospheric air is about
    - (a) 0.034%
    - (b) 0.34%
    - (c) 3.34%
    - (d) 6.5%

11. Ozone layer is essential because it absorbs most of the
    - (a) infrared radiations
    - (b) heat
    - (c) solar radiation
    - (d) ultraviolet-radiation

12. Which of the following is a man made artificial ecosystem?
    - (a) Grassland ecosystem
    - (b) Agro ecosystem
    - (c) Ecosystem of artificial lakes and dams
    - (d) Forest ecosystem

13. Soil best suited for plant growth is
    - (a) Clay
    - (b) Loam
    - (c) Sandy
    - (d) Gravel

14. Which of the following is a biodegradable waste?
    - (a) Radioactive wastes
    - (b) Aluminium cans
    - (c) DDT
    - (d) Cattle dung

15. Association of animals when one species is harmed and the other one is unaffected, is known as
    - (a) Colony
    - (b) Mutualism
    - (c) Commensalism
    - (d) Amensalism

16. Which is the first national park established in India?
    - (a) Bandipur national park
    - (b) Corbett national park
    - (c) Kanha national park
    - (d) Periyar national park

17. Among the most dangerous non-biodegradable waste is
    - (a) cow-dung
    - (b) plastic articles
    - (c) garbage
    - (d) radioactive waste

18. Which group of vertebrates comprises the highest number of endangered species ?
    - (a) Birds
    - (b) Mammals
    - (c) Fishes
    - (d) Reptiles

19. Which one of the following is an example of *ex-situ* conservation?
    - (a) Wildlife sanctuary
    - (b) Seed bank
    - (c) Sacred groves
    - (d) National park

20. In case CO_2 of earth's atmosphere disappears, the temperature of earth's surface would
    - (a) increase
    - (b) decrease
    - (c) depend on oxygen concentration
    - (d) remain the same

RESPONSE GRID	1. ⓐⓑⓒⓓ	2. ⓐⓑⓒⓓ	3. ⓐⓑⓒⓓ	4. ⓐⓑⓒⓓ	5. ⓐⓑⓒⓓ
	6. ⓐⓑⓒⓓ	7. ⓐⓑⓒⓓ	8. ⓐⓑⓒⓓ	9. ⓐⓑⓒⓓ	10. ⓐⓑⓒⓓ
	11. ⓐⓑⓒⓓ	12. ⓐⓑⓒⓓ	13. ⓐⓑⓒⓓ	14. ⓐⓑⓒⓓ	15. ⓐⓑⓒⓓ
	16. ⓐⓑⓒⓓ	17. ⓐⓑⓒⓓ	18. ⓐⓑⓒⓓ	19. ⓐⓑⓒⓓ	20. ⓐⓑⓒⓓ

Max. Marks : 60   **No. of Qs. 60**   **Time : 35 min.**   Date : ..../........./................

1. If distance covered by a particle is zero, what can you say about its displacement?
   - (a) It may or may not be zero
   - (b) It cannot be zero
   - (c) It is negative
   - (d) It must be zero

2. Appliances based on heating effect of current work on
   - (a) only a.c.
   - (b) only d.c.
   - (c) both a.c. and d.c.
   - (d) none of these

3. As we go up in the atmosphere, the heights of the various regions are in the order
   - (a) ionosphere > troposphere > stratosphere
   - (b) ionosphere > stratosphere > troposphere
   - (c) troposphere > ionosphere > stratosphere
   - (d) stratosphere > troposphere > ionosphere

4. When a drop of oil is spread on a water surface, it displays beautiful colours in daylight because of
   - (a) Dispersion of light
   - (b) Reflection of light
   - (c) Polarization of light
   - (d) Interference of light

5. A balloon filled with CO_2 released on earth would (neglect viscosity of air)
   - (a) climb with an acceleration $9.8 \, m/s^2$
   - (b) fall with an acceleration $9.8 \, m/s^2$
   - (c) fall with a constant acceleration $3.4 \, m/s^2$
   - (d) fall with acceleration and then would attain a constant velocity

6. What temperature is the same on celsius scale as well as on Fahrenheit scale?
   - (a) $-212°C$
   - (b) $-40°C$
   - (c) $-32°C$
   - (d) $32°C$

7. A water tank of height 10 m, completely filled with water is placed on a level ground. It has two holes one at 3 m and the other at 7 m from its base. The water ejecting from
   - (a) both the holes will fall at the same spot
   - (b) upper hole will fall farther than that from the lower hole
   - (c) upper hole will fall closer than that from the lower hole
   - (d) more information is required

8. If a liquid is heated in space under no gravity, the transfer of heat will take place by process of
   - (a) conduction
   - (b) convection
   - (c) radiation
   - (d) can not be heated in the absence of gravity

9. Morning sun is not so hot as the mid day sun because
   - (a) Sun is cooler in the morning
   - (b) Heat rays travel slowly is the morning
   - (c) It is God gift
   - (d) The sun's rays travel a longer distance through atmosphere in the morning

10. The resistance of some substances become zero at very low temperature, then these substances are called
    - (a) good conductors
    - (b) super conductors
    - (c) bad conductors
    - (d) semi conductors

11. The bulbs which emit a bluish light, are
    - (a) filled with argon
    - (b) filled with nitrogen
    - (c) vacuum bulbs
    - (d) coated from inside with a light blue colour

12. When a bar magnet is broken into two pieces?
    - (a) We will have a single pole on each piece
    - (b) Each piece will have two like poles
    - (c) Each piece will have two unlike poles
    - (d) Each piece will be lose magnetism

13. Alternating current is converted to direct current by
    - (a) rectifier
    - (b) dynamo
    - (c) transformer
    - (d) motor

14. Woollen clothes are used in winter season because woollen clothes
    - (a) are good sources for producing heat
    - (b) absorb heat form surroundings
    - (c) are bad conductors of heat
    - (d) provide heat to body continuously

RESPONSE GRID	1. ⓐⓑⓒⓓ	2. ⓐⓑⓒⓓ	3. ⓐⓑⓒⓓ	4. ⓐⓑⓒⓓ	5. ⓐⓑⓒⓓ
	6. ⓐⓑⓒⓓ	7. ⓐⓑⓒⓓ	8. ⓐⓑⓒⓓ	9. ⓐⓑⓒⓓ	10. ⓐⓑⓒⓓ
	11. ⓐⓑⓒⓓ	12. ⓐⓑⓒⓓ	13. ⓐⓑⓒⓓ	14. ⓐⓑⓒⓓ	

15. A sounding horn is rotating rapidly in a horizontal circle, the apparent frequency of the horn observed at the centre of the circle
    (a) will be same
    (b) will decrease
    (c) will increase and sometimes more
    (d) None of these

16. What happens when some charge is placed on a soap bubble?
    (a) Its radius decreases   (b) Its radius increases
    (c) The bubble collapses   (d) None of these

17. The resistance of a thin wire in comparison of a thick wire of the same material
    (a) is low
    (b) is equal
    (c) depends upon the metal of the wire
    (d) is high

18. Alternating current cannot be measured by D.C. ammeter because
    (a) A.C. cannot pass through D.C. ammeter
    (b) average value of current for complete cycle is zero
    (c) A.C. is virtual
    (d) A.C. changes its direction

19. p-n junction is said to be forward biased, when
    (a) the positive pole of the battery is joined to the p-semiconductor and negative pole to the n-semiconductor
    (b) the positive pole of the battery is joined to the n-semiconductor and p-semiconductor
    (c) the negative pole of the battery is connected to n- semiconductor and p- semiconductor
    (d) a mechanical force is applied in the forward direction

20. The effective length of the magnet is
    (a) the complete length of the magnet
    (b) the distance between the two poles of the magnet
    (c) the half of the length of the magnet
    (d) the square of the length of the magnet

21. A moving object can come to rest only if it
    (a) has a frictional force acting on it
    (b) has no net force acting on it
    (c) is completely isolated
    (d) applies an impulse to something else

22. In which of the following are no work done by the force?
    (a) A man walking upon a staircare
    (b) A man carrying a bucket of water, walking on a level road with a uniform velocity

    (c) A drop of rain falling vertically with a constant velocity
    (d) A man whirling a stone tied to a string in circle with a constant speed

23. Two identical beakers are filled with water to the same level at 4°C. If one say A is heated while the other B is cooled, then
    (a) Water level in A will rise
    (b) Water level in A will fall
    (c) Water level in B will rise
    (d) Water level in A and B will rise

24. In a long spring which of the following type of waves can be generated
    (a) Longitudinal only
    (b) Transverse only
    (c) Both longitudinal and transverse
    (d) Electromagnetic only

25. At the moment dew formation starts on a cool night, the air
    (a) Must loose all water vapour
    (b) Must remain unsaturated
    (c) Must get mixed up with some other vapour
    (d) Must become saturated

26. Addition of oxygen to a compound is
    (a) reduction   (b) oxidation
    (c) neutralisation   (d) precipitation

27. A compound formed by the reaction of an acid with base is
    (a) salt   (b) indicator
    (c) vitamins   (d) All of these

28. Which of the following compounds is known as methyl ethyl ketone?
    (a) CH_3COCH_3 (b) $CH_3COCH_2CH_3$
    (c) $CH_3CH_2COCH_2CH_3$ (d) CH_3CH_2CHO

29. Solder is an alloy of
    (a) Cu, Mn and Ni   (b) Cu and Sn
    (c) Sn and Pb   (d) Pb and Bi

30. Which one of the following is a chief ore of zinc?
    (a) Calamine   (b) Zincite
    (c) Zinc blend   (d) White vitriol

31. The IUPAC name of the compound given below is
    $CH_3CH_2COCH_2CH_3$
    (a) 1-pentanone   (b) 2-pentanone
    (c) 2-carboxybutane   (d) 3-pentanone

32. Which of the following compounds could belong to the same homologous series?
    (I) $C_2H_6O_2$ (II) C_2H_6O
    (III) C_2H_6 (IV) CH_4O
    (a) I, II   (b) II, III
    (c) III, IV   (d) II, IV

33. The longest period in the periodic table is
    (a) 1
    (b) 5
    (c) 7
    (d) 6

34. Which one of the following is a Dobereiner's triad?
    (a) Cl_2, Mg and Na
    (b) O_2, N_2 and Cl_2
    (c) Cl_2, Br_2 and I_2
    (d) H_2, He and Ne

35. Pure water is obtained from sea water by
    (a) filtration
    (b) distillation
    (c) evaporation
    (d) All of these

36. Barium carbonate is a/an
    (a) compound
    (b) mixture
    (c) element
    (d) alloy

37. Rutherford's scattering experiment is related to the size of the
    (a) nucleus
    (b) atom
    (c) electrons
    (d) neutrons

38. Excess of silicon in cement
    (a) increase setting time
    (b) decrease setting time
    (c) increase hardness
    (d) helps in hydrolysis

39. Hard glass having the same ingredients as soft glass excepts
    (a) hard glass have Na in place of K
    (b) hard glass having K in place of Na
    (c) hard glass having both Na and K
    (d) None of the above

40. A complete fertilizer provides
    (a) N, P, K
    (b) S, K, N
    (c) S, B, K
    (d) N, S, P

41. Global climate is threatened by increase in concentration of
    (a) Oxygen
    (b) Nitrogen
    (c) Water vapours
    (d) Green house gas

42. Spraying of D.D.T. on crops produces pollution of
    (a) Air only
    (b) Air and soil only
    (c) Air, soil and water
    (d) Air and water only

43. Vitamin B_{12} contains metal
    (a) Ca (II)
    (b) Zn (II)
    (c) Fe (II)
    (d) Co (III)

44. The separation technique which involves the difference in their densities is
    (a) sublimation
    (b) separation by separating funnel
    (c) centrifugation
    (d) both (b) and (c)

45. Pick up the odd one out
    (a) Brass
    (b) Air
    (c) Sand
    (d) Graphite

46. In multicellular organisms, ______ refers to the production of progeny possessing features more or less similar to those of parents.
    (a) growth
    (b) reproduction
    (c) metabolism
    (d) consciousness

47. Heart is three - chambered in reptiles, exception is
    (a) Turtle
    (b) *Chameleon*
    (c) *Naja* (Cobra)
    (d) Crocodile

48. Stem tendrils are found in
    (a) cucumber
    (b) pumpkins
    (c) grapevines
    (d) All of these

49. The supportive skeletal structures in the human external ears and in the nose tip are examples of
    (a) ligament
    (b) areolar tissue
    (c) bone
    (d) cartilage

50. Building block of nucleic acid is
    (a) nucleotide
    (b) nucleoside
    (c) amino acid
    (d) fatty acid

51. Which of the following is the most acceptable theory for movement of water through plants?
    (a) Cohesion theory
    (b) Passive transport
    (c) Root pressure
    (d) Capillarity

52. Translation of food in flowering plants occurs in the form of
    (a) starch
    (b) glyceraldehyde
    (c) glucose
    (d) sucrose

53. pH of saliva is
    (a) 6.5
    (b) 8
    (c) 7
    (d) 9.5

54. As blood becomes fully O_2 saturated, haemoglobin is combining with____ molecule(s) of oxygen.
    (a) 1
    (b) 2
    (c) 4
    (d) 8

55. Coronary artery disease (CAD) is often referred to as
    (a) Heart failure
    (b) Cardiac arrest
    (c) Atherosclerosis
    (d) Angina

56. The part of an eye which acts like diaphragm of a photographic camera, is
    (a) Pupil
    (b) Iris
    (c) Lens
    (d) Cornea

RESPONSE GRID

33. ⓐⓑⓒⓓ	34. ⓐⓑⓒⓓ	35. ⓐⓑⓒⓓ	36. ⓐⓑⓒⓓ	37. ⓐⓑⓒⓓ
38. ⓐⓑⓒⓓ	39. ⓐⓑⓒⓓ	40. ⓐⓑⓒⓓ	41. ⓐⓑⓒⓓ	42. ⓐⓑⓒⓓ
43. ⓐⓑⓒⓓ	44. ⓐⓑⓒⓓ	45. ⓐⓑⓒⓓ	46. ⓐⓑⓒⓓ	47. ⓐⓑⓒⓓ
48. ⓐⓑⓒⓓ	49. ⓐⓑⓒⓓ	50. ⓐⓑⓒⓓ	51. ⓐⓑⓒⓓ	52. ⓐⓑⓒⓓ
53. ⓐⓑⓒⓓ	54. ⓐⓑⓒⓓ	55. ⓐⓑⓒⓓ	56. ⓐⓑⓒⓓ	

57. The most common carrier of communicable diseases is
    (a) cockroach   (b) mosquito
    (c) housefly   (d) spider

58. Weeds are
    (a) microbes   (b) unwanted herbs
    (c) insects   (d) fungal pests

59. Red data book contains list of
    (a) endangered species of plants and animals
    (b) extinct animals and plants
    (c) exotic plants and birds
    (d) rare species of plants and animals

60. The period during which foetus remains within mother's womb
    (a) ovulation   (b) puberty
    (c) gestation   (d) adolescence

101 SPEED TEST

72

Max. Marks : 60   **No. of Qs. 60**   **Time : 35 min.**   **Date : ..../......../................**

1. Sudden fall of atmospheric pressure in a large amount indicates
   (a) Storm
   (b) Rain
   (c) Fair weather
   (d) Cold waves

2. A transistor is essentially
   (a) A current operated device
   (b) Power driven device
   (c) A voltage operated device
   (d) Resistance operated device

3. Which of the following velocity time graph is not possible?

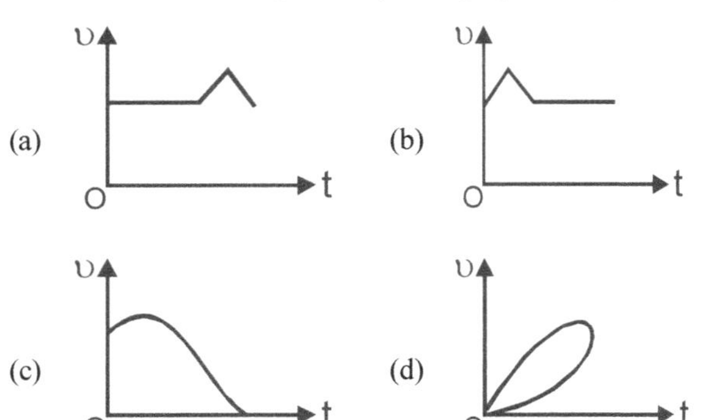

   (a)   (b)   (c)   (d)

4. Which of the following is used in optical fibres ?
   (a) Total internal reflection   (b) Scattering
   (c) Diffraction   (d) Refraction

5. When a sound wave goes from one medium to another, the quantity that remains unchanged is
   (a) Frequency   (b) Amplitude
   (c) Wavelength   (d) Speed

6. Echo is a type of
   (a) reflected sound
   (b) refracted sound
   (c) neither reflected sound nor refracted sound
   (d) None of these

7. For electroplating a spoon, it is placed in the voltmeter at
   (a) the position of anode
   (b) the position of cathode
   (c) exactly in the middle of anode and cathode
   (d) anywhere in the electrolyte

8. Which one of the following substances is the magnetic substances?
   (a) Mercury   (b) Iron
   (c) Gold   (d) Silver

9. To convert mechanical energy into electrical energy, one can use
   (a) DC dynamo   (b) AC dynamo
   (c) motor   (d) both (a) and (b)

10. A vibrating body
    (a) will always produce sound
    (b) may or may not produce sound if the amplitude of vibration is low
    (c) will produce sound which depends upon frequency
    (d) None of the above

11. What happens when a heavy object and a light object are allowed to fall from the certain height in the absence of air?
    (a) Heavy object reaches the ground later than the lighter object
    (b) Lighter object reaches the ground later than the heavier object
    (c) Both heavy and light objects reach the ground simultaneously
    (d) None of these

12. $1 \text{ kWh} = \underline{\hspace{1cm}} \text{MJ}$.
    (a) 36   (b) 0.36
    (c) 3.6   (d) 360

13. Two similar buses are moving with same velocity on a straight road. One of them is empty and the other is loaded with passengers
    (a) Both buses are stopped by the application of same force
    (b) Empty bus will be stopped by applying large force
    (c) Loaded bus will be stopped by applying less force
    (d) Empty buses will be stopped by applying less force and loaded bus will be stopped by appplying large force

14. When a copper ball is heated, the largest percentage increase will occur in its
    (a) diameter   (b) area
    (c) volume   (d) density

RESPONSE GRID	1. ⓐⓑⓒⓓ	2. ⓐⓑⓒⓓ	3. ⓐⓑⓒⓓ	4. ⓐⓑⓒⓓ	5. ⓐⓑⓒⓓ		
	6. ⓐⓑⓒⓓ	7. ⓐⓑⓒⓓ	8. ⓐⓑⓒⓓ	9. ⓐⓑⓒⓓ	10. ⓐⓑⓒⓓ		
	11. ⓐⓑⓒⓓ	12. ⓐⓑⓒⓓ	13. ⓐⓑⓒⓓ	14. ⓐⓑⓒⓓ			

15. A piece of cloth looks red in sun light. It is held in the blue portion of a solar spectrum, it will appear
   (a) red
   (b) black
   (c) blue
   (d) white
16. Conductivity increases in the order of
   (a) Al, Ag, Cu
   (b) Al, Cu, Ag
   (c) Cu, Al, Ag
   (d) Ag, Cu, Al
17. Magnetic lines do not intersect one-another because
   (a) they are at a distance
   (b) they are in the same direction
   (c) they are parallel to another
   (d) at the point intersection there will be two direction of the magnetic force which is impossible
18. *n-p-n* transistors are preferred to *p-n-p* transistors because:
   (a) they have low cost
   (b) they have low dissipation energy
   (c) they are capable of handling large power
   (d) electrons have high mobility than holes and hence high mobility of energy
19. Work is always done on a body when
   (a) A force acts on it
   (b) It moves through a certain distance
   (c) It experiences an increase in energy through a mechanical influence
   (d) None of the above
20. A body travelling with a speed more than the velocity of sound in air is said to travel with
   (a) supersonic speed
   (b) hypersonic speed
   (c) ultrasonic speed
   (d) infrasonic speed
21. What is the material for electric fuse?
   (a) Cu
   (b) Constantan
   (c) Tin-lead alloy
   (d) Nichrome
22. A bar magnet of magnetic moment 80 units is cut into two halves of equal length, the magnetic moment of each half will be
   (a) 80 units
   (b) 40 units
   (c) 60 units
   (d) 20 units
23. Mud houses are cooler in summer and warmer in winter because
   (a) Mud is a good conductor of heat
   (b) Mud is a super conductor of heat
   (c) Mud is a bad conductor of heat
   (d) None of these
24. The waves produced by motor boat sailing in water are
   (a) transverse
   (b) longitudinal
   (c) Longitudinal and transverse
   (d) None of these

25. The resolving limit of a heating human eye is about
   (a) 1'
   (b) 1"
   (c) $1°$
   (d) $\frac{1}{60}$"
26. Select the correct statement from the codes given below
   1. Cut glasses are lead glasses.
   2. The main raw material for the preparation of soda glass in Na_2CO_3.
   3. Quicklime is CaO.
   (a) 1 and 2
   (b) 2 and 3
   (c) 1 and 3
   (d) Only 2
27. Antacids are commonly used to get rid of acidity in the stomach. A commonly used antacid is
   (a) sodium hydrogen phthalate
   (b) magnesium hydroxide
   (c) calcium hydroxide
   (d) manganese acetate
28. Match the Column-I with the Column-II.

	Column-I		Column-II
A.	Primary pollutants	1.	PAN, O_3, Cl
B.	Secondary pollutants	2.	H_2SO_4
C.	Bhopal gas tragedy due to leakage of	3.	SO_2, CO
D.	Stone leprosy	4.	Methyl isocyanate

Codes:

	A	B	C	D
(a)	3	1	4	2
(b)	1	4	2	3
(c)	4	2	3	1
(d)	2	3	1	4

29. Match List-I with List-II.

	List-I		List-II
A.	Glass	1.	Fat and caustic alkali
B.	Soap	2.	Cellulose fibre and gelatin
C.	Paper	3.	Silicates of calcium and aluminium
D.	Cement	4.	Silica

Codes:

	A	B	C	D
(a)	3	2	1	4
(b)	4	2	1	3
(c)	3	1	2	4
(d)	4	1	2	3

<table>
<tr><td rowspan="3">RESPONSE GRID</td><td>15. ⓐⓑⓒⓓ</td><td>16. ⓐⓑⓒⓓ</td><td>17. ⓐⓑⓒⓓ</td><td>18. ⓐⓑⓒⓓ</td><td>19. ⓐⓑⓒⓓ</td></tr>
<tr><td>20. ⓐⓑⓒⓓ</td><td>21. ⓐⓑⓒⓓ</td><td>22. ⓐⓑⓒⓓ</td><td>23. ⓐⓑⓒⓓ</td><td>24. ⓐⓑⓒⓓ</td></tr>
<tr><td>25. ⓐⓑⓒⓓ</td><td>26. ⓐⓑⓒⓓ</td><td>27. ⓐⓑⓒⓓ</td><td>28. ⓐⓑⓒⓓ</td><td>29. ⓐⓑⓒⓓ</td></tr>
</table>

30. Consider the following statements
    1. The chlorine gas is used for the manufacture of bleaching powder.
    2. Bleaching powder is used for disinfecting.
    3. Bleaching powder is used for bleaching cotton and linen in the textile industry.
    Which of the statements given above are correct?
    (a) 1 and 2
    (b) 1 and 3
    (c) 2 and 3
    (d) 1, 2 and 3

31. Which among the following is a chemical change?
    (a) A wet towel dries in the sun
    (b) Lemon juice added to tea causing its colour to change
    (c) Hot air rises over a radiator
    (d) Coffee is brewed by passing steam through ground coffee.

32. Match the Column-I with the Column-II.

	Column-I		Column-II
A.	Molarity (M)	1.	is the concentration unit for ionic compounds which dissolve in a polar solvent to give pair of ions.
B.	Molality (m)	2.	is number of gram equivalents of substance dissolve per litre of the solution
C.	Formality (F)	3.	is the number of moles of the solute dissolved in 1000 g of the solvent
D.	Normality (N)	4.	is the number of moles of solute present in 1 L of the solution

    Codes:

	A	B	C	D
(a)	3	1	2	4
(b)	1	2	4	3
(c)	2	4	3	1
(d)	4	3	1	2

33. Match Column-I (Colloidal dispersion) with Column-II (Nature of the dispersion) and select the correct answer using the codes given below the columns.

	Column-I		Column-II
A.	Milk	1.	Solid in liquid
B.	Clouds	2.	Liquid in gas
C.	Paints	3.	Solids in solids
D.	Jellies	4.	Liquids in liquids
		5.	Liquid in solid

    Codes:

	A	B	C	D
(a)	4	2	1	5
(b)	1	5	3	2
(c)	4	5	1	2
(d)	1	2	3	5

34. Match Column-I with Column-II

	Column-I		Column-II
A.	Proton	1.	Rutherford
B.	Electron	2.	Chadwick
C.	Neutron	3.	Thomson
D.	Nucleus	4.	Goldstein

    Codes:

	A	B	C	D
(a)	4	3	2	1
(b)	3	2	1	4
(c)	2	1	4	3
(d)	1	4	3	2

35. Which one of the following non-metals is not a poor conductor of electricity?
    (a) Sulphur
    (b) Selenium
    (c) Bromine
    (d) Phosphorus

36. Consider the following statements:
    Glass can be etched or scratched by
    1. diamond
    2. hydrofluoric acid
    3. aqua regia
    4. conc. sulphuric acid
    Which of these statements are correct?
    (a) 1 and 4
    (b) 2 and 3
    (c) 1 and 2
    (d) 2 and 4

37. Which one of the following fuels causes minimum environmental pollution?
    (a) Diesel
    (b) Coal
    (c) Hydrogen
    (d) Kerosene

38. Which one of the following elements is alloyed with iron to produce steel which can resist high temperature and also have high hardness and abrasion resistance?
    (a) Aluminium
    (b) Chromium
    (c) Nickel
    (d) Tungsten

39. Cinnabar is an ore of
    (a) Hg
    (b) Cu
    (c) Pb
    (d) Zn

40. A substance which reacts with gangue to form fusible material is called
    (a) Flux
    (b) Catalyst
    (c) Ore
    (d) Slag

41. Which of the following compound has the functional group – OH ?
    (a) 1, 2-ethandiol
    (b) 2-butanone
    (c) Nitrobenzene
    (d) Ethanal

42. Who developed the long form of periodic table?
    (a) Lothar Meyer
    (b) Neils Bohr
    (c) Mendeleev
    (d) Moseley

43. The first group elements are called
    (a) alkali metals (b) alkaline earth metals
    (c) noble gases (d) halogen
44. Calcium sulphate hemihydrate is commonly known as
    (a) plaster of paris (b) gypsum
    (c) ferous sulphate (d) None of these
45. Which of the following is a redox reaction?
    (a) $CaCO_3 \rightarrow CaO + CO_2$
    (b) $H_2 + CuO \rightarrow Cu + H_2O$
    (c) $CaO + 2HCl \rightarrow CaCl_2 + H_2O$
    (d) $NaOH + HCl \rightarrow NaCl + H_2O$
46. An organism considered to be between living and non-living is
    (a) Bacterium (b) Fungi
    (c) Virus (d) Yeast
47. Green plants take carbon dioxide from
    (a) air (b) water
    (c) soil (d) manures
48. Which one of these also acts as a sense organ in addition to being a part of the digestive system?
    (a) Teeth (b) Tongue
    (c) Oesophagus (d) Villi
49. The liver stores food in the form of
    (a) glucose (b) glycogen
    (c) albumen (d) ATP
50. First National Park established in India is
    (a) Gir Sanctuary for Asiatic lion
    (b) Jim Corbett National Park, Uttarakhand
    (c) Bharatpur Bird Sanctuary
    (d) National Botanical Garden, Kolkata
51. Which of the following is a forest product?
    (a) Plastics (b) Wax
    (c) Petroleum (d) Medicinal plants
52. In adult man, normal BP is
    (a) 100/80 mm Hg (b) 120/80 mm Hg
    (c) 100/120 mm Hg (d) 80/120 mm Hg
53. Which of the following organ supports foetus?
    (a) Oviduct (b) Ovary
    (c) Embryo (d) Uterus
54. Rabi crops include
    (a) wheat (b) paddy
    (c) corn (maize) (d) melons
55. Which of the following hormone helps female sex characters?
    (a) Adrenalin (b) Testosterone
    (c) Calcitonin (d) Oestrogen
56. Which of the following is considered as the soldiers of body?
    (a) Lungs (b) Capillaries
    (c) Red blood cells (d) White blood cells
57. Camouflage can be seen in
    (a) stick insect (b) parrot
    (c) monkey (d) fish
58. Which of the following is a gill breather?
    (a) Frog (b) Earthworm
    (c) Tadpole (d) Amoeba
59. Red muscle fibres are rich in
    (a) Golgi bodies (b) Mitochondria
    (c) Lysosomes (d) Ribosomes
60. Greenhouse effect is caused by the increase in the level of
    (a) Carbon dioxide (b) Oxygen
    (c) Nitrogen (d) Water vapour

RESPONSE GRID	**43.** ⓐⓑⓒⓓ	**44.** ⓐⓑⓒⓓ	**45.** ⓐⓑⓒⓓ	**46.** ⓐⓑⓒⓓ	**47.** ⓐⓑⓒⓓ
	48. ⓐⓑⓒⓓ	**49.** ⓐⓑⓒⓓ	**50.** ⓐⓑⓒⓓ	**51.** ⓐⓑⓒⓓ	**52.** ⓐⓑⓒⓓ
	53. ⓐⓑⓒⓓ	**54.** ⓐⓑⓒⓓ	**55.** ⓐⓑⓒⓓ	**56.** ⓐⓑⓒⓓ	**57.** ⓐⓑⓒⓓ
	58. ⓐⓑⓒⓓ	**59.** ⓐⓑⓒⓓ	**60.** ⓐⓑⓒⓓ		

PRE-HISTORIC PERIOD

101 SPEED TEST

73

Max. Marks : 20 **No. of Qs. 20** **Time : 20 min.** **Date : ..../........./.................**

1. The Megaliths of South India are mainly associated with
   - (a) Mesolithic age
   - (b) Neolithic age
   - (c) Chalcolithic age
   - (d) Iron age
2. From among the following, which pair is not matched?
   - (a) Patanjali – Mahabhashya
   - (b) Hal – Gatha Saptshati
   - (c) Bhadrabahu – Brihat Katha Manjari
   - (d) AshvaGhose – Harsh Charit
3. The period of social evolution which represents the hunting-gathering stage is/are the
   - (a) Palaeolithic Age
   - (b) Mesolithic Age
   - (c) Palaeolithic and Mesolithic Age
   - (d) Neolithic Age
4. Which of the following is not evident at Mohenjodaro?
   - (a) Pasupati seal
   - (b) Great granary and great bath
   - (c) Multi-pillared assembly hall
   - (d) Evidence of double burials
5. Which one of the following is not a part of early Jains literature?
   - (a) Therigatha
   - (b) Acarangasutra
   - (c) Sutrakritanga
   - (d) Brihatkalpasutra
6. The Nagara, the Dravida and the Vesara are the
   - (a) three main racial groups of the Indian subcontinent
   - (b) three main linguistic divisions into which the languages of India can be classified
   - (c) three main styles of Indian temple architecture
   - (d) three main musical Gharanas prevalent in India
7. Which one of the following gives the correct chronological order of the vedas?
   - (a) Rigveda, Samaveda, Atharvaveda, Yajurveda
   - (b) Rigveda, Samaveda, Yajurveda, Atharvaveda
   - (c) Atharvaveda, Yajurveda, Samaveda, Rigveda
   - (d) Rigveda, Yajurveda, Samaveda, Atharvaveda
8. The Anguttara Nikhaya which gives information about Mahajanapadas is a part of which Buddhist book?
   - (a) Suttapitaka
   - (b) Vinayapitaka
   - (c) Abhidhammapitaka
   - (d) Jatakas
9. Which amongst the following civilization was not contemporary with the Harappan civilization ?
   - (a) Greek civilization
   - (b) Egyptian civilization
   - (c) Mesopotamian civilization
   - (d) Chinese civilization
10.

List I	List II
(A) Paleolithic age	(1) Sites are found in Chhotangpur's plateau
(B) Mesolithic age	(2) Copper on bronze tools used
(C) Neolithic age	(3) Flint was used
(D) Chalcolithic age	(4) Wheat and barley were grown

   - (a) A – 2 ; B – 4 ; C – 3 ; D – 1
   - (b) A – 3 ; B – 1 ; C – 4 ; D – 2
   - (c) A – 4 ; B – 2 ; C – 3 ; D – 1
   - (d) A – 1 ; B – 3 ; C – 4 ; D – 2
11. The Neolithic settlement of Mehrgarh is located on the bank of which river?
   - (a) Bolan
   - (b) Belan
   - (c) Khurram
   - (d) Gomal
12. The only Neolithic settlement in the Indian subcontinent dating back to 7000 BC lies in
   - (a) Rajasthan
   - (b) Kashmir
   - (c) Sindh
   - (d) Baluchistan
13. The goddess of vegetative fertility, worshipped during the Chalcolithic period of Jorwe culture, was
   - (a) Sakapurni
   - (b) Satakarani
   - (c) Sambhuti
   - (d) Sakambhari
14. Millet was the main foodcrop of which of the following (pre-historic) civilisations?
   - (a) Greek
   - (b) Egyptian
   - (c) Chincese
   - (d) Sumerian
15. In the Indian subcontinent, the Neolithic Age is believed to have begun by
   - (a) 11000 BC
   - (b) 9000 BC
   - (c) 7000 BC
   - (d) 5000 BC
16. All bronze age civilisation were basically
   - (a) agriculture
   - (b) trading
   - (c) commercial
   - (d) farming
17. Excellent cave paintings of Mesolithic age are found at
   - (a) Bhimbetka
   - (b) Attranjikhera
   - (c) Mirzapur
   - (d) Mehrgarh
18. Which of the following is not a principal tool of the Early Stone Age?
   - (a) Scrapper
   - (b) Handaxe
   - (c) Cleaver
   - (d) Chopper
19. Which Neolithic site is not found in Belan valley of Uttar Pradesh?
   - (a) Chopani-Mando
   - (b) Koldihawa
   - (c) Mahagara
   - (d) Chachar
20. Jorwe pottery type seen in the Chalcolithic period is predominantly of?
   - (a) Black on Red ware
   - (b) Black and Red
   - (c) Red ware
   - (d) Ochre colour ware

<table>
<tr><td rowspan="4">RESPONSE GRID</td><td>1. ⓐⓑⓒⓓ</td><td>2. ⓐⓑⓒⓓ</td><td>3. ⓐⓑⓒⓓ</td><td>4. ⓐⓑⓒⓓ</td><td>5. ⓐⓑⓒⓓ</td></tr>
<tr><td>6. ⓐⓑⓒⓓ</td><td>7. ⓐⓑⓒⓓ</td><td>8. ⓐⓑⓒⓓ</td><td>9. ⓐⓑⓒⓓ</td><td>10. ⓐⓑⓒⓓ</td></tr>
<tr><td>11. ⓐⓑⓒⓓ</td><td>12. ⓐⓑⓒⓓ</td><td>13. ⓐⓑⓒⓓ</td><td>14. ⓐⓑⓒⓓ</td><td>15. ⓐⓑⓒⓓ</td></tr>
<tr><td>16. ⓐⓑⓒⓓ</td><td>17. ⓐⓑⓒⓓ</td><td>18. ⓐⓑⓒⓓ</td><td>19. ⓐⓑⓒⓓ</td><td>20. ⓐⓑⓒⓓ</td></tr>
</table>

INDUS VALLEY CIVILISATION

101 SPEED TEST

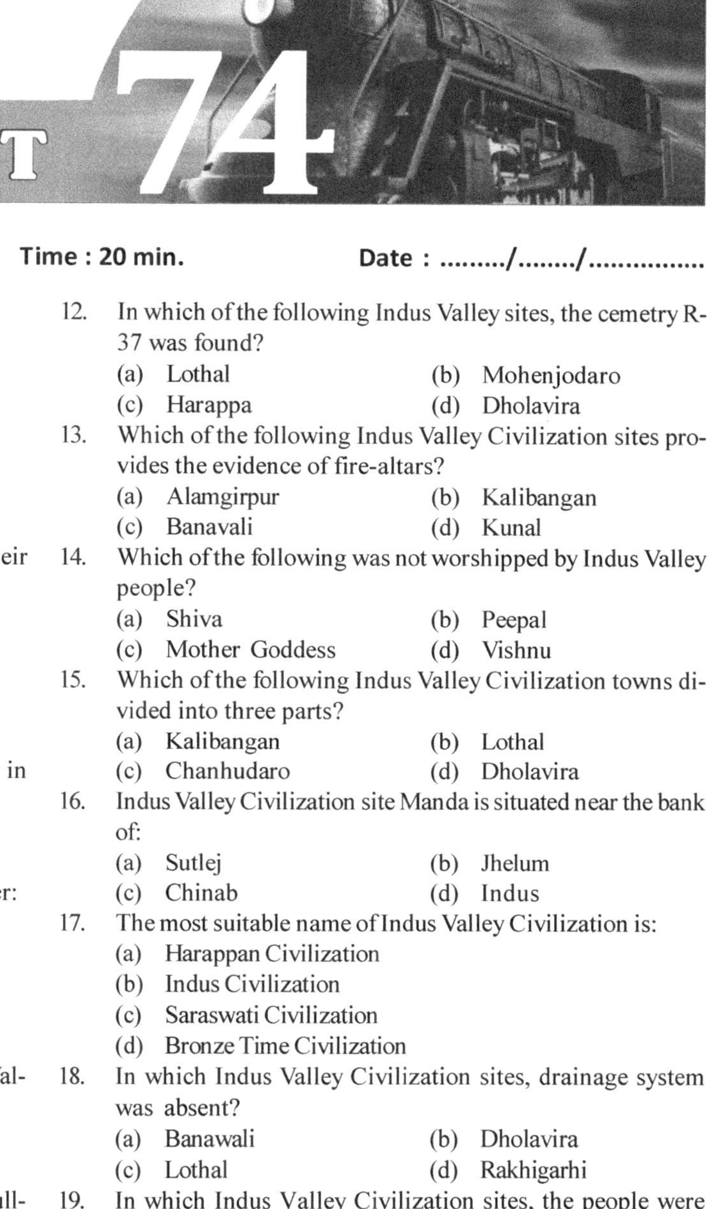

74

Max. Marks : 20   **No. of Qs. 20**   **Time : 20 min.**   **Date : ..../........./................**

1. Indus Valley Civilization was discovered in:
   (a) 1911   (b) 1921   (c) 1931   (d) 1941
2. Almost the people of Indus Valley Civilization were:
   (a) Nigroid   (b) Proto-Austroloid
   (c) Mediterranean   (d) Nordic
3. Indus Valley Civilization belongs to:
   (a) Pre-historical   (b) Historical period
   (c) Proto-historical   (d) Post-historical
4. The people of Indus Valley Civilization usually built their houses of:
   (a) Pucca bricks   (b) Wood
   (c) Stone   (d) None of these
5. Indus Valley Civilization was discovered by:
   (a) Dayaram Sahni   (b) R.D. Banerji
   (c) Cunningham   (d) Wheeler
6. Which of the following showed the greatest uniformity in Indus Civilization settlement?
   (a) Town planning   (b) Bricks
   (c) Religious practices   (d) Building
7. The dockyard at Lothal was well connected with the river:
   (a) Ghaggar   (b) Bhogavo
   (c) Narmada   (d) Tapti
8. The Indus Valley Civilization people traded with the:
   (a) Romans   (b) Parthians
   (c) Mesopotamians   (d) Chinese
9. The best drainage system (water management) in Indus Valley Civilization was:
   (a) Harappa   (b) Lothal
   (c) Mohenjodaro   (d) Kalibangan
10. In which of the following Indus Valley sites the famous Bull-seal was found?
    (a) Harappa   (b) Mohenjodaro
    (c) Lothal   (d) Chanhudaro
11. Which of the following Indus Valley Civilization site was located on the Iranian border?
    (a) Surkotada   (b) Sutkagen Dor
    (c) Kot Diji   (d) Balakot

12. In which of the following Indus Valley sites, the cemetry R-37 was found?
    (a) Lothal   (b) Mohenjodaro
    (c) Harappa   (d) Dholavira
13. Which of the following Indus Valley Civilization sites provides the evidence of fire-altars?
    (a) Alamgirpur   (b) Kalibangan
    (c) Banavali   (d) Kunal
14. Which of the following was not worshipped by Indus Valley people?
    (a) Shiva   (b) Peepal
    (c) Mother Goddess   (d) Vishnu
15. Which of the following Indus Valley Civilization towns divided into three parts?
    (a) Kalibangan   (b) Lothal
    (c) Chanhudaro   (d) Dholavira
16. Indus Valley Civilization site Manda is situated near the bank of:
    (a) Sutlej   (b) Jhelum
    (c) Chinab   (d) Indus
17. The most suitable name of Indus Valley Civilization is:
    (a) Harappan Civilization
    (b) Indus Civilization
    (c) Saraswati Civilization
    (d) Bronze Time Civilization
18. In which Indus Valley Civilization sites, drainage system was absent?
    (a) Banawali   (b) Dholavira
    (c) Lothal   (d) Rakhigarhi
19. In which Indus Valley Civilization sites, the people were known water reservoir technique?
    (a) Banawali   (b) Kalibangan
    (c) Dholavira   (d) Chanhudaro
20. Which of the following Indus Valley Civilization sites gives evidence of a Lipstick?
    (a) Chanhudaro   (b) Banawali
    (c) Mohenjodaro   (d) Kalibangan

RESPONSE GRID					
	1. (a)(b)(c)(d)	2. (a)(b)(c)(d)	3. (a)(b)(c)(d)	4. (a)(b)(c)(d)	5. (a)(b)(c)(d)
	6. (a)(b)(c)(d)	7. (a)(b)(c)(d)	8. (a)(b)(c)(d)	9. (a)(b)(c)(d)	10. (a)(b)(c)(d)
	11. (a)(b)(c)(d)	12. (a)(b)(c)(d)	13. (a)(b)(c)(d)	14. (a)(b)(c)(d)	15. (a)(b)(c)(d)
	16. (a)(b)(c)(d)	17. (a)(b)(c)(d)	18. (a)(b)(c)(d)	19. (a)(b)(c)(d)	20. (a)(b)(c)(d)

101 SPEED TEST

75

Max. Marks : 20   **No. of Qs. 20**   **Time : 20 min.**   Date : ..../........./................

1. Which one of the following is the correct chronological order of the given rulers of ancient India?
   (a) Ashoka—Kanishka—Milinda
   (b) Milinda—Ashoka—Kanishka
   (c) Ashoka—Milinda—Kanishka
   (d) Milinda—Kanishka—Ashoka

2. Which of the following languages was used in Ashoka's Edicts?
   (a) Vasudeva   (b) Pali
   (c) Brahmi   (d) Sanskrit

3. Which of the following metals were mostly used for minting coins during the Mauryan period?
   (a) Bronze and gold   (b) Gold and lead
   (c) Silver and copper   (d) Lead and silver

4. Which of the following pairs is correctly matched?
   (a) Jatakas - Mauryan chronology and genealogy
   (b) Puranas - Ashoka's efforts to spread Buddhism to Sri Lanka
   (c) Dipavamsa - socio-economic conditions of the Mauryan period
   (d) Dighanikaya - Influence of Buddhist ideas on Mauryan polity

5. The Nagas in the Post-Mauryan period ruled from?
   (a) Ganga Valley   (b) Indus Valley
   (c) Brahmaputra Valley   (d) Godavari Valley

6. Which of the following statements about Mauryan society is untrue?
   (a) Megasthenes divided Indian society into seven classes
   (b) Slavery was absent in India
   (c) There was a reduction in gap between the Vaishyas and the Shudras
   (d) Megasthenes says that scarcity and famine were known to Indians

7. Which ruler did Chandrragupta Maurya enter into an alliance to defeat the nandas?
   (a) Parvataka   (b) Selucus Nikator
   (c) Nagasena   (d) Rudrasimha

8. Choose the correct pair.
   (a) Ellora caves - Saka
   (b) Mahabalipuram - Rashtrakutas
   (c) Meenakshi temple - Pallavas
   (d) Khajuraho – Chandellas

9. Who was the founder of Maurya dynasty?
   (a) Chandragupta II   (b) Chandragupta Maurya
   (c) Vishnugupta   (d) Ashoka

10. In the Mauryan Period tax evasion was punished with:
    (a) Death   (b) Confiscation of goods
    (c) Imprisonment   (d) None of the above

11. Kautilya's Arthashastra's chapter on Kantak-Shodhana is mostly devoted to:
    (a) Regulation of profits, wages and prices
    (b) Regulation against adulteration of goods
    (c) Strict control of artisans and traders by the state
    (d) None of the above

12. In the Mauryan Government women could be employed as:
    (a) Royal Bodyguards
    (b) Superintendents of weaving establishments
    (c) Intelligence agents & spices
    (d) All the above

13. Which one of the following rulling dynasties of South India was the biggest rival of the Cholas?
    (a) The Pandyas
    (b) The Chalukyas of Kalyani
    (c) The Gangas of Orissa
    (d) Chalukyas of Vakataka

14. Who of the following Chola kings assumed the title of the Mummadi Chola?
    (a) Vijayalaya   (b) Rajaraya
    (c) Rajendra I   (d) None of the above

15. In the Chola kingdom, a very large village administered as a single unit was called:
    (a) Nadu   (b) Kurram
    (c) Kottram   (d) All the above

16. Who was the founder of Mauryan empire?
    (a) Chandragupta Maurya   (b) Vijayalaya
    (c) Raja Raja   (d) Samudragupta

17. What was the another name of Chanakya?
    (a) Kautilya   (b) Mahagupta
    (c) Sivagupta   (d) Veeragupta

18. Who helped Chandragupta Maurya to defeat Nandas?
    (a) Kamandaka   (b) Sudraka
    (c) Kalhana   (d) Chanakya

19. Who ruled whole of North India before Chandragupta
    (a) Nandas   (b) Guptas
    (c) Harsha   (d) Satavahanas

20. Period of rule of Chandragupta Maurya
    (a) 300-280 B.C.   (b) 324-300 B.C.
    (c) 380-360 B.C.   (d) 310-290 B.C.

RESPONSE GRID	1. (a)(b)(c)(d)	2. (a)(b)(c)(d)	3. (a)(b)(c)(d)	4. (a)(b)(c)(d)	5. (a)(b)(c)(d)
	6. (a)(b)(c)(d)	7. (a)(b)(c)(d)	8. (a)(b)(c)(d)	9. (a)(b)(c)(d)	10. (a)(b)(c)(d)
	11. (a)(b)(c)(d)	12. (a)(b)(c)(d)	13. (a)(b)(c)(d)	14. (a)(b)(c)(d)	15. (a)(b)(c)(d)
	16. (a)(b)(c)(d)	17. (a)(b)(c)(d)	18. (a)(b)(c)(d)	19. (a)(b)(c)(d)	20. (a)(b)(c)(d)

THE GUPTA PERIOD

101 SPEED TEST

76

Max. Marks : 20 | **No. of Qs. 20** | **Time : 20 min.** | **Date : ..../......../................**

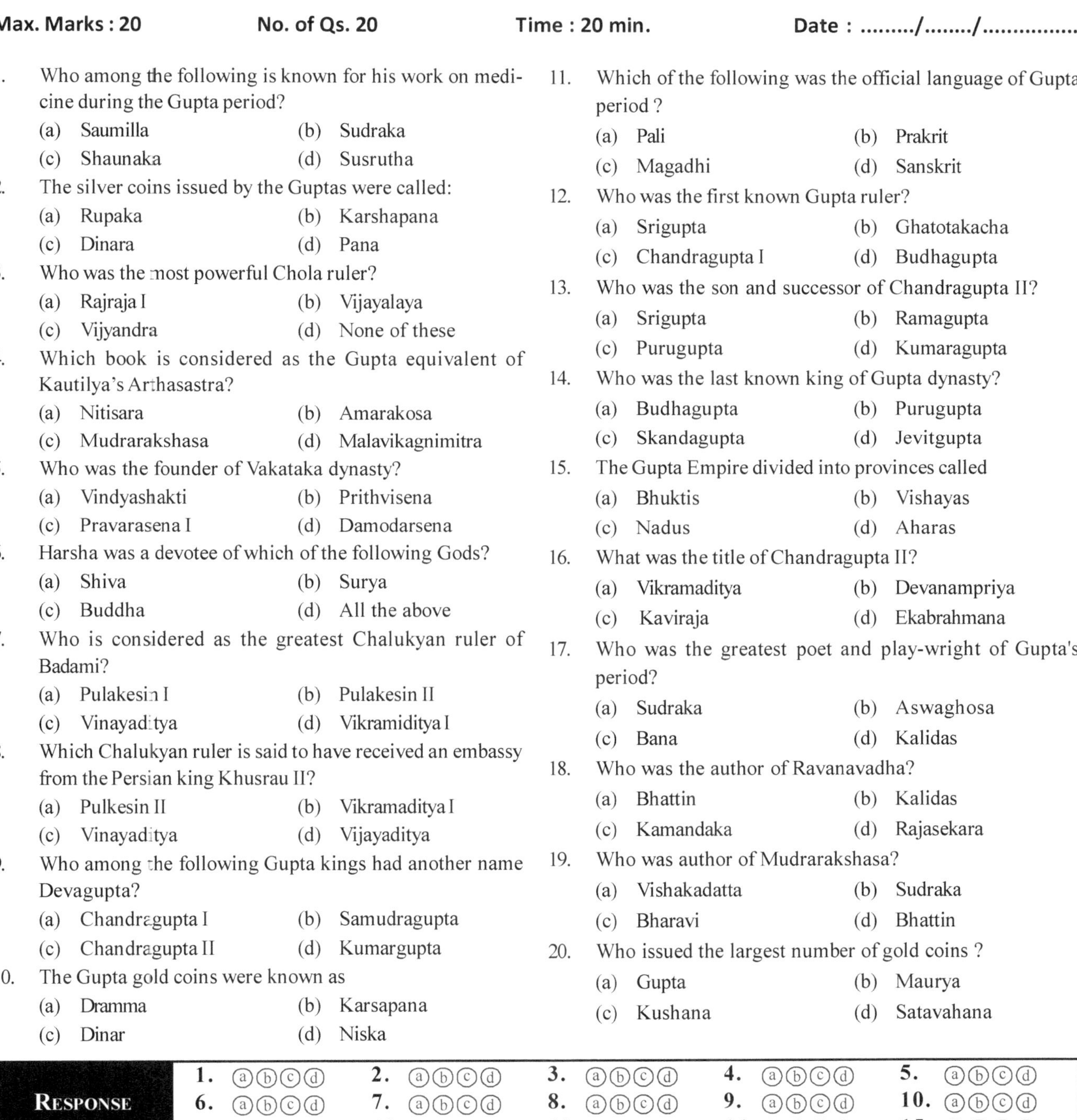

1. Who among the following is known for his work on medicine during the Gupta period?
   - (a) Saumilla
   - (b) Sudraka
   - (c) Shaunaka
   - (d) Susrutha

2. The silver coins issued by the Guptas were called:
   - (a) Rupaka
   - (b) Karshapana
   - (c) Dinara
   - (d) Pana

3. Who was the most powerful Chola ruler?
   - (a) Rajraja I
   - (b) Vijayalaya
   - (c) Vijyandra
   - (d) None of these

4. Which book is considered as the Gupta equivalent of Kautilya's Arthasastra?
   - (a) Nitisara
   - (b) Amarakosa
   - (c) Mudrarakshasa
   - (d) Malavikagnimitra

5. Who was the founder of Vakataka dynasty?
   - (a) Vindyashakti
   - (b) Prithvisena
   - (c) Pravarasena I
   - (d) Damodarsena

6. Harsha was a devotee of which of the following Gods?
   - (a) Shiva
   - (b) Surya
   - (c) Buddha
   - (d) All the above

7. Who is considered as the greatest Chalukyan ruler of Badami?
   - (a) Pulakesin I
   - (b) Pulakesin II
   - (c) Vinayaditya
   - (d) Vikramiditya I

8. Which Chalukyan ruler is said to have received an embassy from the Persian king Khusrau II?
   - (a) Pulkesin II
   - (b) Vikramaditya I
   - (c) Vinayaditya
   - (d) Vijayaditya

9. Who among the following Gupta kings had another name Devagupta?
   - (a) Chandragupta I
   - (b) Samudragupta
   - (c) Chandragupta II
   - (d) Kumargupta

10. The Gupta gold coins were known as
    - (a) Dramma
    - (b) Karsapana
    - (c) Dinar
    - (d) Niska

11. Which of the following was the official language of Gupta period ?
    - (a) Pali
    - (b) Prakrit
    - (c) Magadhi
    - (d) Sanskrit

12. Who was the first known Gupta ruler?
    - (a) Srigupta
    - (b) Ghatotakacha
    - (c) Chandragupta I
    - (d) Budhagupta

13. Who was the son and successor of Chandragupta II?
    - (a) Srigupta
    - (b) Ramagupta
    - (c) Purugupta
    - (d) Kumaragupta

14. Who was the last known king of Gupta dynasty?
    - (a) Budhagupta
    - (b) Purugupta
    - (c) Skandagupta
    - (d) Jevitgupta

15. The Gupta Empire divided into provinces called
    - (a) Bhuktis
    - (b) Vishayas
    - (c) Nadus
    - (d) Aharas

16. What was the title of Chandragupta II?
    - (a) Vikramaditya
    - (b) Devanampriya
    - (c) Kaviraja
    - (d) Ekabrahmana

17. Who was the greatest poet and play-wright of Gupta's period?
    - (a) Sudraka
    - (b) Aswaghosa
    - (c) Bana
    - (d) Kalidas

18. Who was the author of Ravanavadha?
    - (a) Bhattin
    - (b) Kalidas
    - (c) Kamandaka
    - (d) Rajasekara

19. Who was author of Mudrarakshasa?
    - (a) Vishakadatta
    - (b) Sudraka
    - (c) Bharavi
    - (d) Bhattin

20. Who issued the largest number of gold coins ?
    - (a) Gupta
    - (b) Maurya
    - (c) Kushana
    - (d) Satavahana

RESPONSE GRID	1. ⓐⓑⓒⓓ	2. ⓐⓑⓒⓓ	3. ⓐⓑⓒⓓ	4. ⓐⓑⓒⓓ	5. ⓐⓑⓒⓓ
	6. ⓐⓑⓒⓓ	7. ⓐⓑⓒⓓ	8. ⓐⓑⓒⓓ	9. ⓐⓑⓒⓓ	10. ⓐⓑⓒⓓ
	11. ⓐⓑⓒⓓ	12. ⓐⓑⓒⓓ	13. ⓐⓑⓒⓓ	14. ⓐⓑⓒⓓ	15. ⓐⓑⓒⓓ
	16. ⓐⓑⓒⓓ	17. ⓐⓑⓒⓓ	18. ⓐⓑⓒⓓ	19. ⓐⓑⓒⓓ	20. ⓐⓑⓒⓓ

101 SPEED TEST 77

Max. Marks : 20   **No. of Qs. 20**   **Time : 20 min.**   **Date : ..../........./................**

1. Who among the following were famous jurists of medieval India?
   - (a) Vijnanesvara
   - (b) Hemadri
   - (c) Rajasekhara
   - (d) Jimutavahana

2. Which one of the following dynasties built the Khajuraho temple?
   - (a) Chandellas
   - (b) Chauhans
   - (c) Paramaras
   - (d) Tomars

3. Under whose rule, was Ajmer the capital?
   - (a) Mauryas
   - (b) Chauhans
   - (c) Guptas
   - (d) Pallavas

4. Which chola ruler completed the conquest of Sri Lanka?
   - (a) Vijayalaya I
   - (b) Rajaraja I
   - (c) Rajendra I
   - (d) Parantaka I

5. Who is considered as the greatest Chola ruler?
   - (a) Parantaka I
   - (b) Rajaraja I
   - (c) Rajendra I
   - (d) Klulottanga I

6. Which Rashtrakuta king composed the works 'Kavirajamarga', 'Ratnamalika' and 'Passanotaramalika'?
   - (a) Amoghavarsa I
   - (b) Krishna I
   - (c) Indra III
   - (d) Krishna III

7. Buddhism was confined to which areas in the early medieval period?
   - (a) Western India
   - (b) Eastern India
   - (c) Central India
   - (d) Southern India

8. The Palas patronized which form of Buddhism?
   - (a) Hinayana
   - (b) Mahayana
   - (c) Sarvastavadin
   - (d) All of these

9. Kalhana's Rajatarangini,
   - (a) Written in 12th century under the patronage of Sriharsa and Jaisingh
   - (b) Is an acount of history of Kashmir upto 12th century
   - (c) It was written in Sanskrit
   - (d) All the above

10. Lingaraja temple at Bhubaneswar is built, in
    - (a) Nagara style
    - (b) Vesara style
    - (c) Dravidian style
    - (d) Rock - cut

11. Which dynasty initiated the dravidian style of architecture?
    - (a) Pallavas
    - (b) Cholas
    - (c) Vijayanagar
    - (d) Chalukyas of Kalyani

12. The most important feature of Chola administration was
    - (a) absolute despotism of the monarch
    - (b) mandala mudalis at the provincial level
    - (c) autonomous assembly in a district
    - (d) autonomous village assemblies in agraharas

13. Temples in Chola period were,
    - (a) Centres of religious activity
    - (b) Centres of education
    - (c) Centres of economic activity
    - (d) All of the above

14. Who among the following is said to be the pioneer of guerilla warfare in the Deccan region?
    - (a) Shivaji
    - (b) Shah ji Bhosle
    - (c) Malik Ambar
    - (d) Maloji Bhosale

15. Who among the following established the Dal Khalsa?
    - (a) Guru Gobind Singh
    - (b) Guru Arjun Dev
    - (c) Kanpur Singh
    - (d) Bhai Mani Singh

16. Kohinoor Diamond was found probably from which among the following mines?
    - (a) Golconda
    - (b) Kalahandi
    - (c) Panna
    - (d) Bijapur

17. Who propounded the ideal of "Hindu-pad-padshahi"?
    - (a) Baji Rao I
    - (b) Balaji Vishwanath
    - (c) Balaji Baji Rao
    - (d) Mahadji Scindia

18. Who among the following poets used to write the Urdu Ghazals with the pen name "Asad"?
    - (a) Mir Taqi Mir
    - (b) Dushyant
    - (c) Mirza Ghalib
    - (d) Amir Khusrow

19. In which of the following half century, maximum number of Famines attacked India?
    - (a) 1750-1800
    - (b) 1800-1850
    - (c) 1850-1900
    - (d) 1900-1950

20. Who founded the Pala dynasty?
    - (a) Devapala
    - (b) Gopala
    - (c) Dharmapala
    - (d) Mahipal

RESPONSE GRID

1. ⓐⓑⓒⓓ	2. ⓐⓑⓒⓓ	3. ⓐⓑⓒⓓ	4. ⓐⓑⓒⓓ	5. ⓐⓑⓒⓓ
6. ⓐⓑⓒⓓ	7. ⓐⓑⓒⓓ	8. ⓐⓑⓒⓓ	9. ⓐⓑⓒⓓ	10. ⓐⓑⓒⓓ
11. ⓐⓑⓒⓓ	12. ⓐⓑⓒⓓ	13. ⓐⓑⓒⓓ	14. ⓐⓑⓒⓓ	15. ⓐⓑⓒⓓ
16. ⓐⓑⓒⓓ	17. ⓐⓑⓒⓓ	18. ⓐⓑⓒⓓ	19. ⓐⓑⓒⓓ	20. ⓐⓑⓒⓓ

THE DELHI SULTANATE

101 SPEED TEST — 78

Max. Marks : 20 **No. of Qs. 20** **Time : 20 min.** **Date : ..../........./...............**

1. Who was the first ruler of the Slave dynasty?
   (a) Qutubuddin Aibak (b) Iltutmish
   (c) Sultan Mahmud (d) Balban

2. Who abolished Iqta system?
   (a) Qutubuddin Aibak (b) Iltutmish
   (c) Balban (d) Alauddin Khilji

3. Which Sultan of Delhi founded and built the Fort of Siri?
   (a) Iltutmish (b) Balban
   (c) Alauddin Khilji (d) Ghiyasuddin Tughlaq

4. Who founded Agra?
   (a) Iltutmish (b) Firoz Tughlaq
   (c) Sikander Lodhi (d) Ibrahim Lodhi

5. Which Muslim ruler played Holi for the first time in Medieval India?
   (a) Muhammad Bin Tughlaq (b) Humayun
   (c) Akbar (d) Jahangir

6. Who was the last ruler of the Tughlaq dynasty of the Delhi Sultanate?
   (a) Firoz Shah Tughlaq
   (b) Ghiyas-ud-din Tughlaq Shah II
   (c) Nasir-ud-din Mahmud
   (d) Nasrat Shah

7. Which one of the following is the correct chronological order of the Afghan rulers to the throne of Delhi?
   (a) Sikandar Shah-Ibrahim Lodi-Bahlol Khan Lodi
   (b) Sikandar Shah-Bahlol Khan Lodi-Ibrahim Lodi
   (c) Bahlol Khan Lodi-Sikandar Shah-Ibrahim Lodi
   (d) Bahlol Khan Lodi-Ibrahim Lodi-Sikandar Shah

8. Vasco da Gama discovered the sea-route to India in which one of the following years ?
   (a) A.D. 1498 (b) A.D. 1492
   (c) A.D. 1494 (d) A.D. 1453

9. When did Delhi first become capital of a kingdom?
   (a) At the time of Tomar dynasty
   (b) Tughlaq dynasty
   (c) Lodhi dynasty
   (d) None of these

10. Which sultan first did campaign in South India?
    (a) Alauddin Khalji (b) Raziyya
    (c) Qutabdin Aibak (d) None of these

11. Who was the first Delhi sultan to plan for the construction of canals?
    (a) Alauddin Khalji (b) Iltutmish
    (c) Ghiyasuddin Tughluq (d) Feroz Shah Tughluq

12. Which sultan built Hauz Khas, a pleasure resort?
    (a) Mohammed-bin-Tughluq (b) Feroz Shah Tughluq
    (c) Jalaluddin Khalji (d) Sikander Lodhi

13. The first Muslim ruler of Delhi was
    (a) Iltutmish (b) Qubacha
    (c) Yalduz (d) Qutbuddin Aibak

14. Who introduced Arab currency for the first time in India?
    (a) Iltutmish (b) Balban
    (c) Razia Sultana (d) Qutbuddin Aibak

15. What was the period of Qutbuddin Aibak as Delhi Sultan?
    (a) 1206-1210 A.D. (b) 1209-1234 A.D.
    (c) 1234-1254 A.D. (d) 1254-1256 A.D.

16. Which of the following were conquered by the Qutbuddin Aibak ?
    (a) Meerut (b) Ranthambore
    (c) Gujrat, Bihar and Bengal (d) All the above

17. What was the period of Feroz Shah Tughluq as Delhi Sultan?
    (a) 1345-1356 A.D. (b) 1356-1376 A.D.
    (c) 1351-1388 A.D. (d) 1367-1387 A.D.

18. Who was called Sultanate Akbar ?
    (a) Feroz Shah Tughluq
    (b) Muhammad Bin Tughluq
    (c) Alauddin Khilji
    (d) Ghiyas-ud-din Tughluq

19. The Sultan who established marriage bureaus?
    (a) Balban (b) Iltutmish
    (c) Kaikubad (d) Feroz Shah Tughluq

20. Which of the following taxes were levied by the Feroz Shah Tughluq?
    (a) Kharaj (b) Khams
    (c) Jakat and Zijya (d) All the above

RESPONSE GRID

1. (a)(b)(c)(d)	2. (a)(b)(c)(d)	3. (a)(b)(c)(d)	4. (a)(b)(c)(d)	5. (a)(b)(c)(d)
6. (a)(b)(c)(d)	7. (a)(b)(c)(d)	8. (a)(b)(c)(d)	9. (a)(b)(c)(d)	10. (a)(b)(c)(d)
11. (a)(b)(c)(d)	12. (a)(b)(c)(d)	13. (a)(b)(c)(d)	14. (a)(b)(c)(d)	15. (a)(b)(c)(d)
16. (a)(b)(c)(d)	17. (a)(b)(c)(d)	18. (a)(b)(c)(d)	19. (a)(b)(c)(d)	20. (a)(b)(c)(d)

THE MUGHAL EMPIRE

101 SPEED TEST — 79

Max. Marks : 20   **No. of Qs. 20**   **Time : 20 min.**   **Date : ..../........./................**

1. Who was the founder of Mughal dynasty?
   (a) Babur
   (b) Humayun
   (c) Akbar
   (d) Shahjahan
2. Which of the following works shows Humayun's interest in astronomy and astrology?
   (a) Tarikh-i-Salatin-i-Afghana
   (b) Tarikh-i-Rashidi
   (c) Qanun-i-Humayuni
   (d) Tazkirat-ul-Waqiat
3. In which language did Babar wrote his Autobiography?
   (a) Farsee
   (b) Arabi
   (c) Turki
   (d) None of these
4. Where is Babur's tomb situated?
   (a) Kabul
   (b) Lahore
   (c) Delhi
   (d) Ayodhya
5. Who was favoured by Prime Minister Mir Khalifa as Babur's successor instead of Humayun?
   (a) Mirza Suleiman
   (b) Mirza Kamran
   (c) Mirza Askari
   (d) Mehdi Khwaja
6. Who among the following was the first Mughal ruler to adopt the custom of Tuladan?
   (a) Humayun
   (b) Akbar
   (c) Jahangir
   (d) Shahjahan
7. During the Mughal period, what was Narnal or light artillery?
   (a) One carried on elephant back
   (b) One carried on camel back
   (c) One carried by man
   (d) None of these
8. Who built Red Fort at Delhi?
   (a) Shajahan
   (b) Jahangir
   (c) Humayun
   (d) Aurangzeb
9. Who was the architect of Tajmahal?
   (a) Ahmdulla
   (b) Ustad Ahmad Lahari
   (c) Usman Khan
   (d) Utbi
10. The Mughal emperor who built Moti Musjicl at Agra?
    (a) Babar
    (b) Humayun
    (c) Jahangir
    (d) Shajahan
11. Which of the following is incorrect?
    (a) As a result of Akbar's treatment of the Rajputas they contributed richly to the military achievement of his reign
    (b) As a result of Akbar's treatment of Rajputas they contributed to the administrative achievement of his reign
    (c) As a result of Akbar's treatment of the Rajputas, the orthodox Muslim Ulema shed their religious dogmation and began to love the Hindus
    (d) As a result of Akbar's treatment of the Rajputas, the Ranapratap could not mobilise the support of the Rajputas against the Mughals
12. Who was "Chin Qilich Khan"?
    (a) He was a general of Babur
    (b) He was a provincial governor under Aurangazeb
    (c) He was the first independent Nawab of Bengal
    (d) He was the governor of Mughal Deccan Area
13. Which of the following about the duties of the Dewan in the time of Akbar is correct?
    (a) He posted news-writers and spices in different provinces.
    (b) He recommended the appointment of provincial dewans and guided and controlled them
    (c) All orders of appointment to Mansabs of all ranks passed through his office
    (d) He gave authoritative ruling ion conflicting interpretations of Shara
14. Din-a-Ilahi was introduced by Akbar in—
    (a) 1575A.D.
    (b) 1579A.D.
    (c) 1582A.D.
    (d) 1585AD.
15. Who said "Those men who have strong dislike for paintings, I have strong dislike for them"?
    (a) Akbar
    (b) Babar
    (c) Jahangir
    (d) ShahJahan
16. Who was the Mughal Emperor at the time of Nadir Shah's attack?
    (a) Rafi-ud-darjat
    (b) Muhammad Shah
    (c) Ahmad Shah
    (d) Alamgir II
17. What according to Jadunath Sarkar was the reason of the downfall of Aurangzeb?
    (a) Religious policy
    (b) Military helpness
    (c) Rajput policy
    (d) Shivaji
18. Who was famous for laying many gardens?
    (a) Babur
    (b) Humayun
    (c) Akbar
    (d) Jahangir
19. Who introduced the Rank of 'Zat and Sawar'?
    (a) Akbar
    (b) Aurangzeb
    (c) Shah Jahan
    (d) Jahangir
20. Which were the two kingdoms conquerred by Akbar?
    (a) Khandesh and Bijapur
    (b) Bijapur and Ahmednagar
    (c) Ahmednagar
    (d) Berar and Ahmednagar

<table>
<tr><td rowspan="4">RESPONSE GRID</td><td>1. ⓐⓑⓒⓓ</td><td>2. ⓐⓑⓒⓓ</td><td>3. ⓐⓑⓒⓓ</td><td>4. ⓐⓑⓒⓓ</td><td>5. ⓐⓑⓒⓓ</td></tr>
<tr><td>6. ⓐⓑⓒⓓ</td><td>7. ⓐⓑⓒⓓ</td><td>8. ⓐⓑⓒⓓ</td><td>9. ⓐⓑⓒⓓ</td><td>10. ⓐⓑⓒⓓ</td></tr>
<tr><td>11. ⓐⓑⓒⓓ</td><td>12. ⓐⓑⓒⓓ</td><td>13. ⓐⓑⓒⓓ</td><td>14. ⓐⓑⓒⓓ</td><td>15. ⓐⓑⓒⓓ</td></tr>
<tr><td>16. ⓐⓑⓒⓓ</td><td>17. ⓐⓑⓒⓓ</td><td>18. ⓐⓑⓒⓓ</td><td>19. ⓐⓑⓒⓓ</td><td>20. ⓐⓑⓒⓓ</td></tr>
</table>

Max. Marks : 20   **No. of Qs. 20**   **Time : 20 min.**   **Date : ..../......../................**

1. In the beginning, the motive of British East India Company was
   - (a) Trade and territory
   - (b) Trade, not territory
   - (c) Only territory
   - (d) None of the above

2. Which one of the following was the first English ship that came to India?
   - (a) Elizabeth
   - (b) Titanic
   - (c) Red Dragon
   - (d) Mayflower

3. The British East India Company was formed during the reign of
   - (a) Henry VIII
   - (b) James I
   - (c) Charles I
   - (d) Elizabeth I

4. What was the name of the first ship of East India Company of England which reached here on August 24, 1600 AD?
   - (a) Edward
   - (b) Hector
   - (c) Henary
   - (d) William

5. Vasco da Gama discovered the sea route to India in which one of the following years?
   - (a) 1453
   - (b) 1492
   - (c) 1494
   - (d) 1498

6. Which one of the following European trading companies adopted the "Blue Water Policy" in India?
   - (a) Dutch company
   - (b) French company
   - (c) Portuguese company
   - (d) British East India company

7. Which one of the following states was a Milk-cow for the British?
   - (a) Hyderabad
   - (b) Punjab
   - (c) Mysore
   - (d) Awadh

8. From which year, did the British start striking Indian coins with the portrait of the British king?
   - (a) 1835
   - (b) 1858
   - (c) 1860
   - (d) 1758

9. Eden Gardens of Calcutta was built in 1840. It was named 'Eden' after the name of a sister of a Governor General of India. Who was the Governor General?
   - (a) Lord William Bentinck
   - (b) Charles Metacalfe
   - (c) Lord Auckland
   - (d) Lord Allenbourough

10. The first newspaper published in India was
    - (a) The Calcutta Chronicle
    - (b) The Calcutta Gazette
    - (c) The Indian Gazette
    - (d) The Bengal Gazette

11. Which Maratha state was the last to accept the subsidiary alliance of the British?
    - (a) Gaikwad
    - (b) Sindhia
    - (c) Holkar
    - (d) Bhonsle

12. Between which stations was the first railway line opened in India?
    - (a) Calcutta to Raniganj
    - (b) Bombay to Pune
    - (c) Calcutta to Jamshedpur
    - (d) Bombay to Thane

13. Who of the following laid the first rail line in India?
    - (a) Lord Ellenborough
    - (b) Lord Canning
    - (c) Lord Dufferin
    - (d) Lord Dalhousie

14. Who was the father of Civil Service?
    - (a) Lord Minto
    - (b) Lord Wellesley
    - (c) Lord William Bentinck
    - (d) Lord Cornwallis

15. Who among the following was the first Governor General of India?
    - (a) Robert Clive
    - (b) Lord Canning
    - (c) Lord William Bentinck
    - (d) Lord Wellesley

16. Who was the first Governor General of Bengal?
    - (a) Lord Clive
    - (b) Warren Hastings
    - (c) Lord Wellesley
    - (d) Lord Hastings

17. In which year, Raja Ram Mohan Roy founded the Brahmo Samaj?
    - (a) 1822
    - (b) 1828
    - (c) 1830
    - (d) 1833

18. Which one of the following settlements did comprise Zamindar as middleman to collect the land revenue?
    - (a) Mahalwari settlement
    - (b) Ryotwari settlement
    - (c) Permanent settlement
    - (d) None of the above

19. Who was the Governor General of India at the time of Sindh-annexation?
    - (a) Lord Auckland
    - (b) Lord Mayo
    - (c) Lord Dalhousie
    - (d) Lord Ellenborough

20. Who gave the slogans 'Delhi Chalo' and 'Jai Hind'?
    - (a) Mahatma Gandhi
    - (b) Subhash Chandra Bose
    - (c) J. L. Nehru
    - (d) Rasebehari Bose

RESPONSE GRID	1. ⓐⓑⓒⓓ	2. ⓐⓑⓒⓓ	3. ⓐⓑⓒⓓ	4. ⓐⓑⓒⓓ	5. ⓐⓑⓒⓓ
	6. ⓐⓑⓒⓓ	7. ⓐⓑⓒⓓ	8. ⓐⓑⓒⓓ	9. ⓐⓑⓒⓓ	10. ⓐⓑⓒⓓ
	11. ⓐⓑⓒⓓ	12. ⓐⓑⓒⓓ	13. ⓐⓑⓒⓓ	14. ⓐⓑⓒⓓ	15. ⓐⓑⓒⓓ
	16. ⓐⓑⓒⓓ	17. ⓐⓑⓒⓓ	18. ⓐⓑⓒⓓ	19. ⓐⓑⓒⓓ	20. ⓐⓑⓒⓓ

Max. Marks : 20   **No. of Qs. 20**   **Time : 20 min.**   **Date : ..../........./................**

1. Who gave the slogan 'Swaraj is my birth right and I shall have it ?
   (a) Bhagat Singh
   (b) Sukhdev
   (c) Bal Gangadhara Tilak
   (d) Rajguru

2. Who was called as 'Grand Old Man of India'?
   (a) Dadabhai Naoroji
   (b) Bal Gangadhara Tilak
   (c) Lala Lajpat Rai
   (d) Gopala Krishna Gokale

3.. The Age of Moderates in Indian Freedom Struggle was
   (a) 1890-1910
   (b) 1885-1905
   (c) 1900-1910
   (d) 1909-1919

4. Who was the first president of the Muslim league?
   (a) Ali Khan
   (b) Ali Jinna
   (c) Asfanulla Khan
   (d) Agakhan

5. When did the capital transfered from Calcutta to Delhi?
   (a) 1910
   (b) 1911
   (c) 1912
   (d) 1913

6. Who established Anusheelan Samiti?
   (a) Barindra Kumar Ghosh
   (b) Jatindranath Banerjee
   (c) Pramod Mitter
   (d) All the above

7. Annie Besant belonged to
   (a) Gadar Party
   (b) Arya Samaj
   (c) Theosophical Society
   (d) Prarthana Samaj

8. Who was the first woman president of Indian National Congress?
   (a) Sarojini Naidu
   (b) J.B.Krupalani
   (c) Annie Besant
   (d) Arun Asaf Ali

9. The Chauri Chaura incident took place on
   (a) 3rd March 1922
   (b) 5th May 1922
   (c) 13th March 1922
   (d) 5th February, 1922

10. Who was the secretary of Swaraj Party?
    (a) Bala Gangadhara Tilak
    (b) Aravind Kumar Ghosh
    (c) Chandra Sekar Azad
    (d) Motilal Nehru

11. The Simon commission was appointed in
    (a) 1934
    (b) 1928
    (c) 1925
    (d) 1930

12. When was the partition of Bengal officially announced?
    (a) 11th November, 1905
    (b) 16th October, 1905
    (c) 19th December, 1905
    (d) 21th April,1905

13. Who announced the Queen Victoria as the Crown of India?
    (a) Lord Wellesley
    (b) Lord Cornwallis
    (c) Lord Lytton
    (d) Lord Hastings

14. Swaraj as goal of Congress was declared in 1905 at
    (a) Benaras Congress session
    (b) Surat Congress session
    (c) Calcutta Congress session
    (d) Bombay Congress session

15. Where was the imperial Darbar held?
    (a) Delhi
    (b) Calcutta
    (c) Madras
    (d) Bombay

16. Which of the following period was called as Gandhian Era?
    (a) 1910-1947
    (b) 1929-1940
    (c) 1920-1947
    (d) 1932-1947

17. The activity of the Congress during the period of Moderate was summed up as
    (a) Prayer
    (b) Petition
    (c) Protest
    (d) All the above

18. Who shot dead Michael O' Dwyer, the Lt. Governor of Punjab at the time of the Jallianwala Bagh Massacre?
    (a) Udham Singh
    (b) Kartar Singh Sarabha
    (c) Bhagat Singh
    (d) Madanlal Dhingra

19. Bardoli Satyagraha was led by–
    (a) Mahatma Gandhi
    (b) Vallabhbhai Patel
    (c) Jawaharlal Nehru
    (d) Subhash Chandra Bose

20. The Mantra of "Do or Die", was given by–
    (a) Jawaharlal Nehru
    (b) Subhash Chandra Bose
    (c) Mahatma Gandhi
    (d) Binoba Bave

RESPONSE GRID	1. ⓐⓑⓒⓓ	2. ⓐⓑⓒⓓ	3. ⓐⓑⓒⓓ	4. ⓐⓑⓒⓓ	5. ⓐⓑⓒⓓ
	6. ⓐⓑⓒⓓ	7. ⓐⓑⓒⓓ	8. ⓐⓑⓒⓓ	9. ⓐⓑⓒⓓ	10. ⓐⓑⓒⓓ
	11. ⓐⓑⓒⓓ	12. ⓐⓑⓒⓓ	13. ⓐⓑⓒⓓ	14. ⓐⓑⓒⓓ	15. ⓐⓑⓒⓓ
	16. ⓐⓑⓒⓓ	17. ⓐⓑⓒⓓ	18. ⓐⓑⓒⓓ	19. ⓐⓑⓒⓓ	20. ⓐⓑⓒⓓ

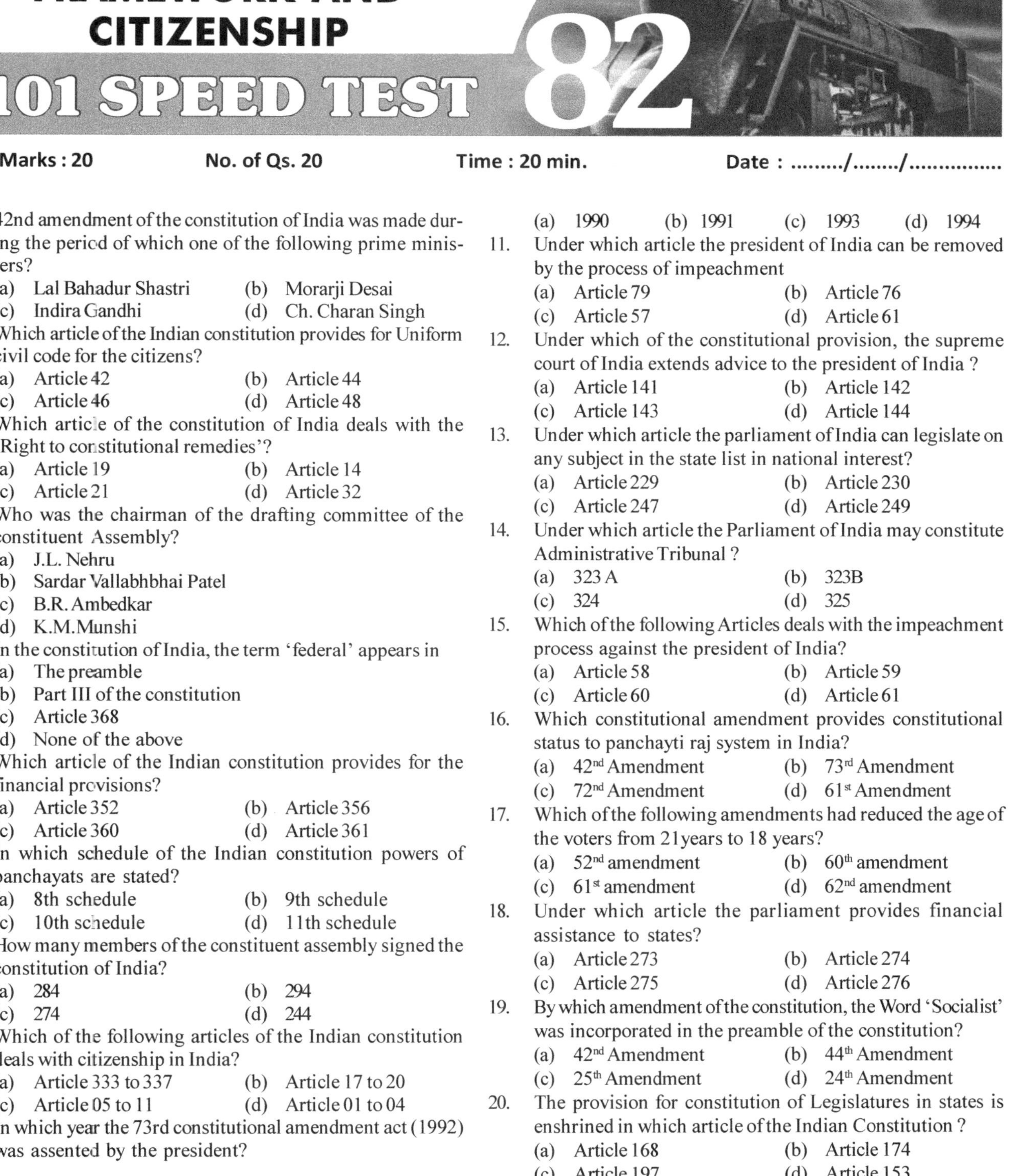

CONSTITUTIONAL FRAMEWORK AND CITIZENSHIP

101 SPEED TEST 82

Max. Marks : 20   **No. of Qs. 20**   **Time : 20 min.**   **Date : ..../......../...............**

1. 42nd amendment of the constitution of India was made during the period of which one of the following prime ministers?
   (a) Lal Bahadur Shastri   (b) Morarji Desai
   (c) Indira Gandhi   (d) Ch. Charan Singh
2. Which article of the Indian constitution provides for Uniform civil code for the citizens?
   (a) Article 42   (b) Article 44
   (c) Article 46   (d) Article 48
3. Which article of the constitution of India deals with the 'Right to constitutional remedies'?
   (a) Article 19   (b) Article 14
   (c) Article 21   (d) Article 32
4. Who was the chairman of the drafting committee of the constituent Assembly?
   (a) J.L. Nehru
   (b) Sardar Vallabhbhai Patel
   (c) B.R. Ambedkar
   (d) K.M.Munshi
5. In the constitution of India, the term 'federal' appears in
   (a) The preamble
   (b) Part III of the constitution
   (c) Article 368
   (d) None of the above
6. Which article of the Indian constitution provides for the financial provisions?
   (a) Article 352   (b) Article 356
   (c) Article 360   (d) Article 361
7. In which schedule of the Indian constitution powers of panchayats are stated?
   (a) 8th schedule   (b) 9th schedule
   (c) 10th schedule   (d) 11th schedule
8. How many members of the constituent assembly signed the constitution of India?
   (a) 284   (b) 294
   (c) 274   (d) 244
9. Which of the following articles of the Indian constitution deals with citizenship in India?
   (a) Article 333 to 337   (b) Article 17 to 20
   (c) Article 05 to 11   (d) Article 01 to 04
10. In which year the 73rd constitutional amendment act (1992) was assented by the president?
    (a) 1990   (b) 1991   (c) 1993   (d) 1994
11. Under which article the president of India can be removed by the process of impeachment
    (a) Article 79   (b) Article 76
    (c) Article 57   (d) Article 61
12. Under which of the constitutional provision, the supreme court of India extends advice to the president of India ?
    (a) Article 141   (b) Article 142
    (c) Article 143   (d) Article 144
13. Under which article the parliament of India can legislate on any subject in the state list in national interest?
    (a) Article 229   (b) Article 230
    (c) Article 247   (d) Article 249
14. Under which article the Parliament of India may constitute Administrative Tribunal ?
    (a) 323 A   (b) 323B
    (c) 324   (d) 325
15. Which of the following Articles deals with the impeachment process against the president of India?
    (a) Article 58   (b) Article 59
    (c) Article 60   (d) Article 61
16. Which constitutional amendment provides constitutional status to panchayti raj system in India?
    (a) 42nd Amendment   (b) 73rd Amendment
    (c) 72nd Amendment   (d) 61st Amendment
17. Which of the following amendments had reduced the age of the voters from 21 years to 18 years?
    (a) 52nd amendment   (b) 60th amendment
    (c) 61st amendment   (d) 62nd amendment
18. Under which article the parliament provides financial assistance to states?
    (a) Article 273   (b) Article 274
    (c) Article 275   (d) Article 276
19. By which amendment of the constitution, the Word 'Socialist' was incorporated in the preamble of the constitution?
    (a) 42nd Amendment   (b) 44th Amendment
    (c) 25th Amendment   (d) 24th Amendment
20. The provision for constitution of Legislatures in states is enshrined in which article of the Indian Constitution ?
    (a) Article 168   (b) Article 174
    (c) Article 197   (d) Article 153

RESPONSE GRID					
	1. ⓐⓑⓒⓓ	2. ⓐⓑⓒⓓ	3. ⓐⓑⓒⓓ	4. ⓐⓑⓒⓓ	5. ⓐⓑⓒⓓ
	6. ⓐⓑⓒⓓ	7. ⓐⓑⓒⓓ	8. ⓐⓑⓒⓓ	9. ⓐⓑⓒⓓ	10. ⓐⓑⓒⓓ
	11. ⓐⓑⓒⓓ	12. ⓐⓑⓒⓓ	13. ⓐⓑⓒⓓ	14. ⓐⓑⓒⓓ	15. ⓐⓑⓒⓓ
	16. ⓐⓑⓒⓓ	17. ⓐⓑⓒⓓ	18. ⓐⓑⓒⓓ	19. ⓐⓑⓒⓓ	20. ⓐⓑⓒⓓ

Max. Marks : 20   **No. of Qs. 20**   **Time : 20 min.**   **Date :** ..../........./................

1. Fundamental Right to ______has been deleted by the ______ Amendment Act.
   (a) Form associations; 44th   (b) Property; 44th
   (c) against exploitation; 42nd (d) private property; 42nd

2. ______ decides about the reasonableness of the restrictions placed on Fundamental Rights?
   (a) Parliament   (b) President
   (c) Supreme Court   (d) Special Tribunal

3. Right against exploitation prohibits children below
   (a) 14 years from working in family businesses
   (b) 14 years of age from working in hazardous occupations
   (c) 14 years from working on family farms
   (d) All of the above

4. ______ in the Constitution elaborates the concept of a welfare state?
   (a) Preamble   (b) Directive Principles
   (c) Fundamental Rights   (d) Fundamental Duties

5. ______ Constitutional Amendment gave a position of primacy to all Directive Principles over Fundamental Rights?
   (a) 24th   (b) 25th
   (c) 36th   (d) 42nd

6. Fundamental Duties were included in the Constitution to:
   (a) give more importance to the Fundamental Rights
   (b) stop subversive and unconstitutional activities
   (c) prevent abuse of Fundamental Rights
   (d) give more power to the executive

7. Fundamental Duties of a citizen EXCLUDE
   (a) promoting communal harmony
   (b) developing a scientific temper
   (c) safeguarding public property
   (d) protecting children from hazardous work.

8. The Constitution calls upon parents to provide opportunities for education to their children between the ages of six and fourteen years under
   (a) Article 21A   (b) Article 29
   (c) Article 45   (d) Article 51A

9. Which of the following was the first to put in place a right to Information Act?
   (a) Goa
   (b) Karnataka
   (c) Tamil Nadu
   (d) The Central Government

10. Which of the following Articles of the Indian Constitution deal with the Directive Principles of State Policy?
    (a) 26 to 41   (b) 31 to 56
    (c) 36 to 51   (d) 41 to 66

11. India has borrowed the concept of fundamental Rights from the Constitution of
    (a) UK   (b) USA
    (c) Russia   (d) Ireland

12. The permanent president of constituent assembly was
    (a) Dr. Ambedkar   (b) Dr. Rajendra Prasad
    (c) K.M. munshi   (d) J.L. Nehru

13. Under which constitutional Amendment has education for children aged 6 to 14 years become Fundamental Right?
    (a) 93rd Amendment   (b) 86th Amendment
    (c) 91st Amendment   (d) 92nd Amendment

14. Which one of the following committees recommended the inclusion of fundamental duties in the Indian Constitution?
    (a) Barua Committee
    (b) Ramaswamy Committee
    (c) Sikri Committee
    (d) Swarn Singh Committee

15. Which one of the following fundamental rights was described by Dr. Ambedkar as the heart and soul of the constitution ?
    (a) Right to freedom against Exploitation
    (b) Right to freedom of Religion
    (c) Right to equality
    (d) Right to constitutional Remedies

16. According to the Indian constitution, which one is not included in the fundamental right to equality?
    (a) Equality before law   (b) Social equality
    (c) Equality of opportunity (d) Economic equality

17. After which amendment the right to acquire, hold and dispose off property is no longer a fundamental Right?
    (a) 42nd Amendment   (b) 44th Amendment
    (c) 43rd Amendment   (d) 40th Amendment

18. According to which amendment no law giving effect to the Directive principle Article 36(b) and (c) can be challenged as violative of Fundamental Rights?
    (a) 42nd   (b) 27th
    (c) 40th   (d) 25th

19. Which of the following articles of Indian constitution enunciates fundamental duties?
    (a) Article 35   (b) Article 51(A)
    (c) Article 32   (d) Article 14

20. Under which article of Indian constitution a High Court can issue writs to protect the fundamental rights?
    (a) Article 15   (b) Article 32
    (c) Article 35   (d) Article 226

RESPONSE GRID					
	1. (a)(b)(c)(d)	2. (a)(b)(c)(d)	3. (a)(b)(c)(d)	4. (a)(b)(c)(d)	5. (a)(b)(c)(d)
	6. (a)(b)(c)(d)	7. (a)(b)(c)(d)	8. (a)(b)(c)(d)	9. (a)(b)(c)(d)	10. (a)(b)(c)(d)
	11. (a)(b)(c)(d)	12. (a)(b)(c)(d)	13. (a)(b)(c)(d)	14. (a)(b)(c)(d)	15. (a)(b)(c)(d)
	16. (a)(b)(c)(d)	17. (a)(b)(c)(d)	18. (a)(b)(c)(d)	19. (a)(b)(c)(d)	20. (a)(b)(c)(d)

101 SPEED TEST

84

Max. Marks : 20　　　**No. of Qs. 20**　　　**Time : 20 min.**　　　**Date : ..../........./................**

1. Indian system of government is based on _____ pattern.
   - (a) French
   - (b) American
   - (c) British
   - (d) Swedish

2. Executive authority of the Union is vested by the Constitution in the
   - (a) Prime Minister
   - (b) President
   - (c) Cabinet
   - (d) Central Legislature

3. Where can impeachment proceedings against the President are initiated ?
   - (a) In Lok Sabha
   - (b) Joint sitting of the two Houses called for this purpose
   - (c) In either House of Parliament
   - (d) In the Supreme Court

4. ___ elects the Vice-President?
   - (a) Electoral college which elects the President
   - (b) Members of the Rajya Sabha and Lok Sabha
   - (c) Electoral college consisting of members of Parliament
   - (d) Members of Parliament in a joint meeting

5. Vice-President's letter of resignation is addressed to:
   - (a) Deputy Chairman of Rajya Sabha
   - (b) Chief Justice of India
   - (c) President of India
   - (d) Speaker of the Lok Sabha

6. The President sends his resignation letter to
   - (a) Chief Justice of India
   - (b) Speaker
   - (c) Vice-President
   - (d) Prime Minister

7. If there vacancy in the offices of both President and Vice-President, who function as President?
   - (a) Chief Justice of India
   - (b) Chief Justice of the Delhi High Court.
   - (c) Any person appointed by Parliament
   - (d) All of the Above

8. Prime Minister is
   - (a) elected by Lok Sabha
   - (b) elected by the Parliament
   - (c) appointed by the President
   - (d) nominated by the party with a majority in the Lok Sabha

9. Salary and perks of the Prime Minister are decided by the
   - (a) Constitution
   - (b) Cabinet
   - (c) Parliament
   - (d) President

10. Policy of the Government is shaped by
    - (a) Ministers
    - (b) Prime Minister
    - (c) Cabinet
    - (d) Special Committees

11. The Prime Minister
    - (a) is head of the government
    - (b) is the leader of Lok Sabha
    - (c) can change the portfolios of Ministers
    - (d) all of the above

12. One-third of the members of Rajya Sabha retire every
    - (a) year
    - (b) two years
    - (c) three years
    - (d) six years

13. Term of Rajya Sabha was fixed by the
    - (a) President
    - (b) Constitution
    - (c) Parliament
    - (d) Cabinet

14. President jointly addresses both houses of parliament
    - (a) Once an year
    - (b) Commencement of each session
    - (c) At the invitation of the Houses
    - (d) During the first session every year

15. If the Vice-President acts as President he gets the emoluments of the:
    - (a) President
    - (b) Vice-President
    - (c) Chairman of Rajya Sabha
    - (d) President and what he was getting as Chairman of Rajya Sabha

16. If the Chairman of Rajya Sabha becomes acting President, his duties as a Chairman are performed by
    - (a) Continues as Chairman
    - (b) a newly elected Chairman
    - (c) Deputy Chairman
    - (d) member of Rajya Sabha deputed by the Chairman

17. Position of the Vice-president of India matches that of the Vice-President of
    - (a) USA
    - (b) Russia
    - (c) Italy
    - (d) New Zealand

18. Parliament does not have the power to remove:
    - (a) Comptroller and Auditor General
    - (b) Supreme Court Judges
    - (c) Chairman of UPSC
    - (d) High Court Judges

19. Members of Rajya Sabha are:
    - (a) Elected indirectly
    - (b) All are nominated
    - (c) Elected both directly and indirectly
    - (d) Elected by members of State Legislative assemblies and Legislative Councils

20. _____ Lok Sabha had been constituted by the end of 2000?
    - (a) Ten
    - (b) Eleven
    - (c) Twelve
    - (d) Thirteen

RESPONSE GRID

1. ⓐⓑⓒⓓ	2. ⓐⓑⓒⓓ	3. ⓐⓑⓒⓓ	4. ⓐⓑⓒⓓ	5. ⓐⓑⓒⓓ
6. ⓐⓑⓒⓓ	7. ⓐⓑⓒⓓ	8. ⓐⓑⓒⓓ	9. ⓐⓑⓒⓓ	10. ⓐⓑⓒⓓ
11. ⓐⓑⓒⓓ	12. ⓐⓑⓒⓓ	13. ⓐⓑⓒⓓ	14. ⓐⓑⓒⓓ	15. ⓐⓑⓒⓓ
16. ⓐⓑⓒⓓ	17. ⓐⓑⓒⓓ	18. ⓐⓑⓒⓓ	19. ⓐⓑⓒⓓ	20. ⓐⓑⓒⓓ

STATE GOVERNMENT

101 SPEED TEST 85

Max. Marks : 20   **No. of Qs. 20**   **Time : 20 min.**   **Date : ..../........./................**

1. Chief executive head of a State is:
   (a) Governor
   (b) President
   (c) Chief Minister
   (d) Prime Minister
2. In appointing a Governor, the President consults the Chief Minister of the State as this is:
   (a) constitutionally imperative
   (b) a convention
   (c) as Parliament has legislated to the effect
   (d) A duty of the President
3. Dual role of the Governor means:
   (a) Constitutional and real executive
   (b) Head of a state and head of government under certain circumstances
   (c) Belonging both to Central and State executive
   (d) Constitutional ruler and represents the Centre
4. Governor does not appoint:
   (a) judges of the High Court
   (b) Chief Minister of the State
   (c) Chairman of the State Public Service Commission
   (d) Advocate-General of the State
5. Vidhan Sabha is:
   (a) the upper house of State Legislature
   (b) Indirectly elected
   (c) subject to dissolution
   (d) unimportant at State level
6. A post under a State is held during the pleasure of the
   (a) President
   (b) Governor
   (c) Parliament
   (d) State Legislature
7. The members of State Legislative Assemblies are elected for a period of
   (a) 2 years
   (b) 6 years
   (c) 5 years
   (d) 3 years
8. The oath of office is administered to the Governor by the
   (a) Chief Justice of India
   (b) President
   (c) Chief Justice of High Court
   (d) Speaker of Legislative Assembly
9. _____ has a separate Constitution?
   (a) Nagaland
   (b) Mizoram
   (c) J & K
   (d) Pondicherry
10. The Chief Minister of a state is
    (a) elected by the State Legislature
    (b) appointed by the Governor
    (c) appointed by the President
    (d) None of the above

11. Governor holds office
    (a) for 5 years
    (b) for a period fixed by the Parliament
    (c) during the pleasure of the President
    (d) till he enjoys the confidence of the Parliament
12. In India there is a single constitution for the union and the states with the exception of
    (a) Sikkim
    (b) Jammu and Kashmir
    (c) Nagaland
    (d) Tamil Nadu
13. There is a constitutional requirement to have a minister is charge of tribal welfare for the states of
    (a) Assam, Nagaland and Manipur
    (b) Himachal Pradesh, Haryana and Rajasthan
    (c) Bihar, Madhya Pradesh and Odisha
    (d) Manipur, Tripura and Meghalaya
14. What is the maximum permissible strength of the legislative assembly (Vidhan Sabha) of any state ?
    (a) 400 members
    (b) 425 members
    (c) 500 members
    (d) 545 members
15. J & K Constitution was framed by:
    (a) Constituent Assembly which framed India's Constitution
    (b) Constituent Assembly set up by the Parliament
    (c) Constituent Assembly set up by the State
    (d) the State Legislature
16. Article 154 states that the Governor can exercise his executive authority either directly or through officers subordinate to him. The word subordinates includes:
    (a) All the ministers and the Chief Minister
    (b) All the ministers except the Chief Minister
    (c) Only the Chief Minister and the Deputy Chief Minister
    (d) Only the Cabinet Ministers
17. Governor of which State has been vested with special powers for scheduled tribes?
    (a) Arunachal Pradesh
    (b) Assam
    (c) Maharashtra
    (d) West Bengal
18. Ministers salaries in a State are determined by:
    (a) the Constitution
    (b) Parliament
    (c) State Legislature
    (d) Governor
19. Which was the first state created as a separate state on the linguistic basis in 1953?
    (a) Punjab
    (b) Maharashtra
    (c) Andhra Pradesh
    (d) Kerala
20. The State Reorganization Commission was constituted in
    (a) 1953
    (b) 1956
    (c) 1950
    (d) 1952

RESPONSE GRID	1. ⓐⓑⓒⓓ	2. ⓐⓑⓒⓓ	3. ⓐⓑⓒⓓ	4. ⓐⓑⓒⓓ	5. ⓐⓑⓒⓓ
	6. ⓐⓑⓒⓓ	7. ⓐⓑⓒⓓ	8. ⓐⓑⓒⓓ	9. ⓐⓑⓒⓓ	10. ⓐⓑⓒⓓ
	11. ⓐⓑⓒⓓ	12. ⓐⓑⓒⓓ	13. ⓐⓑⓒⓓ	14. ⓐⓑⓒⓓ	15. ⓐⓑⓒⓓ
	16. ⓐⓑⓒⓓ	17. ⓐⓑⓒⓓ	18. ⓐⓑⓒⓓ	19. ⓐⓑⓒⓓ	20. ⓐⓑⓒⓓ

86

Max. Marks : 20   **No. of Qs. 20**   **Time : 20 min.**   **Date : ..../........./................**

1. Panchayati Raj has received a constitutional status with ____Amendment Act
   - (a) 72nd
   - (b) 73rd
   - (c) 74th
   - (d) 75th
2. Three-tier Panchayats are:
   - (a) uniformly applicable to all States
   - (b) applicable only to States with population above 50 lakh
   - (c) need not be strictly followed in States with population below 20 lakh
   - (d) has been replaced with a four tier system
3. List of items reserved for the Panchayats are given in the:
   - (a) Eleventh Schedule
   - (b) Twelfth Schedule
   - (c) Seventh Schedule
   - (d) State List
4. Elections to Panchayats are held:
   - (a) every four years
   - (b) every five years
   - (c) when the State Government decides
   - (d) at center's directive
5. A person should be ____ years to stand in a panchayat election
   - (a) 21 years
   - (b) 18 years
   - (c) 25 years
   - (d) 30 years
6. __________ conducts elections to Panchayats and municipalities?
   - (a) State Government
   - (b) Central Government
   - (c) State Election Commission
   - (d) Central Election Commission
7. Electorate for a Panchayat is at:
   - (a) Taluka board
   - (b) all adults of 21 years and above in a village
   - (c) village and selected Members of Parliament and State Legislature
   - (d) Gram Sabha.
8. Direct elections to all tiers of the Panchayat were held first after the 73rd Amendment came into force in ____?
   - (a) Andhra Pradesh
   - (b) Rajasthan
   - (c) Karnataka
   - (d) Madhya Pradesh
9. Chairperson of a municipality is
   - (a) nominated by the State Government
   - (b) directly elected by the voters
   - (c) elected in the manner specified by the State Legislature
   - (d) to be a person with experience in municipal administration

10. If a Panchayat is dissolved, elections are to be held within
    - (a) 1 month
    - (b) 3 months
    - (c) 6 months
    - (d) 1 year
11. Which of the following is a committee on Panchayati Raj institutions?
    - (a) Balwantray Mehta Committee
    - (b) G.V.K. Rao Committee
    - (c) L.M. Singhvi Committee
    - (d) Ashok Mehta Committee
12. Panchayati Raj is a system of:
    - (a) Local government
    - (b) Local administration
    - (c) Local self-government
    - (d) Rural local self-government
13. At ______ years the individual can vote for panchyats.
    - (a) 18
    - (b) 21
    - (c) 25
    - (d) 19
14. Which is correctly matched?
    - (a) Amendment procedure – Article 268
    - (b) Duties of Prime Minister – Article 74
    - (c) President's rule – Article 365
    - (d) Inter-State Council – Article 264
15. Which is the first executive tier of the Panchayati Raj system from below ?
    - (a) Gram Sabha
    - (b) Gram Panchayat
    - (c) Mandal Parishad
    - (d) Panchayat Samiti
16. What is the intermediate tier of the Panchayati Raj System called?
    - (a) Zilla Parishad
    - (b) Taluka Panchayat
    - (c) Panchayat Samiti
    - (d) Gram Sabha
17. Which of the following Articles of the Constitution of India makes a specific mention of village panchayats?
    - (a) Article 19
    - (b) Article 21
    - (c) Article 40
    - (d) Article 246
18. Which one among the following pairs is *not* correctly matched?
    - (a) Union List : Banking
    - (b) State List : Agriculture
    - (c) Concurrent List: Marriage
    - (d) Residuary List : Education
19. The Panchayati Raj was launched on –
    - (a) 2 Oct, 1952
    - (b) 2 Oct , 1950
    - (c) 2 Oct, 1959
    - (d) 2 Oct, 1948
20. The Panchayati Raj was first launched in
    - (a) Rajasthan
    - (b) Andhra Pradesh
    - (c) Uttar Pradesh
    - (d) Punjab

RESPONSE GRID	1. ⓐⓑⓒⓓ	2. ⓐⓑⓒⓓ	3. ⓐⓑⓒⓓ	4. ⓐⓑⓒⓓ	5. ⓐⓑⓒⓓ
	6. ⓐⓑⓒⓓ	7. ⓐⓑⓒⓓ	8. ⓐⓑⓒⓓ	9. ⓐⓑⓒⓓ	10. ⓐⓑⓒⓓ
	11. ⓐⓑⓒⓓ	12. ⓐⓑⓒⓓ	13. ⓐⓑⓒⓓ	14. ⓐⓑⓒⓓ	15. ⓐⓑⓒⓓ
	16. ⓐⓑⓒⓓ	17. ⓐⓑⓒⓓ	18. ⓐⓑⓒⓓ	19. ⓐⓑⓒⓓ	20. ⓐⓑⓒⓓ

JUDICIARY & MISCELLANEOUS

101 SPEED TEST

87

Max. Marks : 20   **No. of Qs. 20**   **Time : 20 min.**   **Date : ..../......../...............**

1. A High Court consists of a Chief Justice and
   (a) at least 5 other judges
   (b) such other judges as specified by the Constitution
   (c) such other judges as decided by the Parliament
   (d) such other judges as determined by the President

2. Andaman & Nicobar Islands comes under?
   (a) Madras High Court
   (b) Tamil Nadu High Court
   (c) Andhra Pradesh High Court
   (d) Calcutta High Court

3. Chandigarh comes under:
   (a) Delhi High Court
   (b) Punjab and Haryana High Court
   (c) Allahabad High Court
   (d) Chandigarh High Court

4. _____ does not have a High Court of its own?
   (a) Sikkim   (b) Bihar
   (c) Himachal Pradesh   (d) Manipur

5. Supreme Court was set up:
   (a) by an act of Parliament
   (b) by the Constitution
   (c) under the Government of India Act, 1935
   (d) by a Presidential order

6. The District and sessions Judge works directly under the control of:
   (a) District Collector   (b) Governor of the state
   (c) Law Minister of the state (d) High Court of the state

7. The Chief Justice of the High Court is appointed by
   (a) the Governor of the state
   (b) the President of India
   (c) the Chief Minister of the state
   (d) the Chief Justice of India

8. What is the number of Judges (including Chief Justice) in the Supreme Court of India as provided in the Constitution of India?
   (a) 20   (b) 24   (c) 26   (d) 28

9. How many types of emergencies has the Constitution envisaged?
   (a) One   (b) Two   (c) Three   (d) Five

10. First general elections in India were held in
    (a) 1949   (b) 1950   (c) 1951   (d) 1947

11. Regional Commissioners are appointed by the:
    (a) President   (b) Election Commission
    (c) Parliament   (d) Governor

12. Originally the Constitution recognised _____ languages.
    (a) 2   (b) 14   (c) 15   (d) 23

13. While Hindi is the official language, English has been permitted for official use till:
    (a) 1995   (b) 2001
    (c) 2010   (d) forever

14. Who held the power to increase the number of judges in the Supreme Court?
    (a) Prime minister   (b) President
    (c) Parliament   (d) Ministry of Law

15. How many courts are there at apex level?
    (a) One   (b) Two
    (c) Three   (d) None

16. In which year High Courts was first established?
    (a) 1862   (b) 1860
    (c) 1972   (d) 1980

17. Mid-day meal given in government -aided schools because of :-
    (a) Supreme Court   (b) High Court
    (c) PIL   (d) All of these

18. Sanctioned strengths of judges in High Courts are –
    (a) 10   (b) 25   (c) 34   (d) 54

19. Who presided the Supreme Court?
    (a) Subordinate   (b) District Court
    (c) Chief Justice   (d) All of these

20. How many levels of court are there in India?
    (a) One   (b) Two   (c) Three   (d) four

<table>
<tr><td rowspan="4">RESPONSE GRID</td><td>1. ⓐⓑⓒⓓ</td><td>2. ⓐⓑⓒⓓ</td><td>3. ⓐⓑⓒⓓ</td><td>4. ⓐⓑⓒⓓ</td><td>5. ⓐⓑⓒⓓ</td></tr>
<tr><td>6. ⓐⓑⓒⓓ</td><td>7. ⓐⓑⓒⓓ</td><td>8. ⓐⓑⓒⓓ</td><td>9. ⓐⓑⓒⓓ</td><td>10. ⓐⓑⓒⓓ</td></tr>
<tr><td>11. ⓐⓑⓒⓓ</td><td>12. ⓐⓑⓒⓓ</td><td>13. ⓐⓑⓒⓓ</td><td>14. ⓐⓑⓒⓓ</td><td>15. ⓐⓑⓒⓓ</td></tr>
<tr><td>16. ⓐⓑⓒⓓ</td><td>17. ⓐⓑⓒⓓ</td><td>18. ⓐⓑⓒⓓ</td><td>19. ⓐⓑⓒⓓ</td><td>20. ⓐⓑⓒⓓ</td></tr>
</table>

INDIAN ECONOMY

101 SPEED TEST — 88

Max. Marks : 20   **No. of Qs. 20**   **Time : 20 min.**   **Date : ..../........./................**

1. Who among the following first made economic planning for India?
   - (a) M. N Roy
   - (b) Dadabhai Naoroji
   - (c) M Vishveshwarya
   - (d) Jawaharla Nehru
2. 'Planned Economy of India' was written by
   - (a) M. Vishveshwarya
   - (b) Dadabhai Naoroji
   - (c) Shriman Narayan
   - (d) Jawaharla Nehru
3. 'Sarvodaya Plan' was prepared by
   - (a) Jaiprakash Narayan
   - (b) Mahatma Gandhi
   - (c) Binoba Bhave
   - (d) Jawaharlal Nehru
4. Planning commission of India was established in
   - (a) 1948
   - (b) 1950
   - (c) 1952
   - (d) 1951
5. National Development Council (NDC) was constituted in
   - (a) 1948
   - (b) 1950
   - (c) 1952
   - (d) 1947
6. Planning in India was started in:
   - (a) 1951
   - (b) 1950
   - (c) 1952
   - (d) None of these
7. 'Gadgil Formula' is concerned with
   - (a) 4th plan
   - (b) 6th plan
   - (c) 1st plan
   - (d) 3rd plan
8. 'Mukherjee Committee' was constituted during
   - (a) 5th plan
   - (b) 4th plan
   - (c) 6th plan
   - (d) 8th plan
9. Who made the first attempt to estimate the National Income of India?
   - (a) Dadabhai Naoroji
   - (b) RC Dutt
   - (c) V K R V Rao
   - (d) PC Mahalanobis
10. Which of the following bank is a commercial bank?
    - (a) SBI
    - (b) Regional Rural Banks (RRBs)
    - (c) Cooperative Bank
    - (d) All of the above
11. The Imperial bank of India was established in
    - (a) 1945
    - (b) 1931
    - (c) 1921
    - (d) 1936
12. Mumbai Stock Exchange was set up in
    - (a) 1875
    - (b) 1948
    - (c) 1952
    - (d) 1891
13. UTI is now controlled by
    - (a) IDBI
    - (b) Finance Ministry
    - (c) RBI
    - (d) SBI
14. State Bank of India (SBI) came into existence in
    - (a) 1948
    - (b) 1955
    - (c) 1935
    - (d) 1949
15. NABARD was established in
    - (a) 1982
    - (b) 1964
    - (c) 1980
    - (d) 1990
16. IDBI was established in
    - (a) 1964
    - (b) 1972
    - (c) 1982
    - (d) 1955
17. RBI was nationalized in
    - (a) 1949
    - (b) 1935
    - (c) 1969
    - (d) 1955
18. The largest bank of India is
    - (a) RBI
    - (b) SBI
    - (c) Central Bank
    - (d) Bank of India
19. The headquarter of RBI is in
    - (a) Mumbai
    - (b) Delhi
    - (c) Kolkata
    - (d) Chennai
20. SEBI (Securities and Exchange Board of India) was constituted in
    - (a) 1986
    - (b) 1982
    - (c) 1988
    - (d) 1992

RESPONSE GRID				
1. ⓐⓑⓒⓓ	2. ⓐⓑⓒⓓ	3. ⓐⓑⓒⓓ	4. ⓐⓑⓒⓓ	5. ⓐⓑⓒⓓ
6. ⓐⓑⓒⓓ	7. ⓐⓑⓒⓓ	8. ⓐⓑⓒⓓ	9. ⓐⓑⓒⓓ	10. ⓐⓑⓒⓓ
11. ⓐⓑⓒⓓ	12. ⓐⓑⓒⓓ	13. ⓐⓑⓒⓓ	14. ⓐⓑⓒⓓ	15. ⓐⓑⓒⓓ
16. ⓐⓑⓒⓓ	17. ⓐⓑⓒⓓ	18. ⓐⓑⓒⓓ	19. ⓐⓑⓒⓓ	20. ⓐⓑⓒⓓ

Max. Marks : 20 **No. of Qs. 20** **Time : 20 min.** **Date : ..../........../.................**

1. The planet nearest to the sun is
   - (a) Mercury
   - (b) Earth
   - (c) Venus
   - (d) Pluto

2. Which planet takes the longest time to go around the sun?
   - (a) Earth
   - (b) Jupiter
   - (c) Uranus
   - (d) Neptune

3. The planet which is called twin sister of the Earth is
   - (a) Mercury
   - (b) Venus
   - (c) Mars
   - (d) Uranus

4. The largest planet in our solar system is
   - (a) Earth
   - (b) Uranus
   - (c) Jupiter
   - (d) Saturn

5. Which of the following is the nearest star of Earth?
   - (a) Sirius
   - (b) Sun
   - (c) Rigel
   - (d) Vega

6. The deepest lake of the world is
   - (a) Baikal
   - (b) Crater
   - (c) Nyasa
   - (d) Tanganyika

7. Which one of the following is an example of a block mountain?
   - (a) Aravalli
   - (b) Andes
   - (c) Black Forest
   - (d) Caucasus

8. The biggest island of the Indian Ocean is
   - (a) Maldives
   - (b) Madagascar
   - (c) Lakshadweep
   - (d) Sumatra

9. U-shaped valley develops in
   - (a) Karst region
   - (b) Glacial region
   - (c) Desert region
   - (d) All of these

10. Volcanic eruptions do not occurs in the
    - (a) Baltic sea
    - (b) Black sea
    - (c) Caribbean sea
    - (d) Caspian sea

11. Quartzite is metamorphosed from
    - (a) Limestone
    - (b) Obsidian
    - (c) Sandstone
    - (d) Shale

12. Black Forest mountain is an example of
    - (a) Folded mountain
    - (b) Block mountain
    - (c) Volcanic mountain
    - (d) Residual mountain

13. Epicentre is concerned with
    - (a) Earthquake
    - (b) Volcano
    - (c) Cyclone
    - (d) Land sliding

14. Which is the largest planet?
    - (a) Neptune
    - (b) Jupiter
    - (c) Earth
    - (d) Venus

15. Which planet does not have satelite?
    - (a) Mars
    - (b) Neptune
    - (c) Uranus
    - (d) Venus

16. Which of the following planets has largest number of satellites or moons?
    - (a) Jupiter
    - (b) Neptune
    - (c) Earth
    - (d) Saturn

17. Which of the following planets is called "Blue planet"?
    - (a) Venus
    - (b) Earth
    - (c) Uranus
    - (d) Mercury

18. The approximate diameter of Earth is
    - (a) 4200 km
    - (b) 6400 km
    - (c) 3400 km
    - (d) 12800 km

19. Which one of the following planets is the brightest?
    - (a) Mars
    - (b) Mercury
    - (c) Venus
    - (d) Jupiter

20. What is meant by the term "Midnight Sun"?
    - (a) Twilight
    - (b) Rising sun
    - (c) Very bright moon
    - (d) Sun shining in the polar circle for long time

RESPONSE GRID	1. ⓐⓑⓒⓓ	2. ⓐⓑⓒⓓ	3. ⓐⓑⓒⓓ	4. ⓐⓑⓒⓓ	5. ⓐⓑⓒⓓ
	6. ⓐⓑⓒⓓ	7. ⓐⓑⓒⓓ	8. ⓐⓑⓒⓓ	9. ⓐⓑⓒⓓ	10. ⓐⓑⓒⓓ
	11. ⓐⓑⓒⓓ	12. ⓐⓑⓒⓓ	13. ⓐⓑⓒⓓ	14. ⓐⓑⓒⓓ	15. ⓐⓑⓒⓓ
	16. ⓐⓑⓒⓓ	17. ⓐⓑⓒⓓ	18. ⓐⓑⓒⓓ	19. ⓐⓑⓒⓓ	20. ⓐⓑⓒⓓ

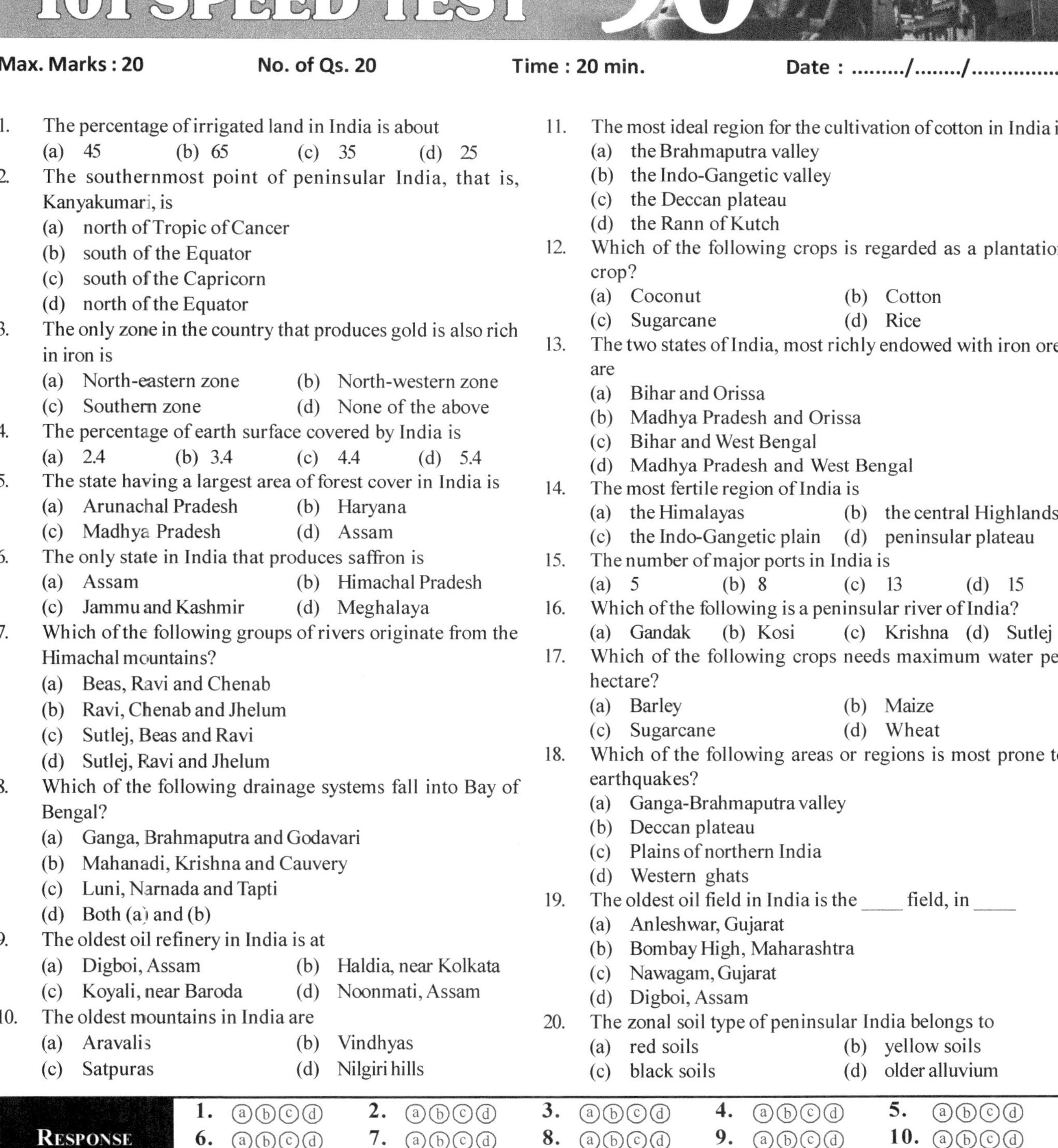

GEOGRAPHY OF INDIA

101 SPEED TEST 90

Max. Marks : 20   **No. of Qs. 20**   **Time : 20 min.**   **Date : ..../........./................**

1. The percentage of irrigated land in India is about
   (a) 45   (b) 65   (c) 35   (d) 25
2. The southernmost point of peninsular India, that is, Kanyakumari, is
   (a) north of Tropic of Cancer
   (b) south of the Equator
   (c) south of the Capricorn
   (d) north of the Equator
3. The only zone in the country that produces gold is also rich in iron is
   (a) North-eastern zone   (b) North-western zone
   (c) Southern zone   (d) None of the above
4. The percentage of earth surface covered by India is
   (a) 2.4   (b) 3.4   (c) 4.4   (d) 5.4
5. The state having a largest area of forest cover in India is
   (a) Arunachal Pradesh   (b) Haryana
   (c) Madhya Pradesh   (d) Assam
6. The only state in India that produces saffron is
   (a) Assam   (b) Himachal Pradesh
   (c) Jammu and Kashmir   (d) Meghalaya
7. Which of the following groups of rivers originate from the Himachal mountains?
   (a) Beas, Ravi and Chenab
   (b) Ravi, Chenab and Jhelum
   (c) Sutlej, Beas and Ravi
   (d) Sutlej, Ravi and Jhelum
8. Which of the following drainage systems fall into Bay of Bengal?
   (a) Ganga, Brahmaputra and Godavari
   (b) Mahanadi, Krishna and Cauvery
   (c) Luni, Narnada and Tapti
   (d) Both (a) and (b)
9. The oldest oil refinery in India is at
   (a) Digboi, Assam   (b) Haldia, near Kolkata
   (c) Koyali, near Baroda   (d) Noonmati, Assam
10. The oldest mountains in India are
    (a) Aravalis   (b) Vindhyas
    (c) Satpuras   (d) Nilgiri hills

11. The most ideal region for the cultivation of cotton in India is
    (a) the Brahmaputra valley
    (b) the Indo-Gangetic valley
    (c) the Deccan plateau
    (d) the Rann of Kutch
12. Which of the following crops is regarded as a plantation crop?
    (a) Coconut   (b) Cotton
    (c) Sugarcane   (d) Rice
13. The two states of India, most richly endowed with iron ore, are
    (a) Bihar and Orissa
    (b) Madhya Pradesh and Orissa
    (c) Bihar and West Bengal
    (d) Madhya Pradesh and West Bengal
14. The most fertile region of India is
    (a) the Himalayas   (b) the central Highlands
    (c) the Indo-Gangetic plain   (d) peninsular plateau
15. The number of major ports in India is
    (a) 5   (b) 8   (c) 13   (d) 15
16. Which of the following is a peninsular river of India?
    (a) Gandak   (b) Kosi   (c) Krishna   (d) Sutlej
17. Which of the following crops needs maximum water per hectare?
    (a) Barley   (b) Maize
    (c) Sugarcane   (d) Wheat
18. Which of the following areas or regions is most prone to earthquakes?
    (a) Ganga-Brahmaputra valley
    (b) Deccan plateau
    (c) Plains of northern India
    (d) Western ghats
19. The oldest oil field in India is the _____ field, in _____
    (a) Anleshwar, Gujarat
    (b) Bombay High, Maharashtra
    (c) Nawagam, Gujarat
    (d) Digboi, Assam
20. The zonal soil type of peninsular India belongs to
    (a) red soils   (b) yellow soils
    (c) black soils   (d) older alluvium

RESPONSE GRID	1. ⓐⓑⓒⓓ	2. ⓐⓑⓒⓓ	3. ⓐⓑⓒⓓ	4. ⓐⓑⓒⓓ	5. ⓐⓑⓒⓓ
	6. ⓐⓑⓒⓓ	7. ⓐⓑⓒⓓ	8. ⓐⓑⓒⓓ	9. ⓐⓑⓒⓓ	10. ⓐⓑⓒⓓ
	11. ⓐⓑⓒⓓ	12. ⓐⓑⓒⓓ	13. ⓐⓑⓒⓓ	14. ⓐⓑⓒⓓ	15. ⓐⓑⓒⓓ
	16. ⓐⓑⓒⓓ	17. ⓐⓑⓒⓓ	18. ⓐⓑⓒⓓ	19. ⓐⓑⓒⓓ	20. ⓐⓑⓒⓓ

WORLD GEOGRAPHY

101 SPEED TEST

91

Max. Marks : 20   **No. of Qs. 20**   **Time : 20 min.**   **Date : ..../........./................**

1. Which is the largest lake of the world?
   - (a) Film
   - (b) Literature
   - (c) Sports
   - (d) Science
2. Which is the deepest lake in the world?
   - (a) Victoria
   - (b) Caspian
   - (c) Baikal
   - (d) Dead sea
3. The highest lake of the world is
   - (a) Tanganyaka
   - (b) Great Slave
   - (c) Titicaca
   - (d) Huron
4. Which lake has the highest salinity (more saline lake) in the world?
   - (a) Van lake
   - (b) Salt lake
   - (c) Dead sea
   - (d) Caspian sea
5. The largest plateau of the world is
   - (a) Mongolia plateau
   - (b) Greenland plaetau
   - (c) Tibbet plateau
   - (d) Gobi plateau
6. The highest rainfall in the world occurs at
   - (a) Mawsynram
   - (b) Cherrapunji
   - (c) Congo
   - (d) Lima
7. The longest mountain range of the world is
   - (a) Himalayas
   - (b) Rockies
   - (c) Andes
   - (d) None of these
8. Which country is known as land of lakes?
   - (a) Norway
   - (b) Sweden
   - (c) Finland
   - (d) Scotland
9. The largest producer of coffee in the world is
   - (a) Venezuella
   - (b) Colombia
   - (c) Brazil
   - (d) Ethiopia
10. 'Great Barrier Reef', the largest coral reef of the world lies off the coast of
    - (a) Australia
    - (b) Japan
    - (c) China
    - (d) West Indies
11. The highest volcanic peak of the world is
    - (a) Chimborazo
    - (b) Kilimanzaro
    - (c) Catopaxi
    - (d) Mauna Loa
12. Which salt is found in largest quantity in oceanic water?
    - (a) Sodium chloride
    - (b) Calcium chloride
    - (c) Magnesium chloride
    - (d) Sodium chloride
13. Which is the largest continent of the world?
    - (a) Africa
    - (b) North America
    - (c) Asia
    - (d) Europe
14. Which continent has the largest population in the world?
    - (a) Asia
    - (b) Europe
    - (c) North America
    - (d) South America
15. Which gas has the largest proportion in the atmosphere?
    - (a) Oxygen
    - (b) Hydrogen
    - (c) Carbon dioxide
    - (d) Nitrogen
16. The highest peak of Africa is
    - (a) Mount Kenya
    - (b) Mount Kilimanjaro
    - (c) Mount Catopaxi
    - (d) Mount Chimborazo
17. River nile originates from
    - (a) Lake Victoria
    - (b) Lake Chad
    - (c) Red Sea
    - (d) Gulf of Aden
18. Which is the largest gold mining centre?
    - (a) Johannesburg
    - (b) Pretoria
    - (c) Transvaal
    - (d) Kimberley
19. Which is the largest diamond mining centre?
    - (a) Durban
    - (b) Kimberley
    - (c) Johannesburg
    - (d) Port Elizabeth
20. The largest river of the world is
    - (a) Hwang Ho
    - (b) Nile
    - (c) Amazon
    - (d) Zaire

RESPONSE GRID	1. ⓐⓑⓒⓓ	2. ⓐⓑⓒⓓ	3. ⓐⓑⓒⓓ	4. ⓐⓑⓒⓓ	5. ⓐⓑⓒⓓ
	6. ⓐⓑⓒⓓ	7. ⓐⓑⓒⓓ	8. ⓐⓑⓒⓓ	9. ⓐⓑⓒⓓ	10. ⓐⓑⓒⓓ
	11. ⓐⓑⓒⓓ	12. ⓐⓑⓒⓓ	13. ⓐⓑⓒⓓ	14. ⓐⓑⓒⓓ	15. ⓐⓑⓒⓓ
	16. ⓐⓑⓒⓓ	17. ⓐⓑⓒⓓ	18. ⓐⓑⓒⓓ	19. ⓐⓑⓒⓓ	20. ⓐⓑⓒⓓ

NATIONAL & INTERNATIONAL AWARDS

101 SPEED TEST 92

Max. Marks : 20 **No. of Qs. 20** **Time : 20 min.** **Date : ..../......../................**

1. Dada Saheb Phalke Award constituted in 1969 for which field?
   - (a) Film
   - (b) Literature
   - (c) Sports
   - (d) Science

2. Jnanpith Award is given for which field?
   - (a) Journalism
   - (b) Music
   - (c) Science
   - (d) Literature

3. Highest award given to civilian in India is
   - (a) Bharat Ratna
   - (b) Padma Vibhushan
   - (c) Sharam Award
   - (d) Padma Bhushan

4. In which year National Film Awards were initiated?
   - (a) 1952
   - (b) 1953
   - (c) 1954
   - (d) 1955

5. Which of the following is different from the others?
   - (a) Kirti Chakra
   - (b) Ashok Chakra
   - (c) Vir Chakra
   - (d) Shaurya Chakra

6. Bharat Ratna, Padma Vibhushan and Padma Shree are given on the eve of
   - (a) Republic Day
   - (b) Independence Day
   - (c) Gandhi Jayanti
   - (d) Pravasi Bhartiya Divas

7. The award is given for extraordinary act of bravery in the field of Naval, Air and Army is
   - (a) Arjuna Award
   - (b) Paramvir Chakra
   - (c) Kalinga Award
   - (d) Ashok Chakra

8. The award given for sports coaching is
   - (a) Dronacharya Award
   - (b) Arjuna Award
   - (c) Bhatnagar Award
   - (d) Shankar Award

9. The award is given in the field of agriculture
   - (a) Bhatnagar Award
   - (b) Bourlog Award
   - (c) Dhanwantari Award
   - (d) Kaling Award

10. The highest peace time gallantry award is
    - (a) Ashok Chakra
    - (b) Param Vir Chakra
    - (c) Kirti Chakra
    - (d) Vir Chakra

11. The Nobel prize was instituted by which country?
    - (a) USA
    - (b) UK
    - (c) Russia
    - (d) Sweden

12. The Academy award is also known as
    - (a) Oscar Award
    - (b) BAFTA Award
    - (c) Matthews Award
    - (d) Palm d'ore

13. Pulitzer prize was established in
    - (a) 1917
    - (b) 1918
    - (c) 1922
    - (d) 1928

14. Nobel prize are distributed annually at
    - (a) Manila
    - (b) New York
    - (c) Stockholm
    - (d) Geneva

15. BAFTA prize is distributed by
    - (a) UK
    - (b) Russia
    - (c) India
    - (d) USA

16. Which of the following is an award instituted by UNESCO?
    - (a) Kalinga Award
    - (b) Pulitzer prize
    - (c) Stirling prize
    - (d) Pritzker prize

17. The Nobel prize awarding ceremony takes place on
    - (a) 10th Dec.
    - (b) 12th Oct.
    - (c) 10th Nov.
    - (d) 15th Dec.

18. Which of the following award is given by World Economic Forum?
    - (a) Crystal Award
    - (b) Kalinga prize
    - (c) Pulitzer Award
    - (d) Abel prize

19. International Gandhi Peace prize is instituted in
    - (a) 1995
    - (b) 1996
    - (c) 1997
    - (d) 1998

20. Oscar awards is instituted in
    - (a) 1928
    - (b) 1929
    - (c) 1930
    - (d) 1932

<table>
<tr><td rowspan="4">RESPONSE GRID</td><td>1. ⓐⓑⓒⓓ</td><td>2. ⓐⓑⓒⓓ</td><td>3. ⓐⓑⓒⓓ</td><td>4. ⓐⓑⓒⓓ</td><td>5. ⓐⓑⓒⓓ</td></tr>
<tr><td>6. ⓐⓑⓒⓓ</td><td>7. ⓐⓑⓒⓓ</td><td>8. ⓐⓑⓒⓓ</td><td>9. ⓐⓑⓒⓓ</td><td>10. ⓐⓑⓒⓓ</td></tr>
<tr><td>11. ⓐⓑⓒⓓ</td><td>12. ⓐⓑⓒⓓ</td><td>13. ⓐⓑⓒⓓ</td><td>14. ⓐⓑⓒⓓ</td><td>15. ⓐⓑⓒⓓ</td></tr>
<tr><td>16. ⓐⓑⓒⓓ</td><td>17. ⓐⓑⓒⓓ</td><td>18. ⓐⓑⓒⓓ</td><td>19. ⓐⓑⓒⓓ</td><td>20. ⓐⓑⓒⓓ</td></tr>
</table>

BOOKS AND AUTHORS

101 SPEED TEST — 93

Max. Marks : 20   **No. of Qs. 20**   **Time : 20 min.**   **Date : ..../........./.................**

1. Which of the following books is written by Kalidasa?
   - (a) Raghuvansham
   - (b) Mitakshara
   - (c) Rajtarangini
   - (d) Arthashastra
2. The book 'Meghdootam' is written by
   - (a) Panini
   - (b) Shudrak
   - (c) Kalidasa
   - (d) Vishkhadatta
3. Which of the following books is written by Kautilya?
   - (a) Daybhag
   - (b) Rajtarangini
   - (c) Arthashastra
   - (d) Mitakshara
4. The book 'Avanti Sundari' is written by
   - (a) Kautilya
   - (b) Dandi
   - (c) Ved Vyas
   - (d) Ashwaghosh
5. Who is the author of 'one night at the call centre'?
   - (a) Vikram Seth
   - (b) Chetan Bhagat
   - (c) Anurag Mathur
   - (d) Robin Sharma
6. The book 'Jhansi Ki Rani' was written by
   - (a) Devkinandan Khatri
   - (b) Sharat Chand Chaudhary
   - (c) Vrindavanlal Verma
   - (d) Mahadevi Verma
7. The book 'Gaban' and 'Godan' were written by
   - (a) Prem Chand
   - (b) Jai Shankar Prasad
   - (c) Amrit Lal Nagar
   - (d) Vrindavanlal Verma
8. 'A Voice for Freedom' is a book written by
   - (a) Corazon Aquino
   - (b) Nayantara Sahgal
   - (c) Aung San Suu Kyi
   - (d) Benazir Bhutto
9. Aurobindo was the author of
   - (a) Discovery of India
   - (b) Hindu view of life
   - (c) Yogashastra
   - (d) Savitri
10. 'Alice in Wonderland' the famous TV serial is based on a book written by
    - (a) Father Discoste
    - (b) Thomas Hardy
    - (c) Charles Dickens
    - (d) Lewis Caroll
11. Who is the writer of 'Swamy and Friends'?
    - (a) Munshi Premchand
    - (b) Raman
    - (c) Max Muller
    - (d) R. K. Narayan
12. The author of controversial book 'Lajja' is a citizen of
    - (a) Pakistan
    - (b) Indonesia
    - (c) Bangladesh
    - (d) India
13. The creator of 'Sherlock Holmes' was
    - (a) Arthur Conan Doyle
    - (b) Ian Fleming
    - (c) Dr. Watson
    - (d) Shakespeare
14. Who is the author of book 'We Indians'?
    - (a) Nirad C. Choudry
    - (b) Subramaniya Swamy
    - (c) Khushwant Singh
    - (d) Muluk Raj Anand
15. 'India of our Dreams' is a book written by
    - (a) Dr. S. Radhakrishnan
    - (b) Dr. C. Subramanian
    - (c) M.V. Kamath
    - (d) Dr. Rajendra Prasad
16. Who has won the Gyan Peeth Award for her book 'Yama'?
    - (a) Maheswari Devi
    - (b) Asha Poorna Devi
    - (c) Amrita Preetam
    - (d) Mahadevi Verma
17. The book 'Gulliver's Travels' was written by
    - (a) Alexandra Dumas
    - (b) Charles Lamb
    - (c) Charles Dickens
    - (d) Jonathan Swift
18. The celebrated novel 'The Godfather' was authored by
    - (a) Harold Robbins
    - (b) John Milton
    - (c) Victor Hugo
    - (d) Mario Puzo
19. The author of the book 'Waiting for the Mahatma' is
    - (a) R.K. Narayan
    - (b) N.A. Palkhiwala
    - (c) Amrita Pritam
    - (d) Manohar Malgonkar
20. Who is the author of 'India Wins Freedom'?
    - (a) Dominique Lapierre
    - (b) Maulana Azad
    - (c) Khan Abdul Gaffar Khan
    - (d) Jawaharlal Nahru

	RESPONSE GRID				
1. ⓐⓑⓒⓓ	2. ⓐⓑⓒⓓ	3. ⓐⓑⓒⓓ	4. ⓐⓑⓒⓓ	5. ⓐⓑⓒⓓ
6. ⓐⓑⓒⓓ	7. ⓐⓑⓒⓓ	8. ⓐⓑⓒⓓ	9. ⓐⓑⓒⓓ	10. ⓐⓑⓒⓓ
11. ⓐⓑⓒⓓ	12. ⓐⓑⓒⓓ	13. ⓐⓑⓒⓓ	14. ⓐⓑⓒⓓ	15. ⓐⓑⓒⓓ
16. ⓐⓑⓒⓓ	17. ⓐⓑⓒⓓ	18. ⓐⓑⓒⓓ	19. ⓐⓑⓒⓓ	20. ⓐⓑⓒⓓ

Max. Marks : 20   **No. of Qs. 20**   **Time : 20 min.**   Date : ..../........./...............

1. India first won the Olympic Hockey gold at
   (a) Amsterdam
   (b) Los Angeles
   (c) Mumbai
   (d) Tokyo

2. The Olympic Games 2016 will be held in
   (a) Rio de Janerio
   (b) London
   (c) Tokyo
   (d) Madrid

3. Which country won the Cricket World Cup in 2011?
   (a) India
   (b) Pakistan
   (c) Australia
   (d) England

4. Rangaswami Cup is associated with
   (a) Wrestling
   (b) Football
   (c) Hockey
   (d) Golf

5. 'Grand Slam' is associated with the game of
   (a) Lawn Tennis
   (b) Hockey
   (c) Football
   (d) Swimming

6. 'Subroto Cup' is associated with
   (a) Badminton
   (b) Cricket
   (c) Chess
   (d) Football

7. The Indian Football team made its first appearance at Olympics in
   (a) 1940
   (b) 1948
   (c) 1950
   (d) 1951

8. Who was the first ODI captain for India?
   (a) Ajit Wadekar
   (b) Bishan Singh Bedi
   (c) Kapil Dev
   (d) Vinoo Mankad

9. Wankhede Stadium is situated in
   (a) Mumbai
   (b) Delhi
   (c) Lucknow
   (d) Bangalore

10. 'Ashes' is the term associated with which of the following sports?
    (a) Cricket
    (b) Badminton
    (c) Basketball
    (d) Football

11. The normal length of a football ground must be
    (a) 110 – 120 m
    (b) 100 – 110 m
    (c) 90 – 100 m
    (d) 120 – 130 m

12. The 'Dronacharya Award' is given to
    (a) Coaches
    (b) Sportspersons
    (c) Umpires
    (d) Sports Editors

13. Which of the following is correctly matched?
    (a) Cricket : Bogey
    (b) Boxing : Bully
    (c) Chess : Checkmate
    (d) Tennis : Smas

14. Who was the first Indian to win an individual medal in Olympics?
    (a) PT Usha
    (b) Karnam Malleshwari
    (c) Deepika Kumari
    (d) Sania Nehwal

15. Who was the first Indian woman who won the gold medal in Asian Games?
    (a) PT Usha
    (b) Sunita Rani
    (c) Shiny Abraham
    (d) Kamaljeet Sandhu

16. In which Indian state did the game of 'Polo' originates?
    (a) Nagaland
    (b) Manipur
    (c) Mizoram
    (d) Kerala

17. When did the Wimbledon Grand Slam Tennis tournament start?
    (a) 1857
    (b) 1877
    (c) 1897
    (d) 1898

18. How many players are there in Kho-Kho?
    (a) 9
    (b) 10
    (c) 8
    (d) 7

19. In which Olympic Games, Hockey was introduced for the first time
    (a) London, 1908
    (b) Stockholm, 1912
    (c) St. Louis, 1904
    (d) Paris, 1900

20. The sportsperson Sunil Chhetri is associated with
    (a) Football
    (b) Shooting
    (c) Cricket
    (d) Hockey

RESPONSE GRID	1. ⓐⓑⓒⓓ	2. ⓐⓑⓒⓓ	3. ⓐⓑⓒⓓ	4. ⓐⓑⓒⓓ	5. ⓐⓑⓒⓓ
	6. ⓐⓑⓒⓓ	7. ⓐⓑⓒⓓ	8. ⓐⓑⓒⓓ	9. ⓐⓑⓒⓓ	10. ⓐⓑⓒⓓ
	11. ⓐⓑⓒⓓ	12. ⓐⓑⓒⓓ	13. ⓐⓑⓒⓓ	14. ⓐⓑⓒⓓ	15. ⓐⓑⓒⓓ
	16. ⓐⓑⓒⓓ	17. ⓐⓑⓒⓓ	18. ⓐⓑⓒⓓ	19. ⓐⓑⓒⓓ	20. ⓐⓑⓒⓓ

CURRENT AFFAIRS

101 SPEED TEST 95

Max. Marks : 40   **No. of Qs. 40**   **Time : 20 min.**   **Date : ..../........./................**

1. In the Union Budget 2018, the Union government has announced to build a tunnel through the Sela Pass. The Sela pass is located in which state?
   - (a) Sikkim
   - (b) Arunachal Pradesh
   - (c) Manipur
   - (d) Himachal Pradesh

2. Which country is the partner country at the 32nd Surajkund International Crafts Mela 2018?
   - (a) Uzbekistan
   - (b) Turkmenistan
   - (c) Kyrgyzstan
   - (d) Oman

3. Who has been honoured with the 2018 Sahitya Akademi Bhasha Samman award?
   - (a) Thakazhi Sivasankara Pillai
   - (b) Rahul Sankarnarayan
   - (c) Shesh Anand Madhukar
   - (d) Visvanatha Satyanarayana

4. Mary Kom has won gold in which weight category at the 2018 India Open boxing Tournament?
   - (a) 64kg category
   - (b) 60kg category
   - (c) 54kg category
   - (d) 48kg category

5. Who has been appointed the new vice-chancellor of Banaras Hindu University (BHU)?
   - (a) Neeraj Tripathi
   - (b) B A Chopade
   - (c) Kuldeep Mehta
   - (d) Ajay Singh

6. Srihari Natraj has grabbed gold medal in 100-metre Backstroke category in swimming at the Khelo India School Games. He hails from which state?
   - (a) Madhya Pradesh
   - (b) Uttarakhand
   - (c) Maharashtra
   - (d) Karnataka

7. Which state government has launched Zero Budget Natural Farming (ZBNF) project to promote organic farming?
   - (a) Punjab
   - (b) Himachal Pradesh
   - (c) West Bengal
   - (d) Assam

8. The 2018 Data Privacy Day (DPD) is observed on which date?
   - (a) January 30
   - (b) January 31
   - (c) January 29
   - (d) January 28

9. What is the theme of the 2018 World Leprosy Day (WLD)?
   - (a) Zero Child Leprosy
   - (b) Leprosy defeats, Live transform
   - (c) Zero Disabilities in girls and boys
   - (d) To live is to help to live

10. What is the India's rank in the 2017 EIU Global Democracy Index?
    - (a) 42nd
    - (b) 64th
    - (c) 33rd
    - (d) 21st

11. Anu Kumar has grabbed the first gold medal of the Khelo India School Games in 1500 metres. He hails from which state?
    - (a) Uttar Pradesh
    - (b) Jharkhand
    - (c) Uttarakhand
    - (d) Rajasthan

12. The Indian Railways is expected to receive its first high-speed electric locomotive by ___________
    - (a) December 2018
    - (b) June 2018
    - (c) July 2018
    - (d) March 2018

13. Kalamandalam Geethanandan of Kerala passed away recently. He was a renowned ___________ artist
    - (a) Koodiyattam
    - (b) Ottanthulal
    - (c) Theyyam
    - (d) Kathakali

14. Who has been conferred with the 'Times Power Women of the Year 2017' (Pune) for Global PR?
    - (a) Shabnam Asthana
    - (b) Amrit Ahuja
    - (c) Jayoti Lahiri
    - (d) Bela Rajan

15. Rail transport company Alstom has its headquarter in which country?
    - (a) Japan
    - (b) China
    - (c) Germany
    - (d) France

16. What is the estimated rate of India's GDP growth for the fiscal 2016-17 as predicted by Central Statistics Office (CSO)?
    - (a) 7.1 Percent
    - (b) 7.3 Percent
    - (c) 6.75 Percent
    - (d) 6.9 Percent

17. Which ministry has launched the Stree Swabhiman Initiative to ensure and maintain Women Health and Hygiene?
    - (a) Ministry of Social Justice and Empowerment
    - (b) Ministry of Health and Family Welfare
    - (c) Ministry of Women and Child Development
    - (d) Ministry of Information Technology and Electronics

18. Who has been conferred with the Badminton Association of India (BAI) Lifetime Achievement Award 2018?
    - (a) Prakash Padukone
    - (b) Syed Modi
    - (c) Dipankar Bhattacharjee
    - (d) Arvind Bhat

19. Which among the following stadiums will host the finals of the 2020 ICC World T20 of both the men's and women's?
    - (a) Salt Lake Stadium, India
    - (b) Melbourne Cricket Ground (MCG), Australia
    - (c) Bidvest Wanderers Stadium, South Africa
    - (d) Lord's Cricket Ground, United Kingdom

20. The Delhi Soccer Association (Football Delhi) has announced to celebrate which legendary football players birthday as Football Day in Delhi as a mark of honor?
    - (a) Jeje Lalpekhlua
    - (b) Baichung Bhutia
    - (c) Sunil Chhetri
    - (d) I. M. Vijayan

21. The 2018 Asian Champions Trophy will be hosted by which country?
    (a) Qatar
    (b) Oman
    (c) Saudi Arabia
    (d) United Arab Emirates
22. Which country will host the 21st Commonwealth Games?
    (a) Kuala Lumpur, Malaysia
    (b) Birmingham, England
    (c) Glasgow, Scotland
    (d) Gold Coast, Australia
23. India's first ever 'Khadi Haat' has launched in which city?
    [a] Lucknow
    (b) Patna
    (c) Ahmedabad
    (d) New Delhi
24. Who has won the 2018 women's singles title in the Australian Open 2018?
    (a) Caroline Wozniack   (b) Serena Williams
    (c) Elina Svitolina   (d) Simona Halep
25. The 2018 International Bird Festival will be held in which National park of India?
    (a) Dudhwa National Park
    (b) Kaziranga National Park
    (c) Dudhwa National Park
    (d) Bandhavgarh National Park
26. Which state is hosting the 2018 National Handloom Expo (NHE)?
    (a) Manipur
    (b) Assam
    (c) Arunachal Pradesh
    (d) Jharkhand
27. Which union minitry has launched "Stree Swabhiman" initiative?
    (a) Ministry of Electronics and Information Technology
    (b) Ministry of Social Justice and Empowerment
    (c) Ministry of Women and Child Development
    (d) Ministry of Health and Family Welfare
28. Which state's tableau has won the best tableau award at the 69th Republic Day Parade 2018?
    (a) Assam
    (b) Maharashtra
    (c) Karnataka
    (d) Chhattisgarh
29. Who has won the 2018 men's Singles title in the Australian Open 2018?
    (a) Marin Cilic
    (b) Novak Djokovic
    (c) Rafael Nadal
    (d) Roger Federer
30. Which union ministry to set up social media communication hubs in districts?
    (a) Ministry of Information and Broadcasting
    (b) Ministry of Law and Justice
    (c) Ministry of Panchayati Raj
    (d) Ministry of Women and Child Development
31. What is the India's GDP growth prediction for FY19, according to 2018 Economic Survey of India?
    (a) 6.5 to 7.25%
    (b) 7 to 7.5%
    (c) 6.9 to 7.2%
    (d) 7.5 to 8.0%
32. Which International organisation will launch a new Global Centre for Cybersecurity to safeguard the world from hackers?
    (a) World Economic Forum
    (b) International Telecommunication Union
    (c) UNICEF
    (d) International Maritime Organization
33. Which state government has launched Mahatma Gandhi Sarbat Vikas Yojna (MGSVY) for distressed sections?
    (a) Karnataka
    (b) Punjab
    (c) Meghalaya
    (d) Kerala
34. What is the theme of the 8th National Voters' Day (NVD-2018)?
    (a) Ethical Voting
    (b) Empowering young and future events
    (c) Accessible Elections
    (d) Authentic Elections & Voting
35. Who has authored the book 'Staniya Svasasan Mei Addhi Aabadhi'?
    (a) V K Singh
    (b) Inderjit Singh
    (c) Thawar Chand Gehlot
    (d) Sadhana Pandey
36. Who has created a national record in the 63kg women's category at the 33rd Women Senior National Weightlifting Championships?
    (a) Amandeep Kaur
    (b) S Thasana Chanu
    (c) Karnam Malleswari
    (d) Rakhi Halder
37. Which Bollywood personality has been honoured with the 24th Crystal Award at the World Economic Forum (WEF-2018)?
    (a) Deepika Padukone
    (b) Aamir Khan
    (c) Shah Rukh Khan
    (d) Priyanka Chopra
38. What is the theme of the 48th annual meeting of the World Economic Forum (WEF-2018)?
    (a) Mastering the Fourth Industrial Revolution
    (b) Responsive and Responsible Leadership
    (c) Creating a Shared Future in a Fractured World
    (d) Together create a United World
39. Which country to host the 6th edition of ICC Women's World Twenty20 2018?
    (a) Australia   (b) England
    (c) New Zealand   (d) West Indies
40. Which Union ministry has launched the 'Protocol for Star Rating of Garbage-Free Cities'?
    (a) Ministry of Information and Broadcasting
    (b) Ministry of Corporate Affairs
    (c) Ministry of Housing and Urban Affairs
    (d) Ministry of Law and Justice

RESPONSE GRID					
	21. ⓐⓑⓒⓓ	22. ⓐⓑⓒⓓ	23. ⓐⓑⓒⓓ	24. ⓐⓑⓒⓓ	25. ⓐⓑⓒⓓ
	26. ⓐⓑⓒⓓ	27. ⓐⓑⓒⓓ	28. ⓐⓑⓒⓓ	29. ⓐⓑⓒⓓ	30. ⓐⓑⓒⓓ
	31. ⓐⓑⓒⓓ	32. ⓐⓑⓒⓓ	33. ⓐⓑⓒⓓ	34. ⓐⓑⓒⓓ	35. ⓐⓑⓒⓓ
	36. ⓐⓑⓒⓓ	37. ⓐⓑⓒⓓ	38. ⓐⓑⓒⓓ	39. ⓐⓑⓒⓓ	40. ⓐⓑⓒⓓ

Max. Marks : 60   **No. of Qs. 60**   **Time : 30 min.**   **Date : ..../........./.................**

1. The highest altitude (4411 metres above sea leavel) is of:
   (a) Daocheng Yading Airport (b) Heathrow Airport
   (c) Kathmandu Airport   (d) Bangda Airport

2. Article 1 of the Indian Constitution declares "India that is Bharat" is a:
   (a) Union of States
   (b) Federal State with Unitary features
   (c) Unitary State with federal features
   (d) Federal State

3. Which was the first super computer purchased by India for medium range weather forecasting?
   (a) CrayXMP-14   (b) Medha-930
   (c) CDC Cyber 930-11   (d) Param

4. The Government of India Act, 1935 was based on:
   (a) Simon Commission
   (b) Lord Curzon Commission
   (c) Dimitrov Thesis
   (d) Lord Clive's report

5. Rajiv Gandhi International Airport is situated in:
   (a) Jammu and Kashmir   (b) New Delhi
   (c) Mangalore   (d) Hyderabad

6. Who founded the Indian National Party in Berlin during 1914?
   (a) Subhash Chandra Bose (b) W.C. Banerjee
   (c) Surendranath Benerjee (d) Champakaraman Pillai

7. In India, Special Economic Zones were established to enhance:
   (a) Free trade
   (b) Foreign Investment
   (c) Employment
   (d) Technology Development

8. During Quit India Movement, 'Parallel Government' was constituted at:
   (a) Varanasi   (b) Allahabad
   (c) Lucknow   (d) Ballia

9. The Poona Pact (1932) was an agreement between:
   (a) Nehru and Ambedkar   (b) Gandhi and Ambedkar
   (c) Malaviya and Ambedkar (d) Gandhi and Nehru

10. On which side did Japan fight in the First World War?
    (a) none, it wag neutral
    (b) with Germany against United Kingdom
    (c) against Russia on its own
    (d) with United Kingdom against Germany

11. "Rainbow Coalition" is a term derived from the politics and policies of:
    (a) Pranab Mukherjee   (b) Barack Obama
    (c) Mitt-Romney   (d) A.B. Vajpayee

12. The layer of the atmosphere in which Radio Waves are reflected back is called:
    (a) Ionosphere   (b) Troposhere
    (c) Stratosphere   (d) Exosphere

13. Provisions of citizenship in Indian Constitution, became applicable in
    (a) 1950   (b) 1949   (c) 1951   (d) 1952

14. Who gave the title of "Sardar" to Ballabh Bhai Patel?
    (a) Mahatma Gandhi   (b) Vinoba Bhave
    (c) Women of Bardoli   (d) Peasants of Gujrat

15. The National Emergency in India declared by the President of India due to the external aggression or armed revolt through
    (a) Article-352   (b) Article-356
    (c) Article-360   (d) Article-368

16. Who was the viceroy when Delhi became the capital of British India?
    (a) Load Curzon   (b) Lord Minto
    (c) Lord Hardinge   (d) Lord Waveli

17. The first Indian Satellite Aryabhatta was launched in
    (a) 1972   (b) 1975   (c) 1977   (d) 1979

18. Where is the shore based steel plant located?
    (a) Tuticorin   (b) Salem
    (c) Vishakhapatnam   (d) Mangalore

19. Recently the Chief Minister of Odisha, Naveen Patnaik, released a book on his father titled 'The Tall Man Biju Patnaik'. Who is the author of the book?
    (a) Sundar Ganesan   (b) Sampad Patnaik
    (c) Debabrata Mohanty   (d) Prem Nath Pandey

20. Which of the following is the coldest planet in solar system?
    (a) Mercury   (b) Saturm
    (c) Uranus   (d) Pluto

RESPONSE GRID					
1. ⓐⓑⓒⓓ	2. ⓐⓑⓒⓓ	3. ⓐⓑⓒⓓ	4. ⓐⓑⓒⓓ	5. ⓐⓑⓒⓓ
6. ⓐⓑⓒⓓ	7. ⓐⓑⓒⓓ	8. ⓐⓑⓒⓓ	9. ⓐⓑⓒⓓ	10. ⓐⓑⓒⓓ
11. ⓐⓑⓒⓓ	12. ⓐⓑⓒⓓ	13. ⓐⓑⓒⓓ	14. ⓐⓑⓒⓓ	15. ⓐⓑⓒⓓ
16. ⓐⓑⓒⓓ	17. ⓐⓑⓒⓓ	18. ⓐⓑⓒⓓ	19. ⓐⓑⓒⓓ	20. ⓐⓑⓒⓓ

21. Which of the following is the highest peak in Great Himalayas?
    (a) Mt. Everest
    (b) Kanchenjungha
    (c) Nanda Devi
    (d) Nanga Parvat
22. Rajya Subha is required to return Money Bill Passed by the Lok Sabha within
    (a) 7 days
    (b) 14 days
    (c) 28 days
    (d) 90 days
23. The Balwant Rai Mehta Committe was associated with
    (a) Industrial Policy
    (b) Banking Reforms
    (c) Panchayati Raj
    (d) Nanga Center-State relations
24. The 21st edition of India International Seafood Show (IISS) 2018 has been organised in which state of India?
    (a) Tamil Nadu
    (b) West Bengal
    (c) Goa
    (d) Andhra Pradesh
25. The Russian Revolution took place in the year
    (a) 1905
    (b) 1909
    (c) 1917
    (d) 1927
26. Name the India's first indigenously developed vaccine which has received the "pre-qualified" tag by the World Health Organisation
    (a) Rubevac Vaccine
    (b) Norovac Vaccine
    (c) Pneumovac Vaccine
    (d) Rotavac Vaccine
27. Pandit Jawaharlal Nehru, the first Prime Minister of India, was born in the year:
    (a) 1859
    (b) 1869
    (c) 1879
    (d) 1889
28. The Constituent Assembly adopted the Indian Constitution on:
    (a) January 26, 1950
    (b) August 15, 1947
    (c) January 30, 1950
    (d) November 26, 1949
29. Radha Reddy and Raja Reddy are the propounders of which classical dance?
    (a) Kuchipudi
    (b) Odissi
    (c) Kathak
    (d) Kathakali
30. In which state the folk dance 'Ghoomar' is performed?
    (a) Gujarat
    (b) Rajasthan
    (c) Orissa
    (d) Nagaland
31. Thaipusam festival is celebrated by which of the following communities?
    (a) Tamil
    (b) Telugu
    (c) Marathi
    (d) Malayalam
32. The annual "Royal Kathima Ceremony" is associated with which of the following religions?
    (a) Jainism
    (b) Buddhism
    (c) Parsi
    (d) Sikhism
33. The most potent greenhouse gas among the following is _____?
    (a) Carbon dioxide
    (b) Methane
    (c) Water Vapor
    (d) Ozone
34. Which among the following river does not flow from east to west?
    (a) Tapti
    (b) Narmada
    (c) Krishna
    (d) Mahi
35. In the context to India's wild life, the flying fox is a __?
    (a) Bat
    (b) Vulture
    (c) Stork
    (d) Kite
36. The Sangai Festival is organized in __:
    (a) Assam
    (b) Manipur
    (c) Mizoram
    (d) Nagaland
37. The "Ninety East Ridge" is a submarine volcanic ridge located in __?
    (a) Pacific Ocean
    (b) Atlantic Ocean
    (c) Indian Ocean
    (d) Arctic Ocean
38. Who among the following propounded the 'Safety Valve Theory' of the foundation of Congress?
    (a) Lala Lajpat Rai
    (b) Anand Mohan Bose
    (c) Surendra Nath Banerjee
    (d) Bipin Chandra Pal
39. Which among the following great revolutionaries was the brain behind the 'Chittagong Armoury Raid'?
    (a) Ganesh Ghosh
    (b) Chandrashekhar Azad
    (c) Surya Sen
    (d) Lala Hardayal
40. Both the processes of transfer of power and the partition of India were hurried through in _____ days.
    (a) 68
    (b) 72
    (c) 83
    (d) 94

RESPONSE GRID	21. Ⓐⓑⓒⓓ	22. Ⓐⓑⓒⓓ	23. Ⓐⓑⓒⓓ	24. Ⓐⓑⓒⓓ	25. Ⓐⓑⓒⓓ
	26. Ⓐⓑⓒⓓ	27. Ⓐⓑⓒⓓ	28. Ⓐⓑⓒⓓ	29. Ⓐⓑⓒⓓ	30. Ⓐⓑⓒⓓ
	31. Ⓐⓑⓒⓓ	32. Ⓐⓑⓒⓓ	33. Ⓐⓑⓒⓓ	34. Ⓐⓑⓒⓓ	35. Ⓐⓑⓒⓓ
	36. Ⓐⓑⓒⓓ	37. Ⓐⓑⓒⓓ	38. Ⓐⓑⓒⓓ	39. Ⓐⓑⓒⓓ	40. Ⓐⓑⓒⓓ

41. Who is custodian of the Indian Constitution?
    (a) President of India
    (b) Chief Justice of India
    (c) Prime Minister of India
    (d) Chairman of Raja Sabha
42. Panchayati Raj System was implemented first in the pair of states
    (a) Andhra Pradesh and Rajasthan
    (b) Assam and Bihar
    (c) Arunachal Pradesh and Uttar Pradesh
    (d) Punjab and Chandigarh
43. Which has become a legal right under 44th Amendment?
    (a) Right to Education
    (b) Right of Property
    (c) Right of Judicical Remedies
    (d) Right to Work
44. Which hill station is called as the 'Queen of the Satpuras'?
    (a) Pachmarhi   (b) Nilgiri
    (c) Mahenderagiri   (d) Cardamom
45. Who among the following were adjudged the World's Most Admired Persons in a poll conducted by YouGov for The Times in January 2014?
    (a) Bill Gates, Anna Hazare and Sachin Tendulkar
    (b) Narendra Modi, Barack Obama and Pope Francis
    (c) Queen Elizabeth, Angelina Jolie and Amitabh Bachchan
    (d) All of the above
46. Operation flood is related to the production of
    (a) Wool   (b) Dairy
    (c) Egg   (d) None of these
47. Which of the following high dignitaries, who are not members of Parliament, has the right to address it?
    (a) Chief Justice of India
    (b) Attorney General of India
    (c) Solicitor General of India
    (d) Chief Election Commissioner of India
48. In 1937, an educational conference endorsing Gandhi's proposals for 'basic education' through the vernacular medium was held at
    (a) Surat   (b) Bombay
    (c) Ahmedabad   (d) Wardha
49. "What is the Third Estate?" pamphlet associated with the French Revolution, was writen by:
    (a) Marquis-Lafayette (b) Edmund Burke
    (c) Joseph Foulon   (d) Abbe Sieyes
40. As a part of the Republic Day 2018 celebrations, 6 days Bharat Parv event has been organized at which of the given places?
    (a) India Gate   (b) Red Fort
    (c) Rashtrapati Bhavan (d) Qutub Minar
51. The Agra Municipal Corporation has released the logo of Smart City Agra featuring Taj Mahal along with _______
    (a) Tiger   (b) Lotus Flower
    (c) Peacock Feather   (d) National Flag

52. Who is the author of the book "A Cricketing Life"?
    (a) Christopher Martin Jenkins
    (b) Sunil Gavaskar
    (c) Kapil Dev
    (d) Tony Greig
53. Who is the Chairman of the 14th Finance Commission?
    (a) D. Subba Rao
    (b) Montek Singh Ahluwalia
    (c) M. Govinda Rao
    (d) Dr. YV Reddy
54. Which of the following does not form a part of the Foreign Exchange Reserves of India?
    (a) Gold
    (b) SDRs
    (c) Foreign currency assets
    (d) Foreign currency and securities held by the banks and corporate bodies
55. Which one of the following is issued by the court in case of an illegal detention of a person?
    (a) Habeas Corpus   (b) Mandamus
    (c) Certiorari   (d) Quo Warranto
56. Under which Article of the Indian Constitution, the decision of the Central Administrative Tribunal can be challenged in the Supreme Court?
    (a) 323A   (b) 329
    (c) 343 C   (d) 343 K
57. In which year was "Jana Gana Mana" adopted as the National Anthem?
    (a) 1948   (b) 1949
    (c) 1950   (d) 1951
58. By which Charter Act, the East India Company's monopoly of trade with China came to an end?
    (a) Charter Act of 1793   (b) Charter Act of 1813
    (c) Charter Act of 1833   (d) Charter Act of 1853
59. How many workers have been selected to be honored with the Prime Minister's Shram Awards for the year 2016?
    (a) 47   (b) 29
    (c) 32   (d) 50
60. Name the movie to win the Best Film Award at the 63rd Filmfare Awards 2018
    (a) Hindi Medium   (b) Bareilly Ki Barfi
    (c) Secret Superstar (d) Tumhari Sulu

<table>
<tr><td rowspan="4">RESPONSE GRID</td><td>41. ⓐⓑⓒⓓ</td><td>42. ⓐⓑⓒⓓ</td><td>43. ⓐⓑⓒⓓ</td><td>44. ⓐⓑⓒⓓ</td><td>45. ⓐⓑⓒⓓ</td></tr>
<tr><td>46. ⓐⓑⓒⓓ</td><td>47. ⓐⓑⓒⓓ</td><td>48. ⓐⓑⓒⓓ</td><td>49. ⓐⓑⓒⓓ</td><td>50. ⓐⓑⓒⓓ</td></tr>
<tr><td>51. ⓐⓑⓒⓓ</td><td>52. ⓐⓑⓒⓓ</td><td>53. ⓐⓑⓒⓓ</td><td>54. ⓐⓑⓒⓓ</td><td>55. ⓐⓑⓒⓓ</td></tr>
<tr><td>56. ⓐⓑⓒⓓ</td><td>57. ⓐⓑⓒⓓ</td><td>58. ⓐⓑⓒⓓ</td><td>59. ⓐⓑⓒⓓ</td><td>60. ⓐⓑⓒⓓ</td></tr>
</table>

Max. Marks : 50   **No. of Qs. 50**   **Time : 30 min.**   **Date : ..../........./.................**

1. The following is formed by revolving rectangle about one of its sides which remains fixed
   (a) Cylinder
   (b) Sphere
   (c) Hemi sphere
   (d) Cone

2. The following is the method for development of a sphere.
   (a) Parallel line method
   (b) Radial line method
   (c) Triangulation method
   (d) Approximate method

3. The development of lateral surfaces of a pentagonal pyramid is
   (a) Five squares
   (b) Five Rectangles
   (c) Five triangles
   (d) None of the above

4. The following is (are) the method(s) of projecting the pictorial views.
   (a) Axonometric projection
   (b) Oblique projection
   (c) Perspective projection
   (d) All of the above

5. Which among following first generation of computers had ?
   (a) Vacuum Tubes and Magnetic Drum
   (b) Integrated Circuits
   (c) Magnetic Tape and Transistors
   (d) All of above

6. Which of the following are components of Central Processing Unit (CPU) ?
   (a) Arithmetic logic unit, Mouse
   (b) Arithmetic logic unit, Control unit
   (c) Arithmetic logic unit, Integrated Circuits
   (d) Control Unit, Monitor

7. A compressed spring possesses
   (a) Kinetic Energy
   (b) Elastic Potential Energy
   (c) Gravitational Potential Energy
   (d) Sound Energy

8. If a bulb uses energy of 100 J and remains on for 25 s, power consumed by bulb will be
   (a) 125 W
   (b) 4 W
   (c) 2500 W
   (d) 75 W

9. For two objects A and B, if mass of A is same as mass of B and speed of A is twice as much as that of B, statement that is correct is
   (a) Kinetic energy of A = kinetic energy of B; because, kinetic energy is independent of speed of object.
   (b) since kinetic energy is inversely proportional to speed of object, kinetic energy of A < kinetic energy of B
   (c) Kinetic energy of A = 1 ? 4 × Kinetic energy of B
   (d) Kinetic energy of A = 4 × Kinetic energy of B

10. When spring or rubber band is released it converts potential energy into
    (a) Mechanical Energy
    (b) Electrical Energy
    (c) Thermal energy
    (d) Kinetic energy

11. When an object is raised to a certain height above ground, it possesses
    (a) Chemical Potential Energy
    (b) Elastic Potential Energy
    (c) Gravitational Potential Energy
    (d) Kinetic energy

12. The dimensional formula of coefficient of viscosity is
    (a) $[MLT^{-1}]$
    (b) $[M^{-1}L^2T^{-2}]$
    (c) $[ML^{-1}T^{-1}]$
    (d) none of these

13. Dimensional formula of latent heat
    (a) $M0L^2T^{-2}$
    (b) MLT^{-2}
    (c) ML^2T^{-2}
    (d) $ML2T^{-2}$

14. If length of pendulum is increased by 2%. The time period will
    (a) increases by 1%
    (b) decreases by 1%
    (c) increases by 2%
    (d) decreases by 2%

15. $[ML^{-1}T^{-2}]$ is the dimensional formula of
    (a) force
    (b) Coefficient of friction
    (c) Modulus of elasticity
    (d) Energy

16. Digital stopwatches show reading up to
    (a) 2 decimal places
    (b) 3 decimal places
    (c) 1 decimal place
    (d) 4 significant figures

17. Large masses such as mass of a truck is usually measured in
    (a) grams
    (b) tones
    (c) liters
    (d) Newton

18. Small masses such as mass of a pen is usually measured in
    (a) tones
    (b) liters
    (c) grams
    (d) Newton

19. Mass per unit volume is called substance's
    (a) weight
    (b) inertia
    (c) density
    (d) force

20. Gravitational force acting per unit mass on object is known as
    (a) gravitational field strength
    (b) gravitational field weakness
    (c) Earth's power
    (d) stress

21. Mass is property of a body that can not be changed by its
    (a) location
    (b) speed
    (c) shape
    (d) all of above

22. Inertia of an object with more mass is
    (a) greater
    (b) equal
    (c) zero
    (d) smaller

<table>
<tr><td rowspan="5">RESPONSE GRID</td><td>1. ⓐⓑⓒⓓ</td><td>2. ⓐⓑⓒⓓ</td><td>3. ⓐⓑⓒⓓ</td><td>4. ⓐⓑⓒⓓ</td><td>5. ⓐⓑⓒⓓ</td></tr>
<tr><td>6. ⓐⓑⓒⓓ</td><td>7. ⓐⓑⓒⓓ</td><td>8. ⓐⓑⓒⓓ</td><td>9. ⓐⓑⓒⓓ</td><td>10. ⓐⓑⓒⓓ</td></tr>
<tr><td>11. ⓐⓑⓒⓓ</td><td>12. ⓐⓑⓒⓓ</td><td>13. ⓐⓑⓒⓓ</td><td>14. ⓐⓑⓒⓓ</td><td>15. ⓐⓑⓒⓓ</td></tr>
<tr><td>16. ⓐⓑⓒⓓ</td><td>17. ⓐⓑⓒⓓ</td><td>18. ⓐⓑⓒⓓ</td><td>19. ⓐⓑⓒⓓ</td><td>20. ⓐⓑⓒⓓ</td></tr>
<tr><td>21. ⓐⓑⓒⓓ</td><td>22. ⓐⓑⓒⓓ</td><td></td><td></td><td></td></tr>
</table>

23. Weight of an object usually measured by
    (a) screw gauge
    (b) physical balance
    (c) beam balance or calibrated electronic balance
    (d) spring balance/compression balance

24. On Moon, 1 kg mass experiences force of
    (a) 1.6 N   (b) 10 N
    (c) 100 N   (d) 5.8 N

25. Speed of a body in particular direction can be called
    (a) acceleration   (b) displacement
    (c) velocity   (d) distance

26. Distance travelled by a body in time 't' is
    (a) instantaneous speed   (b) average velocity
    (c) average acceleration   (d) instantaneous acceleration

27. When speed of object changes, velocity
    (a) remains same   (b) also changes
    (c) decreases   (d) increases

28. A velocity-time graph can give you
    (a) Velocity of moving object
    (b) Acceleration of moving object
    (c) Displacement of moving object
    (d) All of above

29. Speed is defined as
    (a) The change of distance with respect to time
    (b) The rate of change of distance
    (c) Distance moved per unit time
    (d) All of above

30. Speed of light in vacuum is
    (a) 0.3×10^7 m s^{-1} (b) 3×10^7 m s^{-1}
    (c) 30×10^7 m s^{-1} (d) None of above

31. An example of bad thermal insulator is
    (a) potassium   (b) paper
    (c) cork   (d) wool

32. An example of conductor of heat is
    (a) paper   (b) cloth
    (c) air   (d) aluminum

33. In thermometer element which is used to show temperature is
    (a) copper   (b) zinc
    (c) mercury   (d) platinum

34. Which of the following is the fastest process of heat transfer?
    (a) conduction   (b) convection
    (c) radiation   (d) insulation

35. What would be the thermal resistance of an ideal conductor?
    (a) Zero   (b) One
    (c) Infinity   (d) Ten

36. Which of the following instrument will be used to measure alternating current?
    (a) Moving iron voltmeter
    (b) Permanent magnet type ammeter
    (c) Induction type ammeter
    (d) Moving iron (attraction type) ammeter

37. The internal impedance of an accurate voltmeter should be
    (a) As low as possible   (b) Low
    (c) Negligible   (d) Very high

38. Which of the following is the poorest conductor of electricity?
    (a) Silver   (b) Copper
    (c) Aluminium   (d) Carbon

39. The power factor at resonance in R-L-C parallel circuit is
    (a) 0.5 lagging   (b) 0.5 leading
    (c) Unity   (d) Zero

40. The cells are connected in series to
    (a) Increase the current output
    (b) Increase the voltage output
    (c) Decrease the internal resistance
    (d) Decrease the amount of charging voltage required

41. The material used for fuse must have
    (a) Low melting point and low specific resistance
    (b) Low melting point and high specific resistance
    (c) High melting point and low specific resistance
    (d) Low melting point with any specific resistance

42. Which of the following simple machines are combined to make scissors?
    (a) gear and pulley   (b) lever and gear
    (c) lever and wedge   (d) wedge and pulley

43. Which is a simple machine?
    (a) candle   (b) water
    (c) chair   (d) pulley

44. Which example of a simple machine is a lever?
    (a) ramp   (b) screw
    (c) pulley   (d) pliers

45. Which answer lists only simple machines?
    (a) television, computers, levers
    (b) lever, screw, wheel
    (c) screw, car, tires
    (d) lawn mower, edger, leaf blower

46. The person or organization responsible for rehabilitation is:
    (a) an employee's doctor
    (b) the insurance company
    (c) the employer
    (d) the employee, when better

47. When an employee is injured and takes time off work, it is recommended that contact with the injured employee:
    (a) be limited to legal representatives until the claim status (reject or accept) is decided by the insurance agent
    (b) be made by the supervisor and manager direct to the employee as soon as possible after the absence
    (c) resume between the manager and employee once the doctor provides a medical certificate and a return-to-work date
    (d) should be mainly between the insurance agent and rehabilitation provider, to ensure the best treatment and full rest for the injured employee

48. Layer of atmosphere in which Ozone layer lies is
    (a) exosphere   (b) mesosphere
    (c) troposphere   (d) stratosphere

49. Greenhouse gases which is present in very high quantity is
    (a) propane   (b) ethane
    (c) carbon dioxide   (d) methane

50. Exchange of outgoing and incoming radiations that keep Earth warm is known as
    (a) greenhouse effect   (b) radiation effect
    (c) infrared effect   (d) ozone layer depletion

<table>
<tr><td rowspan="5">RESPONSE GRID</td><td>23. ⓐⓑⓒⓓ</td><td>24. ⓐⓑⓒⓓ</td><td>25. ⓐⓑⓒⓓ</td><td>26. ⓐⓑⓒⓓ</td><td>27. ⓐⓑⓒⓓ</td></tr>
<tr><td>28. ⓐⓑⓒⓓ</td><td>29. ⓐⓑⓒⓓ</td><td>30. ⓐⓑⓒⓓ</td><td>31. ⓐⓑⓒⓓ</td><td>32. ⓐⓑⓒⓓ</td></tr>
<tr><td>33. ⓐⓑⓒⓓ</td><td>34. ⓐⓑⓒⓓ</td><td>35. ⓐⓑⓒⓓ</td><td>36. ⓐⓑⓒⓓ</td><td>37. ⓐⓑⓒⓓ</td></tr>
<tr><td>38. ⓐⓑⓒⓓ</td><td>39. ⓐⓑⓒⓓ</td><td>40. ⓐⓑⓒⓓ</td><td>41. ⓐⓑⓒⓓ</td><td>42. ⓐⓑⓒⓓ</td></tr>
<tr><td>43. ⓐⓑⓒⓓ</td><td>44. ⓐⓑⓒⓓ</td><td>45. ⓐⓑⓒⓓ</td><td>46. ⓐⓑⓒⓓ</td><td>47. ⓐⓑⓒⓓ</td></tr>
<tr><td></td><td>48. ⓐⓑⓒⓓ</td><td>49. ⓐⓑⓒⓓ</td><td>50. ⓐⓑⓒⓓ</td><td></td><td></td></tr>
</table>

STAGE I
FULL TEST-1

101 SPEED TEST 98

Max. Marks : 75   **No. of Qs. 75**   **Time : 60 min.**   Date : ..../........./...............

1. Under which Article of the Constitution of India, can the fundamental rights of the members of the Armed Forces be specifically restricted?
   - (a) Article 33
   - (b) Article 19
   - (c) Article 21
   - (d) Article 25

2. The Uttaramerur inscription provides information on the administration of the
   - (a) Chalukyas
   - (b) Satavahanas
   - (c) Pallavas
   - (d) Cholas

3. Who among the following were presented with MBEC (Member of the Most Excellent Order of the British Empire) in January 2014?
   - (a) Singer - Songwirter Adele
   - (b) Musician - PJ Harvey
   - (c) Broadcaster - Aled Jones
   - (d) All of the above

4. Who presides over the Joint Session of Indian Parliament?
   - (a) Speaker of Lok Sabha
   - (b) President of India
   - (c) Chairperson of Rajya Sabha
   - (d) Seniormost Member of Parliament

5. Who is the author of the book "No Full Stops in India"?
   - (a) R.K. Narayan
   - (b) Ved Mehta
   - (c) Nirad C. Choudhuri
   - (d) Mark Tolly

6. Who said "Rama Rajya through Grama Rajya"?
   - (a) Mahatma Gandhi
   - (b) Vinoda Bhave
   - (c) Jayaprakash Narayan
   - (d) Jawaharlal Nehru

7. Where do we find the ideals of Indian democracy in the Constitution?
   - (a) The Preamble
   - (b) Part III
   - (c) Part IV
   - (d) Part I

8. Comptroller and Auditor General of India is appointed by the
   - (a) Prime Minister
   - (b) President
   - (c) Finance Minister
   - (d) Lok Sabha

9. Which Article of the Indian Consitution directs the State Governments to organise Village Panchayats?
   - (a) Article 32
   - (b) Article 37
   - (c) Article 40
   - (d) Article 51

10. The Attorney General of India has the right of audience in
    - (a) the Supreme Court
    - (b) any High Court
    - (c) any Sessions Court
    - (d) any Court of Law within India

11. The capital of the ancient Chola kingdom was
    - (a) Uraiyur
    - (b) Kaveripoompattinam
    - (c) Thanjavur
    - (d) Medurai

12. Arrange the dynasties of Delhi Sultanate given below in chronological order:
    1. Khilji
    2. Tughlaq
    3. Sayyad
    4. Slave
    - (a) 4, 1, 3, 2
    - (b) 1, 4, 2, 3
    - (c) 1, 2, 3, 4
    - (d) 4, 1, 2, 3

13. Which was the earliest settlement of the Dutch in India?
    - (a) Masulipatnam
    - (b) Pulicat
    - (c) Surat
    - (d) Ahmedabad

14. During British rule, who was instrumental for the introduction of the Ryotwari system in the then Madras Presidency?
    - (a) Macartney
    - (b) Elphinstone
    - (c) Thomas Munro
    - (d) John Lawrence

15. Who amongst the following was not associated with the Unification of Italy?
    - (a) Cavour
    - (b) Garibaldi
    - (c) Mussolini
    - (d) Mazzini

16. Of the two bulbs in a house, one glows brighter than the other. Which of the two has a large resistance?
    - (a) the bright bulb
    - (b) the dim bulb
    - (c) both have the same resistance
    - (d) the brightness does not depend upon the resistance.

17. Spherical reflectors used in solar devices to
    - (a) concentrate the energy
    - (b) multiply the energy
    - (c) store the energy
    - (d) none of these

18. The laws of electromagnetic induction have been used in the construction of a
    (a) galvanometer   (b) voltmeter
    (c) electric motor   (d) generator

19. Weight of an astronaut on the surface of the earth is W_1 and his weight on the surface of the moon is W_2, then
    (a) $W_1 < W_2$ (b) $\dfrac{W_1}{W_2} = \dfrac{1}{6}$
    (c) $W_2 < W_1$ (d) $\dfrac{W_2}{W_1} = 1/6$

20. In an a.c. circuit, the current
    (a) is in phase with the voltage
    (b) leads the voltage
    (c) lags the voltage
    (d) any of the above depending on the circumstances

21. To obtain toned and double toned milk from full cream milk we can
    (a) filtrate it   (b) churn it
    (c) distillate it   (d) centrifuge it

22. Which one of the following is a physical change :
    (a) burning of magnesium
    (b) exposure of iron to air and moisture
    (c) dissolution of sugar in water
    (d) formation of a compound

23. Select a heterogeneous mixture out of the following :
    (a) air   (b) solution
    (c) emulsion   (d) alloy

24. A mole does not signify
    (a) atomic mass unit   (b) 6.022×10^{23} ions
    (c) 22.4 litres of a gas at STP (d) gram molecular mass

25. Which of the following non-metals is a liquid?
    (a) Carbon   (b) Bromine
    (c) Phosphorus   (d) Sulphur

26. Name most abundant element in earth crust. Is it metal or non metal?
    (a) Oxygen, Non-metal   (b) Aluminium, Metal
    (c) Silicon, Metalloid   (d) Iron, Metal

27. An aqueous solution with pH = 0 is
    (a) strongly acidic   (b) strongly basic
    (c) neutral   (d) sweakly acidic

28. Curd cannot be stored in
    (i) Brass vessel   (ii) Copper vessel
    (iii) Steel   (iv) Bronze
    (a) (i), (ii), (iii)   (b) (ii), (iii), (iv)
    (c) (i), (ii), (iv)   (d) (i), (iii), (iv)

29. Which one of the following vitamins is essential for coagulation of blood?
    (a) Vitamin - A   (b) Vitamin - B12
    (c) Vitamin - K   (d) Vitamin - D

30. Gypsum ($CaSO_4.2H_2O$) is added to clinker during cement manufacturing to
    (a) decrease the rate of setting of cement
    (b) bind the particle of calcium silicate
    (c) facilitate the formation of colloidal gel
    (d) impact strength to cement

31. The elements B, S and Ge are
    (a) non-metals
    (b) metalloids
    (c) metals
    (d) metal, non-metal and metalloid respectively

32. Which of the following statements is not correct with respect to the trend while going from left to right across the periods of the periodic table?
    (a) The elements become less metallic in nature.
    (b) The number of valence electrons increases.
    (c) The atoms lose their electrons more easily.
    (d) The oxides become more acidic.

33. Which is the first member of alkyne homologous series?
    (a) Methane   (b) Propane
    (c) Ethene   (d) Ethyne

34. The general formula of esters is
    (a) ROR   (b) RCOR
    (c) R-COOH   (d) RCOOR

35. The pH of fresh milk is 6. When it turns sour, the pH
    (a) becomes < 6   (b) remains the same i.e., 6
    (c) becomes > 6   (d) becomes neutral, i.e., 7

36. Sodium stearate is a salt and is used
    (a) in gunpowder   (b) in paint
    (c) to make soap   (d) to make fertilizer

37. Two thick layers of white fur are present as an adaptive feature in
    (a) Polar bear   (b) Arctic hare
    (c) Penguin   (d) Fish

38. Conversion of sugar into alcohol by yeast is
    (a) Pasteurisation   (b) Sterilization
    (c) Fermentation   (d) *Protozoan*

39. In cells, food combines with oxygen and releases
    (a) Energy   (b) Water
    (c) Carbon dioxide   (d) All of these

40. Which one of the following is a cause of soil erosion?
    (a) Heavy rain   (b) Drought
    (c) Overgrazing   (d) All of these

RESPONSE GRID

18. ⓐⓑⓒⓓ	19. ⓐⓑⓒⓓ	20. ⓐⓑⓒⓓ	21. ⓐⓑⓒⓓ	22. ⓐⓑⓒⓓ
23. ⓐⓑⓒⓓ	24. ⓐⓑⓒⓓ	25. ⓐⓑⓒⓓ	26. ⓐⓑⓒⓓ	27. ⓐⓑⓒⓓ
28. ⓐⓑⓒⓓ	29. ⓐⓑⓒⓓ	30. ⓐⓑⓒⓓ	31. ⓐⓑⓒⓓ	32. ⓐⓑⓒⓓ
33. ⓐⓑⓒⓓ	34. ⓐⓑⓒⓓ	35. ⓐⓑⓒⓓ	36. ⓐⓑⓒⓓ	37. ⓐⓑⓒⓓ
38. ⓐⓑⓒⓓ	39. ⓐⓑⓒⓓ	40. ⓐⓑⓒⓓ		

41. Actual gas exchange takes place in the
    (a) trachea (b) bronchi
    (c) larynx (d) alveoli

42. A list of endangered species of wildlife in India is topped by
    (a) Tiger (b) Lion
    (c) White tiger (d) Alligators

43. Which one of the following brings oxygen-rich blood from the heart to the other parts of the body?
    (a) Vein (b) Artery
    (c) Capillary (d) Venules

44. Hydrochloric acid is present in
    (a) Stomach (b) Small intestine
    (c) Large intestine (d) Liver

45. The path that leads from the throat to the lungs is known as
    (a) Trachea (b) Oesophagus
    (c) Epiglottis (d) Larynx

46. Puberty in males is reached at the age of
    (a) 10 years (b) 15 years
    (c) 18 years (d) 21 years

47. Which one of the following is not the method of vegetative propagation?
    (a) Fragmentation (b) Cutting
    (c) Grafting (d) Tissue culture

48. Raising both, plant crop and livestock on farm is called
    (a) Mixed farming (b) Intercropping
    (c) Mixed cropping (d) Rotation of crops

49. Which tree out of the following is not a source of timber?
    (a) Neem (b) Pine
    (c) Teak (d) Sal

50. The master gland in human beings is
    (a) Thyroid (b) Pituitary
    (c) Adrenal (d) Pancreas

51. Find the value of $(0.\dot{6}\dot{3} + 0.\dot{3}\dot{7})$.
    (a) 1/3 (b) 100/99
    (c) 99/100 (d) 100/33

52. The value of $\left[\dfrac{1}{\sqrt{9}-\sqrt{8}}\right]-\left[\dfrac{1}{\sqrt{8}-\sqrt{7}}\right]+\left[\dfrac{1}{\sqrt{7}-\sqrt{6}}\right]$
    $-\left[\dfrac{1}{\sqrt{6}-\sqrt{5}}\right]+\left[\dfrac{1}{\sqrt{5}-\sqrt{4}}\right]$ is
    (a) 6 (b) 5 (c) −7 (d) −6

53. The greatest number which will divide 116, 221, 356 leaving the same remainder in each case is
    (a) 15 (b) 5
    (c) 10 (d) 20

54. The value of $\dfrac{1}{4+\dfrac{1}{4+\dfrac{1}{4+...}}}$ is
    (a) 0.351 (b) 0.452
    (c) 1.258 (d) 0.235

55. Find the value of $\sqrt{2+\sqrt{2+\sqrt{2+\dots\dots\dots}}}$
    (a) 2 (b) − 1
    (c) Both (a) and (b) (d) None of these

56. The third proportional to $\sqrt{3}+1$, $\sqrt{3}+2$ is
    (a) $\dfrac{5+3\sqrt{3}}{2}$ (b) $\dfrac{3+5\sqrt{3}}{2}$
    (c) $\dfrac{3+3\sqrt{3}}{2}$ (d) $\dfrac{5+5\sqrt{3}}{2}$

57. The ratio of the number of boys and girls in a college of 441 students is 5 : 4. How many girls should join the college so that the ratio becomes 1 : 1?
    (a) 50 (b) 49
    (c) 320 (d) 94

58. 5 men and 6 boys finish a piece of work in 4 days; 4 men and 3 boys in 6 days. In how many days would 3 men and 6 boys finish the same work?
    (a) 5 days (b) $\dfrac{36}{7}$ days
    (c) 4 days (d) $\dfrac{29}{7}$ days

59. Pipes A and B can fill a cistern in 10 and 12 hours respectively and pipe C can empty it in 6 hours. If all the three are simultaneously opened, then the time required for the tank to be full is
    (a) 20 hours (b) 60 hours
    (c) 80 hours (d) 40 hours

60. A can finish a work in 24 hours, B in 40 hours and C in 60 hours. They all begin together but A alone continues to work till the end, while B leaves 2 hours and C leaves 7 hours before completion. In what time is the work finished?
    (a) 10 hours (b) 12 hours
    (c) 14 hours (d) 16 hours

61. Select the related word from the given alternates

Spider : Insect : : Crocodile : ?

(a) Reptile   (b) Mammal

(c) Frog   (d) Carnivore

62. In below question four words have been given out of which three are alike in some manner and the fourth one is different. Choose out the odd one

(a) Sailor   (b) Tailor

(c) Goldsmith   (d) Blacksmith

63. Find out right letters for the questions marks :
A M B N E I F J C O D P G K ??

(a) M N   (b) L M

(c) I E   (d) None of these

64. Find the wrong number in the series. 6, 9, 15, 22, 51, 99

(a) 99   (b) 51   (c) 22   (d) 15

65. If MOTHER is coded as 'NPUIFS' select the appropriate code from the answer choices, for the word in capital letters: ZENITH

(a) AFOGHJ   (b) BGPKVJ

(c) AFOJUI   (d) AFOGHI

66. If AEIOU is written as BCJMV, how XCKYB can be written in that code?

(a) YALWC   (b) ADNZE

(c) YELAC   (d) YBLXC

67. Introducing Kamla, Mahesh said : His father is the only son of my father. How was Mahesh related to Kamla ?

(a) Brother   (b) Father

(c) Uncle   (d) Son

68. Siddharth and Murali go for jogging from the same point. Siddharth goes towards the east covering 4 kms. Murali proceeds towards the West for 3 kms. Siddharth turns left and covers 4 kms and Murali turns to the right to cover 4 kms. Now what will be the distance between Siddharth and Murali?

(a) 14 kms   (b) 6 kms

(c) 8 kms   (d) 7 kms

69. A meaningful word starting with R is made from the first, second, fourth, fifth and eighth letters of the word CREATIVE. Which of the following is the middle letter of the word?

(a) E   (b) T

(c) C   (d) A

70. If the day after tomorrow is Sunday, what day was tomorrow's day before yesterday?

(a) Friday   (b) Thursday

(c) Monday   (d) Tuesday

71. A's annual income is reduced from Rs.75,000 to Rs.60,000, while B's income is increased from Rs.60,000 to Rs.75,000. The percentage of decrease in A's income to the percentage of increase in B's income as a percentage is

(a) 125%   (b) 75%

(c) 133%   (d) 80%

72. The distance between two stations A & B is 300 km. A train leaves from the station A with speed 30 kmph. At the same time another train leaves from the station B with speed 45 kmph. The distance of the point where both the trains meet, from the point A is

(a) 100 km   (b) 120 km

(c) 180 km   (d) 200 km

73. Against a stream running at 2 km/ hr, a man can row 9 km in 3 hours. How long would he take in rowing the same distance down the stream?

(a) 9/7 hours   (b) 7/9 hours

(c) 1.5 hours   (d) 3 hours

74. The number of bricks, each measuring 25 cm × 12.5 cm × 7.5 cm, needed to construct a wall 12 m long, 2 m high and 46.2 cm thick, is

(a) 4731   (b) 2304

(c) 9216   (d) 6912

75. The area of a right angled isosceles triangle whose hypotenuse is equal to 270 m is

(a) $19000 \, m^2$ (b) $18225 \, m^2$

(c) $17256 \, m^2$ (d) $18325 \, m^2$

Max. Marks : 75   **No. of Qs. 75**   **Time : 60 min.**   **Date :** ..../........./................

1. Which of the following commissions is not a Constitutional body?
   (a) Union Public Service Commission
   (b) Staff Selection Commission
   (c) Election Commission
   (d) Finance Commission

2. National Income in India is estimated by the
   (a) product and income methods
   (b) product method
   (c) income method
   (d) expenditure method

3. Gandhara art was the combination of
   (a) Indian and Persian styles of sculptures
   (b) Indian and Chinese styles of sculptures
   (c) Indian and Greek styles of sculptures
   (d) None of these

4. Mohammed Gawan was a famous Wazir and Vakil in the kingdom of
   (a) Mysore   (b) Bahmani
   (c) Gujarat   (d) Kashmir

5. Duncan Passage separates
   (a) Little Andamans and Car Nicobar Islands
   (b) North and Middle Andamans
   (c) Middle and South Andamans
   (d) South Andamkans and Little Andamans

6. The President of India has the discretionary power to
   (a) impose President's Rule in a state
   (b) appoint the Prime Minister
   (c) appoint the Chief Election Commissioner
   (d) declare Financial Emergency

7. The script of the Indus Valley Civilization is
   (a) Kharosthi   (b) Undeciphered
   (c) Brahmi   (d) Tamil

8. Which one of the following literary pieces was written by Krishna Devaraya?
   (a) Kaviraja Marga   (b) Ushaparinayam
   (c) Anukta Malyada   (d) Katha Saristhaga

9. Name three important forms of Satyagraha.
   (a) Non-cooperation, civil disobedience and boycott
   (b) Boycott, civil disobedience and rebellion
   (c) Non-cooperation, revolution and referendum
   (d) Revolution, plediscite and boycott

10. When the East India Company was formed, the Mughal emperor in India was
    (a) Jehangir   (b) Humayun
    (c) Aurangzeb   (d) Akbar

11. Which one of the following events did not take place during the Viceroyalty of Lord Curzon?
    (a) Establishment of the Department of Archaeology
    (b) Second Delhi Durbar
    (c) Formation of Indian National Congress
    (d) Partition of Bengal

12. Who among the following played a prominent role during the "Reign of Terror" in France?
    (a) Voltaire   (b) Marat
    (c) Robespierre   (d) Montesquieu

13. The famous slogan 'No taxation without representation' has been taken from :
    (a) French Revolution
    (b) British Civil war
    (c) Indian National Movement
    (d) American war of indep-en-dence

14. Who amongst the following is known as the father of the Russian Revolution?
    (a) Karenski   (b) Trotsky
    (c) Karl Marx   (d) Lenin

15. In which session, did Congress declare 'Purna Swaraj' as, its goal–
    (a) Lahore session, 1929   (b) Nagpur session, 1920
    (c) Allahabad session, 1942 (d) Wardha session, 1942

16. Kerosene oil rises up in a wick of a lantern because of
    (a) Diffusion of the oil through the wick
    (b) Surface tension
    (c) Buoyant force of air
    (d) the gravitational pull of the wick

17. A solid ball of metal has a spherical cavity inside it. The ball is heated. The volume of cavity will
    (a) decrease
    (b) increase
    (c) remain unchanged
    (d) have its shape changed

18. Which of the following is not a unit of time?
    (a) solar year   (b) tropical year
    (c) leap year   (d) light year

19. When light is refracted into a medium,
    (a) Its wavelength and frequency both increase
    (b) Its wavelength increases but frequency remains unchanged
    (c) Its wavelength decreases but frequency remains unchanged
    (d) Its wavelength and frequency both decrease
20. The device used for producing electric current is called a
    (a) generator   (b) galvanometer
    (c) ammeter   (d) motor
21. When current is passed through an electric bulb, its filament glows, but the wire leading current to the bulb does not glow because
    (a) less current flows in the leading wire as compared to that in the filament
    (b) the leading wire has more resistance than the filament
    (c) the leading wire has less resistance than the filament
    (d) filament has coating of fluorescent material over it
22. Wrist watches are made antimagnetic by shielding their machinery with
    (a) plastic sheets
    (b) a metal of high conductivity
    (c) a magnetic substance of low permeability
    (d) a magnetic substance of high permeability
23. An object will continue moving uniformly when
    (a) the resultant force on it is increasing continuously
    (b) the resultant force is at right angles to its rotation
    (c) the resultant force on it is zero
    (d) the resultant force on it begins to decrease
24. In ordinary talk, the amplitude of vibration is approximately
    (a) 10^{-12} m   (b) 10^{-11} m
    (c) 10^{-8} m   (d) 10^{-7} m
25. A block of metal weighs 5 N in air and 2 N when immeresed in a liquid. The buoyant force is
    (a) 3 N   (b) 5 N
    (c) 7 N   (d) zero
26. The bulk modulus of a perfectly rigid body, is equal to
    (a) Infinity   (b) Zero
    (c) Some finite value (d) Non-zero constant
27. Magnification produced by a rear view mirror fitted in vehicles
    (a) is less than one
    (b) is more than one
    (c) is equal to one
    (d) can be more than or less than one depending upon the position of the object in front of it.
28. A bimetallic strip consists of brass and iron. When it is heated it bends into an arc with brass on the convex and iron on the concave side of the arc. This happens because
    (a) brass has a higher specific heat capacity than iron
    (b) density of brass is more than that of iron
    (c) it is easier to bend an iron strip than a brass strip of the same size
    (d) brass has a higher coefficient of linear expansion than iron

29. Before jumping in water from above a swimmer bends his body to
    (a) Increase moment of inertia
    (b) Decrease moment of inertia
    (c) Decrease the angular momentum
    (d) Reduce the angular velocity
30. Which one of the following heating element is used in electric press?
    (a) copper wire   (b) nichrome wire
    (c) lead wire   (d) iron wire
31. Which of the following processes will not produce new magnetic poles?
    (a) cutting a bar magnet in half
    (b) turning on a current in a solenoid
    (c) running a current through a straight wire
    (d) placing an iron rod in contact with a magnet
32. The intrinsic semiconductor becomes an insulator at
    (a) 0°C   (b) 0 K
    (c) 300 K   (d) –100°C
33. No matter how far you stand from a mirror, your image appears erect. The mirror may be
    (a) plane   (b) concave
    (c) convex   (d) none of these
34. When a potential difference is applied across the ends of a linear-metallic conductor:
    (a) the free electrons are set in motion from their position of rest
    (b) the free electrons are accelerated continuously from the lower potential end to the higher potential end of the conductor
    (c) the free electrons acquire a constant drift velocity from the lower potential end to the higher potential end of the conductor
    (d) the vibrating atomic ions in the conductor start vibrating more vigorously
35. Out of gravitational, electrostatic, vander waal and nuclear forces, which are able to provide attractive force between two neutrons
    (a) electrostatic and gravitational
    (b) electrostatic and nuclear
    (c) vander waal and nuclear
    (d) nuclear and gravitational
36. Which of the following must be known in order to determine the power output of an automobile?
    (a) Final velocity and height
    (b) Mass and amount of work performed
    (c) Force exerted and distance of motion
    (d) Work performed and elapsed time of work
37. When ice water is heated,
    (a) its volume first decreases then increases
    (b) its density decreases
    (c) its density first increases, then decreases
    (d) its density first decreases, then increases

38. Whenever the magnetic flux linked with a coil changes, an induced e.m.f.is produced in the circuit. The e.m.f. lasts
    (a) for a short time
    (b) for a long time
    (c) for ever
    (d) so long as the change in flux takes place

39. A motor starter has a
    (a) Variable resistance
    (b) Variable capacitance
    (c) Variable inductance
    (d) Both (a) and (b)

40. A person looking at a mesh of crossed wires is able to see the vertical wires more distinctly than the horizontal wires. This problem is due to
    (a) myopia
    (b) hypermetropia
    (c) astigmatism
    (d) cataract

41. The composition of which of the following does not change with temperature :
    (a) compound   (b) true solution
    (c) colloidal solution (d) suspension

42. Shaving cream is a colloidal solution of
    (a) gas in liquid   (b) liquid in liquid
    (c) solid in liquid   (d) gas in solid.

43. Law of definite proportion was given by :
    (a) John Dalton   (b) Lavoisier
    (c) Joseph Proust   (d) Ritcher

44. Which of the following elements have the same number of protons and neutrons in their atom?
    (a) hydrogen   (b) beryllium
    (c) carbon   (d) nitrogen

45. Who proposed the "Law of Octaves"?
    (a) John Newlands
    (b) J.W.Dobereiner
    (c) Lothar Meyer
    (d) Both (a) and (c)

46. Baking powder is a mixture of $NaHCO_3$ and :
    (a) Ascorbic acid   (b) Tartaric acid
    (c) Citric acid   (d) Formic acid

47. The reaction $Pb(OH)_2 + HNO_3 \rightarrow Pb(OH)NO_3 + H_2O$ shows that $Pb(OH)NO_3$ is :
    (a) an acid salt
    (b) a basic salt
    (c) a base
    (d) an acid

48. An important ore of magnesium is
    (a) malachite   (b) cassiterite
    (c) carnallite   (d) galena

49. The most commonly used in the pure form or as an alloy in domestic appliances is
    (a) aluminium   (b) iron
    (c) copper   (d) zinc

50. Smog is a common pollutant in places having
    (a) High temperature
    (b) Low temperature
    (c) Excessive SO_2 in the air
    (d) Excessive ammonia in the air

51. $\left(\dfrac{147 \times 147 + 147 \times 143 + 143 \times 143}{147 \times 147 \times 147 - 143 \times 143 \times 143} \right) = ?$
    (a) $\dfrac{1}{4}$ (b) 290
    (c) $\dfrac{1}{290}$ (d) 4

52. Find the greatest number that will divide 115, 149 and 183 leaving remainders 3, 5, 7 respectively.
    (a) 14   (b) 16
    (c) 18   (d) 20

53. The largest four-digit number which when divided by 4, 7 and 13 leaves a remainder of 3 in each case,is:
    (a) 8739   (b) 9831
    (c) 9834   (d) 9893

54. The average attendance in a school for the first 4 days of the week is 30 and for the first 5 days of the week is 32. The attendance on the fifth day is
    (a) 32   (b) 40
    (c) 38   (d) 36

55. When the price of a pressure cooker increased by 15%, the sale of pressure cookers decreased by 15%. What was the net effect on the sales?
    (a) 15% decrease   (b) no effect
    (c) 2.25% increase   (d) 2.25% decrease

56. From the salary of an officer, 10% is deducted as house rent, 20% of the rest, he spends on conveyance, 20% of the rest he pays as income tax and 10% of the balance, he spends on clothes. Then , he is left with ₹ 15,552. Find his total salary.
    (a) ₹25,000   (b) ₹30,000
    (c) ₹35,000   (d) ₹ 40,000

57. The single discount which is equivalent to successive discount of 20%, 15% and 10% is.
    (a) 32.7%   (b) 34.2%
    (c) 36.2%   (d) 38.8%

<table>
<tr><td rowspan="3">RESPONSE GRID</td><td>38. ⓐⓑⓒⓓ</td><td>39. ⓐⓑⓒⓓ</td><td>40. ⓐⓑⓒⓓ</td><td>41. ⓐⓑⓒⓓ</td><td>42. ⓐⓑⓒⓓ</td></tr>
<tr><td>43. ⓐⓑⓒⓓ</td><td>44. ⓐⓑⓒⓓ</td><td>45. ⓐⓑⓒⓓ</td><td>46. ⓐⓑⓒⓓ</td><td>47. ⓐⓑⓒⓓ</td></tr>
<tr><td>48. ⓐⓑⓒⓓ</td><td>49. ⓐⓑⓒⓓ</td><td>50. ⓐⓑⓒⓓ</td><td>51. ⓐⓑⓒⓓ</td><td>52. ⓐⓑⓒⓓ</td></tr>
<tr><td></td><td>53. ⓐⓑⓒⓓ</td><td>54. ⓐⓑⓒⓓ</td><td>55. ⓐⓑⓒⓓ</td><td>56. ⓐⓑⓒⓓ</td><td>57. ⓐⓑⓒⓓ</td></tr>
</table>

58. A person sells 36 oranges per rupee and suffers a loss of 4%. Find how many oranges per rupee to be sold to have a gain of 8%?
   (a) 30   (b) 31   (c) 32   (d) 33

59. A man sold two steel chairs for ₹ 500 each. On one he gains 20% and on other, he loses 12%. How much does he gain or lose in the whole transaction?
   (a) 1.5% gain   (b) 2% gain
   (c) 1.5% loss   (d) 2% loss

60. For a certain article, if discount is 25%, the profit is 25%. If the discount is 10%, then the profit is
   (a) 10%   (b) 20%   (c) 35%   (d) 50%

61. Divide ₹ 671 among A, B, C such that if their shares be increased by ₹ 3, ₹ 7 and ₹ 9 respectively, the remainder shall be in the ratio 1 : 2 : 3.
   (a) ₹112, ₹223, ₹336   (b) ₹114, ₹221, ₹336
   (c) ₹112, ₹227, ₹332   (d) ₹114, ₹223, ₹334

62. A and B together can do a job in 12 days. B alone can finish it in 28 days. In how many days can A alone finish the work?
   (a) 21 days   (b) 19 days
   (c) 20 days   (d) None of these

63. A can finish a work in 18 days and B can do the same work in half the time taken by A. Then, working together, what part of the same work they can finish in a day?
   (a) $\dfrac{1}{6}$ (b) $\dfrac{1}{9}$
   (c) $\dfrac{2}{5}$ (d) $\dfrac{2}{7}$

64. 12 men complete a work in 18 days. Six days after they had started working, 4 men joined them. How many days will all of them take to complete the remaining work ?
   (a) 10 days   (b) 12 days
   (c) 15 days   (d) 9 days

65. A train does a journey without stoppage in 8 hours, if it had travelled 5 km/h faster, it would have done the journey in 6 hours 40 minutes. Find its original speed.
   (a) 25 km/h   (b) 40 km/h
   (c) 45 km/h   (d) 36.5 km/h

DIRECTIONS (Q.66 & 67): *Select the related letter/word/ number from the given alternatives.*

66. GAME : 71135 : : BIRD : ?
   (a) 41892   (b) 29148
   (c) 29184   (d) 29814

67. 20 : 7980 : : 12 : ?
   (a) 1800   (b) 1717
   (c) 1716   (d) None of these

68. A child is looking for his father. He went 90 m in the East before turning to his right, He went 20 m before turning to his right again to look for his father at his uncle's place 30 m from this point. His father was not there. From here he went 100 m to the North before meeting his father in a street. How for did the son meet his father from the starting point?
   (a) 80 m   (b) 100 m
   (c) 140 m   (d) 260 m

69. From the given alternative words select the one which cannot be formed using the letters of the given word JERUSALEM
   (a) EASE   (b) SALE
   (c) MAIL   (d) RULE

70. In a certain language, SWITH is written as TVJSI, then how will PLANE will be written?
   (a) KQFBM   (b) FMBQM
   (c) QKBMF   (d) RSNOT

71. If REQUEST is written as S2R52TU, then how will ACID be written?
   (a) 1394   (b) IC94
   (c) BDJE   (d) None of these

72. If O = 16, FOR = 42, then what is FRONT equal to?
   (a) 61   (b) 65
   (c) 73   (d) 78

73. In question below given two statements followed by two conclusions numbered I and II. You have seem to be at variance from commonly known facts and then decide which of the given conclusion logically follows from the two given statements, disregarding commonly known facts.
   Statements : All tomatoes are red.
   All grapes are tomatoes.
   Conclusions : I. All grapes are red.
   II. Some tomatoes are grapes.
   (a) Only conclusion I follows
   (b) Only conclusion II follows
   (c) Either conclusion I or II follows
   (d) Both conclusion I and II follow

74. A series is given with one term missing. Choose the correct alternative from the given ones that will complete the series.
   2, 3, 5, 7, 11, ?, 17
   (a) 12   (b) 13
   (c) 14   (d) 15

75. The diagram represent the student who are singers, dancers and poets.

Study the diagram and identify the region which represent the students who are both poets and singers but not dancer.
   (a) P + T + S   (b) T
   (c) T + V + R + S   (d) P + T + U + S

STAGE II
FULL TEST-1

101 SPEED TEST

100

Max. Marks : 100   **No. of Qs. 100**   **Time : 90 min.**   **Date : ..../........./................**

DIRECTIONS (1-2) : *In each of the following questions, select the related letters/word/numbers from the given alternatives.*

1. Fish : Scales : : Bear : ?
   - (a) Feathers
   - (b) Leaves
   - (c) Fur
   - (d) Skin
2. BDAC : FHEG : : NPMO:?
   - (a) RQTS
   - (b) QTRC
   - (c) TRQS
   - (d) RTQS

DIRECTIONS (3-4) : *In each of the following questions, find the odd number / letters/ word from the given alternatives.*

3. (a) Prod
   - (b) Sap
   - (c) Jab
   - (d) Thrust
4. (a) JKOP
   - (b) MNST
   - (c) CABD
   - (d) OPWX

DIRECTIONS: *Arrange the following words as per order in the dictionary.*

5. Which one-set of letters when sequentially placed at the gaps in the given letter series shall complete it?
   __cb__cab__baca__cba__ab
   - (a) cabcb
   - (b) abccb
   - (c) bacbc
   - (d) bcaba
6. 4, 196, 16, 169, ?, 144, 64
   - (a) 21
   - (b) 81
   - (c) 36
   - (d) 32
7. Find the wrong number in the series.
   6, 9, 15, 22, 51, 99
   - (a) 99
   - (b) 51
   - (c) 22
   - (d) 15
8. In a row of girls, Kamala is 9th from the left and Veena is 16th from the right. If they interchange their positions, Kamla becomes 25th from the left. How many girls are there in the row?
   - (a) 34
   - (b) 36
   - (c) 40
   - (d) 41
9. Among her children, Ganga's favourites are Ram and Rekh(a) Rekha is the mother of Sharat, who is loved most by his uncle Mithun. The head of the family is Ram Lal, who is succeeded by his sons Gopal and Mohan. Gopal and Ganga have been married for 35 years and have 3 children. What is the relation between Mithun and Mohan?
   - (a) Uncle
   - (b) Son
   - (c) Brother
   - (d) No relation
10. Suresh was born on 4th October 1999. Shashikanth was born 6 days before Suresh. The Independence Day of that year fell on Sunday. Which day was Shashikanth born?
    - (a) Tuesday
    - (b) Wednesday
    - (c) Monday
    - (d) Sunday
11. Five boys A, B, C, (d) E are sitting in a park in a circle. A is facing South-West, D is facing South-East, B and E are right opposite A and D respectively and C is equidistant between D and (b) Which direction is C facing'?
    - (a) West
    - (b) South
    - (c) North
    - (d) East
12. In a certain office, $\frac{1}{3}$ of the workers are women, $\frac{1}{2}$ of the women are married and $\frac{1}{3}$ of the married women have children. If $\frac{3}{4}$ of the men are married and $\frac{2}{3}$ of the married men have children, then what part of workers are without children?
    - (a) $\frac{5}{18}$
    - (b) $\frac{4}{9}$
    - (c) $\frac{11}{18}$
    - (d) $\frac{17}{36}$
13. If a man on a moped starts from a point and rides 4 km South, then turns left and rides 2 km to turn again to the right to ride 4 km more, towards which direction is he moving?
    - (a) North
    - (b) West
    - (c) East
    - (d) South
14. If in a certain code HYDROGEN is written as JCJZYSSD, then how can ANTIMONY be written in that code?
    - (a) CPVKOQPA
    - (b) CRZQWABO
    - (c) ERXMQSRC
    - (d) GTZOSUTE

	1. ⓐⓑⓒⓓ	2. ⓐⓑⓒⓓ	3. ⓐⓑⓒⓓ	4. ⓐⓑⓒⓓ	5. ⓐⓑⓒⓓ
RESPONSE GRID	6. ⓐⓑⓒⓓ	7. ⓐⓑⓒⓓ	8. ⓐⓑⓒⓓ	9. ⓐⓑⓒⓓ	10. ⓐⓑⓒⓓ
	11. ⓐⓑⓒⓓ	12. ⓐⓑⓒⓓ	13. ⓐⓑⓒⓓ	14. ⓐⓑⓒⓓ	

15. If DELHI is coded as 73541 and CALCUTTA as 82589662, then how can CALICUT be coded?
    (a) 5279431   (b) 5978013
    (c) 8251896   (d) 8543691

DIRECTION : *In each of the following questions. Select the missing number from the given responses.*

16.

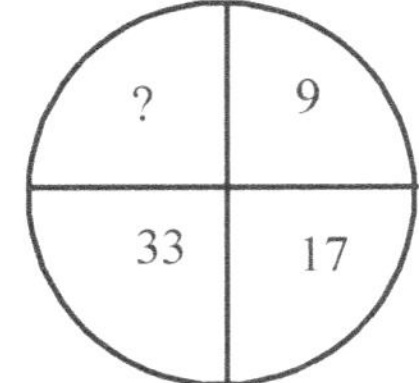

    (a) 60   (b) 68
    (c) 55   (d) 65

17. If '−' stands for '÷' '+' stands for '×' , '÷' for '−' and '×' for '+', which one of the following equations in correct?
    (a) $30 - 6 + 5 \times 4 \div 2 = 27$
    (b) $30 + 6 - 5 \div 4 \times 2 = 30$
    (c) $30 \times 6 \div 5 - 4 + 2 = 32$
    (d) $30 \div 6 \times 5 + 4 - 2 = 40$

18. Some equations have been solved on the basis of a certain system. Find the correct answer for the unsolved equation on that basis. If $9 * 7 = 32$, $13 * 7 = 120$, $17 * 9 = 208$, then $19 * 11 = ?$
    (a) 150   (b) 180
    (c) 210   (d) 240

19. If MEKLF is coded as 91782 and LLLJK as 88867, then how can IGHED be coded?
    (a) 97854   (b) 64521
    (c) 53410   (d) 75632

20. Shan is 55 years old, Sathian is 5 years junior to Shan and 6 years senior to Balan. The youngest brother of Balan is Devan and he is 7 years junior to him. So what is the age difference between Devan and Shan?
    (a) 18 years   (b) 15 years
    (c) 13 years   (d) 7 years

21. Vinod introduces Vishal as the son of the only brother of his father's wife. How is Vinod related to Vishal?
    (a) Cousin   (b) Brother
    (c) Son   (d) Uncle

22. If John celebrated his victory day on Tuesday, 5th January 1965, when will he celebrate his next victory day on the same day?
    (a) 5th January 1970   (b) 5th January 1971
    (c) 5th January 1973   (d) 5th January 1974

23. Five girls M, N, O, P and Q are standing in a row. p is on the right of Q, N is on the left of Q, but is on the right of M, P is on the left of O. Who is standing on the extreme right?
    (a) Q   (b) N
    (c) O   (d) P

24. Sita is elder than Swapn(a) Lavanya is elder than Swapna but younger than Sit(a) Suvarna is younger than both Hari and Swapna, Swapna is elder than Hari. Who is the youngest ?
    (a) Sita   (b) Lavanya
    (c) Suvarna   (d) Hari

25. If in a certain code, RAMAYANA is written as PYKYWYLY, then how MAHABHARATA can be written in that code?
    (a) NBIBCIBSBUB   (b) LZGZAGZQZSZ
    (c) MCJCDJCTCVC   (d) KYFYZFYPYRY

26. If the sum of two numbers be multiplied by each number separately, the products so obtained are 247 and 114. The sum of the numbers is
    (a) 19   (b) 20
    (c) 21   (d) 23

27. The L.(c)M. of three different numbers is 120. Which of the following *cannot* be their H.(c)F.?
    (a) 8   (b) 12
    (c) 24   (d) 35

28. A number when divided by 49 leaves 32 as remainder. This number when divided by 7 will have the remainder as
    (a) 4   (b) 3
    (c) 2   (d) 5

29. In an examination a student scores 4 marks for every correct answer and loses 1 mark for every wrong answer. If he attempts all 75 questions and secures 125 marks, the number of questions he attempts correctly is
    (a) 35   (b) 40
    (c) 42   (d) 46

30. A copper wire is bent in the shape of a square of area 81 cm^2. If the same wire is bent form of a semicircle, the radius (in cm) of the semicircle is

    (Take $\pi = \dfrac{22}{7}$)

    (a) 16   (b) 14
    (c) 10   (d) 7

31. A bicycle wheel makes 5000 revolutions in moving 11 km. Then the radius of the wheel (in cm) is

    (Take $\pi = \dfrac{22}{7}$)

    (a) 70   (b) 35
    (c) 17.5   (d) 140

<table>
<tr><td rowspan="4">RESPONSE
GRID</td><td>15. ⓐⓑⓒⓓ</td><td>16. ⓐⓑⓒⓓ</td><td>17. ⓐⓑⓒⓓ</td><td>18. ⓐⓑⓒⓓ</td><td>19. ⓐⓑⓒⓓ</td></tr>
<tr><td>20. ⓐⓑⓒⓓ</td><td>21. ⓐⓑⓒⓓ</td><td>22. ⓐⓑⓒⓓ</td><td>23. ⓐⓑⓒⓓ</td><td>24. ⓐⓑⓒⓓ</td></tr>
<tr><td>25. ⓐⓑⓒⓓ</td><td>26. ⓐⓑⓒⓓ</td><td>27. ⓐⓑⓒⓓ</td><td>28. ⓐⓑⓒⓓ</td><td>29. ⓐⓑⓒⓓ</td></tr>
<tr><td>30. ⓐⓑⓒⓓ</td><td>31. ⓐⓑⓒⓓ</td><td></td><td></td><td></td></tr>
</table>

32. A shopkeeper allows a discount of 10% to his customers and still gains. 20%. Find the marked price of the article which costs ₹ 450.
   (a) ₹ 600   (b) ₹ 540
   (c) ₹ 660   (d) ₹ 580
33. What single discount is equivalent to two successive discounts of 20% and 15%?
   (a) 35%   (b) 32%
   (c) 34%   (d) 30%
34. What number should be added to or subtracted from each term of the ratio 17 : 24 so that it becomes equal to 1 : 2?
   (a) 5 is subtracted   (b) 10 is added
   (c) 7 is added   (d) 10 is subtracted
35. The ratio of weekly incomes of A and B is 9 : 7 and the ratio of their expenditures is 4 : 3. If each saves ₹ 200 per week, then the sum of their weekly incomes is
   (a) ₹ 3,600   (b) ₹ 4,200
   (c) ₹ 4,800   (d) ₹ 5,600
36. The mean of 50 numbers is 30. Later it was discovered that two entries were wrongly entered as 82 and 13 instead of 28 and 31. Find the correct mean.
   (a) 36.12   (b) 30.66
   (c) 29.28   (d) 38.21
37. The cost price of an article is 40% of the selling price. What percent of the cost price is the selling price?
   (a) 140%   (b) 200%
   (c) 220%   (d) 250%
38. If 90% of A = 30% of B and B = 2x % of A, then the value of x is
   (a) 450   (b) 400
   (c) 300   (d) 150
39. When the price of sugar decreases by 10%, a man could buy 1 kg more for ₹ 270. Then the original price of sugar per kg is
   (a) ₹ 25   (b) ₹ 30
   (c) ₹ 27   (d) ₹ 32
40. If the price of sugar is raised by 25%, find by how much percent a householder must reduce his consumption of sugar so as not to increase his expenditure?
   (a) 10   (b) 20
   (c) 18   (d) 25
41. The simple interest on a sum for 5 years is one fourth of the sum. The rate of interest per annum is
   (a) 5%   (b) 6%
   (c) 4%   (d) 8%
42. X sells two articles for ₹ 4,000 each with no loss and no gain in the interaction. If one was sold at a gain of 25% the other is sold at a loss of
   (a) 25%   (b) $18\frac{2}{9}\%$
   (c) $16\frac{2}{3}\%$ (d) 20%

43. A reduction of 20% in the price of sugar enables me to purchase 5 kg more for ₹ 600. Find the price of sugar per kg before reduction of price.
   (a) ₹ 24   (b) ₹ 30
   (c) ₹ 32   (d) ₹ 36
44. First and second numbers are less than a third number by 30% and 37% respectively. The second number is less than the first by
   (a) 7%   (b) 4%
   (c) 3%   (d) 10%
45. The least number, which is to be added to the greatest number of 4 digits so that the sum may be divisible by 345, is
   (a) 50   (b) 6
   (c) 60   (d) 5
46. The sum of two numbers is 24 and their product is 143. The sum of their squares is
   (a) 296   (b) 295
   (c) 290   (d) 228
47. L.(c)M. of two numbers is 120 and their H.(c)F. is 10. Which of the following can be the sum of those two numbers?
   (a) 140   (b) 80
   (c) 60   (d) 70
48. A student was asked to divide a number by 6 and add 12 to the quotient. He, however, first added 12 to the number and then divided it by 6, getting 112 as the answer. The correct answer should have been
   (a) 124   (b) 122
   (c) 118   (d) 114
49. The sides of a triangles are in the ratio 2:3:4. the perimeter of the triangle is 18cm. The area (in cm^2) of the triangle is
   (a) 9   (b) 36
   (c) $\sqrt{42}$ (d) $3\sqrt{15}$
50. The cost price of an article is 64% of the marked price. The gain percentage after allowing a discount of 12% on the marked price is
   (a) 37.5%   (b) 48%
   (c) 50.5%   (d) 52%
51. The Drafting of the Constitution was completed on:
   (a) 26th January, 1950
   (b) 26th December, 1949
   (c) 26th November, 1949
   (d) 30th November, 1949
52. The judges of the Supreme Court retire at the age of :
   (a) 60 years   (b) 65 years
   (c) 62 years   (d) 58 years
53. Who among the following British persons admitted the Revolt of 1857 as a national revolt?
   (a) Lord Dalhousie
   (b) Lord Canning
   (c) Lord Ellenborough
   (d) Disraeli

RESPONSE GRID	32. ⓐⓑⓒⓓ	33. ⓐⓑⓒⓓ	34. ⓐⓑⓒⓓ	35. ⓐⓑⓒⓓ	36. ⓐⓑⓒⓓ
	37. ⓐⓑⓒⓓ	38. ⓐⓑⓒⓓ	39. ⓐⓑⓒⓓ	40. ⓐⓑⓒⓓ	41. ⓐⓑⓒⓓ
	42. ⓐⓑⓒⓓ	43. ⓐⓑⓒⓓ	44. ⓐⓑⓒⓓ	45. ⓐⓑⓒⓓ	46. ⓐⓑⓒⓓ
	47. ⓐⓑⓒⓓ	48. ⓐⓑⓒⓓ	49. ⓐⓑⓒⓓ	50. ⓐⓑⓒⓓ	51. ⓐⓑⓒⓓ
	52. ⓐⓑⓒⓓ	53. ⓐⓑⓒⓓ			

54. The lowest layer of the atmosphere is:
    (a) Stratosphere   (b) Thermosphere
    (c) Troposphere   (d) Mesosphere
55. The Konkan Railway connects:
    (a) Goa – Mangalore
    (b) Roha – Mangalore
    (c) Kanyakumari – Mangalore
    (d) Kanyakumari – Mumbai
56. Saliva helps in the digestion of:
    (a) Fats   (b) Starch
    (c) Proteins   (d) Vitamins
57. The longest bone in the human body is:
    (a) Ulna   (b) Humerus
    (c) Femur   (d) Tibia
58. The time period of a pendulum when taken to the Moon would:
    (a) remain the same   (b) decrease
    (c) become zero   (d) increase
59. Which of the following could be used as fuel in propellant or rockets?
    (a) Liquid Hydrogen + Liquid Nitrogen
    (b) Liquid Oxygen + Liquid Argon
    (c) Liquid Nitrogen + Liquid Oxygen
    (d) Liquid Hydrogen + Liquid Oxygen
60. White lung disease is prevalent among the workers of:
    (a) Paper industry   (b) Cement industry
    (c) Cotton industry   (d) Pesticide industry
61. An artificial ecosystem is represented by:
    (a) pisciculture tank   (b) agricultural land
    (c) zoo   (d) aquarium
62. The constituents of automobile exhaust that can cause cancer is are:
    (a) Oxides of nitrogen
    (b) Carbon monoxide
    (c) Polycyclic hydrocarbons
    (d) Lead
63. The optimum dissolved oxygen level (in mg/litre) required for survival of aquatic organisms is:
    (a) 4 – 6   (b) 2 – 4
    (c) 8 – 10   (d) 12 – 16
64. Which of the following folk/tribal dances is associated with Uttar Pradesh?
    (a) Veedhi   (b) Thora
    (c) Tamasha   (d) Rauf
65. Which of the following books has been written by Atiq Rahim?
    (a) Earth and Ashes   (b) This savage Rite
    (c) The red Devil   (d) Witness the Night
66. If a computer has more than one processor then it is known as?
    (a) Uni-processor   (b) Multiprocessor
    (c) Multithreaded   (d) Multiprogramming

67. Where is RAM located?
    (a) Expansion Board   (b) External Drive
    (c) Mother Board   (d) All of above
68. Full form of URL is ?
    (a) Uniform Resource Locator
    (b) Uniform Resource Link
    (c) Uniform Registered Link
    (d) Unified Resource Link
69. Wavelength of infrared radiations is
    (a) zero   (b) finite
    (c) shorter   (d) longer
70. Number of atoms in ozone molecules are
    (a) 2   (b) 3
    (c) 4   (d) 1
71. Layer which saves life from harmful effects of UV radiations is known as
    (a) ozone layer   (b) alpha layer
    (c) gamma layer   (d) infrared layer
72. Under the OSH Act, employers are responsible for providing a ______
    (a) Safe workplace   (b) Land
    (c) Insurance   (d) Estimation
73. Safety and Health Achievement Recognition Program (SHARP) recognizes ______
    (a) Small employers who operate safety and health management system
    (b) Large employers who operate safety and health management system
    (c) All employers who operate safety and health management system
    (d) Workers who operate safety and health management system
74. In the case of fatal accident, when should be a report filed for nearest OSHA office?
    a) Within 24 hours   b) Within 48 hours
    c) Within 8 hours   d) Within 4 hours
75. A seesaw on a playground is an example of what type of simple machine?
    (a) screw   (b) wedge
    (c) lever   (d) wheel and axle
76. Which simple machine is used to hold objects together?
    (a) screw   (b) hammer
    (c) wedge   (d) pulley
77. Which could help a person in a wheelchair get from the street onto the sidewalk?
    (a) wheel and axle   (b) inclined plane
    (c) screw   (d) lever

<table>
<tr><td rowspan="4">RESPONSE GRID</td><td>54. ⓐⓑⓒⓓ</td><td>55. ⓐⓑⓒⓓ</td><td>56. ⓐⓑⓒⓓ</td><td>57. ⓐⓑⓒⓓ</td><td>58. ⓐⓑⓒⓓ</td></tr>
<tr><td>59. ⓐⓑⓒⓓ</td><td>60. ⓐⓑⓒⓓ</td><td>61. ⓐⓑⓒⓓ</td><td>62. ⓐⓑⓒⓓ</td><td>63. ⓐⓑⓒⓓ</td></tr>
<tr><td>64. ⓐⓑⓒⓓ</td><td>65. ⓐⓑⓒⓓ</td><td>66. ⓐⓑⓒⓓ</td><td>67. ⓐⓑⓒⓓ</td><td>68. ⓐⓑⓒⓓ</td></tr>
<tr><td>69. ⓐⓑⓒⓓ</td><td>70. ⓐⓑⓒⓓ</td><td>71. ⓐⓑⓒⓓ</td><td>72. ⓐⓑⓒⓓ</td><td>73. ⓐⓑⓒⓓ</td></tr>
<tr><td></td><td>74. ⓐⓑⓒⓓ</td><td>75. ⓐⓑⓒⓓ</td><td>76. ⓐⓑⓒⓓ</td><td>77. ⓐⓑⓒⓓ</td><td></td></tr>
</table>

78. Which of the following voltmeters should be selected for most accurate reading?
    (a) 100 V, 1 A
    (b) 100 V, 100 ohms/volt
    (c) 100 V, 1 mA
    (d) 100 V, 100 mA

79. Two resistors of 2 k-ohm value each and 1 watt rating are connected in series. The net resistance and wattage value will be
    (a) 4 k-ohm, 2 watt
    (b) 1 k-ohm, ½ watt
    (c) 4 k-ohm, 1 watt
    (d) 2 k-ohm, 2 watt

80. Sheath is used in the cables to
    (a) Prevent the moisture from entering the cable
    (b) Provide the strength to the cable
    (c) Avoid the chances of the rust on the strands
    (d) Provide proper insulation

81. Specific heat is -
    (a) the specific temperature at which the substance is in solid state.
    (b) the energy needed to increase the temperature of 1 gram of a substance by 1 degree Celsius.
    (c) the amount of heat conducted in 1 minute.
    (d) the heat needed to increase the temperature of 1 gallon of water by 1 degree Fahrenheit.

82. How will a metal container full of hot water in vaccum lose heat?
    (a) by conduction
    (b) by convection
    (c) by radiation
    (d) will stay hot for ever

83. A cup of hot tea on a metal table in a room loses heat by
    (a) Conduction
    (b) Convection
    (c) Radiation
    (d) All the above

84. What would happen to a hole in a metal sheet when the sheet is heated?
    (a) It decreases in size
    (b) It increases in size
    (c) No change is seen
    (d) First increases and then decreases

85. Negative acceleration is also known as
    (a) Retardation
    (b) Relaxation
    (c) Escalation
    (d) All of above

86. A car covers a distance of 5 km in 5 mins, its average speed is equal to
    (a) 1 km/h
    (b) 25 km/h
    (c) 60 km/h
    (d) None of above

87. Gradient of a displacement-time graph gives
    (a) Velocity of moving object
    (b) Distance travelled by object
    (c) Acceleration of moving object
    (d) None of above

88. Smallest division on stopwatch is
    (a) 0.1 s
    (b) 0.05 s
    (c) 0.01 s
    (d) 1 s

89. On Earth, gravitational field strength is about
    (a) $20 \, N \, kg^{-1}$
    (b) $10 \, N \, kg^{-1}$
    (c) $15 \, N \, kg^{-1}$
    (d) $30 \, N \, kg$

90. Weight or amount of gravitational force acting on an object is dependent on its
    (a) height
    (b) mass
    (c) shape
    (d) energy

91. A tablet has a mass of 90 g. If g is $10 \, N \, kg^{-1}$, then its weight would be
    (a) 0.9 N
    (b) 900 N
    (c) 90 N
    (d) 9 N

92. Rectagular prism is an example of
    (a) Objects having isometric lines
    (b) Object having non-isometric lines
    (c) Object having curved surfaces
    (d) None of the above

93. The isometric projection of a sphere is a
    (a) Circle
    (b) Ellipse
    (c) Hyperbola
    (d) Parabola

94. The isometric axis are inclined at ___ degree to each other.
    (a) 60
    (b) 90
    (c) 120
    (d) 150

95. The following are the methods for drawing isometric views except
    (a) Box method
    (b) Offset method
    (c) Centre lines method
    (d) Parallel line metho(d)

96. Which tool can be used to draw a 90 degree angle?
    (a) 30/60 triangle
    (b) protractor
    (c) drafting machine
    (d) all of the above

97. A block of ice
    (a) cannot radiate heat
    (b) can radiate heat but cannot absorb heat
    (c) can absorb heat but cannot radiate heat
    (d) can radiate as well as absorb heat

98. The range of normal human hearing is in the range of
    (a) 10 Hz to 80 Hz
    (b) 50 Hz to 80 Hz
    (c) 50Hz to 15000 Hz
    (d) 15000 Hz and above

99. Soap and detergents are the source of organic pollutants like
    (a) glycerol
    (b) polyphosphates
    (c) sulphonated hydrocarbons
    (d) All of these

100. The effects of radioactive pollutants depends upon
    (a) Rate of diffusion
    (b) energy releasing capacity
    (c) rate of deposition of the contaminant
    (d) all of these

<table>
<tr><td rowspan="5">RESPONSE GRID</td><td>78. (a)(b)(c)(d)</td><td>79. (a)(b)(c)(d)</td><td>80. (a)(b)(c)(d)</td><td>81. (a)(b)(c)(d)</td><td>82. (a)(b)(c)(d)</td></tr>
<tr><td>83. (a)(b)(c)(d)</td><td>84. (a)(b)(c)(d)</td><td>85. (a)(b)(c)(d)</td><td>86. (a)(b)(c)(d)</td><td>87. (a)(b)(c)(d)</td></tr>
<tr><td>88. (a)(b)(c)(d)</td><td>89. (a)(b)(c)(d)</td><td>90. (a)(b)(c)(d)</td><td>91. (a)(b)(c)(d)</td><td>92. (a)(b)(c)(d)</td></tr>
<tr><td>93. (a)(b)(c)(d)</td><td>94. (a)(b)(c)(d)</td><td>95. (a)(b)(c)(d)</td><td>96. (a)(b)(c)(d)</td><td>97. (a)(b)(c)(d)</td></tr>
<tr><td>98. (a)(b)(c)(d)</td><td>99. (a)(b)(c)(d)</td><td>100. (a)(b)(c)(d)</td><td></td><td></td></tr>
</table>

STAGE II
FULL TEST-2

101 SPEED TEST

Max. Marks : 100   **No. of Qs. 100**   **Time : 90 min.**   **Date : ..../........./................**

DIRECTIONS (Qs. 1-2) : *In each of the following questions, select the one which is different from the other three responses.*

1. (a) Heat   (b) Light
    (c) Bulb   (d) Electricity
2. (a) Wave   (b) Current
    (c) Tide   (d) Storm
3. Which one set of letters when sequentially placed at the gaps in the given letter series shall complete it ?
    a_b_a__n_bb_abbn
    (a) abnabb   (b) bnbban
    (c) bnbbna   (d) babban
4. Which one number is **wrong** in the given series ?
    126, 98, 70, 41, 14
    (a) 98   (b) 70   (c) 126   (d) 41

DIRECTIONS (Qs. 5-6) : *In each of the following questions, a series is given with one term missing. Choose the correct alternative from the given ones that will complete the series.*

5. 3, 4, 7, 11, 18, 29, _?_
    (a) 31   (b) 39
    (c) 43   (d) 47
6. 975, 864, 753, 642, _?_
    (a) 431   (b) 314   (c) 531   (d) 532
7. Ashok's mother was 3 times as old as Ashok 5 years ago. After 5 years she will be twice as old as Ashok How old is Ashok today ?
    (a) 10 years   (b) 15 years
    (c) 20 years   (d) 25 years
8. M is the son of P. Q is the grand daughter of O who is the husband of P. How is M related to O?
    (a) Son   (b) Daughter
    (c) Mother   (d) Father
9. In a row of boys, Srinath is 7th from the left and Venkat is 12th from the right. If they interchange their positions, Srinath becomes 22nd from the left. How many boys are there in the row ?
    (a) 19   (b) 31   (c) 33   (d) 34

10. If the day before yesterday was Sunday, what day will it be three days after the day after tomorrow ?
    (a) Sunday   (b) Monday
    (c) Wednesday   (d) Saturday
11. If HOSPITAL is written as 32574618 in a certain code, how would POSTAL be written in that code?
    (a) 752618   (b) 725618
    (c) 725168   (d) 725681
12. Find the missing number from the given responses.
    173 (24) 526
    431 (18) 325
    253 (?) 471
    (a) 22   (b) 42   (c) 30   (d) 06
13. After interchanging ÷ and +, 12 and 18, which one of the following equations becomes correct?
    (a) $(90 \times 18) + 18 = 60$ (b) $(18 + 6) \div 12 = 2$
    (c) $(72 \div 18) \times 18 = 72$ (d) $(12 + 6) \times 18 = 36$
14. If SPARK is coded as TQBSL, what will be the code for FLAME?
    (a) GMBNF   (b) GNBNF
    (c) GMCND   (d) GMBMF
15. A child is looking for his father, he went 90 metres in the east before turning to his right. He went 20 metres before turning to his right again to look for his father at his uncle's place 30 metres from this point. His father was not there. From here he went 100 metres to his north before meeting his father in a street. How far did the son meet his father from the starting point ?
    (a) 80m   (b) 100m   (c) 260m   (d) 140m
16. What is the number missing from the third target?

5	9	15
16	29	?
49	89	147

    (a) 45   (b) 48   (c) 51   (d) 54
17. In a classroom, there are 5 rows, and 5 children A, B, C, D and E are seated one behind the other in 5 seperate rows as follows :

<table>
<tr><td rowspan="4">RESPONSE
GRID</td><td>1. ⓐⓑⓒⓓ</td><td>2. ⓐⓑⓒⓓ</td><td>3. ⓐⓑⓒⓓ</td><td>4. ⓐⓑⓒⓓ</td><td>5. ⓐⓑⓒⓓ</td></tr>
<tr><td>6. ⓐⓑⓒⓓ</td><td>7. ⓐⓑⓒⓓ</td><td>8. ⓐⓑⓒⓓ</td><td>9. ⓐⓑⓒⓓ</td><td>10. ⓐⓑⓒⓓ</td></tr>
<tr><td>11. ⓐⓑⓒⓓ</td><td>12. ⓐⓑⓒⓓ</td><td>13. ⓐⓑⓒⓓ</td><td>14. ⓐⓑⓒⓓ</td><td>15. ⓐⓑⓒⓓ</td></tr>
<tr><td>16. ⓐⓑⓒⓓ</td><td>17. ⓐⓑⓒⓓ</td><td></td><td></td><td></td></tr>
</table>

A is sitting behind C, but in front of B.

C is sitting behind E, D is sitting in front of E.

The order in which they are sitting from the first row to the last is

(a) DECAB   (b) BACED

(c) ACBDE   (d) ABEDC

18. K is a place which is located 2 km away in the north-west direction from the capital P, R is another place that is located 2 km away in the south-west direction from K. M is another place and that is located 2 km away in north-west direction from R. T is yet another place that is located 2 km away in the south-west direction from M. In which direction is T located in relation to P?

(a) South-west   (b) North-west

(c) West   (d) North

19. Find out which of the diagrams given in the alternatives correctly represents the relationship stated in the question. Sharks, Whales, Turtles

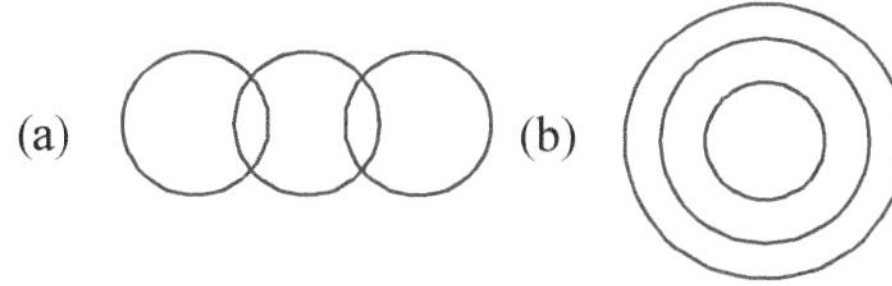

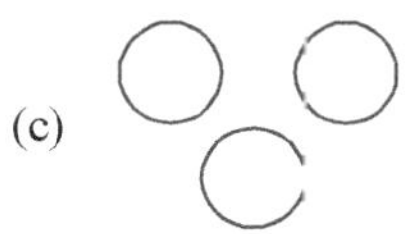

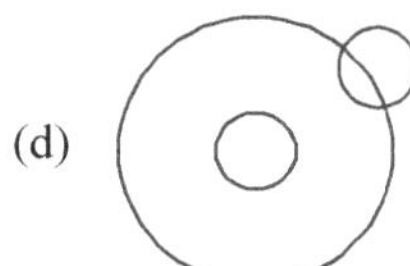

20. If the day after tomorrow is Sunday, what day was tomorrow's day before yesterday?

(a) Friday   (b) Thursday

(c) Monday   (d) Tuesday

21. A man is 3 years older than his wife and four times as old as his son. If the son becomes 15 years old after 3 years, what is the present age of the wife ?

(a) 60 years   (b) 51 years

(c) 48 years   (d) 45 years

22. X and Y are brothers. R is the father of Y. S is the brother of T and maternal uncle of X. What is T to R?

(a) Mother   (b) Wife

(c) Sister   (d) Brother

23. Suresh is 7 ranks ahead of Ashok in the class of 39 students. If Ashok's rank is 17th from the last, what is Suresh's rank from the start ?

(a) 16th   (b) 23th

(c) 24th   (d) 15th

24. If HONESTY is written as 5132468 and POVERTY as 7192068, how is HORSE written in a certain code?

(a) 50124   (b) 51042

(c) 51024   (d) 52014

25. In a certain code SISTER is written as RHRSDQ. How is UNCLE written in that code ?

(a) TMBKD   (b) TBMKD

(c) TVBOD   (d) TMKBD

26. The H.C.F. and L.C.M. of two numebrs are 8 and 48 respectively. If one of the numbers is 24, then the other number is

(a) 48   (b) 36

(c) 24   (d) 16

27. The greatest number, which when subtracted from 5834, gives a number exactly divisible by each of 20, 28, 32 and 35, is

(a) 1120   (b) 4714

(c) 5200   (d) 5600

28. A number, when divided by 114, leaves remainder 21. If the same number is divided by 19, then the remainder will be

(a) 1   (b) 2

(c) 7   (d) 17

29. The number 0.121212.... in the form $\dfrac{p}{q}$ is equal to

(a) $\dfrac{4}{11}$ (b) $\dfrac{2}{11}$

(c) $\dfrac{4}{33}$ (d) $\dfrac{2}{33}$

30. Two numbers are in the ratio 3 : 4. Their L.C.M. is 84. The greater number is

(a) 21   (b) 24

(c) 28   (d) 84

31. A drum of kerosene is $\dfrac{3}{4}$ full. When 30 litres of kerosene is drawn from it, it remains $\dfrac{7}{12}$ full. The capacity of the drum is

(a) 120 l (b) 135 l

(c) 150 l (d) 180 l

32. By what least number should 675 be multiplied so as to obtain a perfect cube number ?

(a) 3   (b) 5

(c) 24   (d) 40

33. If a and b are two odd positive integers, by which of the following integers is $(a^4 - b^4)$ always divisible ?

(a) 3   (b) 6

(c) 8   (d) 12

34. If the ratio of cost price and selling price of an article be as 10 : 11, the percentage of profit is

(a) 8   (b) 10

(c) 11   (d) 15

35. A manufacturer marked an article at Rs. 50 and sold it allowing 20% discount. If his profit was 25% then the cost price of the article was
   (a) Rs. 40
   (b) Rs. 35
   (c) Rs. 32
   (d) Rs. 30

36. A shopkeeper earns a profit of 12% on selling a book at 10% discount on the printed price. The ratio fo the cost price and the printed price of the book is
   (a) 45 : 56
   (b) 45 : 51
   (c) 47 : 56
   (d) 47 : 51

37. By selling a bicycle for ₹ 2,850, Aa shopkeeper gains 14%. If the profit is reduced to 8%, then the selling price will be
   (a) ₹ 2,600
   (b) ₹ 2,700
   (c) ₹ 2,800
   (d) ₹ 3,000

38. If A's income is 50% less than that of B's, then B's income is what per cent mroe than that of A?
   (a) 125
   (b) 100
   (c) 75
   (d) 50

39. Two natural numbers are in the ratio 3 : 5 and their product is 2160. The smaller of the numbers is
   (a) 36
   (b) 24
   (c) 18
   (d) 12

40. If 60% of A = $\dfrac{3}{4}$ of B, then A : B is
   (a) 9 : 20
   (b) 20 : 9
   (c) 4 : 5
   (d) 5 : 4

41. Two successive price increases of 10% and 10% of an article are equivalent to a single price increase of
   (a) 19%
   (b) 20%
   (c) 21%
   (d) 22%

42. An equilateral triangle of side 6 cm has its corners cut off to form a regular hexagon. Area (in cm^2) of this regular hexagon will be
   (a) $3\sqrt{3}$
   (b) $3\sqrt{6}$
   (c) $6\sqrt{3}$
   (d) $\dfrac{5\sqrt{3}}{2}$

43. The length (in metres) of the longest rod that can be put in a room of dimensions 10 m × 10 m × 5 m is
   (a) $15\sqrt{3}$
   (b) 15
   (c) $10\sqrt{2}$
   (d) $5\sqrt{3}$

44. If ₹1000 is divided between A and B in the ratio 3 : 2, then A will receive
   (a) ₹400
   (b) ₹500
   (c) ₹600
   (d) ₹800

45. A sum of money at compound interest doubles itself in 15 years. It will become eight times of itself in
   (a) 45 years
   (b) 48 years
   (c) 54 years
   (d) 60 years

46. If the circumference of a circle is decreased by 50% then the percentage of decrease in its area is
   (a) 25
   (b) 50
   (c) 60
   (d) 75

47. What annual payment will discharge a debt of ₹6,450 due in 4 years at 5% per annum simple interest ?
   (a) ₹1,400
   (b) ₹1,500
   (c) ₹1,550
   (d) ₹1,600

48. The average of the first 100 positive integers is
   (a) 100
   (b) 51
   (c) 50.5
   (d) 49.5

49. In a family, the average age of a father and a mother is 35 years. The average age of the father, mother and their only son is 27 years. What is the age of the son ?
   (a) 12 years
   (b) 11 years
   (c) 10.5 years
   (d) 10 years

50. If 5 men or 7 women can earn ₹ 5,250 per day, how much would 7 men and 13 women earn per day ?
   (a) ₹ 11,600
   (b) ₹ 11,700
   (c) ₹ 16,100
   (d) ₹ 17,100

51. A concave lens always forms an image which is
   (a) real and erect
   (b) virtual and erect
   (c) real and inverted
   (d) virtual and inverted

52. A vitamin requires cobalt for its activity. The vitamin is
   (a) Vitamin B_{12}
   (b) Vitamin D
   (c) Vitamin B_2
   (d) Vitamin A

53. One of the constituents of tear gas is
   (a) Ethane
   (b) Ethanol
   (c) Ether
   (d) Chloropicrin

54. The propagation of sound waves in a gas involves
   (a) adiabatic compression and refraction
   (b) isothermal compression and rarefaction
   (c) isochoric compression and rarefaction
   (d) isobaric compression and rarefaction

55. Plasma membrane in eukaryotic celle is made up of
   (a) Phospholipid
   (b) Lipoprotein
   (c) Phospholpo-protein
   (d) Phospho-protein

56. Which one of the following is also called the 'power plants' of the cell ?
   (a) Golgi body
   (b) Mitochondrion
   (c) Ribosome
   (d) Lysosome

57. Which of the following is not a property of heavy water ?
   (a) Boiling point of heavy water is lower than that of ordinary water
   (b) Density of heavy water is higher than that of ordinary water
   (c) Freezing point of heavy water is higher than that of ordinary water
   (d) It produces corrosion

RESPONSE

35. ⓐⓑⓒⓓ	36. ⓐⓑⓒⓓ	37. ⓐⓑⓒⓓ	38. ⓐⓑⓒⓓ	39. ⓐⓑⓒⓓ
40. ⓐⓑⓒⓓ	41. ⓐⓑⓒⓓ	42. ⓐⓑⓒⓓ	43. ⓐⓑⓒⓓ	44. ⓐⓑⓒⓓ
45. ⓐⓑⓒⓓ	46. ⓐⓑⓒⓓ	47. ⓐⓑⓒⓓ	48. ⓐⓑⓒⓓ	49. ⓐⓑⓒⓓ
50. ⓐⓑⓒⓓ	51. ⓐⓑⓒⓓ	52. ⓐⓑⓒⓓ	53. ⓐⓑⓒⓓ	54. ⓐⓑⓒⓓ
55. ⓐⓑⓒⓓ	56. ⓐⓑⓒⓓ	57. ⓐⓑⓒⓓ		

58. Heat transfer horizontally within the atmosphere is called
    (a) Conduction (b) Convection
    (c) Absorption (d) Advection
59. Who is rightly called the "Father of Local Self Government" in India ?
    (a) Lord Mayo (b) Lord Ripon
    (c) Lord Curzon (d) Lord Clive
60. The Directive Principles of State Policy was adopted from the
    (a) British Constitution (b) Swiss Constitution
    (c) U.S. Constitution (d) Irish Constitution
61. The Prime Minister of India is
    (a) Elected (b) Appointed
    (c) Nominated (d) Selected
62. The monetary policy is India is formulated by
    (a) Central Government
    (b) Industrial Financial Corporation of India
    (c) Reserve Bank of India
    (d) Industrial Development Bank of India
63. WTO basically promotes
    (a) Financial support (b) Global peace
    (c) Unilateral trade (d) Multilateral trade
64. Price theory is also known as
    (a) Macro Economics
    (b) Development Economics
    (c) Public Economics
    (d) Micro Economics
65. The bats can fly in the dark because
    (a) they can see the objects in darkness
    (b) they have weak legs and are likely to be attacked by predators
    (c) they generate flashes of light
    (d) they generate ultrasonic sound waves
66. A circle will appear on an isometric drawing as a(n) __________ .
    (a) Ellipse (b) cycloid
    (c) circle (d) parabola
67. Which type of line is particular to section drawings?
    (a) Break lines (b) phantom lines
    (c) extension lines (d) cutting plane lines
68. A drawing instrument set usually contains all of the following, except:
    (a) bow compass (b) scale
    (c) dividers (d) extra leads
69. Which type of line has precedence over all other types of lines?
    (a) A hidden line (b) a center line
    (c) a visible line (d) none of the above

70. Which one of following is not the vector quantity?
    (a) Torque (b) displacement
    (c) velocity (d) speed
71. Dimensions of impulse are
    (a) $[M L^{-2} T^{-3}]$ (b) $[ML^{-2}]$
    (c) $[M L T^{-1}]$ (d) $[MLT^{-2}]$
72. The dimension of gravitational constant G is
    (a) $[ML^{-2}T^{-3}]$ (b) $[ML^{-2}]$
    (c) $[ML^{-2}T^2]$ (d) $[M^{-1}L^3T^{-2}]$
73. Light year is unit of
    (a) time (b) speed
    (c) distance (d) none of these
74. Density of pure water is
    (a) $19300 \, kg \, m^{-3}$ (b) $1000 \, kg \, m^{-3}$
    (c) $920 \, kg \, m^{-3}$ (d) $13600 \, kg \, m^{-3}$
75. Density of an object with mass m and volume V can be calculated by
    (a) V/m (b) m/V
    (c) m+V (d) mV
76. Mass of jar containing air is 320 g, mass of evacuated jar is 305 g, mass of jar with water is 1090 g and density of water is 1 g cm-3. What is density of air?
    (a) 15 g (b) 785 g
    (c) 325 g (d) $1.27 \times 10^{-3} \, g \, cm^{-3}$
77. Weight of an object depends on strength of
    (a) hotness (b) magnetic force
    (c) gravitational pull (d) biological pull
78. Work done by a force of 1 N which moves an object a distance of 1 m in a specified direction is termed as
    (a) 1 Joule (b) 1 Pascal
    (c) 1 Watt (d) 1 Ohm
79. When an object is raised to a certain height above ground, it possesses
    (a) Chemical Potential Energy
    (b) Elastic Potential Energy
    (c) Gravitational Potential Energy
    (d) Kinetic energy
80. Moving wind and waves, flying bird and spinning bowling ball use
    (a) Potential Energy (b) Mechanical Energy
    (c) Kinetic Energy (d) Thermal Energy
81. From physics point of view, work is being done by
    (a) A man carrying a heavy pile of books in a stationary position
    (b) A boy rote learning for his physics exam
    (c) A girl working on her Math homework
    (d) None of them

82. Region surrounding Earth where gravity is experienced is known as
    (a) potential field   (b) ozone layer
    (c) magnetic field   (d) gravitational field

83. Negative acceleration is also known as
    (a) Retardation   (b) Relaxation
    (c) Escalation   (d) All of above

84. The average speed of an object is defined to be
    (a) One half of the sum of the maximum and the minimum speeds.
    (b) distance it travels multiplied by the time it takes.
    (c) the distance it travels divided by the time it takes.
    (d) the speed determined over an infinitesimally small time interval.

85. If we use plus and minus signs to indicate the directions of velocity and acceleration in one dimension, in which of the following situations does the object speed up?
    (a) negative velocity and negative acceleration
    (b) positive velocity and negative acceleration
    (c) positive velocity and zero acceleration
    (d) negative velocity and positive acceleration

86. If a substance is hot, its particles
    (a) move more faster than the cooler object
    (b) move more slower than the cooler object
    (c) move at the same rate as the cooler object
    (d) may move faster it slower than the cooler object

87. Which of the following has highest heat capacity?
    (a) Water   (b) air
    (c) Soil   (d) None of the above

88. The process of transfer of heat in liquids & gases is called as:
    (a) Conduction   (b) Radiation
    (c) Convection   (d) Absorption

89. A wooden spoon is dipped in a cup of ice cream. Its other end.
    (a) becomes cold by the process of radiation.
    (b) becomes cold by the process of conduction.
    (c) "does not become cold."
    (d) becomes cold by the process of convection.

90. In case of Short Circuit ______ Current will flow in the Circuit.
    (a) Zero.   (b) Very Low
    (c) Normal.   (d) Infinite

91. Siemens or Mho (℧) is the unit of ____________?
    (a) Conductance   (b) Admittance
    (c) Both 1 & 2   (d) None of the above

92. Which part of the lever supplies the force to move something?
    (a) Effort   (b) fulcrum
    (c) load   (d) None of these.

93. Simple machines make work easier by trading ______ for force.
    (a) Friction   (b) motion
    (c) work   (d) distance

94. Which simple machine makes up a pencil sharpener? (The one mounted on the wall)
    (a) inclined-plane   (b) lawn-tractor
    (c) pulley   (d) wheel and axle

95. OSHA was created to ______
    (a) Data analysis
    (b) To reduce hazards
    (c) Ecological development
    (d) EIA analysis

96. Safety and Health Achievement Recognition Program (SHARP) recognizes ______
    (a) Small employers who operate safety and health management system
    (b) Large employers who operate safety and health management system
    (c) All employers who operate safety and health management system
    (d) Workers who operate safety and health management system

97. The pollution which does not persistent harm to life supporting system is
    (a) Noise pollution
    (b) Radiation pollution
    (c) Organochlorine pollution
    (d) All of these

98. Which of the following is not an air pollutant ?
    (a) Smoke   (b) Carbon Dioxide
    (c) Nitrogen Gas   (d) Sulphur Dioxide

99. Documents, Movies, Images and Photographs etc are stored at a?
    (a) Application Sever   (b) Web Sever
    (c) Print Server   (d) File Server

100. Who was the father of Internet?
    (a) Chares Babbage   (b) Vint Cerf
    (c) Denis Riche   (d) Martin Cooper

HINTS & SOLUTIONS

1. Number System

1. (a) $1.236 \times 10^{15} - 5.23 \times 10^{14}$

$= 10^{14}(12.36 - 5.23) = 7.13 \times 10^{14}$

2. (a) $\dfrac{\sqrt{5}}{2} - \dfrac{10}{\sqrt{5}} + \sqrt{125} = \dfrac{\sqrt{5}}{2} - \dfrac{10}{\sqrt{5}} + \dfrac{5\sqrt{5}}{1}$

$= \dfrac{5 - 20 + 10 \times 5}{2\sqrt{5}} = \dfrac{35\sqrt{5}}{10} = 3.5 \times 2.236 = 7.826$

3. (a) Units digit in $(7^4) = 1$. Therefore, units digit in $(7^4)^8$ i.e.

7^{32} will be 1. Hence, units digit in

$(7)^{35} = 1 \times 7 \times 7 \times 7 = 3$

Again, units digit in $(3)^4 = 1$

Therefore, units digit in the expansion of

$(3^4)^{17} = (3)^{68} = 1$

$\Rightarrow$ Units digit in the expansion of

$(3^{71}) = 1 \times 3 \times 3 \times 3 = 7$

and units digit in the expansion of $(11^{35}) = 1$

Hence, units digit in the expansion of

$7^{35} \times 3^{71} \times 11^{55} = 3 \times 7 \times 1 = 1$

4. (d) Let the missing figure in the expression be x.

$\dfrac{16}{7} \times \dfrac{16}{7} - \dfrac{x}{7} \times \dfrac{9}{7} + \dfrac{9}{7} \times \dfrac{9}{7} = 1$

$\Rightarrow 16 \times 16 - 9x + 9 \times 9 = 7 \times 7$

$\Rightarrow 9x = 16 \times 16 + 9 \times 9 - 7 \times 7 = 256 + 81 - 49 = 288$

$\Rightarrow x = \dfrac{288}{9} = 32$

5. (a) By remainder theorem,

9^6 will have the remainder 1 as 9 has the remainder 1.

Also $\dfrac{9^6 + 7}{8}$ will have the same remainder as

$\dfrac{(1)^6 + 7}{8}$ which has the remainder equal to 0.

6. (c) $\dfrac{9 + \sqrt{2}}{\sqrt{5} + \sqrt{3}} + \dfrac{6 - \sqrt{2}}{\sqrt{5} - \sqrt{3}}$

$= \dfrac{9(\sqrt{5} - \sqrt{3}) + \sqrt{2}(\sqrt{5} - \sqrt{3}) + 6(\sqrt{5} + \sqrt{3}) - \sqrt{2}(\sqrt{5} + \sqrt{3})}{(\sqrt{5} + \sqrt{3})(\sqrt{5} - \sqrt{3})}$

$= \dfrac{1}{2}(9\sqrt{5} - 9\sqrt{3} + \sqrt{10} - \sqrt{6} + 6\sqrt{5} + 6\sqrt{3} - \sqrt{10} - \sqrt{6})$

$= \dfrac{1}{2}(15\sqrt{5} - 3\sqrt{3} - 2\sqrt{6})$

$= \dfrac{1}{2}[15 \times 2.236 - 3 \times 1.732 - 2 \times 2.449]$

$= \dfrac{1}{2}[33.540 - 5.196 - 4.898] = 11.723$

7. (c) Let the hundred's, ten's and unit's digit of the required number be x, y and z respectively.

Then the number $= 100x + 10y + z$ ...(1)

And sum of digits $= x + y + z$ ...(2)

According to the question,

$(1) - (2)$ gives $99x + 9y = 9(11x + y)$

which is always divisible by 9.

8. (b) Let the original number of persons be x.

Then, $\dfrac{6500}{x} = \dfrac{6500}{x + 15} + 30$

or $\dfrac{6500}{x} = \dfrac{6500 + 30x + 450}{x + 15}$

or $x^2 + 15x - 3250 = 0$

or $x = 50$

9. (d) On dividing we find that when $\dfrac{11109999}{1111}$

Quotient is 9999 and remainder is 1110.

10. (c) Let the whole number be x

According to question

$x + 20 = \dfrac{69}{x}$

$\Rightarrow x^2 + 20x = 69$

$\Rightarrow x^2 + 20x - 69 = 0$

$\Rightarrow x^2 + 23x - 3x - 69 = 0$

$\Rightarrow x(x + 23) - 3(x + 23) = 0 \Rightarrow (x + 23)(x - 3) = 0$

$\therefore$ $x = 3$ or -23, Hence, 3 is only whole number.

11. (c) Given, numbers are 50, 35 and 35.

Now, place value of 3 is 30 and 30 in the numbers 35 and 35 respectively.

$\therefore$ Sum of the place values $= 30 + 30 = 60$

12. (d) Two digit numbers which are divisible by 3 are

12, 15, 18, 21, 24,------, 99.

Now, This is an A.P where $a = 12$, $d = 3$ and $a_n = 99$.

As we know, $a_n = a + (n - 1)d$

$\Rightarrow 99 = 12 + (n - 1)3 = 9 + 3n$

$\Rightarrow 90 = 3n \Rightarrow n = 30$.

Hence, there are 30 numbers which are divisible by 3.

13. (d) Let the unit and ten places of two digit number be x and y respectively.

Then number will be $10y + x$

According to question

$2(10y + x) = 9(10x + y)$ ...(i)

and $x + y = 9$ ...(ii)

From equation (i) and (ii), we get

$x = 1$ and $y = 8$

Hence number $= 81$

14. (d)

15. (d) We know that first 45 even numbers are

2, 4, 6, 8, 10, 12, ..., 90

Product of these number is

$2 . 4 . 6 . 8 . 10 . 12 .... 90$

$= 2^{45}[1 . 2 . 3 . 4 . 5 . 6 . 7 . 8 . 9 . 10 . 11 .... 45]$

$= 2^{45}[(5 . 20) . 1 . 2 . 3 . 4 . 6 . 7 . 8 . 9 . 10 . 11$

$\qquad\qquad\qquad .... 18 . 19 . 21 . 22 .... 45]$

$2^{45}[(100) . 1 . 2 . 3 . 4 . 6 . 7 .... 18 . 19 . 21 . 22 .... 45]$

Now the product will consist 0 at hundred place.

16. (d) Unit digit in 7^{95}

$= [$Unit digit in $(7^4)^{23} \times 7^3]$

$= [1 \times 343] = 343$

Unit digit in 3^{58}

$= [$Unit digit in $(3^4)^{14} \times 3^2]$

$= [1 \times 9] = 9$

So unit digit in $7^{95} - 3^{58}$
= Unit digit in [343 – 9]
= Unit digit in 334 = 4
So the answer is 4.

17. (c) Product of first 40 odd natural number
$= 1 \cdot 3 \cdot 5 \cdot 7 \cdot 9 \ldots \ldots 79.$
$= 15 \cdot (7 \cdot 9 \cdot \ldots \ldots 79)$
$= 15 \times$ an odd number
So there will be 5 at unit place.
So answer is 5.

18. (b) Let greater number = x
smaller number = y
∴   x + y = 90   ...(1)
and   x – 3y = 14   ...(2)
By equation (1) + (2)
x = 71, y = 19
∴   smaller numgber = 19
greater number = 71

19. (a) Let numbers be 5x and 3x
∴ $5x - 3x = 18$
       $2x = 18$
        $x = 9$
∴   Numbers are 5×9 and 3×9
45 and 27

20. (b) Let numbers be x, x + 8, x + 16
∴   x + x + 8 + x + 16 = 888
      3x = 864
       x = 288
∴   Numbers are = 288, 296, 304

2. HCF & LCM

1. (c) Let the numbers be x and 4x.
Then, $84 \times 21 = x \times 4x$

or $4x^2 = 1764$

or $x^2 = 441$ or x = 21

$\Rightarrow 4x = 4 \times 21 = 84$
Thus the larger number = 84

2. (d) Product of numbers = HCF × LCM

$\Rightarrow$ The other number $= \dfrac{4800 \times 160}{480} = 1600$

3. (a) Let the number are 3 x, 4 x and 5 x.
So, LCM (3 x, 4 x, 5 x) = 60 x
       60 x = 2400
          x = 40
Hence three numbers are 3×40, 4×40 and 5×40
Since the HCF means highest common factor.
So, the HCF = 40

4. (a) We know that product of two numbers
          = LCM × HCF of those numbers
So, product of numbers = 11 × 385
           $= 11 \times 7 \times 5 \times 11$
Since one of them lies between 75 and 125
So this number would be = 11 × 7 = 77
So the number is 77.

5. (a) It is given that the remainder is 25 in each case when we
divide 1305, 4665 and 6905 by k.
So, subtracting 25 from each of the numbers, we get 1280,
4640 and 6880.
HCF (1280, 4640 and 6880) = 160
So the greatest number is 160.
So k = 160

Sum of its digit = 1 + 6 + 0 = 7
So the answer is 7.

6. (b) Here 48 – 38 = 60 – 50 = 72 – 62 = 108 – 98 = 140 – 130
                 = 10
Hence required number
    = (LCM of 48, 60, 72, 108 and 140) – 10
    = 15120 – 10
    = 15110

7. (d) Clearly, HCF is 1

8. (c) LCM $= \dfrac{\text{LCM of } 1, 5, 2, 4}{\text{HCF of } 3, 6, 9, 27} = \dfrac{20}{3}$

9. (b) L.C.M. = (a, b) $= \dfrac{a \times b}{\text{HCF}(a, b)} = \dfrac{1800}{12} = 150$

10. (c) The maximum number of boys or girls alone in a group will
be equal to the H.C.F. of 264 and 408.
           = 24

11. (b) The time after which they will toll together again must be a
multiple of 21, 28 and 30.
Hence, the L.C.M. of 21, 28 and 30 = 420 seconds which is
the required time.

12. (d) Let the numbers be 3x and 4x
Then, HCF = x, so x = 4
So the numbers are 12 and 16
LCM of 12 and 16 = 48

13. (b) Product of two co-prime numbers is equal to their LCM.
So LCM = 117

14. (c) $\dfrac{5}{3} + \dfrac{3}{4} = \dfrac{29}{12} < 5$

$\dfrac{7}{3} + \dfrac{11}{5} = \dfrac{68}{15} < 5$

$\dfrac{11}{14} + \dfrac{8}{3} = \dfrac{33 + 32}{12} = \dfrac{65}{12} > 5$

$\dfrac{13}{5} + \dfrac{11}{6} = \dfrac{133}{30} < 5$

15. (c) So the largest length of rod will be the H.C.F. of length and
breadth.
HCF = 5
Length of rod = 5 m.

16. (c) Time gap between two consecutive ticks

$\dfrac{58}{57}$ sec. and $\dfrac{609}{608}$ sec.

∴ Required time = LCM of $\dfrac{58}{57}$ and $\dfrac{609}{608}$

$= \dfrac{\text{LCM of 58 and 609}}{\text{HCF of 57 and 608}} = \dfrac{1218}{19}$ sec

17. (a) Required time = LCM of 200, 300, 360, 450 sec
            = 1800 sec.

18. (d) The required number must be a factor of (11284 – 7655) or
3629.
Now, 3629 = 19 × 191
∴ 191 is the required number.

19. (c) Bells will toll together again at a time, which is obtained by
taking L.C.M. of their individual tolling intervals.
L.C.M. of 9, 12 and 15 = 180 min
They will toll together again after 180 min, i.e. 3 hours.
Time = 8 + 3 = 11 a.m.

20. (b) LCM of 6, 5, 7, 10 and 12 = 420 seconds

$$= \frac{420}{60} = 7 \text{ minutes}.$$

Therefore, in one hour (60 minutes), then will fall together

8 times $\left(\dfrac{60}{7}\right)$ excluding the one at the start.

3. Simplification

1. (a) as $x = \dfrac{1}{2+\sqrt{3}} = 2 - \sqrt{3}$

$x - 2 = -\sqrt{3}$

Squaring both sides, we get

$(x-2)^2 = (-\sqrt{3})^2 \Rightarrow x^2 + 4 - 4x = 3 \Rightarrow x^2 - 4x + 1 = 0$

Now, $x^3 - x^2 - 11x + 3 = x^3 - 4x^2 + x - 3x^2 - 12x + 3$

$x(x^2 - 4x + 1) + 3(x^2 - 4x + 1)$

$x \times 0 + 3(0)$

$0 + 0 = 0$

2. (d) $x = 3\sqrt{3} + \sqrt{26}$

$$\frac{1}{x} = \frac{1}{3\sqrt{3}+\sqrt{26}} \times \frac{3\sqrt{3}-\sqrt{26}}{3\sqrt{3}-\sqrt{26}}$$

$$\frac{3\sqrt{3}-\sqrt{26}}{(27)-(26)} = 3\sqrt{3} - \sqrt{26}$$

$$\therefore \quad \frac{1}{2}\left(x + \frac{1}{x}\right) = \frac{1}{2}\left[(3\sqrt{3}+\sqrt{26}) + (3\sqrt{3}-\sqrt{26})\right]$$

$$= \frac{1}{2} \times 6\sqrt{3} = 3\sqrt{3}$$

3. (a) $x = 2 + 2^{1/3} + 2^{2/3}$

$x - 2 = 2^{1/3} + 2^{2/3} = 2^{1/3}(1 + 2^{1/3})$

$\Rightarrow (x-2)^3 = [2^{1/3}(1 + 2^{1/3})]^3$

$\Rightarrow x^3 - 8 - 3.x^2.2 + 3.x.2^2 = 2(1+2^{1/3})^3$

$\Rightarrow x^3 - 8 - 6x^2 + 12x = 2(1 + 2 + 3.1^2.2^{1/3} + 3.1.2^{2/3})$

$\Rightarrow x^3 - 6x^2 + 12x - 8 = 2[3 + 3.2^{1/3} + 3.2^{2/3}]$

$\quad = 6(1 - 2^{1/3} + 2^{2/3})$

$= 6(x-1) \qquad \dots(i)$

$$\left[\begin{array}{l} \because \quad x = 2 + 2^{\frac{1}{3}} + 2^{\frac{2}{3}} \\[2mm] \therefore \quad x - 1 = 1 + 2^{\frac{1}{3}} + 2^{\frac{2}{3}} \end{array} \right]$$

$\Rightarrow x^3 - 6x^2 - 12x - 8 = 6x - 6$

$\Rightarrow x^3 - 6x^2 - 12x - 6x - 8 + 6 = 0$

$\Rightarrow x^3 - 6x^2 - 6x - 2 = 0$

4. (c) $x = 1.272727\ldots$ Since two digits are repeating, we multiply x by 100 to get

$100x = 127.2727\ldots$

So, $100x = 126 + 1.272727\ldots = 126 + x$

Therefore, $100x - x = 126, \Rightarrow 99x = 126 \Rightarrow x = \dfrac{126}{99} = \dfrac{14}{11}$

5. (a) $2^{x+4}.3^{x+1} = 288$

$2^4.2^x.3^x.3^1 = 288$

$6^x = \dfrac{288}{48} = 6$

$x = 1$

6. (c) $\left(1+\dfrac{1}{2}\right)\left(1+\dfrac{1}{3}\right)\left(1+\dfrac{1}{4}\right)\ldots\left(1+\dfrac{1}{n}\right)$

$$\frac{3}{2} \times \frac{4}{3} \times \frac{5}{4} \times \ldots \times \frac{(n+1)}{n}$$

$$= \frac{n+1}{2}$$

7. (a) $a = 2+\sqrt{3}$ $\qquad b = 2-\sqrt{3}$

$\quad a^2 = 4+3+4\sqrt{3}$ $\qquad b^2 = 4+3-4\sqrt{3}$

$\quad = 7+4\sqrt{3}$ $\qquad\qquad = 7-4\sqrt{3}$

$$\frac{1}{a^2} + \frac{1}{b^2} = \frac{1}{7+4\sqrt{3}} + \frac{1}{7-4\sqrt{3}}$$

$$= \frac{7-4\sqrt{3}+7+4\sqrt{3}}{49-48}$$

$$= 14$$

8. (a)   9. (c)

10. (b) $\dfrac{1}{x+1} + \dfrac{1}{x+4} = 0$

$x + 4 = -(x+1)$

$2x = -5$

$x = \dfrac{-5}{2} = -2\dfrac{1}{2}$

11. (a) $\dfrac{x}{pq} + \dfrac{x}{qr} + \dfrac{x}{pr} = p+q+r$

$x\left(\dfrac{r+p+q}{pqr}\right) = p+q+r$

$\therefore \quad x = pqr$

12. (d) $\dfrac{12x+1}{4} = \dfrac{13x-1}{5} + 3$

$60x + 5 = 52x - 4 + 15$

$8x = 15 - 4 - 5$

$8x = 6$

$x = \dfrac{6}{8} = \dfrac{3}{4}$

$\therefore \quad x = \dfrac{3}{4}$

13. (c) $a + 2b = 1.6$ $\qquad\qquad\qquad\qquad\qquad \dots(1)$

$$\frac{7}{a+\dfrac{b}{2}} = 10$$

$$\frac{14}{2a+b} = 10$$

$2a + b = 1.4$ $\qquad\qquad\qquad\qquad\qquad \dots(2)$

By equation (1) and (2)

$a = 0.4, b = 0.6$

14. (a) Ratio of amount of coins

$$= \frac{2}{2} : \frac{3}{4} : \frac{4}{10}$$

$$= 20 : 15 : 8$$

Amount of 50p $= \dfrac{129 \times 20}{43} = 60$

Amount of 25p $= \dfrac{129 \times 15}{43} = 45$

Amount of 10p $= \dfrac{129 \times 8}{43} = 24$

∴ Number of each types of coins
$= 60 \times 2, 45 \times 4, 24 \times 10$
$= 120, 180, 240$

15. (c) Let incomes $= 4x$ and $5x$

∴ $\dfrac{4x - 50}{5x - 50} = \dfrac{7}{9}$

$36x - 450 = 35x - 350$
$x = 100$

∴ Income $= 400, 500$

16. (a) $6x + 3y = 7xy$ ...(1)
$3x + 9y = 11xy$ ...(2)
By equations (1) and (2)

$x = 1, \qquad y = \dfrac{3}{2}$

17. (a) In a Δ, sum of internal angles $= 180°$

∴ $\angle A + \angle B + \angle C = 180°$ ....(1)

It is given that $\angle A = \angle B + \angle C$ ....(2)

From (1) and (2)
$\angle A + \angle A = 180°$
$\Rightarrow \quad 2\angle A = 180°$
$\Rightarrow \quad \angle A = 90°$

Let $\quad \angle B = 4x$
$\quad\quad \angle C = 5x$

∴ $\angle B + \angle C = 90°$
$4x + 5x = 90°$
$x = 10°$

∴ $\angle B = 40°$
$\angle C = 50°$

∴ Angles are $90°, 40°, 50°$

18. (d) 'a' is a natural number.

∴ $a^2 + \dfrac{1}{a^2} = a^2 + \dfrac{1}{a^2} - 2 + 2$

$= a^2 + \dfrac{1}{a^2} - 2.a.\dfrac{1}{a} + 2$

$a^2 + \dfrac{1}{a^2} = \left(a - \dfrac{1}{a}\right)^2 + 2$

Now, $\left(a - \dfrac{1}{a}\right)^2$ is always greater than or equal to zero.

∴ $a^2 + \dfrac{1}{a^2} \geq 2$

19. (b)   20. (b)

---

4. Surds, Indices

1. (d) $\left(\dfrac{-1}{216}\right)^{-\frac{2}{3}} = \left(\dfrac{-1}{6^3}\right)^{-\frac{2}{3}} = \left(-\dfrac{1}{6}\right)^{-2} = (-6)^2 = 36$

2. (d) $\left(\dfrac{1}{4}\right)^{-2} = (4)^2 = 16$

3. (c) $13^{\frac{1}{5}}.17^{\frac{1}{5}} = (13 \times 17)^{\frac{1}{5}} = 221^{\frac{1}{5}} = \sqrt[5]{221}$

4. (b) $\left(\dfrac{2^a}{2^b}\right)^{a+b} \left(\dfrac{2^b}{2^c}\right)^{b+c} \left(\dfrac{2^c}{2^a}\right)^{c+a}$

$$= (2^{a-b})^{a+b} \cdot (2^{b-c})^{b+c} \cdot (2^{c-a})^{c+a}$$

$$2^{(a^2-b^2)+(b^2-c^2)+(c^2-a^2)} = 2^0 = 1$$

5. (b) We have,

$$\frac{x^{a(b-c)}}{x^{b(a-c)}} \div \left(\frac{x^b}{x^a}\right)^c$$

$$= \frac{x^{ab-ac}}{x^{ba-bc}} \div (x^{b-a})^c$$

$$= x^{(ab-ac)-(ba-bc)} \times \frac{1}{x^{(b-a)c}}$$

$$= x^{ab-ac-ba+bc} \times \frac{1}{x^{bc-ac}} = x^{-ac+bc} \cdot x^{ac-bc}$$

$$= x^{ac+bc+ac-bc} = x^0 = 1$$

6. (c) $\left[\left\{\left(\dfrac{1}{7^2}\right)^{-2}\right\}^{\frac{-1}{3}}\right]^{\frac{1}{4}} = 7^m$

$\Rightarrow \left[\{(7^{-2})^{-2}\}^{-1/3}\right]^{\frac{1}{4}} = 7^m$

$\Rightarrow \left[(7^4)^{-1/3}\right]^{\frac{1}{4}} = 7^m$

$\Rightarrow (7^{-4/3})^{1/4} = 7^m$

$\Rightarrow 7^{-1/3} = 7^m$

∴ $m = -1/3$

7. (c) $\left(1 + \dfrac{1}{2}\right)\left(1 + \dfrac{1}{3}\right)\left(1 + \dfrac{1}{4}\right).....\left(1 + \dfrac{1}{n}\right)$

$$\frac{3}{2} \times \frac{4}{3} \times \frac{5}{4} \times .....\times \frac{n+1}{n}$$

$$= \frac{n+1}{2}$$

8. (d) $\sqrt[3]{\left(\dfrac{1}{64}\right)^2} = \left[\left(\dfrac{1}{64}\right)^2\right]^{\frac{1}{3}} = \left(\dfrac{1}{64}\right)^{\frac{2}{3}}$

$\left(\dfrac{1}{4}\right)^{3\times\frac{2}{3}} = \left(\dfrac{1}{4}\right)^2 = \dfrac{1}{16}$

9. (c) $\dfrac{2^{(n+2)} - 2(2^n)}{2^{(2n-2)}} = \dfrac{2^n \cdot 2^2 - 2.2^n}{2^2 \cdot 2^{2n}} = \dfrac{2.2^n(2-1)}{2^2.2^{2n}}$

$= \dfrac{1}{2.2^n} = \dfrac{1}{2^{(n+1)}}$

10. (c) $\left[5\left(8^{\frac{1}{3}} + 27^{\frac{1}{3}}\right)^3\right]^{\frac{1}{4}} = \left[5\left((2^3)^{\frac{1}{3}} + (3^3)^{\frac{1}{3}}\right)^3\right]^{\frac{1}{4}}$

$= \left[5(2+3)^3\right]^{\frac{1}{4}} \qquad = \left[5(5)^3\right]^{\frac{1}{4}}$

$= \left[5^4\right]^{\frac{1}{4}} = 5$

11. (c) $3\sqrt{2} + \sqrt[4]{16\times 4} + \sqrt[4]{625\times 4} + \sqrt[6]{2^3}$

$= \sqrt{2} + \sqrt[4]{2^4 \times 2^2} + \sqrt[4]{5^4 \times 2^2} + \sqrt[6]{2^3}$

$= 3\sqrt{2} + 2\sqrt[4]{2^2} + 5\sqrt[4]{2^2} + \sqrt[6]{2^3}$

$= 3\sqrt{2} + 2\sqrt{2} + 5\sqrt{2} + \sqrt{2}$

$= (3+2+5+1)\sqrt{2} = 11\sqrt{2}$

12. (b) Geven Exp. $= \dfrac{1}{1+a+b^{-1}} + \dfrac{1}{1+b+c^{-1}} + \dfrac{1}{1+c+a^{-1}}$

$= \dfrac{1}{1+a+b^{-1}} + \dfrac{b^{-1}}{1+b^{-1}c^{-1}+b^{-1}} + \dfrac{a}{a+ac+1}$

$= \dfrac{1}{1+a+b^{-1}} + \dfrac{b^{-1}}{1+b^{-1}+a} + \dfrac{a}{a+b^{-1}+1}$

$= \dfrac{1+a+b^{-1}}{1+a+b^{-1}} = 1$

$\because \ abc = 1 \Rightarrow (bc)^{-1} = a \Rightarrow b^{-1}c^{-1} = a \ \text{and} \ ac = b^{-1}$

13. (c) $\dfrac{(243)^{\frac{n}{5}} \times 3^{2n+1}}{9^n \times 3^{n-1}} = \dfrac{\left[(3)^5\right]^{\frac{n}{5}} \times 3^{2n+1}}{(3^2)^n \times 3^{n-1}}$

$= \dfrac{3^n \times 3^{2n+1}}{3^{2n} \times 3^{n-1}} \quad \left[a^m \times a^n = a^{m+n}\right]$

$= \dfrac{3^{3n+1}}{3^{3n-1}} \qquad \left[\dfrac{a^n}{a^m} = a^{n-m}\right]$

$= 3^2 = 9$

14. (b) If $27^k = \dfrac{9}{3^k}$

$\Rightarrow 3^{3k} = \dfrac{9}{3^k} \Rightarrow 3^{4k} = 9 \qquad [a^m \times a^n = a^{m+n}]$

$\Rightarrow 9^{2k} = 9 \Rightarrow k = \dfrac{1}{2} \qquad \left[a^m = a^n \text{ then } m = n\right]$

$\Rightarrow \dfrac{1}{k^2} = 4$

15. (c) $\dfrac{3^x}{1+3^x} = \dfrac{1}{9}$

$\Rightarrow 3^x \cdot 9 = 1+3^x \Rightarrow 3^x(9-1) = 1$

$\Rightarrow 3^x = \dfrac{1}{8} \Rightarrow 9^x = \dfrac{1}{64}$

$\therefore \dfrac{9^x}{1+9^x} = \dfrac{\frac{1}{64}}{1+\frac{1}{64}} = \dfrac{1/64}{65/64} = \dfrac{1}{65}$

16. (c) $a = x^{\frac{1}{3}} + x^{-\frac{1}{3}}$

Cubing both sides, we get

$a^3 = x + \dfrac{1}{x} + 3(x^{\frac{1}{3}} + x^{-\frac{1}{3}})$

$a^3 = x + \dfrac{1}{x} + 3a$

$a^3 - 3a = x + x^{-1}$

17. (a)

18. (c) $4^{\sqrt{x}^{\sqrt{x}}} = 256 = 4^4$

$\Rightarrow \sqrt{x}^{\sqrt{x}} = 4 = 2^2 \Rightarrow \sqrt{x} = 2 \Rightarrow \qquad x = 4$

19. (d) Let $3^{x^2} = a$ and $3^{x+6} = b$

the given equation reduces to
$a^2 - 2ab + b^2 = 0 \Rightarrow (a-b)^2$
$\Rightarrow a = b$

$\therefore \ 3^{x^2} = 3^{x+6} \qquad [a^m = a^n \text{ then } m = n]$
$\Rightarrow x^2 = x+6 \Rightarrow x^2 - x - 6 = 0$
$\Rightarrow x^2 - 3x + 2x - 6 = 0 \Rightarrow x(x-3) + 2(x-3) = 0$
$\Rightarrow (x-3)(x+2) = 0 \Rightarrow x = 3 \text{ or } x = -2$

20. (c) $\dfrac{(991)^3 + (9)^3}{(991)^2 - 991\times 9 + (9)^2}$

As $\dfrac{a^3 + b^3}{a^2 - ab + b^2} = \dfrac{(a+b)(a^2 - ab + b^2)}{(a^2 - ab + b^2)}$

$= a + b$

$\therefore \quad 991 + 9 = 1000$

5. Square Roots & Cube Roots

1. (c) Resolve 136 into prime factors and make group of two of each prime factor

$$136 = 2 \times 2 \times 2 \times 17$$

$$136 = (2 \times 2) \times 2 \times 17$$

We find that 2 and 17 doesn't appear in group of two. So, 136 has to be multiplied with 34 to make it a perfect square.

2. (c) Resolving 3888 into its prime factors, we find that

$$3888 = 2 \times 2 \times 2 \times 2 \times 3 \times 3 \times 3 \times 3 \times 3$$

$$3888 = (2 \times 2) \times (2 \times 2) \times (3 \times 3) \times (3 \times 3) \times 3$$

Here we find that prime factor 3 is appearing alone.
So, if we divide 3888 by 3, we will get a perfect square number

3. (b) Let one number = a

$\therefore$　　Second number = $4\,a$

$\Rightarrow$　　$4a \times a = 1936$

$\Rightarrow$　　$a^2 = \dfrac{1936}{4} = 484$

$\Rightarrow$　　$a^2 = 484$

$\Rightarrow$　　$a = 2 \times 11 = 22$

and $4a = 4 \times 22 = 88$

$\therefore$ Numbers are 22 and 88.

4. (d) Least number which is divisible by 4, 6, 10, 15 is LCM (4, 6, 10, 15)

LCM (4, 6, 10, 15) = 60

$60 = 2 \times 2 \times 3 \times 5$

Here we find that 3 and 5 occurs alone.

So, if we multiply 60 by $3 \times 5 = 15$, we get a perfect square no.

$\therefore$ $60 \times 3 \times 15 = 900$

900 is the least square no. which is divisible by 4, 6, 10, 15.

5. (c) Least six digit number is 100000, which is not a perfect square because it has odd number of zeroes.

First let us extract the square number hidden in it.

```
           316
      ┌─────────────
    3 │ 10 00 00
      │  9
      ├─────────────
   61 │   1 00
      │     61
      ├─────────────
  626 │   39 00
      │   37 56
      └─────────────
             1 54
```

$\therefore$　We find that $100000 > (316)^2$ by 154
Next square number $(317)^2 > 100000$

$\therefore$　$(316)^2 < 100000 < (317)^2$

$\therefore$　If we add $(317)^2 - 100000 = 489$ to 100000
We get least six digit perfect sq. no.

$\therefore$　Least four digit perfect square no. is 100489.

6. (b) Let us extract the square root from 24136.

```
           155
      ┌─────────────
    1 │ 2 41 36
      │ 1
      ├─────────────
   25 │ 141
      │ 125
      ├─────────────
  305 │ 1636
      │ 1525
      └─────────────
           111
```

$\therefore$　24136, is 111 more than $(155)^2$. So if we subtract 111 from 24136, we will get a perfect sq. number.

7. (b)

```
                155
       ┌─────────────
     1 │  2 41 36
    ×1 │  1
       ├─────────────
    25 │  141
    ×5 │  125
       ├─────────────
   305 │  1636
    ×5 │  1525
       └─────────────
            111
```

$\therefore$　$24136 < (156)^2$
$24136 < 24336$

$\therefore$　we add $24336 - 24136 = 200$
so that it becomes a perfect square

8. (a) Let the side of square field = 'a' m

$\therefore$ Area of square field = a^2 sq. m
$a^2 = 22500$ m^2

$\Rightarrow a = 150$ m

Speed of cycling = 15 km / hr

$$= \frac{15 \times 1000}{60 \times 60} = \frac{25}{6} \text{ m/s.}$$

Now, total distance to be covered along the boundary
$$= 4 \times 150 = 600 \text{ m}$$

$\because \dfrac{25}{6}$ m is covered in 1 sec.

$\therefore$ 600 m is covered in $\dfrac{600}{25} \times 6 = 144$ sec = 2 min 24 sec.

9. (c) $\sqrt{388 + \sqrt{127 + \sqrt{289}}}$

$= \sqrt{388 + \sqrt{127 + 17}}$　　$\left[\because \sqrt{289} = 17 \right]$

$= \sqrt{388 + \sqrt{144}}$　　$\left[\because \sqrt{144} = 12 \right]$

$= \sqrt{388 + 12} = \sqrt{400}$

$= 20$　　$\left[\because \sqrt{400} = 20 \right]$

10. (b) Gardener arranges $(3984 - 15) = 3969$ plants in different rows to form a square.

Let no. of plants in each row be 'x'

$\therefore$ $x \times x = 3969$

$x^2 = 3969 \Rightarrow x = 63$

11. (a) Area $= \pi r^2 = \dfrac{3168}{7}$

$r^2 = \dfrac{3168}{7} \times \dfrac{7}{22} = 144$

$r = \sqrt{144} = 12\,m$

Diameter = 24 m

12. (d)   13. (a)

14. (b)

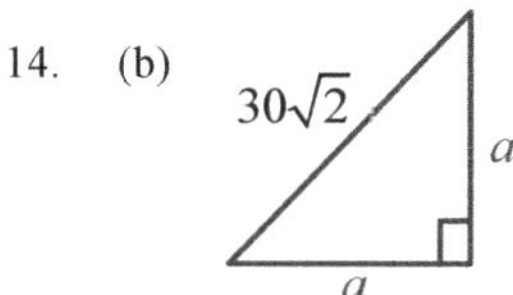

$$\left(30\sqrt{2}\right)^2 = a^2 + a^2$$
$$1800 = 2a^2$$
$$a^2 = 900$$
$$a = 30\,m$$

15. (c)   Expressing 7200 as its prime factors
$$7200 = 2 \times 2 \times 2 \times 2 \times 2 \times 3 \times 3 \times 5 \times 5$$
$$7200 = (2 \times 2 \times 2) \times (2 \times 2) \times (3 \times 3) \times (5 \times 5)$$
We find that prime factors 2, 3 & 5 appear in groups of two, so to make the given no. perfect cube, we must multiply it with $2 \times 3 \times 5 = 30$

16. (d)   Let the ratio of numbers be x.
∴   numbers are $2x$, $3x$ & $4x$.
$$\therefore \quad (2x)^3 + (3x)^3 + (4x)^3 = 33957$$
$$\Rightarrow \quad 8x^3 + 27x^3 + 64x^3 = 33957$$
$$\Rightarrow \quad 99x^3 = 33957$$
$$\Rightarrow \quad x^3 = \frac{33957}{99}$$
$$\Rightarrow \quad x^3 = 343 \Rightarrow x = 7$$
∴   Numbers are $2 \times 7, 3 \times 7, 4 \times 7$
i.e. 14, 21, 28

17. (d) $\sqrt[3]{392} \times \sqrt[3]{448} = \sqrt[3]{2 \times 2 \times 2 \times 7 \times 7}$
$$\times \sqrt[3]{2 \times 2 \times 2 \times 2 \times 2 \times 2 \times 7}$$
$$= \sqrt[3]{(2 \times 2 \times 2) \times (2 \times 2 \times 2) \times (2 \times 2 \times 2) \times (7 \times 7 \times 7)}$$
$$= 2 \times 2 \times 2 \times 7 \qquad \left[\because \sqrt[3]{p} \times \sqrt[3]{q} = \sqrt[3]{pq} \right]$$
$$= 56$$

18. (d)   Volume of given cube $= 8 \times 6 \times 4 = 192 \text{ cm}^3$
$$5^3 < 192 < 6^3$$
$$125 < 192 < 216$$
∴   we add $216 - 192 = 24 \text{ cm}^3$ volume

19. (b)   Let volume of cubes $= a^3$ and b^3
$$\therefore \quad \frac{a^3}{b^3} = \frac{343}{1331} = \left(\frac{7}{11}\right)^3$$
$$\frac{a}{b} = \frac{7}{11}$$
or $a : b = 7 : 11$

20. (c)   Let the natural number be 'x'.
$$\therefore \quad x^3 - x^2 = 48$$
$$\Rightarrow \quad x^2(x-1) = 48$$
$$\Rightarrow \quad 4^2(4-1) = 48$$
$$\therefore \quad x = 4$$

6. Ratio, Proportion & Partnership

1.   (a)   Let the required numbers are $5x$ and $4x$
then $5x \times \dfrac{40}{100} = 12$

$$\Rightarrow x = \frac{12 \times 100}{5 \times 40} = 6$$

50% of second number $= 4x \times \dfrac{50}{100} = 4 \times 6 \times \dfrac{1}{2} = 12$

2.   (d)

3.   (b)   Let the fraction be $\dfrac{2x}{3x}$

Now, $\dfrac{2x-6}{3x} = \dfrac{2}{3} \times \dfrac{2x}{3x}$

$$\Rightarrow 2x - 6 = \frac{4x}{3}$$
$$\Rightarrow 6x - 18 = 4x$$
$$\Rightarrow 2x = 18$$
$$\Rightarrow x = 9$$
∴ Numerator $= 2x = 2 \times 9 = 18$

4.   (d)   Let $A = 2x$, $B = 3x$, $C = 4x$
$$\therefore \frac{A}{B} = \frac{2}{3}, \frac{B}{C} = \frac{3}{4}, \frac{C}{A} = \frac{4}{2} = \frac{2}{1}$$

Now, $\dfrac{A}{B} : \dfrac{B}{C} : \dfrac{C}{A} = \dfrac{2}{3} : \dfrac{3}{4} : \dfrac{2}{1}$

$$= \frac{2}{3} \times 12 : \frac{3}{4} \times 12 : \frac{2}{1} \times 12$$
$$= 8 : 9 : 24$$

5.   (d)   Let number of boys $= 4x$
number of girls $= 5x$
$$\therefore \quad \frac{4x}{5x - 100} = \frac{6}{7}$$
$$30x - 600 = 28x$$
$$2x = 600$$
$$x = 300$$
number of boys $= 4 \times 300 = 1200$

6.   (c)

7.   (c)   Let number be x
$$\therefore \quad \frac{21 - x}{38 - x} = \frac{55 - x}{106 - x}$$
$$2226 - 21x - 106x + x^2 = 2090 - 38x - 55x + x^2$$
$$34x = 136$$
$$x = 4$$
∴   The number is 4

8.   (d)   Let x be the required third proportional
$$\therefore \quad \frac{a^2 - b^2}{(a+b)^2} = \frac{(a+b)^2}{x}$$
$$\Rightarrow x = \frac{(a+b)^4}{a^2 - b^2} = \frac{(a+b)^3 (a+b)}{(a+b)(a-b)} = \frac{(a+b)^3}{(a-b)}$$

9.   (d) $\dfrac{5x - 3y}{5y - 3x} = \dfrac{3}{4}$

$$\Rightarrow \frac{5 - 3\left(\dfrac{y}{x}\right)}{5\left(\dfrac{y}{x}\right) - 3} = \frac{3}{4}$$

$$\Rightarrow 20 - 12\left(\frac{y}{x}\right) = 15\left(\frac{y}{x}\right) - 9$$

$$\Rightarrow 27\left(\frac{y}{x}\right) = 29 \Rightarrow \frac{y}{x} = \frac{29}{27}$$

10. **(d)** Let no. of one-rupee, 50 paise and 25 paise coins be $3x$, $4x$ and $5x$ respectively
$\therefore 3x \times 1 + 4x \times 0.5 + 5x \times 0.25 = 93.75$
$\Rightarrow 3x + 2x + 1.25x = 93.75$
$\Rightarrow 6.25x = 93.75$
$\Rightarrow x = 15$
$\therefore$ No. of coins are 45, 60, 75

11. **(c)** Let the ratio be k
$\therefore \qquad a + b = 6k,\ b + c = 7k,\ c + a = 8k$
$\Rightarrow (a + b) + (b + c) + (c + a) = 6k + 7k + 8k$
$\Rightarrow 2(a + b + c) = 21k$

$$\Rightarrow k = \frac{2 \times 14}{21} = \frac{4}{3}$$

$\therefore \quad c = (a + b + c) - (a + b)$

$$= 14 - 6 \times \frac{4}{3}$$

$$= 14 - 8 = 6$$

12. **(a)** Let monthly salaries be $2x$, $3x$ and $5x$
$\therefore 5x = 2x + 1200 \Rightarrow 3x = 1200$
$\Rightarrow x = 400$
$\therefore \qquad$ Monthly salary of B = 1200
$\therefore \qquad$ Annual salary of B = 14400

13. **(b)** In 30L mixture ratio of milk and water = 7 : 3
$\therefore \qquad$ Milk = 21L, Water = 9L
Let added water = xL

$$\therefore \qquad \frac{21}{9 + x} = \frac{3}{7}$$

$27 + 3x = 147$
$\quad 3x = 120$
$\quad\ x = 40$
$\therefore$ 40L water added

14. **(c)** Let numbers be $3x$, $4x$, $5x$
$\therefore \quad (3x)^2 + (4x)^2 + (5x)^2 = 1250$
$9x^2 + 16x^2 + 25x^2 = 1250$
$50x^2 = 1250$
$x^2 = 25$
$x = 5$
$\therefore \quad$ Numbers are = 15, 20, 25
Sum = 15 + 20 + 25 = 60

15. **(b)** Let the three numbers be a, b, c.

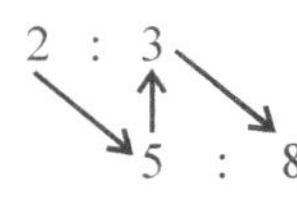

= 10 : 15 : 24

16. **(d)**

17. **(a)** Let the number of seats for mathematics, physics and biology be $5x$, $7x$ and $8x$ respectively.
No of increased seats are (140% of $5x$), (150% of $7x$) and (175% of $8x$)

i.e. $\left(\frac{140}{100} \times 5x\right)$, $\left(\frac{150}{100} \times 7x\right)$ and $\left(\frac{175}{100} \times 8x\right)$

i.e. $7x$, $\dfrac{21}{2}x$, $14x$

$\therefore \quad$ Required ratio $7x : \dfrac{21}{2}x : 14x$
$\qquad$ i.e. $14x : 21x : 28x$
$\qquad = 2 : 3 : 4$

18. **(a)** Let Age of A = $3x$
Age of B = x

$$\therefore \qquad \frac{3x + 15}{x + 15} = \frac{2}{1}$$

$3x + 15 = 2x + 30$
$x = 15$
$\therefore \quad$ Present Age of A = 45 years
$\quad$ Present Age of B = 15 years

19. **(a)** Sides are in the ratio $\dfrac{1}{2} : \dfrac{1}{3} : \dfrac{1}{4}$
$\qquad$ i.e. $6 : 4 : 3$
Let the ratio be x
$\therefore$ sides are $6x$, $4x$ and $3x$
Given that $6x + 4x + 3x = 104$
$\Rightarrow 13x = 104$
$\Rightarrow x = 8$
$\therefore$ longest side = $6x = 6 \times 8 = 48$ cm

20. **(c)** Given $\dfrac{x + 4}{3x + 15} = \left(\dfrac{2}{3}\right)^3 = \dfrac{8}{27}$

$27x + 108 = 24x + 120$
$3x = 12$
$\quad x = 4$

7. Average & Problems on ages

1. **(b)** Total age of the family of five members = $24 \times 5 = 120$
Total age of the family of five members before 8 years
$= 120 - 5 \times 8 = 120 - 40 = 80$

So, Required average age = $\dfrac{80}{5} = 16\,\text{yr}$

2. **(b)** Third number
$= 924 - (2 \times 2015 + 2 \times 196) = 924 - (403 + 392)$
$= 924 - 795 = 129$

3. **(b)** Actual average marks
$= \dfrac{65 \times 150 + 152 - 142}{65} = \dfrac{9750 + 10}{65} = 150.15$

4. **(b)** Difference of marks = $72 + 61 - 48 - 65 = 20$

Correct average marks = $68 + \dfrac{20}{20} = 68 + 1 = 69$

5. **(c)** A + B + C = $3 \times 84 = 252$ kg
A + B + C + D = $4 \times 80 = 320$ kg
$\therefore$ D = $320 - 252 = 68$ kg
$\therefore$ E = $68 + 3 = 71$ kg
Now, $\dfrac{320 - A + 71}{4} = 79$
$\therefore$ A = 75 kg

6. **(c)** $6 \times 49 + 6 \times 52 - 11 \times 50 = 294 + 312 - 550 = 56$

7. **(d)** Total of 30 observation = $45 \times 30 = 1350$
Total of 33 observation $= 1350 + 42 + 44 + 48$
$\qquad\qquad\qquad\qquad\qquad = 1484$

New average = $\dfrac{1484}{33} = 44.97$

8. **(a)** Let numbers be a and b

$$\therefore \qquad \frac{a + b}{2} = 14.5$$

$a + b = 29$ ...(1)

$\sqrt{ab} = 10$

$ab = 100$ ...(2)

By equation (1) and (2)

$a = 25, b = 4$

$\therefore$ Numbers are 25, 4

9. (b) Average $= 30 - 10 = 20$

10. (b) By the theorem: Average speed $= \dfrac{3 \times 40 \times 30 \times 15}{40 \times 30 + 30 \times 15 + 40 \times 15}$

$= \dfrac{3 \times 40 \times 30 \times 15}{2250} = 24$ km/hr

11. (b) Average age $= 28.5$

$\therefore$ Total age $= 28.5 \times 2 = 57$

$\therefore$ Daughter's age $= \dfrac{5}{19} \times 57 = 15$ years

12. (b) Son's age $= \dfrac{5(9-1)}{(9-4)} = 8$ yrs

$\therefore$ Father's age $= 4 \times 8 = 32$ yrs

13. (b) Son's age $= \dfrac{5(7-1) + 5(3-1)}{7-3} = 10$ yrs

From the first relationship of ages, if F is the age of the father then $F + 5 = 3(10 + 5)$

$\therefore$ $F = 40$ yrs

14. (c) Let the ratio of proportionality be x, then

$4x \times x = 196$ or, $4x^2 = 196$ or, $x = 7$

Thus, Father's age $= 28$ yrs, Son's age $= 7$ yrs

After 5 yrs, Father's age $= 33$ yrs.

Son's age $= 12$ yrs

$\therefore$ Ratio $= 33 : 12 = 11 : 4$

15. (c) Let the present age be x yrs. Then

125% of $(x - 10) = x$; and $83\dfrac{1}{3}\%$ of $(x + 10) = x$

$\therefore$ 125% of $(x - 10) = 83\dfrac{1}{3}\%$ of $(x + 10)$

$\dfrac{5}{4}(x - 10) = \dfrac{5}{6}(x + 10)$

or, $\dfrac{5}{4}x - \dfrac{5}{6}x = \dfrac{50}{6} + \dfrac{50}{4}$

or, $\dfrac{5x}{12} = \dfrac{250}{12}$ $\therefore$ $x = 50$ yrs.

16. (d) Let the mother's age be y years.

$\therefore$ The age of father $= (y + 9)$ years

The age of son $= \dfrac{y}{2}$ years

The age of daughter $= \left(\dfrac{y}{2} - 7\right)$ years

Now according to the given condition,

$(y + 9) = 3\left(\dfrac{y}{2} - 7\right)$

$\Rightarrow y + 9 = \dfrac{3y - 42}{2}$ $\Rightarrow 2y + 18 = 3y - 42$

$\Rightarrow y = 60$ years

17. (c) Let the ages of Abhay and his father 10 years ago be x and 5x years respectively. Then,

Abhay's age after 6 years $= (x + 10) + 6 = (x + 16)$ years.

Father's age after 6 years $= (5x + 10) + 6 = (5x + 16)$ years.

$\therefore$ $(x + 16) = \dfrac{3}{7}(5x + 16) \Leftrightarrow 7(x + 16) = 3(5x + 16)$

$\Leftrightarrow 7x + 112 = 15x + 48$

$\Leftrightarrow 8x = 64 \Leftrightarrow x = 8$.

Hence, Abhay's father's present age $= (5x + 10) = 50$ years.

18. (d) 16 years ago, let $T = x$ years and $G = 8x$ years

After 8 years from now, $T = (x + 16 + 8)$ years and $G = (8x + 16 + 8)$ years.

$\therefore$ $8x + 24 = 3(x + 24) \Leftrightarrow 5x = 48$.

8 years ago, $\dfrac{T}{G} = \dfrac{x+8}{8x+8} = \dfrac{\dfrac{48}{5}+8}{8 \times \dfrac{48}{5}+8} = \dfrac{88}{424} = \dfrac{11}{53}$

19. (a) Let the ages of children be x, $(x + 3)$, $(x + 6)$, $(x + 9)$ and $(x + 12)$ years.

Then, $x + (x + 3) + (x + 6) + (x + 9) + (x + 12) = 50$

$\Leftrightarrow 5x = 20 \Leftrightarrow x = 4$.

$\therefore$ Age of the youngest child $= x = 4$ years.

20. (d) Let the present ages of the father and son be 2x and x years respectively.

Then, $(2x - 18) = 3(x - 18) \Leftrightarrow x = 36$.

$\therefore$ Required sum $= (2x + x) = 3x = 108$ years.

8. Percentage

1. (a) y exceeds x by $= \dfrac{25}{100 - 25} \times 100 = 33\dfrac{1}{3}\%$

2. (c)

3. (d) 96% of 20 kg $= \dfrac{96}{100} \times 20 = 19.2$ kg [wt. of water]

Let 'x' kg of water in evaporated, then

$19.2 - x = 95\%$ of $(20 - x)$

$\Rightarrow 19.2 - x = \dfrac{95 \times (20 - x)}{100}$

$\Rightarrow 1920 - 100x = 1900 - 95x$

$\Rightarrow 5x = 20$

$\Rightarrow x = 4$ kg

$\therefore$ Reduced wt $= 20 - 4 = 16$ kg

4. (d) Ratio of men and women $= 1000 : 1075 = 40 : 43$

No. of men in total population $= \dfrac{40}{83} \times 155625$

$= 75000$

No. of women in total population $= 155625 - 75000$

$= 80625$

No. of literate men $= 40\%$ of 75000

$= \dfrac{40 \times 75000}{100} = 30000$

No. of literate women $= 24\%$ of 80625

$= \dfrac{24 \times 80625}{100} = 19350$

$\therefore$ Total no. of literate people $= 30000 + 19350$

$= 49350$

$\therefore$ Required $\% = \dfrac{49350}{155625} \times 100\% = \dfrac{2632}{83}\% = 31\dfrac{59}{83}\%$

5. (c)

6.   **(c)**   Let the man at first had ₹ x

Money lost by man $= 12.5$ of x

$$= \frac{25}{2} \times \frac{1}{100} \times x = \frac{x}{8}$$

$\therefore$ Remaining money $= x - \dfrac{x}{8} = \dfrac{7x}{8}$

Money spent $= 70\%$ of $\dfrac{7x}{8}$

$$= \frac{70}{100} \times \frac{7x}{8} = \frac{49}{80}x$$

Money left with man $= \dfrac{7x}{8} - \dfrac{49}{80}x = \dfrac{21}{80}x$

According to question

Money left $= \dfrac{21}{80}x = 210$

$$\Rightarrow x = \frac{210 \times 80}{21} = 800$$

$\therefore$ At first man had ₹ 800.

7.   **(c)** $\left(30 - 20 - \dfrac{30 \times 20}{100}\right) = 4\%$ Increase

8.   **(c)**   % error

$$= \left(5 + 3 + \frac{5 \times 3}{100}\right)$$

$= 8 + .15$

$= 8.15\%$

9.   **(b)**   Number of girls $= \dfrac{2500 \times 20}{100} = 500$

Number of boys $= 2000$

Number of fail boys $= \dfrac{2500 \times 5}{100} = 100$

Number of fail girls $= \dfrac{500 \times 40}{100} = 200$

Total no. of pass students $= 2500 - 300 = 2200$

Pass % $= \dfrac{2200}{2500} \times 100 = 88\%$

10.   **(a)**   Let the original income per year $=$ ₹ x

$\therefore$ Savings $= 20\%$ of $x = \dfrac{20}{100}x$

After increase his new income $= x + \dfrac{10}{100}x = \dfrac{110}{100}x$

New saving $= 20\%$ of $\dfrac{110}{100}x = \dfrac{20}{100} \times \dfrac{110}{100}x = \dfrac{22}{100}x$

Increase in savings $= \dfrac{22}{100}x - \dfrac{20}{100}x = \dfrac{2}{100}x$

$\therefore$ % increase $= \dfrac{\frac{2}{100}x}{\frac{20}{100}x} \times 100\% = 10\%$

11.   **(a)**   Total increase $= 20 + 20 + \dfrac{20 \times 20}{100} = 44\%$

$\therefore$ Reduce in number $= \dfrac{44}{144} \times 100 = 30\dfrac{5}{9}\%$

12.   **(d)**   Let the maximum marks in the examination $= x$

According to question,

20% of $x + 5 = 30\%$ of $x - 20$

$$\Rightarrow \frac{x}{5} + 5 = \frac{3x}{10} - 20$$

$$\Rightarrow \frac{3x}{10} - \frac{x}{5} = 25$$

$$\Rightarrow \frac{x}{10} = 25$$

$$\Rightarrow x = 250$$

Passing marks $= 20\%$ of $250 + 5 = \dfrac{20}{100} \times 250 + 5 = 55$

$\therefore$ % passing marks $= \left(\dfrac{55}{250} \times 100\right)\% = 22\%$

13.   **(d)**   Total marks to score $= \dfrac{150 \times 60}{100} = 90$

Marks obtained in first 75 questions

$$= \frac{75 \times 1 \times 80}{100} = 60$$

$\therefore$ Marks to be obtained in next 75 questions

$$= 90 - 60 = 30$$

$\therefore$ % of questions to be answered correctly

$$= \left(\frac{30 \times 1 \times 100}{75}\right)\% = 40\%$$

14.   **(b)**   **15.**   **(c)**

16.   **(b)**   Let the required quantity of water $= x$ litres

According to the questions,

$$70 \times \frac{10}{100} + x = (70 + x) \times \frac{12.5}{100}$$

$$\Rightarrow \quad x = 2$$

17.   **(d)**   **18.**   **(a)**

19.   **(a)**   Let the working houre/day (initially) $= x$

wages /hr $=$ ₹ y

$\therefore$ Daily income $= xy$

After increase

Working hr/day $= x + \dfrac{20}{100}x = \dfrac{6x}{5}$

Wages/hr $= y + \dfrac{15}{100}y = \dfrac{23}{20}y$

Daily income $= \dfrac{6x}{5} \times \dfrac{23}{20}y = \dfrac{138}{100}xy$

% increase in daily income $= \left[\left(\dfrac{\frac{138}{100}xy - xy}{xy}\right) \times 100\right]\%$

$$= \left(\frac{38}{100} \times 100\right)\% = 38\%$$

20. (c) Let the marked price $= ₹\, x$

After a discount of 20% price $= x - \dfrac{20}{100}x = ₹\, \dfrac{4x}{5}$

After a 10% discount on new price

$= \dfrac{4x}{5} - \dfrac{10}{100} \times \dfrac{4x}{5}$

$= ₹\, \dfrac{4x}{5} - \dfrac{2x}{25}$

$= ₹\, \dfrac{18x}{25}$

As given $\dfrac{18x}{25} = 108$

$\Rightarrow x = \dfrac{108 \times 25}{18} = ₹\, 150$

9. Profit & Loss

1. (b) Let marked price $= ₹\, x$

$\therefore$ selling price (S.P) $= x - \dfrac{25}{100}x$

$SP = ₹\, \dfrac{3}{4}x$

Let cost price (CP) $= ₹\, y$
Profit $= 20\%$

$\therefore \quad \dfrac{20}{100}y = 40$

$\Rightarrow y = 200$
$\therefore$ selling price (SP) $= 200 + 40 = ₹\, 240$

$\therefore \quad \dfrac{3}{4}x = 240 \Rightarrow x = \dfrac{240 \times 4}{3} = 320$

2. (d) Error in measurement $= 100 - 80 = 20$ cm

$\therefore \quad \% \text{ gain} = \left(\dfrac{\text{Error}}{\text{True value-Error}} \times 100 \right)\%$

$\% \text{ gain} = \left(\dfrac{20}{100 - 20} \right) \times 100\%$

$= \dfrac{20 \times 100}{80}\%$

$= 25\%$

3. (c) Let the original price of each article $= ₹\, 100$
$\therefore$ new price $= ₹\, 105$
Original selling price of 100 articles $= 100 \times 100 = 10{,}000$
Selling price of the article at new price $= 97.5 \times 105$
$\qquad\qquad\qquad\qquad\qquad\qquad = ₹\, 10237.50$

[No of article sold $= 97.5$]
$\therefore$ Profit $= 10237.50 - 10{,}000 = 237.50$

$\therefore \% \text{ profit} = \left(\dfrac{237.50}{10{,}000} \times 100 \right)\% = 2.4\%$

4. (b)   5. (a)

6. (c) Loss $\% = \dfrac{x^2}{100}\% = \left(\dfrac{x}{10} \right)^2 \%$

$\% \text{ Loss} = \left(\dfrac{10}{10} \right)^2 = 1\%$

7. (c) Price $= \dfrac{20 \times 10}{(100 - 20) \times 5} = \dfrac{20 \times 10}{80 \times 5} = 50 \text{ paise}$

8. (c) Let CP for A $= ₹\, x$
$\therefore \qquad$ CP for B $= ₹\, 1.2x$
and CP for C $= ₹\, 1.5x$
$\therefore \qquad 1.5\,x = 225$

$\Rightarrow \qquad x = \dfrac{225}{1.5} = ₹\, 150$

$\therefore \qquad$ CP for A $= ₹\, 150$

9. (c) $CP = \dfrac{5000 \times (100 - 4)}{(100 + 20)} = \dfrac{5000 \times 96}{120} = ₹4000$

10. (b) Let CP $= ₹\, x$

First SP $= 115\%$ of $x = \dfrac{23}{20}x$

second CP $= 90\%$ of $x = \dfrac{9x}{10}$

second SP $= 120\%$ of $\dfrac{9x}{10} = \dfrac{120}{100} \times \dfrac{9x}{10}$

$= \dfrac{27x}{25}$

It is given that

$\dfrac{23x}{20} - \dfrac{27x}{25} = 28$

$\Rightarrow \quad \dfrac{115x - 108x}{100} = 28$

$\Rightarrow \quad x = \dfrac{28 \times 100}{7} = ₹\, 400$

11. (d) Marked percentage above CP

$= \dfrac{\text{Discount \% + Profit\%}}{100 - \text{Discount\%}} \times 100$

$= \dfrac{10 + 8}{100 - 10} \times 100$

$= \dfrac{18}{90} \times 100 = 20\%$

12. (c) M.P $= \dfrac{266 \times 100}{95} = ₹280$

Now SP $= ₹280$
$\qquad P = 12\%$

$CP = \dfrac{280 \times 100}{112} = ₹250$

13. (c)

14. (c) Let CP = ₹ 100

∴ Gain on $\dfrac{1}{4}$ th i.e. ₹ 25 = ₹ 2.5

∴ SP = ₹ 27.5

Loss on $\dfrac{3}{4}$ th i.e. ₹ 75 = 20% of 75 = ₹ 15

∴ Selling price (SP) = 75 – 15 = ₹ 60.

∴ Total SP = 60 + 27.5 = 87.5

∴ Loss = 100 – 87.5 = ₹ 12.5

∴ % Loss $= \left(\dfrac{12.5}{100} \times 100\right)$

% Loss = 12.5%

15. (c)

16. (a) Let the original price = ₹ x

∴ CP $= \dfrac{15}{16}x$

SP $= x + \dfrac{10}{100}x = \dfrac{11}{10}x$

∴ % gain $= \dfrac{\dfrac{11}{10}x - \dfrac{15}{16}x}{\dfrac{15}{16}x} \times 100\%$

$= \dfrac{52}{3}\% = 17.33\%$

17. (c)

18. (a) Let the required profit per cent be x%
Then (110% of 2000) + [(100 + x)% of 2000]
$\qquad\qquad\qquad = 116\%$ of 40000

⇒ $\left(\dfrac{110}{100} \times 2000\right) + \left(\dfrac{100+x}{100} \times 2000\right) = \dfrac{116}{100} \times 4000$

⇒ 2200 + 2000 + 20x = 4640 ⇒ 20x = 440 ⇒ x = 22%

19. (c) SP of 1 kg of mixture = ₹ 66 per kg
Profit = 10%

CP of 1 kg of mxiture $= ₹\left(\dfrac{100}{110} \times 66\right) = ₹\ 60$

By the rule of alligation we have
Cost of 1 kg of rise of Ist kind Cost of 1 kg of rice of IInd kind

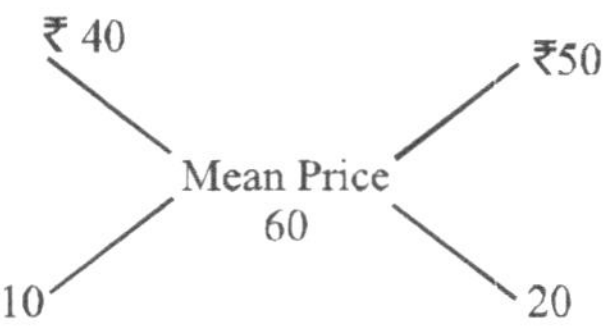

Reqduired ratio = 10 : 20 = 1 : 2

20. (d) Total cost price of mobile phone and refrigerator
= ₹ (12000 + 10000) = ₹ 22000
SP of mobile phone = (88% of 12000)

$= ₹\left(\dfrac{88}{100} \times 12000\right) = ₹\ 10560$

SP of refrigerator = 108% of 10000

$= ₹\left(\dfrac{108}{100} \times 10000\right) = ₹\ 10800$

Total SP of both the articles = ₹ (10560 + 10800)
= ₹ 21360
Loss = ₹ (22000 – 21360) = ₹ 640.

1. (c) 18 men complete the same work in $= \dfrac{30 \times 27}{18} = 45$ days

18 men complete the double work in = 45 × 2 = 90 days.

2. (d) Let required number of binders be 'x'
Less books, less binders (direct)
More days, less binders (indirect)

$\left.\begin{array}{llll}\text{Books} & 900 & :660 \\ \text{Days} & 12 & :10\end{array}\right\} :: 18 : x$

$900 \times 12 \times x = 660 \times 10 \times 18$

$x = \dfrac{660 \times 10 \times 18}{900 \times 12} = 11$

3. (a) Let number of days = x

∴ $\dfrac{8400}{7 \times 36} = \dfrac{8100}{x \times 9}$

$x = \dfrac{8100 \times 7 \times 36}{8400 \times 9} = 27\,\text{days}$

4. (b) Let numbers of ream = x

∴ $\dfrac{26}{13 \times 1000} = \dfrac{x}{500 \times 17}$

$x = 170$ reams

5. (a) Let number of days = x

∴ $\dfrac{9}{5 \times 18} = \dfrac{x}{66 \times 15}$

$x = 99$ days

6. (c) Let cost = x

∴ $\dfrac{112.50}{810 \times 70} = \dfrac{x}{840 \times 63}$

∴ $x = ₹105$

∴ Cost of half former = ₹52.5

7. (a) 27 men mow 225 hectares in 15 days

∴ 1 man mow 225 hectares in (15 × 27) days (indirect)

∴ 1 man mow 1 hectares in $\dfrac{15 \times 27}{225}$ days (direct)

1 man mow 165 hectares in $\dfrac{15 \times 27}{225} \times 165$ days (direct)

∴ 33 men mow 165 hectares in $\dfrac{15 \times 27 \times 165}{225 \times 33} = 9$ days

8. (a) Number of man $= \dfrac{30 \times 6 \times 9}{25 \times 8} \times 10$

= 81 men

9. (a) More men, less time (Indirect)
Let original number of men = x

No of Men	No of Days
x	10
$x - 5$	12

$\dfrac{x}{x-5} = \dfrac{12}{10}$

⇒ $10x = 12x - 60$

⇒ $2x = 60 \Rightarrow x = 30$

10. (d) 10 mason 8 hrs 50 m wall 25 days
1 mason 8 hrs 50 m wall 25 × 10 days
1 mason 1 hr 50 m wall 25 × 10 × 8 days

1 mason 1 hr 1 m wall $\dfrac{25 \times 10 \times 8}{50}$ days

1 mason 1 hr 36 m wall $\dfrac{25 \times 10 \times 8 \times 36}{50}$ days

1 mason 6 hr 36 m wall $\dfrac{25 \times 10 \times 8 \times 36}{50 \times 6}$ days

15 mason 6 hr 36 m wall $\dfrac{25 \times 10 \times 8 \times 36}{50 \times 6 \times 15}$ days
= 16 days

11. (c) $(X + Y)$'s one day work = $\dfrac{1}{72}$

$(Y + Z)$'s one day work = $\dfrac{1}{120}$

$(Z + X)$'s one day work = $\dfrac{1}{90}$

∴ $2(X + Y + Z)$'s one day work = $\dfrac{1}{72} + \dfrac{1}{120} + \dfrac{1}{90}$

$= \dfrac{5 + 3 + 4}{360} = \dfrac{12}{360} = \dfrac{1}{30}$

∴ $(X + Y + Z)$'s one day work = $\dfrac{1}{2} \times \dfrac{1}{30} = \dfrac{1}{60}$

∴ They will complete the work in 60 days.

12. (d)

13. (a)

14. (d) A can do 1 work in 10 days

B can do 1 work in $\dfrac{9 \times 5}{3}$ days = 15 days

C can do 1 work in $\dfrac{8 \times 3}{2}$ days = 12 days

∴ $(A + B + C)$'s one day work = $\dfrac{1}{10} + \dfrac{1}{15} + \dfrac{1}{12}$

$= \dfrac{6 + 4 + 5}{60} = \dfrac{15}{60} = \dfrac{1}{4}$

∴ They will complete the work in 4 days.

15. (b) Given $(6 M + 8 B) \times 10 = (26 M + 48 B) \times 2$
⇒ $60 M + 80 B = 52 M + 96 B$
⇒ $8 M = 16 B$
⇒ $1 M = 2 B$
∴ $15 M + 20 B = 30 B + 20 B = 50 B$
$6 M + 8 B = 12 B + 8 B = 20 B$

Now Boys   Days
      20   10
      50↓   x (Let)

∴ $x = \dfrac{20 \times 10}{50} = 4$ days

16. (b)   **17. (a)**   **18. (b)**

19. (b)

20. (d) 1 Man = 3 Boys and 1 Woman = 2 Boys
∴ 24 Men + 20 Women + 16 Boys
$= (24 \times 3) + (20 \times 2) + 16$
$= 72 + 40 + 16$
$= 128$ Boys
27 Men + 40 Women + 15 Boys $= (27 \times 3) + (40 \times 2) + 15$
$= 81 + 80 + 15 = 176$ Boys.

Now,

No. of Boys	Duration	Wages
128 ↑	1 ↑	224
176	52	x (Let)

∴ $x = \dfrac{176}{128} \times \dfrac{52}{1} \times 224$

$x = ₹\ 16,016$

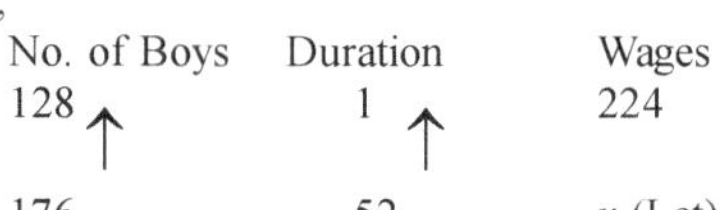

1. (b) Let the required number of working hours/day = x

Pumps 4 : 3 ⎫
Days   1 : 2 ⎬ :: 8 : x

∴ $4 \times 1 \times x = 3 \times 2 \times 8$

⇒ $x = \dfrac{3 \times 2 \times 8}{4} = 12$

2. (c) Part of the cistern filled by first pipe in 1 minute = $\dfrac{1}{6}$

Part of the cistern filled by second pipe in 2 minutes = $\dfrac{1}{7}$

Part of the cistern filled in first 2 minutes = $\dfrac{1}{6} + \dfrac{1}{7} = \dfrac{13}{42}$

Part of the cistern filled in 6 minutes = $\dfrac{3 \times 13}{42} = \dfrac{39}{42}$

Remaining part = $1 - \dfrac{39}{42} = \dfrac{3}{42} = \dfrac{1}{14}$

∴ Time taken to fill $\dfrac{1}{14}$ parts = $\dfrac{6}{14} = \dfrac{3}{7}$

∴ Total time = $6 + \dfrac{3}{7} = 6\dfrac{3}{7}$ minutes

3. (c) P takes to turns
then Q takes 60 × 3 = 180 turns

No. of turns for boths = $\dfrac{1}{60} + \dfrac{1}{180} = \dfrac{4}{180}$

= 45 turns

4. (d) Work done by both pipes in 1 min = $\dfrac{1}{12} + \dfrac{1}{15} = \dfrac{9}{60}$

Work done in 3 min = $\dfrac{9}{60} \times 3 = \dfrac{9}{20}$

Remaining work = $1 - \dfrac{9}{20} = \dfrac{11}{20}$

B fill 1 tank in 15 min

B fill $\dfrac{11}{20}$ part in = $15 \times \dfrac{11}{20} = \dfrac{33}{4}$ = 8 min 15 sec.

5. **(c)** Let both pipes open for x min.

$$\therefore \quad \left(\frac{1}{12}+\frac{1}{16}\right)\times x + \frac{1}{16}\times 4 = 1$$

$$\frac{7x}{48}=\frac{3}{4}$$

$$x = \frac{36}{7}\ \text{min}$$

$$\text{Total time} = 4+\frac{36}{7}=\frac{64}{7}$$

$$= 9\frac{1}{7}\ \text{min}$$

6. **(b)** Part filled by (A + B + C) in 3 minutes

$$= 3\left(\frac{1}{30}+\frac{1}{20}+\frac{1}{10}\right)=3\times\frac{11}{60}=\frac{11}{20}$$

Part filled by C in 3 minutes $=\dfrac{3}{10}$

$$\therefore \quad \text{Required ratio} = \frac{\dfrac{3}{10}}{\dfrac{11}{20}}=\frac{3}{10}\times\frac{20}{11}=\frac{6}{11}$$

7. **(a)**

$$\frac{18}{24}+\frac{18-x}{32}=1$$

$$\frac{18-x}{32}=\frac{1}{4}$$

$x = 10$ min

$\therefore$ B close before $18-10 = 8$ min.

8. **(b)** Pipe A has 1H work $=\dfrac{1}{6}$

Pipe A has 3 H work $=\dfrac{1}{2}$

4 pipes fill in 1 H $=\dfrac{1}{6}+\dfrac{1}{6}+\dfrac{1}{6}+\dfrac{1}{6}=\dfrac{2}{3}$ part

$\dfrac{1}{2}$ part they fill in $=\dfrac{3}{4}$ min = 45 min

Total time = 3H 45 min

9. **(d)** (A + B) pipes 1 H work $=\dfrac{1}{12}+\dfrac{1}{15}=\dfrac{9}{60}$

(A + C) pipes 1 H work $=\dfrac{1}{12}+\dfrac{1}{20}=\dfrac{8}{60}$

[(A + B) + (A + C)] pipes 2 H work $=\dfrac{17}{60}$

(2×5) H work $=\dfrac{17}{60}\times 3 =\dfrac{17}{20}$

Remaining work $= 1-\dfrac{17}{20}=\dfrac{3}{20}$

Total time = 6 + 1 = 7H.

10. **(a)** Diameter of three pipes say A, B, C are in the ratio

$$1:\frac{4}{3}:2$$

The ratio of flow can in the ratio $1^2:\left(\dfrac{4}{3}\right)^2:2^2$

$$= 1:\frac{16}{9}:4$$

Time taken by each pipe separately to fill the tank

$$= 1:\frac{9}{16}:4$$

If the pipe with diameter 2 cm takes 61 min. to fill the tank, then pipe A will take 61×4 minutes and pipe B will take

$$61\times 4\times\frac{9}{16}=\frac{61\times 9}{4}\ \text{min}$$

$\therefore$ In 1 min all the 3 pipes will fill

$$=\frac{1}{61}+\frac{1}{61\times 4}+\frac{4}{61\times 9}=\frac{4\times 9 + 9 + 4\times 4}{61\times 4\times 9}$$

$$=\frac{1}{36}\ \text{of the tank}$$

$\therefore$ Time taken by all the three pipes to fill the tank = 36 mins.

11. **(c)**

12. **(a)** Let it takes t minutes to completely fill the tank.

$$\text{Now,}\ \frac{t}{6}+\frac{t}{8}+\frac{t-6}{12}=1$$

$$\text{or}\ \frac{4t+3t+2t-12}{24}=1$$

or $9t - 12 = 24$
or $9t = 36 \Rightarrow t = 4$ min.

13. **(d)** Let the time be t hours after 6 am.

$$\therefore\quad \frac{1}{15}\times t+\frac{(t-1)}{20}+\frac{(t-2)}{30}+\frac{(t-3)}{60}=1$$

$\therefore$ $4t + 3(t-1) + 2(t-2) + (t-3) = 60$

$\therefore$ $t = 7$ hours $\therefore$ It is filled at 1 pm

14. **(c)** Net part filled in 1 hour $=\left(\dfrac{1}{5}+\dfrac{1}{6}-\dfrac{1}{12}\right)=\dfrac{17}{60}$.

$\therefore$ The tank will be full in $\dfrac{60}{17}$ hrs i.e., $3\dfrac{9}{17}$ hrs.

15. **(a)** Let cistern will be full in x min. Then,
part filled by A in x min + part filled by B in (x − 1) min + part filled by C in (x − 2) min = 1

$$\Rightarrow \frac{x}{3}+\frac{x-1}{4}+\frac{x-2}{6}=1\ \Rightarrow 9x=19\Rightarrow x=\frac{19}{9}=2\frac{1}{9}\text{min}$$

16. **(d)** Capacity of the tank = (12 × 13.5) litres = 162 litres.
Capacity of each bucket = 9 litres.

$$\text{Number of buckets needed} =\left(\frac{162}{9}\right)=18.$$

17. **(a)** Radius of the pipe (r) = 4 cm. = 0.04 meter
Volume of water flowing out per sec
$= \pi r^2 \times$ rate of flow

$$=\frac{22}{7}\times 0.04^2\times 3\ \text{cu meters} = 0.0151\ \text{cubic m}$$

Time taken to fill the tank $= 40 \times 30 \times \dfrac{8}{0.0151}$ sec

$= \dfrac{40 \times 30 \times 8}{0.01} \times \dfrac{1}{3600}$ hours $= 176.6$ hours

18. (d) A + B fill in 6 hrs.

B + C fill in 10 hrs.

A + C fill in $7\dfrac{1}{2} = \dfrac{15}{2}$ hrs

$\therefore$ 2 (A + B + C) fill in

$$\dfrac{6 \times 10 \times \dfrac{15}{2}}{6 \times 10 + 6 \times \dfrac{15}{2} + 10 \times \dfrac{15}{2}} = \dfrac{6 \times 5 \times 15}{180} = \dfrac{5}{2}$$

$\therefore$ A + B + C filled the tank in 5 hrs.

Now, A[= (A + B + C) – (B + C)] fill in $\dfrac{10 \times 5}{10 - 5} = 10$hrs.

Similarly, B fill in $\dfrac{\dfrac{15}{2} \times 5}{\dfrac{15}{2} - 5} = 15$ hrs and C fill in

$\dfrac{5 \times 6}{6 - 5} = 30$ hrs.

19. (b) Work of both tap for 1 hour $= \dfrac{1}{2} - \dfrac{1}{3} = \dfrac{1}{6}$

Hence, both tap will fill the cistern in 6 hours.

20. (c) In 1 hour, empty part $= \dfrac{1}{8}$ th.

When tap is turned on, then

empty part in 1 hour $= \dfrac{1}{12}$ th .

$\therefore$ Part of cistern emptied, due to leakage in

1 hour $= \dfrac{1}{8} - \dfrac{1}{12} = \dfrac{3 - 2}{24} = \dfrac{1}{24}$ th

Now, In 1 min, cistern fill $= 6$ lit

$\therefore$ In $\dfrac{1}{60}$ hr, cistern fill $= 6$ lit.

$\therefore$ Cistern can hold $= 6 \times 60 \times 24$ litre $= 8640$ litre.

12. Time, Speed & Distance

1. (b) Total distance covered $= 300 + 500 = 800$ km.

Total time taken to cover 800 km

$= \dfrac{300}{45} + \dfrac{500}{60} = \dfrac{20}{3} + \dfrac{25}{3} = \dfrac{45}{3} = 15$hr.

$\therefore$ Average speed $= \dfrac{800}{15} = \dfrac{160}{3} = 53\dfrac{1}{3}$ kmph

2. (a) Let distance AB $= x$ units

Let $\dfrac{3}{5}x$ distance is covered in t_1 time and $\dfrac{2}{5}x$ distance

is covered in t_2 time

$\therefore$ 3a $= \dfrac{\dfrac{3}{5}x}{t_1} \Rightarrow t_1 = \dfrac{x}{5a}$ $\qquad$ ...(1)

and $2b = \dfrac{\dfrac{2}{5}x}{t_2} \Rightarrow t_2 = \dfrac{x}{5b}$ $\qquad$ ...(2)

Total time taken in going from B to A and back at speed of 5c

$t = \dfrac{2x}{5c}$

Now, $t = t_1 + t_2$

$\therefore \dfrac{2x}{5c} = \dfrac{x}{5a} + \dfrac{x}{5b}$

$\Rightarrow \dfrac{2}{c} = \dfrac{1}{a} + \dfrac{1}{b}$

3. (a) Distance $=$ Average speed $\times$ time

$= \dfrac{2 \times 21 \times 24}{21 + 24} \times 10$

$= \dfrac{2 \times 21 \times 24}{45} \times 10 = 224$ km

4. (d)

5. (b) Let B takes x H

then A takes $\left(x + \dfrac{1}{2}\right)$ H

$\therefore \left(x + \dfrac{1}{2}\right) 3 = x \times 4$

$6x + 3 = 8x$

$2x = 3$

$x = \dfrac{3}{2}$

$\therefore$ A takes $= \dfrac{3}{2} + \dfrac{1}{2}$

$= 2$ Hrs.

6. (a) Let speed of car P be x km/hr and car Q be 4 km/hr.

When cars are moving in opposite directions

$\dfrac{120}{x + y} = 1 \Rightarrow x + y = 120$ $\qquad$ ...(1)

When cars are moving in same direction

$\dfrac{120}{x - y} = 6 \Rightarrow 6x - 6y = 120$

$\Rightarrow x - y = 20$ $\qquad$ ...(2)

From (1) and (2)

$x = 70$ km/hr, $y = 50$ km/hr

$\therefore$ speed of car $P = 70$ km/hr.

7. (c) Average speed $= \dfrac{\text{Total distance}}{\text{Total time}}$

$= \dfrac{600 + 800 + 500 + 100}{\dfrac{600}{80} + \dfrac{800}{40} + \dfrac{500}{400} + \dfrac{100}{50}} = 65\dfrac{5}{123}$ km / h

8. (d) Let total time taken = x H
$$\therefore \quad 14x - 10x = 20$$
$$4x = 20$$
$$x = 5H$$
$$\therefore \quad \text{Actual distance} = 5 \times 10 = 50 \text{ km}$$

9. (a) Stoping per hour $= \dfrac{54 - 45}{45} \times 60$
$$= \dfrac{9}{45} \times 60 = 12 \text{ min}$$

10. (d) Let distance travelled on foot = x km
$$\therefore \quad \dfrac{x}{4} + \dfrac{61 - x}{9} = 9$$
$$9x + 244 - 4x = 324$$
$$5x = 80$$
$$x = 16 \text{ km}$$
$$\therefore \quad \text{Distance travelled on foot} = 16 \text{ km}$$

11. (c) Let actual speed = x
$$\therefore \quad \dfrac{5}{7} x \times \dfrac{6048}{3600} = 42$$
$$x = \dfrac{42 \times 7 \times 3600}{5 \times 6048}$$
$$x = 35 \text{ km/h}$$

12. (c) Let the distance be x km.
According to question
$$\dfrac{x}{7\frac{1}{2}} - \dfrac{x}{8} = 4$$
$$\Rightarrow \quad \dfrac{2x}{15} - \dfrac{x}{8} = 4$$
$$\Rightarrow \quad \dfrac{16x - 15x}{120} = 4$$
$$\Rightarrow \quad x = 480 \text{ km}$$

13. (b) Distance travelled per H = 35, 37, 39
$$S_n = \dfrac{n}{2}\big[2a + (n-1)d\big]$$
$$n = 12, \ a = 35, \ d = 2$$
$$= \dfrac{12}{2}\big[2 \times 35 + (12 - 1) \times 2\big]$$
$$= 6[70 + 22]$$
$$= 6 \times 92 = 552 \text{ km}$$

14. (c) Time $= 4.5 \times \dfrac{5}{18} x + 3.75 \times \dfrac{5}{18} \times x = 726$
$$1.25x + 1.04x = 726$$
$$x = 317 \text{ sec}$$
$$= 5.28 \text{ min}$$

15. (b) Distance from his house
$$= \dfrac{\text{Product of speed}}{\text{Difference of speed}} \times \text{total time}$$
$$= \dfrac{\dfrac{5}{2} \times \dfrac{7}{2}}{1} \times \dfrac{12}{60}$$
$$= \dfrac{35}{4} \times \dfrac{1}{5} = \dfrac{7}{4} = 1.75 \text{ km}$$

16. (d) Let total distance = x km
$$\therefore \quad \dfrac{x}{3} + \dfrac{x}{2} = 5$$
$$x = 6 \text{ km}$$

17. (a) Let time taken from village to post office (one side) = t hrs
Time taken for whole journey = 5 hrs 48 min
$$= 5 \text{ hr } \dfrac{48}{60} \text{ hr} = 5\dfrac{4}{5} \text{ hrs.}$$
Now, $25 \times t = 4\left(5\dfrac{4}{5} - t\right)$
$$\Rightarrow \quad 25t = \dfrac{29 \times 4}{5} - 4t \Rightarrow 29t = \dfrac{29 \times 4}{5}$$
$$\Rightarrow \quad t = \dfrac{4}{5} \text{ hrs}$$
$$\therefore \quad \text{Distance} = 25 \times \dfrac{4}{5} = 20 \text{ km}$$

18. (c) Let distance travelled at 100 km/hr be 'x' km.
$$\therefore \quad \text{Distance travelled at 50 km/hr is } (170 - x) \text{ km.}$$
Total time taken to cover 170 km is 2 hrs.
$$\therefore \quad \dfrac{x}{100} + \dfrac{170 - x}{50} = 2$$
$$\Rightarrow \quad x + 340 - 2x = 200$$
$$\Rightarrow \quad x = 140 \text{ km}$$
$$\therefore \quad \text{Distance travelled at 100 km/hr is 140 km.}$$

19. (b) Let the truck travels for 't' hour at 60 km/hr.
$$\therefore \quad 60 \times t + 30 \times (6 - t) = 240$$
$$\Rightarrow \quad 60t + 180 - 30t = 240$$
$$\Rightarrow \quad 30t = 60$$
$$\Rightarrow \quad t = 2 \text{ hr.}$$
$$\therefore \quad \text{Truck travels 2 hours at 60 km/hr.}$$

20. (d) Let initial speed = x km/h
$$\therefore \quad \dfrac{200}{x} - \dfrac{200}{x + 10} = 1$$
$$x(x + 10) = 2000$$
$$x^2 + 10x - 2000 = 0$$
$$x = 40 \text{ km/h}$$
$$\therefore \quad \text{Initial speed of car} = 40 \text{ km/h.}$$

13. Trains

1. (a) Let speed of first train = x km/h
speed of second train = y km/h
$$\therefore \quad \text{In same direction} = 18 = \dfrac{90 + 90}{x - y}$$
$$x - y = 10 \qquad \qquad \text{...(1)}$$
In opposite direciton $= 9 = \dfrac{90 + 90}{x + y}$
$$x + y = 20 \qquad \qquad \text{...(2)}$$
By (1) and (2)
$$x = 15, \ y = 5$$
$$\therefore \quad \text{speed of second train} = 5 \text{ km/h}$$

2. (c) Let the length of train be 'x' m
Speed of train be 'y' m/sec
$$\text{Given speed} = \dfrac{\text{distance}}{\text{time}}$$

$$y = \frac{x}{4} \qquad \text{...(1)}$$

and $\qquad y = \dfrac{x+75}{9} \qquad \text{...(2)}$

From (1) and (2)

$$\frac{x}{4} = \frac{x+75}{9}$$

$\Rightarrow \quad 9x = 4x + 300$

$\Rightarrow \quad x = 60$ m

$\therefore \quad y = \dfrac{60}{4} = 15$ m/sec

3. (b) $\quad t = \dfrac{500+500}{\left(45+30\right)\times\dfrac{5}{18}}$

$\qquad = \dfrac{1000\times18}{75\times5} = 48\sec$

4. (d) Let first train travel x km

$\therefore \quad \dfrac{x}{50} = \dfrac{x+120}{60}$

$6x = 5x + 600$

$x = 600$

$\therefore$ Distance between A and B is

$600 + 600 + 120 = 1320$km.

5. (a) Speed of first train $= \dfrac{120}{10} = 12$ m/s

Speed of second train $= \dfrac{120}{15} = 8$ m/s

$\therefore \quad t = \dfrac{120+120}{12+8} = \dfrac{240}{20} = 12\sec$

6. (b) Let slower speed $= u$ km/hr

As the distance is fixed

$u \times 8 = (u+5) \times \dfrac{20}{3}$ [$\because$ 6 hr 40 min $= 6$hr $+ \dfrac{40}{60}$ hr

$\qquad\qquad\qquad\qquad\qquad = 6\dfrac{2}{3} = \dfrac{20}{3}$ hrs]

$\Rightarrow 24$ u $= 20$ u $+ 100$

$\Rightarrow 4$ u $= 100$

$\Rightarrow$ u $= 25$ km/hr

7. (d) Let time taken by VB express $= x$h

$\therefore \quad \left(x+2\right)\times 60 = x \times 80$

$60x + 120 = 80x$

$20x = 120$

$x \quad = 6$h

$\therefore$ Required distance $= 6 \times 80$

$= 480$ km.

8. (b) Distance travelled by slower train in 18 sec

$= 30 \times \dfrac{5}{18} \times 18 = 150$m

Distance travelled by faster train in 18 sec

$= 58 \times \dfrac{5}{18} \times 18 = 290$m

$\therefore$ The length of faster train $= 290 - 150 = 140$m

9. (d) $\quad t = \dfrac{300+200}{\left(90+60\right)\times\dfrac{5}{18}}$

$\qquad = \dfrac{500\times18}{150\times5} = 12\sec$

10. (a) Given, speed $= 65$ km/hr, distance $= 1300$ km

$\therefore$ Time $= \dfrac{1300}{65} = 20$ hrs.

$\therefore 24 - 20 = 4$ hrs are spent at 4 junctions in stoppage

$\therefore$ Time taken by the train to halt at each station

$\qquad = \dfrac{4\times60}{8} = 30$ min

11. (d) Let speed of good train $= x$ km/h

$\therefore \quad t = \dfrac{187.5}{\left(50+x\right)\times\dfrac{5}{18}}$

$450 + 9x = 187.5 \times \dfrac{18}{5}$

$450 + 9x = 675$

$\qquad x = 25$

$\therefore$ Speed of good train $= 25$ km/h

12. (b) Length of train $= 12 \times 15 = 180$ m

time $= 18$ sec

speed $= \dfrac{180}{18} = 10$ m/sec

Now length of train $= 10 \times 15 = 150$ m

Speed $= 10$ m/sec

Ttime $= \dfrac{150}{10} = 15\sec$

13. (d) Speed of train relative to jogger $= 45 - 9 = 36$ km/hr

$= 36 \times \dfrac{5}{18} = 10$ m/sec

Distance to be covered $= 240 + 120 = 360$ m.

$\therefore$ Time taken $= \dfrac{360}{10} = 36$ sec

14. (b)

15. (c) Let the speeds of two trains be 'x' m/sec and 'y' m/sec respectively.

Length of first train $= 27$ x metres

Length of second train $= 17$ y metres

$\therefore \quad \dfrac{27x+17y}{x+y} = 23$

$\Rightarrow 27x + 17$ y $= 23x + 23y$

$\Rightarrow 4x = 6y$

$\Rightarrow \dfrac{x}{y} = \dfrac{3}{2} \Rightarrow x : y = 3 : 2$

16. (a) Let the speed of the goods train be x kmph.

Distance covered by goods train in 10 hours

$\qquad$ = Distance covered by express train in 4 hours.

$\therefore 10x = 4 \times 90$ or $x = 36$.

So, speed of goods train $= 36$ kmph.

17. (a) Due to stoppages, it covers 20 km less .

Time taken to cover $20\,\text{km} = \dfrac{20}{80}\,\text{h} = \dfrac{1}{4}\,\text{h}$

$= \dfrac{1}{4} \times 60\,\text{min} = 15\,\text{min}$

18. (b) Let the distance between the two stations be x km.

Then, $\dfrac{x}{50} - \dfrac{10}{6} = \dfrac{x}{30} - \dfrac{50}{6}$

$\Rightarrow \dfrac{x}{50} - \dfrac{1}{6} = \dfrac{x}{30} - \dfrac{5}{6}$

or $\dfrac{x}{30} - \dfrac{x}{50} = \dfrac{2}{3}$ or $x = 50\,\text{km}$

Thus distance between the station A and B = 50 km

19. (d) Let the speed of the second train be x km/h
The relative speed = (50 + x) km/h
These trains will cross each other in a time equivalent of covering a distance equal to 108 + 112, i.e. 220 meters in 6 seconds, running a speed of (50 + x) km/h

$\therefore \quad \dfrac{1}{50+x} \times \dfrac{220}{1000} = \dfrac{6}{3600} \Rightarrow x = 82$

$\therefore$ The speed of the second train = 82 km/h.

20. (b) Let the length of the bridge be x m.

Now, $(x + 100) = 72 \times 25 \times \dfrac{5}{18} = 500$

$\Rightarrow x = 500 - 100 = 400\,\text{m}$

14. Boats & Streams

1. (b) Downstream speed = 15 + 5 = 20 km/h.

$\therefore$ Required distance $= 20 \times \dfrac{24}{60} = 8\,\text{km}.$

2. (b) Let man's rowing speed in still water = x km/hr
Let speed of current = y km/hr

Downstream speed $= x + y = \dfrac{36}{6} = 6$ ...(1)

Upstream speed $= x - y = \dfrac{24}{6} = 4$ ...(2)

(1) – (2)
$2y = 2 \Rightarrow y = 1$

$\therefore$ speed of current = 1 km/hr.

3. (d) Let the speed of the stream be x km/h.
Then, upstream speed = (15 – x) km/h.
and downstream speed = (15 + x) km/h.

Now, $\dfrac{30}{(15+x)} + \dfrac{30}{(15-x)} = 4.5$

Checking with options, we find that x = 5 km/h.

4. (a) Let speed of the boat in still water be x km/h and speed of the current be y km/h.
Then, upstream speed = (x – y) km/h
and downstream speed = (x + y) km/h

Now, $\dfrac{24}{(x-y)} + \dfrac{28}{(x+y)} = 6$ ...(i)

and $\dfrac{30}{(x-y)} + \dfrac{21}{(x+y)} = \dfrac{13}{2}$ ...(ii)

Solving (i) and (ii), we have
x = 10 km/h and y = 4 km/h

5. (a) Let the rate against the current be x km/hr. Then,

$\dfrac{12-x}{2} = 1.5 \Rightarrow 12 - x = 3 \Rightarrow x = 9\,\text{km}/\text{hr}$

6. (d) Let speed of boat = 36x km/h
Speed of current = 5x km/h

$\therefore \quad (36x + 5x) \times \dfrac{310}{60} = (36x - 5x) \times t$

$t = \dfrac{41 \times 310}{60 \times 31} = \dfrac{41}{6} = 6\text{H}\ 50\,\text{min}$

7. (d) Let the distance between the two parts = 'x' km
Let the speed of steamer in still water = 'y' km/hr

$\therefore \quad \dfrac{x}{y+2} = 4 \Rightarrow x = 4y + 8$ ...(1)

$\dfrac{x}{y-2} = 5 \Rightarrow x = 5y - 10$ ...(2)

From (1) and (2)
$4y + 8 = 5y - 10$
$\Rightarrow y = 18$
$\therefore$ From (1)
$x = 4 \times 18 + 8 = 80\,\text{km}.$

8. (c) Let speed of boat in still water = x km/h
speed of current = y km/h
$\therefore \quad (x + y) \times t = (x - y) \times 2t$
$x = 3y$
$x : y = \ 3 : 1$

9. (d) Let speed in downstream = (x + y)
speed in upstream = (x – y)

$\therefore \quad \dfrac{d}{x+y} + \dfrac{d}{x-y} = \dfrac{21}{4}$ ...(1)

As $\dfrac{2d}{x-y} = 7$

$\therefore \quad \dfrac{2d}{x+y} = \dfrac{21}{4} \times 2 - 7$

$= \dfrac{7}{2}\,\text{hours}$

10. (b) Let rate of stream = x kmph

$\therefore \quad \dfrac{20}{8+x} = \dfrac{12}{8-x}$

$160 - 20x = 96 + 12x$
$64 = 32x$
$x = 2$
$\therefore$ Rate of stream = 2 kmph

11. (a) Rate of stream = 1.5 km/hr
Let speed of man in still water = u km/hr
and distance = d
$\therefore$ downstream speed = (u + 1.5) km/hr
upstream speed = (u – 1.5)km/hr

$\therefore$ From question $\dfrac{2d}{u+1.5} = \dfrac{d}{u-1.5}$

$\Rightarrow 2u - 3 = u + 1.5$
$\Rightarrow u = 4.5\,\text{km/hr}$

12. (c) Let speed in downstream = (x + y)
Speed in upstream = (x – y)

$\therefore \quad 4(x+y) = 40$

$x + y = 10 \qquad\qquad ...(1)$

and $3(x-y) = 24$

$x - y = 8 \qquad\qquad ...(2)$

By (1) and (2)

$x = 9, y = 1$

$\therefore$ speed in still water is 9 km/h

13. (c)

14. (a) Let speed in still water $= x$ km/h

Speed of stream $= 2$ km/h

$\therefore \quad \dfrac{10}{x+2} + \dfrac{10}{x-2} = \dfrac{55}{60}$

$10x + 10x = \dfrac{11}{12}\left(x^2 - 4\right)$

$11x^2 - 240x - 44 = 0$

$x = 22$

$\therefore$ speed in still water $= 22$ km/h

15. (b) Let upstream rate $= x$ km//hr,

downstream rate $= y$ km/hr

$\therefore \quad \dfrac{24}{x} + \dfrac{36}{y} = 6 \qquad\qquad ...(1)$

$\dfrac{36}{x} + \dfrac{24}{y} = \dfrac{13}{2} \qquad\qquad ...(2)$

Add (1) and (2), we get

$60\left(\dfrac{1}{x} + \dfrac{1}{y}\right) = \dfrac{25}{2} \Rightarrow \dfrac{1}{x} + \dfrac{1}{y} = \dfrac{5}{24} \qquad ...(3)$

Subtract (1) from (2)

$12\left(\dfrac{1}{x} - \dfrac{1}{y}\right) = \dfrac{1}{2} \Rightarrow \dfrac{1}{x} - \dfrac{1}{y} = \dfrac{1}{24} \qquad ...(4)$

Add (3) and (4)

$\dfrac{2}{x} = \dfrac{6}{24} \Rightarrow x = 8$

From (3) $y = 12$

$\therefore$ Velocity of current $= \dfrac{1}{2}(y-x) = \dfrac{1}{2}(12-8) = 2$ km/hr

16. (a) Let speed in downstream $= (x+y)$

Speed in upstream $= (x-y)$

$\therefore \quad (x+y) = 2(x-y)$

$x = 3y$

$x : y = 3 : 1$

17. (c) Downstream speed $= 14 + 4 = 18$ km/hr

Upstream speed $= 14 - 4 = 10$ km/hr

Let the distance between A and B $= 'x'$ km

$\therefore \quad \dfrac{x}{18} + \dfrac{\frac{x}{2}}{10} = 19$

$\therefore \quad \dfrac{x}{18} + \dfrac{x}{20} = 19$

$\dfrac{10x + 9x}{180} = 19$

$\dfrac{19x}{180} = 19 \Rightarrow x = 180$ km

18. (b) Speed of the boat downstream $= \dfrac{120}{5} = 24$ km/h

Ratio of speeds of boat and stream $= 2 : 1$

$\therefore$ Speed of the stream $= \dfrac{1}{3} \times 24 = 8$ km/h

19. (c) Let speed of boat in still water $= x$ km/hr

Let speed of stream $= y$ km/hr

Let distance covered $= d$ km

$\therefore \quad \dfrac{d}{x+y} = \dfrac{45}{60} = \dfrac{3}{4} \qquad ...(1)$

$\dfrac{d}{x-y} = \dfrac{75}{60} = \dfrac{5}{4} \qquad ...(2)$

Form (1) & (2),

$\dfrac{x-y}{x+y} = \dfrac{3}{5} \Rightarrow 5x - 5y = 3x + 3y$

$\Rightarrow 2x = 8y \Rightarrow \dfrac{y}{x} = \dfrac{1}{4}$

$\therefore$ ratio of speed of the stream to boat in still water $= 1 : 4$

20. (b) Let the distance $= d$ km

Time taken to row upstream $'t_1' = \dfrac{d}{5-3} = \dfrac{d}{2} \qquad ...(1)$

Time taken to row downstream $'t_2' = \dfrac{d}{5+3} = \dfrac{d}{8} \qquad ...(2)$

$t_1 + t_2 = 5$ (Given)

$\therefore \quad \dfrac{d}{2} + \dfrac{d}{8} = 5$

$\Rightarrow \dfrac{4d + d}{8} = 5 \Rightarrow d = 8$ km

$\therefore$ Distance of the place $= 8$ km.

15. Simple Interest & Compound Interest

1. (c) A $= ₹\,220$; P $= ₹\,200$; R $= ?$

$n = 1$ year.

$A = P\left(1 + \dfrac{R}{100}\right)^n$

$220 = 200\left(1 + \dfrac{R}{100}\right)^n$

$1 + \dfrac{R}{100} = \dfrac{220}{200}$

$R = 10\%$.

2. (d) P $= ₹\,12500$. N $= 2$ years, Rate $= 10\%$. When interest is payable yearly

$A = 12500\left(1 + \dfrac{10}{100}\right)^2 = ₹\,15125$

When interest is payable half yearly

$A = 12500\left(1 + \dfrac{5}{100}\right)^4 = ₹\,15193.82$

Difference = ₹ (15193.82 – 15125)

$\qquad\qquad$ = ₹ 68.82

3. **(b)** Nanoo's interest for an year at 10% compunded half yearly

$$= 400\left(1+\frac{5}{100}\right)^2 - 400$$

$$= \frac{400\times21\times21}{20\times20} - 400$$

$$= ₹\,441 - 400 = ₹\,41$$

Meenu's interest at simple interest

$$= \frac{400\times10\times1}{100} = ₹\,40$$

Thus, Nanoo paid 41 – 40 = ₹ 1 more

4. **(a)** For the first year S.I. and C.I. are same. The difference is therefore equal to the interest on S.I. for one year at 8%.

$$\therefore\ \text{S.I. for 1 year} = \frac{160\times100}{8} = ₹\,2000$$

Hence the principal $= \dfrac{2000\times100}{8} = ₹\,25000$

When the interest is compounded half yearly, C.I. for two years

$$= 25000\left(1+\frac{4}{100}\right)^4 - 25000$$

$$= ₹\,29246.50 - 25000$$
$$= ₹\,4246.50$$

S.I. for 2 years = ₹ 4000

Difference in interests = ₹ 4246.50 – 4000
$\qquad\qquad\qquad\qquad\quad$ = ₹ 246.50

5. **(c)** In 2 years, ₹ 1 will become $\left(1+\dfrac{15}{100}\right)^2$ times of itself

$$= \left(\frac{115}{100}\right)^2 \text{ times of itself} = \frac{13225}{10000} \text{ times of itself}$$

$$\therefore\ \text{ Increase} = \frac{13225}{10000} - 1 = \frac{3225}{10000} = 32.25\%$$

6. **(b)** Let population become 9261 in 'x' years.

$$\frac{\text{Amount}}{\text{Principal}} = \left(1+\frac{\text{Rate}}{100}\right)^{\text{Time}}$$

$$\therefore\ \frac{9261}{8000} = \left(\frac{21}{20}\right)^x$$

$$\therefore\ \left(\frac{21}{20}\right)^3 = \left(\frac{21}{20}\right)^x$$

$$\therefore\ \text{Time} = 3 \text{ years}$$

7. **(b)** $(1+r) = 1+\dfrac{1}{25} = \dfrac{26}{25}$

Let Mohan and Sohan receives ₹ x and ₹ y respectively at present.

$$\text{Then } \frac{x}{y} = \left(\frac{26}{25}\right)^{2-3} = \left(\frac{26}{25}\right)^{-1} = \frac{25}{26}$$

$\therefore$ Mohan's share $= \dfrac{25}{51} \times ₹\,5100 = ₹\,2500$

8. **(c)** Let rate of increase in population = r% p.a.

$$\text{Then } 4800 = 3600\left(1+\frac{r}{100}\right)^5$$

$$\therefore\ \left(1+\frac{r}{100}\right)^5 = \frac{4800}{3600} = \frac{4}{3}$$

Population in the next 5 years will become

$$4800 \times \frac{4}{3} = 6400.$$

9. **(d)** Remaining part $= 1-\left(\dfrac{1}{3}+\dfrac{1}{6}\right) = \dfrac{1}{2}$

Average rate % per annum (R)

$$= \left(\frac{1}{3}\times3\right) + \left(\frac{1}{6}\times6\right) + \left(\frac{1}{2}\times8\right) = 6\%$$

SI = ₹ 600

T = 2 years, P = ?

$$I = \frac{PTR}{100}$$

$$P = \frac{100\times I}{TR}$$

$$= \frac{100\times600}{2\times6}$$

$$= ₹\,5000.$$

10. **(c)** $\qquad A = P\left(1+\dfrac{TR}{100}\right)$

$$81 = 72\left(1+\frac{T\times\dfrac{25}{4}}{100}\right)$$

$$\frac{16+T}{16} = \frac{81}{72}$$

$$16 + T = 18$$
$$T = 2 \text{ years.}$$

11. **(d)**

Bhanu $\qquad\qquad$ Madhuri

T_1 = 3 years $\qquad$ T_2 = 10 years

R_1 = 12% $\qquad\quad$ R_2 = 24%

Let P = 100

$$\frac{A_1}{A_2} = \frac{100+T_1R_1}{100+T_2R_2}$$

$$= \frac{100+3\times12}{100+10\times24}$$

$$= \frac{136}{340} = \frac{2}{5}$$

$$\therefore\ A_1 : A_2 = 2 : 5$$

12. **(b)**

Gopi	Krishna
P = ₹ 1800	P = ₹ 1200
R = 12%	R = 18%
T = 2 years	T = 3 years

$$I_1 = \frac{PTR}{100} \qquad I_2 = \frac{PTR}{100}$$

$$= \frac{1800 \times 2 \times 12}{100} \qquad = \frac{1200 \times 3 \times 18}{100}$$

$$= ₹\,432 \qquad\qquad = ₹\,648$$

$I_1 : I_2 = 432 : 648 = 2 : 3.$

13. **(b)** $(1 + r) = 1 + \dfrac{1}{40} = \dfrac{41}{40}$

$\therefore$ Amount $= 1600 \times \dfrac{41}{40} \times \dfrac{41}{40} = 1681$

$\therefore$ Compound interest $= ₹\,1681 - ₹\,1600 = ₹\,81$

14. **(b)** Amount $= 25000 \times \left(1 + \dfrac{20}{100}\right)^2 \times \left(1 + \dfrac{10}{100}\right)^1$

$$= 25000 \times \left(\dfrac{6}{5}\right)^2 \times \dfrac{11}{10} = 39600$$

$\therefore$ Compound interest $= 39600 - 25000 = 14600.$

15. **(a)** $2^2 = 4.$

$\therefore$ The amount will become 4 times in $2 \times 5 = 10$ years.

16. **(d)** Let principal $= ₹\,100$

Amount after two years $= 100 \times \left(\dfrac{11}{10}\right)^2 = ₹121$

$\therefore$ Compound interest for second year
$$= ₹\,121 - ₹\,110 = ₹\,11$$
But actual compound interest for second year
$$= ₹\,132 \text{ (i.e. 12 times of } ₹\,11)$$
$\therefore$ Principal $= 12 \times ₹\,100 = ₹\,1200$

17. **(b)** $(1 + r)^3 = \dfrac{18522}{16000} = \dfrac{9261}{8000} = \left(\dfrac{21}{20}\right)^3 = \left(1 + \dfrac{1}{20}\right)^3$

$\therefore$ Rate of interest $= \dfrac{1}{20} = 5\%$

18. **(a)** $\text{C.I.} = 2000\left[\left(1 + \dfrac{8}{100 \times 4}\right)^{4 \times \frac{9}{12}} - 1\right]$

$P = 2000$, $R = 8\%$ p.a., $t = 9$ months $= \dfrac{9}{12}$ year

$\text{C.I.} = 2000\left[\left(1 + \dfrac{8}{100 \times 4}\right)^{4 \times \frac{9}{12}} - 1\right]$ $(n = 4)$

$$= 2000\left[\left(\dfrac{102}{100}\right)^3 - 1\right] = ₹\,122.$$

$\therefore$ the compound interest is ₹122

19. **(c)** Let x be lent at 5% and $(1200 - x)$ at 4%

Then we have, $\dfrac{x \times 5 \times 2}{100} + \dfrac{(1200 - x) \times 4 \times 2}{100} = 106$

$\Rightarrow\ x = 500.$

20. **(a)** Difference $= \dfrac{\text{Sum} \times r^2 (300 + r)}{(100)^3}$

$$= \dfrac{8000 \times 2.5 \times 2.5(300 + 2.5)}{100 \times 100 \times 100}$$

$$= \dfrac{8 \times 25 \times 25 \times 3025}{100 \times 100 \times 100} = \dfrac{121}{8} = ₹\,15.125$$

16. Mensuration

1. **(a)** Let the sides of triangle are $3x$, $4x$ and $5x$ respectively.
$\therefore$ Perimeter $= 3x + 4x + 5x = 12x$
$\therefore 12x = 36$ (given)
$\therefore x = 3$ cm
So sides are 9 cm, 12 cm and 15 cm
The sides follow the relation $15^2 = 12^2 + 9^2$
$\therefore$ Triangle is a right angled triangle.

$\therefore$ area of $\Delta = \dfrac{1}{2} \times 9 \times 12 = 54$ cm^2

Area can also be calculated using Heron's formula

$$s = \dfrac{9 + 12 + 15}{2} = 18 \text{ cm}$$

$\therefore$ Area $= \sqrt{18(18-9)(18-12)(18-15)} = \sqrt{18 \times 9 \times 6 \times 3}$

$$= \sqrt{9 \times 2 \times 9 \times 3 \times 2 \times 3}$$

Area $= 9 \times 2 \times 3 = 54$ cm^2

2. **(d)**

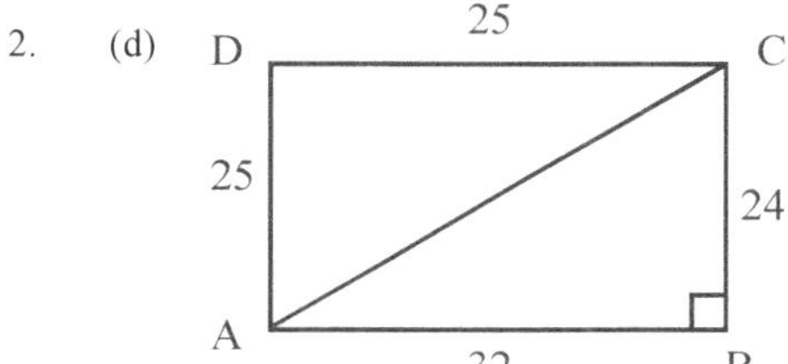

Let ABCD is the plot with sides shown. Join AC
As $\angle$ ABD $= 90°$

$\therefore$ AC $= \sqrt{AB^2 + BC^2} = \sqrt{32^2 + 24^2}$
$\quad$ AC $= 40$ m

Area of ΔABC $= \dfrac{1}{2} \times 32 \times 24$

Area of ΔABC $= 384$ m^2 $\qquad$ ...(1)

Area of ΔACD $= \sqrt{s(s - AC)(s - CD)(s - AD)}$

s = semiperimeter of ΔACD

$$s = \dfrac{25 + 25 + 40}{2} = 45$$

$\therefore$ Area of ΔACD

$$= \sqrt{45(45 - 40)(45 - 25)(45 - 25)} = 300\,m^2$$

Area of plot ABCD = Area of ΔABC + Area of ΔACD
$$= 384 + 300 = 684 \text{ m}^2$$

3. **(c)** Length of room = 6.75 m = 675 cm
Breadth of room = 5.75 m = 575 cm
Square tiles are to be used to pave the room.
The side of the square (tile) must be a factor of both length & breadth of the room
∴ HCF of 675 and 575 = 25 cm

∴ No of tiles = $\dfrac{\text{Area of room}}{\text{Area of one tile}}$

No of tiles = $\dfrac{675 \times 575}{25 \times 25} = 621$

4. **(d)** Let side of square = 100 units
Area of squre = $100 \times 100 = 10000$ square units
Length of rectangle = 120 units
Breadth of rectangle = 80 units
Area of rectangle = $120 \times 80 = 9600$ units
∴ Area of rectangle = 96% Area of square

5. **(b)** Let the length and breadth of plot are $5x$ and $3x$ respectively
∴ Perimeter of plot = $2(5x + 3x) = 16x$
According to question
$16x \times 7.5 = 3000$

$\Rightarrow x = \dfrac{3000}{16 \times 7.5} = 25$

∴ Length of plot $5x = 125$ m
Breadth of plot $3x = 75$ m
∴ Difference = $125 - 75 = 50$ m

6. **(d)** Area of square = $9 \times 9 = 81$ cm^2
Area of rectangle = $81 \times 6 = 486$ cm^2
Let length and breadth of rectangle be 'l' and 'b'
∴ $l \times b = 486$ ...(1)
Also $l = 6b$ ...(2)
From (1) and (2)
$6b \times b = 486$

$b^2 = \dfrac{486}{6} = 81$

$\Rightarrow b = 9$ cm
∴ $l = 6b = 54$ cm
Perimeter = $2(l + b) = 2(54 + 9) = 2 \times 63$
Perimeter = 126 cm

7. **(c)** Let length of rectangle = $5x$
breadth of rectangle = $4x$
∴ $5x - 4x = 20$
$x = 20$
∴ Length = $5 \times 20 = 100$m
breadth = $4 \times 20 = 80$m
perimeter = $2(l + b)$
$= 2(100 + 80) = 2 \times 180$
$= 360$ m

8. **(d)** Let ABCD is a square whose side is 'a' units.
DB is its diagonal and DBQP is square drawn on diagonal DB of square ABCD

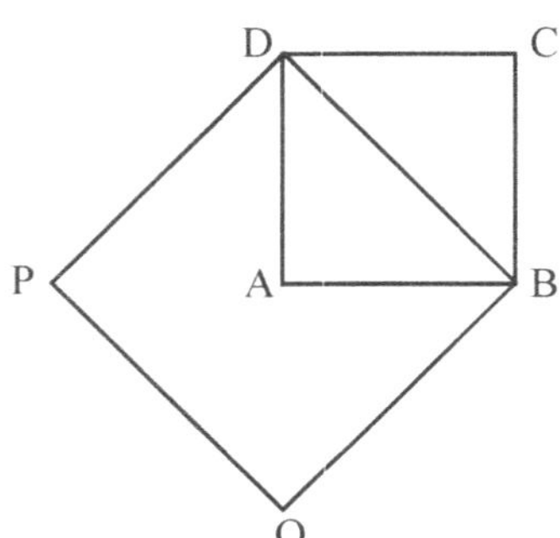

Area of ABCD = a × a = a^2 ...(1)
From $\triangle$ABD
$DB^2 = AB^2 + AD^2$
$DB^2 = a^2 + a^2$
$\Rightarrow DB = a\sqrt{2}$
Area of square DBQP = $a\sqrt{2} \times a\sqrt{2} = 2a^2$ ...(2)
From (1) and (2)
Area of square : Area of square DBQP = $a^2 : 2a^2 = 1 : 2$

9. **(a)**

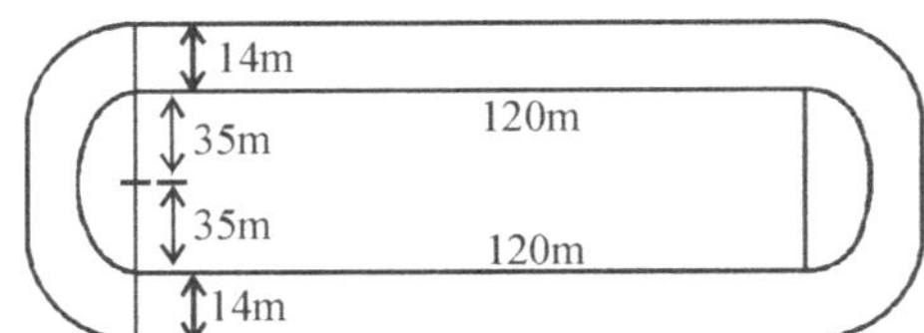

The area of the track

$= (120 \times 98 - 120 \times 70) + 2 \cdot \dfrac{1}{2}\pi\left[49^2 - 35^2\right]$

$= 3360 + 3696 = 7056 \text{m}^2$

10. **(a)**

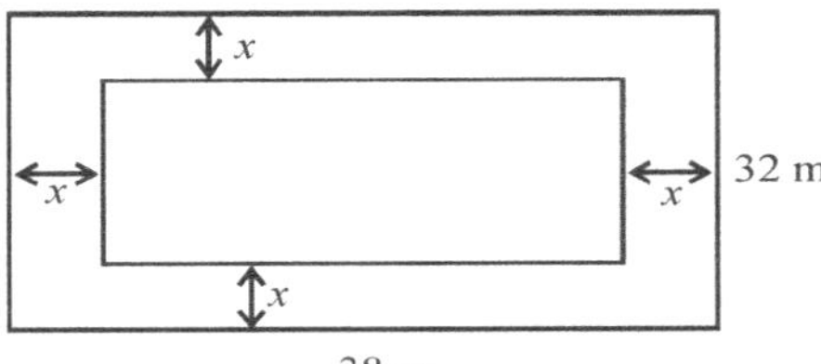

Let the width of path = x m
∴ $(38 - 2x)(32 - 2x) = 616$
$1216 - 140x + 4x^2 = 616$
$4x^2 - 140x + 600 = 0$
$x^2 - 35x + 150 = 0$
∴ $x = 30, \ x = 5$
Hence, the width of path = 5 m

11. **(b)** Let the original radius = r
∴ Area $A = \pi r^2$
increased area $A' = \pi(r + 1)^2$
Now, $A' = A + 22$
$\pi(r + 1)^2 = \pi r^2 + 22$
$\Rightarrow \pi[(r + 1)^2 - r^2] = 22$
$\Rightarrow \pi[(r + 1 + r)(r + 1 - r)] = 22$
$\Rightarrow \pi(2r + 1) = 22$

$2r + 1 = \dfrac{22 \times 7}{22}$ $\qquad \left[\because \pi = \dfrac{22}{7}\right]$

$\Rightarrow 2r + 1 = 7$
$\Rightarrow 2r = 6$
$\Rightarrow r = 3$ cm

12. **(d)** $2\pi R_1 = 88$ $\qquad 2\pi R_2 = 132$

$R_1 = \dfrac{88 \times 7}{44} = 14\,\text{cm}$ $\qquad R_2 = \dfrac{132 \times 7}{44} = 21\,\text{cm}$

Area of Ring = $\pi\left(21^2 - 14^2\right)$

$= \dfrac{22}{7} \times 245$

$= 770 \text{ cm}^2$

13. (b) Area of square field = $63 \times 63 = 3969$ m^2

Area of field grazed by horses = $4 \times \dfrac{\pi r^2 \theta}{360}$

$= \dfrac{22}{7} \times \dfrac{63}{2} \times \dfrac{63}{2} \times \dfrac{90}{360} \times 4$

$= 3118.5$ m^2

Required area = $3969 - 3118.5 = 850.5$ m^2

14. (c)

15. (c) The area of the shaded region
$= 2 \times$ Area of sector – Area of square
$= (50\pi - 100)$ units

16. (b) Area of a sector $= \pi r^2 \times \dfrac{\theta}{360}$

$\therefore$ Area of sector OCBO $= \pi \times 8^2 \times \dfrac{45}{360} = 8\pi \, m^2$

Area of sector OADO $= \pi \times 6^2 \times \dfrac{45}{360} = \dfrac{9\pi}{2} m^2$

$\therefore$ Area of shaded region $= \left(8\pi - \dfrac{9\pi}{2}\right) m^2$

$= \dfrac{7\pi}{2} m^2 = \dfrac{7 \times 22}{2 \times 7} m^2$

Area of shaded region $= 11$ m^2

17. (a) Let r_1 be the radius of hemisphere and r_2 be the radius of the cone.
Given that volume of hemisphere = volume cone.

$\dfrac{2}{3}\pi r_1^3 = \dfrac{1}{3}\pi r_2^2 h \Rightarrow \dfrac{2}{3}\pi 6^3 = \dfrac{1}{3}\pi r_2^2 \times 75$

$\Rightarrow r_2^2 = \dfrac{2 \times 6 \times 6 \times 6}{75} = \dfrac{12}{5} = 2.4$ cm

18. (a) Radius (r) of garden roller = $\dfrac{1.4}{2} = 0.7$ m.

Height (h) of garden roller = 2 m
$\therefore$ Area covered in 1 revolution = $2\pi rh$, (Surface Area)
$= 2 \times \pi \times 0.7 \times 2 = 8.8$ m^2
$\therefore$ Area covered in 5 revolutions $= 8.8 \times 5$
$= 44.0$ m^2

19. (b) Let radius = r
Slant height = $5x, 4x$
$\therefore$ Curved surface area of smaller cane = $\pi r \times 4x$
$4\pi r x = 200$
$\pi r x = 50$
curved surface area of larger cane = $\pi r \times 5x$
$= 5\pi rx = 5 \times 50$
$= 250$ cm^2

20. (a) Let increase in level = h cm
$\therefore$ Volume of increase water = $4x$
Volume of spherical balls

$\pi(5)^2 \times h = \dfrac{4}{3}\pi(11^3 \times 4)$

$h = \dfrac{16}{75}$ cm

---

1. (c) $0.\overline{6} = \dfrac{6}{9}$

$0.\overline{7} = \dfrac{7}{9}$

$0.\overline{8} = \dfrac{8}{9}$

$0.\overline{6} + 0.\overline{7} + 0.\overline{8} = \dfrac{6}{9} + \dfrac{7}{9} + \dfrac{8}{9} = \dfrac{21}{9} = \dfrac{7}{3}$

2. (a) We know that product of two numbers
$\qquad$ = LCM $\times$ HCF of those numbers
So, product of numbers = 11×385
$\qquad = 11 \times 7 \times 5 \times 11$
Since one of them lies between 75 and 125
So this number would be = $11 \times 7 = 77$
So the number is 77.

3. (c) Product of first 40 odd natural number
$= 1 \cdot 3 \cdot 5 \cdot 7 \cdot 9 \,............\, 79.$
$= 15 \cdot (7 \cdot 9 \cdot \,............\, 79)$
$= 15 \times$ an odd number
So there will be 5 at unit place.
So answer is 5.

4. (b) 20 & 30

5. (c) $\sqrt{388 + \sqrt{127 + \sqrt{289}}}$

$= \sqrt{388 + \sqrt{127 + 17}} \qquad \left[\because \sqrt{289} = 17\right]$

$= \sqrt{388 + \sqrt{144}} \qquad \left[\because \sqrt{144} = 12\right]$

$= \sqrt{388 + 12} = \sqrt{400}$

$= 20 \qquad \left[\because \sqrt{400} = 20\right]$

6. (d) $\dfrac{5x - 3y}{5y - 3x} = \dfrac{3}{4}$

$\Rightarrow \dfrac{5 - 3\left(\dfrac{y}{x}\right)}{5\left(\dfrac{y}{x}\right) - 3} = \dfrac{3}{4}$

$\Rightarrow 20 - 12\left(\dfrac{y}{x}\right) = 15\left(\dfrac{y}{x}\right) - 9$

$\Rightarrow 27\left(\dfrac{y}{x}\right) = 29 \Rightarrow \dfrac{y}{x} = \dfrac{29}{27}$

7. (a) Let age of A = $3x$ yrs
Age of B = x yrs

$\therefore \dfrac{3x + 15}{x + 15} = \dfrac{2}{1}$

$3x + 15 = 2x + 30$
$x = 15$
$\therefore$ Age of A = $3 \times 15 = 45$ yrs
Age of B = 15 yrs

8. (b) $\left(\dfrac{x^b}{x^c}\right)^{b+c-a} \times \left(\dfrac{x^c}{x^a}\right)^{c+a-b} \times \left(\dfrac{x^a}{x^b}\right)^{a+b-c}$

$\left(x^{b-c}\right)^{b+c-a} \times \left(x^{c-a}\right)^{c+a-b} \times \left(x^{a-b}\right)^{a+b-c}$

$= x^{b^2-c^2-ab+ac+c^2-a^2-bc+ab+a^2-b^2-ac+bc}$

$= x^0 = 1$

9. (a) Let the sides of triangle are $3x$, $4x$ and $5x$ respectively.

$\therefore$ Perimeter $= 3x + 4x + 5x = 12x$

$\therefore 12x = 36$ (given)

$\therefore x = 3$ cm

So sides are 9 cm, 12 cm and 15 cm

The sides follow the relation $15^2 = 12^2 + 9^2$

$\therefore$ Triangle is a right angled triangle.

$\therefore$ area of $\Delta = \dfrac{1}{2} \times 9 \times 12 = 54$ cm^2

Area can also be calculated using Heron's formula

$s = \dfrac{9+12+15}{2} = 18$ cm

$\therefore$ Area $= \sqrt{18(18-9)(18-12)(18-15)} = \sqrt{18 \times 9 \times 6 \times 3}$

$= \sqrt{9 \times 2 \times 9 \times 3 \times 2 \times 3}$

Area $= 9 \times 2 \times 3 = 54$ cm^2

10. (b) Let radius of sphere $= r$ cm

$\therefore$ Surface area (S) $= 4\pi r^2$

$4\pi r^2 = 2464 \Rightarrow r^2 = \dfrac{2464}{4 \times 22} \times 7 \Rightarrow r = 14$ cm

Volume of sphere (V) $= \dfrac{4}{3}\pi r^3 = \dfrac{4}{3} \times \dfrac{22}{7} \times (14)^3$

$= 11498.67$ cm^3

11. (a) Let l, b, h are sides of cuboid

$\therefore$ $lb = 120$ cm^2, $bh = 72$ cm^2, $lh = 60$ cm^2

Volume of cuboid $= lbh$

$= \sqrt{120 \times 72 \times 60}$

$= 720$ cm^3

12. (c) Let the distance be x km.

According to question

$\dfrac{x}{7\frac{1}{2}} - \dfrac{x}{8} = 4$

$\Rightarrow \dfrac{2x}{15} - \dfrac{x}{8} = 4$

$\Rightarrow \dfrac{16x - 15x}{120} = 4$

$\Rightarrow x = 480$ km

13. (b) Using Distance $= \dfrac{\text{Product of speed}}{\text{Difference of speed}} \times \text{total time}$

$= \dfrac{3\frac{1}{2} \times 2\frac{1}{2}}{1} \times \dfrac{12}{60}$

$= 1.75$ km

14. (c) Let the length of train be 'x' m

Speed of train be 'y' m/sec

Given speed $= \dfrac{\text{distance}}{\text{time}}$

$y = \dfrac{x}{4}$ ...(1)

and $y = \dfrac{x+75}{9}$ ...(2)

From (1) and (2)

$\dfrac{x}{4} = \dfrac{x+75}{9}$

$\Rightarrow 9x = 4x + 300$

$\Rightarrow x = 60$ m

$\therefore y = \dfrac{60}{4} = 15$ m/sec

15. (d) Let speed of boat $= 36x$

speed of current $= 5x$

$\therefore$ time taken $= \dfrac{(36x + 5x) \times 5\frac{10}{60}}{(36x - 5x)}$

$= 6$ hours 50 min

16. (a) $3 \div \left[(8-5) \div \left\{ (4-2) \div \left(2 + \dfrac{8}{13} \right) \right\} \right]$

$= 3 + \left[3 \div \left\{ 2 \div \dfrac{34}{13} \right\} \right]$

$= 3 \div \left[3 \div \left\{ 2 \times \dfrac{13}{34} \right\} \right] = 3 \div \left[3 \div \dfrac{13}{17} \right]$

$= 3 \div \left[3 \times \dfrac{17}{13} \right] = 3 \div \dfrac{51}{13} = 3 \times \dfrac{13}{51} = \dfrac{13}{17}$

17. (a) $1 + \dfrac{1}{1 + \dfrac{1}{1 + \dfrac{1}{9}}} = 1 + \dfrac{1}{1 + \dfrac{1}{\dfrac{10}{9}}} = 1 + \dfrac{1}{1 + \dfrac{9}{10}}$

$= 1 + \dfrac{1}{\dfrac{19}{10}} = 1 + \dfrac{1}{1 + \dfrac{1}{\dfrac{10}{9}}} = 1 + \dfrac{1}{1 + \dfrac{9}{10}} = 1 + \dfrac{10}{19} = \dfrac{29}{19}$

18. (c) Let CP $= ₹ x$

then, if SP $= ₹ 350$

Profit $= $ SP $-$ CP $= ₹ (350 - x)$

if SP $= ₹ 340$ then, profit $= ₹ (340 - x)$

$\therefore (350 - x) - (340 - x) = \dfrac{5}{100}x$

$\Rightarrow 10 = \dfrac{5}{100}x \Rightarrow x = 200$

19. (b) SP = ₹ 1, Loss = 20%

$$\Rightarrow CP = \left(\frac{100}{80} \times 1\right) \Rightarrow CP = ₹\frac{5}{4}$$

Now, $CP = ₹\frac{5}{4}$, gain, 20%

$$\Rightarrow SP = \frac{120}{100} \times \frac{5}{4} = ₹\frac{3}{2}$$

For $₹\frac{3}{2}$, he must sell 12 oranges

For ₹ 1, he must sell $\left(12 \times \frac{2}{3}\right) = 8$ oranges.

20. (a) Simple Interest for 1.5 years
= Rs. (873 − 756) = Rs. 117
Since, Simple Interest for 2 years

$$= \frac{117}{1.5} \times 2 = Rs.\,156$$

Principal
756 − 156 = Rs. 600
Rate of interest

$$= \frac{156 \times 100}{600 \times 2} = 13\%$$

18. Arithmetic Section Test-II

1. (b) $? = (41)^2 + (38)^2 \times (0.15)^2$
$1681 + 1444 \times 0.0225$
$1681 + 32.49 = 1713.49$

2. (c) $? = 434.43 + 43.34 + 3.44 + 4 + 0.33 = 485.54$

3. (b) $1008 \times \frac{7}{8} - 968 \times \frac{3}{4}$
$882 − 726 = 156$

4. (b) Suppose the number is x.

$$x - \frac{x}{7} = 180 \Rightarrow \frac{7x - x}{7} = 180$$

$$\Rightarrow \frac{6x}{7} = 180 \Rightarrow x = \frac{180 \times 7}{6}$$

$x = 210$

5. (b) $(0.064) \times (0.4)^7 = (0.4)^? \times (0.0256)^2$
$(0.4)^3 \times (0.4)^7 = (0.4)^? \times (0.4)^{4 \times 2}$
$(0.4)^{3+7} = (0.4)^? \times (0.4)^8$

$$\frac{(0.4)^{10}}{(0.4)^8} = (0.4)^?$$

$(0.4)^{10-8} = (0.4)^?$
$2 = ?$

6. (a) $? = \left(\sqrt{6} - 1\right)^2 - 2\sqrt{6} = 6 + 1 + 2\sqrt{6} - 2\sqrt{6} = 7$

7. (d) $\sqrt{\frac{210.25}{100}} + \sqrt{\frac{21025}{10000}} \Rightarrow \frac{145}{10} + \frac{145}{100} \Rightarrow 14.5 + 1.45 = 15.95$

8. (d) $\because 1.\overline{34} = \frac{133}{99}$

$$4.\overline{12} = \frac{371}{90}$$

$$1.\overline{34} + 4.\overline{12} = \frac{133}{99} + \frac{371}{90} = \frac{4081 + 1330}{990} = \frac{5411}{990}$$

9. (b) $\dfrac{2}{1} - \dfrac{11}{39} + \dfrac{5}{26}$

$$= \frac{156 - 22 + 15}{78} = \frac{149}{78} = 1\frac{71}{78} = 1 + \frac{71}{78}$$

10. (b) $\dfrac{-6p - 9}{3} = \dfrac{2p + 9}{5}$

$-30p - 45 = 6p + 27$
$-36p = 72$
$p = -2$

11. (d) Given Expression =

$$\sqrt{2 \times \sqrt{2 \times \sqrt{2 \times \sqrt{2 \times 2^{1/2}}}}}$$

$$= \sqrt{2 \times \sqrt{2 \times \sqrt{\left(2 \times 2^{3/4}\right)}}}$$

$$= \sqrt{2 \times \sqrt{2 \times 2^{7/8}}} = \sqrt{2 \times 2^{15/16}} = 2^{31/32}$$

12. (d) $CI - SI = P\left(\dfrac{R}{100}\right)^2$

$$P = \frac{144 \times 100 \times 100}{15 \times 15}$$

$P = ₹6400$

13. (c) Using $CI - SI = \dfrac{R \times SI}{2 \times 100}$

$$410 - 400 = \frac{R \times 400}{2 \times 100}$$

$$R = \frac{10}{2} = 5\%$$

14. (a) Let AD = x and BC = 4 cm (given)

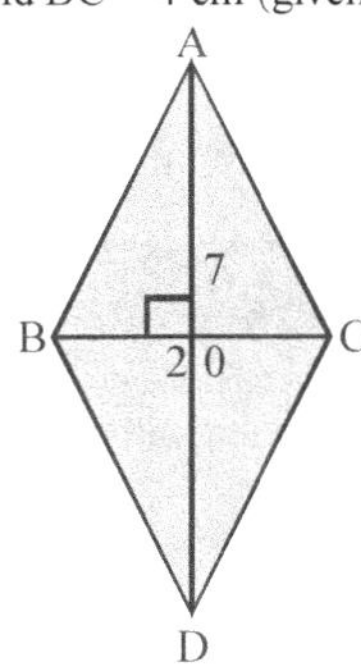

Then $\dfrac{1}{2} \times x \times 4 = 28$ or $x = 14$ cm.

Clearly, $AO = \dfrac{14}{2} = 7$ cm

By Pythagorus theorem,
$AO^2 + BO^2 = AB^2$
or $7^2 + 2^2 = 53$ or $AB = \sqrt{53}$

$\therefore$ perimeter = $4AB = 4\sqrt{53}$

15. (a) $\dfrac{\sqrt{3}}{2} \times \text{side} = \sqrt{6}$

    $\text{side} = 2\sqrt{2}$ cm.

    $\text{area} = \dfrac{\sqrt{3}}{4} \times (\text{side})^2 = \dfrac{\sqrt{3}}{4} \times (2\sqrt{2})^2 = 2\sqrt{3}$ cm^2

16. (c) $2\pi r = \dfrac{30}{\pi}$

    $2r = \dfrac{30}{\pi^2}$

17. (c) $\dfrac{1}{5} : \dfrac{1}{x} = \dfrac{1}{x} : \dfrac{100}{125}$

    $\Rightarrow \left(\dfrac{1}{x} \times \dfrac{1}{x} \right) = \left(\dfrac{1}{5} \times \dfrac{100}{125} \right) = \dfrac{4}{25}$

    $\Rightarrow \dfrac{1}{x^2} = \dfrac{4}{25} \Rightarrow x^2 = \dfrac{25}{4} \Rightarrow x = \dfrac{5}{2} = 2.5.$

18. (d) Let the required number of days be x. Then, less men, more days.

    $\therefore 27 : 36 :: 18 : x$

    $\Rightarrow 27 \times x = 36 \times 18$

    $\Rightarrow x = \dfrac{36 \times 18}{27} \Rightarrow x = 24$

19. (c) Total age of 3 boys = (25×3) years = 75 years.
    Ratio of their ages = 3 : 5 : 7.

    Age of the yongest boy = $\left(75 \times \dfrac{3}{15} \right)$ = 15 years.

20. (b) Let the remaining food will last for x days.
    95 men had provisions food for 195 days. 65 men had provisions food for x days. Less men, more days

    $\therefore 65 : 95 :: 195 : x$

    $\Rightarrow (65 \times x) = (95 \times 195)$

    $\Rightarrow x = \dfrac{95 \times 195}{65} = 285$ days

19. Analogy-I

1. (c) The words in each pair are synonyms of each other.
2. (d) Chairman is the highest authority in a conference. Similarly, editor is the highest authority in a newspaper agency.
3. (d) The part of a kitchen, used for storing grains, utensils, etc. is called a pantry.
   Similarly, the part of a kitchen, used for washing utensils, is called a scullery.
4. (a) Second is a disease which affects the first.
5. (a) First develops from the second.
6. (b) Second is the act of cutting the first.
7. (d) Second is a measure of the boundary of the first.
8. (b) First moves in the second by capillary action.
9. (d) First causes the second.
10. (b) The direction indicated by the second word in each pair lies 135° clockwise to that indicated by the first word.
11. (b) Clearly, $42 = 7 \times 6$ and $56 = 7 \times (6 + 2)$.
    Similarly, $110 = 11 \times 10$.
    So, required number = $11 \times (10 + 2) = 11 \times 12 = 132$.

12. (c) The relationship is $(x^2 - 1) : [(x + 4)^2 + 1]$.
    Since, $168 = (13)^2 - 1$, so required number = $(13 + 4)^2 + 1 = (17)^2 + 1 = 290$.
13. (c) $2 \times 2 \times 2 - 1 = 8 - 1 = 7$ Similarly,
    $3 \times 3 \times 3 - 1 = 27 - 1 = 26$
14. (d) First two letters of the first term are in reverse order in the second term and so are the next two letters.
15. (b) Fifth and third letters of the first term are first and second letters of the second term and first two letters of the first term are third and fourth letters of the second term.
16. (d) There is a gap of one letter between each corresponding letters of 'QYGO' and 'SAIQ'
17. (d) There is a gap of three letters between each corresponding letters of 'YAWC' and 'UESG'.
18. (d) 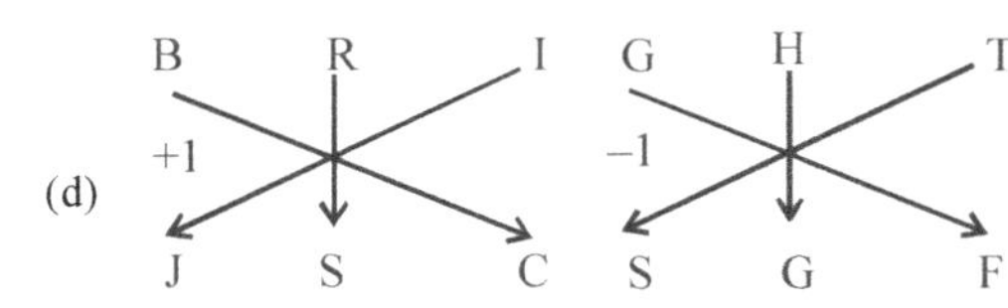
    Similarly,
    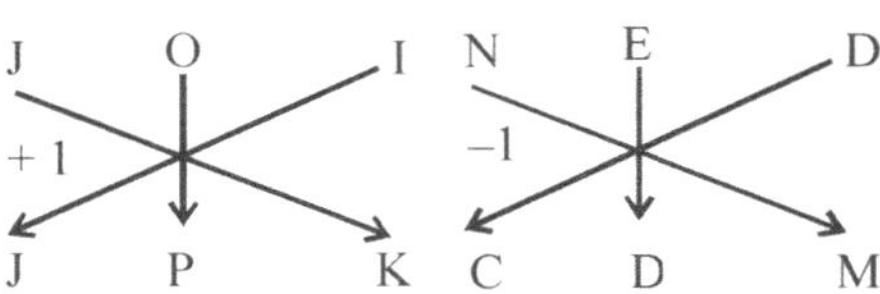
19. (a) The second number is the product of the digits of the first.
20. (d) The first is found in the form of the second.

20. Analogy-II

1. (a) They are synonymous.
2. (e) 'Delicious' is the adjective used for 'Taste'. Similarly, 'Melodious' is the adjective used for 'Voice'.
3. (a) A successful finish of 'Education' equips one with 'Diploma'. Similary, a successful finish in 'Sports' equips one with 'Trophy'.
4. (d) The clock makes a journey of time.
5. (c) Cure ensures removal of illness in the same way as remedy insures removal of grief.
6. (c) Jewellery consists of Necklace ie 'Necklace' is a kind of 'Jewellery'. Similarly, 'Shirt' is a kind of 'Apparel'.
7. (d) **Bouquet** is a bunch of **flowers**. Similarly, **Sentence** is a set of **words** that is complete in itself.
8. (e) From SECTOR TO RTERBN; The second letter becomes third, fourth becomes second, and last becomes first. Also, after subtracting one letter from the first, we get fourth, from third, we get fifth and from fifth we get last.
9. (d) When **Income** is more than expenditure, it bears **Profit.** But when **Expenditure** is more than income, then **loss** occurs.
10. (d) **Wire** is the medium to transmit **Electricity.** Similarly, **Pipe** is the medium to carry **Water**.
11. (b) Here, the first is the working place of the second.
12. (a) Words are arranged in alphabetical order but from right to left. If becomes UTSOMC.
13. (d) As   Similarly,

    $P \xrightarrow{+8} X \qquad J \xrightarrow{+8} R$

    $R \xrightarrow{+8} Z \qquad L \xrightarrow{+8} T$

    $L \xrightarrow{+8} T \qquad F \xrightarrow{+8} N$

    $N \xrightarrow{+8} V \qquad H \xrightarrow{+8} P$

14. (b) Fifth and third letters of the first term are first and second letters of the second term and first two letters of the first term are third and fourth letters of the second term.

15. (d) As,   Similarly,

$A \xrightarrow{+14} O$ $S \xrightarrow{+14} G$

$C \xrightarrow{+18} U$ $U \xrightarrow{+18} M$

$F \xrightarrow{+20} Z$ $X \xrightarrow{+20} R$

$J \xrightarrow{+0} J$ $B \xrightarrow{+0} B$

16. (d) As,   Similarly,

$A \xrightarrow{+7} H$ $M \xrightarrow{+7} T$

$C \xrightarrow{+6} I$ $O \xrightarrow{+6} U$

$E \xrightarrow{+7} L$ $Q \xrightarrow{+7} X$

17. (c) The words in each pair are synonyms.

18. (d) As,   Similarly

$C \xrightarrow{+2} E$ $F \xrightarrow{+2} H$

$G \xrightarrow{+2} I$ $J \xrightarrow{+2} L$

19. (a) The largest ocean is Pacific Ocean.
Similarly, the largest island is Greenland.

20. (d) Tuberculosis is a disease of lungs.
Similarly, Cataract is a disease of eyes.

21. Classification

1. (b) All except Autorickshaw have four wheels.
2. (c) All except Knee are parts of hand.
3. (a) All except Ear are internal organs.
4. (b) All except Instruct denote learning process.
5. (c) All except Deliberation indicate research.
6. (d) All except Rice are cash crops, while rice is a food crop.
7. (d) All except Wife are elderly people.
8. (a) All except electricity are means of communication
9. (b) All except Flower are types of plants.
10. (b) All except Axe are tools used by a carpenter.
11. (a) In all other groups, the first and second as well as the third and fourth letters are consecutive.
12. (b) All other groups contain four consecutive letters in reverse alphabetical order.
13. (a) In all other groups, the first and second as well as the third and fourth letters are consecutive and the third letter is nine steps ahead of the second.
14. (c) In all other groups, the number of letters skipped between two consecutive letters increases by one from left to right.
15. (d) In all other pairs, second is a part of the first.
16. (b) In all other pairs, second is the result of the first.
17. (b) The words in all other pairs are synonyms.
18. (c) $(9 - 7)^2 = 4$, $(13 - 7)^2 = 36$, $(11 - 7)^2 = 16$, but $(9 - 5)^2 \neq 25$.
19. (d) The difference in all the other cases is 12.
20. (c) The product in all other cases is 96.

22. Series-I

1. (b) The first and second letters in each group more two steps in forward direction, while the third term moves one step forward. Working on this pattern, the next term would be GHT.
2. (d) The first letter of each group moves + 1 steps, second letter moves – 1 step and the third letter moves – 2 steps. Thus, the next group of letters would be roa.

3. (a) 13   25   51   101   203   **405**
    ×2–1   ×2+1   ×2–1   ×2+1   ×2–1

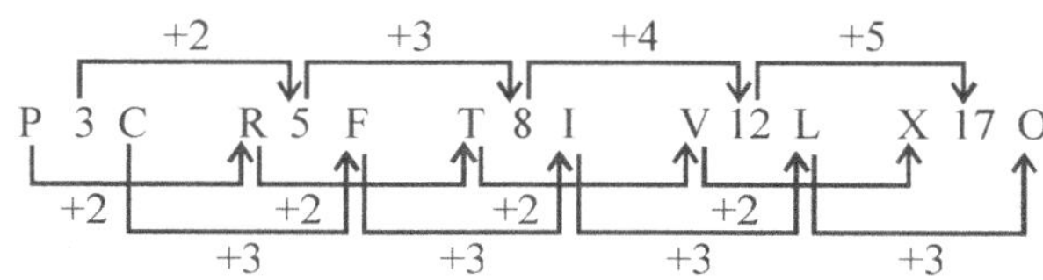

4. (d) 4   8   28   80   244   **728**
    ×3–4   ×3+4   ×3–4   ×3+4   ×3–4

5. (c) P 3 C   R 5 F   T 8 I   V 12 L   X 17 O
    (+2, +3, +4, +5 across; +2 and +3 within)

6. (b) 198   194   185   169   **144**
    -2^2 -3^2 -4^2 -5^2

7. (c) The first, third, fifth .... and second, fourth .... terms are groups of consecutive natural numbers.

8. (b) 5   6   8   9   11   **12**
    +1   +2   +1   +2   +1

9. (c) The series progress with a difference of – 5.

10. (b) 0   2   6   12   20   **30**
    +2   +4   +6   +8   +10

11. (a) 5   7   9   11   13   **15**
    +2   +2   +2   +2   +2

12. (d) 125   80   45   20   **05**
    –45   –35   –25   –15

13. (c) 198   202   211   227   **252**
    $+2^2$ $+3^2$ $+4^2$ $+5^2$

14. (a) In three consecutive letters, a, b, c are each repeated once. Hence the series would be.
c̲ ab / a̲ b c̲ / b c a̲ / c a b̲

15. (a) The series is aabb/aa̲bb̲/aabb
The missing letters are thus aabab

16. (d) 10   18   34   **66**   130   258
    +8   +16   +32   +64   +128

17. (d) A M B N,   E I F J,   C O D P,   G K **H L**
    (+1 pattern)

In each group of 4 letters, 1st and 3rd letters, 2nd and 4th letters alternatively increased. Hence, the missing letter would be HL.

18. (d) A   G   L   P   S   **U**
    +6   +5   +4   +3   +2

19. (a) 625   5   125   25   25   **125**   5
    (×5, ×5; ÷5, ÷5, ÷5)

20. (c) 2   12   30   56   **90**   132   182
(1^2+1) (3^2+3) (5^2+5) (7^2+7) (9^2+9) (11^2+11) (13^2+12)

23. Series-II

1. (c)

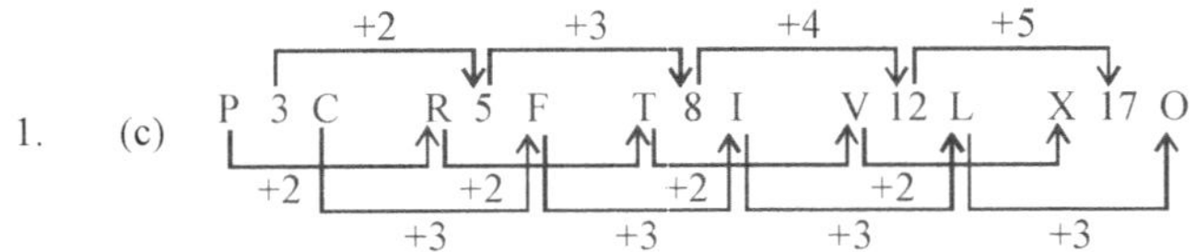

2. (b) C is the 3rd letter, F sixth, I ninth so next letter will be 12th, i.e. L.

The middle numerics are the squares of 2, 3, 4 and so on. So next numeric would be 25.

The last letter follow the order : U is 3rd letter after R, X is 3rd after U. So, R would be 3rd letter after 'O'.

∴ Missing term = L25O.

3. (c) First number is increasing by 5, 7, 9, 11, 13....

Second letter is decreasing by 1 position. Third number is increasing by 2.

4. (d) The sequence is as follows :

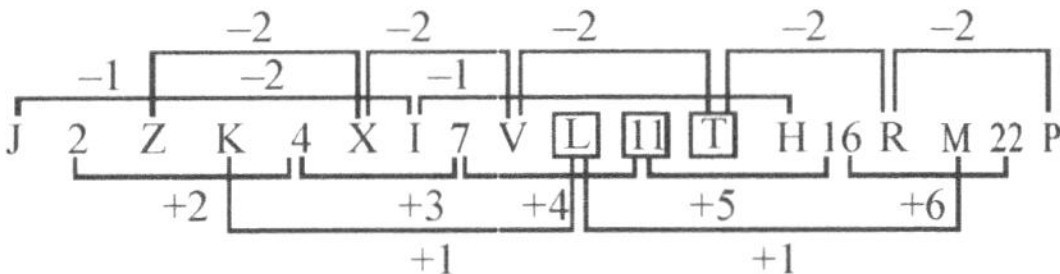

5. (c)

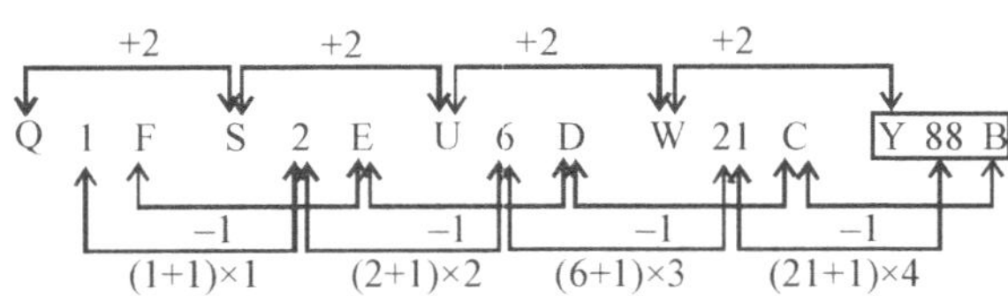

6. (c)

K-11   M-13   P-16   T-20   Y-25

with +2, +3, +4, +5

7. (b)

C – 2   E – 3   G – 4   I –5   K–6

+1, +1, +1, +1 and + 2, + 2, – 2, + 2

8. (c)

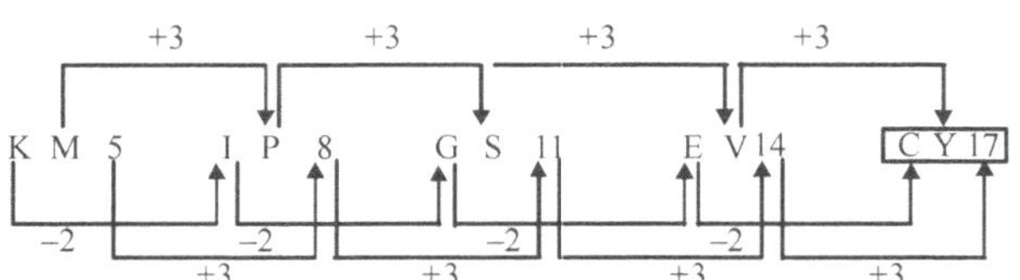

9. (d)

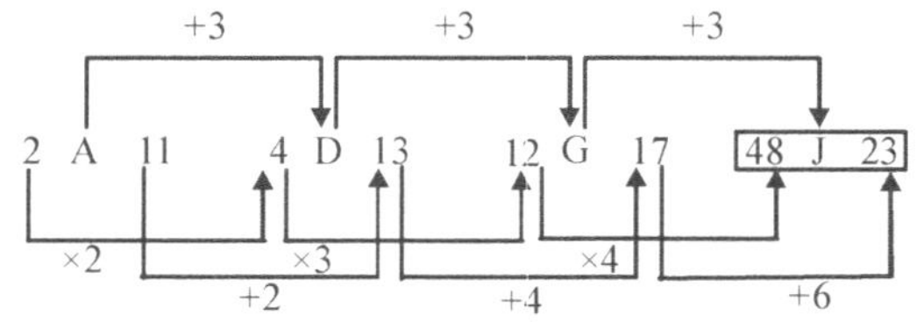

10. (d)

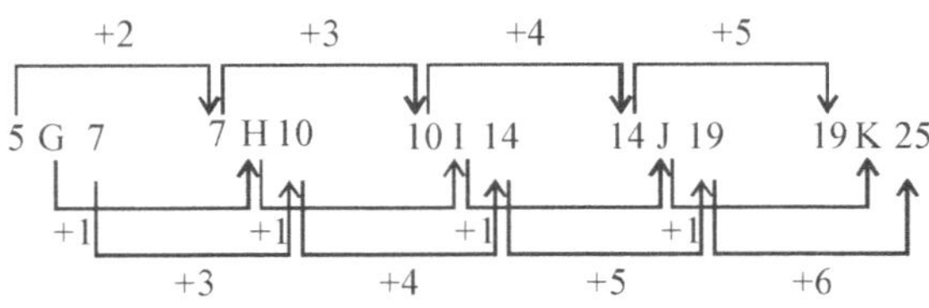

11. (c)

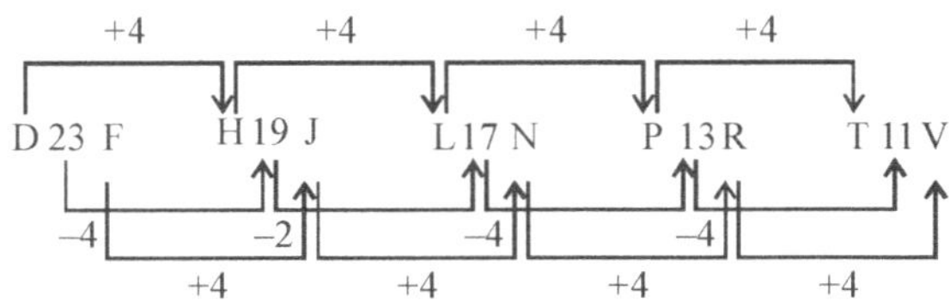

12. (c)

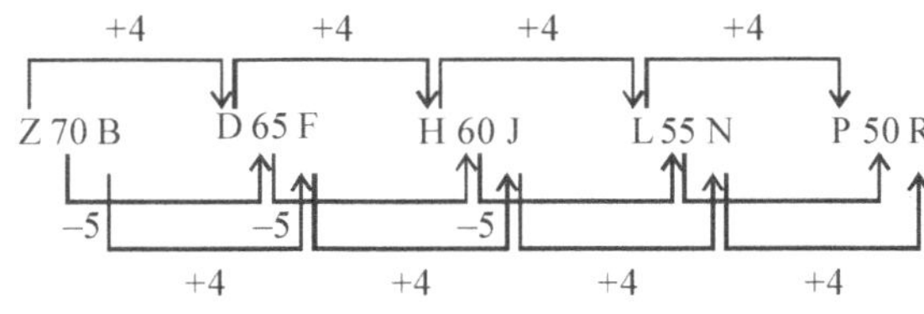

13. (c)

Z 70 B   D 65 F   H 60 J   L 55 N   P 50 R
with +4 and –5 patterns

14. (c)

A $\xrightarrow{+5}$ F $\xrightarrow{+5}$ K $\xrightarrow{+5}$ **P**

3 $\xrightarrow{+2}$ 5 $\xrightarrow{+2}$ 7 $\xrightarrow{+2}$ **9**

E $\xrightarrow{+5}$ J $\xrightarrow{+5}$ O $\xrightarrow{+5}$ **T**

15. (c)

D $\xrightarrow{+6}$ J $\xrightarrow{+6}$ P $\xrightarrow{+6}$ V $\xrightarrow{+6}$ **B**

9 $\xrightarrow{\times 3}$ 27 $\xrightarrow{\times 3}$ 81 $\xrightarrow{\times 3}$ 243 $\xrightarrow{\times 3}$ **729**

Y $\xrightarrow{-6}$ S $\xrightarrow{-6}$ M $\xrightarrow{-6}$ G $\xrightarrow{-6}$ **A**

16. (a) The first letter of each term is moved three steps forward and the second letter is moved three steps backward to obtain the corresponding letters of the next term.

17. (c)

C $\xrightarrow{+2}$ E $\xrightarrow{+2}$ G $\xrightarrow{+2}$ I $\xrightarrow{+2}$ **K**

2 $\xrightarrow{+3}$ 5 $\xrightarrow{+7}$ 12 $\xrightarrow{+15}$ 27 $\xrightarrow{+31}$ **56**

E $\xrightarrow{+3}$ H $\xrightarrow{+3}$ K $\xrightarrow{+3}$ N $\xrightarrow{+3}$ **Q**

18. (a)

Z $\xrightarrow{-1}$ Y $\xrightarrow{-1}$ X $\xrightarrow{-1}$ W $\xrightarrow{-1}$ V

A $\xrightarrow{+1}$ B $\xrightarrow{+1}$ C $\xrightarrow{+1}$ D $\xrightarrow{+1}$ E

5   4   6   3   **7**   So, VE₇
with –1 and +1 patterns

19. (b)

```
0    3    8    15    24    35
  +3   +5   +7   +9   +11
    +2   +2   +2   +2
```

The two consecutive letters are pairs of opposite letters.

$b \leftrightarrow y; c \leftrightarrow x; d \leftrightarrow w$

Therefore, ? = w – 35

20. (c)

```
C —+2→ E —+2→ G —+2→ I —+2→ [K 11] —+2→ [M 13]
3 —+2→ 5 —+2→ 7 —+2→ 9 —+2→ 11 —+2→ 13
```

24. Coding and Decoding-I

1. (d) P S I C H O L A Z Y
0 1 2 3 4 5 6 7 8 9
875.50 = ZAO.OP

2. (d) Q K T B F M = 4 5 2 8 6 3

3. (c) G($), A(÷), M(*), E(%) B(#), E(%), A(÷), D(×) MADE = * ÷ × %

4. (b)
B   O   R   N
–1 +1 –1 +1
A   P   Q   O   N
L   A   C   K
–1 +1 –1 +1
K   B   B   L   K

Similarly,
G   R   I   D
–1 +1 –1 +1
F   S   H   E   D

5. (b) Split the word STREAMLING into two groups consisting of equal letters. You get STREA and MLING. Now, reverse both the groups. You get AERTS and GNILM. Now, write each letter of first group two places forward. You get CGTVU. Write each letter of second group one place forward. You get HOJMN. Now, join both the groups without changing the order of letters. You get CGTVUHOJMN.
Similarly, PERIODICAL is coded as
PERIODICAL → OIREPLACID → QKTGRMBDJE

6. (d) Divide the word into two halves. Now, reverse the order of the letters of the first half and replace odd positioned letters with one letter forward and even positioned letter with one letter backward as in English alphabet.
For the second half letters, the odd-positioned letters are coded as one letter forward and even-positioned letters are coded as one letter backward' as in English alphabet.

7. (c) The series is W/WY/WYB/WYBG/WYBGR

8. (a) Here, each letter of the word CLOUD is written as three letters forward and one letter backward alternately. Following this CLOUD becomes FKRTG. After that, reverse the order of the result obtained in the previous operation. Thus, FKRTG becomes GTRKF.
Similarly, SIGHT will change its form as follows:
SIGHT → VHJGW → WGJHV

9. (c)
A   R   O   M   A   T   I   C
+1 –1 +1 –1 +1 –1 +1 –1
B   Q   P   L   B   S   J   B

Similarly,
B   R   A   I   N
+1 –1 +1 –1 +1
C   Q   B   H   O

10. (d) The colour of human blood is red. Here *white* means *red*. Therefore *white* is our answer.

Do not opt for *black* because *red* means *black* implies that black is called red.

11. (d)

12. (d) C R E A T I V E
When the letters in both the halves are reversed, we get
A E R C E V I T
+1 –1 +1 –1 +1 –1 +1 –1
B D S B F U J S
Next, the letters have been written as one place forward and one place backward alternately.
Similarly, TRIANGLE is coded as follows:
T R I A N G L E
A I R T E L G N
+1 –1 +1 –1 +1 –1 +1 –1
B H S S F K H M
Hence, code for TRIANGLE is BHSSFKHM

13. (a)
O V E R   O P E N
+1 +1 +1 +1 – 1 Similarly, +1 +1 +1 +1– 1
P W F S Q   P Q F O M

14. (d) We know colour of blood is red. Here, *red* is called *sky*. Therefore, our correct answer is '*sky*'.

15. (c)
P O E T R Y
× / –1 –1 –1 –1 –1 –1
Q O N D S Q X

Similarly,
O V E R
× / –1 –1 –1 –1
P N U D Q

Similarly, MORE will be coded as follows:
M O R E
× / –1 –1 –1 –1
N L N Q D

16. (d)
M O T H E R S
+2 –2 +2 –1 +2 –2 +2
O M V G G P U
Similarly, BROUGHT be coded as follows:
B R O U G H T
+2 –2 +2 –1 +2 –2 +2
D P Q T I F V

17. (d) The first three letters of the word are reversed. Thus PENCIL becomes NEPCIL. Now add 4 to odd-positioned letters and subtract 2 from even-positioned ones. Similarly, BROKEN becomes ORBKEN. Then we do the calculations: O + 4, R – 2, B + 4, K – 2, E + 4, N – 2, *i.e.* SPFIIL.

18. (d) Odd-placed letters are coded as two places forward and even-placed letters are coded as four places forward as in English alphabet.

19. (b) A real tough one! If we number the letters of the word from 1 to 6, first rearrange the letters in the order 615243. Next, to this reversed order of letters, apply the following alternately: move three letters ahead; go one letter backward.
Thus NUMBER first becomes RNEUBM. Then
R + 3 = U, N – 1 = M,
E + 3 = H, U – 1 = T, B + 3 = E, M – 1 = L. So the final code is UMHTEL.
Similarly, SECOND → DSNEOC → GRQDRB

20. (c) The letters at odd-numbered positions (1st, 3rd, ...) move two letters backward. While those at even numbered positions (2nd, 4th, ...) move three letters forward.

25. Coding and Decoding-II

1. (a)

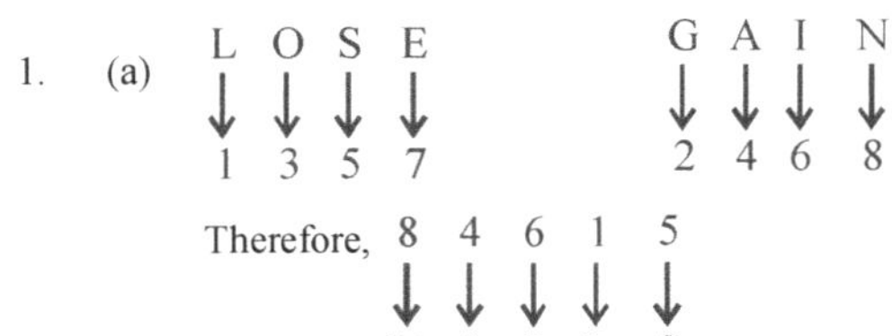

Therefore,

$$8 \quad 4 \quad 6 \quad 1 \quad 5$$
$$\downarrow \quad \downarrow \quad \downarrow \quad \downarrow \quad \downarrow$$
$$N \quad A \quad I \quad L \quad S$$

2. (a)

3. (c) The word is divided into three equal sections, and the letters of first and third sections are written backwards.

Similarly,

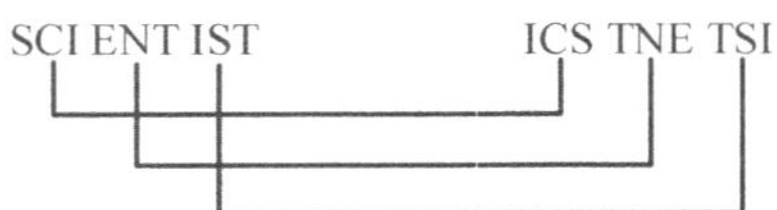

4. (d)   5. (c)

6. (c)

$$C \quad A \quad L \quad C \quad U \quad T \quad T \quad A$$
$$\downarrow \quad \downarrow \quad \downarrow \quad \downarrow \quad \downarrow \quad \downarrow \quad \downarrow \quad \downarrow$$
$$8 \quad 2 \quad 5 \quad 8 \quad 9 \quad 6 \quad 6 \quad 2$$

Therefore,

$$C \quad A \quad L \quad I \quad C \quad U \quad T$$
$$\downarrow \quad \downarrow \quad \downarrow \quad \downarrow \quad \downarrow \quad \downarrow \quad \downarrow$$
$$8 \quad 2 \quad 5 \quad 1 \quad 8 \quad 9 \quad 6$$

7. (a)

8. (a)

Therefore,

$$\pi \propto \gamma \quad \chi \quad \varepsilon \quad \lambda \quad \omega$$
$$\downarrow \quad \downarrow \quad \downarrow \quad \downarrow \quad \downarrow \quad \downarrow \quad \downarrow$$
$$V \quad A \quad G \quad U \quad E \quad L \quad Y$$

ω may be the code for Y.

9. (b) The letters have been written in the reverse order in the code
1 2 3 4 5 6 7 8 9 10 11
I N S T I T U T I O N
Its code is
11 10 9 8 7 6 5 4 3 2 1
N O I T U T I T S N I
Therefore,
1 2 3 4 5 6 7 8 9 10
P E R F E C T I O N
Its code would be
10 9 8 7 6 5 4 3 2 1
N O I T C E F R E P

10. (c)

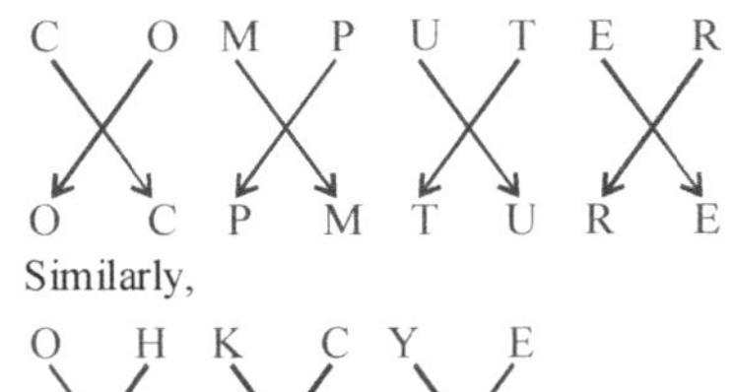

Similarly,

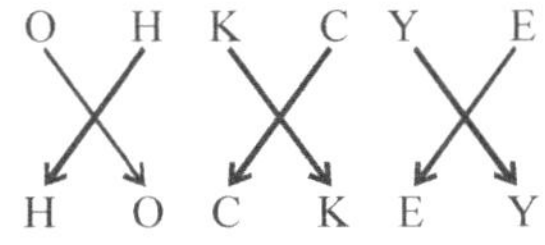

11. (d)

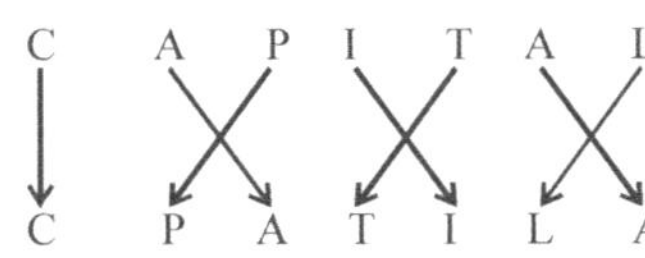

Similarly,

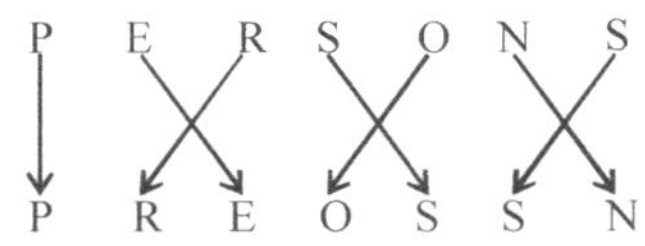

12. (b)
$S \Rightarrow 19 + 1 = 20$
$I \Rightarrow 9 + 1 = 10$
$S \Rightarrow 19 + 1 = 20$
$T \Rightarrow 20 + 1 = 21$
$E \Rightarrow 5 + 1 = 6$
$R \Rightarrow 18 + 1 = 19$
Similarly,
$B \Rightarrow 2 + 1 = 3$
$R \Rightarrow 18 + 1 = 19$
$O \Rightarrow 15 + 1 = 16$
$T \Rightarrow 20 + 1 = 21$
$H \Rightarrow 8 + 1 = 9$
$E \Rightarrow 5 + 1 = 6$
$R \Rightarrow 18 + 1 = 19$

13. (b)
$$P \quad E \quad A \quad R$$
$$\downarrow \quad \downarrow \quad \downarrow \quad \downarrow$$
$$G \quad F \quad D \quad N$$
Therefore,
$$R \quad E \quad A \quad P$$
$$\downarrow \quad \downarrow \quad \downarrow \quad \downarrow$$
$$N \quad F \quad D \quad G$$

14. (a)
$$F \quad L \quad A \quad T \quad T \quad E \quad R$$
$$\downarrow \quad \downarrow \quad \downarrow \quad \downarrow \quad \downarrow \quad \downarrow \quad \downarrow$$
$$7 \quad 2 \quad 3 \quad 8 \quad 8 \quad 5 \quad 9$$
$$M \quad O \quad T \quad H \quad E \quad R$$
$$\downarrow \quad \downarrow \quad \downarrow \quad \downarrow \quad \downarrow \quad \downarrow$$
$$4 \quad 6 \quad 8 \quad 1 \quad 5 \quad 9$$
Therefore,
$$M \quad A \quad M \quad M \quad O \quad T \quad H$$
$$\downarrow \quad \downarrow \quad \downarrow \quad \downarrow \quad \downarrow \quad \downarrow \quad \downarrow$$
$$4 \quad 3 \quad 4 \quad 4 \quad 6 \quad 8 \quad 1$$

15. (c)

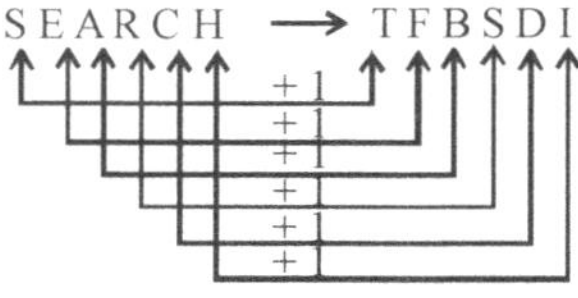

Similarly,

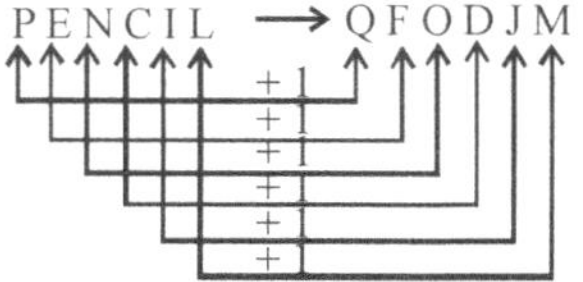

16. (c) 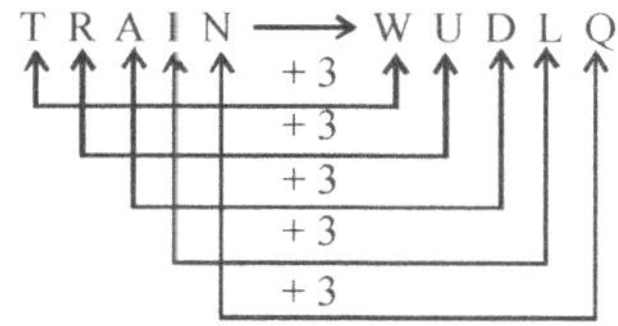

Similarly,

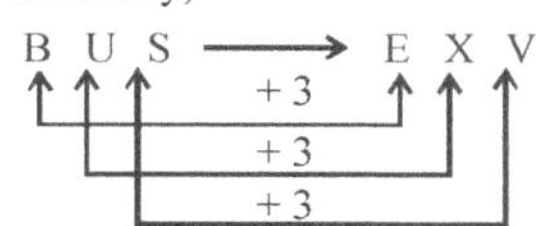

17. (d) $A \Rightarrow 27 - 1 = 26$
$S \Rightarrow 27 - 19 = 8$
$H \Rightarrow 29 - 8 = 19$
$A \Rightarrow 27 - 1 = \dfrac{26}{79}$

Similarly,
$V \Rightarrow 27 - 22 = 5$
$I \Rightarrow 27 - 9 = 18$
$N \Rightarrow 27 - 14 = 13$
$A \Rightarrow 27 - 1 = 26$
$Y \Rightarrow 27 - 25 = 2$
$B \Rightarrow 27 - 2 = 25$
$H \Rightarrow 27 - 8 = 19$
$U \Rightarrow 27 - 21 = 6$
$S \Rightarrow 27 - 19 = 8$
$H \Rightarrow 27 - 8 = 19$
$A \Rightarrow 27 - 1 = 26$
$N \Rightarrow 27 - 14 = \dfrac{13}{180}$

18. (a) 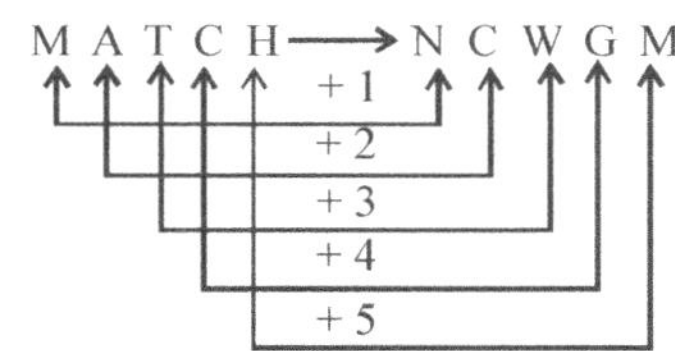

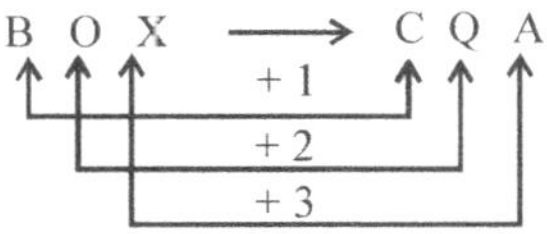

Therefore,

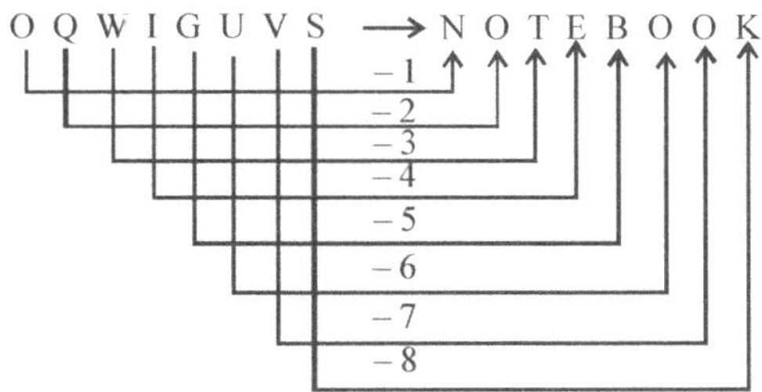

19. (b) 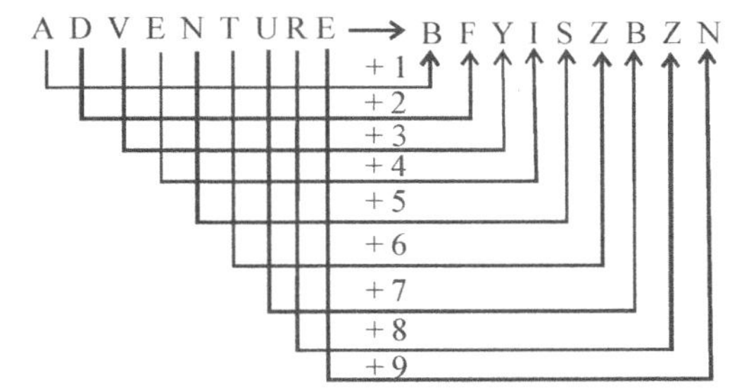

Similarly,

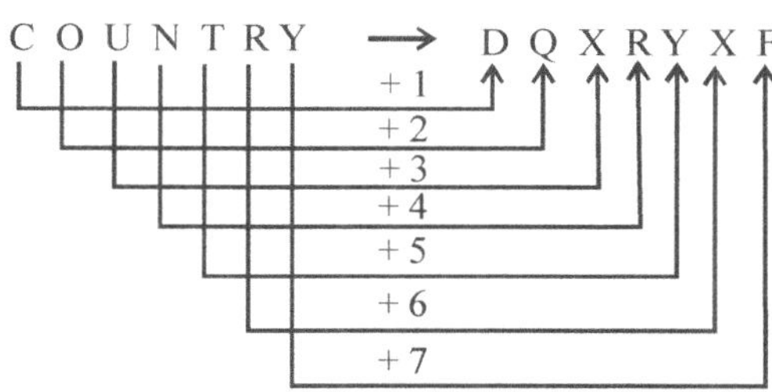

20. (c) 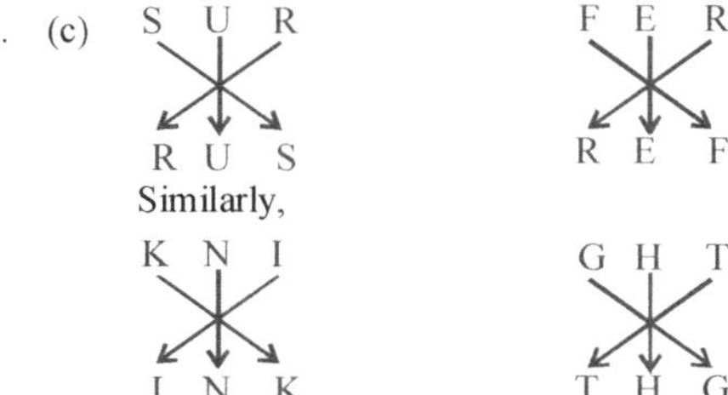

Similarly,

26. Word Formation

1. (d) Here specific letters are E, M, A and L. Words formed with these letters are as follows
   1. LAME   2. MALE   3. MEAL
   Since, no. of words formed by the given letters is more than two, our answer is choice (d).

2. (b) Here, given number is **95137248.** When the number is arranged in ascending order number becomes as follows 12345789. Now, look at the pairs: 35. What do you observe? These pairs are those pairs each of which has as many digits between them in the number as when they are arranged in ascending order.

3. (a) 
   E X T R A
   When E and A are arranged in alphabetical order then i.e. AE, E will be second.

4. (d) SING, SIGN

5. (a) INDIAN = 17 + 27 + 7 + 17 + 1 + 27 = 96

6. (d) Selected letters of the given word are R, H, A and E. By using each letter only once we can make the following words:
   1. HEAR   2. HARE
   This is more than one.

7. (d) The letters are: P, L, A, E. Meaningful words: PALE, LEAP, PEAL.

8. (c) C R E D I B I L I T Y

9. (b) P O W E R F U L
   E F L O P R U W
   only U remains unchanged.

10. (d) PI, RU and ON.
    P R O D U C T I O N

11. (d) The specified letters are D, I, T and E. Words formed by these letters are as follows:
    (i) EDIT   (ii) DIET
    (iii) TIDE   (iv) TIED

12. (b) Here specified letters are: E, A, S, M and T. Words formed from these letters are as follows:
    1. STEAM   2. MATES
    3. TEAMS

13. (d) After interchanging, the order of the letters in the word becomes as follows:
    S G N I K R O W
    Thus, the third letter to the left of R is N.

14. (d) Here specified letters are: R, I, A and L. Words formed with these letters are:
1. RAIL   2. LIAR   3. LAIR

15. (a) S P O N T A N E O U S

In each shown pairs there is one letter less than the number of letters between them in English alphabet.

16. (d) A, R, D, I, Y. We can make DIARY, DAIRY

17. (b) PUMPKIN

18. (d) The third, fifth, seventh and tenth letters of the word PROJECTION are O, E, T and N respectively. The words formed are NOTE and TONE.

19. (d) Clearly, we have :
COMPREHENSION → (COM) (PREHENS) (ION)
→ COMIONSNEHERP
The middle letter is the seventh letter, which is S.

20. (b) The words are HE, ART, LESS

27. Blood Relation

1. (b) E is the husband of D.
C is the brother of D.
Therefore, C is the brother-in-law of E.

2. (d) Female members: Mother, 3 daughter-in-law, one daughter, Four grand daughters.
Thus, there are nine female members.

3. (a) C and D are children of A and B. B is mother of C and D.
Therefore, B is sisters-in-law of E.

4. (a) O is the husband of P. M is the son of P.
Therefore, M is the son of O.

5. (b) R is father of X and Y.
S is maternal uncle of X and Y.
Considering the given options, it may be assumed that T is wife of R.

6. (c) C is the daughter of B and A is father of B.
Therefore, C is niece of E.

7. (a) Wife of Vinod's father means the mother of Vinod.
Only brother of Vinod's mother means maternal uncle of Vinod.
Therefore, Vinod is cousin of Vishal.

8. (c) Shubha is granddaughter of Sheela, who is sister of Pramod.
Rahul is son of Pramod.
Therefore, Rahul is uncle of Sheela.

9. (a) Husband ⇒ One
Wife ⇒ One
Five married sons
⇒ 5 × 2 = 10
Number of children
⇒ 5 × 4 = 20
Total number of members
= 1 + 1 + 10 + 20 = 32

10. (c) Grandson of Arun's mother means either son or nephew of Arun. Therefore, Arun is the father-in-law of that girl.

11. (b) The relations describe in the question can be represented as follows:

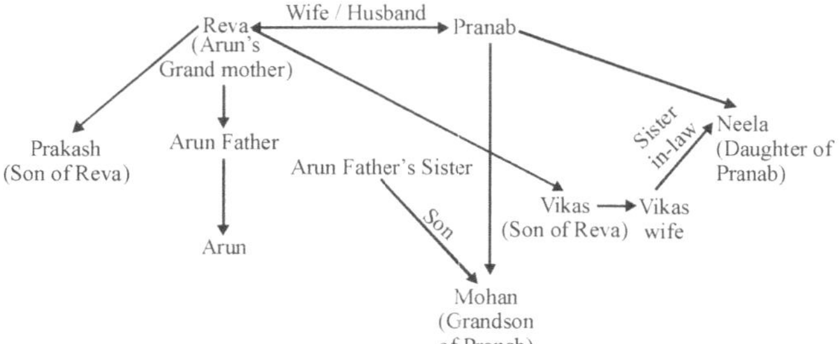

Thus wife of Vikas is sister in-law of Neela.

12. (c)

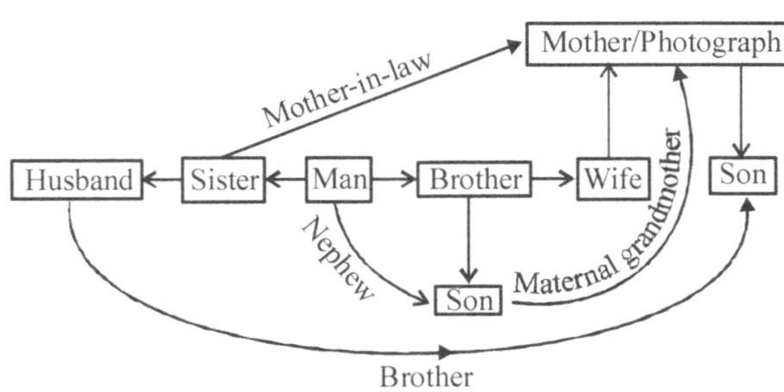

13. (d) Boy = son of Urmila's grandfather's only daughter
= son of Urmila's paternal aunt
= Urmila's cousin
Hence, Urmila is also the boy's cousin.

14. (d) It is possible that Ashok is married, that he has no child, etc.

15. (c)

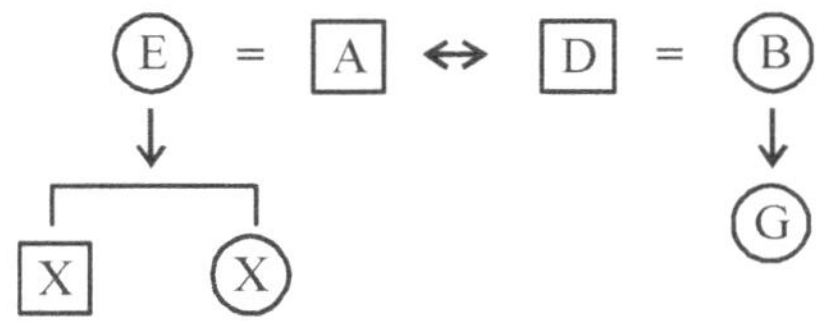

16. (d) Girl = the only daughter of Arun's grandfather's son.
= the only daughter of Arun's father or uncle
= Arun's sister or cousin

17. (b) Boy = Grandson of Rasika's grandmother's only son = Grandson of Rasika's father = Rasika's nephew

18. (d) '↔' → brothers, '=' → couple, '↓' →offspring, '□' → male, 'O' → female, 'X' → unknown

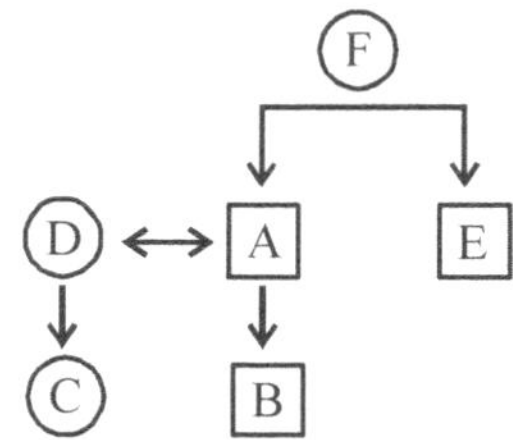

Clearly, C and F are the remaining members to be adjusted in place of two x. since, there are 3 children out of which two are girls, i.e. G and F, so clearly the third children C is a boy. So C is the son of E and A.

19. (b) 'O' → Female, '□' →Male, '↔' → Couple, '↓' → Offspring

Since, there is only 1 married couple, so D must be married to A, as D is the mother of two and B is the son of A. Also, as number of males and females are equal, so F must be a female.

20. (d) '□' → Male, 'O' → Female
'↓' → offspring, '=' → couple
'↔' → Sibbling

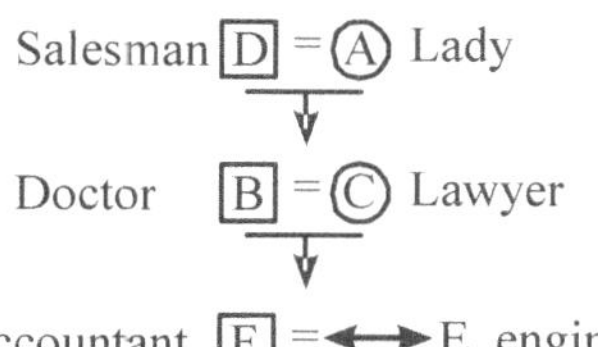

As, sex of E is not clear, so E can be brother or sister of F. Hence, relation between E and F can't be established.

28. Directions & Distance

1. (b) 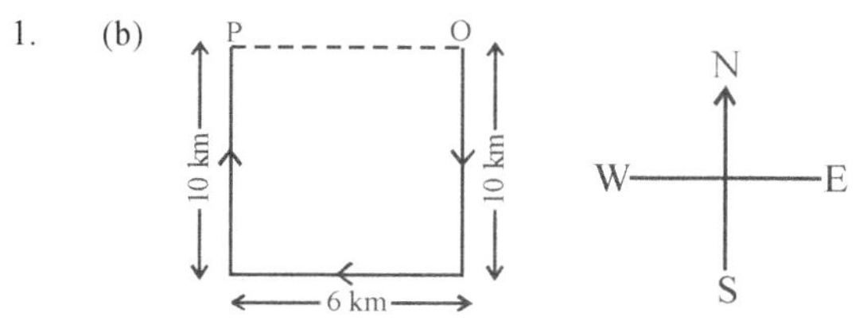

2. (a) 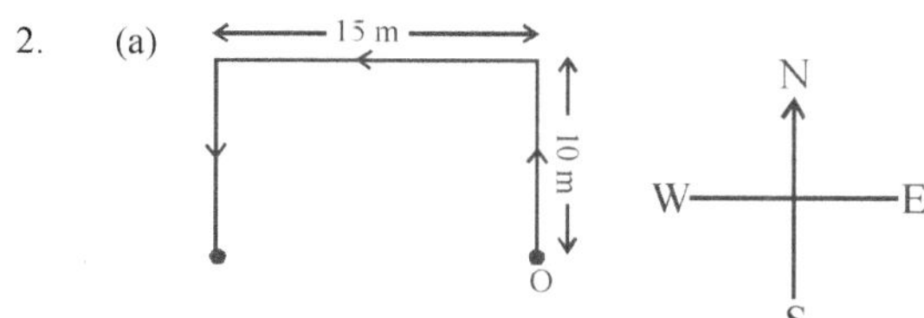

3. (b) 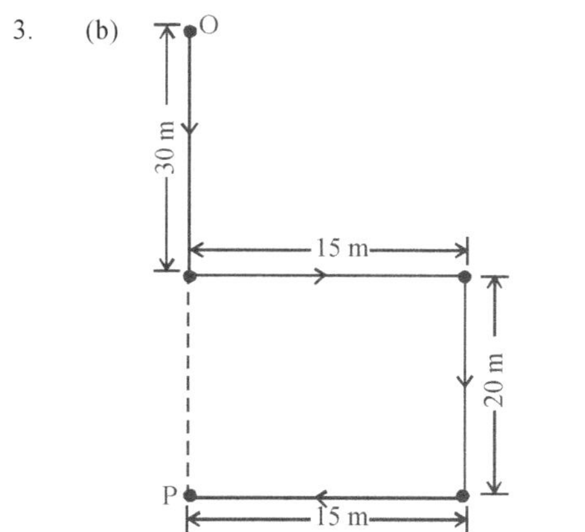

OP = 30 m + 20 m = 50 m

4. (b) 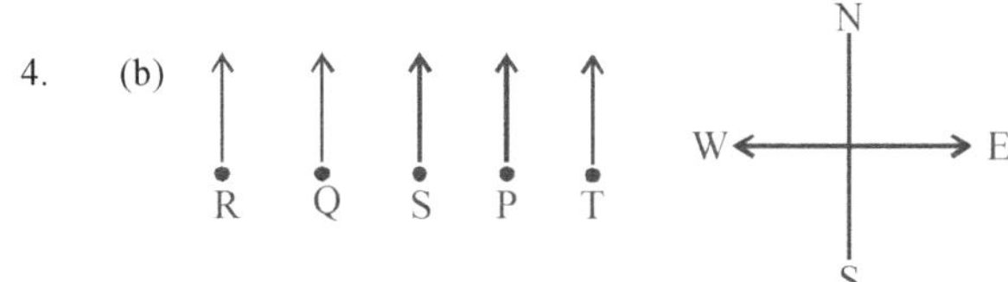

5. (c) 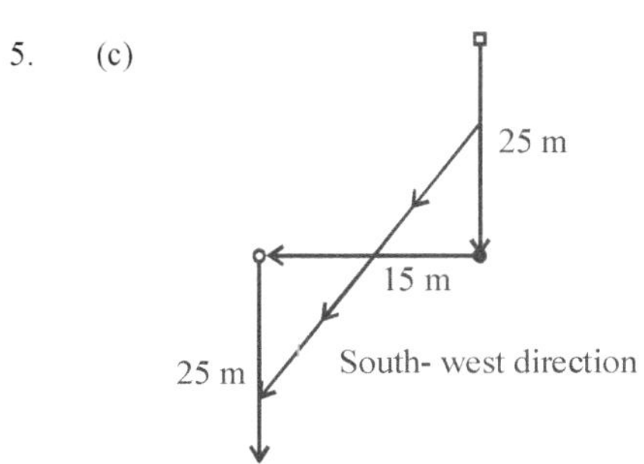

6. (d) 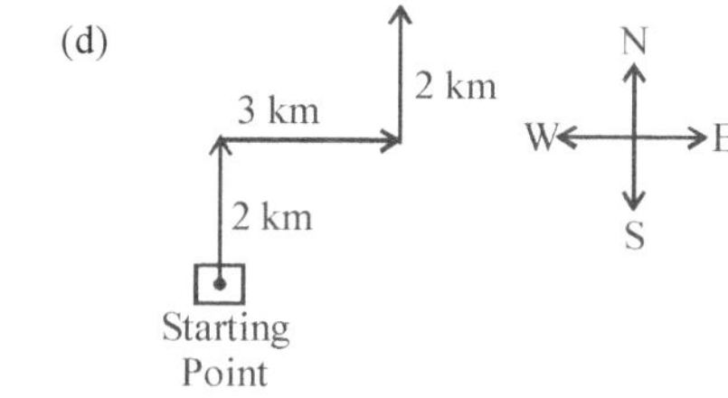

Clearly, he is facing towards north.

7. (a) 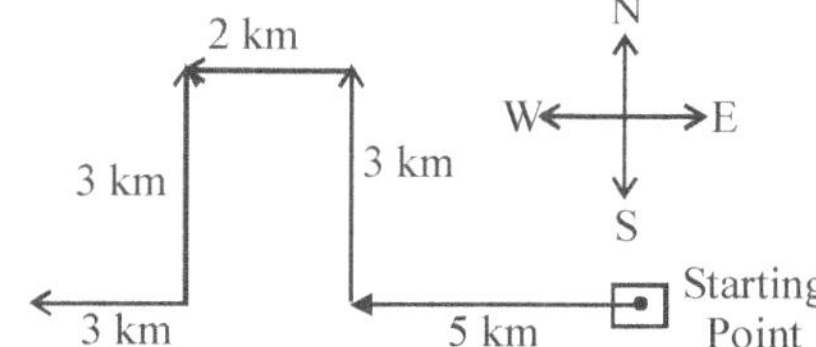

It is clear from the diagram that Kamu is to the west of her house.

8. (b) 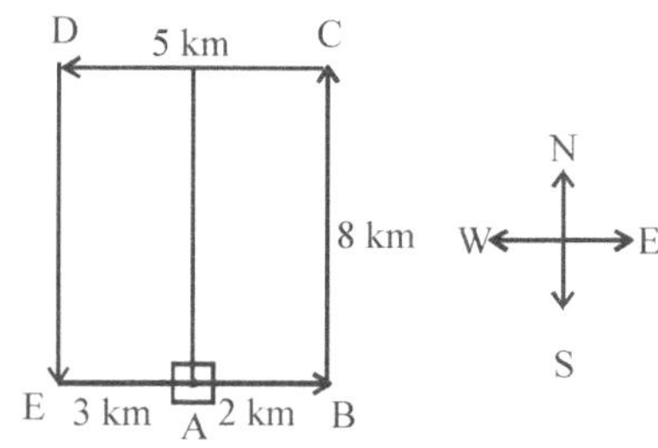

9. (b) 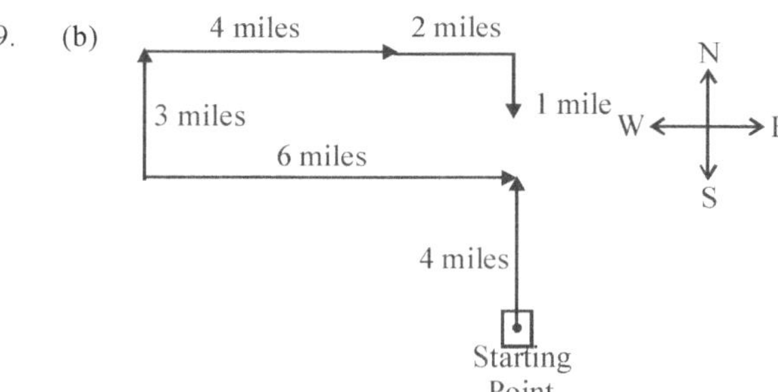

Now the man is facing towards south.

10. (b) 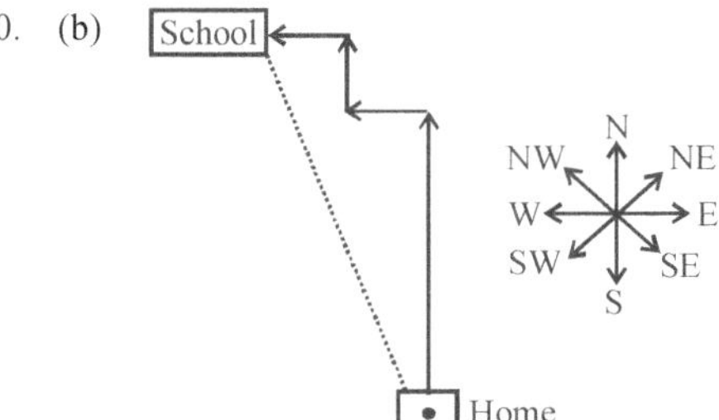

It is clear from the diagram that school is in North-West direction with respect to home.

11. (d) 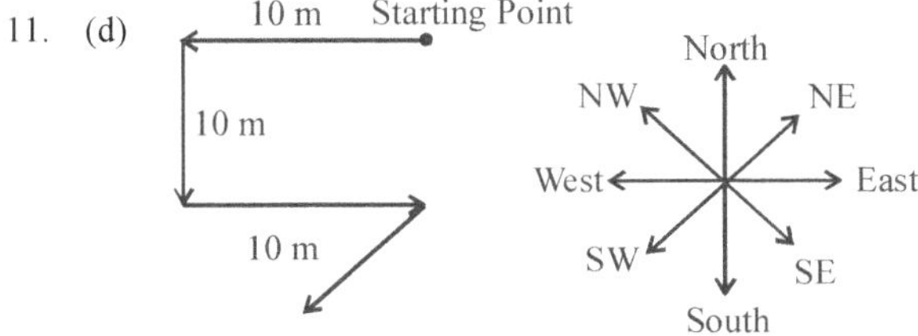

12. (a)
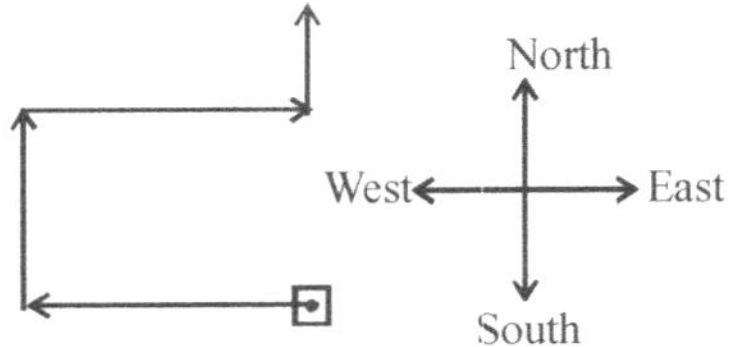

Now he is walking towards North

13. (a)

14. (d)
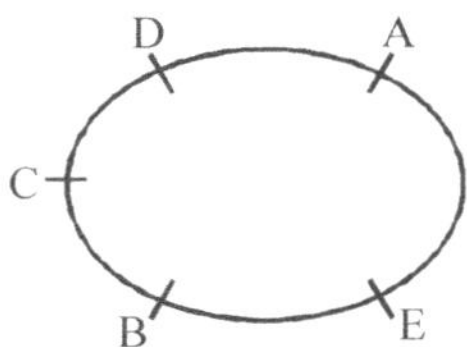

C is facing towards East.

15. (b)
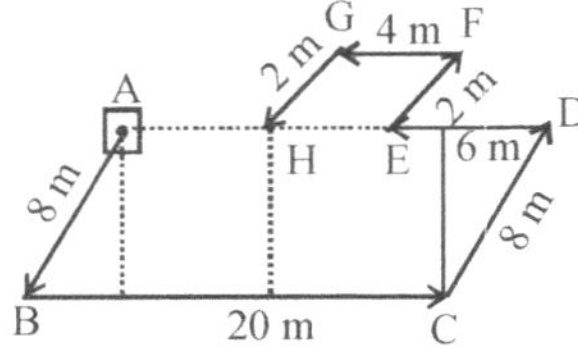

AH = 20 – (4 + 6) = 10 m

16. (d)
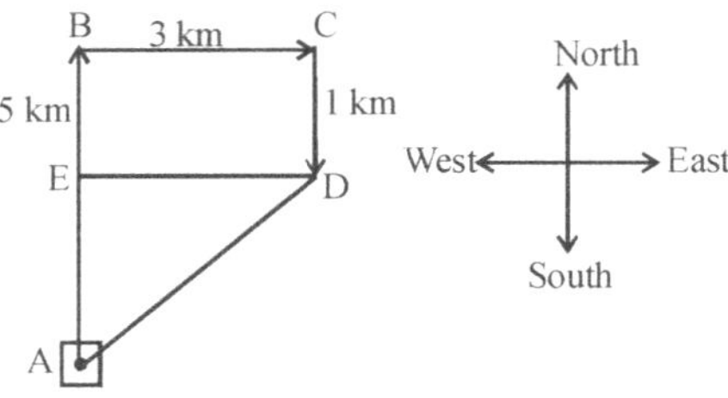

Required distance $AD = \sqrt{(AE)^2 + (DE)^2}$

$= \sqrt{(4)^2 + (3)^2}$

$= \sqrt{16 + 9} = \sqrt{25} = 5$ km

17. (d)
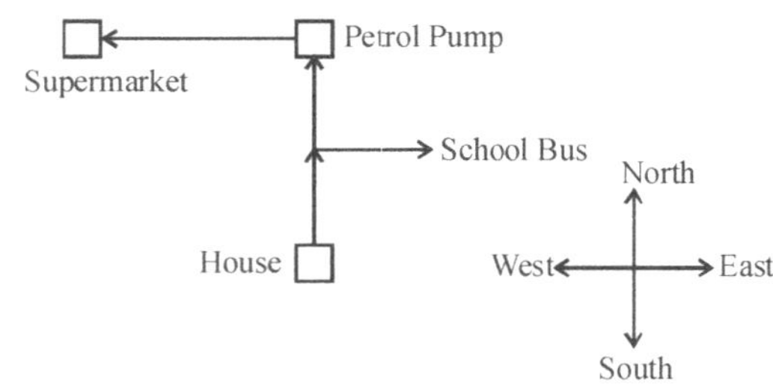

Supermarket is in the west from the petrol pump.

18. (a) In the morning an object casts its shadow to the West. In the evening an object casts its shadow to the east. Therefore, Gol Gumbaz is to the eastern side of Bara Kaman.

19. (b)
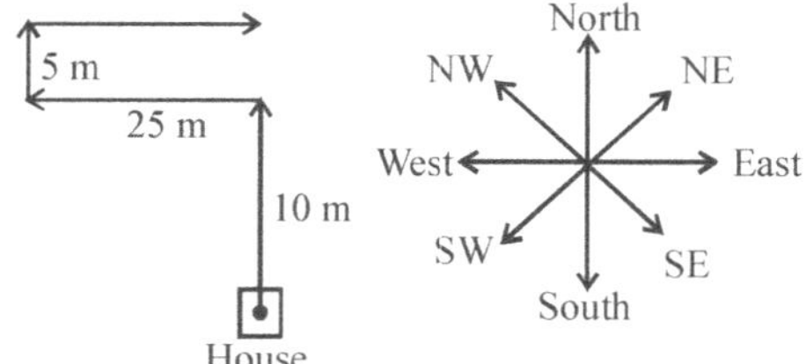

He is facing East.

20. (b)
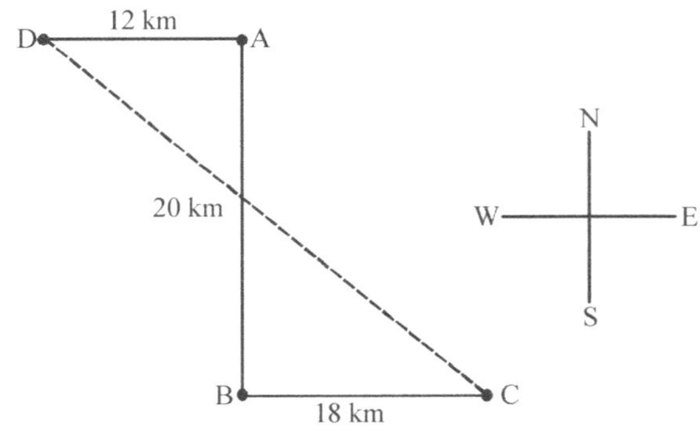

29. Clock & Calendar

1. (a) Day before yesterday was Thursday.
   Today is Saturday.
   Tomorrow will be Sunday.

2. (c) Total number of days
   = 27 + 365 + 365 + 365 + 339 = 1461 days
   Now, 1461 ÷ 7 = 5 Odd days
   Therefore, 5th December, 1997 would be
   Sunday + 5 = Friday

3. (a) 30th September 1998 ⇒ Wednesday
   30th September 1999 ⇒ Thursday
   30th September 2000 ⇒ Saturday
   Because 2000 is a Leap Year and there is one extra day in the month of February.
   30th September 2001 ⇒ Sunday
   30th September 2002 ⇒ Monday
   30th September 2003 ⇒ Tuesday

4. (b) Each second-space equals 1°.
   A clock gains five minutes every hour.

   It means the clock gains $\dfrac{5}{60}$ minutes in one minute.

   $\dfrac{5}{60} \times 360 = 30$

   The second hand will traverse 360.5° in one minute.

5. (b) 5th January 1965 ⇒ Tuesday
   5th January 1966 ⇒ Wednesday
   5th January 1967 ⇒ Thursday
   5th January 1968 ⇒ Friday
   5th January 1969 ⇒ Sunday
   Since, 1968 is a Leap Year.
   5th January 1970 ⇒ Monday
   5th January 1971 ⇒ Tuesday

6. (c) At 9'O clock, the minute hand is 9 × 5 = 45 minute – spaces behind the hour hand. Therefore, the minute hand will have to gain 45 – 30 = 10 minute space over the hour hand.
   ∴ Gain of 55 minute spaces equals 60 minutes.
   ∴ Gain of 15 minute spaces equals

   $= \dfrac{60}{55} \times 15 = \dfrac{180}{11} = 16\dfrac{4}{11}$

   Therefore, hour and minute hands of a clock point in opposite

   direction after 9'O clock at $16\dfrac{4}{11}$ minutes past 9.

7. (b) Shashikant was born on 29th September 1999.
   15th August, 1999 was Sunday.
   Days upto 29th September from 15 August.
   16 + 29 = 45 days = 6 weeks 3 old days.
   Sunday + 3 = Wednesday.

8. (a) Hands of clock will be together at $32\dfrac{8}{11}$ minutes past 6.

There are 30 minute spaces between hour and minute hand at 6 O' clock.
The minute hand gains 55 minutes in 60 minutes.
∴ It will gain 30 minutes in

$$\dfrac{60}{55}\times 33 = 32\dfrac{8}{11} \text{ minutes}$$

9. (a) The year 1996 was a Leap Year.
Number of days remaining in the 1996.
= 366 – 26 = 340 days
= 48 weeks 4 odd days
1997, 1998 and 1999 together have 3 odd days.
2000 was a Leap year
Days upto 15th August 2000
31 + 29 + 31 + 30 + 31 + 30 + 31 + 15 = 228 days

$$\dfrac{228}{7} = 32 \text{ weeks 4 odd days}$$

Now, total number of odd days = 4 + 3 + 4 = 11

$$\dfrac{11}{7} = 1 \text{ week 4 odd days}$$

15th August 2000 was 4 days beyond Friday i.e., Tuesday.

10. (c) LCM of 16 and 18
= 2 × 8 × 9 = 144
Both Cuckoos will come out together again at
12.00 + 2.24 = 2.24 pm

11. (c)

The minute hand points West, it means the clock has been rotated through 90° clockwise. Therefore, hour hand will point North-West.

12. (b) In a year, number of weeks = 52 extra day = 1
From 2002 to 2008, there are 6 years.
So number of extra days = 6 (1) = 6
While 2004 and 2008 are leap years, having one more extra day apart from the normal extra day.
Thus, number of extra days = 6 + 1 + 1 = 8
Out of these 8 extra days, 7 days form a week and so 1 day remains.
Hence, March 1, 2002 is 1 day less then March 1, 2008 i.e., it is Friday.

13. (c) In one hour, hour hand and minute hand are at right angles 2 times.
Time = 10 p.m – 1 p.m = 9 hr.
∴ No. of times, when both hands are perpendicular to each other in 9 hr = 9 × 2 = 18

14. (a) Since, in one hour, two hands of a clock coincide only once, so, there will be value.

Required time $T = \dfrac{2}{11}(H\times 30 + A°)$ minutes past H.

Here H = initial position of hour hand = 3
(Since 3 o'clock)
A° = required angle = 0°   (Since it coincides)

$$T = \dfrac{2}{11}(3\times 30 + 0) \text{ minutes past 3}$$

$$= 16\dfrac{4}{11} \text{ minutes past 3.}$$

15. (c) On 31st December, 2005 it was Saturday.
Number of odd days from the year 2006 to the year 2009
= (1 + 1 + 2 + 1) = 5 days
∴ On 31st December 2009, it was Thursday.
Thus, on 1st Jan, 2010 it is Friday.

16. (d) Count the number of odd days from the year 2007 onwards from the year 2007 onwards to get the sum equal to 0 odd day.

Year	2007	2008	2009	2010	2011	2012	2013	2014	2015	2016	2017
Odd day	1	2	1	1	1	2	1	1	1	2	1

17. (b) Each day of the week is repeated after 7 days
So, after 63 days, it will be Monday.
∴ After 61 days, it will be Saturday.

18. (c) 17th June, 1998 = (1997 years + Period from 1.1.1998 to 17.6.1998)
Odd days in 1600 years = 0
Odd days in 300 years = (5 × 3) ≡ 1
97 years has 24 leap years + 73 ordinary years.
Number of odd days in 97 years = (24 × 2 + 73) = 121
= 2 odd days.
Jan. Feb. March April May June
(31 + 28 + 31 + 30 + 31 + 17) = 168 days
= 24 weeks = 0 odd day
Total number of odd days = (0 + 1 + 2 + 0) = 3
Given day is Wednesday.

19. (d) No. of days between 21st July, 1947 and 21 st July, 1999
= 52 years + 366 days.
= 13 beap years + 39 ordinary years + 366 days
= (13 × 2) odd days + 39 odd days + 2 odd days
= (26 + 39 + 2) odd days = 67 odd years = 4 odd days.
= (7 – 4) = 3 days before the week day on 21st July, 1999 = Saturday.

20. (b) Time between 1 p.m. on Tuesday to 1 p.m. on Thursday = 48 hrs. The watch gains (1 + 2) = 3 minutes in 48 hrs.
it gains 1 min, in 16 hrs.
Hence, it will show correct time at 5 a.m. on Wednesday.

30. Logical Venn Diagram-I

1. (d) Some politicians may be poets and vice-versa.
Some politicians may be women and vice-versa.
No poet can be women as women poet is called poetess.

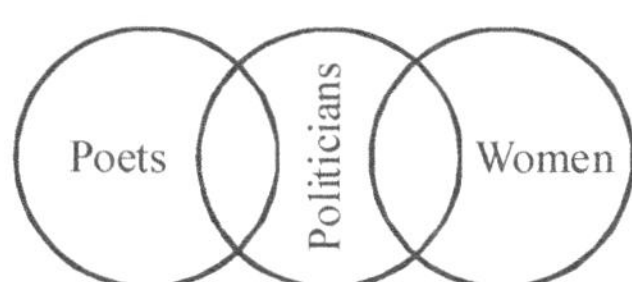

2. (b) 20% of 80 = $\dfrac{20}{100}\times 80 = 16$

50% of remaining

$$= (80 – 16)\times \dfrac{50}{100} = 32$$

The families which do not own any vehicle.
= 80 – (32 + 16)
= 80 – 48 = 32

3. (c) Judge is different from both the thief and criminal.
The thief comes under the class criminal.

4. (c) 25 have VCRs and each VCR owner also has a TV.
Therefore, the TV owners who have not VCRs 75 – 25 = 50.
Now, 10 have all the three. Therefore, 50 – 10 = 40 have only TV.

5. (a) Some teachers may be graduates and vice-versa.
All teachers and all graduates are human beings.

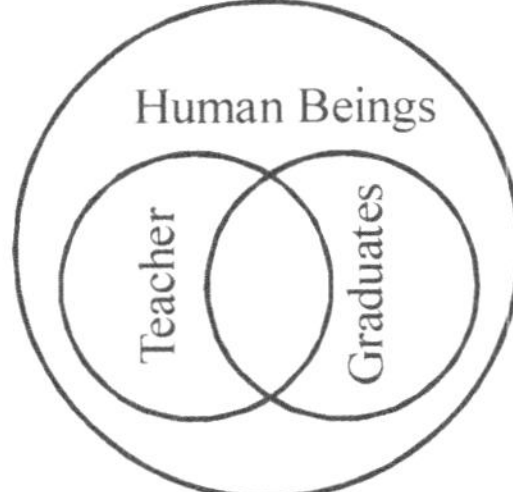

6. (d) Snake is different from Lizard, but both are reptiles.

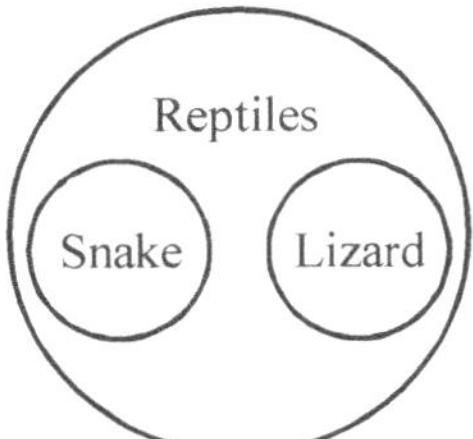

7. (c) Tiger is different from Lion. Both are Animals.

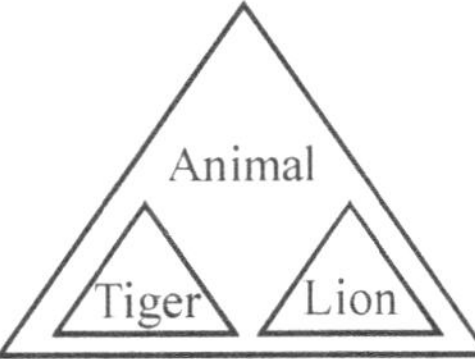

8. (a) 12 students take Maths and Physics but not 'Spanish.

9. (c) Every thing is composed of molecules. Sun is different from Moon.

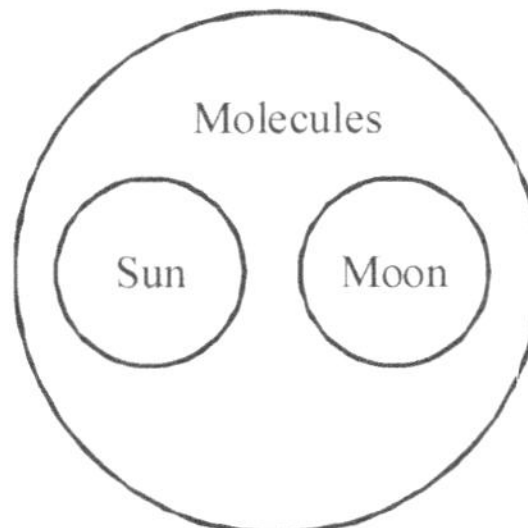

10. (b) The required region should be common to circle and square and outside the triangle. Such region is marked '2'.

31. Logical Venn Diagram-II

1. (b) Some bio-products are food while some other bio-products are poison.

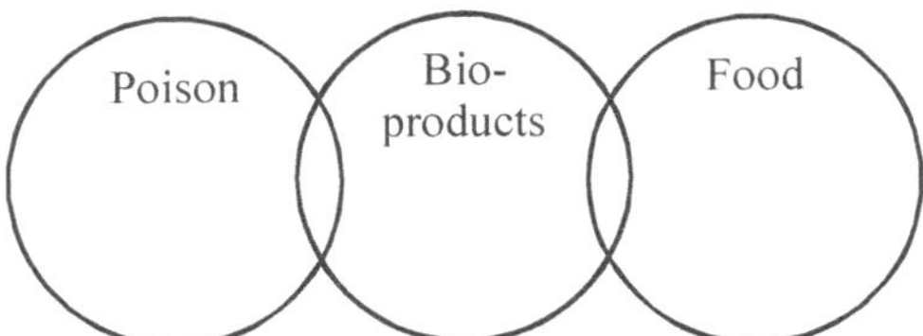

2. (d) The required portion should be common to the triangle and the circle. Such portion is marked 'C'.

3. (c) Pen is different from Pencil. But both are stationery items.

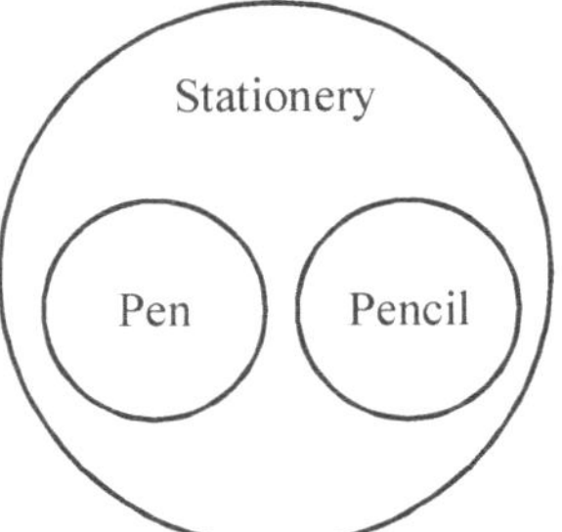

4. (b) Pea is different from kidney bean. But both are Leguminous seeds.

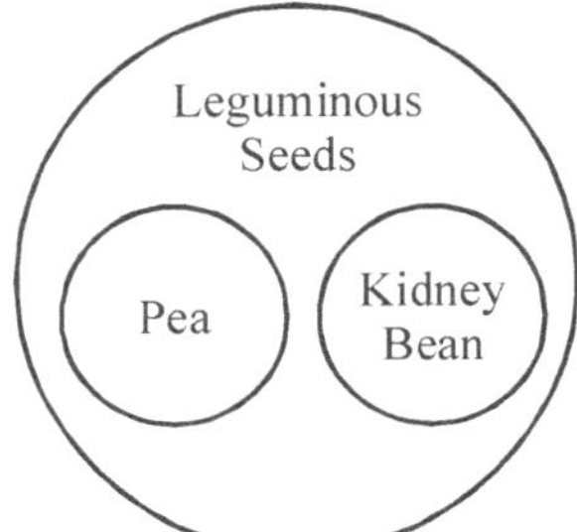

5. (a) Some boys are students
Some students are boys.
Some students are athletes.
Some athletes are students.
Some boys are athletes.
Some athletes are boys.
Some boys who are students are athletes.
Some students who are boys are athletes.
Some athletes who are students are boys.

6. (d) 3 + 6 = 9

7. (c) 

8. (b) All mothers are women.
All women are people.

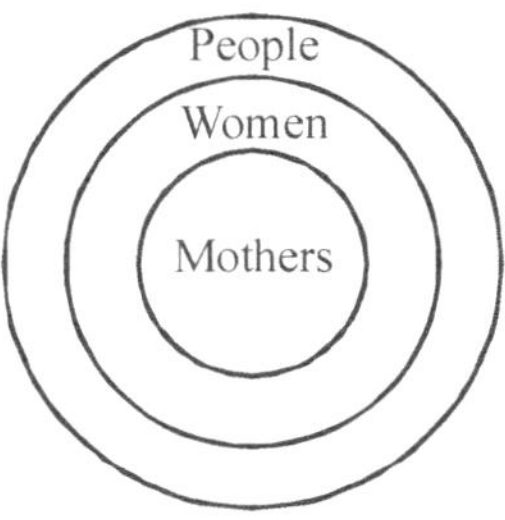

9. (d) 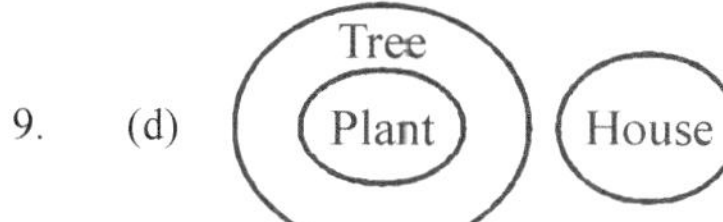

10. (b) Herring is type of fish, fish belongs to the class of animals.
11. (c) Nurse and Patient are differents but both are parts of Hospitals.
12. (c) Nose and hand are differents but both are parts of body.
13. (b) All diamonds rings are rings, all rings are ornaments.
14. (d) Table are furniture but book are differents.
15. (c) Chess and table tennis are differents but both are indoor games.

32. Syllogisms

1. (d) Both the Premises are Universal Affirmative (A-type). These two Premises are not aligned. Now take the Converse of one of the Premises to align them.

   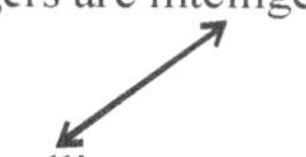

   A + I ⇒ No Conclusion.

2. (b) First Premise is Universal Affirmative and the second Premise is Universal Negative (E-type).

   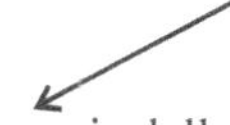

   A + E ⇒ E-type of Conclusion
   "No student is dull"
   This is conclusion II.

3. (b) Both the Premises are Universal Affirmative (A-type).

   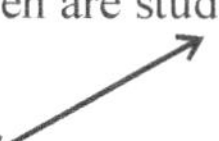

   A + A ⇒ A -type of Conclusion.
   "All children are players."
   This is Conclusion II.

4. (a) It is clear that Anand is not a teacher. Anand may be student or clerical staff.

5. (d) Both the Premises are Particular Affirmative (I-type). No conclusion follows from the two particular Premises.

6. (d) From general statements, Universal Conclusion cannot be drawn.

7. (b) 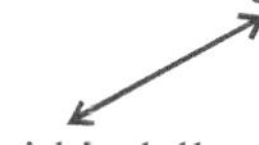

   A + E ⇒ E-type of Conclusion
   "No student is dull"
   This is Conclusion II.
   All students, without exception are girls. Therefore, there are no boys who are students.

8. (b) First Premise is Universal Affirmative (A-type).
   Second Premise is Particular Affirmative (I-type).

I + A ⇒ I-type of Conclusion
"Some women are aged"
This is Conclusion II.

9. (c) Both the Premises are Universal Affirmative (A-type).

   A + A ⇒ A-type of Conclusion
   "All skaters are runners."
   Conclusion I is Converse of it.
   Conclusion II is Implication of the first Premise.

10. (c) First Premise is Universal Affirmative (A-type).
    Second Premise is Particular Affirmative (I-type).

   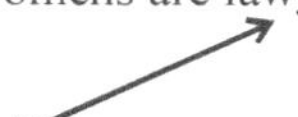

    I + A ⇒ I-type of Conclusion
    "Some womens are liars".
    This is Conclusion I.

11. (b) Both the Premises are Universal Affirmative (A-type).

    A + A ⇒ A-type of Conclusion
    "All stones are tigers."
    This is Conclusion I.
    Conclusion IV is Converse of it.

12. (c) First Premise is Universal Affirmative (A-type).
    Second promise is particular affirmative (I-type)

   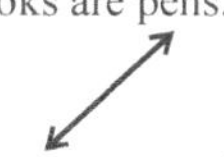

    A + I ⇒ No Conclusion
    Conclusion III is Converse of the second Premise.
    Conclusion IV is Converse of the first Premise.

13. (a) 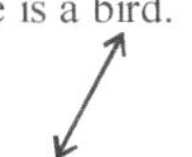

    I + A ⇒ I-type of Conclusion
    "Some villages are towns".
    This is Conclusion III.

14. (a) Statement I is Particular Affirmative (I-type)
    Statement II is Universal Affirmative (A-type).

    A + I ⇒ No Conclusion
    Conclusion I is Converse of the Statement I.

15. (d) From both the Statements it is clear that only Ravi has five pens in the class. Therefore, only Conclusion IV follows.

16. (b) The first and second Premises are Particular Affirmative (I-type).
The third Premises is Universal Affirmative (A-type).

Some beautifuls are honest.

All honest are sensitives.
I + A ⇒ I-type of Conclusion
"Some beautifuls are sensitives."
Conclusion I is Converse of it.

17. (a) First Premise is Particular Affirmative (I-type).
Second Premise is Universal Affirmative (A-type)

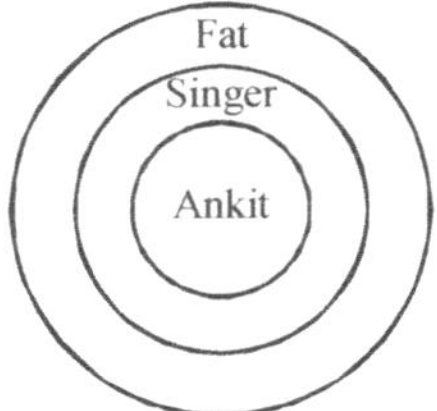

All centuries are decades.

Some decades are years.
A + I ⇒ No Conclusion
Conclusion II is Converse of the first Premise.
Conclusions I and III form Complementary Pair. Therefore, either I or III follows.

18. (a) All the singers are fat and Ankit is a singer. So, Ankit is fat.

19. (a) First Premise is Particular Affirmative (I-type).
Second Premise is Universal Negative (E-type).

Some cats are dogs.

No dog is a toy.
I + E ⇒ O – type of Conclusion
"Some cats are not toys"
This is Conclusion III.
Conclusion I is Converse of the first Premise.

20. (c) Statement I consists of two Particular Affirmative (I-type) Premises.
Statement II consists of two Universal Affirmative (A-type) Premises.

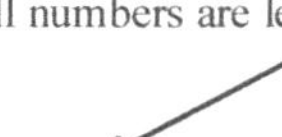

Some locks are numbers.

All numbers are letters.
I + A ⇒ I – type of Conclusion
"Some locks are letters".
This is Conclusion II.

All numbers are letters.

All letters are words.
A + A ⇒ A – type of Conclusion
"All numbers are words".
Conclusion I is Converse of it.

33. Non verbal reasoning

1. (d) In each step the elements of the upper row shift from left to right in cyclic order while elements of the lower row shift from right to left in cyclic order.

2. (b) In each step, the whole figure rotates by 45° ACW. The middle element interchanges with elements on either side alternately while the third element is replaced by a new one.

3. (c) In each step the whole figure rotates by 90° ACW while one of the end elements is replaced alternately on either side.

4. (a) In the first step the elements shift from the upper left to lower right → middle left → upper right → lower left → upper left. In the next step the elements shift one step CW in cyclic order.

5. (d) In each step the upper element rotates by 90° ACW. The lower element gets inverted and a curve is added to it on the upper side.

6. (c) In alternate steps the elements shift one-and-a-half sides CW while one of the elements beginning from the ACW end gets replaced by a new one in each step.

7. (b) In each step the whole figure rotates by 90° CW while one element is added in each step alternately on CW and ACW end.

8. (b) In each step the whole figure rotates by 90° ACW and an arc is added on the CW side.

9. (b) In each step the triangles rotate by 90° CW. The shading of the right triangle changes alternately. The shadings of the middle and left triangles change in each step in a set order.

10. (a) In each step the quadrilateral rotates by 90° ACW while it shifts half a side CW alternately.

34. General Intelligence & Reasoning Section Test-I

1. (a) A square is a two-dimensional figure consisting of sides whereas a cube is a three-dimensional figure. Similarly, circle is a two-dimensional figure and a sphere is a three-dimensional figure.

2. (d) The first is found in the form of the second.

3. (d) Lotus is grown in water (Mud).

4. (d) The number 49 is a perfect square of a natural number.

5. (d) 1, 12, 123, 1234, 12345, 123456, 123456 [7]

6. (c) ABCD, ABCDE, ABCDEF, PQRS, PQRST, PQRST [U]

7. (c) 

8. (b) Meaningful words are : ARE, ART, ATE

9. (a) Teacher write on blackboard with chalk, here chalk is called book, hence here the code of chalk is book.

10. (d)

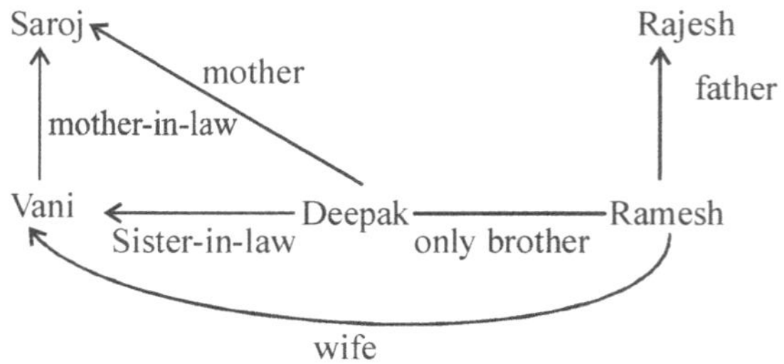

35. General Intelligence & Reasoning Section Test-II

1. (c)

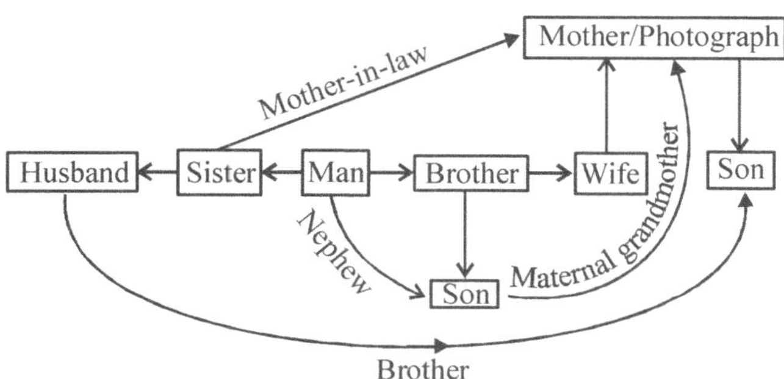

2. (a) As,

$$D \xrightarrow{+2} F \qquad I \xrightarrow{+2} K$$
$$O \xrightarrow{+2} Q \qquad \text{and} \qquad N \xrightarrow{+2} P$$

Similarly,

$$A \xrightarrow{+2} C$$
$$T \xrightarrow{+2} V$$

3. (b) W R O M B T → 7 1 9 4 8 3
4. (d) The colour of blood is red and here red means orange.
5. (b)

6. (c)

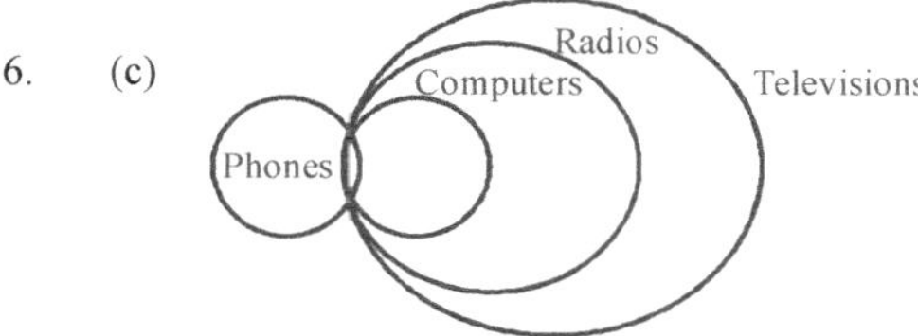

Conclusions :
I. Not True
II. True

7. (b) Clearly the school is in north-east

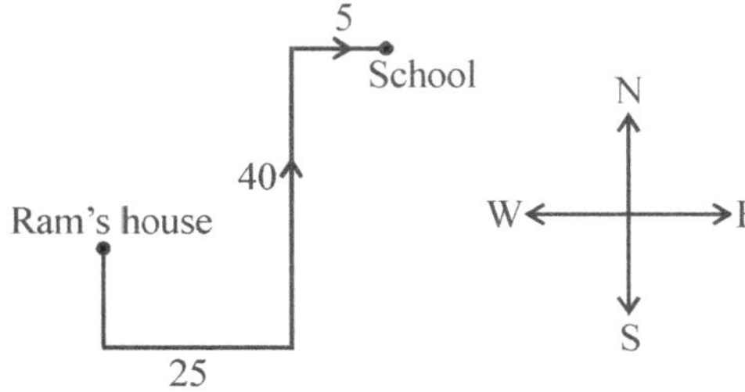

8. (b) SKILL, KILLS
9. (c) Word :
W A L K I N G
Alphabetical order :
A G I K L N W
So, the positions of K and N remain unchanged.
10. (d) The series is abcab, bcabc, cabca.

36. Mechanics-I

1. (a) Acceleration due to gravity independent of mass $h = \dfrac{1}{2}gt^2$

both will reach simultaneously.
2. (d)   3. (b)   4. (a)
5. (a) Washing machine works on the principle of centrifugation.

Centrifugation is a process that involves the use of the centrifugal force for the separation of mixtures with a centrifuge, used in industry and in laboratory settings. More-dense components of the mixture migrate away from the axis of the centrifuge, while less-dense components of the mixture migrate towards the axis.

6. (b)
7. (d) When a motorcar makes a sharp turn at a high speed, we tend to get thrown to one side because we tend to continue in our straight line motion and an unbalanced force is applied by the engine of the motorcar changes the direction of motion of the motorcar. So, we slip to one side of the seat due to the inertia of our body.

8. (d)   9. (a)
10. (c) $v^2 = u^2 + 2gh \Rightarrow v = \sqrt{u^2 + 2gh}$

So, for both the cases velocity will be equal.

11. (b) At a particular time, two values of velocity are not possible.
12. (b) The bullet will hit the monkey. If it drops, because at the time of firing, the direction of bullet was towards the monkey. After this the downward accleration 'g' is same for both monkey & bullet. Hence the direction of bullet during its motion is always towards the droping monkey & at the cross section of the path followed by the monkey & path followed by the bullet. The bullet will hit the monkey.
Note : If monkey does not drop at the time of firing the bullet, the bullet will never hit the monkey.

13. (a) The car over turn, when reaction on inner wheel of car is zero, i.e., first the inner wheel of car leaves the ground (where G is C.G of car, h is height of C.G from the ground, f_1 & f_2 are frictional force exerted by ground on inner & outer wheel respectively).

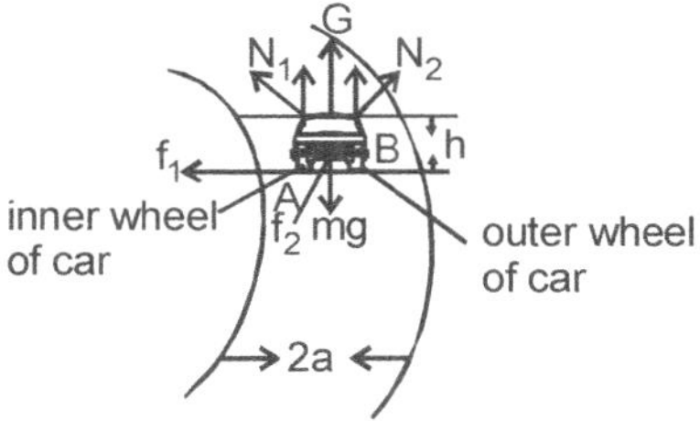

The max. speed for no over turning is

$$v_{max} = \sqrt{\frac{gra}{h}}$$

where r is radius of the path followed by car for turn & 2a is distance between two wheels of car (i.e., AB)

14. (c,d) As it is clear from the solutions 27 (if road is banked) & 28 (if road is horizontal), that if necessary centripetal force is not provided to moving body, then it starts skidding because contrifugal force is not balanced by centripetal force. It is occurs, when the speed is greater than certain velocity v_{max} for given banking of road & radius of path (in case of banking friction less road $v_{max} = \sqrt{\tan\theta\, rg}$) & for given static friction & radius of path (in case of horizontal friction road $v_{max} = \sqrt{\mu_s\, rg}$). If we consider both banking of road & friction also, then max velocity by which the car safely turn withour skidding is $v_{max} = \sqrt{\dfrac{rg(\mu + \tan\theta)}{1 - \mu\tan\theta}}$. Hence both options (c) & (d) are correct.

15. (d) Friction can be decreased by all the given methods.
16. (c)   17. (a)   18. (a)   19. (a)
20. (d)

37. Mechanics-II

1. (d)   2. (b)   3. (a)   4. (c)
5. (d) The weight of an object is the force with which it is attracted towards the earth. W = mg
6. (d)
7. (c) The boy does not exert a torque to rotating table by jumping, so angular momentum is conserved i.e., $= \dfrac{d\vec{L}}{dt} = 0 \Rightarrow \vec{L} =$ constant
8. (d) An athlete runs some distance before taking a long jump, because by doing this, he picks up the inertia of motion, which helps him in taking a longer jump.
9. (b) The change in momentum in metal ball after the collision with a wall is
$\Delta P = m(v_2 - v_1) = m(0 - v_1) = -mv_1$
the change in momentum in rubber wall is
$\Delta P' = m(v_2' - v_1) = m(-v_1 - v_1) = -2mv_1 \qquad (\because v_2' = v_1)$
hence $\Delta P' > \Delta P$
10. (a)
11. (a) There are no external horizontal forces acting on the 'man plus boat' system. (The forces exerted by the man and the boat on each other are internal forces for the system.) Therefore, the centre of mass of the system, which is initially at rest, will always be at rest.
12. (a)   13. (c)   14. (c)   15. (a)
16. (a)   17. (c)   18. (d)
19. (d) As displacement S = 0, work done W = FS = 0
20. (a) As gravity g = 0
    ∴ Weight W = mg = 0
    but mass is not zero.

38. Properties of matter

1.   (b) Ice is lighter than water. When ice melts, the volume occupied by water is less than that of ice. Due to which the level of water goes down.
2. (b)
3. (a, d) Pressure is smaller where velocity is higher and velocity is higher where area is smaller.
4. (d)   5. (b)   6. (b)   7. (a)
8. (c)   9. (d)   10. (c)   11. (b)
12. (b)   13. (c)   14. (d)
15. (d) As cross-section areas of both the tubes A and C are same and tube is horizontal. Hence according to equation of continuity $v_A = v_C$ and therefore according of Bernoulli's theorem $P_A = P_C$ i.e. height of liquid is same in both the tubes A and C.
16. (a)   17. (b)
18. (a) Because dimension of invar does not vary with temperature.
19. (a)
20. (d) Volume conservation or incompressibility is an imprtant property of a liquid.

39. Heat

1. (a) The area of circular hole increases when we heat the metal sheet & expansion of metal sheet will be independent of shape & size of the hole.
2. (a)
3. (c) Melting point (M.P.) of ice decrease with increase of pressure (because ice contracts on melting). Hence some ice melts. When we press two block of ice together such that after releasing the pressure two block join & this penomenon is called regelation.

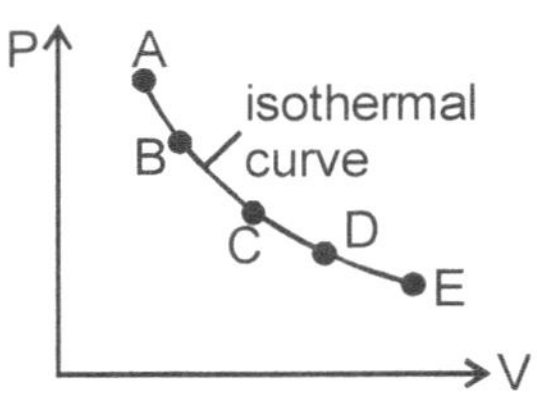

4.   (b)
5. (c) $\dfrac{dP}{dT} = \dfrac{JL_{vap}}{T(V_2 - V_1)}$ in case of boiling V_2 is always greater than V_1, so with decrease in pressure, B.P. (boiling point) also decreases & we feel difficulty in cooking at high altitude.
6. (a)   7. (a)   8. (c)   9. (c)
10. (c)   11. (b)   12. (a)   13. (a)
14. (c)   15. (b)
16. (d) Water has maximum density at 4°C.
17. (c) Water has maximum density at 4°C, so if the water is heated above 4°C or cooled below 4°C density decreases, i.e., volume increases. In other words, it expands so it overflows in both the cases.

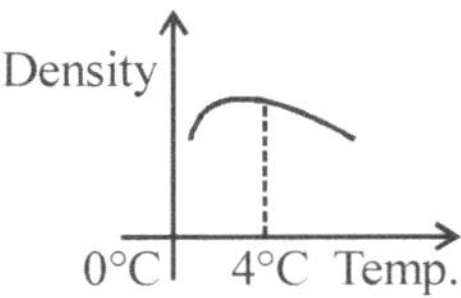

18. (a) Heat taken by ice to melt at 0°C is
$Q_1 = mL = 540 \times 80 = 43200$ cal
Heat given by water to cool upto 0°C is
$Q_2 = ms\Delta\theta = 540 \times 1 \times (80 - 0) = 43200$ cal
Hence heat given by water is just sufficient to melt the whole ice and final temperature of mixture is 0°C.
Short trick : For these types of frequently asked questions you can remember the following formula
$$\theta_{mix} = \dfrac{m_w \theta_w - \dfrac{m_i L_i}{c_w}}{m_i + m_w}$$ (See theory for more details)
If $m_w = m_i$ then $\theta_{mix} = \dfrac{\theta_w - \dfrac{L_i}{c_w}}{2} = \dfrac{80 - \dfrac{80}{1}}{2} = 0°C$
19. (c)
20. (d) Due to large specific heat of water, it releases large heat with very small temperature change.

40. Sound

1. (b)   2. (a)   3. (b)   4. (b)
5. (c)   6. (d)   7. (b)
8. (d) Time lost in covering the distance of 2 km by the second waves $t = \dfrac{d}{v} = \dfrac{2000}{330} = 6.06$ sec $\approx$ 6 sec.
9. (d) Velocity of sound in steel in maximum out of the given materials water and air. In vacuum sound cannot travel, it's speed is zero.
10. (b)   11. (c)
12. (d) The sound of different source are said to differ in quality. The number of overtones and their relative intensities determines the quality of any musical sound.
13. (b) The frequency of note 'Sa' is 256 Hz while that of note 'Re' and 'Ga' respectively are 288 Hz and 320 Hz

14.	(c)	15.	(a)	16.	(b)	17.	(c)	
18.	(a)	19.	(b)					

20. (d) Speed of sound decreases when we go from solid to gaseous state and increases with increase in temperature. It also depends upon properties of the medium through which it travels.

41. Ray Optics

1.	(a)	2.	(a)	3.	(c)	4.	(b)	

5. (b) The star is considered to be a point source of light for its distance from the earth. Apparent change in position of its image due to atmospheric refraction causes twinkling of stars.

6. (c) Interference at thin films causes colouring of soap bubble.

7. (d) Because, the focal length of eye lens can not decreased beyond a certain limit.

8.	(a)	9.	(a)	10.	(c)	11.	(b)	
12.	(b)	13.	(a)	14.	(b)			

15. (d) Objects are invisible in liquid of R.I. equal to that of object.

16. (d)

17. (c) If eye is kept at a distance d then $MP = \dfrac{(D-d)}{f_0 f_e}, MP$ decreases

18. (c) 19. (d)

20. (d) Visible region decreases, so the depth of image will not be seen.

42. Wave Optics

1. (b) As the star is accelerated towards earth, its apparent frequency increases, apparent wavelength decreases. Therefore, colour of light changes gradually to violet.

2. (c) Interference at thin films causes colouring of soap bubble.

3. (b) Infrared radiation is detected by pyrometer.

4. (d) Interference is shown by electromagnetic as well as mechanical waves.

5. (c) The intensity of illumination is given by

$$I = \frac{P\cos\theta}{r^2}$$

where P = power of the source
r = distance between source and point
θ = angle of incidence
when θ = 0, I will be maximum. Hence, the rays from the sun are incident normally on the earth surface.

6. (d) Laser beams are perfectly parallel. so that they are very narrow and can travel a long distance without spreading. This is the feature of laser while they are monochromatic and coherent these are characteristics only.

7. (c)

8. (a) Light is electromagnetic in nature it does not require any material medium for its propagation.

9. (b) Due to expansion of universe, the star will go away from the earth thereby increasing the observed wavelength. Therefore the spectrum will shift to the infrared region.

10. (a)

11. (c) Polarisation is not shown by sound waves.

12. (b) Shifting towards violet region shows that apparent wavelength has decreased. Therefore the source is moving towards the earth.

13.	(a)	14.	(c)	

15. (c) β-rays are beams of fast electrons.

16.	(d)	17.	(d)	

18. (d) Ground wave and sky wave both are amplitude modulated wave and the amplitude modulated signal is transmitted by a transmitting antenna and received by the receiving antenna at a distance place.

19. (b) Infrared radiations reflected by low lying clouds and keeps the earth warm.

20. (b) Ozone layer absorbs most of the UV rays emitted by sun.

43. Electrostatics

1. (c) Positive charge is due to deficiency of electrons.

2. (a)

3. (d) Ebonite is the best insulator.

4. (d) The weight can be increased slightly, if it acquire negative charge & weight can be decreased slightly, if it acquires positive charge.

5.	(c)	6.	(a)	7.	(a)	

8. (a) When a lamp is connected to D.C. line with a capacitor. It will form an open circuit. Henc, the lamp will not glow.

9. (c)

10. (c) Since both are metals so equal amount of charge will induce on them.

11. (d) Negative charge means excess of electron which increases the mass of sphere B.

12. (c) Because in case of metallic sphere either solid or hollow, the charge will reside on the surface of the sphere. Since both spheres have same surface area. So they can hold equal maximum charge.

13. (b) Every system tends to decrease its potential energy to attain more stability when we increase charge on soap bubble its radius increases $\left[U \propto \dfrac{1}{r}\right]$.

14. (a) In case of spherical metal conductor the charge quickly spreads uniformly over the entire surface because of which charges stay for longer time on the spherical surface. While in case of non-spherical surface, the charge concentration is different at different points due to which the charges do not stay on the surface for longer time.

15. (b) When a positively charged body connected to earth , electrons flows from earth to body and body becomes neutral.

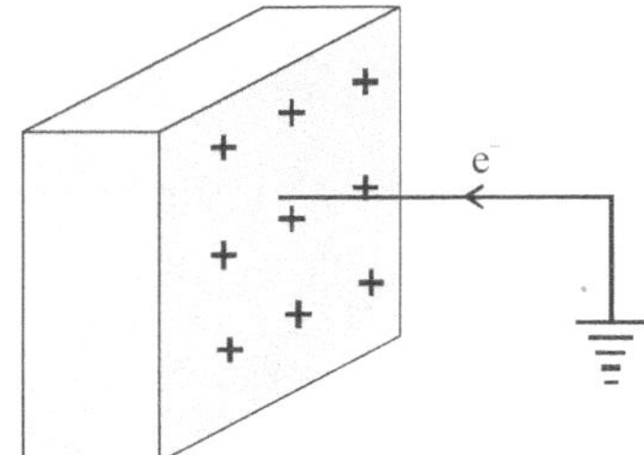

16. (b)

17. (b) In charging half of energy supplied by the battery is lost in the form of heat.

18. (d)

19. (d) Electric charge is quantised. It is an integral multiple of e = 1.60×10^{-19} C

20. (a)

44. Current Electricity

1.	(d)	2.	(c)	

3. (a) Parameters of electricity supply are different in different countries. In India they are:
Potential Difference of 220 V, Frequency of 50 hertz and Current Rating of 5A/15A.

4. (b)

5. (b) In a parallel circuit, the voltage across each of the components is the same, and the total current is the sum of the currents through each component. The wiring for most homes is parallel .In parallel circuit each branch receives equal current. If one branch in the circuit is broken, electric current will still flow in other branches.

6. (c) Human body, though has a large resistance of the order, of KΩ (say 10 kΩ), is very sensitive to minute currents even as low as a few mA. Electrons, excites and disorders the nervous system of the body and hence one fails to control the activity of the body.

7. (c) $R \propto \dfrac{1}{\tau}$; where τ = Relaxation time

When lamp is switched on, temperature of filament increases, hence τ decreases so R increases

8. (d)

9. (a) To convert a galvanometer into a voltmeter, a high value resistance is to be connected in series with it.

10. (a) Internal resistance $\propto \dfrac{1}{\text{Temperature}}$

11. (d) Energy consumed in kWh = $\dfrac{\text{watt} \times \text{hour}}{1000}$

$\Rightarrow$ For 30 days, $P = \dfrac{10 \times 50 \times 10}{1000} \times 30 = 150\,\text{kWh}$

12. (d) Colliding electrons lose their kinetic energy as heat.

13. (c) Power loss in transmission $P_L = \dfrac{P^2 R}{V^2} \Rightarrow P_L \propto \dfrac{1}{V^2}$

14. (a) Watt-hour meter measures electric energy.

15. (c) $i \propto \dfrac{1}{R}$ and $P \propto \dfrac{1}{R} \Rightarrow i \propto P$ i.e., in parallel bulb of higher power will draw more current.

16. (c)   17. (c)

18. (b) As temperature increases resistance of filament also increases.

19. (a) An ideal cell has zero resistance.

20. (d)

45. Alternating Current and Electromagnetic Induction

1. (c)   2. (d)   3. (c)   4. (c)
5. (c)   6. (c)   7. (a)   8. (a)
9. (c)   10. (c)

11. (b) In dc ammeter, a coil is free to rotate in the magnetic field of a fixed magnet.

If an alternating current is passed through such a coil, the torque will revese it's direction each time the current changes direction and the average value of the torque will be zero.

12. (d) Brightness $\propto$ P$_{consumed}$ $\propto \dfrac{1}{R}$. For bulb , $R_{ac} = R_{dc}$, so brightness will be equal in both the cases.

13. (d)   14. (a)   15. (c)

16. (b) $X_C = \dfrac{1}{2\pi v C} \Rightarrow X_C \propto \dfrac{1}{v}$

17. (a) $L \propto N^2$ i.e., $\dfrac{L_1}{L_2} = \left(\dfrac{N_1}{N_2}\right)^2 \Rightarrow L_2 = L_1 \left(\dfrac{N_2}{N_1}\right)^2 = 4L_1$

18. (c) Eddy currents are set up when a plate swings in a magnetic field. This opposes the motion.

19. (d) $e = Bvl \Rightarrow e \propto v \propto gt$

20. (d)

46. Magnetism

1. (b)   2. (d)   3. (c)   4. (a)
5. (a) Soft iron has low coercivity.
6. (a) Diamagnetism is the universal property of all substances.
7. (c) Ferrites; e.g. CoFe2 O4 and NiFe2 O4 are used for coating magnetic tapes.

8. (a)   9. (c)   10. (c)   11. (a)
12. (c)   13. (c)   14. (c)   15. (d)
16. (a)   17. (c)

18. (c) Near the magnetic poles, H = 0, therefore, magnetic compass will not work.

19. (d) The direction of magnetic lines of force of a bar magnet is from north to south pole.

20. (c) For each half M = m $\times$ 2 ℓ becomes half and volume V = a $\times$ 2 l also becomes half therefore, I = M/V, remains constant.

47. Semiconductor Electronics

1. (c) Electric conduction, in a semi conductors occurs due to both electrons & holes.

2. (d) In extrinsic semi conductor the number of holes are not equal to number of electrons i.e.,

$n_p \neq n_e$

In P - type $n_p > n_e$

In N - type $n_e > n_p$

But over all both P & N - type semi conductor are uncharged.

3. (a)   4. (c)

5. (b) The electrical conductivity of a semiconductor at 0 K is zero. Hence resistivity (= 1/electrical conductivity) is infinity.

6. (d) The temperature coefficient of resistance of a semiconductor is negative. It means that resistance decrease with increase of temperature.

7. (b) The r.m.s. value of a.c. component of wave is more than d.c. value due to barrier voltage of p-n junction used as rectifier

8. (c) Zener diode is used as a voltage regulator i.e. for stabilization purposes

9. (b) In the reverse biasing of p-n junction, the voltage applied supports the barrier voltage across junction, which increases the width of depletion layer and hence increases its resistance

10. (c) The power amplifier handles large power

11. (c) The size (or length) of collector is large in comparison to emitter (base is very small in comarison to both collector & emitter) to dissipate the heat.

12. (d) In forward biasing, the diode conducts. For ideal junction diode, the forward resistance is zero; therefore, entire applied voltage occurs across external resistance R i.e., there occur no potential drop, but potential across R is V in forward biased.

13. (b) [Hint At 0K (–273°C) motion of free electron stop i.e., there is no electron in conduction band therefore at 0K intrinsic semiconductor becomes insulator.]

14. (c)

15. (b) Since $n_e > n_h$, the semiconductor is N-type

16. (c)

17. (a) ac $\to$ Rectifier $\to$ dc

18. (a) A positive feedback from output to input in an amplifier provides oscillations of constant amplitude.

19. (a) Aluminium is trivalent impurity

20. (c)

48. Nature of Matter

1. (c) Rusting of iron is a chemical change. In this process iron is converted into rust (hydrated iron oxide, $Fe_2O_3.xH_2O$) in the presence of water and oxygen.

2. (c)   3. (d)

4. (d) During combustion of a candle heat is evolved. Hence it is an exothermic process.

5. (b)   6. (d)   7. (c)

8. (b) German silver contains copper, zinc and nickel. Copper and zinc are major constituents of brass.

9. (c)   10. (a)   11. (c)   12. (c)

13. (a) is correct because physical properties such as magnetism, can be used to separate parts of a mixture.

14. (a) is correct because the component of this mixture will separate over time. B and C are colloids and apple juice is a solution.
15. (c) is correct because the particles that make up pure substances are identical throughout the substance.
16. (b)
17. (b) Brass is an alloy that is an example of solid-solid solution.
18. (a) Atoms that make up an element or molecules that make up a compound are identical.
19. (a)   20. (b)

49. Structure of atom

1. (d)
2. (b) Hydrogen nuclei (1 proton, 0 neutron) on trapping neutron become deuterium (1 proton, 1 neutron)
3. (c)   4. (d)   5. (b)   6. (c)
7. (d)   8. (a)   9. (a)   10. (d)
11. (a) Atomic number of hydrogen = no. of protons = 1
Mass number of hydrogen = no. of protons + no. of neutrons
= 1 + 0 = 0
12. (a)   13. (c)   14. (b)   15. (c)
16. (a)
17. (c) Neutron was discovered by Chadwick.
18. (b) Sequence in terms of increasing mass-
Electron < proton < hydrogen atom < alpha particle
19. (c) H contains one proton and one electron only
20. (a) Isobars are the species which contains same mass number but different atomic number. Therefore isobars possess different chemical properties.

50. Classification of elements

1. (d) Hydrogen is a non-metal but it is placed with alkali metals in periodic table.
2. (b)   3. (d)   4. (c)   5. (b)
6. (c) Fluorine is the most electronegative element in the periodic table.
7. (d) Caesium (Cs) is the most electropositive element in the periodic table.
8. (c)   9. (b)
10. (b) Element with atomic no. 36 (Krypton) has electronic configuration $3d^{10}\,4s^2\,4p^6$ belongs to p-block.
11. (d)   12. (c)
13. (c) Group 17 elements are halogens.
14. (b)   15. (b)   16. (c)   17. (d)
18. (a)
19. (a) Rare earth elements consists of Lanthanoids and actinoids is the first element of rare earth metals.
20. (b)

51. Acids and Bases

1. (d)   2. (a)
3. (a) Baking soda is $NaHCO_3$.
4. (b)   5. (a)   6. (b)
7. (d) All bases are not alkali. Alkali is a basic, ionic salt of an alkali metal or an alkaline earth metal element.
8. (d)   9. (b)   10. (d)   11. (a)
12. (d)   13. (a)
14. (b) Vanilla can be used as an Olfactory indicator. Olfactory indicators change there odour in acidic or basic media.
15. (b)   16. (c)
17. (b) An antacid is basic in nature and hence changes the colour of pH paper to greenish blue.
18. (a)   19. (b)
20. (c) Hydrochloric acid helps in digestion of food. It is secreted by the walls of the stomach.

52. Neutralisation and Salts

1. (d) Sodium acetata (CH_3COONa) is water forms NaOH which is a strong base and hence makes the solution basic.

2. (a)   3. (b)   4. (d)   5. (d)
6. (c)   7. (d)   8. (a)
9. (c) Lime is CaO. It doesn't give CO_2 with dil.acid.
10. (a)
11. (b) Antacids like $NaHCO_3$ or $Mg(OH)_2$ are used for treating indigestion.
12. (a)   13. (d)
14. (c) $$Ca(OH)_2 + Cl_2 \longrightarrow CaOCl_2 + H_2O$$
Slaked lime   Bleaching powder
15. (b) Sodium carbonate is bitter in taste. Its bitterness is neutralized by adding tartaric acid in baking powder.
16. (c)   17. (a)
18. (c) Baking soda is $NaHCO_3$. It doesn't have water of crystallisation.
19. (a)   20. (b)

53. Occurence and extraction of metals

1. (c) In electrolytic refining of copper, the common elements present in anode mud are:
Selenium, tellurium, silver, gold, platinum and antimony. These elements are very less reactive. Thus they are not affected during purification process.
2. (a)   3. (a)   4. (a)   5. (c)
6. (b) $ZnO + C \longrightarrow Zn + CO$
7. (c) Iron pyrites is FeS_2.
8. (d)   9. (a)   10. (d)   11. (c)
12. (a)   13. (c)   14. (c)   15. (a)
16. (a)   17. (b)
18. (d) Cassiterite is a tin oxide mineral, SnO_2.
19. (d)   20. (b)

54. Properties and uses of metals and non-metals

1. (b)   2. (c)   3. (a)   4. (d)
5. (d)   6. (d)   7. (b)   8. (d)
9. (d) Graphite is also known as black lead.
10. (d)   11. (b)   12. (b)   13. (b)
14. (d)   15. (b)   16. (d)
17. (d) Smelting involves the reduction of the ore to the molten metal at a high temperature. For the extraction of less electropositive metal powerful reducing agents such as C, H_2, CO water gas, Na, K, Mg, Al may be used.
18. (c)
19. (d) Calomel : Hg_2Cl_2
Blue vitriol : $CuSO_4 \cdot 7H_2O$
Gypsum : $CaSO_4 \cdot 2H_2O$
Normal salt : NaCl
20. (c)

55. Air pollution

1. (a)   2. (d)   3. (a)   4. (c)
5. (a)   6. (c)   7. (a)   8. (a)
9. (c)   10. (c)   11. (b)
12. (c) SO_2 produces sulphuric acid

$$SO_2 + O_2 + H_2O \xrightarrow[\text{Soot particles}]{NO_x} H_2SO_4$$

Presence of hydrocarbons, NO_x and soot particles increases the oxidation of SO_2. Acidity in rain is created due to the presence of oxides of sulphur and nitrogen in the rain.
13. (d) The ozone layer is mainly damaged by chlorofluoro carbons.
14. (c)
15. (b) Gasoline mixed with tetra ethyl lead is the main source of lead in the atmosphere
16. (d) Troposphere is the lowest zone and thermosphere is the upper most zone of the atmosphere

13. (c) Higher concentration of NO_2 in air may leads respiratory infections and bronchitis specially in newborn child.

14. (d)   16. (a)

15. (d) Gradual warming of the atmosphere due to trapping of long wave radiations (infrared raditions) is called global warming. Global warming may cause the polar ice caps to melt, raising sea levels and possibly flooding many low-lying areas of land.

56. Water Pollution

1. (c)   2. (a)   3. (c)   4. (b)

5. (a) The degree of pollution is directly proportional to BOD. Therefore more the organic pollution (specially sewage), more would be BOD of water.

6. (b)   7. (d)   8. (b)

9. (d) Fluoride pollution causes dental fluorosis.

10. (c)   11. (d)   12. (c)   13. (c)

14. (c) Thermal power plants require a large quantity of water for cooling. The water after cooling is left in the water body. The temperature of the left water is generally very high and affects aquatic life.

15. (c) BOD means number of miligrams of O_2 required for decomposition of one litre of waste by decomposing microorganisms (bacteria).

16. (d)   17. (c)   18. (b)

19. (b) Due to addition of domestic sewage, phosphates, nitrates etc. in water body, the water body becomes rich in nutrients especially phosphates and nitrates ions, as a result of nutrient enrichment water bodies become highly productive or eutrophic and this phenomena is called eutrophication.

20. (c)

57. General Concepts of Chemistry

1. (d) Equivalent wt. of oxalic acid $= \dfrac{\text{molar mass}}{\text{basicity}}$

$$= \frac{126}{2} = 63$$

2. (b) Atomic wt. = equivalent wt. $\times 3 = 9 \times 3 = 27$

3. (b) Reduction involves addition of electrons and oxidation involves loss of electrons.

4. (b) A reducing agent is a substance which is oxidised and show loss of electrons.

5. (a)   6. (b)

7. (b) $2Pb(NO_3)_2(s) \longrightarrow 2PbO(s) + 4NO_2(g) + O_2(g)$

Oxidation reaction

8. (a) $Fe(s) + CuSO_4(aq) \longrightarrow FeSO_4(aq) + Cu(s)$

Reduction reaction

9. (d)   10. (a)   11. (a)   12. (a)

13. (d) $N_1V_1 = N_2V_2 : 20 \times \dfrac{1}{10} = \dfrac{1}{20} \times V; V = 40\text{ml}.$

14. (a) $\because$ 40 gm NaOH contains 16 gm of oxygen.

$\therefore$ 100 gm of NaOH contains

$$= \frac{16}{40} \times 100 = 40\% \text{ oxygen}$$

15. (b)

16. (a) $M = \dfrac{w \times 1000}{\text{m.wt} \times \text{Volume in ml}} = \dfrac{10.6 \times 1000}{106 \times 500} = 0.2\ M.$

17. (a) No. of mole

$$= \frac{\text{mass of substance}}{\text{molecular mass of substance}}$$

$$0.1 = \frac{W}{M_{CH_4}}; 0.1 = \frac{W}{16} \quad \left(\because M_{CH_4} = 16\right) \Rightarrow W = 1.6\text{gm}$$

18. (b)   19. (a)

Reduction

20. (c) $FeCl_3 + H_2S \longrightarrow FeCl_2 + HCl + S$

Oxidation

In the given reaction H_2S is undergoing oxidation, hence behave as reducing agent.

58. Man Made Materials-I

1. (d)

2. (d) If glass is cooled suddenly it develops strain and are likely to fall in pieces. To avoid it, the fusion mixture is cooled slowly. The process of slow cooling is known as annealing.

3. (c) Ordinary glass is a mixture of sodium and calcium silicate.

4. (b)   5. (a)   6. (c)

7. (c) When pure silica or quartz is heated to high temperature in an electric vaccum furnace, a transparent glass like substance called silica glass, quartz glass or vitrified silica is obtained.

8. (d)   9. (a)   10. (c)

11. (a) Cement + Sand + Water = Mortar

12. (b)   13. (a)   14. (c)   15. (d)

16. (a) Constituents of cement are lime stone, clay (provides silica and alumina) and gypsum in small amount.

17. (d)   18. (c)   19. (c)   20. (d)

59. Man-made materials-II

1. (d) NPK is a mixed fertilizer whereas urea, CAM (Calcium Ammonium Molybdate) and Ammonium sulphate are straight fertilizers.

2. (b)   3. (c)

4. (b) Temporary hardness can be removed by boiling.

5. (d)

6. (b) Lime being alkaline is applied to acidic soil.

7. (d) Triple superphosphae is a phosphatic fertilizer (single fertilizer).

8. (a)

9. (c) $CaCN_2$ (nitrolim), NH_4NO_3 (ammonium nitrate) and NH_2CONH_2 (urea) are examples of nitrogenous fertilizers.

10. (a)

11. (c) Nitrogen fixing bacteria present in root nodules of gram fix the atmospheric nitrogen.

12. (a) Hydrolysis of ammonium sulphate results in the formation of H_2SO_4 which makes the soil acidic.

13. (d)   14. (a)   15. (a)   16. (a)

17. (a)   18. (d)

19. (a) Vitamin B is water soluble vitamin where as other are of at soluble vitamins.

20. (b)

60. General Organic Chemistry

1. (a)

Hydrocarbons	Molecular weights
methane (CH_4)	16
ethane (C_2H_6)	30
propane (C_3H_8)	44
Butane (C_4H_{10})	58

2. (b)

3. (b) Normal butane $\Rightarrow H_3C$—CH_2—CH_2—CH_3

Isobutane $\Rightarrow H_3C$—$\overset{\displaystyle CH_3}{\underset{\displaystyle |}{CH}}$—$CH_3$

4. (d)   5. (a)   6. (d)   7. (c)

8. (c)   9. (a)   10. (d)   11. (b)

12. (a) $\overset{\displaystyle OH}{\underset{\displaystyle |}{CH_2}}$—$\overset{\displaystyle OH}{\underset{\displaystyle |}{CH_3}}$

1, 2 – ethandiol

13. (d) Alicyclic compounds are aliphatic cyclic compounds that are not aromatic.

For example: cyclopropane, cyclobutane etc.

14. (b)   15. (c)   16. (a)   17. (c)

18. (d)   19. (a)   20. (c)

61. Cells

1. (c)   2. (a)

3. (c) Lysosomes are organelles that contain digestive enzymes (acid hydrolases). They digest excess or worn out organelles, food particles, and engulfed viruses or bacteria. The membrane surrounding a lysosome prevents the digestive enzymes inside from destroying the cell.

4. (a) In cell biology, a mitochondrion is a membrane-enclosed organelle, found in most eukaryotic cells. Mitochondria are sometimes described as "cellular power plants," because they generate most of the cell's supply of ATP, used as a source of chemical energy.

5. (b) Adenosine 5'-triphosphate (ATP) is a multifunctional nucleotide that is most important as a "molecular currency" of intracellular energy transfer. ATP transports chemical energy within cells for metabolism. It is produced as an energy source during the processes of photosynthesis and cellular respiration and consumed by many enzymes and a multitude of cellular processes including biosynthetic reactions, motility and cell division.

6. (d) Plastids are major organelles found in plants and algae. Plastids are responsible for photosynthesis, storage of products like starch and for the synthesis of many classes of molecules such as fatty acids and terpenes which are needed as cellular building blocks and/or for the function of the plant.

7. (b) Mitochondria are present in animals as well as in plants that contain DNA but in plants, plastids are also present that have their own DNA and ribosomes.

8. (c) Ribosomes are present in prokaryotic as well as in eukaryotic cells.

9. (b) Cell division is a process by which a cell, called the parent cell, divides into two cells, called daughter cells. In meiosis however, a cell is permanently transformed and cannot divide again. Cell division takes from 3 minutes to 6 hours to complete. The primary concern of cell division is the maintenance of the original cell's genome. Before division can occur, the genomic information which is stored in chromosomes must be replicated, and the duplicated genome separated cleanly between cells.

10. (d)   11. (c)   12. (b)   13. (a)
14. (b)   15. (d)   16. (c)

17. (c) Ribosomes are the workhouses of protein biosynthesis, the process of translating messenger RNA (mRNA) into protein. The mRNA comprises a series of codons that dictate to the ribosome the sequence of the amino acids needed to make the protein. Using the mRNA as a template, the ribosome translates each codon of the mRNA, pairing it with the appropriate amino acid. This is done using molecules of transfer RNA (tRNA) containing a complementary anticodon on one end and the appropriate amino acid on the other.

18. (a)

19. (a) In prokaryotes, the nucleoid is an irregularly shaped region within the cell where the genetic material is localised.

20. (c) The main arena of various types of activities of a cell is cytoplasm. It forms the living protoplasm of a cell excluding the nucleus. It consists of proteins, fats, carbohydrates, nucleic acids, vitamins, waste metabolites and all organelles.

62. Tissues

1. (a) Muscle tissue is separated into three distinct categories: visceral or smooth muscle, which is found in the inner linings of organs; skeletal muscle, which is found attached to bone in order for mobility to take place; and cardiac muscle which is found in the heart. Vascular tissue is a complex tissue found in vascular plants, meaning that it is composed of more than one cell type. The primary components of vascular tissue are the xylem and phloem. Connective tissue - It holds everything together. Blood is a connective tissue.

2. (b) A stoma is a tiny opening or pore, found mostly on the underside of a plant leaf, and used for gas exchange. The pore is formed by a pair of specialized sclerenchyma cells known as guard cells which are responsible for regulating the size of the opening.

3. (d) The matrix comprises the other major constituent of bone. It has inorganic and organic parts. The inorganic is mainly crystalline mineral salts and calcium, which is present in the form of hydroxyapatite. The matrix is initially laid down as unmineralized osteoid. Mineralisation involves osteoblasts secreting vesicles containing alkaline phosphatase. This cleaves the phosphate groups and acts as the foci for calcium and phosphate deposition.

4. (b)

5. (c) Sclerenchyma tissues are found in hard parts of plant body, in cortex, pith, hypodermis, in the pulp of fruits. Young cells are living and they have protoplasm. But matured cells becomes dead due to deposition of secondary walls. They give mechanical support, strength and rigidity to the plant body.

6. (d)   7. (c)   8. (c)

9. (c) Inner bark of a woody plant is phloem & function of phloem is to transport food from the leaves to the other parts of the plant. Xylem is another transporting duct of plant that transport minerals & water from the roots to the leaves.

10. (c)   11. (c)

12. (b) Collenchymas provides malleability and flexibility to certain parts of the plants.

13. (d)   14. (b)

15. (b) Parenchyma containing chloroplasts are called chlorenchyma and is found in green leaves and some green aerial organs. The cells of chlorenchyma tissues contain chloroplast and hence perform the function of photosynthesis. It provides mechanical strength and flexibility to the plant.

16. (d)   17. (b)   18. (c)
19. (b)   20. (d)

63. PLANT PHYSIOLOGY

1. (d) The oxygen released during photosynthesis of green plants comes from the breakdown of water *i.e.,* photolysis of water during light phase of photosynthesis.

2. (d)

3. (b) Leghaemoglobin is an oxygen scavenger. The enzyme that catalyses the fixation of nitrogen functions under anaerobic conditions. Leghaemoglobin combines with oxygen and protects Nitrogenase.

4. (d) Gram would be preferred for sowing in order to enrich the soil with nitrogen. It is because gram is a leguminous crop. The root nodules of leguminous crop contains *Rhizobium*, a symbiotic bacterium that helps in fixing of nitrogen from atmosphere.

5. (b)
6. (c) Diffusion of water across a semi permeable membrane is called osmosis. Due to osmosis raisins when put in plain water swells up whereas when put again in brine solution, they shrivel up.
7. (c)   8. (c)   9. (c)   10. (d)
11. (b)   12. (b)
13. (d) Calcium activates enzymes, is a structural component of cell walls, influences water movement in cells and is necessary for cell growth and division. Some plants must have calcium to take up nitrogen and other minerals. Calcium is easily leached. Calcium, once deposited in plant tissue, is immobile (non-translocatable) so there must be a constant supply for growth. Deficiency causes stunting of new growth in stems, flowers and roots. Symptoms range from distorted new growth to black spots on leaves and fruit. Yellow leaf margins may also appear.
14. (b)   15. (a)
16. (b) There are about seven nutrients essential to plant growth and health that are only needed in very small quantities. These are manganese, boron, copper, iron, chlorine, molybdenum, and zinc. Though these are present in only small quantities, they are all necessary.
17. (c)   18. (b)   19. (c)   20. (b)

64. HUMAN PHYSIOLOGY

1. (a) Glycogen is stored in liver and muscles in human beings. Carbohydrates are used primarily as source of chemical energy to be metabolized immediately into glucose or stored as glycogen. The synthesis of glycogen is called glycogenesis.
2. (c)   3. (b)   4. (b)
5. (d)   6. (b)
7. (b) Frog has lungs as its main respiratory organs but during hibernation & aestivation and during its habitat in water it respires through skin.
8. (d)   9. (c)
10. (b) Human skeleton is mainly formed of bones and cartilages. It is formed of 206 bones in adult man.
11. (d)   12. (a)   13. (a)   14. (c)
15. (a)   16. (c)   17. (c)
18. (d) Tongue forms the floor of the oral cavity and it helps in the act of swallowing, help in mixing saliva with the food, help in speaking etc.
19. (c)   20. (a)

65. GENETICS AND EVOLUTION

1. (d)
2. (a) DNA occur mainly in nucleus, forming major chemical proportion of chromosomes. Some amount of DNA is also present in cytoplasm (mitochondria and plastids).
3. (c) Genetics is the study of principles and mechanism of heredity and variations.
4. (d)
5. (a) Loss of a prehensile tail is associated with the gradual development of erect posture and bipedal gait.
6. (c)
7. (d) Hershey and Chase (1952) worked on *Escherichia coli* and conclusively proved that DNA is the genetic material.
8. (d)
9. (d) The most significant trend in evolution of modern man (*Homo sapiens*) from his ancestors is development of brain capacity.

10. (d)   11. (b)   12. (b)   13. (b)
14. (a)   15. (b)   16. (b)   17. (d)
18. (b)   19. (d)   20. (d)

66. DIVERSITY IN LIVING ORGANISMS

1. (c) Aristotle who lived sometime around 384 BC to 322 BC is considered to be the Father of Biology. He was the student of Plato. Theophrastus and Alexander the great were the students of Aristotle. According to the Encyclopedia Britannica, "Aristotle was the first genuine scientist in history" due to his writings in wide scientific fields.
2. (c) Cockroach has blood known as haemocoel, snails and kangaroos also have blood in their bodies. But *Hydra* does not contain any blood but still it respires. It does not have any respiratory organs but it respires and thus exchanges gases throughout its body.
3. (a) *Agaricus* is an edible, gilled fungus belonging to class Basidiomycetes. It is commonly known as field mushroom.
4. (b) *Cycas* are naked seed plant, placed in gymnosperm. *Spirogyra* are algae which have chlorophyll, so make their food. *Funaria* is bryophyte rise in moist soils. *Chlorella* is a algae, rich in protein, fats and carbohydrates, vitamins and minerals. *Chlorella* purifies the air in nuclear submarines, space vehicles. Astronaut use this algae as food and moreover.
5. (b) The branch of biology under which morphological, anatomical, pathological, genetic studies of fungi are done, comes under the field of Mycology. While Phycology, Ethology, Microbiology deal with Algae, Animal behavior and microbes respectively.
6. (c) Jelly fish belongs to the genus *Aurelia* of phylum Cnidaria.
7. (c) Bryophytes includes simplest and primitive land plants. They are called amphibians of plant kingdom. They produce spores and embryo but lack seeds and vascular tissues.
8. (d) Lichen is a composite symbiotic association of a fungal member (mycobiont) and an algal or cyanobacterial member (phycobiont). The phycobiont is photosynthetic and syntheses carbohydrates, which is consumed by the mycobiont. The mycobiont provides mechanical support to the alga and also helps absorbing the minerals from the substrata.
9. (a) The title, Seahorse has been given to 54 species of marine fish in the genus *Hippocampus*.
10. (c) *Ginkgo* is a living fossil. Its ancestors are unchanged for the last many hundred years. However its relatives have got extinct.
11. (c) *Selaginella* the spikemosses is a genus of the family Selaginellaceae. It is stored by dipping its roots in water.
12. (d) Cold blooded animals do not use internally generated energy to regulate their body temperature. On the other hand warm blooded animals such as human beings have internal mechanisms that maintain their body temperature within a certain range, regardless of the ambient temperature of surroundings. Fish, frog and lizard are all cold blooded organisms.
13. (b)
14. (a) Mushroom is actually the fruiting body of the fungus, which is produced to bear millions of germinative spores. Most mushrooms belong to the *Basidiomycota* and *Agaricomycetes*.

15. (b) Arthropoda is the largest phylum in the animal kingdom in terms of both number of taxa and biomass.

16. (d) To inhibit water loss or to conserve water most of the desert species have waxy leaves that keep them water proof when stomata are closed. Water is further conserved by reducing surface area so most succulents have few leaves or no leaves. Some desert plants have thorns instead of leaves. Thorns do not let the water go out.

17. (b) Pitcher plant is an insectivorous plant. It feeds on living creatures including insects and small mammals. These plant attracts the prey with a smell of rotting meat. The victim is dissolved by some chemical enzymes.

18. (a)   19. (a)   20. (a)

67. HUMAN DISEASES

1. (a) The organ which is affected by hepatitis is the liver. There is inflammation of the liver and the disease is characterized by the presence of inflammatory cells in the tissue of the liver.

2. (a) Malaria is a mosquito-borne infectious disease of humans and other animals. It is caused by parasitic protozoan of the genus *Plasmodium*.

3. (d) The long term effect of alcoholism may lead to 'Liver cirrhosis' which is characterized by replacement of liver tissue by fibrosis and regenerative nodules.

4. (c) Emphysema is chronic obstructive pulmonary disease in which the air sacs (alveoli) in the lungs are damaged. Due to which most of the body parts do not get oxygen.

5. (b) Beri-beri is a disease caused by the deficiency of vitamin B_1 (thiamin). East-Asian countries in which people eat predominately polished rice Beri-beri is a prolonged problem.

6. (a) When there is oxygen deficit in the muscles, the later start converting the pyruvate into lactic acid due to which some side-effects occur like acidification of muscles and their fatigue.

7. (d) Haemophilia lowers blood plasma clotting factor levels of the coagulation factors needed for a normal process of blood clotting. If bleeding occurs in normal injuries does not stop itself.

8. (d) Diphtheria is caused by a bacterium *Corynebacterium diphtheriae*, Polio is a fatal viral disease, small pox is also a viral disease. Rabies is also viral disease.

9. (b) *P. vivax* is one of the six species of malaria parasites that commonly infect humans. It is responsible for the 65% of malarial cases in Asia.

10. (b) Gout is a painful medical condition in which needle-like uric acid crystals precipitate in the joints, skin, capillaries and other tissues. This is caused when the quantity of uric acid is excessive in the blood plasma.

11. (a) The normal platelet count in human being is 150,000 to 250,000 per microletre. In Dengue fever the viral attack is primarily on platelets. Their count is reduced to a significant number in the fever. It can reach below 50,000 per microlitre which can prove to be fatal.

12. (b) *Mycobacterium* is a genus of actinobacteria, known to cause tuberculosis and leprosy in humans.

13. (d) Vitamin K takes part in the blood clotting in humans. Out of the three forms of Vitamin K, Vitamin K_1, or phylloquinone is responsible to maintain healthy blood clotting. The natural source of it is in green vegetables.

14. (d) Iodine is given as a supplement in the common salt used in cooking to combat Iodine deficiency syndromes in humans as iodine as such is present in small quantity in the sea water.

15. (d) Lungs are supposed to be least damaged by harmful radiations.

16. (d) Foot and mouth disease in cattle is caused mainly by virus. In 2010-2011 Japan, Korea and Bulgaria had got their cattle with this disease.

17. (c) During dehydration the body loses much of the fluids, sodium chloride and other minerals. Thus electrolytes' solution is given to such a patient to replenish the lost minerals and salts.

18. (a) Night blindness is medically known as Nyctalopiain which the rod cells in the retina gradually lose their ability to respond to the light. Vitamin-A deficiency in the diet of humans is one of the causes of night blindness.

19. (b) Polio is caused by a enterovirus which is a member of the family of Picornaviridae. Bird flu is caused by virus H1N1 or H5N1.

20. (c) Arsenic-74 is used in the diagnosis of certain tumours.

68. PLANT DISEASES

1. (c)   2. (d)

3. (d) Red Rot of Sugarcane caused by *Colletotrichum falcatum*. Canes become wrinkled. They have reddish areas with white cross-bands. Alcoholic smell comes out of them. Midribs of leaves have oblong red lesions.

4. (b)

5. (d) Sesame or Brown leaf spot of rice caused by *Helminthosporium oryzae*. Bengal famine of 1942-43 was due to it.

6. (b) *Claviceps purpurea* develops sclerotia in the ears of cereals, especially rye. The sclerotia yield ergot which is medicinally useful in treating migraine, enlarged prostate glands and uterine haemorrhages.

7. (b) Early blight of Potato is caused by fungus *Alternaria solani*. Leaflets have small oval brown spots with concentric rings.

8. (b)   9. (a)   10. (a)

11. (b) Smuts are pathogenic basidiomycetes which possess thick-walled black-coloured resting spores called chlamydospores, teleutospores or smut spores. Smuts are of two types, loose and covered. In loose smuts the spores are exposed from the beginning, *e.g.*, loose smut of wheat (*Ustilago tritici*). In covered smuts, the spores remain covered till before liberation, *e.g.*, bunt of wheat (*Tilletia tritici*).

12. (d)

13. (b) A poisonous mushroom is called toadstool. It often possesses white basidiospores *e.g., Amanita polloides / A. caesarea* (Death cap/Caesar's mushroom).

14. (b) Tikka disease produces dark brown necrotic circular spots on the leaflets of Groundnut. This disease is caused by *Cercospora arachidicola* and *Cercospo-ridium personatum*.

15. (d)   16. (a)   17. (d)   18. (c)

19. (b) Plant hormone Gibberellins discovered from the fungus *Gibberella fujikuroi* as its infection produces bakane disease (sterile plants with excessive growth) in Rice.

20. (c)

69. BIOLOGY IN HUMAN WELFARE

1. (d) Mycorrhizal associations play vital role in plant nutrition. They greatly increase the efficiency of nutrient and water uptake; enhance resistance to pathogens, and buffer plant species against several environmental stresses and drought resistance. Mycorrhizal also improve plant growth and survival in soils contaminated by heavy metals.
2. (a)
3. (b) *Nostoc* fix atmospheric nitrogen and are used as inoculations for paddy crop.
4. (c)   5. (c)   6. (c)
7. (a)   8. (b)
9. (b) Ethanol production in India from maize, sugarcane, starch, corn grain etc. Maize is easily available and maize is not costly for product as to economic concern.
10. (b)   11. (d)   12. (a)   13. (b)
14. (b)   15. (a)   16. (b)   17. (a)
18. (c) The first effective bioherbicide was a mycoherbicide (a fungus which destroys weeds) developed in 1981. The herbicide belongs to *Phytophthora* which controls the growth of milk weed vines in citrus orchards.
19. (a) *Jatropha* is a genus of flowering plants in the spurge family, euphorbiaceae. Currently the oil from *Jatropha curcas* seeds is used for making biodiesel fuel in Phillipines and in Brazil.
20. (b)

70. ECOLOGY & ENVIRONMENT AWARENESS

1. (c)   2. (d)
3. (b) Above 80 dB sound becomes hazardous.
4. (d) Fluorides of carbon is the major pollutant from jet plane emission.
5. (b)
6. (d) The Taj mahal is threatened by environmental pollution, especially by acid rain due to sulphur dioxide emitted from Mathura refinery.
7. (b) CFCs reacts with ozone and cause its depletion. That is why CFCs are not recommended to be used in refrigerators.
8. (a)
9. (a) *E. coli* lives in the human intestine. If they are present in water it indicates that the water is polluted. *E.coli* coliform count test is done.
10. (a) The content of CO_2 in atmospheric air is 0.034%. The main contributors to air are N_2 and O_2.
11. (d)   12. (b)
13. (b) Loam soil is best suited for plant growth because it possesses good aeration, nutritive salts and good water retaining capacity.
14. (d)   15. (d)   16. (b)   17. (d)
18. (b)
19. (b) *Ex-situ* conservation is the conservation of selected organism in places outside their natural homes. They include off site collection and gene banks. *In situ* conservation, on the other hand, is the conservation of endangered species in their natural habitat. Biosphere reserves, National parks, Wildlife sanctuaries and Sacred groves all are examples of *in situ* conservation.
20. (b) In case CO_2 of earth's atmosphere disappears, the temperature of earth's surface would decrease.

71. General Science Section Test - I

1. (d) Distance covered by a particle is zero only when it is at rest. Therefore, its displacement must be zero.
2. (c) As H $\propto$ I^2, so for heating effect both a.c. and d.c. can be used.
3. (b) (i) Due to Ionosphere, we recieve signals on distant part of earth.
(ii) In troposphere, aeroplane flies.

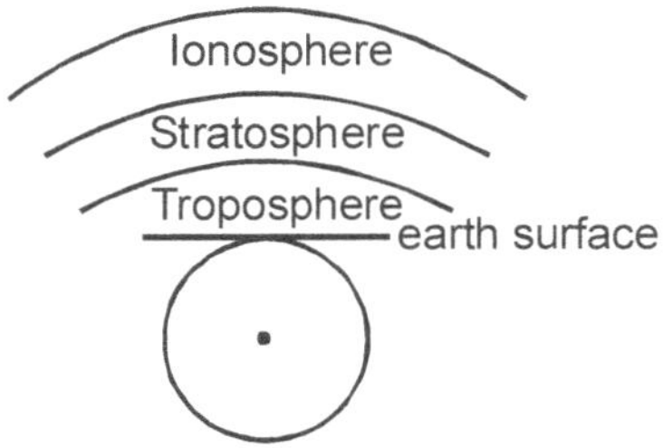

4. (d) The colours are seen due to interference of light. The colours seen in reflected light are complementry with the colours seen in transmitted light.
5. (c) If B is upthrust of air on balloon, and a is downward acceleration, then
$$Mg - B = Ma$$
$$\Rightarrow a = \frac{Mg - B}{M} = g - \frac{V\rho_{air}g}{V\rho_{CO_2}}$$
$$= \left(1 - \frac{V\rho_{air}}{V\rho_{CO_2}}\right)g = \left(1 - \frac{28.8}{44}\right) \times 9.8 \text{ m/s}^2 = 3.4 \text{ m/s}^2$$

6. (b) $\dfrac{C}{5} = \dfrac{F - 32}{9}$
Here C = F
$$\frac{C}{5} = \frac{C - 32}{9} \Rightarrow 9C = 5C - 160$$
$4C = -160 \Rightarrow C = -40°C.$
Thus at $-40°C$ and $-40°$ F the temperture is same.

7. (a) Velocity of water from hole A
$$v_1 = \sqrt{2gh}$$
Velocity of water from hole B
$$v_2 = \sqrt{2g(H_0 - h)}$$
Time of reaching the ground from hole B
$$t_1 = \sqrt{2(H_0 - h)/g}$$
Time of reaching the ground from hole A
$$t_2 = \sqrt{2h/g}$$

8. (c)   9. (d)   10. (b)   11. (a)
12. (c)   13. (a)
14. (c) In winter, the temperature of surrounding is low compared to the body temperature (37.4°C). Since, woollen clothes are bad conductors of heat, so they keep the body warm.
15. (a)
16. (b) The radius of soap bubble increases because of outward force acting on the bubble due to charging.

17. (d)   18. (b)
19. (a) For forward biasing of *p-n* junction, the positive terminal of external battery is to be connected to *p*-semiconductor and negative terminal of battery to the n-semiconductor.
20. (b)   21. (a)   22. (b)
23. (d) At 4°C, water expands either it is cooled or heated.
24. (c)   25. (d)   26. (b)
27. (a)   28. (b)   29. (c)   30. (d)
31. (d) The functional group is in the 3rd carbon atom in the chain.
32. (d) Organic compounds which can be represented by a general formula, differ from each other by a fixed group of atoms, and have a gradation of properties form a homologous series.
33. (d)
34. (c) Cl - 35.5
Br - 80
I - 127

Average of the atomic mass $= \dfrac{35.5 + 127}{2} = 81.2 = 80$

35. (b) Pure water is obtained from sea water by distillation. This technique is applied only for the purification of those liquids which boil without decomposition at atmospheric pressure and contain non-volatile impurities.
36. (a) Barium carbonate, $BaCO_3$ is a compound.
37. (a) On the basis of results of α-ray scattering experiment, Rutherford postulated that atom consists of two parts (i) nucleus and (ii) extra nuclear part.
38. (b)
39. (a) Hard glass contains Na while soft glass contains potassium.
40. (a)
41. (d) Because this will cause the melting of polar ice caps resulting in a rise of nearly 60 feet on the sea level. Coastal regions and low lying areas all over the world will go under water.
42. (c)
43. (d) Co (III) Transition metal is present in vitamin B_{12}.
44. (d)   45. (d)
46. (b) Reproduction ensures the continuity of the species, generation after generation. Genetic variation is created and inherited during reproduction.
47. (d) Crocodile belongs to class Reptilia. They have usually three chambered heart but crocodile have four chambered heart.
48. (d) Tendrils are thread - like sensitive structures which can coil around a support and help the plant in climbing. E.g., Cucumber and grapevines.
49. (d) Cartilage is a type of connective tissue which is present in human external ears and in the nose tip.
50. (a)
51. (a) Cohesion of water and transpiration pull theory is the most widely accepted theory put forth by **Dixon** and **Jolly** in 1894, and further supported by **Renner (1911, 1915)**, **Curtis** and **Clark** (1951), **Bouner** and **Golston** (1952), **Kramer** and **Kozlowski** (1960). It is also known as **Dixons cohesion theory,** or **Cohesion tension theory**.
52. (d)
53. (a) pH of saliva is 6.5.
54. (c) Haemoglobin has 4 subunits, each of which binds to 1 molecule of O_2 for a total of 4 molecules of O_2 bound to 1 haemoglobin molecules.
55. (c) Coronary Artery Disease (CAD) or Atherosclerosis is a disorder in which the deposition of calcium, fat, cholesterol and fibrous tissue occurs in coronary arteries which makes the lumen of arteries narrower and thereby affect the blood supply.

56. (b)
57. (c) All communicable diseases are caused by micro-organisms. They spread through contact, air, water, food or insects (flies and mosquitoes). Insects are called the carriers of diseases.
58. (b) Weeds are plants, other than the crop plants, growing alongwith the crop. Weeds grow vigorously and draw more nutrition from the soil than the crop plants. This makes the soil poor in minerals and deprives the crop of its minerals needs.
59. (a) A list of threatened species of plants and animals in different parts of the world has been prepared and issued by World Conservation Union (WCU) assigning responsibility of protecting these species to the respective Governments.
60. (c)

72. General Science Section Test - II

1. (a) When, storm comes then velocity of wind increases sharply, so atmospheric pressure decreases suddenly.
2. (c) A transistor is a current operating device in which the emitter current controls the collector current.
3. (d) is not possible, because at a particular time t, displacement cannot have two values.
4. (a) The basic principle of communication in fibre optics is based on the phenomenon of total internal reflection.
5. (a)   6. (a)
7. (b) In electroplating, the metallic ions are positive, which are deposited on cathode.
8. (b)   9. (d)   10. (c)   11. (c)
12. (c)   13. (d)
14. (c) When a copper ball is heated, it's size increases. As volume $\propto$ (radius)^3 and Area $\propto$ (radius)^2, so percentage increase will be largest in it's volume. Density will decrease with rise in temperature.
15. (b)
16. (b) Silver is the best conductor of electricity.
17. (d)   18. (d)   19. (c)   20. (a)
21. (c)   22. (b)
23. (c)
24. (c) On the surface of water, transverse waves and longitudinal waves inside water.
25. (a)   26. (c)   27. (b)   28. (a)
29. (d)   30. (d)   31. (b)   32. (d)
33. (a)   34. (a)
35. (b) Grey Selenium conducts electricity. It is better conductor of electricity in light than in darkness, its conductivity varying directly with the intensity of light.
36. (c) Diamond is the hardest element on the earth and is used to cut or scratch glass whereas hydrofluoric acid is used for writing on the glass.
37. (c) Coal, Diesel and Kerosene on combustion releases CO_2, SO_2 and other Nitrogen oxides in the atmosphere unlike 'Hydrogen' which is having highest fuel value (150 kJ/g) and is least harmful to the environment among fuels.
38. (b) The hardness of steel directly proportional to the percentage of chromium. Chromium is alloyed with Iron to produce steel which can resist high temperature and also have high hardness and abrasion resistance.
39. (a)
40. (a) $\text{Gangue}\,(\text{Impurity}) + \text{flux} \rightarrow \text{Slag}$
(Infusible)   (Fusible)

41. (a) 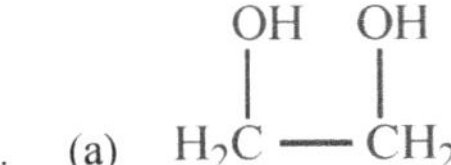

42. (b) Neils Bohr developed the long form of periodic table on the basis of Moseley's principle.

43. (a) Oxides of these metals dissolve in water to give strong alkalies.

44. (a)   45. (b)

46. (c) Viruses are the minute organisms and are considered as organisms between living and non-living. Outside the living cells of the host the virus is simply an inactive particle, similar to a non-living object. Once inside the body of the host, it becomes active and starts multiplying, showing a character of living objects.

47. (a) Green plants take carbon dioxide from air. Leaves take in carbon dioxide and release oxygen through the tiny pores called stomata. The stomata are present on the underside of leaves.

48. (b) Tongue is a thick muscular organ which makes the floor of the mouth. It consists of four types of taste buds - salty, sweet, sour and bitter to sense the taste of bud. Thus, it also acts as a sense organ.

49. (b)   50. (b)   51. (d)

52. (b) In normal person, the normal blood pressure is 120/80 mm Hg. The normal systolic (pumping) pressure is 120 mm Hg and normal diastolic (resting) pressure is 80 mm Hg.

53. (d)

54. (a) Rabi crops grown in winter season from November to April. Examples are Wheat, gram, peas, mustard and linseed etc.

55. (d) Ovaries in female produce two hormones-
   (i) Oestrogen which helps in regulating whole set of female sex characters, including formation of ova.
   (ii) Progesterone to regulate reproductive (menstrual) cycle.

56. (d) White corpuscles are like soldiers because they fight off the body's enemies -- harmful bacteria and disease. White blood cells attack and kill germs in the body, and they also carry away dead cells.

57. (a) Camouflage is the structural adaptation that enables species to blend with their surroundings; allows a species to avoid detection by predators. Stick insects can camouflage themselves to blend themselves with the branch of trees.

58. (c) Fish and tadpole have gills as respiratory organs. Gills have filaments which are like the teeth of a hair comb. These filaments are full of small capillaries carrying blood. Water enters through the mouth and flows over the gills.

59. (b)   60. (a)

73. PRE-HISTORIC PERIOD

1. (d)   2. (c)   3. (c)   4. (d)

5. (a) Therigatha was a part of the Buddhist literature.

6. (c) Nagara, Dravida and Vesara are three main styles of Indian temple architecture.

7. (d)   8. (a)   9. (d)   10. (b)

11. (a)   12. (d)   13. (d)   14. (c)

15. (c)   16. (a)   17. (a)   18. (a)

19. (d)   20. (a)

74. INDUS VALLEY CIVILISATION

1. (b) The Indus Valley was discovered by Dayaram Sahni in 1921. It is one of the world's earliest urban civilizations alongside with its contemporaries, Mesopotamia and Ancient Egypt. The Indus Valley covers modern day Pakistan and the northwest of India.

2. (c) Indus Valley Civilization had been a combination of diverse racial elements. Certain anthropological investigations and examinations of the human remains show that four racial types existed in this civilization namely Proto-Australiod, Mediterranean, Alpinoid and the Mongoloid. Most of the people belong to Mediterranean race.

3. (c)

4. (a) Houses of Indus Valley Civilization were one or two stories high, made of baked (Pucca) bricks, with flat roofs. Each was built around a courtyard, with windows overlooking the courtyard. The outside walls had no windows. Each home had its own private drinking well and its own private bathroom. Clay pipes led from the bathrooms to sewers located under the streets.

5. (a) Harappan civilization was discovered in 1921–22 when two of its most important sites were excavated. The first was excavated by Dayaram Sahni and the second by R.D. Banerji.

6. (a) The greatest uniformity is noticed in the layouts of the towns, streets, structures, brick size, drains, etc. Almost all the major sites (Harappa, Mohenjodaro, Kalibangan and others) are divided into two parts–a citadel on higher mound on the western side and a lower town on the eastern side of the Indus Valley Civilization settlement.

7. (b)

8. (c) The people of Indus Valley Civilization mainly traded with the Mesopotamians. Dilmun and Makan were intermediate trading stations between Meluha and Mesopotamia. Meluha is the earliest name of Indus area.

9. (b)

10. (a) On the site of Indus Valley Civilization, the famous Bull-seal was found in Harappa. The Bull-seal shows a humped bull displaying a strong and energetic bull. The figure has been made well, a proof of the fine artistic skills acquired by the people of that time. Seals are mainly in square or rectangular shape. This Bull-seal dates to around 2450-2200 BC.

11. (b) Sutkagen Dor is the westernmost known archaeological site of Indus Valley Civilization. It is located about 480 km west of Makran coast near the Iran border in Balochistan province of Pakistan. Sutkagen Dor would have been on the trade route from Lothal in Gujarat to Mesopotamia and was probably heavily involved in the fishing trade similar to that which exists today in the coast along Balochistan.

12. (c) There are over fifty-five burial sites in the Indus Valley were found in Harappa. The burials are interpreted primarily as reflections of social structure and hierarchy. The strongest evidence for this interpretation would be burial sites in Harappa, cemetery R-37 and Cemetery H. R-37 is the smaller site compared to Cemetery H, and has about 200 burials. Archeologists believe it was a restricted cemetery that was used by a particular group or family that lived in Harappa.

13. (b) Kalibangan – is an archaeological site where ploughed field, bones of camel, circular and rectangular graves, distinctive fire (Vedic) altars with provision of ritual bathing have been found.

14. (d) The numerous seals and figurines discovered in the excavations carried out at various sites connected with the Harappan culture point out to the religious beliefs of the Indus Valley people.
Worship of Mother Goddess: A large number of excavated terracotta figurines are those of a semi-nude figure which is identified with some female energy or Shakti or Mother Goddess, who is the source of all creation.

Worship of Pashupati or Lord Shiva: The Pashupati seal in which the three-faced male god is shown seated in a yogic posture, surrounded by a rhino and a buffalo on the right, and an elephant and a tiger on the left, make the historians conclude that the people of those days worshipped Lord Shiva. Discovery of a large number of conical or cylindrical stones shows that the people worshipped lingam, the symbol of Lord Shiva.

Worship of Trees: The worship of trees was widespread. The Pipal tree was considered most sacred.

Other Objects of Worship: People also worshipped animals, such as the bull, buffalo and tiger. Besides animals, these people also worshipped the Sun, the Fire and the Water.

There was no evidence of the God Vishnu worshipped by the people of Indus Valley Civilization.

15. (d) The Indus Valley Civilization town Dholavira is divided into three parts. The citadel, middle town and the lower town were the three pre-existing planned geometrical divisions in Dholavira. The middle town had its own defense mechanism, planned streets, gateways, wells and roads. Most of the buildings were built with stones.

16. (c) Indus Valley Civilization site Manda is situated on the right bank of Chenab river in the foot hills of Pir Panjal range, 28 km northwest of Jammu. Manda is the north site of Indus civilization. It was discovered by J.P. Joshi in 1982.

17. (a) Harappan Civilization is the most suitable name for Indus Valley Civilization because Harappa lies in the centre of Indus Civilization. It was also an urban trade centre.

18. (a)

19. (c) Dholavira had a series of water storing tanks and step wells, and its water management system has been called 'unique'. The unique feature is the sophisticated water conservation system of channels and reservoirs, the earliest found anywhere in the world and completely built of stone.

20. (a) The Indus Valley Civilization site Chanhudaro finds indicate the use of lipstick.

75. THE MAURYAN EMPIRE

1.	(c)	2.	(c)	3.	(c)	4.	(d)
5.	(a)	6.	(b)	7.	(a)	8.	(d)
9.	(b)	10.	(a)	11.	(c)	12.	(d)
13.	(d)	14.	(d)	15.	(c)	16.	(a)
17.	(a)	18.	(d)	19.	(a)	20.	(b)

76. THE GUPTA PERIOD

1. (d) Susrutha Samitha was written by Susrutha. He was said to have been the best surgeon during the Gupta period.

2.	(a)	3.	(a)	4.	(a)	5.	(a)
6.	(d)	7.	(b)	8.	(a)		

9. (c) The Gupta king, Chandragupta II had another name Devagupta. Chandragupta II was the third, and most significant of the Gupta kings (C.375–C.415). Inheriting a large empire, he extended his control to Gujarat (north of Bombay) and Malwa (central India). To strengthen his southern flank, he made marriage arrangements for his daughters with southern dynasties. In different inscriptions, Chandragupta II also named as Devasri and Devaraja in various inscriptions.

10. (c) The Gupta gold coins were known as Dinar. The world's first coins were Greek, made in Lydia about 640 BC. The earliest Indian coins were silver, and it was not until about 100 AD that the Kushan emperor Vima Kadaphises introduced the first Indian gold coin, which was a gold dinar bearing the image of Shiva. So India's history of issuing gold coins dates back almost 2,000 years.

11. (d) Sanskrit was the official language of Gupta period. Scholars of this period include Varahamihira and Aryabhatta, who is believed to be the first to come up with the concept of zero, postulated the theory that the Earth moves round the Sun, and studied solar and lunar eclipses. Kalidasa, who was a great playwright, who wrote plays such as Shakuntala, which is said to have inspired Goethe, and marked the highest point of Sanskrit literature is also said to have belonged to this period.

12. (a) Srigupta was the first known Gupta ruler. The Gupta empire was an ancient Indian empire, founded by Maharaja Sri Gupta, which existed from approximately 320 to 550 CE and covered much of the Indian Subcontinent. The peace and prosperity created under the leadership of the Guptas enabled the pursuit of scientific and artistic endeavours. This period is called the Golden Age of India.

13.	(d)	14.	(d)	15.	(a)	16.	(a)
17.	(d)	18.	(a)	19.	(a)	20.	(a)

77. EARLY MEDIEVAL INDIA

1. (c) He was a sanskrit poet and dramatist.

2. (a) Khajuraho is a village in the Indian state of Madhya Pradesh, located in Chhatarpur District, about 385 miles southeast of Delhi, the capital city of India. The Khajuraho group of monuments has been listed as a UNESCO World Heritage site. Khajuraho temples were constructed between 950 and 1050 AD. During the reign of Chandel Empire.

3. (b) Ajmer (Rajasthan) was the capital of Chauhan kings in the 12th century and later became the 'subs' headquarters under the Mughals.

4.	(c)	5.	(c)	6.	(a)	7.	(b)
8.	(b)	9.	(d)	10.	(a)	11.	(a)
12.	(d)	13.	(d)	14.	(c)	15.	(c)
16.	(a)	17.	(b)	18.	(c)	19.	(c)
20.	(b)						

78. THE DELHI SULTANATE

1. (a) Qutubuddin Aibak was purchased by Muhammad Ghori who later made him his Governor. After the death of Ghori, Aibak took up sovereign powers on 24th June 1206 founding the Slave Dynasty in India.

2. (b) Alauddin Khilji abolished Iqta system. He was son-in-law and nephew of Jalaluddin Khilji. He succeeded the throne in 1296 after killing Jalaluddin Khilji.

3. (c) Alauddin Khilji, Sultan of Delhi, built the fort of Siri during 1297–1307. The main objective of the construction of this fort to protect Delhi from invasion of Mongol.

4. (c) In 1504, Sikandar Shah Lodi founded Agra. He transferred the capital from Delhi to Agra. He was the most capable monarch of the Lodi dynasty. He sacked the temples of Mathura and converted the buildings to muslim uses. He charged Jaziya and pilgrim's tax from the Hindus with severity. He was against taking out tazias in procession during Muharram.

5. (a)
6. (c) Ghiyasuddin Tughlaq founded Tughlaq dynasty in 1320 AD (CE). Nasiruddin Mahmud was the last ruler of Tughlaq dynasty (1395–1412 AD).
7. (c) Bahlol (1451–1489); Sikandar (1489–1517); Ibrahim (1517–1526)
8. (a) Vasco da Gama reached Calicut in India on May 27, 1498.
9. (a) 10. (a) 11. (c) 12. (b)
13. (d) 14. (a) 15. (a) 16. (d)
17. (c) 18. (a) 19. (d) 20. (d)

79. THE MUGHAL EMPIRE

1. (a) Babur was the founder of Mughal dynasty. Born on February 14, 1483 at Andizhan Babur was the eldest of the three sons of Umar Sheikh Mirza. The Mughal emperor Babur is described as a military genius and a skillful warrior.

2. (c)
3. (c) Babur wrote his autobiography in Turki language. It is an autobiographical work, written in the Chagatai language, known to Babur as "Turki" (meaning Turkic), the spoken language of the Andijan-Timurids. Babur's prose is highly Persianized in its sentence structure, morphology, and vocabulary, and also contains many phrases and smaller poems in Persian.

4. (a) The Bagh-e-Babur garden is the final resting place of the first Mughal emperor, Babur. Although present-day Afghanistan was not Babur's original homeland (he was born in Ferghana in present-day Uzbekistan), he felt sufficiently enamoured of Kabul that he desired to be buried here. When Babur died in 1530, he was initially buried in Agra against his wishes. Between 1539 and 1544, Sher Shah Suri, a rival of Babur's son Humayun, fulfilled his wishes and interred him at Babur's Garden. The headstone placed on his grave read "If there is a paradise on earth, it is this, it is this, it is this."

5. (d) Mehndi Khwaja favoured by prime minister Mir Khalifa as Babur's successor instead of Humayun. Babur's prime minister Mir Khalifa had doubts about Humayun's abilities and tried to raise Mehdi Khwaja, Babur's brother-in-law to the throne.

6. (a)
7. (c) There were several types of Mughal light artillery. If carried on the back of a man, they were called Narnal; if carried on backs of elephants Gajal, if on backs of camels Shutrnal.

8. (a) 9. (b) 10. (d) 11. (c)
12. (d) 13. (b) 14. (c) 15. (c)
16. (b) 17. (b) 18. (d) 19. (a)
20. (c)

80. INITIAL MODERN HISTORY

1. (b)
2. (c) Red Dragon was the first English ship that came to India. The Red Dragon fought the Portuguese at the Battle of Swally in 1612, and made several voyages to the East Indies.

3. (d) The British East India Company was formed during the reign of Elizabeth I. Commonly associated with trade in basic commodities, which included cotton, silk, indigo dye, salt, saltpetre, tea and opium, the Company received a Royal Charter from Queen Elizabeth in 1600, making it the oldest among several similarly formed European East India Companies.

4. (b)

5. (d) Vasco da Gama discovered the sea route to India in 1498. The first Portuguese encounter with India was on 20 May 1498 when Vasco da Gama reached Calicut on Malabar Coast. Vasco da Gama sailed to India for a second time with 15 ships and 800 men, arriving at Calicut on 30 October 1502, where the ruler was willing to sign a treaty.

6. (c) Portuguese trading company adopted the 'Blue Water Policy' in India. Francisco de Almeida became the 1st Portuguese viceroy in India initiated the Blue Water Policy, which aimed at the Portuguese Mastery of the Sea and confined Portuguese relationship with India only for the purpose of trade and commerce.

7. (d)
8. (a) In 1835, the Bitish started striking Indian coins with the portrait of the British king. British India Coins (1862 – 1947) were stuck under the authority of the crown. The new coins minted under the Coinage Act, 1835 had the effigy of William IV on the obverse and the value on the reverse in English and Persian. The coins issued after 1840 bore the portrait of Queen Victoria. The first coinage under the crown was issued in 1862 and in 1877 Queen Victoria assumed the title of the Empress of India. We have tried to cover the Uniform coinage of this period.

9. (c) Lord Auckland was the Governor General when the Eden Gardens of Calcutta was built in 1840. The Gardens came into being when the Governor General; Lord Auckland desired to create a circus and a garden. A pleasure ground with an oblong tank in centre was laid out on this site generally resorted to for riding an recreation. The site was initially named 'Auckland Circus Gardens'.

10. (d) The first newspaper published in India was the Bengal Gazette. James Augustus Hickey published the first newspaper in India on January 29; 1780. It was the liberal policy of the Press Act of 1835, which continued till 1856, that encouraged the growth of newspapers in the country.

11. (c) 12. (d)
13. (d) Lord Dalhousie laid the frist rail line in India. Railways were first introduced to India in 1853 from Bombay to Thane.

14. (d) Lord Cornwallis was the father of Civil Services. The term 'civil service' was used for the first time by the East India Company to distinguish its civilian employee from their military counterparts. Lord Cornwallis started the Civil Service in Indian to effectively administer British territories in India.

15. (c)
16. (b) Warren Hastings was the first Governor General of Bengal. When Warren Hastings assumed the administration of Bengal in 1772, he found it in utter chaos. The financial position of the Company became worse and the difficulties were intensified by famine. Therefore, Warren Hastings realized the immediate need for introducing reforms and was responsible for lot of reforms in Bengal.

17. (b) Raja Ram Mohan Roy founded the Brahmo Samaj in 1828. He founded Brahmo Samaj in order to institutionalise his ideas and mission which aimed at political uplift of the masses through social reform and to that extent can be said to have had nationalist undertones.

18. (c) Permanent settlement comprises Zamindar as middleman to collect the land revenue. The Zamindars were made the owners of the whole land in their Zamindari as long as they paid their dues to the state and they worked as agents of government in collecting the land revenue.

19. (d)
20. (b)

81. INDIAN FREEDOM STRUGGLE

1.	(c)	2.	(a)	3.	(b)	4.	(d)
5.	(b)	6.	(d)	7.	(c)	8.	(c)
9.	(d)	10.	(d)	11.	(b)	12.	(b)
13.	(d)	14.	(a)	15.	(a)	16.	(c)
17.	(d)	18.	(a)	19.	(b)	20.	(c)

82. CONSTITUTIONAL FRAMEWORK AND CITIZENSHIP

1. (c) The Forty-second Amendment of the Constitution of India, officially known as The Constitution (Forty-second Amendment) Act, 1976, was enacted during the Emergency (1975-1977) by the Congress government headed by Indira Gandhi. Most provisions of the amendment came into effect on 3 January 1977, others were enforced from 1 February and Section 27 came into force on 1 April 1977. The 42nd Amendment is regarded as the most controversial constitutional amendment in Indian history. It attempted to reduce the power of the Supreme Court and High Courts to pronounce upon the constitutional validity of laws. It laid down the Fundamental Duties of Indian citizens to the nation. This amendment brought about the most widespread changes to the Constitution until then, and is sometimes called a "mini-Constitution" or the "Constitution of Indira".

2. (b) Article 44 of the Indian constitution provides for uniform civil code for the citizens. Uniform civil code of India is a term referring to the concept of an overarching civil law code in India. A uniform civil code administers the same set of secular civil laws to govern all people irrespective of their religion, caste and tribe. This supersedes the right of citizens to be governed under different personal laws based on their religion or caste or tribe. Such codes are in place in most modern nations. The common areas covered by a civil code include laws related to acquisition and administration of property, marriage, divorce and adoption. The Constitution of India attempts to set a uniform civil code for its citizens as a Directive Principle, or a goal to be achieved.

3. (d) Article 32 of the constitution of India deals with the 'Right to constitutional Remedies'. Remedies for enforcement of rights conferred by this Part
(a) The right to move the Supreme Court by appropriate proceedings for the enforcement of the rights conferred by this Part is guaranteed.
(b) The Supreme Court shall have power to issue directions or orders or writs, including writs in the nature of habeas corpus, mandamus, prohibition, quo warranto and certiorari, whichever may be appropriate, for the enforcement of any of the rights conferred by this Part
(c) Without prejudice to the powers conferred on the Supreme Court by clause (1) and (2), Parliament may by law empower any other court to exercise within the local limits of its jurisdiction all or any of the powers exercisable by the Supreme Court under clause (2)
(d) The right guaranteed by this article shall not be suspended except as otherwise provided for by this Constitution

4. (c) B.R. Ambedkar was the chairman of the drafting committee of the constituent Assembly

5. (d) In the constitution of India, the term 'federal' appears in the part I of the constitution.

6. (c) Article 360 of the Indian constitution provides for provision as the financial emergency. If the President is satisfied that a situation has arisen whereby the financial stability or credit of India or of any part of the territory thereof is threatened, he may by a Proclamation make a declaration to that effect.

7. (d) The powers of panchayats are stated in the 11th schedule of the Indian constitution.

8. (c) There were 294 members of the constituent assembly who signed the constitution of India. The Constitution was drafted by the Constituent Assembly, which was elected by the elected members of the provincial assemblies.

9. (c) Article 05 to 11 of the Indian constitution deals with citizenship in India. The legislation related to this matter is the Citizenship Act 1955, which has been amended by the Citizenship (Amendment) Act 1986, the Citizenship (Amendment) Act 1992, the Citizenship (Amendment) Act 2003, and the Citizenship (Amendment) Act, 2005. Article 9 of Indian Constitution says that a person who voluntarily acquires citizenship of any other country is no longer an Indian citizen. Also, according to The Passports Act, a person has to surrender his Indian passport, it is a punishable offense under the act if he fails to surrender the passport.

10. (c) In 1993, 73rd constitution Amendment act (1992) was assented by the President of India.

11. (d) Under Article 61, the president of India can be removed by the process of impeachment. Under Article 61 of the Constitution, the President of India can be impeached for the violation of the Constitution, which is solely to be decided by the Parliament.

12. (c) Under article 143 of the constitutional provision, the supreme court of India extends advice to the president of India. Concerning **Power of President to consult Supreme Court**, If at any time it appears to the President that a question of law or fact has arisen, or is likely to arise, which is of such a nature and of such public importance that it is expedient to obtain the opinion of the Supreme Court upon it, he may refer the question to that Court for consideration and the Court may, after such hearing as it thinks fit, report to the President its opinion thereon.

13. (d) Under the Article 249, the parliament of India can legislate on any subject in the state list in national interest. Notwithstanding anything in the foregoing provisions of this Chapter, if the Council of States has declared by resolution supported by not less than two thirds of the members present and voting that it is necessary or expedient in national interest that Parliament should make laws with respect to any matter enumerated in the State List specified in the resolution, it shall be lawful for Parliament to make laws for the whole or any part of the territory of India with respect to that matter while the resolution remains in force.

14. (a)　　　　15. (d)

16. (b) 73rd Amendment provides constitutional status to Panchayti Raj System in India.

17. (c) 61st Amendment of the constitution had reduced the age of the voters from 21 years to 18 years. The Sixty-first Amendment of the Constitution of India, officially known as The Constitution (Sixty-first Amendment) Act, 1988, lowered the voting age of elections to the Lok Sabha and to the Legislative Assemblies of States from 21 years to 18 years. This was done by amending Article 326 of the Constitution, which related to elections to the Lok Sabha and the Assemblies.

18. (c) Under the Article 275 the parliament provides financial assistance to states. Such sums of grants as Parliament may by law provide shall be charged on the Consolidated Fund of India in each year as grants in aid of the revenues of such States as Parliament may determine to be in need of assistance, and different sums may be fixed for different States

19. (a)

20. (a) The provision for constitution of Legislatures in states is enshrined in Article 168 of the Indian constitution. Constitution of Legislatures in States
(1) For every State there shall be a Legislature which shall consist of the Governor, and
(a) in the States of Bihar, Madhya Pradesh, Maharashtra, Karnataka and Uttar Pradesh, two houses:
(b) in other States, one House
(2) Where there are two Houses of the Legislature of a State, one shall be known as the Legislative Council and the other as the Legislative Assembly, and where there is only one House, it shall be known as the Legislative Assembly

83. FUNDAMENTAL RIGHTS AND DUTIES

1.	(b)	2.	(c)	3.	(b)	4.	(b)
5.	(d)	6.	(b)	7.	(d)	8.	(d)
9.	(a)						

10. (c) Part IV of the constitution (Articles 36 – 51) contains the Directive principle of state policy.

11. (b)

12. (a) Fundamental duties enshrined in the Indian constitution do not have any legal sanction. The Fundamental Duties of citizens were added to the Constitution by the 42nd Amendment in 1976, upon the recommendations of the Swaran Singh Committee that was constituted by the government earlier that year.

13. (b)

14. (d) Swarn Singh Committee redounded the inclusion of fundamental duties in the Indian Constitution. The Fundamental Duties of citizens were added to the Constitution by the 42nd Amendment in 1976, upon the recommendations of the Swaran Singh Committee that was constituted by the government earlier that year.

15. (d) 16. (c) 17. (b) 18. (a) 19. (b)

20. (d) Under Article 226 of Indian constitution a High Court can issue writes to protect the fundamental Rights. Notwithstanding anything in Article 32 every High Court shall have powers, throughout the territories in relation to which it exercises jurisdiction, to issue to any person or authority, including in appropriate cases, any Government, within those territories directions, orders or writs, including writs in the nature of habeas corpus, mandamus, prohibitions, quo warranto and certiorari, or any of them, for the enforcement of any of the rights conferred by Part III and for any other purpose.

84. POLITICAL SYSTEM

1.	(c)	2.	(b)	3.	(c)	4.	(b)
5.	(c)	6.	(c)	7.	(a)	8.	(c)
9.	(c)	10.	(c)	11.	(d)	12.	(b)
13.	(c)	14.	(d)	15.	(a)	16.	(c)
17.	(a)	18.	(c)	19.	(a)	20.	(d)

85. STATE GOVERNMENT

1.	(a)	2.	(b)	3.	(d)	4.	(a)
5.	(c)	6.	(b)	7.	(c)	8.	(c)
9.	(a)	10.	(b)	11.	(c)	12.	(b)
13.	(d)	14.	(c)	15.	(c)	16.	(a)
17.	(a)	18.	(c)	19.	(c)	20.	(b)

86. PANCHAYATI RAJ

1.	(b)	2.	(c)	3.	(a)	4.	(b)
5.	(a)	6.	(c)	7.	(d)	8.	(d)
9.	(c)	10.	(c)	11.	(d)	12.	(d)
13.	(a)	14.	(c)	15.	(b)	16.	(c)
17.	(c)						

18. (d) Education is included in the concurrent list. Also residuary list/powers are matters not included the Union list, state list or the concurrent list. These are powers under the judiciary.

19. (c)   20. (a)

87. JUDICIARY & MISCELLANEOUS

1.	(d)	2.	(d)	3.	(b)	4.	(d)
5.	(b)	6.	(d)	7.	(b)		

8. (c) The Supreme Court originally consisted of a Chief-Justice and seven other judges. In 1985, the strength was increased. It comprises the chief justice and not more than 25 other judge.

9.	(c)	10.	(c)	11.	(a)	12.	(b)
13.	(d)	14.	(c)	15.	(a)	16.	(a)
17.	(c)	18.	(b)	19.	(c)	20.	(d)

88. INDIAN ECONOMY

1.	(c)	2.	(a)	3.	(a)	4.	(b)
5.	(c)	6.	(a)	7.	(a)	8.	(d)
9.	(a)	10.	(a)	11.	(c)	12.	(a)
13.	(a)	14.	(b)	15.	(a)	16.	(a)
17.	(a)	18.	(a)	19.	(a)	20.	(c)

89. PHYSICAL GEOGRAPHY

1. (a) The planet nearest to the sun is mercury. Mercury is the smallest and closest to the Sun of the eight planets in the Solar System, with an orbital period of about 88 Earth days.

2. (d) Neptune takes the longest time to go around the sun. Neptune orbits the Sun at an average distance of 4.5 billion km. Like all the planets in the Solar System, Neptune follows an elliptical path around the Sun, varying its distance to the Sun at different points along its orbit.

3. (b) The planet which is called twin sister of earth is Venus. Venus is known as the Earth's twin because of its similar size, chemical composition and density. However, due to its toxic atmosphere, Venus is not habitable.

4. (c) The largest planet in our solar system is Jupiter. Jupiter is the fifth planet from the Sun and the largest planet in the Solar System. It is a gas giant with mass one-thousandth of that of the Sun but is two and a half times the mass of all the other planets in the Solar System combined.

5. (b)

6. (a) The deepest lake of the world is Baikal. Lake Baikal is a rift lake in the south of the Russian region of Siberia, between the Irkutsk Oblast to the northwest and the Buryat Republic to the southeast.

7. (c) Black Forest is an example of a block mountain. The Black Forest is a wooded mountain range in Baden-Wurttemberg, southwestern Germany. It is bordered by the Rhine valley to the west and south. The highest peak is the Feldberg with an elevation of 1,493 metres (4,898 ft). The region is almost rectangular with a length of 160 km (99 mi) and breadth of up to 60 km (37 mi).

8. (b) The biggest Island of the Indian ocean is Madagascar. Madagascar, officially the Republic of Madagascar and previously known as the Malagasy Republic, is an island country in the Indian Ocean, off the coast of Southeast Africa.

9. (b) U-shaped valley develops in the Glacial region. Ice causes friction on the sides of the valley.

10. (a)   11. (c)   12. (b)   13. (a)
14. (b)   15. (d)

16. (a) Jupiter has largest number of satellites or moons. The planet Jupiter has 67 confirmed moons. This gives it the largest retinue of moons with "reasonably secure" orbits of any planet in the Solar System.

17. (b) Earth is called the 'Blue Planet' due to the abundant water on its surface. This is because liquid water covers most of the surface of the planet. The Earth has the right mass, chemical composition, and location can support liquid water.

18. (d) The approximately diameter of Earth is 12800 km. The rotation of the planet has slightly flattened it out, so it has a larger diameter at the equator than at the poles. The equatorial diameter of Earth is 12,756 km, its polar diameter is 12,713 km, and its average diameter, which is referred to in common usage, is 12,742 km or 7,926 miles.

19. (c)   20. (d)   20. (c)

90. GEOGRAPHY OF INDIA

1.	(c)	2.	(d)	3.	(c)	4.	(a)
5.	(c)	6.	(c)	7.	(a)	8.	(d)
9.	(a)	10.	(a)	11.	(c)	12.	(a)
13.	(a)	14.	(c)	15.	(c)	16.	(c)
17.	(c)	18.	(a)	19.	(d)	20.	(a)

91. WORLD GEOGRAPHY

1.	(a)	2.	(c)	3.	(c)	4.	(a)
5.	(c)	6.	(a)	7.	(c)	8.	(c)
9.	(c)	10.	(a)	11.	(c)	12.	(a)
13.	(c)	14.	(a)	15.	(d)	16.	(b)
17.	(a)	18.	(a)	19.	(b)	20.	(c)

92. NATIONAL & INTERNATIONAL AWARDS

1. (a) Dada Saheb Phalke award, constituted for the field of film in 1969, the birth centenary year of Dadasaheb Phalke, who is considered as the father of Indian cinema is given to recognize the contribution of film personalities towards the development of Indian Cinema and for distinguished contribution to the medium, its growth and promotion.

2. (d) The Jnanpith award is a literary award which along with the Sahitya Akademi Fellowship is one of the two most prestigious literary honours in the country. The award was instituted in 1961. Any Indian citizen who writes in any of the official languages of India is eligible for the honour.

3. (a) Bharat Ratna is India's highest civilian award. The official criteria for awarding the Bharat Ratna stipulated it is to be conferred "for the highest degrees of national service which includes artistic, literary, and scientific achievements, as well as "recognition of public service of the highest order". The last recipient of the award is the cricketer Sachin Tendulkar for the year 2014.

4. (c) The National Film awards, one of the most prominent film awards in India, were established in 1954. Every year, a national panel appointed by the government selects the winning entry, and the award ceremony is held in New Delhi where the President of India presents the awards.

5. (c) Vir Chakra is an Indian gallantry award presented for acts of bravery in the battlefield while the Ashok Chakra, Kirti Chakra and Shaurya Chakra in addition for separate acts of gallantry are awarded for valour, courageous action or self-sacrifice away from the battlefield.

6. (a)

7. (b) The Param Vir Chakra is India's highest military decoration awarded for the highest degree of valour or self-sacrifice in the presence of the enemy. It can be awarded to officers or enlisted personnel from all branches of the Indian military and can be, and often has been, awarded posthumously.

8. (a) Dronacharya Award is an award presented by the government for excellence in sports coaching. The award comprises bronze statuette of Dronacharya, a scroll of honour and a cash component of Rs.500,000. The award was instituted in 1985. The last recipient of the award is Raj Singh for wrestling in the year 2014.

9. (b) In order to recognize a scientist, who provides a breakthrough for agriculture through a new insight that has created high potential value for the future, the Norman Borlaug Award has been constituted. The nominations for the awards are for a scientist(s) of any discipline of agricultural and allied sciences. The award would be of Rs.10 lakh in cash.

10. (a) The Ashok Chakra is an Indian military decoration awarded for valour, courageous action or self-sacrifice away from the battlefield. It is the peace time equivalent of the Param Vir Chakra, and is awarded for the "most conspicuous bravery or some daring or pre-eminent valour or self-sacrifice" other than in the face of the enemy.

11. (d) The Nobel prize is a set of an international awards bestowed in a number of categories which is given annually to the winners by Swedish and Norwegian Committees in recognition of cultural and/or scientific advances. It was the will of the Swedish inventor Alfred Nobel that established the Nobel prizes in 1895 in Sweden.

12. (a) The Academy award is also known as the Oscar award which is presented for various categories in the Film industry. It was first given in 1929.

13. (a) The Pulitzer Prize is a U.S. award for achievements in newspaper and online journalism, literature, and musical composition. It was established in 1917 and administered by Columbia University in New York City by provisions in the will of American publisher Joseph Pulitzer.

14. (c) The Nobel awards in literature, medicine, physics, chemistry, peace, and economics are given in Stockholm, Sweden. The Peace prize is awarded in Oslo, Norway.

15. (a) The British Academy Film awards are presented in an annual award show hosted by the British Academy of Film and Television Arts (BAFTA). It is given by UK and is considered to be the counter awards for Oscars.

16. (a) The Kalinga Prize for popularization of Science is an international distinction instituted by UNESCO. It was started in 1951 by donation from Mr Bijoyanand Patnaik, founder and president of the Kalinga Foundation Trust in India.

17. (a) The Nobel Award is given on the death anniversary of Alfred Nobel. He had died on 10 December 1896. This award is actually given in his memory.

18. (a) The World Economic Forum gives Crystal award to those artists who have improved the state of the world through their art.

19. (a) International Gandhi Peace prize is given annually by Government of India to those individuals and organizations which contribute towards changes in the political, social or economic reforms via non-violence. It was instituted in 1995.

20. (b)

93. BOOKS AND AUTHORS

1. (a) Raghuvansham is written by Kalidasa. Raghuvansha, a long classical poem of 19 cantos, contains a brilliant account of the illustrious kings of Raghu Dynasty. It is indeed a gallery of brilliant kings - Dilipa, Raghu, Aja, Dasharatha, Rama - painted exquisitely by Kalidasa in which the picture of Rama is undoubtedly the best.

2. (c) Meghdootam is written by Kalidasa. The meghaduta is a poem describing the message of departed Yaksha to his wife, to be conveyed through a cloud. Yaksha, a servant of lord, Kubera, made some mistake in his duty; Kubera punished him with a curse, banishing him from Alaka into exile for a period of one year. Therefore, Yaksha sent his message to his wife through a cloud.

3. (c) Kautilya's Arthashastra is an excellent treatise on statecraft, economic policy and military strategy. it is said to have been written by Kautilya, also known by the name Chanakya or Vishnugupta, the prime minister of India's first great emperor, Chandragupta Maurya.

4. (b)

5. (b) One night @ call centre is written by Chetan Bhagat, published in 2005. The themes involve the anxieties and insecurities of the rising Indian middle class, including questions about career, inadequacy, marriage, family conflicts in a changing India, and the relationship of the young Indian middle class to both executives and ordinary clients whom they serve in U.S.A.

6. (c) Jhansi Ki Rani is written by Vrindavanlal Verma. Vrindavan Lal Verma is the acclaimed author of various books including a National Award winning book titled "Mrignayani".

7. (a) Gaban and Godan were written by Prem chand. Prem Chand was the first Hindi author to introduce realism in his writings. He pioneered the new form - fiction with a social purpose. He supplemented Gandhiji's work in the political and social fields by adopting his revolutionary ideas as themes for his literary writings.

8.	(b)	9.	(d)	10.	(d)	11.	(d)
12.	(c)	13.	(a)	14.	(c)	15.	(c)
16.	(d)	17.	(d)	18.	(d)	19.	(a)
20.	(b)						

94. SPORTS AND GAMES

1. (a) The India national field hockey team had won its first Gold in 1928 at Amsterdam, Nederlands in which India defeated the Nederlands by 3-0. India also won Gold in 1932, 1936, 1948, 1952, 1956, 1964, and 1980.

2. (a) The host city of the Olympic Games 2016 will be Rio de Janeiro, Brazil.

3. (a) India had won the cricket world cup 2011, defeating Sri Lanka by 6 wickets in the final in Wankhede Stadium Mumbai, thus becoming the first country to win the Cricket World Cup final on home soil.

4. (c)

5. (a) The four Grand Slam tournaments, also called Majors, are the most important annual tennis events. The Grand Slam itinerary consists of the Australian Open in mid January, the French Open in May/June, Wimbledon in June/July, and the US Open in August/September.

6. (d) Subroto Cup Football Tournament is an inter-school football tournament in India, named after the Indian Air Force Air Marshal Subroto Mukerjee. Subroto Cup is conducted by the Indian Air Force, with support from India's Ministry of Youth Affairs & Sports.

7. (b) India's first major football international tournament was in 1948 London Olympics, where a predominately barefooted Indian team lost 2–1 to France.

8. (a) India had played her first ODI in 1974 under the captaincy of Ajit Wadekar.

9. (a) Wankhede stadium is in Mumbai. It is in this stadium that India had won the World cup cricket in 2011 against Sri Lanka.

10. (a) The term 'ashes' is associated with cricket.

11. (b) The average length of the football field is $100 - 110$m ($110 - 120$ yards) with width is in the range of 64 to 75 m (70–80 yd).

12. (a) The Dronacharya award is presented by Indian Government to people showing excellence in sports coaching. B.I. Fernandez is the first foreign Coach who was awarded by Dronacharya Award in 2012.

13. (c) Bogey is associated with Golf, Bully is used in hockey, Smas is a vague term. The only correct match here is Chess: Checkmate.

14. (b) Karnam Malleshwari is an Indian weightlifter. She is the first Indian to win an individual medal in Olympics.

15. (d) Kamaljeet Sandhu is a former woman Indian athlete who won gold medal at 1970 Asian Games in 400 m race. She was the first woman to win Gold in any Asian games.

16. (b) The modern game of polo, though was formalised and popularised by the British, is actually derived from Manipur, India, where the game was known as 'Sagol Kangjei', 'Kanjai-bazee', or 'Pulu'.

17. (b)   18. (a)

19. (a) Hockey (as field hockey) was introduced in Olympics for the first time in Summer Olympics London in 1908.

20. (a) Sunil Chhetri is an Indian professional footballer who plays as a striker for Bengaluru FC in the I-League.

95. CURRENT AFFAIRS

1.	(b)	2.	(c)	3.	(c)	4.	(d)
5.	(b)	6.	(d)	7.	(b)	8.	(d)
9.	(c)	10.	(a)	11.	(c)	12.	(d)
13.	(b)	14.	(a)	15.	(d)	16.	(a)
17.	(d)	18.	(a)	19.	(b)	20.	(c)
21.	(b)	22.	(d)	23.	(d)	24.	(a)
25.	(c)	26.	(b)	27.	(a)	28.	(b)
29.	(d)	30.	(a)	31.	(b)	32.	(a)
33.	(b)	34.	(c)	35.	(d)	36.	(d)
37.	(c)	38.	(c)	39.	(d)	40.	(c)

96. GENERAL AWARENESS SECTION

1.	(a)	2.	(a)	3.	(a)	4.	(a)
5.	(d)	6.	(d)	7.	(b)	8.	(d)
9.	(b)	10.	(d)	11.	(b)	12.	(a)
13.	(a)	14.	(a)	15.	(a)	16.	(c)
17.	(b)	18.	(c)	19.	(a)	20.	(d)
21.	(a)	22.	(b)	23.	(c)	24.	(c)
25.	(c)	26.	(d)	27.	(d)	28.	(d)
29.	(a)	30.	(b)	31.	(a)	32.	(b)
33.	(c)	34.	(c)	35.	(a)	36.	(b)
37.	(c)	38.	(a)	39.	(c)	40.	(b)
41.	(b)	42.	(a)	43.	(b)	44.	(a)
45.	(d)	46.	(b)	47.	(b)	48.	(d)
49.	(d)	50.	(b)	51.	(c)	52.	(a)
53.	(d)	54.	(d)	55.	(a)	56.	(a)
57.	(c)	58.	(b)	59.	(d)	60.	(a)

97. BASIC SCIENCE & ENGINEERING SECTION TEST

1.	(a)	2.	(d)	3.	(c)	4.	(d)	5.	(a)
6.	(b)	7.	(b)	8.	(b)	9.	(d)	10.	(d)
11.	(c)	12.	(c)	13.	(a)	14.	(a)	15.	(c)
16.	(a)	17.	(b)	18.	(c)	19.	(c)	20.	(a)
21.	(a)	22.	(a)	23.	(d)	24.	(a)	25.	(c)
26.	(b)	27.	(b)	28.	(d)	29.	(d)	30.	(c)
31.	(a)	32.	(d)	33.	(c)	34.	(c)	35.	(a)
36.	(d)	37.	(d)	38.	(d)	39.	(c)	40.	(b)
41.	(b)	42.	(c)	43.	(d)	44.	(d)	45.	(b)
46.	(c)	47.	(b)	48.	(d)	49.	(c)	50.	(a)

98. STAGE I FULL TEST - 1

1.	(a)	2.	(d)	3.	(d)	4.	(a)
5.	(d)	6.	(a)	7.	(a)	8.	(b)
9.	(c)	10.	(d)	11.	(a)	12.	(d)
13.	(b)	14.	(c)	15.	(c)	16.	(b)
17.	(a)	18.	(d)	19.	(b, c)	20.	(d)
21.	(d)	22.	(c)	23.	(c)	24.	(a)
25.	(b)	26.	(a)	27.	(a)	28.	(c)
29.	(c)	30.	(a)	31.	(b)	32.	(c)
33.	(d)	34.	(d)	35.	(a)	36.	(c)

37. (a) Polar bears have two thick layers of white fur and lots of fat in their body to keep them warm. The white fur blends with snowy background and protect them from their enemies.

38. (c) Fermentation is anaerobic breakdown of carbohydrates by micro-organisms producing alcohol, organic acids and a variety of other products alongwith heat and waste gases. Yeast brings about alcoholic fermentation. It is accompanied by evolution of carbon dioxide.

39. (d)

40. (d) Removal of upper layer of soil by running water, wind or human activities is called soil erosion. Heavy rain, drought, intensive farming, over-grazing, all are causes of soil-erosion.

41. (d)   42. (c)

43. (b) Arteries transport oxygen-rich blood from the heart to the other parts of the body. They have thick elastic walls because blood flows through them under high pressure.

44. (a)

45. (a) Trachea allows air to pass from pharynx to bronchi (lungs).

46. (b) Boys at the age of 14 to 15 years and girls at the age of 11 to 12 years attain puberty (the reproductive maturity). Simultaneously, some major changes in the body of the girls and boys take place which continue upto the age of 19 or 20 to bring about complete maturity.

47. (a) Vegetative propagation is a type of reproduction which occurs from the vegetative parts of a plant such as the stem, the root and the leaf. Cutting, grafting, layering, tissue culture are the methods of artificial vegetative propagation. While fragmentation is a mode of asexual reproduction in which only one parent organism is required for multiplication and formation of new organisms.

48. (a)   49. (a)

50. (b) Pituitary gland is the master gland located underneath the brain. It regulates the functioning of all other glands. It secrets hormones like growth hormone (GH), trophic hormone (TH), prolactin, vasopressin and oxytocin.

51. (b) We have $\dfrac{63}{99} + \dfrac{37}{99} = \dfrac{100}{99}$.

52. (b) By rationalization we have

$$\left[\frac{1}{\sqrt{9}-\sqrt{8}}\right] = \frac{1}{\sqrt{9}-\sqrt{8}} \times \frac{\sqrt{9}+\sqrt{8}}{\sqrt{9}+\sqrt{8}} = \frac{\sqrt{9}+\sqrt{8}}{9-8} = \sqrt{9}+\sqrt{8}$$

Similarly $\left[\dfrac{1}{\sqrt{8}-\sqrt{7}}\right] = \sqrt{8}+\sqrt{7}$ and $\dfrac{1}{\sqrt{7}-\sqrt{6}} = \sqrt{7}+\sqrt{6}$

and so on. The given expression
$= (\sqrt{9}+\sqrt{8}) - (\sqrt{8}+\sqrt{7}) + (\sqrt{7}+\sqrt{6}) - (\sqrt{6}+\sqrt{5}) + (\sqrt{5}+\sqrt{4})$
$= \sqrt{9} + \sqrt{4} = 3 + 2 = 5$.

53. (a) Let 'r' be the remainder $\Rightarrow 221 - r, 116 - r, 356 - r$ are exactly divisible by that number. Now, if two numbers are divisible by a number, then their difference
$\Rightarrow [(221 - r) - (116 - r)], [(356 - r) - (116 - r)].$
and $[(356 - r) - (221 - r)]$ are divisible by that number
$\Rightarrow 105, 135, 240$ are divisible by that number
$= $ HCF of 105, 135, 140 = 15.

54. (d) The equation can be reduced to $X = 1/(4 + X)$ where

$$X = \cfrac{1}{4 + \cfrac{1}{4 + \cfrac{1}{4+...}}}$$

$\Rightarrow X(4 + X) = 1 \Rightarrow X^2 + 4x - 1 = 0$

$\Rightarrow X = \dfrac{-4 \pm \sqrt{16+4}}{2} = \dfrac{-4 \pm 4.47}{2} \Rightarrow X = 0.235$.

55. (a) Let $\sqrt{2+\sqrt{2+\sqrt{2+.........}}} = x$; $2 + \sqrt{2 + \sqrt{2 + ...}} = x^2$
$2 + x = x^2$; $x^2 - x - 2 = 0$; $x^2 - 2x + x - 2 = 0$;
$x(x - 2) + 1(x - 2) = 0$
$\therefore \ x = -1$ or 2

Since x can't take –ve values. Hence x = 2.

56. (a) Let X be the required 3rd proportional, then $\dfrac{\sqrt{3}+1}{\sqrt{3}+2} = \dfrac{\sqrt{3}+2}{X}$

Or $X = \dfrac{\left(\sqrt{3}+2\right)^2}{\sqrt{3}+1} = \dfrac{7+4\sqrt{3}}{\sqrt{3}+1} \times \dfrac{\sqrt{3}-1}{\sqrt{3}-1} = \dfrac{5+3\sqrt{3}}{2}$.

57. (b) Number of boys $= \dfrac{5}{9} \times 441 = 245$.

Number of girls $= \dfrac{4}{9} \times 441 = 196$.

$\therefore$ The number of girls needed to join to make the ratio 1 : 1 is 245 – 196 = 49.
Short-cut : 1 unit = 441/9 = 49
$\therefore$ So number of girls required to make ratio 1 : 1 = 49.

58. (b) $(5M + 6B) \times 4 \equiv 1$ work   ...(a)

$(4M + 3B) \times 6 \equiv 1$ work   ...(b)

Equate these to get : $2M = 3B \Rightarrow M = \dfrac{3B}{2}$.

We want to find X such that $(3M + 6B)X \equiv 1$ ...(c)

By putting $\Rightarrow M = \dfrac{3B}{2}$ in (b) and (c) we get

$\left(4 \times \dfrac{3B}{2} + 3B\right) \times 6 = 1$ or $54B = 1 \Rightarrow B = \dfrac{1}{54}$.

And $\left(3 \times \dfrac{3B}{2} + 6B\right)X = 1 \Rightarrow \dfrac{21B}{2}X = 1$

$\Rightarrow \dfrac{21}{2} \times \dfrac{1}{54}X = 1 \Rightarrow X = \dfrac{108}{21} = \dfrac{36}{7}$ days.

59. (b) In 1 minute the part filled is $1/10 + 1/12 - 1/6 = 1/60$.
Hence tank will be totally filled in 60 hrs.

60. (c) Let the required time = x hours. By the question,

$\dfrac{x}{24} + \dfrac{x-2}{40} + \dfrac{x-7}{60} = 1 \Rightarrow \dfrac{5x + 3x - 6 + 2x - 14}{120} = 1 \Rightarrow 10x - 20 = 120.$ $\therefore x = \dfrac{140}{10} = 14$ hours.

61. (a) Second denotes the class to which the first belongs.

62. (a) : All except Sailor need raw material to work on.

63. (d)

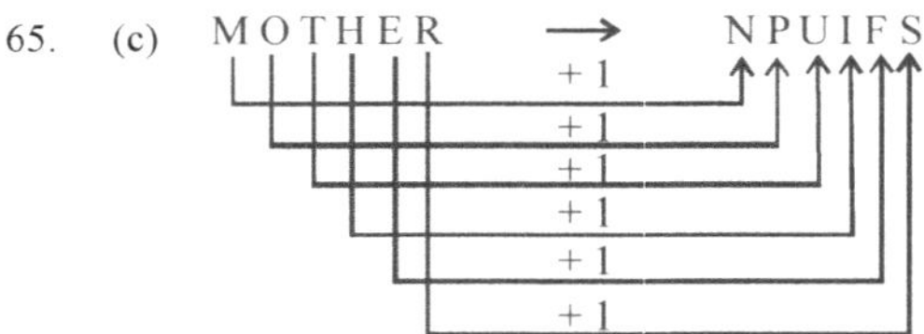

In each group of 4 letters, 1st and 3rd letters, 2nd and 4th letters alternatively increased. Hence, the missing letter would be HL.

64. (c)

65. (c)

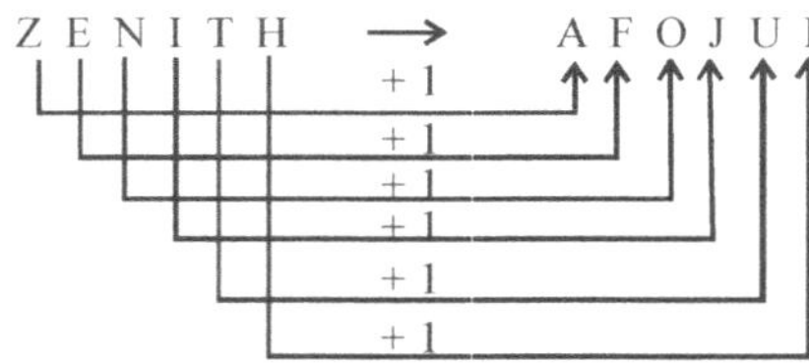

Similarly,

66. (a)

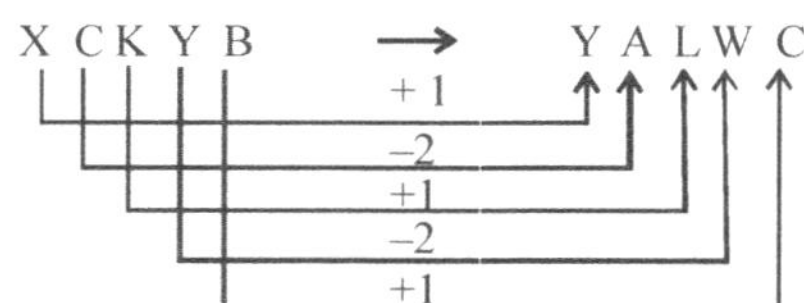

Similarly,

67. (b) The only son of Mahesh's father is Mahesh himself. Father of Kamla is Mahesh and Mahesh is father of Kamla.

68. (d)

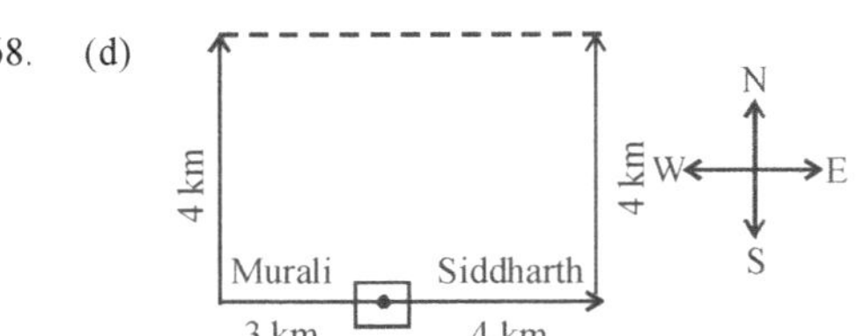

Required distance = 3 + 4 = 7 km

69. (d)

1	2	3	4	5	6	7	8
C	R	E	A	T	I	V	E

Meaningful Word

$\Rightarrow$ R E A C T

70. (b) The day after tomorrow is Sunday.
Therefore, today is Friday.
The day on tomorrow's day before yesterday
= Friday − 1 = Thursday

71. (d) A's decrease = $15000/75000 \times 100 = 20\%$.
B's increase = $15000/60000 \times 100 = 25\%$.
Now, 20 is 80% of 25.

72. (b) Relative speed = 30 + 45 = 75 kmph.
Now time taken for them to meet = 300/75 = 4 hours
In 4 hours, Distance from A = 4 × 30 = 120 km.

73. (a) Let X be the speed of man in still water, the speed of stream = 2 km/hr.
(X − 2) = 9/3 or X = 5.
Now X + 2 = 7, hence time required = 9/7 hours.

74. (a) The number of bricks are

$= \dfrac{\text{volume of the wall}}{\text{volume of the brick}} = \dfrac{1200 \times 200 \times 46.2}{25 \times 12.5 \times 7.5} = 4730.8 = 4731.$

75. (b) Hypotenuse = 270 m
$\Rightarrow$ Hypotenuse^2 = Side^2 + Side^2 = 2 (Side)^2
$\Rightarrow$ Side^2 = $(270)^2/2 = 72900/2 = 36450$
$\Rightarrow$ Required Area = $1/2 \times$ (side)^2.

$= \dfrac{36450}{2} = 18225$ m^2

99. STAGE I FULL TEST - 2

1. (b) Staff Selection Commission is an agency of the Government of India to recruit "staff" for the central government ministries and departments. It is not a constitutional body as it was established in 1975 by an executive decision. Then, it was known as Subordinate Services Commission.

2. (c) There are three methods to estimate national income namely, product method, income method and consumption method. In India, a combination of Income method and the Product (output) method is used for estimating national income.

3. (c) Gandhara style of Buddhist art developed out of a merger of Greek, Syrian, Persian, and Indian artistic influence. This style flourished and achieved its peak during the Kushan period, from the 1st to the 5th centuries.

4. (b) Mahmud Gawan was a minister in Bahamani Empire who expanded and extended the Bahamani Kingdom rapidly. He was appointed as the vakil-us-sultanate under Humayun Shah. He also served in the dual capacity of both amir-i-jumla and wazir-i-kull of the province.

5. (d) Duncan Passage is a strait in the Indian Ocean. It separates Rutland Island (part of Great Andaman) to the north and

6. (b) The President of India can use discretionary powers under the following situations: (i) In appointing the Prime Minister form among the contenders when no single party attains majority after elections to the Lok Sabha; (ii) While exercising a pocket veto; (iii) Returning the Bill passed by the Parliament once for its reconsideration; etc.

7. (b) Although these seals and samples of Indus writing have been floating around the scholastic world for close to 70 years, little progress has been made on deciphering this elegant script. The Indus script is an un-deciphered script.

8. (c) Krishna Deva Raya wrote the book Amukta Malyada (A Garland Dedicated to the Lord) in Telugu. This book describes the pangs of separation suffered by Andal (an incarnation of the goddess Mahala-kshmi).

9. (a) There are three forms of Satyagraha, namely; (i) non-cooperation, (ii) civil disobedience, and (iii) boycott. These were most commonly employed during the freedom struggle in India under leadership of Gandhi.

10. (d) The English East India Company was founded in 1600. Akbar was Mughal Emperor from 1556 until his death in 1605.

11. (c) The Indian National Congress was formed in 1885 when Lord Dufferin was the Viuceroy of India. Allan Octavian Hume brought about its first meeting

12. (c) The Reign of Terror (5 September 1793 – 28 July 1794) was a period of violence that occurred after the onset of the French Revolution, incited by conflict between rival political factions, the Girondins and the Jacobins, and marked by mass executions of "enemies of hte revolution." Robespierre, a French lawyer and politician, was an important figure during the Reign of Terror, which ended a few months after his arrest and execution in July 1794.

13. (d) American war of independence

14. (d) Lenin

15. (a) Lahore session, 1929

16. (b) Kerosene oil rises up in wick of a lantern because of capillary action. If the surface tension of oil is zero, then it will not rise, so oil rises up up in a wick of a lantern due to surface tension.

17. (b) Tropical year is the year in which there is total solar eclipse. Light year represents distance

18. (d)   19. (b,c)   20. (a)
21. (c)   22. (d)   23. (c)
24. (c)   25. (a)   26. (d)
27. (a)

28. (d) It is so because brass has a higher coefficient of linear expansion.

29. (b) In doing so moment of inertia is decreased and hence angular velocity is increased

30. (a)   31. (c)

32. (a) At 0K, motion of free electrons stop. Hence conductivity becomes zero. Therefore, at 0K intrinsic semiconductor becomes insulator.

33. (a, c)   34. (c, d)   35. (c)
36. (d)   37. (a, c)   38. (d)
39. (a)   40. (c)   41. (a)
42. (a)   43. (b)   44. (c)
45. (a)   46. (b)   47. (b)
48. (c)   49. (a)   50. (b)

51. (a) Given exp. $= \left(\dfrac{a^2 + ab + b^2}{a^3 - b^3} \right) = \left(\dfrac{1}{a - b} \right)$, where $a = 147$,

$b = 143 \Rightarrow \left(\dfrac{1}{a - b} \right) = \left(\dfrac{1}{147 - 143} \right) = \dfrac{1}{4}$

52. (b) Required number
= HCF of $(115 - 3)$, $(149 - 5)$ and $(183 - 7)$
= HCF of 112, 144 and 176 = 16

53. (b) Greatest number of 4 digits is 9999. L.C.M. of 4, 7 and 13 is 364.
On dividing 9999 by 364, the remainder obtained is 171.
∴ Greatest number of 4 digits divisible by 4, 7 and $13 = (9999 - 171) = 9828$.
Hence, required number $= (9828 + 3) = 9831$

54. (b) Attendance on the fifth day $= 32 \times 5 - 30 \times 4$
$= 160 - 120 = 40$

55. (d) Net effect on sale $= -\dfrac{(\text{common \% change})^2}{100}$

$= \dfrac{-(15)^2}{100} = 2.25\%$ decrease

56. (b) Let the total salary be ₹ x.
Then, $(100 - 10)\%$ of $(100 - 20)\%$ of $(100 - 20)\%$ of $(100 - 10)\%$ of $x = 15552$

$\Rightarrow \left(\dfrac{90}{100} \times \dfrac{80}{100} \times \dfrac{80}{100} \times \dfrac{90}{100} \times x \right) = 15552$

$\Rightarrow x = \left(\dfrac{15552 \times 10000}{64 \times 81} \right) = 30,000.$

57. (d) Single discount of successive discount 20% and 15%

$= 20 + 15 - \dfrac{26 \times 15}{100} = 35 - 3 = 32$

Now, single discount of successive discount 32% and 10%

$= 32 + 10 - \dfrac{32 \times 10}{100} = 42 - 3.2 = 38.8$

58. (c) Let he sells x oranges per rupee.

$\dfrac{1}{36} : (100 - 4) :: x : (100 + 8)$

$\Rightarrow x = \dfrac{108}{96 \times 36} = \dfrac{1}{32}$

He sells 32 oranges per rupee.

59. (a) S.P. of the 1st chair = ₹ 500
Gain = 20%

∴ C.P. of the 1st chair $= \dfrac{500 \times 100}{100 + 20} = \dfrac{500 \times 100}{120}$

$= \dfrac{1250}{3}$

S.P. of the 2nd chair = ₹ 500
Loss = 12%

∴ C.P. of the 2nd chair $= \dfrac{500 \times 100}{100 - 12} = \dfrac{500 \times 100}{88}$

$$= \frac{500 \times 25}{22} = \frac{250 \times 25}{11} = \frac{6250}{11}$$

Now S.P. of both the chairs = ₹ 1000

C.P. of both the chairs

$$= \frac{1250}{3} + \frac{6250}{11} = \frac{13750 + 18750}{33} = \frac{32500}{33}$$

$$\therefore \text{ Net gain} = 1000 - \frac{32500}{33} = \frac{500}{33}$$

$$\Rightarrow \text{ Gain \%} = \frac{500/33}{32500/33} \times 100 = \frac{500}{32500} \times 100$$

$$= \frac{100}{65} = \frac{20}{13} = 1.5\% \quad \text{(To one place of decimal)}$$

OR

$$\left[\frac{2(100 + x\%)(100 - y\%)}{(100 + x\%) + (100 - x_2\%)} - 100 \right]\%$$

$$\Rightarrow \left[\frac{2(100 + 20)(100 - 12)}{(100 + 20) + (100 - 12)} - 100 \right]$$

$$= \left[\frac{2 \times 120 \times 88}{120 \times 88} - 100 \right] = 1.5\%$$

$$\therefore \text{ Profit \%} = 1.5\%$$

60. **(d)** For same article, $\dfrac{100 - d_1}{100 - d_2} = \dfrac{100 + g_1}{100 + g_2}$

$$\Rightarrow \frac{100 - 25}{100 - 10} = \frac{100 + 25}{100 + g_2} \Rightarrow \frac{75}{90} = \frac{125}{100 + g_2}$$

$$\Rightarrow 100 + g_2 = \frac{90 \times 125}{75} = 150 \Rightarrow g_2 = 50\%$$

61. **(a)** Let A's share be ₹ x,

B's share be ₹ y. Then,

C's share = ₹ [671 – (x + y)]

Now, $x + 3 : y + 7 : 671 - (x + y) + 9 = 1 : 2 : 3$

$$\Rightarrow x + 3 : y + 7 : 680 - (x + y) = 1 : 2 : 3$$

$$\therefore \ x + 3 = \frac{1}{6} \times 690 = 115$$

$$\Rightarrow x = ₹ 112$$

Also $y + 7 = \dfrac{2}{6} \times 690 = 230$

$$\Rightarrow y = ₹ 223$$

$$\therefore \text{ C's share} = ₹ [671 - (112 + 223)] = ₹ 336$$

62. **(a)** (A + B)'s 1 day's work = $\dfrac{1}{12}$ th part of whole work.

B's 1 day's work = $\dfrac{1}{28}$ th part of whole work.

$$\therefore \text{ A's 1 day's work} = \frac{1}{12} - \frac{1}{28} = \frac{1}{21} \text{th part of whole work.}$$

$$\therefore \text{ A alone can finish the work in 21 days}$$

63. **(a)** A's 1 day's work = $\dfrac{1}{18}$ and B's 1 day's work = $\dfrac{1}{9}$.

$$\therefore \ (A + B)\text{'s 1 day's work} = \left(\frac{1}{18} + \frac{1}{9} \right) = \frac{1}{6}.$$

64. **(d)** In 1 day, work done by 12 men = $\dfrac{1}{18}$

In 6 days, work done by 12 men = $\dfrac{6}{18} = \dfrac{1}{3}$

Remaining work = $\dfrac{2}{3}$

Now, $m_1 \times d_1 \times w_2 = m_2 \times d_2 \times w_1$

or $\quad 12 \times 18 \times \dfrac{2}{3} = 16 \times d_2 \times 1$

or $\quad d_2 = \dfrac{4 \times 18 \times 2}{16} = 9 \, \text{days}$

OR

12 men complete the remaining work is
= (18 – 6) = 12 days
1 men complete the remaining work in = 12 × 12 days
(12 + 4) men complete the remaining work in

$$= \frac{12 \times 12}{16} = 9 \text{ days}$$

65. **(a)** Let original speed = S km/h

Here, distance to be covered is constant

$$\therefore S \times 8 = (S + 5)\left(\frac{20}{3} \right)$$

$$\Rightarrow 8S - \frac{20}{3}S = \frac{100}{3} \Rightarrow S = \frac{100}{4} = 25 \text{ km/h}$$

66. **(c)** Forward letter posiitons have been put for each letter. Let us see

G A M E → B I R D

7 1 1 3 5 Similarly, 2 9 1 8 4

67. **(c)** $(x)^3 - x = (12)^3 - 12 = 1716$

68. **(b)** The movements of the child from A to E are as shown in figure.

Clearly, the child meets his father at E.

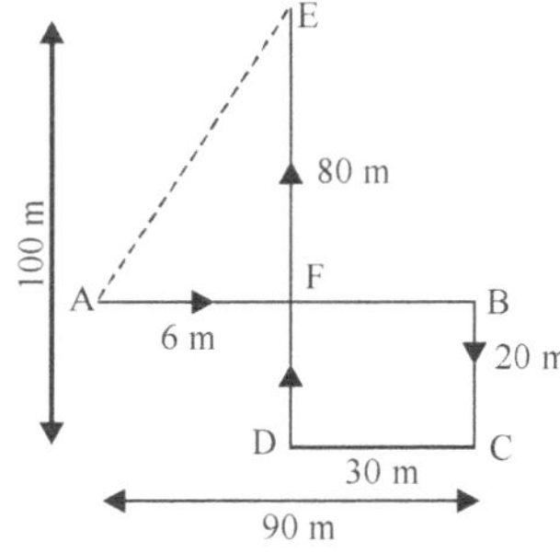

Now, AF = (AB – FB)
= (AB – DC) = (90 – 30) m = 60 m

EF = (DE – DF = (DE – BC)
= (100 – 20) m = 80 m
∴ Required distance

$$= AE = \sqrt{AF^2 + EF^2} = \sqrt{(60)^2 + (80)^2}$$

$$= \sqrt{3600 + 6400} = \sqrt{10000} = 100 \text{ m}$$

69. (c) Due to absence of letter 'I', the word MAIL cannot be formed.

70. (c) As,   Similarly,

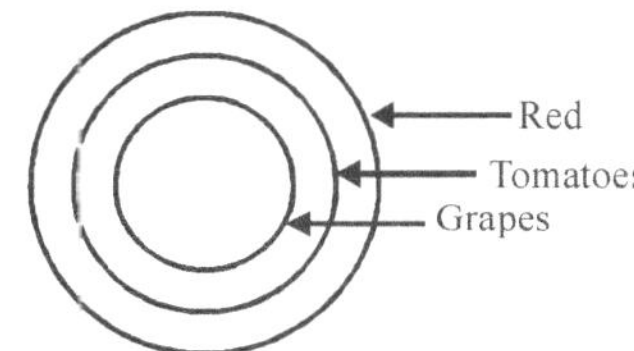

$$S \xrightarrow{+1} T \qquad P \xrightarrow{+1} \boxed{Q}$$
$$W \xrightarrow{-1} V \qquad L \xrightarrow{-1} K$$
$$I \xrightarrow{+1} J \qquad A \xrightarrow{+1} B$$
$$T \xrightarrow{-1} S \qquad N \xrightarrow{-1} M$$
$$H \xrightarrow{+1} I \qquad E \xrightarrow{+1} F$$

71. (d) Clearly, vowels A, E, I, O, U are coded as 1, 2, 3, 4, 5 respectively. Each of the consonants in the word is moved one step forward to give the corresponding letter of the code. So, the code for ACID becomes 1D3E.

72. (d) We have A = 2, B = 3, ..., Z = 27. Then.
FOR = F + O + R = 7 + 16 + 19 = 42.

FRONT = F + R + O + N + T = 7 + 19 + 16 + 15 + 21 = $\boxed{78}$.

73. (d) When all tomatoes are red and all grapes are tomatoes, then all grapes are also red. When all grapes are tomatoes, then some tomatoes must be grapes. Therefore, both conclusion I and II are correct.

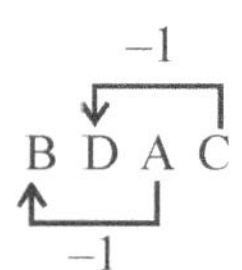

74. (b) Clearly, the given series consists of prime numbers starting from 2. So the missing term is the prime number after 11 which is 13.

75. (b) Area common to singer and poets.

100. STAGE II FULL TEST - 1

1. (c) The body of fish remains covered with scales externally. Similarly, the body of bear remains covered with fur.

2. (d) As,

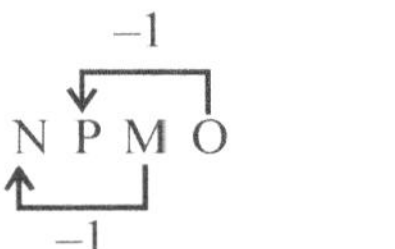

$$\overset{-1}{B \ D \ A \ C} \qquad \overset{-1}{F \ H \ E \ G}$$

Similarly,

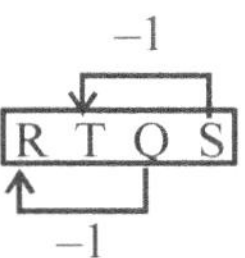

$$\overset{-1}{N \ P \ M \ O} \qquad \overset{-1}{\boxed{R \ T \ Q \ S}}$$

3. (b) **Prod (Verb)** means, 'to push somebdy/something with a finger or a pointed object', 'to encourage', 'to poke'.
Prod (Noun) means 'an act of prodding', 'an act of reminding somebody to take action'.
Sap (Verb) means 'to make somebody/something weak or destroy gradually'.
Sap (Noun) means 'the liquid in a plant that carrries food to all parts of it', 'a stupid person who is easily tricked or treated unfairly'.

Jab (Verb) means 'to push or poke at somebody/something quickly and roughly'.
Jab (Noun) means 'a sudden rough blow'.
Thrust (Verb) means 'to push something/somebody/oneself suddenly or violently'.
Thrust (Noun) means 'an act or movement of thrusting'.
Therefore, Sap is different from others.

4. (b) Except MNST, all others are having a vowel.

5. (c) $\boxed{b}$ cb / $\boxed{a}$ ca / b $\boxed{c}$ b / aca / $\boxed{b}$

cb / a $\boxed{c}$ a / b

6. (c) The pattern is as follows :
$4 = (2)^2$; $16 = (4)^2$; $36 = (6)^2$;
$64 = (8)^2$; $196 = (14)^2$; $169 = (13)^2$;
$144 = (12)^2$;

7. (c) $6 + 3 = 9, 9 + 6 = 15 \ 15 + 12 = \boxed{27}, 27 + 24 = 51, 51 + 48$
$= 99$

8. (c) Here,

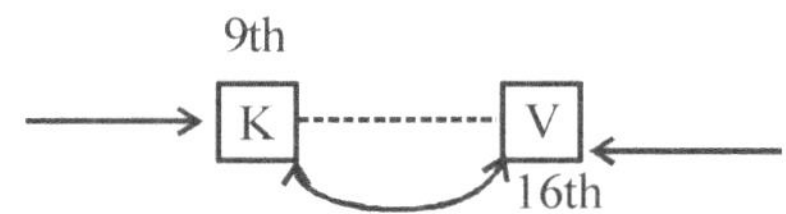

Total number of girls = 25 + 16 – 1 = 40

9. (d)

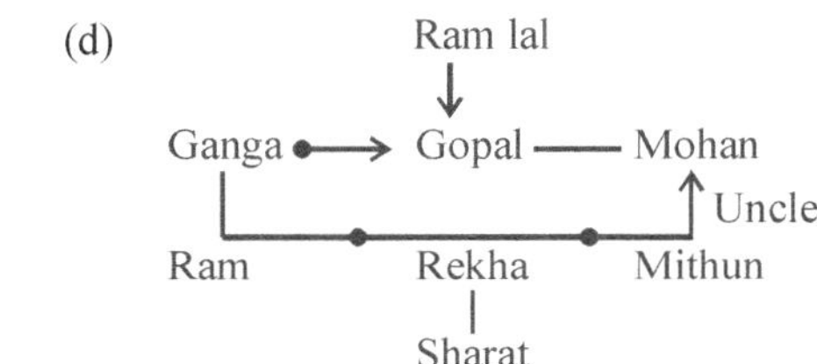

10. (b) Shashikant was born on 29th September 1999.
15th August, 1999 was Sunday.
Days upto 29th September from 15 August
16 + 29 = 45 days = 6 weeks 3 old days
Sunday + 3 = Wednesday.

11. (d)

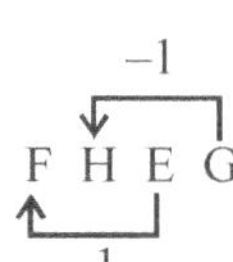

So, C is facing towards East.

12. (c) Suppose total number of workers in the office = x

Number of woman workers = $\dfrac{x}{3}$

∴ Number of man workers

$$= x - \dfrac{x}{3} = \dfrac{3x - x}{3} = \dfrac{2x}{3}$$

Number of married woman workers = $\dfrac{x}{3} \times \dfrac{1}{2} = \dfrac{x}{6}$

Number of married woman workers who have children

$$= \dfrac{x}{6} \times \dfrac{1}{3} = \dfrac{x}{18}$$

Number of married man workers

$$= \frac{2x}{3} \times \frac{3}{4} = \frac{x}{2}$$

Number of married man workers who have children =

$$\frac{x}{2} \times \frac{2}{3} = \frac{x}{3}$$

Number of workers who have children

$$= \frac{x}{3} + \frac{x}{18}$$

$$= \frac{6x + x}{18} = \frac{7x}{18}$$

Number of workers without children

$$= x - \frac{7x}{18} = \frac{18x - 7x}{18} = \frac{11}{18}x$$

13. **(d)** The direction diagram is as follows:
Starting point

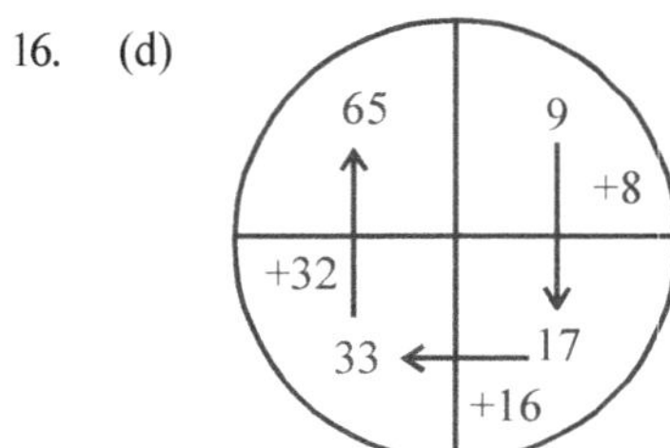

It is clearly shown that he is moving south direction.

14. **(b)** Difference is $+2, +4, +6, +8, +10, +12, +14, +16$

15. **(c)** As, D E L H I
    ↓ ↓ ↓ ↓ ↓
    7 3 5 4 1

and C A L C U T T A
    ↓ ↓ ↓ ↓ ↓ ↓ ↓ ↓
    8 2 5 8 9 6 6 2

Therefore,

C A L I C U T
↓ ↓ ↓ ↓ ↓ ↓ ↓
| 8 | 2 | 5 | 1 | 8 | 9 | 6 |

16. **(d)**

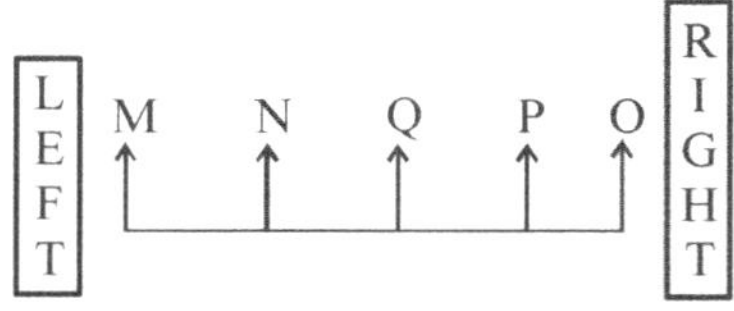

17. **(a)** $30 - 6 + 5 \times 4 \div 2 = 27$
$\Rightarrow 30 \div 6 \times 5 + 4 - 2 = 27$
$\Rightarrow 25 + 4 - 2 = 27$
$30 + 6 - 5 \div 4 \times 2 = 30$
$\Rightarrow 30 \times 6 \div 5 - 4 + 2 = 30$
$\Rightarrow 36 - 4 + 2 \neq 30$
$30 \times 6 \div 5 - 4 + 2 = 32$
$\Rightarrow 30 + 6 - 5 \div 4 \times 2 \neq 32$

18. **(d)** $9 + 7 = 16$; $9 - 7 = 2$
$16 \times 2 = 32$
$13 + 7 = 20$; $13 - 7 = 6$
$20 \times 6 = 120$
$17 + 9 = 26$; $17 - 9 = 8$
$26 \times 8 = 208$
$19 + 11 = 30$; $19 - 11 = 8$
$30 \times 8 = \boxed{240}$

19. **(c)** As, M E K L F
    ↓ ↓ ↓ ↓ ↓
    9 1 7 8 2

and

L L L J K
↓ ↓ ↓ ↓ ↓
8 8 8 6 7

Therefore,

I G H E D
↓ ↓ ↓ ↓ ↓
| 5 | 3 | 4 | 1 | 0 |

(Here, E = 1, F = 2, G = 3, So on.)

20. **(a)** Age of Shan = 55 years
Age of Sathian = 55 – 5 = 50 years
Age of Balan = 50 – 6 = 44 years
Age of Devan = 44 – 7 = 37 years
Difference between the ages of Shan and Devan = 55 – 37 = 18 years.

21. **(a)** Wife of Vinod's father means the mother of Vinod.
Only brother of Vinod's mother means maternal uncle of Vinod.
Therefore, Vinod is cousin of Vishal.

22. **(b)** 5 January 1965 $\Rightarrow$ Tuesday
5 January 1966 $\Rightarrow$ Wednesday
5 January 1967 $\Rightarrow$ Thursday
5 January 1968 $\Rightarrow$ Friday
5 January 1969 $\Rightarrow$ Sunday
Since, 1968 is a leap year.
5 January 1970 $\Rightarrow$ Monday
5 January 1971 $\Rightarrow$ Tuesday

23. **(c)** The arrangement is as follows :

LEFT M N Q P O RIGHT

So, O is standing on the extreme right.

24. **(c)** Sita > Swapna .... (i)
  S   Sw
S > Lavanya > Sw .... (ii)
       L
Hari, Sw > Suvarna .... (iii)
  H   Su

Sw > H .... (iv)
From all the statements :
S > L > Sw > H > Su

25. (d) As,

R	A	M	A	Y	A	N	A
$-2\downarrow$	$-2\downarrow$	$-2\downarrow$	$-2\downarrow$	$-2\downarrow$	$-2\downarrow$	$-2\downarrow$	$-2\downarrow$
P	Y	K	Y	W	Y	L	Y

Similarly,

M	A	H	A	B	H	A	R	A	T	A
$-2\downarrow$	$-2\downarrow$	$-2\downarrow$	$-2\downarrow$	$-2\downarrow$	$-2\downarrow$	$-2\downarrow$	$-2\downarrow$	$-2\downarrow$	$-2\downarrow$	$-2\downarrow$
K	Y	F	Y	Z	F	Y	P	Y	R	Y

26. (a) Let the numbers be x and y.
$$\therefore x(x+y) = 247$$
and $y(x+y) = 114$
$$\Rightarrow x^2 + xy = 247 \text{ and } xy + y^2 = 114$$
On adding;
$$x^2 + xy + xy + y^2 = 247 + 114$$
$$\Rightarrow x^2 + 2xy + y^2 = 361$$
$$\Rightarrow (x+y)^2 = 19^2 \Rightarrow x + y = 19$$

27. (d) HCF must be a factor of LCM from option 35 is not factor of 120.

28. (a) Here, the first divisor i.e. 49 is multiple of second divisor i.e. 7.
∴ Required remainder = Remainder obtained on dividing 32 by 7 = 4

29. (b) Let the number of correct answers be x.
$$\therefore x + 4 - (75 - x) \times 1 = 125$$
$$\Rightarrow 4x - 75 + x = 125$$
$$\Rightarrow 5x = 125 + 75 = 200$$
$$\therefore x = \frac{200}{5} = 40$$

30. (d) Side of a square
$$= \sqrt{81} = 9 \text{ cm}$$
∴ Length of the wire
$$= 4 \times 9 = 36 \text{ cm.}$$
∴ Perimeter of semi-circle $= (\pi + 2)r$
where r = radius
$$\Rightarrow \left(\frac{22}{7} + 2\right)r = 36$$
$$\Rightarrow \frac{36}{7}r = 36$$
$$\Rightarrow r = \frac{36 \times 7}{36} = 7 \text{ cm.}$$

31. (b) Distance covered by wheel in one revolution
= Circumference of wheel
$$= \frac{11000}{5000} = \frac{11}{5} \text{ m}$$
$$= \frac{11}{5} \times 100 \text{ cm} = 220 \text{ cm}$$
$$\therefore 2\pi r = 220$$
$$\Rightarrow 2 \times \frac{22}{7} \times r = 220$$
$$\Rightarrow r = \frac{220 \times 7}{2 \times 22} = 35 \text{ cm}$$

32. (a) Let the marked price of the article be ₹ x.
$$\therefore x \times \frac{90}{100} = \frac{450 \times 120}{100}$$
$$\Rightarrow \frac{9x}{10} = 540$$
$$\Rightarrow x = \frac{540 \times 10}{9} = ₹ 600$$

33. (b) Single equivalent discount
$$= \left(x + y - \frac{xy}{100}\right)\%$$
$$= \left(20 + 15 - \frac{20 \times 15}{100}\right)\% = 32\%$$

34. (d) Let the number x be added
$$\therefore \frac{17 + x}{24 + x} = \frac{1}{2}$$
$$\Rightarrow 34 + 2x = 24 + x$$
$$\Rightarrow 2x - x = 24 - 34$$
$$\Rightarrow x = -10$$
Hence, 10 should be subtracted.

35. (*) Let monthly income of A and B be 9x and 7x
Expenditure = Income − Saving
ATQ
$$\frac{9x - 200}{7x - 200} = \frac{4}{3}$$
$$27x - 6.00 = 28x - 800$$
$$x = 200$$
Sum $= 200 \times 16 = 3200$

36. (c) Requried average
$$= 30 + \frac{(28 + 31 - 82 - 13)}{50}$$
$$= 30 + \left(-\frac{36}{50}\right) = 30 - 0.72 = 29.28$$

37. (d) Let the S.P. of the article = ₹ 100
∴ C.P. = ₹ 40
∴ Required percentage
$$= \frac{100}{40} \times 100 = 250\%$$

38. (d) $$\frac{A \times 90}{100} = \frac{B \times 30}{100}$$
$$\Rightarrow 3A = B$$
$$\Rightarrow 3A = A \times \frac{2x}{100}$$
$$\Rightarrow 300 = 2x \Rightarrow x = 150$$

39. (b)　Let the original price of sugar be ₹ x/kg.

$\therefore$ New price $= ₹\ \dfrac{9x}{10}$ /kg

$\therefore\ \dfrac{\dfrac{270}{\dfrac{9x}{10}} - \dfrac{270}{x}}{} = 1$

$\Rightarrow \dfrac{300}{x} - \dfrac{270}{x} = 1 \Rightarrow \dfrac{30}{x} = 1$

$\Rightarrow x = ₹\ 30/kg$

40. (b)　Percentage decrease $= \dfrac{25}{125} \times 100 = 20$

41. (a)　$\dfrac{\text{Simple Interest}}{\text{Principal}} = \dfrac{1}{4}$

$\therefore$ Rate $= \dfrac{\text{S.I.} \times 100}{\text{Principal} \times \text{Time}}$

$= \dfrac{1 \times 100}{4 \times 5} = 5\ \%\ \text{per annum}$

42. (d)　SP of both articles is same. Profit on one is equal to loss on the other.
If loss per cent be x, then

$25 - x - \dfrac{25x}{100} = 0$

$\Rightarrow 25 - x - \dfrac{x}{4} = 0 \Rightarrow 100 - 4x - x = 0$

$\Rightarrow 5x = 100$
$\Rightarrow x = 20$

43. (b)　Let CP = x, Total ₹ = 600, Sugar bought

$= \dfrac{600}{x}$

ATQ $\dfrac{80x}{100}\left[\dfrac{600}{x} + 5\right] = 600$

$480 + 4x = 600$
$4x = 120$
$x = 30$

44. (d)　Let the third number = 100.
First number = 70
Second number = 63
$\therefore$ Required per cent

$= \dfrac{70 - 63}{70} \times 100 = 10\%$

45. (b)　The largest 4-digit number = 9999

$345)9999(28$
$\quad\ \underline{690}$
$\quad\ 3099$
$\quad\ \underline{2760}$
$\quad\ \ 339$

$\therefore$ Required number $= 345 - 339 = 6$

46. (c)　Let the two numbers be x and y.
$\therefore\ x + y = 24$
and, $xy = 143$
$\therefore\ x^2 + y^2 = (x + y)^2 - 2xy$
$= (24)^2 - 2 \times 143$
$= 576 - 286 = 290$

47. (d)　Let the numbers be 10x and 10y where x and y are prime to each other.
$\therefore$ LCM = 10 xy
$\Rightarrow 10xy = 120$
$\Rightarrow xy = 12$
Posssible pairs $= (3, 4)$ or $(1, 12)$
$\therefore$ Sum of the numbers $= 30 + 40 = 70$

48. (b)　Let the number be x

$\therefore\ \dfrac{x + 12}{6} = 112$

$\Rightarrow x + 12 = 672$
$\Rightarrow x = 672 - 12 = 660$

$\therefore$ Correct answer $= \dfrac{660}{6} + 12$

$= 110 + 12 = 122$

49. (d)　Ratio = 2 : 3 : 4
$= 4 : 6 : 8$
Perimeter = 18 cm

$\therefore$ Semi-perimeter(s) $= \dfrac{4 + 6 + 8}{2} = 9$

$\therefore$ Area of triangle

$= \sqrt{s(s - a)(s - b)(s - c)}$

$= \sqrt{9(9 - 4)(9 - 6)(9 - 8)}$

$= \sqrt{9 \times 5 \times 3 \times 1} = 3\sqrt{15}$ sq. cm.

50. (a)　Marked price of article $= ₹\ 100$ (let)
$\therefore$ C.P. of article $= ₹\ 64$
$\therefore$ S.P. of article $= ₹\ 88$
$\therefore$ Profit per cent

$= \dfrac{88 - 64}{64} \times 100 = 37.5\%$

51. (c)	52. (b)	53. (d)	54. (c)	55. (b)
56. (b)	57. (c)	58. (d)	59. (d)	60. (d)
61. (d)	62. (d)	63. (a)	64. (b)	65. (a)
66. (b)	67. (c)	68. (a)	69. (d)	70. (b)
71. (a)	72. (a)	73. (a)	74. (c)	75. (c)
76. (a)	77. (b)	78. (c)	79. (a)	80. (a)
81. (b)	82. (c)	83. (d)	84. (b)	85. (a)
86. (c)	87. (a)	88. (c)	89. (b)	90. (b)
91. (a)	92. (a)	93. (a)	94. (c)	95. (d)
96. (d)	97. (d)	98. (c)	99. (d)	100. (d)

101. STAGE II FULL TEST - 2

1. (c)　Bulb is an item while all others are phenomena.

2. (c)　Except Tide, all other terms are related to both air and water. But tide is a regular rise and fall in the level of sea, caused by the attraction of the moon and sun.

3. (b) a $\boxed{b}$ b $\boxed{n}$ / a $\boxed{bb}$ n / $\boxed{a}$ bb $\boxed{n}$ / abbn

4. (d) 126   98   70   42   14
         −28   −28   −28   −28

Therefore, the number 41 is wrong the series.

5. (d) $3+1=4$; $3+4=7$;
         $4+7=11$; $7+11=18$
         $11+18=29$; $18+29=\boxed{47}$

6. (c) 975   864   753   642 $\boxed{531}$
         −111   −111   −111   −111

7. (b) Suppose the present age of Ashok is x years and that
         of his mother is y years.
         5 years ago
         $3(x-5)=(y-5)$
         $\Rightarrow 3x-15=y-5$
         $\Rightarrow 3z-y=10$ ...(i)
         5 years hence,
         $2(x+5)=(y+5)$
         $\Rightarrow 2x+10=y+5$
         $\Rightarrow 2x-y=-5$ ...(ii)
         From equations (i) and (ii)
         $x=15$ years

8. (a) O is the husband of P. M is the son of P.
         Therefore, M is the son of O.

9. (c) 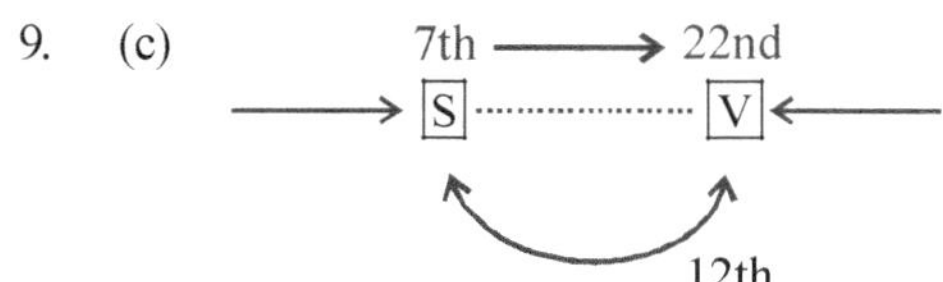

Total number of boys in the row
$=22+12-1=\boxed{33}$

10. (a) Day before yesterday was Sunday.
         Therefore, today is Tuesday.
         Day after tomorrow will be Thursday.
         Thursday + 3 = Sunday

11. (b) As, H O S P I T A L
            ↓ ↓ ↓ ↓ ↓ ↓ ↓ ↓
            3 2 5 7 4 6 1 8

Therefore,

         P O S T A L
         ↓ ↓ ↓ ↓ ↓ ↓
         $\boxed{7\ 2\ 5\ \ 6\ \ 1\ \ 8}$

12. (a) $1+7+3+5+2+6=24$
         $4+3+1+3+2+5=18$
         Therefore,
         $2+5+3+4+7+1=\boxed{22}$

13. (d) $(12+6)\times 18=36 \Rightarrow (18 \div 6)\times 12=36$
         $\Rightarrow 3\times 12\ \boxed{36}$

14. (a) 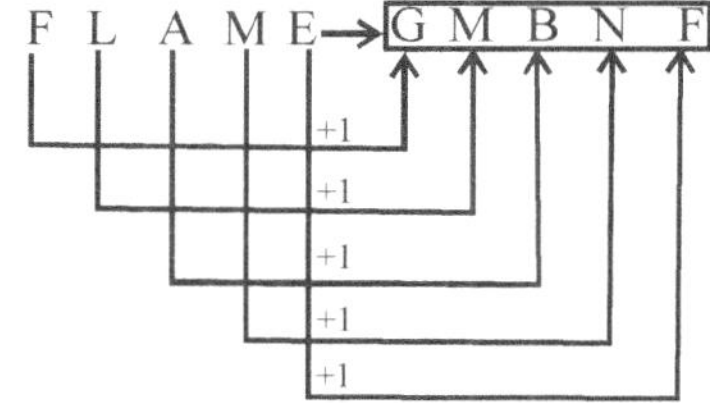

Similarly,

F L A M E → $\boxed{G\ M\ B\ N\ F}$

15. (b)

∴ Required distance = AF

$=\sqrt{(80)^2+(60)^2}$

$\sqrt{6400+3600}=\sqrt{10000}=\boxed{100m}$

16. (b) As, $5\times 3+1=16$
         $16\times 3+1=49$
         $9\times 3+2=29$
         $29\times 3+2=89$
         Therefore,
         $15\times 3+3=\boxed{48}$
         $48\times 3+3=147$

17. (a) 1st Row $\Rightarrow$ D
         2nd Row $\Rightarrow$ E
         3rd Row $\Rightarrow$ C
         4th Row $\Rightarrow$ A
         5th Row $\Rightarrow$ B

18. (c) 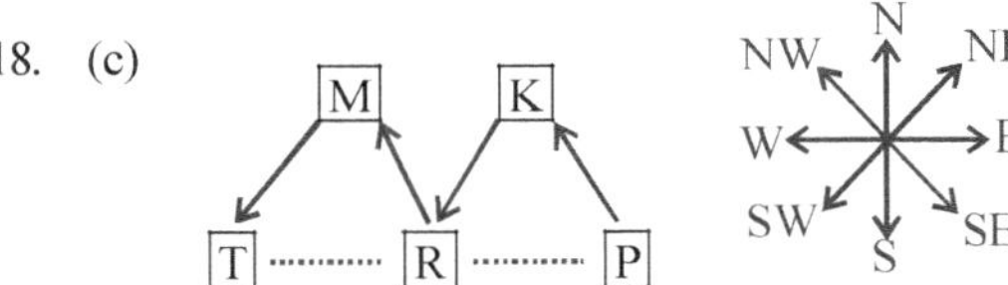

It is clear that T is located to the West of P.

19. (c) Sharks belong to class pisces. Whale is a mammal and Turtle belongs to class reptilia.

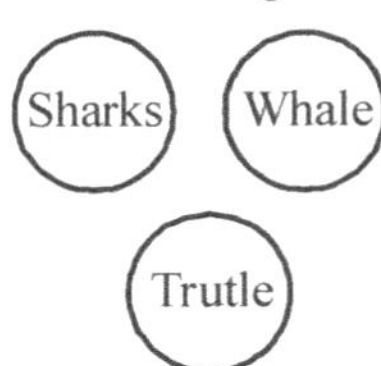

20. (b) The day after tomorrow is Sunday.
Therefore, today is Friday.
The day on tomorrow's day before yesterday = Friday $- 1 =$ Thursday

21. (d) Suppose the present age of son is x years.
Therefore, present age of the father $= 4x$ years
According to question,
$x + 3 = 15$
$\therefore x = 15 - 3 = 12$ years
The present age of father
$= 4x = 4 \times 12 = 48$ years
$\therefore$ The present age of man's wife
$= 48 - 3 = 45$ years

22. (b) R is father of X and Y.
S is maternal uncle of X and Y Considering the given options, it may be assumed that T is wife of R.

23. (a) $\boxed{S}$ $\boxed{A}$
24th   17th

24. (b) As, H O N E S T Y
↓ ↓ ↓ ↓ ↓ ↓ ↓
5 1 3 2 4 6 8

and, P O V E R T Y
↓ ↓ ↓ ↓ ↓ ↓ ↓
7 1 9 2 0 6 8

Therefore,
H O R S E
↓ ↓ ↓ ↓ ↓
5 1 0 4 2

25. (a) As,   S I S T E R ⟶ R H R S D Q

Similarly,

U N C L E ⟶ $\boxed{\text{T M B K D}}$

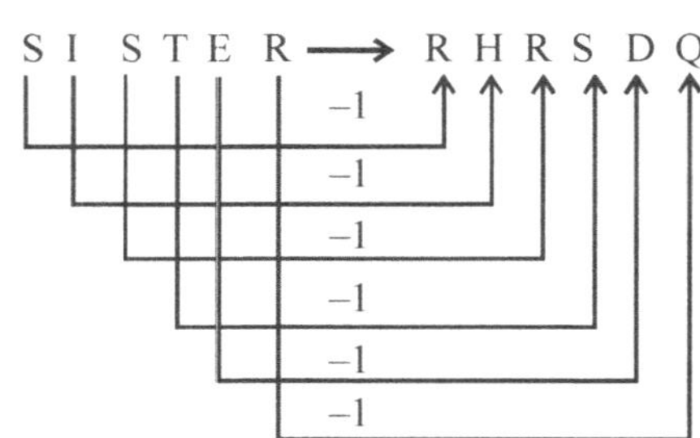

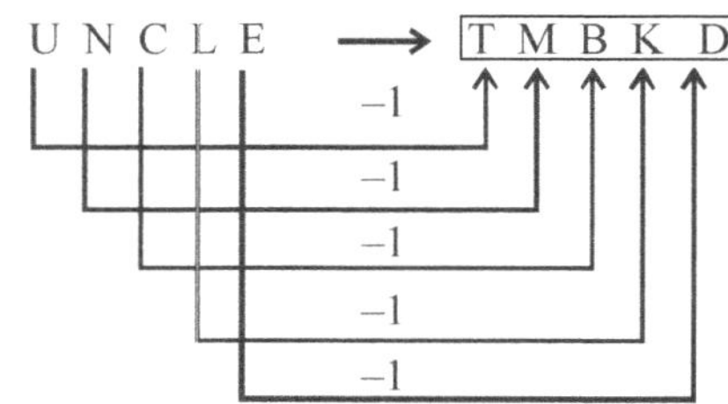

26. (d) $p \times q = HCF \times LCM$
$\therefore$ Second number $= \dfrac{8 \times 48}{24} = 16$

27. (b)
$$
\begin{array}{c|cccc}
2 & 20, & 28, & 32, & 35 \\
\hline
2 & 10, & 14, & 16, & 35 \\
\hline
5 & 5, & 7, & 8, & 35 \\
\hline
7 & 1, & 7, & 8, & 7 \\
\hline
 & 1, & 1, & 8, & 1
\end{array}
$$
$\therefore$ LCM $= 2 \times 2 \times 5 \times 7 \times 8 = 1120$
$\therefore$ Required number
$= 5834 - 1120 = 4714$

28. (b) If the first divisor is a multiple of second divisor.
Then, remainder by the second divisor.
$\therefore$ Remainder $= 21 \div 19 = 2$

29. (c) $0.121212.... = 0.\overline{12} = \dfrac{12}{99} = \dfrac{4}{33}$

30. (c) Let the numbers be 3x and 4x.
$\therefore$ Their LCM $= 12x$
$\therefore 12x = 84$
$\Rightarrow x = \dfrac{84}{12} = 7$
$\therefore$ Larger number
$= 4x = 4 \times 7 = 28$

31. (d) Let the capacity of the drum be x litres.
$\therefore \dfrac{3x}{4} - 30 = \dfrac{7x}{12}$
$\Rightarrow \dfrac{3x}{4} - \dfrac{7x}{12} = 30$
$\Rightarrow \dfrac{9x - 7x}{12} = 30$
$\Rightarrow \dfrac{x}{6} = 30$
$= x = 6 \times 30 = 180$ litres

32. (b) $675 = 5 \times 5 \times 3 \times 3 \times 3 = 5$
No to be multiplied

33. (c) $a^4 - b^4 = (a^2 + b^2)(a + b)(a - b)$
$\therefore$ Required number $= (3 + 1)(3 - 1) = 8$

34. (b) Gain $= 11x - 10x = ₹x$
$\therefore p\% = \dfrac{p \times 100}{p} \times 100 = \dfrac{x}{10x} \times 100 = 10$

35. (c) Marked price $= ₹50$
S.P. after discount $= 80\%$ of 50
$= ₹40$
If the CP of article be $₹x$, then
$\dfrac{125 \times x}{100} = 40$
$\Rightarrow x = \dfrac{40 \times 100}{125} = ₹32$

36. **(a)** Let the CP be ₹100.

∴ SP = ₹112

If the marked price be ₹x, then

90% of x = 112

$$\Rightarrow x = \frac{112 \times 100}{90} = ₹\frac{1120}{9}$$

∴ Required ratio

$$= 100 : \frac{1120}{9}$$

$$= 900 : 1120 = 45 : 56$$

37. **(b)** C.P. of bicycle

$$= \frac{100}{114} \times 2850 = ₹2500$$

S.P. for a profit of 8%

$$= \frac{108}{100} \times 2500 = ₹2700$$

38. **(b)** Required precentage

$$= \frac{50}{100 - 50} \times 100$$

$$= 100\%$$

39. **(a)** Let the numbers be 3x and 5x.

∴ 3x × 5x = 2160

$$\Rightarrow x^2 = \frac{2160}{3 \times 5} = 144 = 12 \times 12$$

$$\Rightarrow x = 12$$

∴ Smaller number

= 3x = 3 × 12 = 36

40. **(d)**
$$\frac{A \times 60}{100} = B \times \frac{3}{4}$$

$$\Rightarrow A \times \frac{3}{5} = B \times \frac{3}{4}$$

$$\Rightarrow \frac{A}{B} = \frac{3}{4} \times \frac{5}{3} = 5 : 4$$

41. **(c)** Single equivalent percentage increase in price

$$= \left(10 + 10 + \frac{10 \times 10}{100}\right)\% = 21\%$$

42. **(c)**

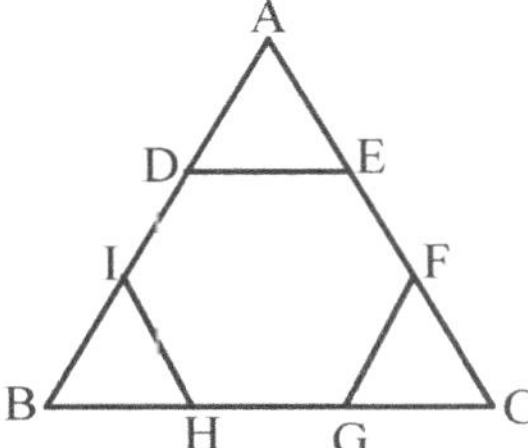

Side of the regular hexagon

$$= \frac{1}{3} \times 6 = 2 \text{ cm}$$

∴ Area of the hexagon $= \dfrac{3\sqrt{3}}{2} a^2$

$$= \frac{3\sqrt{3}}{2} \times 2 \times 2$$

$$= 6\sqrt{3} \text{ sq. cm.}$$

43. **(b)** Length of the longest rod

$$\sqrt{a^2 + b^2 + c^2}$$

$$= \sqrt{10^2 + 10^2 + 5^2}$$

$$= \sqrt{225} = 15 \text{ metre}$$

44. **(c)** A's share

$$= ₹\left(\frac{3}{5} \times 1000\right) = ₹600$$

45. **(a)**
$$A = P\left(1 + \frac{R}{100}\right)^T$$

$$2 = 1\left(1 + \frac{Rate}{100}\right)^{15}$$

Cubing on both sides, we have

$$8 = 1\left(1 + \frac{Rate}{100}\right)^{45}$$

Required time = 45 years

46. **(d)** Circumference = $2\pi r$ (one variable)

∴ The decrease in area $= 50 - 50 + \dfrac{50 \times 50}{100}$

$$= -75\%$$

47. **(b)** Let the annual instalment be ₹x.

$$\therefore \left(x + \frac{x \times 3 \times 5}{100}\right)$$

$$+ \left(x + \frac{x \times 2 \times 5}{100}\right) + \left(x + \frac{x \times 1 \times 5}{100}\right) + x = 6450$$

$$\Rightarrow \frac{115x}{100} + \frac{110x}{100} + \frac{105x}{100} + x = 6450$$

$$\Rightarrow 115x + 110x + 105x + 100x$$

$$= 6450 \times 100$$

$$\Rightarrow 430x = 6450 \times 100$$

$$\therefore x = \frac{6450 \times 100}{430} = ₹1500$$

48. **(c)** $1 + 2 + 3 + \ldots\ldots + n = \dfrac{n(n+1)}{2}$

∴ Average of these numbers

$$\therefore \text{ Average} = \frac{n+1}{2}$$

$$= \frac{100+1}{2} = 50.5$$

49. (b) Father + mother
   $= 2 \times 35 = 70$ years
   Father + mother + son
   $= 27 \times 3 = 81$ years
   $\therefore$ Son's age $= 81 - 70 = 11$ years

50. (d) 5 men $\equiv 7$ women

   $$\therefore 7 \text{ men} \equiv \frac{7}{5} \times 7 = \frac{49}{5} \text{ women}$$

   $$\therefore 7 \text{ men} + 13 \text{ women}$$

   $$= \frac{49}{5} + 13 = \frac{114}{5} \text{ women}$$

   Now,

   $$\because 7 \text{ women} \equiv ₹5250$$

   $$\therefore \frac{114}{5} \text{ women}$$

   $$\equiv \frac{5250}{7} \times \frac{114}{5} = ₹17100$$

51. (b)

52. (a) Vitamin B-12, also called cobalamin, is a water-soluble vitamin that has a key role in the normal functioning of the brain and nervous system, and the formation of red blood cells.

53. (d)   54. (a)   55. (a)

56. (b) Acetic acid, also known as ethanoic acid, is an organic chemical compound best recognized for giving vinegar its sour taste and pungent smell. It is one of the simplest carboxylic acids and has the chemical formula CH_3COOH.

57. (a) Boiling point of heavy water is lower than that or ordinary water

58. (d) Advection is the transfer of heat or matter by the flow of a fluid, especially horizontally in the atmosphere or the sea.

59. (b) The real benchmarking of the government policy on decentralisation can, however, be attributed to Lord Ripon who, in his famous resolution on local self-government on May 18, 1882, recognised the twin considerations of local government: (i) administrative efficiency and (ii) political education.

60. (d)   61. (b)

62. (c) The Reserve Bank of India is India's central banking institution, which controls the monetary policy of the indian rupee. It commenced its operations on 1 April 1935 during the British Rule in accordance with the provisions of the Reserve Bank of India Act, 1934.

63. (d)   64. (d)

65. (d) Bats are good at flying at night because they use sound rather than sight to navigate. Bats send pulses of sound through their mouths or noses, and these pulses echo back outlining the objects in the bats flight path. The ears of a bat are large and oddly constructed but they help it to determine where the echoes are coming from.

66. (a)	67. (d)	68. (b)	69. (c)
70. (d)	71. (c)	72. (d)	73. (c)
74. (b)	75. (b)	76. (d)	77. (c)
78. (a)	79. (c)	80. (c)	81. (d)
82. (d)	83. (a)	84. (b)	85. (b)
86. (a)	87. (a)	88. (c)	89. (c)
90. (d)	91. (c)	92. (a)	93. (d)
94. (d)	95. (b)	96. (a)	97. (a)
98. (c)	99. (d)	100. (b)	